Teaching Science in Elementary and Middle School Classrooms

A PROJECT-BASED APPROACH

Teaching Science in Elementary and Middle School Classrooms

A PROJECT-BASED APPROACH

second edition

Joseph S. Krajcik
THE UNIVERSITY OF MICHIGAN

Charlene M. Czerniak
THE UNIVERSITY OF TOLEDO

Carl F. Berger
THE UNIVERSITY OF MICHIGAN

Boston   Burr Ridge, IL   Dubuque, IA   Madison, WI   New York   San Francisco   St. Louis
Bangkok   Bogotá   Caracas   Kuala Lumpur   Lisbon   London   Madrid   Mexico City
Milan   Montreal   New Delhi   Santiago   Seoul   Singapore   Sydney   Taipei   Toronto

McGraw-Hill Higher Education

A Division of The **McGraw-Hill** *Companies*

TEACHING SCIENCE IN ELEMENTARY AND MIDDLE SCHOOL CLASSROOMS: A PROJECT-BASED APPROACH
Published by McGraw-Hill, a business unit of The McGraw-Hill Companies, Inc., 1221 Avenue
of the Americas, New York, NY, 10020. Copyright © 2003, 1999, by The McGraw-Hill
Companies, Inc. All rights reserved. No part of this publication may be reproduced or distributed
in any form or by any means, or stored in a database or retrieval system, without the prior written
consent of The McGraw-Hill Companies, Inc., including, but not limited to, in any network or
other electronic storage or transmission, or broadcast for distance learning.
Some ancillaries, including electronic and print components, may not be available to customers
outside the United States.

This book is printed on acid-free paper.

1 2 3 4 5 6 7 8 9 0 DOC/DOC 0 9 8 7 6 5 4 3 2

ISBN 0-07-248674-0

Publisher: *Jane Karpacz*
Developmental editor II: *Cara Harvey*
Editorial coordinator: *Christina Lembo*
Marketing manager: *Pamela Cooper*
Media producer: *Lance Gerhart*
Lead project manager: *Susan Trentacosti*
Production supervisor: *Carol A. Bielski*
Senior designer: *Jenny El-Shamy*
Lead supplement producer: *Marc Mattson*
Manager, photo research: *Brian J. Pecko*
Cover images: *Gettyimages*
Typeface: *9/11 Garamond*
Compositor: *GAC Indianapolis*
Printer: *R.R. Donnelley & Sons Co.*

Library of Congress Control Number: 2002107634

www.mhhe.com

Dedication

To Ann, my wife, whose encouragement and support has allowed me to develop as a person and scholar and to my children—Michael, Paul, Ellen—who continuously inspire me to improve and stay young.
Joe

To my parents who helped inspire my love of science and to my husband, David, who was supportive of the time required to write this book.
Charlene

To Sharon, my wife, support, and companion of 48 years, and to my sister, Elsa, for her love of learning and teaching.
Carl

About the Authors

Joseph S. Krajcik
THE UNIVERSITY
OF MICHIGAN

Joseph Krajcik, a Professor of Science Education in the School of Education at the University of Michigan, focuses his research on designing science classrooms so that students engage in finding solutions to meaningful, real-world questions through inquiry and the use of learning technologies. His working philosophy is that such learning environments will help students develop deep understanding of content as well as strategies for generating new understanding. Professor Krajcik focuses his current research efforts by working with teachers and administrators in the Detroit Public Schools and other systems to design instructional materials that can help all students learn science.

Professor Krajcik has authored and co-authored numerous articles or chapters in books. His publications have appeared in *The Journal of Research in Science Teaching, Journal of Learning Sciences, Elementary School Journal, Journal of Computers in Mathematics and Science Education,* and *Educational Researcher.* Professor Krajcik makes frequent presentations at national and international conferences that focus on his research, as well as presentations that translate research findings into classroom practice. His principal teaching responsibilities include graduate science education courses and science education methods. He is an active member of the National Association of Research in Science Teaching (NARST) and the National Science Teachers Association, and reviews manuscripts for a number of journals. His colleagues recognized his leadership abilities and contribution to science education by electing him President of NARST in 1999. In 2001, the American Association for the Advancement of Science recognized Professor Krajcik for his accomplishments in science education by inducting him as a fellow into the Association.

Charlene M. Czerniak
THE UNIVERSITY
OF TOLEDO

Charlene Czerniak is a professor at The University of Toledo in Curriculum and Instruction. She received her Ph.D. in science education from The Ohio State University. A former elementary teacher in Bowling Green, Ohio, she has authored and co-authored over 50 articles. She has also published a book and two chapters in books, and illustrated 12 children's science education books. Her publications have appeared in *The Journal of Research in Science Teaching, Journal of Science Teacher Education, School Science and Mathematics, Science Scope, and Science and Children*. Professor Czerniak has been the author and director of numerous grant funded projects that targeted professional development of science teachers. Most notable is a National Science Foundation grant entitled "Toledo Area Partnership in Education: Support Teachers as Resources in Elementary Science (TAPESTRIES)" which was funded for $5.2 million. She has made frequent presentations at national and regional conferences that focus on her research interests on teachers' beliefs about teaching science. Professor Czerniak's areas of specialty also include professional development for elementary and middle grades teachers, science education reform, and school improvement. She is an active member in the National Association of Research in Science Teaching, the Association for Education of Teachers of Science, the School Science and Mathematics Association, and the National Science Teachers Association, and reviews manuscripts for a number of journals associated with these organizations. She also served as President of the School Science and Mathematics Association.

Carl F. Berger
THE UNIVERSITY OF MICHIGAN

Carl F. Berger is the Director of Academic Information Processes at The University of Michigan, where he is also a Professor in the School of Education. He received his doctorate (Ed.D.) from the University of California–Berkeley, where he was a research scientist from 1966 to 1971. A former junior high school and high school teacher, he was a member of the Science Curriculum Improvement Study author team. He has authored or co-authored over a dozen books. He was selected in 1979 as the outstanding teacher education in the state of Michigan and in 1996 received the Distinguished Contributions to Science Education through Research award from the National Association for Research in Science Teaching (NARST). His special interests are in how children learn science using technology, and in applications of technology in classrooms and program improvement.

Brief Contents

PORTFOLIO ACTIVITIES xvi
PREFACE xx

1. Why and How Should I Teach Science to Children? 2

2. How Do Children Construct Understanding in Science? 36

3. What Is a Driving Question? 76

4. How Are Scientific Investigations Developed? 112

5. How Can Learning Technologies Be Used to

   Support Investigations? 166

6. How Do I Develop Collaboration in the Science Classroom? 198

7. How Do I Develop and Use Benchmark Lessons? 248

8. Why Do We Assess Students in Science? 304

9. How Is Student Understanding Assessed? 334

10. How Do I Manage the Project-Based Science Classroom? 380

11. How Do I Plan a Project-Based Curriculum? 438

12. What Are the Next Steps? 478

GLOSSARY   G
PHOTO CREDITS   CR–1
INDEX   I

Contents

PORTFOLIO ACTIVITIES   xvi

PREFACE   xx

CHAPTER 1
Why and How Should I Teach Science to Children? 2

OVERVIEW OF THE BOOK 4
INTRODUCTION TO THE CHAPTER 6

Scenario 1: Reading About Science 7
Scenario 2: Direct Instruction 8
Scenario 3: Process Science Teaching 8
Scenario 4: Project-Based Science 9

AN OVERVIEW OF PROJECT-BASED SCIENCE 11

Driving Questions 11
Students Engaged in Investigations 12
Communities of Learners
Collaborating Together 12

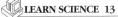
USING TECHNOLOGY TOOLS TO LEARN SCIENCE 13

Creation of Artifacts 13

WHAT IS SCIENCE? 14

Theories 14
Scientific Process 17
The Nature of Science in Project-Based Science Teaching 17

WHY SHOULD YOUNG LEARNERS STUDY SCIENCE? 17

Science Affects Every Aspect of Our Lives 19
Students Acquire Useful Knowledge, Skills, and Attitudes 19
Science Teaches Critical Thinking, Problem Solving, and Decision Making 20

Science Helps Students Take Responsibility for Their Actions 20
Science Develops Scientifically Literate Citizens 20
Positive Science Experiences Are Important in Elementary and Middle School Grades 21

GOALS OF SCIENCE EDUCATION 21

National Science Education Standards 22
Project 2061: Science for All Americans 24
Benchmarks for Science Literacy 24
The National Science Teachers Association Position Statement 25
Summary of National Goals 26

HOW DO THE CURRENT NATIONAL GOALS COMPARE WITH PROJECT-BASED SCIENCE? 28

CHAPTER SUMMARY 31
CHAPTER HIGHLIGHTS 32
REFERENCES 33

CHAPTER 2
How Do Children Construct Understanding in Science? 36

INTRODUCTION 38
STUDENT UNDERSTANDING 38

Scenario 1: What Is Alive? 39
Scenario 2: Boiling Water 39
Scenario 3: Burning Steel Wool 40
Meaningful Understandings 43
Types of Knowledge 44

MODELS OF TEACHING 46

A Receptional Approach to Teaching 47

A Transformational Approach to Teaching 47
SOCIAL CONSTRUCTION OF KNOWLEDGE 48
  The Influence of Jean Piaget 49
  The Influence of Lev Vygotsky 52
A SOCIAL CONSTRUCTIVIST MODEL OF TEACHING 54
  Active Engagement with Phenomena 54
  Use and Application of Knowledge 56
  Multiple Representations 61
  Use of Learning Communities 62
  Authentic Tasks 68
  **USING TECHNOLOGY TOOLS TO
  EXTEND LEARNING** 70

CHAPTER SUMMARY 71
CHAPTER HIGHLIGHTS 72
REFERENCES 73

CHAPTER 3
**What Is a Driving
Question?** 76
INTRODUCTION 78
*Scenario 1: Reading About
Force and Motion* 79
*Scenario 2: Learning About Force and
Motion via an Activity* 79
*Scenario 3: Learning About Motion and
Force Through a Driving Question* 80
WHAT IS A DRIVING QUESTION? 81
  Features of Driving Questions 82
  Examples of Driving Questions 87
HOW DOES THE DRIVING QUESTION DIFFER FROM
OTHER QUESTIONS? 91
HOW IS A DRIVING QUESTION DEVELOPED? 92

Teacher-Generated Driving Questions 92
  **USING TECHNOLOGY TOOLS TO DEVELOP A
  DRIVING QUESTION** 98
  Student-Generated Driving Questions 100
WHAT IS THE VALUE OF THE DRIVING QUESTION? 106
HOW CAN A DRIVING QUESTION BE USED
THROUGHOUT A PROJECT? 108
CHAPTER SUMMARY 109
CHAPTER HIGHLIGHTS 109
REFERENCES 110

CHAPTER 4
**How Are Scientific
Investigations
Developed?** 112
INTRODUCTION 114
*Scenario 1: A Step-by-Step
Activity* 114
Scenario 2: A Trial-and-Error Activity 115
Scenario 3: An Investigation 115
INVESTIGATIONS IN ELEMENTARY AND MIDDLE SCHOOL
SCIENCE INSTRUCTION 117
THE INVESTIGATION WEB 118
  Messing About 120
  Asking and Refining Questions 125
  Hypothesizing 129
  Making Predictions 130
  Finding Information 131
  Planning and Designing 134
  Carrying Out the Procedures 144
  Making Sense of Data 147
  Drawing Conclusions 153

Sharing with Others 155
Moving into the Next Round of
Investigation 158
SUPPORTING STUDENTS' IMPLEMENTATION OF
INVESTIGATIONS 158
CRITERIA FOR ASSESSING THE VALUE OF AN
INVESTIGATION 160
CHAPTER SUMMARY 162
CHAPTER HIGHLIGHTS 163
REFERENCES 164

CHAPTER 5
How Can Learning
Technologies Be Used to
Support Investigations? 166
INTRODUCTION 168
Scenario 1: Technology as a
Mindless Activity 169
Scenario 2: Going to the Computer Lab 169
Scenario 3: Using Technology to Support
Students Doing Investigations 170
ROLE OF TECHNOLOGY IN CONSTRUCTING
SCIENCE UNDERSTANDINGS 171
Learning Technologies to Support Active
Engagement with Phenomena 172
Learning Technologies to Support Using and
Applying Knowledge 179
Learning Technologies as a Source
of Information 181
Learning Technologies to Support the
Creation of Multiple Representations 184
Learning Technologies to Support the
Creation of Learning Communities 188
ROLE OF THE TEACHER 188
INTEGRATING TECHNOLOGY INTO INSTRUCTION 190
Issues to Consider When Incorporating
Technological Tools into Your
Curriculum 190
CHAPTER SUMMARY 192
CHAPTER HIGHLIGHTS 193
REFERENCES 195

CHAPTER 6
How Do I Develop
Collaboration in the
Science Classroom? 198
INTRODUCTION 200
Scenario 1: Group Work with
Little Guidance 200
Scenario 2: Individual Jobs in
Group Work 200
Scenario 3: Using Expert Groups 201
Scenario 4: A Learning Community 202
THE NATURE OF COLLABORATION 203
What Is Collaboration? 203
What Are the Characteristics of
Collaboration? 205
TYPES OF COLLABORATIVE LEARNING 206
Among Students 206
Between Students and Teacher 208
Between Students and the Community 209
CREATING A COLLABORATIVE ENVIRONMENT 210
Forming Groups 210
Developing Collaborative Skills 212
Involving All Students Equitably 224

USING TECHNOLOGY TOOLS TO CREATE A
COLLABORATIVE ENVIRONMENT 228

CHALLENGES THAT ARISE WHEN STUDENTS
COLLABORATE IN SMALL GROUPS 230
A Lack of Collaborative Skills 230
Loafing 230
The Fear of Being Duped and the
Dominating of Others 232
Status Differential 232
Pacts 233
Diversity 233
Socially Induced Incompetence 234
A Belief in the "Right Answer" 234
Lack of Support from Parents, Colleagues,
or Administrators 234
WHY COLLABORATION ALMOST ALWAYS WORKS BETTER
THAN INDIVIDUAL LEARNING 236
Using Multiple Zones of Proximal
Development to Provide Cognitive
Support for a Variety of Learners 236

Effects on Achievement, Problem Solving,
and Understanding 237
Spread of Cognitive Load Among
Learners 238
Promotion of Autonomous,
Motivated Learning 239
Reduction of Anxiety About Learning 239
Inclusion of Groups Traditionally Left
Behind in Science 240
Development of Real Life Skills 241
CHAPTER SUMMARY 243
CHAPTER HIGHLIGHTS 244
REFERENCES 245

CHAPTER 7
How Do I Develop and Use
Benchmark Lessons? 248
INTRODUCTION 250
Scenario 1: Reading About
Insects 250
Scenario 2: Using a Microscope 250
Scenario 3: Observing Insects 251
THE ROLE OF BENCHMARK LESSONS IN
PROJECT-BASED SCIENCE 252
Benchmark Lessons: A Critical Component of
Project-Based Science 252
When to Plan a Benchmark Lesson 255
PLANNING A BENCHMARK LESSON 263
Developing Learning Performances 263
Creating a Lesson Plan for a
Benchmark Lesson 264
USING DEMONSTRATIONS 273
The Purpose for Demonstrations 273
Presenting Demonstrations to Learners 274
Cautions in Giving Demonstrations 275
Discrepant Events 275
Student Demonstrations 276
USING LARGE GROUP DISCUSSIONS 277
Value of Discussions 277
Leading a Discussion 278
Techniques for Improving Classroom
Discussions 278
Keeping Track of Your Comments 280
PRESENTING INFORMATION 280

Metaphors, Similes, and Analogies 282
Diagrams, Graphs, and Pictures 282
Movies, Videos, and Educational
Television 283
Guest Lectures 284
Community Resources 284
Active Strategies 284
USING LITERATURE 287
Children's Literature 288
Magazines and Periodicals for Children 289
USING TECHNOLOGY TOOLS TO ACQUIRE
WRITTEN INFORMATION 289
Making Sense of Written Material 290
USING CONCEPT MAPS 292
Issues to Consider When Using
Concept Maps 292
USING QUESTIONS 294
Types of Questions 294
CHAPTER SUMMARY 298
CHAPTER HIGHLIGHTS 299
REFERENCES 300

CHAPTER 8
Why Do We Assess Students
in Science? 304
INTRODUCTION 306
Scenario 1: Traditional Paper-
and-Pencil Tests 306
Scenario 2: Tests Used in a Project-Based
Environment 306
Scenario 3: Embedded Assessment 308
THE PURPOSE OF ASSESSMENT 309
Large-Scale and High-Stakes Assessment 310
THE NATURE OF CLASSROOM ASSESSMENT 313
Current Assessment Is Responsive
to Context 314
Current Assessment Is a Continuous Process
Embedded in Instruction 315
Current Assessment Is Multidimensional 315
Current Assessment Engages Students in the
Assessment Process 316
Current Assessment Is Valid
and Reliable 316

*Current Assessment Matches Today's
Educational Goals 317*
*Current Assessment Accommodates
Cultural Diversity 318*
*Current Assessment Is Consistent with
Learning Theory 319*
*Current Assessment Measures Meaningful
Understanding 320*
WHAT TO ASSESS 322
WHEN TO ASSESS 325
   **USING TECHNOLOGY TOOLS TO EXAMINE
   ASSESSMENT 329**

CHAPTER SUMMARY 330
CHAPTER HIGHLIGHTS 330
REFERENCES 331

CHAPTER 9
How Is Student
Understanding
Assessed? 334
   INTRODUCTION 336
      *Scenario 1: Gathering
Assessment Information 336*
      *Scenario 2: Assembling Assessment
Information 336*
      *Scenario 3: Making Judgments About
Assessment Information 337*
ASSESSMENT OF STUDENT UNDERSTANDING 338
      Gathering Assessment Information 338
      *Assembling and Presenting Assessment
Information 354*
      *Making Judgments from Assessment
Information 362*
   **USING TECHNOLOGY TOOLS TO ENHANCE
   ASSESSMENT 372**

ANOTHER LOOK AT THE ADVANTAGES OF
EDUCATIONAL ASSESSMENT 372
      Advantages for Teachers 373
      Advantages for Students 373
      Advantages for Parents 374
CHAPTER SUMMARY 376
CHAPTER HIGHLIGHTS 376
REFERENCES 378

CHAPTER 10
How Do I Manage the
Project-Based Science
Classroom? 380
   INTRODUCTION 382
      *Scenario 1: Reading About
Science 382*
      Scenario 2: Direct Science Instruction 383
      Scenario 3: Process Science 384
      Scenario 4: Multiple Investigations 384
CLASSROOM CLIMATE 386
      *A Constructivist Rationale and Framework
for Thinking About Classroom Climate 388*
      *Creating an Effective Classroom
Climate 389*
      Being a Role Model 390
CLASSROOM ORGANIZATION 397
      Arranging the Classroom 397
      Structuring the School Day 403
      Maintaining a Safe Classroom 409
MANAGEMENT STRATEGIES 416
      Before Instruction 416
      During Instruction 423
      After Instruction 429
   **USING TECHNOLOGY TOOLS TO FACILITATE
   CLASSROOM MANAGEMENT 432**

CHAPTER SUMMARY 433
CHAPTER HIGHLIGHTS 433
REFERENCES 435

CHAPTER 11
How Do I Plan a Project-
Based Curriculum? 438
   INTRODUCTION 440
      *Scenario: Planning the
Curriculum 440*
DEVELOPING A PROJECT 441
      *Identifying Concepts, Specifying Learning
Performances, and Matching to Curriculum
Objectives 442*
      Developing the Driving Question 443
      Developing Benchmark Lessons 446
      Developing Investigations 448
      Developing Assessments 450

Developing a Calendar of Activities 452
Developing a Project 452
SELECTING AND OBTAINING RESOURCES 452
Selecting Resources 455
Obtaining Resources 455
INTEGRATED CURRICULUM 460
The Definition of Integration 468
How Project-Based Science Supports
Curriculum Integration 469
A Word of Warning 470
An Example of Curriculum Integration 470
Concept Mapping to Plan Integrated
Projects 472

USING TECHNOLOGY TOOLS TO PLAN
PROJECTS 473

CHAPTER SUMMARY 474
CHAPTER HIGHLIGHTS 475
REFERENCES 476

CHAPTER 12
What Are the Next
Steps? 478
INTRODUCTION 480
SUMMARY OF PROJECT-BASED
SCIENCE 480

BENEFITS OF PROJECT-BASED SCIENCE 482
CHALLENGES OF PROJECT-BASED SCIENCE 483
Teacher Discomfort with Content
Knowledge 484
Teacher Discomfort with the Process
of Science 486
Limited Student Experience 487
Lack of Time 488
Real or Perceived External Pressures 489
CONTINUING YOUR PROFESSIONAL GROWTH 491
Joining Professional Organizations 491
Attending Conferences 492
Subscribing to Publications 492
USING TECHNOLOGY TOOLS FOR PROFESSIONAL
DEVELOPMENT 492

INQUIRY INTO YOUR TEACHING 493
CHAPTER SUMMARY 497
CHAPTER HIGHLIGHTS 497
REFERENCES 498

Glossary G
Photo Credits CR-1
Index I

Portfolio Activities

1.1   What are Your Elementary and Middle School Science Experiences? 7

1.2   What Are the Characteristics and Challenges of Each of the Scenarios? 10

1.3   Where's the Other Film Canister? 15

1.4   Why Should Children Learn Science? 19

1.5   What Are Your Personal Goals for Science Education? 23

1.6   Case Study of an Elementary or Middle Grade Classroom 30

1.7   Questions about Science Teaching 31

2.1   Thinking about Your Own Understanding 42

2.2   Investigate Young Learners' Ideas 42

2.3   Recognizing and Evaluating a Social Constructivist Lesson 50

2.4   Determining Levels of Concreteness and Abstractness 58

2.5   Developing a Social Constructivist Lesson 70

3.1   Comparing the Three Scenarios 82

3.2   Comparing the Three Scenarios Again 88

3.3   Evaluating Various Questions 92

3.4   Generating Driving Questions from Topics 100

3.5   Analyze Classroom Science and Develop Driving Questions 101

3.6   Developing Driving Questions from What Students Know 104

4.1   Going on a Stream Walk 123

4.2   Identifying Testable Questions 130

4.3   Making Hypotheses from Questions 131

4.4   Writing Procedures 137

4.5   Controlling Variables: Paper Dragon Races 138

4.6   Sprouting Bean Plants 143

4.7   Planning and Designing 145

4.8   Performing Your Own
        Investigation 159

4.9   Supporting Implementation of
        Investigations 160

4.10   Comparing Two Investigations 162

5.1   Ways in Which You Have Used
        Technologies for Learning 171

5.2   Why Should Children Use Learning
        Technology? 171

5.3   Using Microcomputer-Based
        Laboratories to Visualize Evaporative
        Cooling 174

5.4   The Value of Using Microcomputer-
        Based Laboratories in the
        Classroom 177

5.5   Using the World Wide Web to Access
        and Visualize Data: Exploring the
        FeederWatch Program 178

5.6   The Value of Using Simulations to
        Help Students Learn Science
        Concepts 180

5.7   The Value of Building Models for
        Helping Students Learn Science
        Concepts 182

5.8   The Value of Searching for Materials
        on the World Wide Web Using Digital
        Libraries 185

5.9   The Value of Creating Multimedia
        Documents 187

5.10   Using Learning Technologies to Help
        Students Learn Science 192

6.1   How Does Collaboration Change the
        Nature of the Classroom? 204

6.2   How Do You Introduce Collaborative
        Skills to Students? 214

6.3   Making T-Charts 215

6.4   How Do Children Build Trust in a
        Group? 218

6.5   What Skills Are Helpful in Collaborative
        Groups? 220

6.6   How Can You Help Students Build
        Understanding? 227

6.7   How Do Roles Facilitate Collaborative
        Learning? 229

6.8   Troubleshooting 235

6.9   How Do I Explain Collaborative
        Learning to Colleagues and
        Parents? 236

6.10   How Do Teachers' Roles Change in a
        Collaborative Classroom? 240

6.11   How Does Collaboration Change the
        Nature of the Classroom? 242

6.12   What Curriculum Resources Use
        Collaborative Strategies? 243

7.1   What Is a Concept? 256

7.2   Building a Concept Map 259

7.3   Developing a Concept Map to Identify
        Benchmark Lessons 261

7.4   Planning and Teaching a Benchmark Lesson 273

7.5   Heating Water in a Paper Cup 276

7.6   The Inverted Jar 277

7.7   Leading a Discussion 280

7.8   Finding Images on the World Wide Web 283

7.9   What Educational Value Do Community Resources Have? 285

7.10   Planning and Teaching Another Benchmark Lesson 288

7.11   How Can I Use a Children's Science Magazine? 290

7.12   Identifying Levels of Questions 297

7.13   Analyzing Your Questioning Style 298

8.1   What Is the Purpose of Assessment? 310

8.2   How Do Teachers' Beliefs about Instruction Affect Their Methods of Assessment? 311

8.3   High-Stakes Testing 313

8.4   How Does Science Reform Affect Assessment Practices? 318

8.5   What Are the Pitfalls of Traditional Testing? 323

8.6   How Can I Choose a Good Assessment Technique to Measure Understanding? 325

8.7   Assessing Learning Performances 328

9.1   Developing a Skills Checklist 341

9.2   Assessing Affective Attributes 343

9.3   Writing a Classroom Test 351

9.4   Developing a Performance-Based Assessment 355

9.5   Creating Your Own Portfolio 363

9.6   Developing a Scoring Rubric 367

9.7   Creating a Report Card 371

9.8   Efficiency of Assessment 375

9.9   What Have You Learned about Assessment? 375

10.1   Managing a Science Classroom 386

10.2   What Makes a Positive Project-Based Science Classroom Climate? 388

10.3   Promoting Positive Affective Factors 393

10.4   Draw a Scientist 395

10.5   Equitable Classroom Practices 397

10.6   Arranging a Project-Based Science Classroom 402

10.7   Preplanning the Number of Minutes Allocated to Subjects 405

10.8   Scheduling 410

10.9   Conducting a Safety Audit 416

10.10   Establishing Ground Rules 418

10.11   Making a Contract 423

10.12   Anticipating Problems 425

10.13   Rethinking Your Views about Managing a Project-Based Science Class 432

11.1   Identifying Concepts, Specifying Learning Performances, and Matching to Curriculum Objectives 444

11.2   Turning Concepts, Learning Performances, and Curriculum Objectives into Driving Questions 446

11.3   Developing Benchmark Lessons 449

11.4   Developing an Investigation 451

11.5   Developing Assessments 452

11.6   Developing a Calendar of Activities 454

11.7   Revisiting Your Project Design 455

11.8   Selecting Good Resources 457

11.9   Finding Resources Using the Web 459

11.10   Identifying Resources in Local Stores 460

11.11   Investigating Your Beliefs about Curriculum Integration 468

11.12   Developing Integrated Curriculum 474

12.1   Benefits of Project-Based Science 484

12.2   Your Challenges 491

12.3   Revisiting Initial Ideas in Your Portfolio 496

12.4   Reexamining Your Portfolio 496

Preface

In *Teaching Science in Elementary and Middle School Classrooms: A Project-Based Approach, Second Edition*, we present an approach to teaching science to all children. We believe that all children should develop an in-depth and meaningful understanding of enduring concepts, principles, and themes of science, as well as the processes of doing science. We define understanding as helping students to see relationships among ideas, finding underlying reasons for these relationships, using these ideas to explain and predict phenomena, and applying their understandings to new situations. Such a focus on science learning emphasizes less the coverage of content and more the in-depth exploration of major ideas and explanation. Moreover, we strongly believe that all students should understand how to apply the processes of scientific inquiry. Finally, we firmly believe that all students should have equitable opportunities to learn science. In this text we focus on helping both the novice and experienced teachers learn how to teach science to elementary and middle grades children.

A PROJECT-BASED APPROACH

To accomplish the goal of helping both new and experienced teachers learn how to teach science, we explore an exciting teaching method referred to as project-based science. A central tenet of this approach is that it engages young learners in exploring important and meaningful questions through a process of investigation and collaboration. Project-based science engages children in asking and refining questions; seeking background information; making predictions; designing investigations; collecting, analyzing, and interpreting data; making explanations; and creating products to share ideas. Project-based science stresses that science teaching should emphasize students actively engaging in science rather than teachers giving science information to students. The teaching of science should de-emphasize the simple recall of facts and focus on students using evidence and strategies for developing and revising explanations of phenomena. As a result, students learn fundamental science concepts and principles that they apply to their daily lives. As stated in the *National Science Education Standards,* inquiry should be the preferred mode of instruction at all grade levels and for all students. "Learning science is something students do, not something that is done to them" (NRC, 1996).

THE AUDIENCE

Although intended primarily for university students studying to become elementary and middle grades teachers, this text is also suitable for practicing teachers striving to find new, exciting approaches to science teaching. Throughout this text, we strive to answer important questions about teaching science to children and we included numerous strategies to support students in inquiry learning that will help both new and experienced teachers. We also pay attention to the important role collaboration plays in inquiry and in developing an understanding of science. Although teaching science to elementary and middle grades students is complex, it is also very rewarding.

ORGANIZATION AND COVERAGE

As in the first edition, various chapters in the book focus on helping students learn science through inquiry, as well as providing support in planning and managing science teaching. We present expanded and updated coverage of many important ideas. In Chapter 1, Why and How Should I Teach Science to Children?, we introduce you to project-based science. Chapter 2, How Do Children Construct Understanding in Science?, focuses on factors that influence students' construction of understanding, including prior experiences, social interactions, and teachers. In Chapter 3, What Is a Driving Question?, we examine one of the central features of project-based science because driving questions initiate, implement, and sustain inquiry. Chapter 4, How Are Scientific Investigations Developed?, explores how to support students engaged in investigations to find solutions to questions that are of interest to them. In Chapter 5, How Can Learning Technologies Be Used to Support Investigations?, we examine the theoretical ideas behind the value of using new learning technologies and explore how teachers can use new technology tools to help students investigate questions important to them. Chapter 6, How Do I Develop Collaboration in the Science Classroom?, discusses types of collaboration between students, teachers, and members of the community. In Chapter 7, How Do I Develop and Use Benchmark Lessons?, we focus on methods and procedures a teacher can use to help students learn fundamental science concepts. Chapter 8, Why Do We Assess Students in Science?, discusses the purpose of assess-

ment and what and when we assess. In Chapter 9, How Is Student Understanding Assessed?, we focus on methods of assessment in a project-based environment, ways that project-based science enhances learning and improves students' scores on high-stakes tests, and advantages of assessment. Chapter 10, How Do I Manage the Project-Based Science Classroom?, discusses classroom climate, classroom organization, and management skills. Chapter 11, How Do I Plan a Project-Based Curriculum?, explains ways that teachers can plan projects that meet a school district's curricular objectives and frameworks. In Chapter 12, What Are the Next Steps?, we summarize features of project-based science, and we discuss benefits and challenges associated with a project environment.

NEW IN THE SECOND EDITION

In the Second Edition, we expanded our focus on certain topics of interest, updated the presentation of material, and included a number of features that will enhance using the materials.

- **National Science Education Standards.** Coverage of National Science Education Standards is integrated throughout the text. Marginal links highlight connections between specific content and the national standards.

- **Coverage of Technology.** The coverage of the use of learning technologies has been expanded. New to the text is a chapter on how technology can support students in inquiry (Chapter 5). In addition, each chapter now has a section that discusses the use of learning technologies as related to the chapter's topics.

- **Coverage of Assessment.** The coverage of assessment has been expanded into two chapters. Chapter 8, *Why Do We Assess Students in Science?*, discusses the purpose of assessment and what and when we assess. In Chapter 9, *How Is Student Understanding Assessed?*, we focus on methods of assessment in a project-based environment, ways that project-based science enhances learning and improves students' scores on high-stakes tests, and advantages of assessment.

- **Portfolio Activities.** The Portfolio Activities provide exercises that explore and expand key content in an applied manner, and help the learner make connections between various ideas. They can be used as class activities, assignments, or assessments and may ultimately be added to the reader's portfolio.

- **Pedagogical System.** The text's pedagogical system has been expanded to provide the student with additional support and resources. The pedagogical system includes: **learning performances** at the beginning of each chapter that focus students on what they will learn through reading and engaging in the activities of the chapter; **chapter outlines**; **scenarios** that provide a look into classrooms and children learning science; marginal **links to the National Science Education Standards**; **Portfolio Activities; print forms; key ideas** listed in the margin; marginal **Web links; chapter summary; chapter highlights** link to the **student materials on the Online Learning Center**; and **key terms** with page references.

- **Online Learning Center.** The new Online Learning Center located at **www.mhhe.com/ krajcik2e** presents important content from the chapter, reviews key terms, provides a chapter assessment, and contains each chapter's Web links. Students will find this Online Learning Center a valuable feature as they learn to teach science.

SUPPLEMENTS

- **For the Instructor.** The text is accompanied by an Instructor's Manual that contains teaching and activity ideas, as well as assessment questions. Additional instructor resources are housed in the instructor's section of the Online Learning Center. at **www.mhhe.com/krajcik2e**.

   Within the text, instructors should watch for the marginal Web links and the printable tables and figures. Both of these reference content available on the Online Learning Center.

- **For the Student.** The Online Learning Center at **www.mhhe.com/krajcik2e** provides the student with study tools and resources.

ACKNOWLEDGMENTS

The ideas in the book would not have been possible without the innovative thinking of colleagues at The University of Michigan and The University of Toledo. We owe much of the theoretical work to Phyllis Blumenfeld, Ron Marx, and Elliot Soloway at The University of Michigan. These educational researchers have worked with Joe to help identify, explore, and expand the ideas of project-based learning. Much of their work in developing the ideas of project-based learning was supported by funding from the National Science Foundation. Colleagues at The University of

Toledo, particularly Mark Templin, Janet Struble, and Rebecca Schneider, inspired Charlene's writing and ideas. Colleagues Andrew Lumpe at Southern Illinois University and Jodi Haney and Lena Ballone at Bowling Green State University continue to influence Charlene's work.

We would also like to acknowledge the many teachers who have expanded our ideas on teaching project-based science. Appreciated are the teachers at Greenhills Middle School—Ann Novak and Chris Gleason—who helped expand Joe's views of supporting students in inquiry within and across projects. Some of the ideas presented in this book stem from their teaching. We appreciate Juanita Clay-Chambers, Chief Curriculum Officer for the Detroit Public Schools, who pushes Joe's thinking about teaching in urban settings. We also appreciate teachers Karen Amatia, Deborah Peek-Brown and Alycia Meriweather from Detroit Public Schools, whose practice has enlarged Joe's thinking of using project-based science in urban classrooms. The contributions of Jon Singer and Barb Hug, former post-doctorate fellows at The University of Michigan, helped expand Joe's thinking about designing project-based environments, contextualizing projects, and supporting students in doing inquiry. Finally, we acknowledge the many graduate students who have worked with us and who have expanded our thinking about teaching and learning. In particular we would like to acknowledge former graduate students at The University of Michigan who help move forward the ideas of project-based science; a few of these include Barbara Crawford, Margaret Roy, Michele Wisnudel-Spitulnik, Ann Rivet, and Becky Schneider.

Our thanks are also extended to the following reviewers for their comments on this text:

Michael Svec, *Furman University*

Paul E. Peknik, Jr., *Iona College*

Cathy Dotson, *Tennessee Temple University*

Ken King, *Northern Illinois University*

Dana L. Zeidler, *University of South Florida*

Chris Muire, *Berry College*

Carmen E. Trisler, *Wittenberg University*

Bruno Hicks, *University of Maine at Fort Kent*

Ann Haley Mackenzie, *Miami University of Ohio*

Joseph D. Sharpe, *Tennessee Technological University*

John A. Craven III, *Queens College*

Carole D. Hillman, *Elmhurst College*

Elaine V. Howes, *Teachers College, Columbia University*

Caryn S. Pugliese, *Slippery Rock University*

C. Sheldon Woods, *DePaul University*

Albert Nous, *University of Pittsburgh*

Finally, we would like to thank the many undergraduate and graduate students in elementary and middle grades education at The University of Toledo and The University of Michigan who used the first edition of the book and gave us feedback on how to improve it. These students provided many suggestions for improving ideas in the book, adding features and revising activities. They also conducted their own project-based investigations and helped shape ideas presented in the book. We also want to thank our current editor, Cara Harvey, for encouraging us to complete this work. Finally, we thank our families who encouraged us in this effort by allowing us to spend numerous extra hours on revising this edition of the book when we could have been with them. Thanks go to Joe's family, wife Ann and children Michael, Paul, and Ellen; Charlene's husband David; and Carl's wife Shari.

Joseph S. Krajcik
Charlene M. Czerniak
Carl F. Berger

Teaching Science in Elementary and Middle School Classrooms

A PROJECT-BASED APPROACH

Chapter 1

Why and How Should I Teach Science to Children?

OVERVIEW OF THE BOOK

INTRODUCTION TO THE CHAPTER

AN OVERVIEW OF PROJECT-BASED SCIENCE

WHAT IS SCIENCE?

WHY SHOULD YOUNG LEARNERS STUDY SCIENCE?

GOALS OF SCIENCE EDUCATION

HOW DO THE CURRENT NATIONAL GOALS
    COMPARE WITH PROJECT-BASED SCIENCE?

CHAPTER LEARNING PERFORMANCES

- *Describe the primary features of project-based science.*
- *Compare and contrast project-based science with reading about science, direct instruction, and process science.*
- *Explain how project-based science reflects the nature of science.*
- *Justify why young learners should learn science.*
- *Summarize the primary features of our national science education goals.*
- *Explain the value of using project-based science to meet national goals and standards, particularly goals of encouraging females and minorities in science.*

OVERVIEW OF THE BOOK

When you think about the prospect of teaching science to children, many questions probably come to your mind: *What characterizes science in elementary and middle grades? How should science be taught to young learners? How can I motivate children to become interested in science? How can I help them learn about science in their everyday world?*

One of the primary goals of science education in schools today focuses on helping all children learn about their world. In *Teaching Science in Elementary and Middle School Classrooms: A Project-Based Approach,* we focus on helping you learn how to teach science to elementary-age and middle school–age children.

To accomplish this goal of helping you learn how to teach science, we present an exciting science teaching method that we refer to as **project-based science**. This teaching approach engages all young learners—regardless of culture, race, or gender—in exploring important and meaningful questions through a process of investigation and collaboration. Throughout this dynamic process, students ask questions, make predictions, design investigations, collect and analyze data, make products, and share ideas. As a result, students learn fundamental science concepts and principles that they apply to their daily lives.

The roots of project-based learning are found in the writings of many distinguished educators including John Dewey, Jerome Bruner, and Robert Karplus.[1] Elements of this approach also can be found in other forms of science teaching: inquiry-based learning, which focuses instruction on students using science process skills such as observing and interpreting data; science, technology, society (STS), which focuses instruction on issues related to societal problems; and problem-driven science, which focuses on science issues. Project-based science stands apart from these other forms of science teaching, however, in that it situates the learning of science in questions that children find meaningful. As a result, it shifts the responsibility of learning to the child.

Support for this approach can be found in the works of contemporary educators including Ann Brown and colleagues (1994), Wolff-Michael Roth (1995), Phyllis Blumenfeld and colleagues (1991), and Richard Roup and colleagues (1992). This approach requires dynamic teaching methods that match the guidelines of today's major science education reports including *The National Science Education Standards* (National Research Council, 1996; 2000), *Project 2061: Science for All Americans* (Rutherford & Ahlgren, 1989), *Benchmarks for Science Literacy* (AAAS, 1993), and the National Science Teachers Association recommendations for elementary science (NSTA, 1991). At the end of this chapter, we will discuss more thoroughly how project-based science works with these national efforts.

Although it has a solid foundation in educational theory, project-based science represents a fundamental shift in how to teach science in most classrooms today. While it is already being used successfully in many schools, you may find this kind of science instruction quite different from what you have experienced in the past. Learning to teach in a way that is different from what you have experienced can be very difficult. As you

---

> ## Key Idea
>
> Project-based science stands apart from these other forms of science teaching because it situates the learning of science in questions that children find meaningful and relevant to their lives.

---

[1] John Dewey was the founder of the progressive education movement that encouraged students to be active learners. In the 1930s, the Lincoln School of Teachers College and other schools used real situations to help students ground their learning. Jerome Bruner, an education theorist, helped establish curriculum reform during the 1960s. His book *Toward a Theory of Instruction* set the stage for much of the modern direction of curricula today. Robert Karplus was a physicist who co-founded The Science Curriculum Improvement Study, a pioneer elementary science program of the 1960s. The program exists today in a third incarnation of the "hands-on, minds-on" movement of that era. We discuss the influence of these individuals in more detail in Chapter 2.

work through this book, most likely you will be changing the way you think about science and science teaching. More importantly, you'll be changing the way you help students learn science. We will assist you with these changes by providing strategies for helping children engage in inquiry that involves important and worthwhile questions.

Although this book does not provide teaching activities to help you learn science content, content understanding is critical to effective science teaching. When appropriate throughout the chapters, we will refer to other references that cover science content or children's science activities.

Chapter 1—"Why and How Should I Teach Science to Children?"—introduces you to project-based science. It also answers the question "What is science?" and discusses why it is important for young children to learn fundamental concepts and principles as well as processes of science. This chapter also presents important information about current national goals in science education and illustrates how project-based science matches these initiatives.

Chapter 2—"How Do Children Construct Understanding in Science?"—focuses on the characteristics of children and the connection of these characteristics with learning science. It pays close attention to factors that influence students' construction of understanding, including prior experiences, social interactions, and teachers.

Driving questions initiate, implement, and sustain inquiry and are thus central to project-based science. Chapter 3—"What Is a Driving Question?"—explores characteristics and issues of driving questions. It provides answers to the questions "What are driving questions?" "Where do they come from?" and "What makes a good driving question?"

Investigation is an essential element of project-based science. Chapter 4—"How Are Scientific Investigations Developed?"—explores how to help students engage in investigations and find solutions to questions that are of interest to them. It examines the various components of investigations, such as asking and refining questions, designing experiments, analyzing data, and presenting findings. It also discusses ways that a teacher can support inquiry and overcome the challenges of implementing investigations.

New technology tools can enhance learning. Chapter 5—"How Can Learning Technologies Be Used to Support Investigations?"—examines the value of using new learning technologies and explores how teachers can use new technology tools to help students investigate questions important to them.

Collaboration in science teaching is frequently much more effective than individual learning. Chapter 6—"How Do I Develop Collaboration in the Science Classroom?"—discusses types of collaboration among students, teachers, and members of the community. It presents ways that a teacher can create a collaborative environment, build the social skills students need to sustain collaboration, hold students accountable during collaboration, and overcome challenges that might arise while implementing collaborative groups.

Chapter 7—"How Do I Develop and Use Benchmark Lessons?"—focuses on methods and procedures to help students learn fundamental science concepts. Benchmark lessons are teacher-directed classroom activities that help students develop understandings essential to project work. Topics covered include questioning strategies, instructional strategies (such as demonstrations and discrepant events), activities, and concept mapping.

Assessing students' understanding lies at the center of the educational process. Chapter 8—"Why Do We Assess Students in Science?"—discusses the purpose of assessment in a science classroom. The chapter also describes characteristics of assessment. We explain what to assess and when to assess. Finally, the chapter presents ideas for using technology tools to examine assessment.

Many teachers today face the realities of high-stakes assessments. Chapter 9—"How Is Student Understanding Assessed?"—focuses on the process of assessment and presents numerous ideas about how to assess students' understanding and skills. Finally, it discusses advantages for teachers, students, and parents in using various assessment strategies.

Managing an elementary or middle grade classroom presents challenges for many teachers, especially new teachers. Chapter 10—"How Do I Manage the Project-Based Science Classroom?"—discusses classroom climate, classroom organization, and management skills. It presents many practical strategies that teachers can use to manage students successfully as they engage in science learning.

Chapter 11—"How Do I Plan a Project-Based Curriculum?"—explains ways that teachers can plan projects that meet school districts' curricular objectives and frameworks. It also shows how existing curriculum materials can be modified to fit in a project environment. Attention is given to integrating science across the curriculum. Finally, the chapter discusses how teachers can find and manage resources.

Finally, Chapter 12—"What Are the Next Steps?"—summarizes features of project-based science and discusses the benefits and challenges of a project environment. The book concludes with a reflection on the principles and ideas explored throughout this book.

Each of these chapters includes portfolio activities to help you engage in learning this exciting way to teach science. First, each chapter starts with several scenarios that are designed to help you envision various classroom scenes. Throughout the text, questions encourage you to stop and think about ideas. Other questions ask you to think about your own experiences as a student to help you construct an understanding of how to teach science. There are activities throughout each chapter that are designed to help you construct meaning from what you're reading. When you complete these activities, you will have portfolio products (or artifacts). You will look more closely at artifacts in Chapters 8 and 9, which concern assessment, and you will re-examine these artifacts in Chapter 12. The book also contains links to Internet sites through the Online Learning Center.

Throughout the book, we discuss how technology can be used to teach science. For example, Chapter 5 discusses how technology enhances learning. Chapter 6 explores how technology can be used to enhance collaboration among members of a community.

INTRODUCTION TO THE CHAPTER

In this chapter, we introduce you to project-based science teaching. Later, we answer the question "What is science?" We explore why young children need to learn science, and we review the goals of science education. Finally, we discuss how project-based science matches today's science education goals.

First, however, to challenge your thinking about science and science teaching, we start this chapter by encouraging you to reflect on your own past experiences as a student of science. This reflection will help you examine your personal views of science teaching and learning. In Portfolio Activity 1.1, you begin the portfolio that you will use throughout this book. Take time now to complete Portfolio Activity 1.1.

As you reflected on your own experiences in Portfolio Activity 1.1, you may have found that you did not have many memories of learning science or that you had good memories of science class. Maybe you did hands-on activities. Perhaps your teacher exhibited excitement about teaching science. By studying science, you may have learned about important questions related to your world. However, your memories may not have

Portfolio Activity 1.1

WHAT ARE YOUR ELEMENTARY AND MIDDLE SCHOOL SCIENCE EXPERIENCES?

Materials Needed:
- Something to write with
- A folder or binder to start a portfolio

A. Think back to your elementary and middle school days. Do you recall your teachers teaching science? What do you remember about learning science in early elementary grades? Middle grades? What kinds of topics did your teachers cover? How did they teach science? Did you take field trips to planetariums, zoos, or science museums? Did you conduct "experiments"? Were you required to complete a science fair project? Take notes in your portfolio about what you remember.

B. What science learning experiences are most vivid in your mind? Do you remember stories such as about Newton "discovering" gravity when an apple fell on his head? Write a short paragraph in your portfolio about your most vivid memories of science learning experiences.

been positive ones; science may have been presented as dull, boring, or difficult to learn. Perhaps your out-of-school memories about science learning, such as that second-grade field trip to the zoo, were the strongest and most positive. The literature shows that many of us did not experience learning science in a dynamic and active manner that included asking questions, collaborating with others to find solutions, and designing investigations (NRC, 1996; Stake & Easley, 1978). As a result, many of us don't have good models of teaching science to use in our own classrooms.

Let's examine several models of science teaching. As you read these scenarios, contrast them with your memories of elementary and middle school science.

Scenario 1: Reading About Science

Maybe your class was like this: Mrs. Patterson[2] said, "Okay, boys and girls, let's turn to page thirty-seven in the science book. Don't forget to write down the bold print science words for your spelling list for the quiz on Friday. Al, would you please read the first paragraph?"

Al sat in the middle of the classroom. You all had figured out the order of reading and who would read next, and you sighed a little relief as you counted the paragraphs and found that yours was beyond the last page of assigned text. At the end of each paragraph, Mrs. Patterson wrote new words on the board. If it was after Wednesday, they would be on next week's spelling list. After looking at the colored pictures in the book and day-dreaming a little, you heard Mrs. Patterson say, "Now turn to page forty-one and answer the first four questions. Make sure to use complete sentences and check your spelling."

Sound familiar? We call this *read about science,* an expression we will sometimes use in upcoming chapters. In classes in which students only read about science, teachers often focus primarily on vocabulary words and facts in the textbook. Although reading about science is one important strategy for learning, it is too often a passive activity as illustrated in this scenario.

[2]All scenarios and names of people in scenarios throughout this book are fictitious. Any similarity to actual teachers, students, or schools is coincidental.

Scenario 2: Direct Instruction

Perhaps your class was like this: Mr. Velasquez stood in front of your class by the hot plate he kept near his desk. Normally, he had his coffee on the plate, but today there was a soda can resting on it. Mr. Velasquez said, "This soda can was empty, but I rinsed it out; and I added about 2 centimeters of water to it. You can see the steam coming out of the top of the can, and some of you can hear the water boiling on the inside. I'm going to take the can off the hot plate with these hot pads and quickly turn it over into this icy pan of water. I want you to watch what happens and try to figure out what is going on." You thought it might explode; after all, it was boiling inside and very hot. As you watched, Mr. Velasquez set the can in the icy water. Almost instantly the sides of the can crumpled inward as though it had been crushed by a giant force. "Well, what do you think?" he asked. As usual, Bobby Wilson's hand shot up. "Yes," said Mr. Velasquez. He didn't wait for anybody else to think. You had some ideas but they had not quite formed in your mind. Bobby Wilson blurted out, "It's the suction; when the can cools down, something on the inside is sucking the can in!" "Well," said Mr. Velasquez, "it does have to do with the can cooling, but you see, as the can cools, the steam turns back to water and that takes up less space. Actually, it is the air on the outside of the can that is pressing in. It is the air pressure that does it." To this day, you remember this dramatic demonstration.

We call this kind of teaching *direct instruction*. It occurs when a teacher provides the direct answers, sometimes after a demonstration. Although demonstrations can be powerful benchmark lessons, in this scenario the teacher merely told the students what they had seen. Students were expected to understand the concept told to them simply because they had witnessed the demonstration.

Scenario 3: Process Science Teaching

Maybe your class was like this: Mr. Haddad said, "Today we're going to find out how high a ball bounces when it is dropped and if the kind of ball makes a difference. This is part of the science process of prediction, and you will be graphing your results. Each pair of you has a ball with a letter on it, a meter stick, and a sheet of graph paper. First, drop the ball from a height of 100 centimeters onto the floor and record the height of the bounce. After you have done this four times, drop it from a different height four times and record your results. Then answer the questions on the board."

You looked up at the board and the questions were as follows:

1. Did the ball bounce back to the same height for each height it was dropped?
2. Graph the height of the bounce on the Y axis and the height from which it was dropped on the X axis. What is the pattern?
3. What would the graph look like if you dropped the ball onto a carpeted floor?

You and your partner didn't quite understand Mr. Haddad's questions, but you had a meter stick and a rubber ball so there would be a lot of things you could try. Anyway, if it got too bad, Mr. Haddad would come around and show you what to do. Graphing always presented two difficulties. One, the last point you would try to plot would always fall just outside the edge of the graph paper and, two, you would always do the whole thing in ink and then, when you'd make a mistake, you'd have to start all over. By the time you finished graphing the data, you had forgotten what you were supposed to find out. Oh well, science was fun and you did some interesting activities.

This kind of science teaching we label *process science teaching*. The primary purpose of the lesson is for students to use science process skills such as observing, predicting, and graphing. Process science lessons can be used as benchmark lessons, but processes should not be presented as separate stand-alone lessons. Rather, processes need to be connected with important concepts. For example, in the lesson described, the processes could have been connected to learning about forces and motion. Then, students would have understood why they were doing the activity.

Scenario 4: Project-Based Science

Maybe your class was like this: You and a couple of friends were looking at the pet rabbit in the cage in your classroom. Normally, the rabbit was eager to eat the carrots you gave him. "Maybe he's sick," you thought. You and your friends *questioned* why the rabbit wasn't eating. With your teacher's encouragement, you and classmates formed teams to *investigate* the sudden change. You had other pets in your classroom (including hamsters, gerbils, a snake, and fish), and your teacher encouraged you to investigate the question "What do pets need to stay healthy?"

Each day, *teams of students* from your class visited one of the classroom pets and provided it with several different foods. You gave the rabbit foods such as carrots, celery, oats, alfalfa, and rabbit pellets purchased from the pet food store. Some teams used computer *technology* to obtain information from the World Wide Web about the needs of various pets. When you heard that one of the members of another team had called the local pet store, and the manager was interested in your class investigation and would come to talk about the needs of pets, you were surprised that members of the *community* would *collaborate* with you in your investigation. You knew you had to come up with some great questions.

After *several weeks* of investigating what pets need to stay healthy, you and your classmates *shared results* in graphic form. A couple of teams included photographs of animals and models of healthy environments in their presentations. You found that different pets need different habitats, special kinds of food, a clean environment, and veterinary care to fight against diseases or infections. In fact, you were able to change a few things in the rabbit's diet to entice him to eat. You still had a question about the needs of your pet iguana at home, but you knew that the classroom rabbit was happy and healthy.

This last scenario is an example of what we call *project-based science*. The primary purpose of the project was for students to collaborate for a substantial length of time in the investigation of an important question that was interesting to them. In the process, students learned science concepts, used technology, and developed products. Take time to complete Portfolio Activity 1.2 now.

Portfolio Activity 1.2

WHAT ARE THE CHARACTERISTICS AND CHALLENGES OF EACH OF THE SCENARIOS?

Materials Needed:
- Something to write with

A. Respond in your portfolio to the following questions about each scenario:

   1. What are the characteristics of the scenario?

   2. What are students doing to help them learn science?

   3. What is the teacher doing to help students learn science?

4. Who is responsible for the learning?

5. How would the teacher evaluate what the students learned?

B. What are the challenges you see in teaching science in each of the scenarios? List them in your portfolio.

C. In your portfolio, write about which scenario seems to provide the most meaningful science experiences for elementary students. What about for middle grade students? Why?

The scenarios you just read are, in some respects, stereotyped. Although we will reflect throughout this book on the science teaching techniques illustrated by these scenarios, you shouldn't completely dismiss any one kind of science teaching based solely on these scenarios. There is no one best way to teach, but there are ways that can produce more student understanding and better motivation and do more to develop lifelong interest in science. Some of the techniques just described are appropriate for benchmark lessons, lessons that teach basic skills or concepts. (To learn more about benchmark lessons, see Chapter 7.) Although project-based science is, for many reasons that will be elaborated on throughout this book, the most effective overall approach to teaching science, you will find times when teacher-directed activities are not only acceptable but preferred. Imagine that, as part of answering a question about water pressure in the school's drinking fountains, you have students investigate how powerful the air pressure is in the water lines. For safety purposes, you wouldn't want an elementary student boiling water in a soda can to demonstrate how air pressure can crush the can. Instead, you might decide to demonstrate the activity yourself so that students could develop an understanding of air pressure and apply it to their investigation of pressure in the water pipes. Demonstrations such as this serve as benchmark lessons that provide important information needed by students.

As you thought about your own science learning experiences, you may have found that you had more than one kind of experience. Indeed, science teaching has gone through several revolutions or evolutions in the last thirty years. So, amid all this change, why has project-based science emerged as such an important way to teach science? In the next section, you'll explore the features of this approach and learn why it is so important.

AN OVERVIEW OF PROJECT-BASED SCIENCE

Project-based science can be used to answer students' and teachers' questions about the world around them. Investigating real-world questions that students find meaningful has long been touted as a viable learning structure; the roots of the idea go back to John Dewey, who is often described as the father of progressive education. Dewey promoted teaching strategies that helped students actively engage in learning about topics relevant to their lives. Because it focuses on students and their interests, project-based science is sensitive to the varied needs of diverse students with respect to culture, race, and gender (Haberman, 1991; Haberman, 1995; Atwater, 1994). Haberman (1995), in describing exemplary or "star" teachers who are successful in teaching children in poverty from diverse cultural backgrounds, states, "Stars do not use direct instruction as their primary method. . . . Stars use some variation of the project method" (p. 13). He adds, "Star teachers find projects that interest children. They then plan with children how they will set about studying the topics. Usually the projects are built around a set of questions or problems that are of vital interest to the children" (p. 34).

Project-based science has several fundamental features. The fourth scenario reflects some of these features, which we will discuss thoroughly throughout the book. However, to provide you with an initial framework, let's examine some of them briefly now. First, driving questions or problems serve to organize and guide instructional tasks and activities. Second, students engage in investigations to answer their questions. Third, communities of students, teachers, and members of society collaborate on the question or problem. Fourth, students use learning technologies to investigate, develop artifacts or products, collaborate, and access information. The result is a series of artifacts or products that address the question or problem.

> **Key Idea**
>
> In project-based science, driving questions serve to organize and guide instructional activities in which students collaborate and use new learning technologies to (1) engage in investigations to answer questions and (2) develop and present artifacts that address the questions.

Driving Questions

Science classes should have children explore solutions to questions (NRC, 1996; 2000). Project-based science calls for a question or problem that is meaningful and important to learners (Blumenfeld et al., 1991; Krajcik et al., 1993). We refer to such a question as a **driving question.** An example is "What is the pH of rainwater in our city?" The driving question is the first step in meeting all of the other key components of project-based science. It sets the stage for planning and carrying out investigations to measure the acidity of rainwater and test the impact acid rain has on living and nonliving things. Once the stage has been set, students might use technology to investigate the question. For example, they might use electronic pH meters and find information on the World Wide Web about acids and bases. As students collaboratively pursue solutions to the driving question, they develop meaningful understanding of key scientific concepts such as acids and bases, pH, and concentration. Hence, instruction is anchored in real-world situations that students find meaningful and from which questions emerge, and it leads to students developing deep understandings. Finally, students can develop concrete representations, such as posters, of the results of their investigations of the driving question. Creating these representations solidifies students' learning.

> **NSES**
>
> **CONNECTING TO**
> **NATIONAL SCIENCE EDUCATION STANDARDS**
>
> **Science Teaching Standards**
> Teachers select science content and adapt and design curricula to meet the interests, knowledge, understanding, abilities, and experiences of students (p. 30).

The source of the questions being asked and investigated distinguishes project-based science from other methods of teaching science. In the fourth scenario, how did the question about the health needs of pets emerge? Often, but not always, the question comes from the student. Sometimes it is possible to set up a learning situation that will lead to a natural question from the students. In one science curriculum, for example, second and third grade students set up a series of aquariums with clear plastic shoe boxes, water, sand, fish, and water plants but no water pumps or filters. As you can imagine, a layer of "black stuff" appears on the bottom of the aquariums in a week or so, and always one or more students asks, "Where does the black stuff on the sand come from?" The teacher can then build with the children a clear set of investigations/experiences to find the answers to this question.

In other situations, teachers may have to present the driving question themselves, but they do so in a real world context, one with which the students can identify and about which they can ask **subquestions**. For instance, if a teacher starts a project with the question "Is our water safe?" students have the potential to ask a number of subquestions such as "Is our water safe to swim in?" "Is our water safe to drink?" and "What can live in our water?" Another example comes from consumer products. For instance, the teacher might set up this question for the class, "Are our products environmentally friendly?" Students' subquestions might include "Is my ink pen environmentally friendly?" "Are my batteries environmentally friendly?" and "Is my chewing gum environmentally friendly?"

All driving questions should be meaningful and important to students. We will discuss the features and benefits of driving questions more thoroughly in Chapter 3.

CONNECTING TO
NATIONAL SCIENCE EDUCATION STANDARDS

Science Teaching Standards
Inquiry into authentic questions generated from student experiences is the central strategy for teaching science (p. 31).

Key Idea

A driving question is meaningful and relevant to students.

Students Engaged in Investigations

Sustained **inquiry** based on important and meaningful questions forms one of the hallmarks of science. In project-based science, students investigate a question over a long period of time rather than engage in short-term activities or **investigations** that are out of the context of real life. Questions such as "What do pets need to stay healthy?" and "Where did the black stuff come from in the bottom of the aquarium?" can provide the basis for long-term investigation. These investigations are meaningful to students and therefore keep the students' attention for long periods of time—sometimes over the course of the entire school year.

Key Idea

In project-based science, students become members of a community collaborating to investigate questions.

Communities of Learners Collaborating Together

As we will discuss in Chapter 2, learning occurs in a social context. Project-based science involves students, teachers, and members of society collaborating to investigate questions. In Chapter 6, we discuss in detail how teachers can develop and implement **collaboration** in the classroom. In this manner, the classroom becomes a community of learners. Students collaborate with others in their classroom and with their teacher to form conclusions, make sense of information, and present findings. The use of telecommunication technology allows students access to a wider community in which they can communicate with knowledgeable individuals, take advantage of more extensive resources, communicate with other students in different parts of the world, and share data with other student scientists and professional scientists.

For instance, students investigating the black stuff in the bottom of the aquarium might interview a local pet store owner. Students investigating the needs of pets might collaborate with experts from a local pet store or veterinary hospital to find answers to their problem. In each situation, students can use the World Wide Web to obtain additional information, and they can use electronic communications to describe their projects to others.

CONNECTING TO
NATIONAL SCIENCE EDUCATION STANDARDS

Science Teaching Standards
Teachers of science guide and facilitate learning. In doing this, teachers orchestrate discourse among students about scientific ideas (p. 32).

USING TECHNOLOGY TOOLS TO LEARN SCIENCE

Technology tools can help transform the science classroom into an environment in which learners actively construct knowledge (Tinker & Papert, 1989; Linn, 1997; White & Fredrickson, 1995). We refer to technology tools that can support students in learning as **learning technologies.**

Using technology tools in project-based science makes the environment more authentic to students. The students can use the computer to access *real* data on the Internet, expand interaction and collaboration with others via networks (such as e-mail), use tools to gather data (such as light and motion probes that are plugged into computer ports), employ graphing and visualization tools to analyze data, and produce multimedia artifacts. In addition, the multimodal and multimedia capabilities of technology make information more accessible, not only physically (by providing easy access to information) but intellectually (by helping students incorporate new information into their understanding) as well (Blumenfeld et al., 1991).

> **Key Idea**
>
> Technology tools can help students carry out investigations and construct understanding.

For example, students actively "construct" knowledge when they use technology such as a computer-based temperature probe to gather data about the temperature of the aquarium with the black stuff at the bottom. Real-time graphing (simultaneous graphing with the temperature probe) makes information intellectually accessible because it allows students to make immediate interpretations of their data. Another example involves the study of weather. Students can study how temperature fluctuates during the day and night by taking continuous temperature readings with an electronic temperature probe. They can download satellite weather maps from the World Wide Web and then predict the weather just as meteorologists do. In these ways, technology makes weather information physically accessible. When children use simple draw programs to create pictures to represent their ideas, technology has helped make their ideas intellectually accessible. By sharing data with others, learners make their information physically accessible to others.

Technology should be used as a tool to support science teaching. Chapter 5 explores how learning technologies support investigations, and we have integrated discussion of its importance throughout all of the chapters of this book.

Creation of Artifacts

Because **artifacts** show what students have learned, they can be used as forms of assessment of students' understanding of science (Marx, Blumenfeld, Krajcik, & Soloway, 1997). Project-based science results in a series of artifacts, or products, that address the driving question and show what children have learned. Often, teachers have students share their artifacts with other class members and with teachers, parents, and members of the community.

The creation and sharing of artifacts serves several purposes. First, artifacts are real and motivating. For example, making a display of appropriate habitats for classroom pets is more enjoyable and, therefore, more motivating than taking a test about animal habitats. The creation and sharing of artifacts also more closely approximates the activities of "real" science. Scientists frequently expose their ideas to public scrutiny through the processes of publishing and presenting their work at conferences. Presenting an artifact to an audience of peers, professionals, and community members provides an outcome for the investigation and gives students an opportunity to talk with others about their work.

Second, artifacts help students develop and represent understanding. Because artifacts (such as physical models, reports, videotapes, and computer programs) are concrete and explicit, they can be shared and critiqued. Such feedback permits learners to reflect, extend their understanding, and revise their artifacts.

Third, artifacts allow students to show what they have learned throughout an investigation, and they document broad learning—sometimes over an entire school year. Because artifacts show learning over time, they track how student understanding develops. For these reasons, artifacts are excellent forms of assessment.

While studying the question "What kind of insects live on our playground?" students could construct maps of where on the playground they found various insects. Students could then compare their maps with the maps of other students in the class (making the investigation real and motivating). By comparing and contrasting their maps, students might construct new knowledge. They might discover that the playground provides several different types of habitats for insects (sandy area, grassy area, wooded area) and that different insects live in different habitats. Finally, students in the class could study these habitats throughout the school year to document changes in insect populations during different seasons, thereby providing a measure of learning over time. We discuss artifacts more thoroughly in Chapters 8 and 9.

WHAT IS SCIENCE?

What do you think **science** is all about? Don't be surprised if you have difficulty answering this question. It is never easy to explain what science is. However, to teach science to children, it is important to develop some understanding of this question. More thorough descriptions of science can be found in the works of Kuhn (1962) and Phillips (1987), but we will spend some time exploring the question "What is science?" here.

Theories

Humans created science to predict, explain, and understand events and phenomena in the natural world. These predictions and explanations are dependent upon the ideas or, more formally, the theories that scientists have developed that are consistent with observations.

Portfolio Activity 1.3   WHERE'S THE OTHER FILM CANISTER?

Materials Needed:

- An assortment of 35 mm film canisters
- A variety of small objects that can be placed inside 35 mm film canisters (there must be two of each item; for example, two paper clips or two marbles)
- Duct tape or packing tape

A. In this activity, each team of students should get a 35 mm film canister and objects to place inside it. Each team should have the same assortment of small objects. The team should place one, two, or three objects but only one of each type of item in its canister and then seal it with duct tape or packing tape.

B. Each team's task is to find a film canister from another team that, when shaken, makes sounds similar to its own canister. NOTE: This can become challenging if teams put more than one small object in each canister.

C. Try to construct a model about what is in each of the other teams' canisters by using an empty film canister and shaking it with the different objects inside to test the theory.

D. What are the various activities or processes that you went through to develop a theory of what is in the film canister? Without opening the cans and looking inside, how sure can you be that your theory is correct?

E. How does this activity resemble the construction of scientific theories to explain real-world phenomena? How do the methods you used resemble the scientific methods you use in your daily life?

Theories represent detailed explanations of how the world works. For instance, the theory of plate tectonics gives us a detailed explanation of the origin of the continents. The fact that this theory has also helped us explain other related phenomena like earthquakes and volcanic activity enhances its strength.

Theories provide predictive and explanatory power, but when theories can no longer explain and make predictions, humans create new theories to replace the old ones. The new theory explains everything the old theory does but also accounts for observations that the old theories could not explain. For instance, chemists once thought that atoms were small indivisible spheres. However, this model of the atom could not explain all observable data related to how atoms behaved nor could it help us explain how various atoms reacted with different atoms. Chemists replaced the indivisible atom with an atom that had various components. Theory construction and the replacement of old theories with new ones also illustrate the tentative nature and the dynamic, recursive process of science. Portfolio Activity 1.3 helps illustrate this point.

In Portfolio Activity 1.3, your theories helped you explain what objects you thought were in the film canisters. Theories influence how we see and interpret (or make sense of) data and the world around us. To understand how our world views influence what we see and how we interpret data, let's examine a theory that influenced interpretations for many years. In 1817, William Bucklund found a giant pointed tooth that resembled the

NSES

**CONNECTING TO
NATIONAL SCIENCE EDUCATION STANDARDS**

Principles and Definitions
The goal of science is to understand the natural world (p. 24).

smaller tooth of a modern-day lizard. He built a theory that the tooth came from a giant lizard. Later, other researchers found giant teeth that were flat. In 1841, Richard Owen put together a theory that the pointed and flat teeth came from giant animals that were extinct, and he named these extinct animals *dinosaurs,* which means "terrible lizards." Because theories shape the way we see the world, for many years scientists believed dinosaurs were giant lizards or cold-blooded reptiles. Scientists believed that dinosaurs buried their eggs and left them to hatch much like many reptiles today lay eggs in the sand and leave them to hatch. Recently, Bob Bakker, a paleontologist, developed a theory that dinosaurs, because of their large rib cages and huge chest area, had very large hearts—and most modern animals with large hearts are warm blooded. Further, he suggested that the large hip sockets and thighs were characteristic of fast-moving animals and similar to the hips and thighs of modern chickens or turkeys. Jack Horner, another paleontologist, found evidence that dinosaurs did not lay eggs and leave them to hatch like reptiles. Instead, they tended to their eggs and reared their young in families (Czerniak, 1995a; Czerniak, 1995b). As you can see, as humans gained more evidence about dinosaurs, our theories changed. Our current theories about dinosaurs are also tentative, and it is quite likely that these too will change some day.

Based on questions that scientists ask about real world problems, they form hypotheses (best guesses). Scientists test these **hypotheses** by collecting data, analyzing data, making conclusions, and communicating findings because to be classified as scientific, the observations, measurements, and conclusions made by one group of scientists must be verified by others.

The understanding that results from science is tentative and changes with new observations, and it is dependent upon the agreement of other scientists. Science allows us to revise ideas, gather more data, or change predictions and test again. In this sense, science is a dynamic, recursive process that results in tentative findings that help explain the way the world works.

In project-based science classrooms, students find solutions to questions by messing about with ideas, asking and refining other questions, finding information, planning and designing, building apparatus, collecting data, analyzing data, making conclusions, and communicating findings. We refer to the process of carrying out an investigation as the *investigation web.* We will discuss this process more thoroughly in Chapter 4, but to briefly illustrate how students investigate questions let's look at how they might find answers to the question "Where does the black stuff on the sand come from?" Students might refine this question by asking additional questions such as "Did the fish leave the black stuff?" "Is the black stuff alive?" "Does it grow?" "Did the black stuff grow because the aquarium was in the sun near the window?" and "Would we still have the black stuff if we added a filter to the aquarium?" Students can look for and find information about aquarium maintenance in books and magazines in the school library, on the World Wide Web, or in pet stores. One group of students might decide to test the idea of whether the black stuff is caused by placing the aquarium in the sun. They might set up several different aquariums in different locations in the room, collect data about the growth of the black stuff, analyze the data, and make a conclusion. These students might communicate their findings by creating a newsletter that tells owners of aquariums what to do to limit the growth of the black stuff in the bottom of their aquariums.

Scientific Process

The process of science involves asking and refining questions, finding information, planning and designing, building the apparatus and collecting data, analyzing data, making conclusions, finding solutions, and communicating findings. In some respects, we employ scientific processes in our daily lives. Trying a variation of a recipe, for example, is an experiment. We might change the ratio of whole wheat to white flour to experiment with making the bread heavier. We might add more sugar to make it sweeter, or we might add more yeast to make if fluffier.

CONNECTING TO
NATIONAL SCIENCE EDUCATION STANDARDS

Principles and Definitions
Inquiry is a multifaceted activity that involves making observations; posing questions; examining books and other sources of information to see what is already known; planning investigations; reviewing what is already known in light of experimental evidence; using tools to gather, analyze, and interpret data; proposing answers, explanations, and predictions; and communicating the results (p. 23).

How many times have we groaned at the results when we realized we changed two or more ingredients (variables) at the same time and couldn't figure out which one (or ones) caused the different results, either bad or good? Inevitably, the confounding results taught us to be more careful and use more scientific ways of testing the recipe so that it could be replicated the next time we made bread. In Chapter 4—"How Are Scientific Investigation Developed?"—we will further explore the process of science.

The Nature of Science in Project-Based Science Teaching

Why have we introduced these ideas about the **nature of science?** Like scientists, students in science classes ask questions and try to find answers that will help them explain their world. Students use investigative processes just as scientists do. Students create artifacts and share these with members of a learning community; likewise, scientists share their research findings with others. Students and scientists alike generate new ideas and questions as a result of their investigations and communication with others. Finally, students develop creativity, open-mindedness, and imagination, qualities essential for successful scientists. Project-based science is a teaching approach that develops learning environments that reflect the nature of science.

WHY SHOULD YOUNG LEARNERS STUDY SCIENCE?

As we watch children play, we realize that they are imaginative tool designers and theory builders. For example, children turn cardboard boxes into space ships or sets of kitchen utensils into medical equipment as they play. Just like scientists construct theories, children construct their view of reality. For example, a child watching a tree's leaves blowing in the wind might construct his or her own belief that trees make wind. Although this is not a scientifically accepted explanation of the phenomenon, the process used to generate the theory is not that far from the processes used by scientists.

Students collect data to help answer questions important to them.

Helping young children learn science can be one of the most enjoyable experiences in teaching. Watching them develop skills and learn concepts and facilitating that development and learning can be empowering experiences. Students have a natural inquisitiveness that generates many questions such as "Why do pumpkins decompose?" "What happens to all the garbage?" "How does my electrical train work?" and "Why does Ming Na run faster than Caitlin?" This is what project-based science is all about—helping students investigate answers to questions like these.

Science is in every elementary and middle school curriculum, and over the last several decades much more attention has been given to elementary and middle level science education. People have written position statements,[3] developed state models or frameworks for science, created new science curriculum materials, and, in many states, written science proficiency tests that are taken as early as the first grade. Science teaching also receives a great deal of attention in the national media. For example, it is not uncommon to read about how this generation's science achievement compares with that of a previous generation or with those of other international countries. The media continually review and examine state proficiency scores and goals for science education. Why has the teaching of science in elementary and middle schools received such substantial attention? Why is it important for children to learn science? In Portfolio Activity 1.4, you will think about this question.

Like you, a child may awake to the sound of an alarm clock. The clock is operated by electricity, and the sound reaches her ears through vibrating air molecules. She showers using water heated by gas and uses soap and shampoo, which are chemicals. She eats cereal or bread that is processed from plants, fortified with vitamins, packaged with technology, and delivered to stores through other technology. Her clothes are made from cotton (a plant) and acrylic (a synthetic fabric). The morning newspaper she reads is made from trees. Headphones bring radio waves to her ears. The music is created by vibrations. Her school bus runs on gasoline burned in a combustion engine. The brakes on the school bus cause it to stop through friction. At school, the child uses computers, and CD-ROMs, and at home she plays with computer toys, she watches videos, and she listens to CDs—all inventions and technology that resulted from basic scientific discoveries about electricity, light, and magnetism. Her day, like yours, contains hundreds of events that are related to science. Each of these situations gives rise to questions that students could ask and investigate: "What chemicals are in our homes?" "What kinds of foods promote better health?" "How does technology improve our lives?"

Because science clearly affects every aspect of our lives, we need a basic understanding of science in order to understand our lives and explain the world. There are also many other reasons for students to learn science. It helps them acquire knowledge and skills that will be useful throughout their lives; it teaches them to think critically, solve

Key Idea

Science study helps students acquire knowledge and skills that will be useful throughout their lives; it develops positive attitudes that foster taking responsibility for one's actions; and it guides students in understanding real life issues.

[3]For example, The National Science Teachers Association 1991 *Position Statement* stresses that science instruction should be a regular part of the school day.

Portfolio Activity 1.4   **WHY SHOULD CHILDREN LEARN SCIENCE?**

Materials Needed:
- A sheet of paper
- Something to write with

A. On a sheet of paper, make three columns. Label the first column "Things I Did Today," label the second column "Related Science Concept," and label the third column "Related Questions." Take about five minutes to reconstruct what you did since you got up this morning. List as many things as you can remember in the first column.

B. In the second column, identify as many related science concepts as you can. For example, you may have used

a curling iron and hair spray to style your hair. The curling iron is heated with electricity, and the hair spray is a chemical, so the related concepts are electricity and chemistry.

C. In the third column, write down related questions for each situation, such as "How can I make hair spray work better?" and "Where does electricity come from?"

D. Reflect upon the list you have constructed. How does it help answer the question "Why should children learn science?" Record your thoughts and your lists in your portfolio.

problems, and make decisions that can improve the quality of their lives; it develops attitudes, such as curiosity or sensitivity to environmental concerns, that foster taking responsibility for one's actions; and it guides students in understanding real life issues and participating in a global society—the hallmark of scientifically literate citizens. Finally, some students will be encouraged by their studies in the elementary and middle level to pursue science studies in high school grades, when the study of science is often optional, and in postsecondary education.

Science Affects Every Aspect of Our Lives

As you saw in Portfolio Activity 1.4, science (or technology that results from the efforts of science) affects every aspect of our lives in the workplace, at home, at school, in transportation, and in entertainment. Young children are especially curious and interested in understanding phenomena in their lives. They ask a lot of "Why?" and "What if?" questions. Much of what they are curious about is related to science.

Students Acquire Useful Knowledge, Skills, and Attitudes

By studying science, children acquire knowledge, skills, and attitudes that will be useful to them throughout their lives as they engage in such activities as choosing lifestyle habits related to food and exercise, conducting everyday activities that affect the environment, making informed voting decisions, and solving everyday problems. For example, knowledge about the systems of the human body and nutrition provides the basis for making informed decisions about the food one eats. Skills such as comparing and contrasting are involved in selecting one food over another. Attitudes, such as curiosity, lead one to seek more information about nutrition and exercise in journals or on the World Wide Web.

Science Teaches Critical Thinking, Problem Solving, and Decision Making

In science, students learn to think critically, solve problems, and make decisions. For example, students investigating the black stuff at the bottom of the aquarium must critically analyze and review possible causes of the growth. They learn to solve the problem by investigating different variables such as the amount of light reaching the aquarium, the pH of the water, the filtration systems, and the types of gravel. Finally, they make decisions regarding the most effective procedures for maintaining the aquarium. This science investigation, of course, is related to real life, because some students also have aquariums in their homes and many students are interested in animals. More importantly, however, through this study students learn skills they can apply to other situations. For example, the next time they encounter an everyday problem, such as trying to figure out why certain plants are not growing well in the garden or why a toy doesn't work properly any more, they will have acquired the skills of analysis, review, investigation, and making conclusions.

Science Helps Students Take Responsibility for Their Actions

As students investigate many scientific questions, they acquire knowledge and develop attitudes that encourage them to take responsibility for their own actions. For example, if students learn in an investigation that motor oil kills plants, their future behavior regarding the disposal of motor oil will be affected.

Science Develops Scientifically Literate Citizens

Science guides students in understanding real-life issues and helps them participate in local, national, and world issues—the hallmarks of scientifically literate citizens. In this new millennium, we find that now, more than at any other time in our history, students face crucial decisions about global issues. These include environmental pollution, AIDS, overpopulation, world hunger, nuclear power, and genetic engineering. Science and engineering have generated solutions to some of these issues: cars with better fuel mileage, more fuel-efficient homes, and great quantities of more nutritious foods. Scientific investigation, invention, and technology have also resulted in discoveries that make life easier for humans, provide cures for diseases, and inspire exploration of new frontiers such as the ocean or space. We need professional scientists to investigate these matters, but we also need a scientifically literate citizenry who can participate in making informed decisions about them. Today's students, more than those of any previous generation, will need to understand basic scientific principles.

Students in project-based science classrooms learn to investigate, understand, and interpret information and interface with people in their own communities. As a result, they are better prepared to deal with the scientific, technological, and social issues that will face them in the future.

NSES

CONNECTING TO NATIONAL SCIENCE EDUCATION STANDARDS

Introduction

The goals for school science that underlie the *National Science Education Standards* are to educate students who are able to experience the richness and excitement of knowing about and understanding the natural world; use appropriate scientific processes and principles in making personal decisions; engage intelligently in public discourse and debate about matters of scientific and technological concern; and increase their economic productivity through the use of the knowledge, understanding, and skills of scientifically literate people in their careers (p. 13).

Positive Science Experiences Are Important in Elementary and Middle School Grades

Most educators agree that science is an essential and crucial subject for all students. The elementary and middle school grades are especially important years for students to construct understanding about the world and develop interest in science so that they will pursue scientific studies as they continue into upper grades where science may become optional (NRC, 1996).

Poor instruction and shallow development of science concepts in elementary and middle school grades are often at fault for persistent, inaccurate beliefs about scientific phenomena. Students come to school with their own ideas about how things in the natural world work, ideas that are not always consistent with the conceptions of experts in the field. For instance, children often believe that a force is needed to keep an object in motion or that mass is lost when substances are burned. Both these ideas make intuitive sense and are consistent with casual observations and life experiences. For instance, when driving a car, the car doesn't keep moving unless we keep our foot on the gas pedal. Typically, we need to apply a force to keep it moving because of the opposing force of friction. When we burn a log in a fireplace, we see that only ashes remain and it appears that other mass is gone. Therefore, we find that many adults, in spite of school instruction in science, still hold ideas that differ from those of scientists (Harvard Private Universe Tapes, 1995).

The elementary and middle grades are also important years for developing curiosity and interest in science. Research by Yager and Yager (1985) has shown that negative attitudes toward science increase by grade level, and students, especially girls, as early as grade three exhibit dislike of and anxiety toward science. The Third International Mathematics and Science Study (TIMSS, 1997, 1998; Schmidt et al., 2001) found similar patterns in students' attitudes toward science. Eighty-five percent of fourth graders indicated that they liked science. However, by the time students reached the twelfth grade, their favorable attitudes toward science had decreased. The percentage of students who liked science ranged from 49 percent to 68 percent, depending upon the discipline, with chemistry on the low end and biology on the high end. The reason students gradually come to dislike science frequently lies in the way science is taught (passively) and the type of curriculum used (not relevant to students' lives). As a teacher, you will be in the position to stimulate student interest in science or extinguish it. Project-based science will help you develop students' interests in science because it involves active investigation of important and meaningful questions.

Children explore their environment.

Third International Mathematics and Science Study (TIMSS)

GOALS OF SCIENCE EDUCATION

In the next two sections of this chapter, we examine the **goals** of science education in the United States and we consider why project-based science enables you to teach in a way that meets those goals. This is an exciting and challenging time in science education history. Many parents, educators, scientists, and public officials are concerned that students will be unable to cope with the massive explosion of knowledge and the tremendous changes that science and technology will bring about in our future. More and more, we're concerned about the ability of our students to develop an understanding of science that they can apply to real life. We all realize that the understandings students develop in school will impact what they are able to do throughout their lives, regardless of their chosen careers. It's not surprising that one fundamental national goal of science education today is to develop a scientifically literate society.

This goal, like our other science education goals, has been affected by a number of forces—history, social changes, governmental concerns about economic competitiveness, research findings, and the powerful influence of science and technology on modern society. Our science education goals have thus changed dramatically during this century, and as we head into the twenty-first century, educators continue to grapple with identifying the appropriate goals for science education.

The success of our national goals strongly depends on the individual goals we set in our classes. Tying national goals to our own classroom goals can be helpful in guiding our students to become scientifically literate citizens. In this section, we examine several reform documents, national policies, and position statements that have established the goals for science education in our country today. Specifically, we summarize the *National Science Education Standards* (National Research Council, 1996), *Project 2061: Science for All Americans* (Rutherford & Ahlgren, 1989), *Benchmarks for Science Literacy* (AAAS, 1993), and *An NSTA Position Statement: Elementary School Science* (NSTA, 1991). Before we do this, however, take a moment to complete Portfolio Activity 1.5 and think about the goals you believe are important for science education.

National Science Education Standards

National Science Education Standards

The National Research Council, with the assistance of the National Academy of Sciences, developed the *National Science Education Standards* (National Research Council, 1996). Subsequent publications (National Research Council, 2000; National Research Council, 2001) explore the national science standards with respect to inquiry and assessment. The goal of the *National Science Education Standards* is to educate *all* students "to experience the richness and excitement of knowing about and understanding the natural world; use appropriate scientific processes and principles in making personal decisions; engage intelligently in public discourse and debate about matters of scientific and technological concern; and increase their economic productivity through the use of the knowledge, understanding, and skills of the scientifically literate person in their careers" (p. 13). To accomplish these goals, the *National Science Education Standards* simultaneously addresses standards for teaching science, the professional development of teachers of science, assessment in science education, K–12 science content, science education programs, and the science education system. These standards represent a consensus of teachers, science educators, scientists, and the public.

The *National Science Education Standards* stresses that science should be inquiry based and adapted to meet the interests, abilities, and experiences of students.

CONNECTING TO
NATIONAL SCIENCE EDUCATION STANDARDS

Overview

The intent of the *Standards* can be expressed in a single phrase: establish science standards for all students. The phrase embodies both excellence and equity. The *Standards* apply to all students, regardless of age, gender, cultural or ethnic background, disability, aspiration, or interest and motivation in science (p. 2).

Portfolio Activity 1.5

WHAT ARE YOUR PERSONAL GOALS FOR SCIENCE EDUCATION?

Materials Needed:
- A sheet of paper
- Something to write with

A. Before reading the section on the goals of science education, brainstorm in small groups the goals that you think are important for science education. Try to reach group consensus. Share your group's goals with the rest of the class.

B. How do the goals of science education differ among your groups? What are the similarities?

C. Think about one national goal already mentioned—the development of scientifically literate citizens. What do you think characterizes a scientifically literate citizen? What does a scientifically literate citizen need to know? What skills does this person need to have? What attitudes should this person possess? How does this goal compare with your group's goals?

D. Record your thoughts in your portfolio.

It emphasizes that science teachers should use strategies that develop science understanding through a community of learners, use resources outside the school that support inquiry, guide and facilitate learning by promoting collaboration and discourse among students, help students become responsible for their own learning, and work with colleagues within science (biology, chemistry, geology, and physical science) and across disciplines (mathematics, language arts, social studies, art, music, and physical education).

Teachers should engage in ongoing assessment of their teaching and of student learning to help themselves, parents, the general public, and policy makers improve instruction. Assessment standards are designed to change the focus of assessment to include what we value most in science education. This means that we need to assess rich, well-structured knowledge, scientific understanding and reasoning, and deep understanding of what students know.

The content standards are based on unifying concepts and processes in science, science as inquiry, physical science, life science, earth and space science, science and technology, science in personal and social perspectives, and the history and nature of science. These unifying concepts are described as the powerful, overarching ideas in science, which include systems, order, change, constancy, and equilibrium.

The *National Science Education Standards* demands that science be taught through processes (such as observing, classifying, measuring, experimenting, and making conclusions) and requires students to use knowledge to reason and think critically. The standards for *physical, life, earth,* and *space science* focus on subject matter, listing the facts, concepts, principles, theories, and models that all students should know in grades K–4, 5–8, and 9–12. The standards for *science and technology* focus on the connections between science and invention and are designed to help students make decisions. The *personal and social perspectives science* standards emphasize the fact that students need to understand the world around them so as to be able to make decisions about personal and societal issues. Finally, the *history and nature of science* standards challenge teachers to teach students about the historical nature of science, emphasizing that it is an ongoing, changing process.

Project 2061: Science for All Americans

Project 2061

Project 2061: Science for All Americans was published by the American Association for the Advancement of Science (Rutherford & Ahlgren, 1989) for the purpose of achieving science literacy nationwide. It was the synthesis of five panel reports on (1) biology and health science; (2) mathematics; (3) technology; (4) physical science, information sciences, engineering; and (5) social and behavioral sciences. *Project 2061* is intended to focus on the meaningful learning of science rather than on sheer coverage of numerous science topics. Its intention is to transform K–12 science while paying attention to all parts of the educational system (goals, curriculum testing, teacher education, and instruction).

Project 2061 is a large-scale, long-term project with several broad goals:

1. In order to ensure scientific literacy, the amount of material covered throughout the academic year needs to be reduced. All children, not only those who have traditionally been successful in science, learn more thoroughly when fewer topics are covered in greater depth. Instead of reading vast amounts of material, students need to think deeply about central concepts, themes, and principles of science.

2. Because the boundaries of science are much grayer than they are portrayed in the science textbooks, emphasis must be placed on showing the integration of and connections among the various science fields as well as with social science, mathematics, language arts, and technology.

3. Because philosophers and historians of science now view science as human enterprise, curriculum and science instruction must illustrate the influence of human thought and action on scientific endeavor and the influence of scientific endeavor on human thought.

4. Because science is more than a culmination of facts, science education must foster scientific ways of thinking, including skepticism, open-mindedness, and creativity. Science teaching for scientific literacy needs to be consistent with the spirit and character of scientific inquiry and with scientific values. Science teaching needs to portray science as a dynamic, recursive enterprise that focuses on explanation of observed phenomena and generation of new questions.

5. Educational reform must be comprehensive, focusing on the learning needs of all children, covering all grades and subjects, and dealing with all components and aspects of the educational system.

Benchmarks for Science Literacy

Benchmarks

The American Association for the Advancement of Science also developed *Benchmarks for Science Literacy* (1993). *Benchmarks* is designed to serve as a curriculum model for curriculum developers, state departments of education, and school systems developing science curriculum. The benchmarks are not instructions on how to teach; they are statements about what *all* students should know or be able to do in science, mathematics, and technology at grades 2, 5, 8, and 12. There are twelve categories of benchmarks: (1) the nature of science, (2) the nature of mathematics, (3) the nature of technology, (4) the

THE SCIENTIFIC WORLD VIEW BENCHMARK			Table 1.1
Grades K–2	**Grades 3–5**	**Grades 6–8**	
When a science investigation is done the way it was done before, we expect to get very similar results. Science investigations generally work the same way in different places.	Results of similar investigations seldom turn out exactly the same.	When similar investigations give different results, the challenge is to judge whether the differences are trivial or significant. Scientific knowledge is subject to modification as new information is found; ideas may change. Some scientific knowledge is very old but still applicable today. Some matters may not be examined usefully in a scientific way.	

physical setting, (5) the living environment, (6) the human organism, (7) human society, (8) the designed world, (9) the mathematical world, (10) historical perspectives, (11) common themes, and (12) habits of mind.

Table 1.1 takes one benchmark, the Scientific World View (AAAS, 1993, pp. 5–8), and shows what is expected of students at the end of second grade, fifth grade, and eighth grade. The benchmark is paraphrased for brevity; you should look at the entire report to see all the thinking of the contributing teachers and researchers.

Notice how the benchmarks become more complex as the grades progress and how a concept becomes elaborated throughout the grades. That means that it is as important for first and second graders to achieve a selected understanding as it is for sixth graders. You should see that this benchmark, like the others in *Benchmarks for Science Literacy*, could be used to provide direction for what students should know and be able to do in science at specific grade levels.

Recently, the American Association for the Advancement of Science developed the *Atlas of Science Literacy* (AAAS and NSTA, 2001). This document is useful in planning curriculum, because it illustrates how concepts are related to each other.

The National Science Teachers Association Position Statement

The National Science Teachers Association (NSTA) publishes position statements on a variety of topics in science education. One position statement provides educators with basic guidelines for elementary science (NSTA, 1991). *An NSTA Position Statement: Elementary School Science* advocates daily science instruction for every elementary child at every grade level. This position statement emphasizes the need to involve children in science at an early age to develop interest in science and prepare children for living in an increasingly scientifically and technologically oriented society. The NSTA position statement stresses problem-solving skills; firsthand investigation and inquiry; broad conceptual themes integrated across the curriculum; and assessment aligned with problem solving, inquiry, process skills, instructional modes, and curriculum objectives.

> ### Key Idea
> National goals form the basis for standards for learning about science and developing scientifically literate citizens.

National Science Teachers Association (NSTA)

Summary of National Goals

In the previous section, we explored four major reform efforts. The *National Science Education Standards, Project 2061, Benchmarks for Science Literacy,* and NSTA's *Position Statement* will influence the character of science education in schools for years to come. These efforts have resulted from the work of some of the best thinkers in science, science education, teaching, and learning. What these people have advocated for science education is consistent with how children learn. Other reports also match closely the recommendations of the four major reform efforts described. What follows is a summary of the common themes of these recommendations. We can cluster these themes under three broad categories: learning, curriculum, and teaching.

Learning

With respect to learning, six major themes are apparent:

1. Students should explore broad **concepts** or "big ideas" instead of isolated facts or skills. A quote from Alvin Toffler's 1970 book *Future Shock* illustrates the need to cover large, conceptual ideas rather than facts:

   > At the rate at which knowledge is growing, by the time the child born today graduates from college, the amount of knowledge in the world will be four times as great. By the time that child is fifty years old, it will be thirty-two times as great, and 97 percent of everything known in the world will have been learned since the time he was born (p. 157).

   Because of the rate of knowledge growth, no individual knows all there is to know and never will. For this reason, teachers should focus on broad topics. For instance, students should explore ecosystems instead of isolated topics such as rivers, plants, and animals. In this way students learn the connections between concepts and principles and are able to apply their understanding to as yet unencountered situations.

2. *All* students should learn to **think critically**, solve problems, and make decisions. Science is for all students, not just those embarking on scientific careers. We live in a world that is scientifically and technologically based. As our children develop into adults, the world will continue to change as a result of scientific and technological decisions. To make informed decisions regarding their own lives and society, children need to have a firm understanding of both the content and process of science so that they may, for example, one day be able to make informed decisions regarding the management of natural resources.

3. Children should **construct meaning** from experiences with concrete materials rather than passively. Literature on child development is clear about the fact that children develop understanding by cognitively engaging in the exploration of phenomena. While some children learn about plants simply by reading about them, most children also need to grow plants and observe their development to construct deep understandings.

4. Students should learn how to **apply** science and technology to everyday life. Science should be relevant to students' lives and not consist solely of learning concepts but also of their applications. Students who study decomposition of matter, for example, might also be asked to create school and home composting systems.

5. Science should foster the development of students' natural **curiosity**, **creativity**, and **interest**. For example, if students are interested in magnets but their textbook only covers matter and energy, the teacher should take advantage of the students' interest in magnetism and set the textbook aside.

6. Science instruction should foster the development of **scientific attitudes**. Students should learn to seek out knowledge, be skeptical, rely on data, accept ambiguity, be willing to modify explanations, cooperate in answering questions and solving problems, respect reason, and be honest. For instance, students typically believe that what they read in a book, hear on television, or read in the newspaper is true. Science instruction can teach students to question what they read and see. Additionally, elementary and middle grades science should aim to promote positive attitudes about science.

Curriculum

With respect to curriculum, three major themes come to the forefront:

1. **Less content** should be covered. Students should be allowed to discover and learn in depth a few major concepts and principles. Instead of covering weather, the human body, magnetism, electricity, chemical change, and the solar system in one year, students might explore only three or four of these major areas.

2. Science should be portrayed to students as **interdisciplinary**, connected to other fields of study. In actual practice, science areas are interwoven. Paul DeHart Hurd, in an article entitled "Why We Must Transform Science" (1991, p. 33), wrote,

    > Science today is characterized by some 25,000 to 30,000 research fields. Findings from these fields are reported in 70,000 journals, 29,000 of which are new since 1978. Traditional disciplines have been hybridized into such new research areas as biochemistry, biophysics, geochemistry, and genetic engineering. . . . These changes in the way modern science is organized have yet to be reflected in science courses. There is little recognition that in recent years the boundaries between the various natural sciences have become more and more blurred and major concepts more unified.

    Topics should be connected. For example, in exploring a question such as "What is in our stream?" students study basic chemical concepts such as concentration and equilibrium as well as perform basic chemical tests for various substances. They explore biology concepts by examining living organisms found in the water. They study earth science concepts such as the water cycle and the watershed. All of these areas are studied in an integrated and unified manner rather than as isolated facts.

3. Students should explore the interrelationships among science, technology, and society. The study of science should highlight the **integration** of technology with societal issues. For example, in investigating "What is in our lake?" students could explore how our waterways get polluted. They might also explore how our society makes decisions and passes laws that govern many of the actions taken by individuals and industries.

Teaching

With respect to teaching, five major themes are apparent:

1.   The teacher serves as a **guide** in the classroom, encouraging student exploration and learning, rather than as an authoritative presenter of knowledge. For instance, instead of lecturing about decomposition and bacteria, a teacher might have students explore why pumpkins decompose by setting up various conditions to investigate decomposition. Students might set up a compost pile at the school, they might build a worm bin for their classroom, or they might create a decomposition column. In these situations, the teacher would serve as a facilitator, setting up the situations, but the students would conduct the actual investigations.

2.   The content of science should be taught as a **process**, involving investigation and answering questions. For example, in the process of exploring why pumpkins decompose, students would ask questions, design plans, collect and analyze data, and make decisions. Assessment should be consistent with this process of inquiry and investigation. In other words, it should measure what is taught. Assessment should also typically be embedded into instruction rather than conducted solely at the end of a chapter or unit.

3.   Science instruction needs to be integrated with instruction in the other discipline areas. Teachers should focus on the relationships among science, language arts, social studies, and mathematics. For instance, a class exploring air pollution might write letters to legislators, create posters expressing their opinions, or make graphs.

4.   Science instruction should encourage students to challenge conceptions and debate ideas. In this process, they form communities of learners who collaborate together. For example, students might work together to challenge each other's ideas about which factors contribute most to the decomposition of leaves.

5.   Science instruction should build upon children's **prior experiences** and knowledge. For instance, if a child believes that air doesn't have mass or take up space, instruction should be designed to foster new understanding. Many of the ideas that children come to school with result from their experiences in play. For instance, a student might develop the idea that gases don't have mass from playing with helium balloons.

HOW DO THE CURRENT NATIONAL GOALS COMPARE WITH PROJECT-BASED SCIENCE?

Now that you have been introduced to the major national goals, you might wonder how they match the goals of project-based science. This approach to science learning is congruent with current goals as represented in projects such as the *National Science Education Standards* (National Research Council, 1996, 2000, 2001), *Project 2061: Science for All Americans* (Rutherford & Ahlgren, 1989), *Benchmarks for Science Literacy* (AAAS, 1993), and *An NSTA Position Statement: Elementary School Science* (NSTA, 1991).

First, all of the national goals stress teaching less content at each grade level. Project-based science is consistent with this emphasis, because its focus is on covering less content in greater depth. Students *investigate authentic questions* that encompass central concepts over an *extended period of time.* The process of *asking and modifying questions, performing investigations,* and *building artifacts* to answer questions might take place over weeks or months. For instance, in order for students to discover what bugs they have in their school yard and when the bugs disappear and reappear, they will have to conduct investigations throughout the entire school year. By covering broader, "big ideas" instead of isolated facts, students in project-based classrooms develop richer, fundamental understandings of major themes or issues. Project-based science takes more time to teach than covering many topics superficially; this method helps teachers use the time they have to teach deeply.

Second, all of the major national goals stress that science should be relevant to students' daily lives and that students should apply their understanding to the real world. Project-based science's driving questions are important, meaningful, and worthwhile. Students apply the solutions they develop to their own life situations. For example, students learning about the black stuff in the bottom of the aquarium learn how to set up and maintain aquariums at home. They learn to make informed decisions regarding pollution in an aquarium.

Third, all of the national goals call for the integration of science throughout the curriculum, within the sciences and across all disciplines. Project-based science promotes this interdisciplinary approach to instruction because, in the investigation of real-world questions, science cannot be separated from other subject areas. For instance, when students explore the quality of water, they combine a number of science disciplines including chemistry (chemicals in the water), biology (effect on plant and animal life), and earth science (polluted water seeping into groundwater supplies below rock layers). Opportunities to connect with other curricular areas also exist. For instance, students might explore public policy governing the pollution of waterways by private industry (social studies). They might create three-dimensional models of their local watersheds (art).

Fourth, the national goals stress that the teacher should serve as a guide to the instruction that takes place in the classroom. In project-based science, the teacher's role is not to impart knowledge to passive learners but to guide students through the processes of modifying driving questions, developing investigations, engaging in explorations, collaborating with others, and creating artifacts. The teacher *facilitates* learning by teaching benchmark lessons, helping students find resources, putting students in touch with members of the community, fostering collaboration, and asking questions that lead to new investigations.

Fifth, national recommendations call for classrooms composed of communities of learners. In project-based science classrooms, students are encouraged to collaborate with other students and with members of the community, debate ideas, challenge the thinking of peers, share ideas, and communicate with people around the world. Teachers in project-based science classrooms see themselves and their students as members of a learning environment.

Sixth, a major focus of the national goals is on the way students learn: Prior experiences should be taken into account and hands-on materials should be used. In project-based science classrooms, teachers identify students' prior knowledge of a concept and use this information to guide lessons and assess learning. Students in project-based science classrooms construct meaning by exploring phenomena. They don't just read about water pollution; they use materials such as secchi disks, pH meters, and water test kits to investigate water quality.

> ## *Key Idea*
> Project-based science is a dynamic teaching approach that helps educators meet the goals and standards set by national reform efforts.

Portfolio Activity 1.6

CASE STUDY OF AN ELEMENTARY OR MIDDLE GRADE CLASSROOM

Materials Needed:
- An elementary or middle school to study

A. Obtain permission from the appropriate officials (usually a school district superintendent, curriculum director, or principal and classroom teacher) at an elementary or middle school to conduct a small case study at the school.

B. Research how the school's course of study, curriculum, instructional practices, and assessment techniques compare with the guidelines proposed by national organizations (such as AAAS, NRC, and NSTA).

C. In your opinion, how well is this school meeting suggested goals? In what ways is it falling short?

D. How well is the school implementing the features of project-based science? In what ways is it failing to implement project-based science ideas?

E. What obstacles might you face trying to implement project-based science in this environment?

F. Record all of these ideas in your portfolio.

Seventh, all of the national goals argue that science should be learned through investigation. Investigation is the core of project-based science. Investigations provide students with the opportunity to ask questions, explore and initiate ideas, plan, seek information, construct designs, collect and interpret data, make inferences, reevaluate their understandings, and construct useful connections among real-life ideas. For example, students investigating the cause of the black stuff at the bottom of the aquarium ask and refine questions about variables related to the growth of the black stuff, design experiments to identify what causes the growth, collect and analyze data about the amount of black stuff, and make decisions about aquarium maintenance.

Eighth, an essential element of the national goals is building interest in science. Meaningful questions are a fundamental part of project-based science as they capitalize upon students' natural curiosity. Students' questions drive the curriculum, leading to investigation of topics that are meaningful and interesting to the students. Because project-based science builds on students' interests, it helps meet the many needs of a diverse classroom.

Ninth, national goals stress the development of scientific attitudes and habits of mind such as accepting ambiguity, being skeptical, and respecting reason. Project-based science supports the development of habits of mind through the processes of investigation (asking questions, developing experiments, collaborating with others, making conclusions, and constructing artifacts).

Tenth, each of the national reports calls for new methods of assessing student understanding in science that are fair, are reliable, and match instructional goals. Project-based science stresses assessment methods that are embedded in the instructional process. Student-developed artifacts, for example, represent students' understandings of the topic they have investigated. For instance, while investigating what insects live on the playground, students might make drawings of insect life cycles. Such activity is developed during the process of investigation, but it also serves as a tool of assessment because it can tell the teacher whether students understand the concept of the investigation.

Portfolio Activity 1.7   **QUESTIONS ABOUT SCIENCE TEACHING**

Materials Needed:
- Paper to write on
- Something to write with

A. Think about the questions you now have about teaching project-based science that you believe you should have the answers to by the time you finish this book.

B. What are your top three or four driving questions about learning to teach elementary or middle school science? Include questions on the goals of science education, why young students should learn science, how science should or should not be emphasized in elementary and middle education, and project-based science.

C. Record your questions in your portfolio.

In Portfolio Activity 1.6, you will conduct a case study of an elementary or middle grade classroom to see for yourself whether classrooms in your region are meeting the fundamental national goals for science and how many of the elements of project-based science are evident in these classrooms.

You probably have many questions at this point about teaching in a project-based science environment. Just as this approach is driven by questions, this book should be driven by questions. Practice asking yourself questions as you work through each section of a chapter. Questions such as "Does this work as well for early elementary grades?" and "What would I have to do to make it work?" are driving questions that are important to teaching. Now that you have been introduced to project-based science, use your questioning ability to become one of the best science teachers in the country. Begin by asking questions about science teaching in Portfolio Activity 1.7.

We hope you have seen how project-based science serves to implement suggested national goals for teaching science. Throughout this book we will explore in greater depth many of the ideas that were introduced in this chapter.

CHAPTER REVIEW   **www.mhhe.com/krajcik2e**

ONLINE LEARNING CENTER

Go to the Online Learning Center at **www.mhhe.com/krajcik2e** to review important content from the chapter and key terms, take a chapter assessment, and link to the chapter's websites.

CHAPTER SUMMARY

Project-based science represents an exciting way to teach science. In project-based science classrooms, students investigate and collaborate with others to seek answers to real-world questions. Using technology, students investigate, develop artifacts, collaborate, and make products to show what they have learned. This method of teaching science motivates students to learn and explore, it parallels what scientists do, and it meets the national goals for and standards of science education. Throughout the remaining chapters of this book, you will encounter more in-depth information about the fundamental features of project-based science and strategies for implementing the approach. In the process, we hope you see how enjoyable teaching science can be.

CHAPTER HIGHLIGHTS

- Project-based science stands apart from other forms of science teaching because it situates the learning of science in questions that children find meaningful and relevant to their lives.
- One way to examine features of project-based science is to contrast it with
  - Reading about science.
  - Direct instruction.
  - Process science teaching.
- Project-based science is sensitive to the varied needs of diverse students with respect to culture, race, and gender.
- Driving questions serve to organize and guide instructional tasks and activities.
- All driving questions should be meaningful and important to students.
- Students engage in investigations to answer their questions.
- Communities of students, teachers, and others collaborate on the question or problem.
- Students use technology to investigate, develop artifacts, collaborate, access information, and actively construct knowledge.
- A series of artifacts or products document what students have learned.
- Scientists test these hypotheses by collecting data, analyzing data, making conclusions, and communicating findings.
- To be classified as scientific, the observations, measurements, and conclusions made by one group of scientists must be verified by others.
- The understanding that results from science is tentative and changes with new observations.
- Science study helps students
  - Acquire knowledge and skills that will be useful throughout their lives.
  - Develop positive attitudes that foster responsibility for one's actions.
  - Guide students in understanding real life issues.
- Science affects every aspect of our lives.
- The study of science helps develop scientifically literate citizens.
- The elementary and middle grades are also important years for developing curiosity and interest in science.
- Science education goals advocate science literacy for *all* students and set forth recommendations about learning, curriculum, and teaching
  - Students should explore broad concepts or "big ideas" instead of isolated facts or skills.
  - *All* students should learn to think critically, solve problems, and make decisions.
  - Children should construct meaning from experiences with concrete materials rather than passively.
  - Students should learn how to apply science and technology to everyday life.
  - Science should foster the development of students' natural curiosity, creativity, and interest.
  - Science instruction should foster the development of scientific attitudes.
  - Less content should be covered in the curriculum.
  - Science should be portrayed to students as interdisciplinary, connected to other fields of study.

- The teacher serves as a guide in the classroom, encouraging student exploration and learning, rather than as an authoritative presenter of knowledge.
  - The content of science should be taught as a process, involving investigation and answering questions.
  - Science instruction should encourage students to challenge and debate ideas.
  - Science instruction should build upon children's prior experiences and knowledge.
- Project-based science is a dynamic teaching approach that helps educators meet the goals and standards set by national reform efforts.

KEY TERMS

Apply (26)

Artifacts (13)

Collaboration (12)

Concepts (26)

Construct meaning (26)

Creativity (27)

Curiosity (27)

Driving question (11)

Goals (21)

Guide (28)

Hypotheses (16)

Inquiry (12)

Integration (27)

Interdisciplinary (27)

Interest (27)

Investigations (12)

Learning technologies (13)

Less content (27)

Nature of science (17)

Prior experiences (28)

Process (28)

Project-based science (4)

Science (14)

Scientific attitudes (27)

Subquestions (12)

Theories (15)

Think critically (26)

REFERENCES

American Association for the Advancement of Science. 1993. *Benchmarks for science literacy.* New York: Oxford University Press.

American Association for the Advancement of Science. 2001. *Atlas of Science Literacy.* Washington, D.C.: American Association for the Advancement of Science and National Science Teachers Association Press.

Atwater, M. M. 1994. Research on cultural diversity in the classroom. In *Handbook of research on science teaching and learning,* ed. D. L. Gabel. New York: Macmillan.

Blumenfeld, P., E. Soloway, R. Marx, J. Krajcik, M. Guzdial, and A. Palincsar. 1991. Motivating project-based learning: Sustaining the doing, supporting the learning. *Educational Psychologist* 26: 369–98.

Brown, A. L., and J. C. Campione. 1994. Guided discovery in a community of learners. In *Classroom lessons: Integrating cognitive theory and classroom practice,* ed. K. McGilly, 229–70. Cambridge, Mass.: MIT Press/Bradford Books.

Czerniak, C. M. 1995a. Dinosaur! *School Science and Mathematics* 95(3): 160–61.

Czerniak, C. M. 1995b. Dinosaurs: Fantastic creatures that ruled the earth. *School Science and Mathematics* 95(3): 161–62.

Haberman, M. 1991. The pedagogy of poverty versus good teaching. *Phi Delta Kappa* 73(4):290–94.

Haberman, M. 1995. *STAR teachers of children in poverty.* West Lafayette, Ind.: Kappa Delta Pi.

Hurd, P. D. 1991, October. Why we must transform science education. *Educational Leadership* 33–35.

Krajcik, J. S. 1993. Learning science by doing science. In *What research says to the science teacher: Science, society and technology,* ed. R. Yager. Washington, D.C.: National Science Teachers Association.

Kuhn, T. S. 1962. *The structure of scientific revolutions.* Chicago, Ill.: The University of Chicago Press.

Linn, M. C. 1997. Learning and instruction in science education: Taking advantage of technology. In *International handbook of science education,* ed. D. Tobin and B. J. Fraser. The Netherlands: Kluwer.

Marx, R. W., P. C. Blumenfeld, J. S. Krajcik, and E. Soloway. 1997. Enacting project-based science: Challenges for practice and policy. *Elementary School Journal* 97:341–58.

National Research Council. 1996. *National science education standards.* Washington, D.C.: National Academy Press.

National Research Council. 2000. *Inquiry and the national science education standards.* Washington, D.C.: National Academy Press.

National Research Council. 2001. *Classroom assessment and the national science education standards.* Washington, D.C.: National Academy Press.

National Science Teachers Association. 1991. *An NSTA position statement: Elementary school science.* Washington, D.C.: NSTA.

Phillips, D. C. 1987. *Philosophy, science, and social inquiry.* Oxford: Permagon Press.

Presidents and Fellows of Harvard College. 1995. *The private universe project.* South Burlington, Vt.: Annenburg/Corporation of Public Broadcasting Mathematics and Science Collection.

Roth, W. M. 1995. *Authentic school science.* The Netherlands: Kluwer.

Roup, R. R., S. Gal, B. Drayton, and M. Pfister, eds. 1992. *LabNet: Toward a community of practice.* Hillsdale, N.J.: Erlbaum.

Rutherford, J., and A. Ahlgren. 1989. *Science for all Americans: Project 2061.* New York: Oxford University Press.

Schmidt, W. H., C. C. McKnight, R. T. Houang, H. C. Wang, D. E. Wiley, L. S. Cogan, and R. G. Wolfe. 2001. *Why schools matter: A cross national comparison of curriculum and learning.* San Francisco: Jossey Bass.

Stake, R. E., and J. A. Easley et al. 1978. *Case studies in science education.* Urbana, Ill.: Center for Instructional Research and Curriculum Evaluation, University of Illinois.

Third International Mathematics and Science Study (TIMSS). 1997.

Third International Mathematics and Science Study (TIMSS). 1998.

Tinker, R. F., and S. Papert. 1989. Tools for science education. In *1988 AETS Yearbook: Information technology and science education,* ed. J. Ellis. Columbus, Ohio: Association for the Education of Teachers in Science.

Toffler, Alvin. 1970. *Future shock.* New York: Bantam Books.

White, B. Y., and J. R. Fredrickson. April 1995. *The Thinker Tools Inquiry Project: Making scientific inquiry accessible to students and teachers. Causal Models Research Group Report 95-02.* Berkeley, Calif.: School of Education, University of California.

Yager, R. E., and S. O. Yager. 1985. Changes in perceptions of science for third, seventh, and eleventh grade students. *Journal of Research in Science Teaching* 22(4):347–58.

We planted our seeds on Wed. April 26th

We have been growing our garden for this many days: ||||| ||||| ||||| |||||

Chapter 2

How Do Children Construct Understanding in Science?

INTRODUCTION

STUDENT UNDERSTANDING

MODELS OF TEACHING

SOCIAL CONSTRUCTION OF KNOWLEDGE

A SOCIAL CONSTRUCTIVIST MODEL OF TEACHING

CHAPTER LEARNING PERFORMANCES

- *Explain the difference between inert and meaningful knowledge.*
- *Describe the three types of knowledge—content, procedural, and metacognitive.*
- *Critique examples of teaching to determine if they represent receptional or transformational approaches to teaching and learning.*
- *Explain what is meant by social constructivism and describe the various features of a social constructivist model of teaching.*
- *Develop a lesson based on the social constructivist model of teaching.*
- *Apply the idea of scaffolding to help children accomplish a difficult learning task.*
- *Discuss how authentic tasks help women and minorities participate and stay interested in science.*

INTRODUCTION

Children face an increasingly scientific and technological world. Information and access to information are growing at an exponential rate. Schools need to prepare our youth to learn and apply all of this scientific knowledge to solve real-world problems. Do students in our schools develop understandings that help them use science? What is a *usable understanding of science*? How can teachers help students develop usable science understanding?

This chapter examines the educational literature that anchors project-based science in the social constructivist theory of learning. We'll consider a social constructivist model of teaching that focuses on active engagement with phenomena, using and applying knowledge, multiple representations, use of learning communities, and the role of authentic tasks. We'll examine types of knowledge and ways to help students develop integrated understandings through the construction of knowledge in social situations. Finally, we will explore a number of techniques to help teachers scaffold students' learning of science. First, however, let's develop a working definition of *understanding*.

STUDENT UNDERSTANDING

What kinds of science understandings do students develop in school? Does school help them develop understandings that are useful for their lives? Unfortunately, a number of research studies (Osborne & Freyberg, 1986; Rutherford & Ahlgren, 1989; AAAS, 1993; and Linn, 1998) indicate that students at the elementary, middle, and high school levels do not develop an understanding of science that is useful for their everyday lives. Most students memorize science terms without understanding, and they memorize how to solve problems (Eylon & Linn, 1988; Osborne & Freyberg, 1986). Students learn bits of factual information and how to solve problems at the end of chapters by using formulas. Scientific facts and algorithmic problem solving make up much of the science curriculum taught in U.S. schools. Most children do not develop rich understanding and cannot apply what they learn to explain scientific phenomena. This kind of knowledge has been defined as *inert knowledge*. The learner with **inert knowledge** lacks connections and relationships between ideas, and cannot retrieve or use knowledge in appropriate situations (Perkins, 1992). For example, a fifth grader might be able to define *atom* but not know how to use the definition to explain properties of matter.

Students' decreased interest in science appears to be a contributing factor to decreased understanding of science. Although most elementary children start school with an interest in the physical world, they soon lose interest in learning about science. As students transition to middle school, their interest in science decreases further and students lose motivation to continue their learning of science. Yager and Penick (1986) summarized the data from various national studies and concluded that "the more years our students enroll in science courses, the less they like it." This conclusion is also supported by the Third International Mathematics and Science Study (TIMSS, 1998), which indicates that interest in science decreases from elementary grades to high school. One possible reason for this decrease in motivation stems from the predominant use of textbooks to teach science and the emphasis on memorizing science facts. Most students need to experience science as an active process of engagement for interest to be high.

Key Idea

School science often results in students developing inert knowledge—disconnected, unusable fragments of ideas.

Let's examine three scenarios that illustrate the variety of understandings students have of scientific ideas.

Scenario 1: What Is Alive?

The first scenario comes from a common biology topic: What is alive? Mr. Ramirez asked his second graders if a seed, such as that from an apple, is alive. Most of his students responded, "No." When Mr. Ramirez probed them to explain their answers, many said that a seed does not move and so cannot be alive.

Young children tend to categorize *alive* and *not alive* according to superficial physical characteristics and to the presence or absence of locomotion (Carey, 1985; Driver, Squires, Rushworth, & Wood-Robinson, 1994). Older students and students more knowledgeable of biology retain aspects of this categorization scheme but seem to broaden their criteria for *life* to include more carefully differentiated ideas of function (autonomous movement is distinguished from simple movement) and ideas about additional functions (growth, metabolism, and reproduction). If we ask older children (seventh or eighth grade) if an apple seed is alive, many will say that it has the "potential" to grow but that it is not alive. This example shows how students do not develop rich ideas about basic biological phenomena.

Scenario 2: Boiling Water

The second scenario centers on a common physical science topic: the boiling and condensing of water. Ms. Beacher asked two of her fourth-grade students, Kristen and Shawn, to make observations of and explain a laboratory setup in which water was boiling in a beaker and condensing on a cool glass surface held above the beaker. Figure 2.1 shows the experimental setup. Kristen said that the water was boiling. Ms. Beacher asked how she knew, and Kristen answered, "Because of the bubbles in the water." Shawn added that water was condensing on the glass surface. Ms. Beacher probed them further to elicit more in-depth responses. She asked, "What is inside the bubbles?" Kristen responded, "Air," and Shawn agreed. Then Ms. Beacher asked, "Well, if there is air in the bubbles, where does the air in the bubbles come from?" Both Kristen and Shawn looked at Ms. Beacher with blank faces. She then asked them, "Shawn, you mentioned that water was condensing on the glass surface. Where does that water come from?" Shawn responded, "It evaporated from the beaker." Ms. Beacher probed further: "Can you tell me what it means to evaporate from the beaker?" Shawn replied, "You know; it came from the beaker."

This scenario shows that the children were able to use scientific terms, but they could not use the terms to explain some everyday phenomena. Children might use terms such as *evaporate, condense,* and *boil.* However, if we use probing questions to elicit from them more in-depth descriptions and explanation of the phenomena, we find that many students don't have a very rich understanding of the terms they use. As the example illustrates, many of them cannot go beyond just using vocabulary terms (Osborne & Cosgrove, 1983). Interestingly enough, the responses of eighth graders are not very different from those of these fourth graders. In their explanation of boiling, some eighth-grade students say that the bubbles in the water are made of air or hydrogen and oxygen gas instead of explaining that the bubbles are filled with water molecules in the gaseous phase.

Figure 2.1

Children cannot frequently explain simple phenomena such as the boiling and condensing of water.

Scenario 3: Burning Steel Wool

The third scenario centers on a common chemistry topic. Ms. Jackson's sixth graders observed a piece of steel wool burning in air. Many of the students explained that a chemical reaction was occurring. However, when Ms. Jackson asked them to predict how the original mass of the steel wool would compare to the mass of material remaining after burning, almost all of the students predicted that the mass of the material remaining after burning would be less than the original mass of the steel wool. Ms. Jackson then asked the students to explain why they thought the mass would decrease. Many of them said that it turned to ash, like paper or wood, when it burned. Next, the students measure the mass of steel wool before burning and then measured it again after burning. They noticed that the mass did not decrease and, in fact, increased (see Figure 2.2). Most children, and adults too, would be surprised at these results. When Ms. Jackson asked the students to explain the increase in mass, some said that the steel wool turned into carbon, which is heavier than steel wool (Anderson, 1986).

Children believe that the residue that remains after steel wool is burned will weigh less than the steel wool.

Once again, the responses of eighth graders do not differ substantially from those of these sixth graders. The example illustrates that students lack understanding of combustion, in which a substance chemically combines with oxygen to form a new substance, iron oxide.

These scenarios illustrate that, when we ask students to qualitatively explain scientific phenomena, students typically use the "correct" words such as *evaporation, condensation,* or *reaction,* but they lack understanding of the underlying scientific concepts (Driver, Squires, Rushworth, & Wood-Robinson, 1994; Osborne & Cosgrove, 1983).

How would you have answered the questions in the three scenarios? Qualitative explanations of scientific phenomena are a challenge, not only for many elementary and middle school students, but also for many high school, undergraduate, and even graduate students. When the three scenarios were replicated in science methods classes and in graduate courses, even students with backgrounds in science had a difficult time giving solid, qualitative explanations of the observed phenomena. Many college students were surprised that the residue of burning the steel wool had more mass than the steel wool, even though they had successfully completed introductory college chemistry. Take time now to complete Portfolio Activity 2.1.

What is *your* reaction to the fact that the mass of a tree comes primarily from carbon dioxide found in the air and water taken from the environment? Many students, even biology majors, seem surprised by this information. Yet this is the basic premise of photosynthesis—a concept that is found in every elementary book and covered in every basic biology class in high school and college.

To learn more about scientific understandings, talk with some children about common physical, chemical, or biological phenomena. Having conversations with children of

Key Idea

Students have meaningful understandings when they can use their knowledge in a variety of different situations to solve problems.

Portfolio Activity 2.1   THINKING ABOUT YOUR OWN UNDERSTANDING

Materials Needed:
- Something to write with
- If available, the *Private Universe Project* tapes (Presidents and Fellows of Harvard College, 1995)

A. Picture a tree seed. Next, picture an entire tree. How did the tree get its mass? Where did it come from? Answer these questions in your portfolio.

B. Contrast your answers with those of a few classmates. What ideas do you and your classmates have about where the mass came from? Try to come to a consensus.

C. Look up the word *photosynthesis* in a science book and read about it. What are your thoughts now about how a tree gets its mass? How do these differ from your initial thoughts? How are they alike?

D. If available, watch some of the episodes of the Harvard *Private Universe Project* series. One of them centers on how a seed grows to be a tree. What are your reactions to students' understandings of science concepts?

E. Think about the types of understandings you have developed about science concepts. How often have you used your science ideas to explain phenomena in your daily life? List as many examples as you can in your portfolio.

Portfolio Activity 2.2   INVESTIGATE YOUNG LEARNERS' IDEAS

Materials Needed:
- Something to write with
- Baking soda
- A 250 ml beaker
- Vinegar
- Water
- Two students of different ages to talk with

A. Set up a conversation with two students of different ages to learn about how they understand some science concepts. You might want to tape your interview. Make sure to find out the following information:

- Age of student.
- Current grade.
- What science topics they remember studying in school or at home.

NOTE: Probing a child to determine his or her conceptual understanding is a difficult process. It is a good idea to practice with a classmate or a friend before you conduct these interviews with students. Tape these practice sessions and study the way you asked questions. In general, observe the following guidelines when interviewing your learners:

1. Avoid using leading questions that suggest responses. For example, don't say, "How do you think this will re-act?" By saying *react,* you lead the students to think something is going to happen.

2. Avoid praise or negative comments. For example, don't say, "Good." Rather, say, "I see."

3. Use phrases that allow a learner to clarify and expand on his or her ideas. Be sure to probe when scientific or technical terminology is used. For example, if the student says, "It will evaporate," ask, "What do you mean by 'it will evaporate'?" To clarify ideas, say things like, "Could you tell me more about what you mean?" Here are other phrases:

- "Please describe that further."
- "What do you mean by…?"
- "Tell me more about…?"
- "Is this what you mean…?"
- "Please explain that further."
- "Hmm. That's interesting. Tell me more about that."
- "What else would you like to tell me about what you observed?"

4. Listen to the learner—use active listening techniques. For example, look at the child when he or she is speaking. Paraphrase what the student says. For example, if the child says, "I think it will disappear," you might say, "Do you mean you wouldn't be able to see it?" Ask for explanations. Summarize what you think the student said.

different ages and comparing their responses can help you discover some surprising things about what they know. Portfolio Activity 2.2 is designed to help you begin talking to children about their science ideas.

Meaningful Understandings

Instead of developing inert knowledge, project-based science helps students develop meaningful understandings. **Meaningful understanding** results from the learner building relationships and connections among ideas and blending personal experiences with more formal scientific knowledge (Bransford, Brown, & Cocking, 1999; Krajcik, 2001). Imagine a child who understands from a prior lesson the relationship between molecules in gaseous, liquid, and solid states. The child learns a new concept about sound vibrations traveling through different substances. The child notices during some activities that sound travels best through solids, next best through liquids, and least well through air. The teacher asks, "Why do you think sound travels best through the solid and least well through the air?" The child answers, "Well, it probably has something to do with what it is made of." The teacher replies, "What did we learn about what all matter is made of?" The child says, "Atoms." The teacher prompts the student by saying, "What do you know about

5. Use the learner's language to rephrase and further probe the learner's response. For example, if a student says, "I won't be able to see it," say, "Why can't you *see* it?" Don't say, "Do you mean it will dissolve?"

6. Provide the learner with ample time to construct a response. Wait at least three to five seconds after asking a question before you say anything more.

7. Establish a calm and accepting atmosphere. Don't rush the conversation by talking hurriedly or being judgmental about responses.

8. If a learner cannot answer a question, try rephrasing the question to find out what the student does know and what his or her thoughts are. For example, if you first ask, "What do you think will happen?" and the child doesn't respond, rephrase the question to say, "What do you think will happen when I put this baking soda into this water and stir it?" However, be careful; don't add more than what the student said.

B. Complete the following tasks with the two students:

Dissolving Change Task. In this task, you will mix a teaspoon of baking soda in 100 ml of water. The baking soda will dissolve in the water.

- Show students a teaspoon of baking soda and a 250 ml beaker with 100 ml water. Ask students to predict what will happen if you mix the baking soda in the water.
- Place the baking soda in the beaker of water and stir. Ask the students to describe what they see. Ask the

students to explain what they observe. Find out what the students mean by the words they use. For instance, if they say, "It dissolved," ask them what they mean by *dissolved*.

- Ask the students what they might see if they could magnify the contents of the beaker 100 million times. Ask the students to draw what they think they would see.

Chemical Change Task. In this task, you will mix a teaspoon of baking soda in vinegar. This is a chemical change; the baking soda will react with the vinegar to form new products.

- Show students a teaspoon of baking soda and a 250 ml beaker with 100 ml of vinegar. Ask students to predict what will happen if you mix the baking soda in the vinegar.
- Place the baking soda in the beaker of vinegar. Ask students to describe what they see. Ask students to explain what they observe. Find out what the students mean by the words they use. For instance, if they say, "It reacted," ask them what they meant by *reacted*.
- Ask what they might see if they could magnify the contents of the beaker 100 million times. Ask the students to draw what they think they would see.

C. Process what you found. Combine your data with the data from other students in your class. Summarize your data. What conclusions can you draw? What educational implications do your conclusions indicate? Record these in your portfolio.

the molecules in different states of matter?" The child answers, "Well, the molecules are close together in solids and far apart in gases." The teacher questions, "And what might this tell you about sound travel?" The child says, "Oh, I get it. In solids the molecules are close, so vibrations happen because the molecules can bump into each other. And that's not true in gases; the molecules can't bump into each other as well because they are too far apart." This student has meaningful understandings: she used her understanding of molecules in different states of matter to come up with a new explanation of the effect of states of matter on sound travel.

Students who have meaningful understandings can use those understandings to solve problems. For instance, a child with meaningful understanding might use Newton's laws of motion to explain why a person needs to wear seat belt when riding in a car. Newton's First Law of Motion states that an object will stay at rest or continue in motion unless acted upon by a force. Therefore, we wear a seat belts so that our bodies don't continue in motion (hit the windshield or get thrown out of the car) if the car comes to a sudden stop.

Figure 2.3, created by Valerie Talsma, illustrates the difference between inert and meaningful understanding. The cell in the lower left corner, Cell A, represents a learner who has very little understanding and whose understandings are not connected to each other. This learner has inert knowledge—disconnected, unusable fragments of facts. The cell in the lower right corner, Cell B, represents a learner with some understanding that is tightly integrated. This learner has the type of understanding we want a student to develop at the third- or fourth-grade level, where their understandings, although limited, should be integrated. The cell in the upper left corner, Cell C, represents a learner who has accumulated knowledge but has not integrated the knowledge. This is the type of understanding that often emerges in schools. The cell in the upper right corner, Cell D, represents a learner who has accumulated knowledge and developed meaningful understandings. This is the rich, integrated understanding that learners achieve in project-based science.

Types of Knowledge

One way to think about integrated and meaningful knowledge is to think about three types of knowledge: content, procedural, and metacognitive (Anderson & Krathwohl, 2001; Perkins, 1992). All three types of knowledge are needed for understandings to become integrated and meaningful.

Content knowledge refers to the central concepts, principles, and theories in an area of study. One example of a central science concept is *force*. An example of a principle is Newton's First Law of Motion. A learner who understands why an object stops moving once it is given a push, for example, has a better foundation to understand central concepts and principles of physics such as *force, acceleration, velocity,* and Newton's three laws of motion.

Content knowledge, however, is only one type of knowledge that students need to develop (Perkins, 1992; Krajcik, 2001). Understanding also depends upon accumulating supporting knowledge that helps the learner know how to learn. This supporting knowledge includes procedural knowledge and metacognitive knowledge. **Procedural knowledge** is essential in helping a student engage in inquiry and in finding solutions to problems. A child uses procedural knowledge to find solutions to questions, design an experiment, and

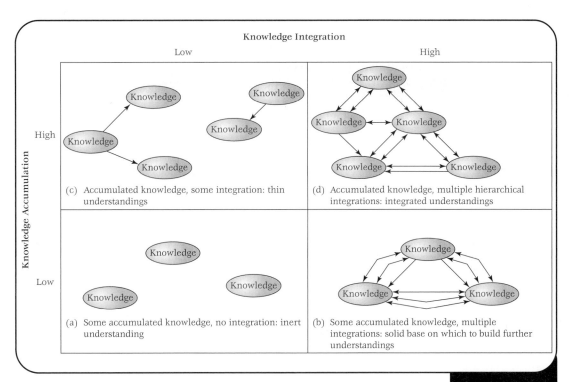

Understanding is a function of knowledge accumulation and knowledge integration. Theoretically, it is possible to accumulate a large number of discrete bits of knowledge without creating relationships between those pieces of knowledge or with only a few weak relationships (Cells A and C). It is also possible to have a limited amount of knowledge of which each piece is well integrated or linked to other knowledge, perhaps in multiple ways (Cell B). Rich, integrated understandings are achieved as knowledge becomes both structured and integrated (Cell D).

Figure 2.3

(Talsma, 1998).

find and evaluate background information related to a question. For instance, knowing how and when to control variables is procedural knowledge. (Chapter 4—"How Are Scientific Investigations Developed?"—discusses the control of variables in more detail.) Procedural knowledge also involves knowing when the evidence is sufficient for a person to draw a valid conclusion.

Metacognitive knowledge (Anderson & Krathwohl, 2001) is knowledge about cognition in general as well as awareness and knowledge about one's own cognition. Anderson and Krathwohl describe three types of metacognitive knowledge: strategic knowledge, knowledge of cognitive tasks, and self-knowledge. *Strategic knowledge* refers to knowing different strategies for learning such as knowing how to use search terms to find information on the World Wide Web. *Knowledge of cognitive tasks* refers to the

Table 2.1

THREE TYPES OF KNOWLEDGE

Type of Knowledge	Definition	Examples
CONTENT	Knowing the central concepts and principles in a domain	In biology, understanding predator and prey relationships; in chemistry, understanding physical and chemical change; in physics, understanding inertia
PROCEDURAL	Knowing how to solve problems and design and carry out investigations	Knowing how to design an experiment; knowing how to analyze data; knowing strategies for monitoring one's progress
METACOGNITION	Knowing different strategies for learning; knowing the difference between different cognitive tasks; knowing one's own strengths and weaknesses in learning	Knowing different strategies for solving problems; knowing that memorizing definitions of terms is not as difficult as explaining what a term means; knowing that one finds it difficult to write careful observations

understanding that cognitive tasks are different such as understanding that data analysis might include transforming the data into a different representation. *Self-knowledge* refers to knowing one's own strength and weaknesses in learning. For instance, a child might realize that he has difficulty spelling science words, so he might need to spend extra time on them.

A child uses metacognitive knowledge to monitor her progress on a report or to decide when to seek help with a procedure. A student with strong metacognitive strategies will be able to track how well he is completing a task, such as following procedures, that is part of an investigation that extends over time. A child with metacognitive knowledge will know when she has collected enough information to make a conclusion.

We present this summary of the three types of knowledge because all three are essential for students to develop the integrated and meaningful understanding needed for continued learning. Limiting a student to content knowledge robs the learner from learning more. Meaningful understandings will occur only if content knowledge is developed in the process of engaging in inquiry. For example, if a child knows only definitions of molecular states, she will not be able to use the understandings and apply them to a new situation related to sound travel. Table 2.1 summarizes the three types of knowledge.

MODELS OF TEACHING

You can think of teaching on a broad continuum from transformational approaches to receptional approaches.

Transformational approaches to teaching and learning involve teachers supporting students to make sense of material. Project-based science is one example of a transformational approach to teaching and learning. In contrast, **receptional approaches** to teaching and learning involve teachers transmitting information and students receiving it. Receptional approaches to teaching and learning have long dominated our school systems. Armstrong (1994) writes, "For most Americans, the word *classroom* conjures up an image of students sitting in neat rows of desks facing the front of the room, where a teacher either sits at a large desk correcting papers or stands near a blackboard lecturing students" (p. 86).

A Receptional Approach to Teaching

Marie, a sixth-grade teacher, believes that children need to be quiet and in their seats to learn the information she is telling them. In a recent lesson in which she taught about sound, she first had the students read from the textbook the chapter on sound. Students read out loud one paragraph at a time. Marie indicated to students what the important concepts were by writing them on the board as they were read. Students wrote definitions of the important vocabulary words—frequency, pitch, amplitude, waves, rarefaction, and compression—in their science journals. Marie attempted to prove to the students that sound is produced by waves by demonstrating the waves that are created by striking a tuning fork and placing it in water. Next, Marie showed the children the different frequencies produced by tuning forks of various pitches. Finally, Marie reinforced the important concepts by showing a videotape covering the same ideas. Students received a homework assignment: They had to answer three questions at the end of the textbook chapter. Marie evaluated the students with a quiz at the end of the week. On this quiz, students were asked to choose the correct definitions for words such as pitch, amplitude, and frequency.

A Transformational Approach to Teaching

Roberta, another sixth-grade teacher, introduced the same sound lesson as Marie in a very different manner. Roberta was investigating with her class the driving question "What Makes Music?" She introduced a benchmark lesson to help students understand basic concepts of sound. First, she handed each child in the class a balloon, a rubber band, and a ruler. The students were instructed to spend the next ten minutes exploring ways to make sounds with each of the objects. At the end of the exploration time, students were asked to discuss their findings with each other in small groups and later share with the whole class what they had discovered about sound. Roberta did not evaluate these ideas but listed all of them on the board. One child said that the balloon was louder than the rubber band. Another said that the ruler changed sound as it was hung off the table at different lengths. A third student said that a loud sound was created when she snapped Randy, her neighbor, with the rubber band. (Oops—the teacher forgot to set some basic ground rules for behavior! See Chapter 10 for more information about classroom management.) Yet another child said that all the objects were moving when the sounds were produced. Roberta wrote the word *vibration* on the board and told the children that that is the term scientists use for such movement.

Then she asked the class to stop and compare each object again. She asked, "Is it true that all the objects need to be moving to produce sound?" The students debated the evidence supporting this conjecture. One student asked how the sounds made by a thick rubber band would differ from those made by a thin one, just as the strings on his guitar made different sounds. Roberta encouraged the students to explore this idea. Through questioning, she guided the students through a comparison of the lengths, thicknesses, and stretched widths of the various objects and a comparison of the pitches. She asked students to think about why the pitch would be different—was there anything different about the vibrations? Using the materials, students explored the question in small groups. By analyzing the evidence they collected, the students explained that the differences in pitch seemed to be caused by variations in how fast the rubber bands were moving.

Roberta introduced the class to the term *frequency* and helped students see how their findings matched the definition of this term. Students were encouraged to think about their own experiences that would support the concept that sound is caused by vibrations and that pitch is caused by variations in the frequency of the vibrations. A student mentioned the digital monitors on her stereo system that visually displayed the frequency of vibrations. Another told about a time that he dropped salt on the top of the TV; the salt "danced" up and down and vibrated while the TV was turned on but was still when the TV was turned off. A third student discussed how she would place her fingers and move her lips to play her clarinet. Yet another talked about watching the pictures on her brother's wall vibrate when he turned up his rock music. Roberta consistently asked students to elaborate on their examples and to explain how the examples supported the question asked. Students were frequently asked to confirm or refute comments made by others in the class. Finally, to evaluate what students learned, Roberta asked them to write down in their journals what they had learned in the lesson.

What can be done to help children develop integrated and meaningful understanding of science? How can we help children apply scientific concepts and principles to solve real world problems that are of interest to them? What can be done to help children develop content, procedural, and metacognitive knowledge? Research findings from the last two decades have shown growing support for the notion that integrated and meaningful types of knowledge are best learned when what occurs in schools is less receptional and more transformational.

SOCIAL CONSTRUCTION OF KNOWLEDGE

How do students come to make sense of material rather than only memorize it? Brown, Collins, and Duguid (1989) argue that "knowledge is . . . in part a product of the activity, context, and culture in which it is developed and used" (p. 32). These researchers see knowledge as contextualized. By **contextualized** they mean that knowledge cannot easily be separated from the situation in which it is developed. Blumenfeld and colleagues (1998) reiterate this notion: "Knowing and doing are not separated; knowledge is not an abstract phenomenon that readily can be transferred from how it is learned in the classroom for use in other situations." This learning model, which suggests that learning cannot be separated from the social context in which it takes place, is often referred to as **social constructivism.**[1]

Unlike the receptional approach to teaching, the transformational approach is consistent with social constructivist theory and project-based science. What are the similarity and differences between the two approaches? Can you identify a constructivist lesson? Portfolio Activity 2.3 will help you explore this idea on your own.

The Influence of Jean Piaget

Jean Piaget

Jean Piaget (1970), arguably the most influential developmental psychologist of the twentieth century, believed that a person's reasoning and intelligence developed like other biological systems—through maturation, or innate biological changes, as well as through the process of equilibration. According to Piaget (1970), an individual actively modifies what he/she knows through interactions with the environment and others. Maturation, in addition to environmental and social interactions, influenced how an individual's reasoning and intelligence developed. **Equilibration** refers to the process of modifying one's mental structures, or schemas, to fit new experiences. **Schemas** can be thought of as blueprints that guide behavior and reasoning but that can be modified.

Piaget tested his ideas about intellectual development on his own and other children and identified four "forms" of thought. These are not lock-step stages tied to specific ages but rather types of thought more or less pronounced at various developmental levels. Even adults learning something new will progress through the various forms of thought. Piaget's four forms of thought are **sensorimotor intelligence** (in which the child interacts with the environment through sensory and muscular activity), **preoperational thought** (characterized by the development of language and rapid conceptual development focused on mastering representations without thorough understanding), **concrete operations** (in which children develop the ability to apply logical thought to problems they come across in their environment), and **formal operations** (in which the child becomes able to apply logical thought to all types of problems—including ones he or she cannot actually experience directly).

Piaget's ideas about biological maturation and interaction with the environment and others had important consequences for curriculum and instructional activities. If an individual does not reach a particular maturation point, it will be impossible for him to develop understanding; similarly, if he lacks appropriate experience, he will not be able to develop the appropriate understanding. Hence, according to Piaget, curricular materials should fit the cognitive development of the student. If, for example, the curriculum aims at exploring abstract ideas, then students whose cognitive development is still at the concrete operational stage may lose their motivation and not succeed in their learning.

Piaget's ideas about adaptation also play a key role in his theory of reasoning and intellectual development. **Adaptation** refers to an individual's attempt to create an accurate view of the world so that she can continue the process of development. Two basic principles allow adaptation to occur: assimilation and accommodation. **Assimilation** refers to

> ### Key Idea
>
> *Adaptation* refers to actively creating an accurate view of world. Adaption occurs through two pricipals: assimilation and accommodation.

[1] This book adopts a social constructivist perspective. Other forms of constructivism are radical constructivism and contextual constructivism. For more information on other variants of constructivism, see Tobin, K., ed. 1993, *The practice of constructivism in science education*, Washington, D.C.: American Association for the Advancement of Science. Also consult Shapiro, B. 1994. *What children bring to light: A constructivist perspective on children's learning in science.* New York: Teachers College Press.

Portfolio Activity 2.3

RECOGNIZING AND EVALUATING A SOCIAL CONSTRUCTIVIST LESSON

Materials Needed:
- Something to write with

A. Read the following classroom descriptions.

1. Marquette, a kindergarten teacher, asks her students to tell her what they want to know about pets. Three students want to know more about dinosaurs, two students want to know how they can get pet rabbits, one inquires about a lizard, and two want to learn more about kittens. As students suggest these animals, she writes the words *dinosaur, rabbit, lizard,* and *kitten* on the board. Marquette does not tell the three students that dinosaurs are not pets; instead, she asks the students what they think about the pets suggested. Quickly a number of students point out that dinosaurs are not pets. Marquette asks the students to elaborate on their reasons for this belief, and then she asks the students who originally suggested dinosaurs what they think. Two agree that they are not pets, but one, Tyrone, says that he has a whole collection of them. Marquette asks this student to explain what he thinks it means to have a pet; he says that a pet is an animal you collect. She asks him if he has ever been to a pet store. He has. She asks whether he has ever seen dinosaurs for sale at the pet store. He agrees that he hasn't. Another student quickly quips that the pets must be alive, and you need to feed and care for them. Tyrone agrees and says that he would like to learn more about lizards that look like the dinosaurs in his collection.

    Marquette leads the class in a discussion about what students would like to know about each animal, and she asks them to suggest how they might learn these things. From this discussion comes the idea that veterinarians and pet store owners would be able to answer a number of their questions. Carlos, a boy in the class, says that his mother is a veterinarian and that he will ask her to come to school to talk. Marquette agrees, and she calls the mother to make arrangements. Mrs. Hernandez comes to school the next week and teaches the students about the nutrition necessary for various types of pets—particularly the lizard, rabbit, and kitten suggested by the students. She also discusses dogs, guinea pigs, hamsters, and gerbils, as instructed by Marquette. The next day, Marquette passes out a worksheet with pictures of animals and the foods they eat. The children are evaluated on their ability to match the proper food with the animal that eats it.

2. Ron, a third-grade teacher, is very interested in space flight and astronomy. He has shared with the students in his class many artifacts, including photographs taken on vacations and trips to the Kennedy Space Center at Cape Canaveral in Florida and the Neil Armstrong Center in Wapakoneta, Ohio. He has shown many movies and videos on space travel, and he has even brought his telescope to school for the students to look through. His students have become quite interested in astronomy and space travel. During science class, a student in the class shares with the others that his parents took him to a planetarium at a nearby university over the weekend. Ron decides this would be a great trip for his class and schedules it. On the trip, students learn about the constellations and apparent movement of stars in the sky throughout the year. Ron finds an activity in a teacher book with a star locating device in it. He has his students make the star finder and asks the students to look for certain constellations in the sky over the next month. Daily, he has students share information they have discovered about the stars and various constellations. At the end of the month, he gives the students a quiz in which they match the constellations with their names. He also quizzes students on the definitions of *star, constellation, sun, orbit, revolution, rotation,* and other important words that are in the textbook.

B. Using the following chart, evaluate the two lessons in terms of how well they meet the criteria for social constructivist lessons. Record the results in your portfolio. Then meet with teammates to discuss your evaluations. Come to a consensus.

C. Neither of these two lessons has all the features of a social constructivist classroom. How could they be revised to contain more of the features?

D. Meet with your classmates to come to a consensus on improving the lessons.

E. Record the results of your meetings and thoughts in your portfolio.

Scale for Evaluating Degree of Constructivist Learning

Active Engagement with Phenomena

Students ask and refine questions related to phenomena.
often _____ _____ _____ _____ _____ _____ seldom

Students predict and explain phenomena.
often _____ _____ _____ _____ _____ _____ seldom

Students mindfully interact with concrete materials.
often _____ _____ _____ _____ _____ _____ seldom

Use and Application of Knowledge

Teachers and students use prior knowledge.
often _____ _____ _____ _____ _____ _____ seldom

Students identify and use multiple resources.
often _____ _____ _____ _____ _____ _____ seldom

Students plan and carry out investigations.
often _____ _____ _____ _____ _____ _____ seldom

Students apply concepts and skills to new situations.
often _____ _____ _____ _____ _____ _____ seldom

Students are given time for reflection.
often _____ _____ _____ _____ _____ _____ seldom

Students take action to improve their own world.
often _____ _____ _____ _____ _____ _____ seldom

Multiple Representations

Students use varied evaluation techniques.
often _____ _____ _____ _____ _____ _____ seldom

Students create products or artifacts to represent understanding.
often _____ _____ _____ _____ _____ _____ seldom

Students revise products and artifacts.
often _____ _____ _____ _____ _____ _____ seldom

Use of Learning Communities

Students use language as a tool to express knowledge.
often _____ _____ _____ _____ _____ _____ seldom

Students express, debate, and come to a resolution regarding ideas, concepts, and theories.
often _____ _____ _____ _____ _____ _____ seldom

Students debate the viability of evidence.
often _____ _____ _____ _____ _____ _____ seldom

Learning is situated in a social context.
often _____ _____ _____ _____ _____ _____ seldom

Knowledgeable others help students learn new ideas and skills that they couldn't learn on their own.
often _____ _____ _____ _____ _____ _____ seldom

Role of Authentic Tasks

Driving questions focus and sustain activities.
often _____ _____ _____ _____ _____ _____ seldom

The topic or question is relevant to the student.
often _____ _____ _____ _____ _____ _____ seldom

Learning is connected to students' lives outside school.
often _____ _____ _____ _____ _____ _____ seldom

Science concepts and principles emerge as needed to answer a driving question.
often _____ _____ _____ _____ _____ _____ seldom

fitting new information into existing mental structures or schemes. For instance, a child who has goldfish will think of a fish as an animal that lives in water. When he learns about whales in school, sees a picture of a whale in a book, or sees a video about whales, he classifies the whale as a fish because it lives in water. **Accommodation** refers to making a permanent change in a mental structure. For instance, as the child gains more knowledge about fish and mammals, he changes his mental structure of a fish as an animal that lives in water. He now has schemas for fish that live in water and mammals that live in water.

Piaget's theory of intellectual development had a major influence on the development of the inquiry-focused curriculum of the 1960s such as the Elementary Science Study (ESS) program. ESS asked young students to interact with materials to build mental structures of key science ideas. For instance, in the *Battery and Bulb* unit, students were given a wire, a bulb, and a battery and were asked to light the bulb. Based on this experience, a student would be better able to build a cognitive structure for a circuit.

Piaget's theory of intellectual development also profoundly influenced Robert Karplus's notion of the learning cycle (Karplus, 1977). The **learning cycle** is an instructional model used in a number of curriculum projects developed in the 1960s and 1970s. According to Karplus, the learning cycle consists of phases of instruction that help students learn by providing them with direct experiences with concrete materials, opportunities to construct understandings about concepts, and chances to apply their understandings to new situations. The learning cycle phases are explored more thoroughly in Chapter 7.

Many psychologists refer to Jean Piaget as the "founder of constructivism." Piaget's ideas on how environment and social interactions influence knowledge construction have had a major impact on the constructivist theories at the foundation of new inquiry-oriented curricula of the 1990s and 2000s and on the use of collaborative learning strategies in science. Piaget regarded socialization as significant in the development of reasoning (Piaget, 1959). He argued that, when learners discuss ideas with their peers, they become aware of the different views of a problem. This confrontation requires them to seek new information and formulate new hypotheses and, over time, to structure a new way of thinking. We discuss collaboration thoroughly in Chapter 6.

The Influence of Lev Vygotsky

Although influenced by Piaget, social constructivist theories in education developed primarily from the works of Lev Vygotsky, a Russian psychologist, who concluded that children construct knowledge or understanding as the result of thinking and doing in social contexts (Vygotsky, 1986). Vygotsky believed that development depends on biological factors (such as brain growth and maturation) and on social and cultural forces (such as the influence of others at home, in school, or on the playground). He also believed that learning takes place in social contexts (such as during playtime with peers, in conversations with classmates, or while parents or teachers are speaking) and that children internalize information they gather in those contexts to form understanding. Children gradually become more independent and autonomous through social interactions with others such as teachers and other adults. Researchers in science education have found evidence to support the social constructivist viewpoint about how children learn science (Brown & Campione, 1994; Driver, 1989; Roth, 1995).

Social constructivism holds that children learn concepts or construct meaning through their interactions with and interpretations of their world, including essential interactions

> ### Key Idea
>
> Social constructivism holds that children learn concepts or construct meaning through their interactions with and interpretations of their world, including essential interactions with others.

with others. From the moment a child is born, she (supported through interactions with others) is constructing knowledge of her environment. Knowledge is not something that is simply memorized; it is constructed by the learner according to her experiences in the world. For example, a child may learn that leaves fall from trees after they turn colors during the autumn by observing this happen several years in a row. Discussions with family members or peers may influence his understanding. For example, a parent might explain that leaves fall when the weather becomes cold. Knowledge is the result of individual interpretations (the child notices they fall after they turn color) and constructions of reality as it occurs in a social context (a parent says this happens when it gets cold).

Children receive information, interpret it, and relate it to other **prior knowledge and experiences.** As a result, they come to school already holding concepts related to concepts teachers will be expecting to help them learn. These prior experiences and conceptions will influence any new knowledge they attempt to acquire. For example, a teacher who attempts to teach a class about why trees drop leaves will encounter any number of prior ideas about this phenomenon in the minds of her students. Some might think the leaves drop because they are dead. Some might think the tree runs out of food. Others might think that the color of the leaves causes them to fall. Some might think trees sleep in the winter. Still others might think that the cold winter winds blow the leaves off. These prior beliefs will affect the teaching and learning going on in the classroom. Because prior knowledge and experiences influence the learning of new knowledge, it is important to reflect frequently on prior experiences. You probably have already noticed that the chapter titles in this book are questions, each chapter begins with reflective questions, and many activities ask you to think about your own experiences. These questions help *you* reflect on *your* ideas.

Because children come to school with prior understandings about their world, their concepts and theories are not always the same as those developed over the years by scientists. As a teacher you might try, for example, to teach elementary students that air is matter and that matter is something that takes up space and has mass. A typical activity in many elementary textbooks demonstrates to children that two deflated balloons will balance on a scale but that one deflated and one inflated balloon will result in the tilt of the inflated balloon toward the ground.[2] This activity provides students with some evidence that air has mass and takes up space—the balloon filled with air has more mass than the one without air.

What if, before showing children the result of this activity, a teacher asked them to predict the event? What do you think young children would predict? Think about some of the prior experiences elementary children may have had with air. Air (helium) in a balloon causes it to float away. Air in a raft or beach ball causes it to float on water. Air cannot be seen. These prior experiences may have convinced students that air is nothing or that air has no mass. They may predict, therefore, that nothing will happen—air is a nonentity, so the

> **Key Idea**
>
> Prior experiences and knowledge influence the learning of new knowledge.

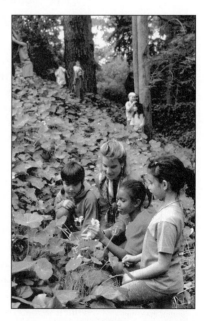

Children learn about their environment by interacting with others.

[2]When doing this demonstration, the balloon must be filled with a source of dry air, so do not blow up the balloon using your mouth. Your lungs and mouth contain much moisture and will add water vapor to the balloon as well as other gases. Instead, use a bicycle pump to blow up the balloon.

inflated and deflated balloons should still balance. Perhaps they will predict that the inflated balloon will float upward and the empty balloon will sink. Young students will probably not be convinced otherwise by a teacher's demonstration.

The teacher needs to create a learning environment that encourages students to revise their own concepts to accept these new formulations. This is not an easy task. Learning is a continuous process that requires many new experiences in which students can construct and reconstruct knowledge by interacting with others and materials. Children need many opportunities to express and explore their ideas. These ideas about social constructivism have a number of implications for teaching science and are the foundations for project-based science.

A SOCIAL CONSTRUCTIVIST MODEL OF TEACHING

The social constructivist theory asserts that children take an active role in constructing meaning; they cannot construct meaning by passively absorbing knowledge transmitted from a teacher. An ancient Chinese proverb captures this idea in three simple lines:

Tell me, and I forget.

Show me, and I remember.

Involve me, and I understand.

Accordingly, teaching based on social constructivist theory focuses on the child as an active builder of knowledge in a community of learners. Social constructivist theory has implications for the way a teacher creates the learning environment, sets up lessons, asks questions, reacts to students' ideas, and carries out lessons. Lorsbach and Tobin (1992) suggest that teaching science using a constructivist approach means that teachers do *not* teach science as "the search for the truth." Instead, they teach science more as scientists really do science—by actively engaging children in the "social process of making sense of experiences." This approach differs greatly from much of what can be seen in "school science" today, where science teaching consists of asking students to memorize terminology and find correct answers.

Table 2.2 lists the main features of this model of learning. We will now explore each of these in depth.

Active Engagement with Phenomena

Children construct understanding in science by actively engaging with phenomena. **Active engagement** describes several experiences: Students ask and refine questions related to phenomena, they predict and explain phenomena, and they mindfully interact with concrete materials. Active engagement, then, is both mental and physical.

Students Ask and Refine Questions and Predict and Explain Phenomena

To actively engage students intellectually, teachers must create a learning environment in which students can *ask questions* freely, *dialogue* with classmates and more knowledgeable others to *refine questions,* and *predict and explain phenomena.* Such cognitive

FEATURES OF THE SOCIAL CONSTRUCTIVIST MODEL OF LEARNING

Table 2.2

ACTIVE ENGAGEMENT WITH PHENOMENA
- Students ask and refine questions related to phenomena.
- Students predict and explain phenomena.
- Students mindfully interact with concrete materials.

USE AND APPLICATION OF KNOWLEDGE
- Teachers and students use prior knowledge.
- Students identify and use multiple resources.
- Students plan and carry out investigations.
- Students apply concepts and skills to new situations.
- Students are given time for reflection.
- Students take action to improve their own world.

MULTIPLE REPRESENTATIONS
- Teachers use varied evaluation techniques.
- Students create products or artifacts to represent understanding.
- Students revise products and artifacts.

USE OF LEARNING COMMUNITIES
- Students use language as a tool to express knowledge.
- Students express, debate, and come to a resolution regarding ideas, concepts, and theories.
- Students debate the viability of evidence.
- Learning is situated in a social context.
- Knowledgeable others help students learn new ideas and skills that they couldn't learn on their own.

AUTHENTIC TASKS
- Driving questions focus and sustain activities.
- The topic or question is relevant to the student.
- Learning is connected to students' lives outside school. Technology tools can help connect learning to life outside of the school.
- Science concepts and principles emerge as needed to answer a driving question.

activities help students make connections and develop in-depth understandings (Brooks & Brooks, 1993). It is through discourse (asking questions, having discussions about important questions, making predictions, and providing explanations) that students come to understand what they know. (The role of questioning and ways to set up project-based learning environments that support questioning are covered in several chapters. Chapter 4 explores the role of predicting and explaining phenomena.)

Imagine a second-grade teacher asks, "How could we find out if the apple seed is alive?" She is stimulating the students to ask questions. Students might ask in return, "Could we plant it?" "Can we cut it open to see if something is growing inside?" "Could we ask a farmer?" The teacher has the students work in groups to discuss and refine these

CONNECTING TO
NATIONAL SCIENCE EDUCATION STANDARDS

Science Teaching Standards

An important stage of inquiry and of student science learning is the oral and written discourse that focuses the attention of the student on how they know what they know and how their knowledge connects to larger ideas, domains, and the world beyond the classroom (p. 36).

questions. They might debate the fact that cutting open the seed could kill it and, therefore, defeat the purpose of their investigation. This thought might lead them to settle on planting the seed to see if it is alive. If the students planted the apple seed, they could predict what would happen next. This could lead to more refined questions such as "Why isn't it sprouting yet?" and "Do we need to water it more?" If the apple seed began to sprout, students could explain that the seed was alive. However, a lively debate could still take place about whether the seed was alive before being planted. It is through the process of asking and refining questions, making predictions, making observations and providing explanations about the apple seed that students begin to understand whether the seed is alive.

Students Mindfully Interact with Concrete Materials

One hallmark of social constructivist teaching is that students mindfully interact with concrete materials. Children retain more of what they are taught if they engage in more active, concrete types of learning. In fact, it is estimated that the more active and concrete their learning, the more they retain (Bruner, 1977).

Dale's Cone of Experience

Dale's Cone of Experience (Dale, 1969) provides teachers with a tool for thinking about teaching strategies. This categorization is not a prescription for determining how actively students are engaged cognitively because, for example, even active reading strategies[3] can make reading about science far less passive. Rather, it provides a framework for thinking about how a particular strategy might use concrete materials. Notice where demonstrations fall on the scale of Dale's Cone of Experience[4] in Figure 2.4. A demonstration is visually oriented; students do not work directly with materials but rather watch the teacher work with materials. Demonstrations, thus, are moderately abstract compared with activities in which students work with concrete materials themselves. Some instructional tools, such as computer applications, can provide different levels of direct student interaction. Thus, computer applications (which were not yet widely used in schools at the time Dale proposed this hierarchy) can fall into several categories. Some computer programs are very abstract—requiring mostly reading or symbol interpretation. However, computer *simulations* fit into the Contrived Experiences category, and programs with interface devices permitting students to investigate with temperature and light probes provide Direct Experiences. Take time to complete Portfolio Activity 2.4.

Use and Application of Knowledge

Key Idea

Students develop meaningful understanding when they use and apply ideas.

To develop meaningful understandings, students need to use and apply their knowledge. This use and application of knowledge is supported by six strategies:

1.   Teachers must consider students' prior knowledge.

---

[3]See, for example, Carr, E. M., and L. E. Aldinger. 1994. *Thinking works: Using cognitive processes in the language arts classroom.* Ann Arbor, Mich.: Exceptional Innovations.

[4]Edgar Dale's Cone of Experience pictured in Figure 2.4 was modified by a personal friend, Rolinda LeMay, to include comments pertaining to level of involvement and percentage of retention.

2. Activities must encourage students to identify and use multiple resources.

3. Activities must involve students in planning and carrying out investigations.

4. Learned concepts and skills must be applied to new situations.

5. Students should be allowed time for reflection.

6. Teachers must help students take action to improve their own world.

CONNECTING TO
NATIONAL SCIENCE EDUCATION STANDARDS

Science Education Program Standards
Learning science is something students do, not something that is done to them. In learning science, students describe objects and events, ask questions, acquire knowledge, construct explanations of natural phenomena, test those explanations in many different ways, and communicate their ideas to others (p. 18).

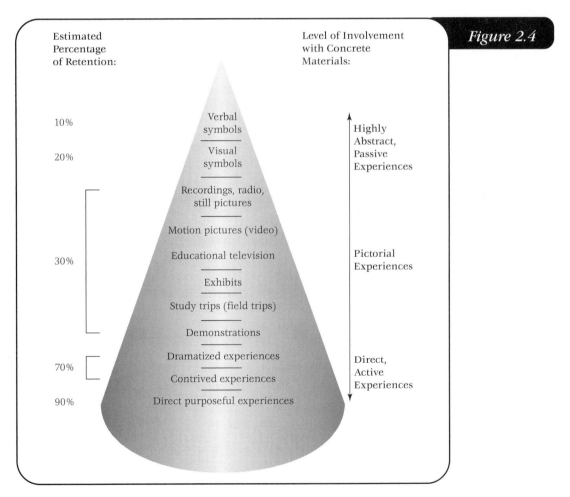

Figure 2.4

Estimated Percentage of Retention:

Level of Involvement with Concrete Materials:

10%   Verbal symbols

20%   Visual symbols

Recordings, radio, still pictures

Motion pictures (video)

Educational television

30%

Exhibits

Study trips (field trips)

Demonstrations

Dramatized experiences

70%   Contrived experiences

90%   Direct purposeful experiences

Highly Abstract, Passive Experiences

Pictorial Experiences

Direct, Active Experiences

Dale's Cone of Experience.

Portfolio Activity 2.4   **DETERMINING LEVELS OF CONCRETENESS AND ABSTRACTNESS**

Materials Needed:
- A copy of Dale's Cone of Experience (Figure 2.4)

A. What follows is a list of a number of strategies for teaching about recycling. Rank each strategy's level of abstraction on a scale of 1 to 5 (1 being very concrete and 5 being very abstract).

1. Watching a television documentary about landfill problems.
2. Watching the teacher sort aluminum, glass, and plastic into three recycling bins.
3. Visiting a recycling center.
4. Burying a piece of plastic, a glass cup, a banana skin, a piece of bread, and an aluminum can; watering the items weekly; and periodically uncovering the items to see if they are decomposing.
5. Painting a poster to promote recycling.
6. Writing a rap song about recycling.
7. Coloring a picture about the ways to limit litter (reuse, recycle, reduce).
8. Starting a compost in the school playground.
9. Arranging in sequence pictures about how long it takes some items to biodegrade.
10. Reading a newspaper article about recycling.
11. Listening to a guest speaker from the local recycling center.
12. Writing a story about the future if people fail to solve landfill problems.
13. Creating a poem about recycling.
14. Sorting items from the school lunch into aluminum, glass, and plastic bins.
15. Starting a school paper recycling program.
16. Keeping track of the amount of waste produced in the classroom for the week and estimating how much would be produced in a year.
17. Role playing what to do if a friend drops a candy wrapper on the ground.
18. Looking at photographs of landfills.

B. Convene with some of your classmates to share your rankings of the teaching strategies. Try to come to a consensus about the rankings.

C. Obtain a variety of teacher resources and activity books. Look in them for lessons to teach about plant growth. In your portfolio, make a list of lessons, activity ideas, or investigations that would be more concrete than the ones in the books. How could you make any abstract strategies more concrete?

Teachers and Students Use Prior Knowledge and Experience

In order for a teacher to help students use and apply their knowledge, she or he must consider what it is that students already know. The following paragraph serves as an illustration of this point:

> It is really actually simple. First, you arrange things into different groups depending upon their makeup. Of course, one pile may be enough depending on how much there is to do. If you have to go somewhere else due to a lack of equipment, that is the next step; otherwise, you are pretty well set. It is important not to overdo any particular part of the job. That is, it is better to do too few things at once than too many. In the short run, this may not seem important, but trouble from doing too many can easily arise. A mistake can be expensive as well. Working the equipment should be self-explanatory, and we need not dwell on it here. Soon, however, it will become just another facet of life. It is difficult to see an end to the necessity for this task in the immediate future, but then one can never tell (Bransford, 1979).

What is this paragraph about? You probably had difficulty understanding it because you were not given any clue about its topic. If you had known from the start that it was about washing clothes, you would have understood it instantly. Reread the paragraph now that you know what it is about. Doesn't it make more sense? In this case, activating your prior knowledge clearly would have enhanced your ability to understand new material.

Constructivist teaching approaches focus on the learner's prior knowledge, because it is the learner who must integrate new ideas into his or her current understandings. Shapiro (1994) writes,

> The role of the teacher [in a constructivist view] is not to simply present new information, correct students' "misconceptions," and demonstrate skills. It is to guide the learner to consider new ways of thinking about phenomena and events. In order to do so, the teacher must have some understanding of what the learner brings to the learning experience, that is, his or her prior ideas, and thoughts (p. 8).

To help students integrate their understandings, teachers must know about their prior understandings. Recall the examples earlier in this chapter of the role played by prior knowledge and experience in learning. Children have had years of experience with leaves falling or with air (blowing, in balloons, in balls) before they come to school to receive formal instruction about these concepts. When teachers attempt to teach students that air has mass, prior experiences may conflict with the new ideas as students try to integrate the new understandings into their conceptual framework of "air." With some awareness of students' past experiences, teachers can help students reconcile what seem to be conflicts between those experiences and new learning. Without this awareness, teachers will still be able to ensure that teaching takes place but not that learning does.

There are many ways to probe for students' prior knowledge. For example, in the washing clothes scenario, a teacher could provide students with a mental organizer (such as telling them they are about to read about washing clothes) and discuss what they know about washing clothes before students read the paragraph. Another strategy is to remind students of an activity or investigation done earlier in the year that has some connection to new learning.

Students Identify and Use Multiple Resources

An important strategy in helping children construct understandings in science is having them identify and use multiple resources. **Multiple resources,** which might be used in the course of answering a driving question, include books, journals, science equipment, supplies, and computers. They reinforce student understanding through different presentation and through emphasis of different information. While a book might explain via text and photographs how a landfill works, a Web page might present a slightly different explanation through illustrations and through interactive charts of statistics on landfill usage and cleanup efforts. When students analyze and synthesize this different information presented in these different ways, they create more solid, integrated understandings.

Students Plan and Carry Out Investigations

The cycle of asking a question, making observations, designing an investigation, collecting data, analyzing results, and asking new questions, which is a key feature of project-based science, requires children to use and apply their understandings. (The investigation web is further explored in Chapter 4.) Assume a class is exploring the question "Where does all our garbage go?" To explore this driving question, students might set up a decomposition column (or other organic matierial), which is a small composter in a 2-liter pop bottle filled with leaves, dirt, banana peels, and worms. Students ask questions such as "Why do worms help the materials in our pop bottles decompose faster?" or "How does moisture affect how fast decomposition occurs?" Students gather information related to their questions from multiple resources such as books, journals, and the World Wide Web. Students plan investigations to answer these questions, considering the materials they will need, how they will collect and analyze the data, and how they will present their findings to the class. They make predictions about what will happen to the items in the bottle. Then students carry out their investigations. They debate whether two pop bottles can provide ample evidence for whether moisture affects the rate of decomposition. Students create artifacts such as posters or multimedia products to represent their understanding of decomposition. Finally, students share and explain ideas about the problem of decomposition as it relates to landfills. This process of asking and refining questions, debating ideas, making predictions, designing experiments, gathering information, collecting and analyzing data, drawing conclusions, and communicating ideas and findings to others helps students construct a solid, integrated understanding of the topic and related concepts.

Students Apply Concepts and Skills to New Situations

Students develop rich, meaningful understandings when they apply their knowledge to new situations. This phenomenon is illustrated as the change in understanding from Cell C to Cell D in Figure 2.3. By applying concepts and skills to new situations, students elaborate on their understandings, form new connections with old ideas, and build connections between new ideas and old ideas. For instance, in the decomposition example, students can apply their knowledge of how oxygen affects decomposition to real world situations such as landfills. Through discussions with others, students can make connections between the understanding that oxygen is needed for decomposition and the awareness that materials don't decompose quickly in a landfill.

Students Are Given Time for Reflection

In science, **reflection** involves thinking about alternative questions, considering hypotheses, contemplating a variety of answers, speculating on outcomes, deliberating on steps that can be taken, and meditating on conclusions found. Reflection takes *time.* Teachers cannot rush through topics, lessons, and examples and expect students to learn new material thoroughly. For this reason, constructivist teachers present fewer topics in the curriculum and spend more time on them. Teachers provide students with time in class to discuss ideas with others, write about experiences, and revise ideas and products. Recall the teacher who had students discuss whether the apple seed was alive. During discussions teachers use the technique of wait-time: They wait three to five seconds after asking a question before calling on a student. In addition, teachers ask *probing* questions, which are questions designed to elicit more details. (Wait-time and probing questions are discussed in more detail in Chapter 7.) Brooks and Brooks (1993) write,

> Classroom environments that require immediate responses prevent these students from thinking through issues and concepts thoroughly, forcing them, in effect, to become spectators as their quicker peers react. They learn over time that there's no point in mentally engaging in teacher-posed questions because the questions will have been answered before they have had the opportunity to develop hypotheses (p. 115).

Students Take Action to Improve Their Own World

The idea of taking action to improve the world has become popular in science education in the last few decades. The Science Technology Society (STS) movement that was popularized in the 1980s is one example. STS focuses on topics such as health, population, resources, pollution, and environment—topics that people must understand in order to become active citizens who make decisions and take actions related to society or to improving their lives.

Children are particularly interested in studying questions that can be applied to their own lives and improve their own world. Adolescents see themselves as emerging adults and feel a particular urgency about the future. Many adolescents are interested in ecological topics and environmental issues (Barnes, Shaw, & Spector, 1989). Adolescents see exploration of these topics as a way of taking action to improve their world. Middle grade students may be interested in more far-reaching *local* issues, such as the health of a local stream. They may be interested in monitoring the quality of the stream and reporting it to a local governmental agency. Young elementary students have less global concerns. They are interested in more personal concerns such as improving the living conditions and nutrition of their pets at home. Children of all ages care about improving the school environment. They can put up bird feeders, plant wildflowers, and organize a litter pickup day. When learning includes taking action to improve their world, children see the importance of it, and the action solidifies their knowledge.

NSES

CONNECTING TO NATIONAL SCIENCE EDUCATION STANDARDS

Science Education Content Standards K–4

As a result of activities in grades K–4, all students should develop understanding of personal health, characteristics and changes in population, types of resources, changes in environments, and science and technology in local challenges (p. 138).

NSES

CONNECTING TO NATIONAL SCIENCE EDUCATION STANDARDS

Science Education Content Standards 5–8

As a result of activities in grades 5–8, all students should develop abilities of technological design and understandings about science and technology (p. 161).

Multiple Representations

Constructivist theory asserts that learning involves developing **multiple representations** of ideas that integrate understanding. In the decomposition activity described earlier, students constructed a decomposition column, wrote about their investigation, and built a poster to express their ideas. Writing, building a poster, and manipulating materials are examples of different representations. These three activities require the translation of understandings into three different formats—concrete, textual, and graphical representations. When students make connections among these representations, they develop integrated understandings that can be applied to new situations.

> ### Key Idea
> When students make connections between various representations, they develop integrated understandings that they can apply to new situations.

Teachers Use Varied Evaluation Techniques

There are two reasons to use varied evaluation techniques. First, different types of evaluation techniques can better assess different types of understanding formed through a variety of intellectual activities. Second, multiple forms of assessment help different learners succeed in demonstrating their understandings.

In project-based science, students develop different types of understandings that each must be assessed, and these understandings may be assessed in a variety of ways. (Assessment and evaluation are covered in detail in Chapters 8 and 9.) For example, how might students demonstrate understanding about water quality in a stream? They might write reports, present artifacts to classmates, take photographs, or create multimedia products that document a stream cleanup effort.

Because different learners will respond to different assessment techniques in different ways, using a variety of assessment techniques ensures that all students are evaluated appropriately. Whereas one child might flourish on a written exam, another might present her ideas more effectively with a poster or three-dimensional model, and yet another might express his ideas better through a written journal. By using a variety of forms of assessment, teachers let students express their understandings in ways consistent with their individual strengths.

Because constructivist theories focus on students' prior experiences to frame teaching and learning, multiple paths (from different students' ideas) to learning emerge. Therefore, assessment also needs to include students' interpretations of their learning. Students' interpretations can be captured with self-evaluation techniques. Teachers can interview students about how they think they have progressed in learning about a topic or skill. Students can also keep journals to track their own progress throughout a project.

Students Create and Revise Products or Artifacts to Represent Understanding

Another approach to helping students create understanding is through the building and revision of artifacts. Artifacts are tangible representations of student understanding that answer a driving question. They include models, reports, videos, and computer programs. They can be thought of as external, intellectual products. Papert (1980, 1993) refers to artifacts as "objects-to-think-with" because they are concrete and explicit and serve as tools of learning. Students build understanding by constructing artifacts and explaining to each other the meaning of their artifacts. Artifacts and products can be critiqued by others—students, teachers, parents, and community members. As a result, learners have many opportunities to reflect on and revise their artifacts, and so they have many opportunities to further enrich their knowledge.

Imagine that students decide to make a poster presentation to explain how they will explore the influence of fertilizer on plant growth. In the process of developing this artifact, students need to select plants and explain their selections, and they need to determine the amount of fertilizer. The students need to provide answers to questions such as "How many plants?" "How much fertilizer?" and "How often?" All of these decisions focus the students' thinking and help develop deeper understanding. Students again have an opportunity for enhanced understanding when their teacher and classmates give them feedback on their poster.

Use of Learning Communities

The social constructivist model holds that students learn in a social context—a learning community. Within such learning communities, language is a primary tool for developing understanding. In this section, we explore five aspects of **learning communities:**

1. students using language as a tool to express knowledge,
2. students using language to come to a resolution about science ideas and theories,
3. students debating the viability of evidence,
4. students learning in a social context, and
5. students learning from knowledgeable others.

We will also discuss ways that knowledgeable others can use scaffolding to help students learn.

Students Use Language as a Tool to Express Knowledge

Children (and adults) learn best when they can talk about and share their ideas with their peers and with concerned adults. Hence, meaningful learning develops as an interplay between the child thinking about ideas (an *intra*personal use of language) and talking with others (an *inter*personal use of language). This interplay helps the child build connections among ideas, integrating understanding. When a child uses the words push or pull to describe force to another child, a learner demonstrates his or her understanding of the concept.

Teachers can help students use language in a variety of ways. One, students can debate ideas. For example, they can debate whether temperature affects the growth of seeds. Two, students can share information in written form. For example, students can create reports to share the results of their investigations with others or exchange journals so that others can read about their investigations. Three, students can learn through oral language. For example, many teachers have students explain their investigations to classmates using artifacts or products.

Students Express, Debate, and Come to a Resolution Regarding Ideas, Concepts, and Theories

Healthy debates are a critical aspect of developing understanding in science. Constructivists define *science* as knowledge that has been publicly debated and accepted by scientists (Shapiro, 1994). Scientists continually obtain new information from investigations, and they debate ideas based on this information. Similarly, in science classrooms, teachers want students to debate ideas, concepts, and theories and come to resolutions about them. The student who believed dinosaurs were pets because he collected them debated this idea with classmates, who offered reasons that dinosaurs were not pets. Finally, all students came to the resolution that dinosaurs were not pets.

Students Debate the Viability of Evidence

Scientists constantly debate the viability of evidence. One group of scientists may speculate that mutations being found in frogs around the world are the result of depleted ozone. Another group of scientists argues that the deformations are a result of pollutants in the environment. The viability of evidence is debated until one supposition or another is supported by most in the scientific community. Just as scientists debate the viability of evidence, students

NSES

CONNECTING TO
NATIONAL SCIENCE EDUCATION STANDARDS

Science Education Program Standards
Thinking critically about evidence includes deciding what evidence should be used and accounting for anomalous data (p. 145).

need to do this in science classrooms. For example, students might debate whether the height of a plant is a good indicator of growth. Some students might argue that number of leaves and color are more important indicators than is height, because height might only indicate that the plant is stretching to reach sunlight (a tropism).

Learning Is Situated in a Social Context

Children do not construct understanding in isolation but in a social context. Parents, friends, teachers, peers, community members, books, television, movies, and cultural customs all affect the construction of student understanding. For example, students learning about decomposition share with classmates their findings from various experiments performed on decomposition columns. They visit local landfills or recycling plants and talk with the managers. They connect to the World Wide Web to talk with other students around the country about the problem of landfills in their region. They talk with peers to see if any use composts at home. Each of these social interactions helps students build integrated understandings. In isolation, these understandings might not be connected, but through social construction of ideas, students link new understandings with old ones.

Knowledgeable Others Help Students Learn New Ideas and Skills That They Couldn't Learn on Their Own

A basic idea that stems from these ideas about language, culture, and community is that more competent others can assist children in accomplishing a more difficult cognitive task than they otherwise could on their own. The development of understanding occurs as a result of social interaction with more knowledgeable others and with peers. Even second graders are able in learning communities to carry out sophisticated investigations under the guidance of a classroom teacher.

Vygotsky (1978) developed the construct of the **zone of proximal development** to represent the hypothetical space between assisted and unassisted performance of a learner, or the distance between the actual developmental level as determined by independent problem solving and the level of potential development as determined through problem solving under adult guidance or in collaboration with more capable peers (1978, pp. 85–86). He studied the difference between concepts learned spontaneously, or out of school, with those learned in school, and he concluded that children learned more when the teacher or more knowledgeable adults assisted them. The presence of a more knowledgeable other appeared to foster the discussion and debate of ideas. Vygotsky concluded that the social interaction between students and teachers or other adults is an important aspect of intellectual development, because the zone of proximal development allows learners to take part in more cognitively challenging tasks and problem solving than they could on their own.

Others have expanded Vygotsky's ideas to include collaborative interactions with peers. Researchers have found that students learn more effectively when working in collaborative groups with advanced or knowledgeable peers than they do working alone. Forman (1989) coined the term **bidirectional zone of proximal development** to describe the expertise levels in collaborative groups and the fluctuations among group members—sometimes members are the teacher and sometimes they are the learner. A collaborative classroom thus becomes an environment that comprises what Vygotsky called multiple zones of proximal development. Students are exposed to overlapping zones as they learn by interacting with many different people—the teacher, peers, and community members. Each person with whom the student interacts can become a support that will enable the student to climb to the next level of learning. This is one reason that collaborative learning is stressed in constructivist classrooms. We discuss collaboration in detail in Chapter 6.

By identifying the learners' zones of proximal development, a teacher can provide the assistance that is needed to move a learner to a higher level of understanding than would be possible without the support. Good teachers have always provided this support by doing things such as modeling ideas for students. The zone of proximal development simply serves to name these types of support so we can talk about them.

Scaffolding. The concept of scaffolding stems from Vygotsky's notion of the zone of proximal development. **Scaffolding** (Bruner, 1977; Wood, Bruner, & Ross, 1976) is a process in which a more knowledgeable individual provides support to another learner to help him or her understand or solve a problem. In scaffolding, the more knowledgeable other directs those aspects of the intellectual task that are initially beyond the capacity of the learner. This allows the learner to take part in intellectual activities that otherwise would be unwelcoming, activities that he or she doesn't completely understand. Imagine a parent helping her child put together a Lego structure. The parent might say, "Let's find all the pieces that are blue." Next the parent might suggest snapping all the blue pieces together. Although the child might not see how the individual steps fit together to build a castle, because the parent has structured the activity, the child can participate in building the structure.

Scaffolds used by knowledgeable others (parents, teachers, other adults, or peers) include modeling, coaching, sequencing, reducing complexity, marking critical features, and using visual tools. In the Lego example, the parent has provided a very important aspect of instruction that is known as *sequencing*. Sequencing, which is just one of the many types of scaffolds that can be used in a classroom, breaks a difficult task into much smaller, manageable subtasks. What follows is a summary of scaffolding strategies that teachers can use to support learning:

> ### Key Idea
> A more knowledgeable individual provides a scaffold to support a learner by helping him or her to take part in intellectually demanding tasks just out of his or her developmental level.

- **Modeling** is the process through which a more knowledgeable person illustrates to the learner how to complete a task. For example, a teacher could demonstrate how to use the concept of *average* to analyze data or how to read a scale. Many science processes can be modeled for students. Some of these processes are *asking questions, planning and designing investigations,* and *forming conclusions.*
- **Coaching** involves providing suggestions to help a student develop knowledge or skills. For example, a teacher might make suggestions to a student about how to make more precise measurements when reading a spring scale. The teacher might suggest, for instance, that the student make sure the scale is calibrated to start at zero before beginning to use the scale. Other forms of coaching include asking thought-provoking questions (such as "How do your data support your conclusion?"), giving students sentence stems (such as "My data support my conclusion because . . ."), and supplying intellectual or cognitive prompts (such as asking students to write down predictions, give reasons, and elaborate answers).
- **Sequencing** is breaking down a larger task into subtasks so a child can focus on completing just one subtask at a time rather than worry about the entire task at once. A teacher might break down the process of investigations into

Figure 2.5

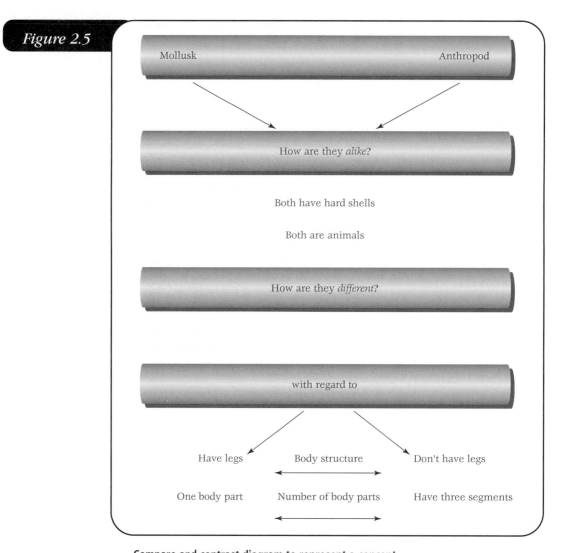

Compare and contrast diagram to represent a concept.

various components, not allowing the learner to proceed to the next step until completing a step. For example, the teacher could require the learner to complete a rough blueprint plan before moving on to building an apparatus.

- **Reducing complexity** involves withholding complex understandings or tasks until the learner has mastered simpler understandings or subtasks. The classical example is helping a child learn to ride a bicycle by using training wheels. In science classrooms, a teacher might use an analogy to reduce the complexity of a concept. For instance, a teacher might compare DNA to the instructions for building a model airplane.

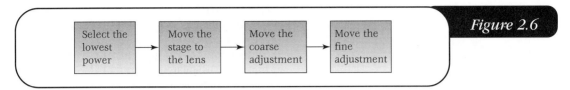

Figure 2.6

Visual tool to represent steps in a task

- **Marking critical features** is highlighting the essential elements of a concept or task. For instance, a teacher might point out to young students that animals called *mammals* all have hair. In teaching a student how to focus a microscope, a teacher might point out that it is important to always start with the lowest-power lens first.
- **Using visual tools** (pictorial prompts) can help students understand their own thinking, processes, concepts, or tasks (Hyerle, 1996; Parks & Black, 1992). Visual tools make abstract ideas more concrete by organizing them or illustrating relationships among them. Although there are many kinds of visual tools, we illustrate two: one designed to help students understand a concept (Figure 2.5) and another designed to help students understand a task (Figure 2.6). *Compare and contrast diagrams* (Parks & Black, 1992) are visual tools that illustrate the relationships among the characteristics of two different objects. Learning the classifications of various animals, for example, requires students to understand similarities or differences among animals. Figure 2.5 is a sample compare and contrast diagram that depicts the similarities and differences between mollusks and arthropods. Steps provide a simple pictorial representation of a task, helping students to visualize it. Figure 2.6 is a simple pictorial representation of the steps to focus a microscope.

Graphic Organizers

Often, it is the teacher who provides the scaffolds during instruction. Other vehicles for scaffolding are peers (same age or older), community members, parent volunteers, and technology. Many teachers find that, at first, they (or knowledgeable others) must provide much support and structure in the classroom. However, gradually, the learner can take more and more responsibility for structuring his or her own learning.

For example, at the beginning of the year, a teacher might model for students how to ask good questions and demonstrate why they are appropriate questions. However, as the year progresses, the teacher expects students to ask their own questions and give justifications for why they are good questions. When students have reached this point, it is still critical that the teacher provide feedback.

For scaffolding to be beneficial to the learner, the following conditions must be present.

- Support must be relevant to the student and the student's task. To be relevant, the support must be related to a task a student needs to complete. For instance, the teacher can reduce the complexity of data analysis by providing a chart for collecting data.
- Support must correspond to the level of help needed by the student. If the support is geared too high for students, it will not match their understanding. If it is too low, it will not be useful. The analogy that DNA is like a set of instructions

for putting together a model airplane might be appropriate for a fifth grader who has put together an airplane. Comparing DNA to the instructions in a computer program, however, would be beyond most fifth graders' experience.

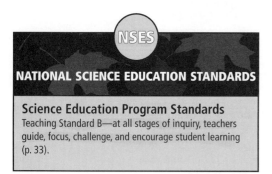

NATIONAL SCIENCE EDUCATION STANDARDS

Science Education Program Standards
Teaching Standard B—at all stages of inquiry, teachers guide, focus, challenge, and encourage student learning (p. 33).

- The support must be given in close proximity in time to the student's request for help. Delaying support might mean that an educational opportunity is lost and that support is not given until a student no longer needs it.
- The student must take action on the opportunity (or apply what he or she has learned). For example, a student needs to apply her understanding of finding averages to her own data.
- Scaffolds need to be **faded**—This means that the support must decrease over time. A child first learning to ride a bike uses training wheels. The training wheels are gradually raised. Next, the training wheels are removed, and the child tries to ride the bike with an adult running alongside the bike. Finally, the child rides the bike on his or her own. In science class, a teacher might start by showing students how to create a bar graph. Next, the class and the teacher co-construct bar charts. After that, students working in groups construct bar graphs with the teacher merely giving them feedback.

Authentic Tasks

Social constructivism also points to the need for students to learn by addressing problems that they see as authentic (Brown, Collins, & Duguid, 1989; Newman, Griffin, & Cole, 1989; Resnick, 1987). To develop meaningful understandings, students must develop knowledge related to real situations. Because deep learning occurs only when a task is situated, tasks must take on meaning beyond what occurs in the school. **Authentic tasks** are those that have meaning for the child beyond the classroom. We'll explore four aspects of authentic tasks: the driving question, the relevance of a question or topic to students, the connection of learning to students' lives outside of school, and the emergence of science concepts and principles when they are needed.

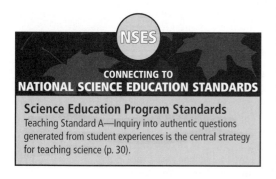

CONNECTING TO
NATIONAL SCIENCE EDUCATION STANDARDS

Science Education Program Standards
Teaching Standard A—Inquiry into authentic questions generated from student experiences is the central strategy for teaching science (p. 30).

Driving Questions Focus and Sustain Activities

Driving questions are a vehicle for bringing authentic tasks into classrooms. (Chapter 3 explores the driving question in greater detail.) In project-based science, the driving question contextualizes learning experiences in the lives of learners, organizes concepts, and drives activities. As students pursue solutions to a driving question, they develop meaningful understandings of key scientific concepts. For instance, the question "What is the pH of rainwater in our city?" allows students to explore concepts such as acids and bases, pH, and concentration. The question also organizes the activities involved in planning and carrying out investigations of the acidity of rainwater and of the impact acid rain has on living and nonliving things. A question such as "How do you light a structure?" allows students to explore principles such as parallel and series circuits, voltage, resistance, current, and power. Activities might be organized around students designing and building structures that they can light.

The Topic or Question Is Relevant to the Student

A guiding principle of constructivism is that problems, questions, and topics must be relevant or pertinent to children. Greenberg (1990) suggests that relevant questions are testable by children, involve the use of equipment in testing ideas, are complex enough to elicit problem-solving approaches, and can be solved through group efforts. Haberman (1995) argues that many students' misbehaviors in schools are caused by not being involved with meaningful learning activities. He stresses that project-based methods can make learning relevant and meaningful. Similarly, Blumenfeld and colleagues (1991), in a summary of the literature, argue that student interest is enhanced when (a) tasks are varied and include novel elements, (b) the problem is authentic and has value, (c) the problem is challenging, (d) there is closure through the creation of an artifact or product, (e) there is choice about what and/or how work is done, and (f) there are opportunities to work with others.

Some people criticize the idea of relevance, arguing that a certain curriculum, whether pertinent to students or not, must be covered in schools. Brooks and Brooks (1993) write that, "relevance does not have to be preexisting for the student. . . . Relevance can emerge through teacher mediation" (p. 35). (For this reason, Chapters 3, 4, and 10 discuss ways teachers can stimulate curiosity and develop relevant investigations.) Few children will come to school interested in the topics of force, momentum, and acceleration. However, a teacher can help make these topics relevant to students by turning the topics into driving questions such as "How do we stay on a skateboard?" or "Why do I have to wear a helmet, knee pads, and wrist protectors when I'm rollerblading?"

> **Key Idea**
> Authentic tasks have meaning for the child beyond the classroom.

Learning Is Connected to Students' Lives Outside School

Children (and adults) usually exert greater effort to study questions that relate to their own lives outside of school. If a lesson being presented to students is not connected to their lives, it is not uncommon for an upper elementary or middle school student to ask, "Why do we need to know this?" Unfortunately, teachers sometimes reply, "Because it is in the book" or "You will need it when you get older." Few children have the patience to study something simply because it is in the book, and most children do not have the cognitive capacity to accept or care that they will need something far in their future. Research on women's and minorities' involvement in science also points out the need to connect science to children's lives outside of school (Barton, 1998; Haberman, 1995). The lack of relevance to life outside of school is believed to be a strong factor in leading girls and minorities away from science.

Most topics in elementary and middle grades curriculum can be situated in students' lives. For example, teachers can connect the concept of insulation to students' lives by emphasizing the role of insulation in coats and gloves, thermos bottles that keep drinks hot or cold, and coolers that keep food from spoiling.

Portfolio Activity 2.5   **DEVELOPING A SOCIAL CONSTRUCTIVIST LESSON**

Materials Needed:
- A video of an elementary or middle grade science lesson or a classroom that you can observe in person
- Materials to develop and teach a lesson
- Video equipment and video
- The rating scale from Portfolio Activity 2.3

A. Obtain a video of an elementary or middle grades science lesson or observe a teacher teaching a science lesson. Use the rating scale from Portfolio Activity 2.3 to evaluate the teaching. What could the teacher do

to make the lesson more consistent with the social constructivist view?

B. Prepare your own lesson to teach a new concept to a child or to a group of peers. Make a video of yourself teaching the lesson. Use the rating scale found in Portfolio Activity 2.3 to analyze how well you employ constructivist approaches to teach the concept.

C. How would you improve upon your lesson if you were to reteach it? Record your ideas in your portfolio.

Science Concepts and Principles Emerge as Needed to Answer a Driving Question

In constructivist classrooms, the concepts and skills presented are used to answer driving questions rather than presented for their own sake. When concepts and principles emerge on an as-needed basis, students can more easily integrate them into their understandings. For example, students learn to read a thermometer so that they can measure the temperature in their decomposition column. They learn about oxygen so that they can understand why worms help the decomposition process. In each of these examples, students aren't learning something because it's in the textbook; they are learning it so that they can solve a problem or apply it to a particular situation. Before continuing, complete Portfolio Activity 2.5.

USING TECHNOLOGY TOOLS TO EXTEND LEARNING

Technology tools extend learning by helping students perform cognitive tasks. Humans have always used cognitive tools to help them learn, engage in intellectual tasks, and make work easier (Salomon & Perkins, 1991). For example, humans used the abacus as early as 500 B.C. for counting and performing calculations. Adding machines and calculators are more modern technological tools for helping us calculate. Concept maps, or diagrams to visualize relationships among ideas or concepts, are used widely in schools to clarify concepts. New technology tools also serve as cognitive tools. Electronic spreadsheets allow accountants to collect and analyze numbers. Graphs allow them to visualize and interpret data.

In science classes today, a wide variety of technology tools are available to help students learn. For example, computers can be used to access data on the World Wide Web, calculate data on spreadsheets, visualize concepts on a diagram or picture, and express ideas as written words. Palms or PDAs can be used to acquire, process, organize, and visually represent information. Temperature, light, and motion probes can help students conduct investigations and learn important concepts that are more difficult to understand without the use of technology. Because technology tools have assumed such an important role in science teaching, we devote Chapter 5 to a more thorough review of technology tools.

CHAPTER REVIEW   www.mhhe.com/krajcik2e

Go to the Online Learning Center at **www.mhhe.com/krajcik2e** to review important content from the chapter and key terms, take a chapter assessment, and link to the chapter's websites.

CHAPTER SUMMARY

In this chapter, we discussed student understanding and examined several scenarios of student understanding. Students need to construct content, procedural, and metcognitive knowledge to develop understanding. Project-based science strives to create meaningful understandings.

The chapter reviewed the historical roots of constructivism and outlined a social constructivist model of teaching. The first feature of this model is active engagement of students with phenomena. In a constructivist classroom, students ask and refine questions, predict and explain phenomena, and engage with concrete materials. The second feature is student use and application of knowledge. In constructivist teaching, teacher and students consciously address prior knowledge, and students identify and use multiple resources, plan and carry out investigations, apply concepts and skills to new situations, devote time to reflection, and take action to improve their own world. The third characteristic is the use of multiple representations of understandings. Multiple representations include varied evaluation techniques and student products or artifacts. The fourth characteristic is the use of learning communities. Learning communities are created when students use language to express knowledge; express, debate, and come to a resolution regarding ideas, concepts, and theories; debate the viability of evidence; learn in a social context; and obtain help from knowledgeable others in learning new ideas and skills that they couldn't learn on their own. The fifth characteristic is the focus on authentic tasks. What makes learning authentic are driving questions that focus and sustain activities, topics or questions that are relevant to the student, learning that is connected to students' lives outside school, and science concepts and principles that emerge as needed to answer a driving question. These five characteristics characterize a transformational as opposed to a receptional approach to teaching.

We discussed the important role teachers play in scaffolding student learning. Scaffolds allow learners to take part in cognitive activities just beyond their reach of cognitive development. Teachers can scaffold learners by modeling, coaching, sequencing, reducing complexity, marking critical features, and using visual tools.

Tasks in school need to be authentic for children to find them meaningful. Four aspects of authentic tasks are driving questions, the relevance of questions or topics to students, the connection of learning to students' lives outside of school, and the emergence of science concepts and principles when they are needed. Technology tools play an important role in making connections to students' lives in science classrooms today.

CHAPTER HIGHLIGHTS

- Meaningful understanding results when learners have built relationships among ideas, can explain these relationships, and can use their ideas to explain and predict phenomena.
- School science often results in students developing inert knowledge—disconnected, unusable fragments of ideas.
- Project-based science leads to students developing meaningful understandings.
- To develop meaningful understanding, students need to develop content, procedural, and metacognitive knowledge.
- Children construct meaning through their interactions with and interpretations of their world, including essential interactions with others.
- The features of social constructivist teaching include
    - active engagement in phenomena,
    - use and application of knowledge,
    - multiple representations,
    - use of learning communities, and
    - authentic tasks.
- Language serves as a tool to develop understanding.
- Teachers scaffold students so they can engage in tasks just out of their cognitive reach.
- Teachers can scaffold learners by
    - modeling,
    - coaching,
    - sequencing,
    - reducing complexity,
    - marking critical features, and
    - using visual tools.
- Tasks in school need to be authentic to have meaning.
- Four aspects of authentic tasks are
    - the driving question,
    - the relevance of a question or topic to students,
    - the connection of learning to students' lives outside of school, and
    - the emergence of science concepts and principles when they are needed.
- Technology tools extend learning in science classrooms.

KEY TERMS

Accommodation (52)

Active engagement (54)

Adaptation (49)

Assimilation (49)

Authentic tasks (68)

Bidirectional zone
   of proximal
   development (64)

Coaching (65)

Concrete operations (49)

Content knowledge (44)

Contextualized (48)

Equilibration (49)

Faded (68)

Formal operations (49)

Inert knowledge (38)

Learning communities (62)

Learning cycle (52)

Learning technologies (70)

Marking critical
   features (67)

Meaningful
   understanding (43)

Metacognitive
    knowledge (45)
Modeling (65)
Multiple
    representations (61)
Multiple resources (59)
Preoperational
    thought (49)
Prior knowledge (53)

Procedural knowledge (44)
Receptional
    approaches (47)
Reducing complexity (66)
Reflection (60)
Scaffolding (63)
Schemas (49)
Sensorimotor
    intelligence (49)

Sequencing (65)
Social constructivism (49)
Transformational
    approaches (47)
Using visual tools (67)
Zone of proximal
    development (64)

REFERENCES

American Association for the Advancement of Science. 1993. *Benchmarks for science literacy.* New York: Oxford University Press.

Anderson, B. 1986. Pupils' explanations of some aspects of chemical reactions. *Science Education* 70(5):549–63.

Anderson, L. W., and D. R. Krathwohl, eds. 2001. *A taxonomy for learning, teaching and assessing: A revision of Bloom's taxonomy of educational objectives.* New York: Longman.

Armstrong, T. 1994. *Multiple intelligence in the classroom.* Alexandria, Va.: Association for Supervision and Curriculum Development.

Barnes, M. B., T. J. Shaw, and B. S. Spector. 1989. *How science is learned by adolescents and young adults.* Dubuque, Iowa: Kendall-Hunt Publishing Company.

Barton, A. C. 1998. *Feminist science education.* New York: Teachers College Press.

Blumenfeld, P., E. Soloway, R. Marx, J. S. Krajcik, M. Guzdial, and A. Palincsar. 1991. Motivating project-based learning: Sustaining the doing, supporting the learning. *Education Psychologist* 26(3 & 4):369–98.

Blumenfeld, P. C., R. W. Marx, H. Patrick, J. S. Krajcik, and E. Soloway. 1998. Teaching for understanding. In *International handbook of teachers and teaching* (pp. 819–878), eds. B. J. Biddle, T. L.

Goode and I. F. Goodson. Dordrecht, The Netherlands: Kluwer.

Bransford, J. D. 1979. *Human cognition: learning, understanding and remembering.* Belmont, Calif.: Wadsworth Publishing Company.

Bransford, J. D., A. L. Brown, and R. R. Cocking, eds. 1999. *How people learn: Brain, mind, experience and school.* Washington, D.C.: National Academy Press.

Brooks, J. G., and M. B. Brooks. 1993. *In search of understanding: The case for constructivist classrooms.* Alexandria, Va.: Association for Supervision and Curriculum Development.

Brown, A. L., and J. C. Campione. 1994. Guided discovery in a community of learners. In *Classroom lessons: Integrating cognitive theory and classroom practice,* ed. K. McGilly, pp. 229–70. Cambridge, Mass.: MIT Press, Bradford Books.

Brown, J. S., A. Collins, and P. Duguid. 1989. Situated cognition of learning. *Educational Researcher* 18:32–42.

Bruner, J. 1977. *The process of education.* Cambridge, Mass.: Harvard University Press.

Carey, S. 1985. *Conceptual change in childhood.* Cambridge, Mass.: Harvard University Press.

Dale, E. 1969. *Audiovisual methods in teaching.* New York: Dryden Press.

Driver, R. 1989. The construction of scientific knowledge in school classrooms. In *Doing science: Images of science in science education,* ed. R. Millar, pp. 83–106. Lewes, East Sussex: Falmar Press.

Driver, R. A. Squires, P. Rushworth, and V. Wood-Robinson. 1994. *Making sense of secondary science.* New York: Routledge.

Dwyer, D. C. 1994. Apple classrooms of tomorrow: What we've learned. *Educational Leadership* 51:4–10.

Eylon, B., and M. C. Linn. 1988. Learning and instruction: An examination of four research perspectives in science education. *Review of Educational Research* 58(3):251–302.

Forman, E. A. 1989. The role of peer interaction in the social construction of mathematical knowledge. *International Journal of Educational Research* 13:55–70.

Greenberg, J. 1990. *Problem-solving situations. Volume I.* Corvallis, Ore.: Grapevine Publications, Inc.

Haberman, M. 1995. *STAR teachers of children in poverty.* West Lafayette, Ind.: Kappa Delta Pi.

Hyerle, D. 1996. *Visual tools for constructing knowledge.* Alexandria, Va.: Association for Supervision and Curriculum Development.

Karplus, R. 1977. Science teaching and the development of reasoning. *Journal of Research in Science Teaching* 14:169–75.

Krajcik, J. S. 2001. Supporting science learning in context: Project based learning. In *Portable technologies: science learning in context,* eds. R. Tinker and J. S. Krajcik, 7–29. New York: Kluwer Academic/Plenum Publishers.

Krajcik, J. S., and M. Starr. 2001. Learning science content in a project-based environment. In *Portable technologies: Learning science in context,* eds. R. Tinker & J. S. Krajcik, 103–20. New York: Kluwer Academic/Plenum Publishers.

Linn, M. C. 1998. The impact of technology on science instruction: Historical trends and current opportunities. In *International handbook of science education,* eds. B. J. Fraser & D. Tobin, 265–94. The Netherlands: Kluwer.

Lorsbach, A., and K. Tobin. Sept. 1992. *Research matters to the science teacher: Constructivism as a referent for science teaching.* Columbus, Ohio: National Association for Research in Science Teaching.

National Research Council. 1996 *National science education standards.* Washington, D.C.: National Academy Press.

Newman, D. P., Griffin, and M. Cole. 1989. *The construction zone: Working for cognitive change in school.* Cambridge, England: Cambridge University Press.

Osborne, R., and P. Freyberg. 1986. *Learning in science: The implications of children's science.* London: Heinemann.

Osborne, R. J., and M. M. Cosgrove. 1983. Children's conceptions of the changes of states of water. *Journal of Research in Science Teaching* 20(9): 825–38.

Papert, S. 1980. *Mindstorms: Children, computers, and powerful ideas.* New York: BasicBooks.

Papert, S. 1993. *The children's machine: Rethinking school in the age of the computer.* New York: BasicBooks.

Parks, S., and H. Black. 1992. *Organizing thinking: Graphic organizers.* Pacific Grove, Calif.: Critical Thinking Press and Software.

Perkins, D. 1992. *Smart schools: Better thinking and learning for every child.* New York: The Free Press.

Piaget, J. 1959. *The language and thoughts of a child* (3rd ed.). London: Routledge and Paul Kegan.

Piaget, J. 1970. Advances in child and adolescent psychology. In *Science of education and the psychology of the child,* 25–41. New York: Orion Press.

Presidents and Fellows of Harvard College. 1995. *The private universe project.* South Burlington, Vt.: Annenburg/Corporation of Public Broadcasting Mathematics and Science Collection.

Resnick, L. B. 1987. Learning in school and out. *Educational Researcher* 16:13–20.

Roth, W. M. 1995. *Authentic school science.* The Netherlands: Kluwer.

Rutherford, J., and A. Ahlgren. 1989. *Science for all Americans: Project 2061.* New York: Oxford University Press.

Salomon, G., D. N. Perkins, et al. 1991. Partners in cognition: Extending human intelligence with intelligent technologies. *Educational Researcher* 20:2–9.

Shapiro, B. 1994. *What children bring to light: A constructivist perspective on children's learning in science.* New York: Teachers College Press.

Talsma, V. 2002. *Student scientific understandings in a ninth grade project-based science classroom: A river runs through it.* Unpublished dissertation. Ann Arbor: University of Michigan.

Third International Mathematics and Science Study (TIMSS). 1998.

Vygotsky, L. 1986. *Thought and language.* Translated by A. Kozulin. Cambridge, Mass.: MIT Press. (Original English translation published 1962.)

Vygotsky, L. S. 1978. *Mind in society: The development of higher psychological processes.* Cambridge, Mass.: Harvard University Press.

Wood, D., J. S. Bruner, and G. Ross. 1976. The role of tutoring in problem solving. *Journal of Child Psychology and Psychiatry* 17:89–100.

Yager, R. E., and J. E. Penick. 1986. Perceptions of four age groups toward science classes, teachers, and the value of science. *Science Education* 70(4):355–64.

Chapter 3

What Is a Driving Question?

INTRODUCTION

WHAT IS A DRIVING QUESTION?

HOW DOES THE DRIVING QUESTION DIFFER FROM
    OTHER QUESTIONS?

HOW IS A DRIVING QUESTION DEVELOPED?

WHAT IS THE VALUE OF THE DRIVING QUESTION?

HOW CAN A DRIVING QUESTION BE USED
    THROUGHOUT A PROJECT?

CHAPTER LEARNING PERFORMANCES

- *Describe driving question.*
- *Explain the features of a driving question.*
- *Create driving questions and defend why they are good driving questions.*
- *Describe how to help children generate driving questions.*
- *Distinguish between driving questions and topic-based questions.*
- *Explain the value of using driving questions to teach science.*

INTRODUCTION

Project-based science has several features, one of which is the driving question (Krajcik, Blumenfeld, Marx, & Soloway, 2000). This chapter will explore the nature of the driving question and attempt to answer a variety of questions about the driving question itself: *What is a driving question? What makes a good driving question? What is the value of a driving question? How do I develop driving questions? And how do I use them to teach science?*

The driving question organizes and drives the diverse activities of a project. Examples of some driving questions are "Will it rain tomorrow?" "Why do I look the way I do?" "What care do our classroom pets need?" "What types of trees grow in our neighborhood?" "How healthy is our stream?" and "Does my community have acid rain?" In the fall of the school year, a good question for many early elementary students might be "Do pumpkins all have the same number of seeds?" This question would give students many opportunities to explore characteristics of pumpkins and the growth of plants.

What characteristics do these example driving questions have in common? Usable driving questions are

1.   Feasible: Students can design and perform investigations to answer the questions.
2.   Worthwhile: The questions contain rich science content, relate to what scientists really do, and can be broken down into smaller questions.
3.   Contextualized: They are pertinent to the world, nontrivial, and important.
4.   Meaningful: They are interesting and exciting to learners.
5.   Ethical: They are not harmful to living organisms or the environment.
6.   Sustainable: They lead to the pursuit of detailed answers over time.[1]

Driving questions also meet the learning and motivational needs of *all* students (Atwater, 1994; Haberman, 1991; Haberman, 1995) and, therefore, are critical for creating learning environments for both boys and girls as well as for children from different cultures and races.

This chapter provides many examples of driving questions that meet the six criteria. The chapter also explores how teachers and students can develop driving questions. The chapter ends with a discussion of the value of using a driving question throughout a project. Before we begin our discussion of the driving question, let's examine three scenarios that describe ways in which teachers might organize science instruction. These scenarios will illustrate the importance of using driving questions to teach children science.

[1]Blumenfeld, Soloway, Marx, Krajcik, Guzdial, & Palinscar, 1991; Krajcik, Blumenfeld, Marx, & Soloway, 1994.

Scenario 1: Reading About Force and Motion

Think about your own elementary and middle school science experiences. Perhaps your science class was like this: Mr. Simmons, your fifth-grade science teacher, started class by saying, "Today we're going to find out about force and motion. Open your books and read pages 121 to 123, which focus on motion and force. Pay attention to the photographs and diagrams." You scanned the pages and read carefully the captions under the graphs and photographs. After about fifteen minutes, Mr. Simmons directed students to work in groups at their tables to answer several questions at the end of the chapter. After another fifteen minutes, Mr. Simmons called on several students to give their responses to the questions.

You followed most of the reading, but occasionally you drifted off, thinking about the conversation you had with Carmella on the phone last night. You weren't sure why you were learning about force and motion. It was fun working with the students at your table to answer the questions. You were pleased that Mr. Simmons said, "Very good," when you responded, "You need a force," to the question, "Why does an object stop moving?" You had picked up the answer from your reading. It was confusing to you because it seemed from your everyday experiences that force must be applied to *keep* something moving. You kept thinking about pedaling your bike and how you needed to keep pedaling to keep moving.[2]

Sound familiar? In Chapter 1, we referred to this method of science instruction as *read about science*. Although students were introduced to new ideas, they experienced science largely as a reading activity. The concepts of science were not linked to the children's everyday lives. Although reading is an important part of science learning, when reading about science is not tied to a larger picture that has meaning for students, it can become a routine and uninteresting way of learning.

Scenario 2: Learning About Force and Motion Via an Activity

Maybe your class was like this: Mrs. Wilson, your fifth-grade teacher, always had you doing activities in science. Mrs. Wilson directed the class to work in groups to test if the mass of a block at the bottom of a ramp influenced how far it would move when hit by a moving toy car. Previously, your class had concluded that the number of washers in a toy car influenced how far it could push a wood block at the bottom of an inclined plane (a ramp supported by two books). Mrs. Wilson wrote on the board, "Does mass influence how far the block will move?" She handed out a sheet with directions on how you should set up and carry out the activity. She also handed out a sheet of paper with two columns on it. The columns were labeled "Number of Blocks (Mass)" and "Distance the Blocks Moved."

You were pretty sure that the more blocks you had, the shorter the distance they would move, so you were not sure why you were doing the activity. It was pretty easy, except for measuring the distance the blocks moved. Sometimes you and your partners disagreed about how far the blocks moved. Overall, the time went by pretty fast. You always looked forward to doing the activities, although you weren't always sure why you were doing them.

[2]This is a classic misconception. The appropriate scientific concept is Newton's First Law of Motion which states that every object continues at rest or in motion, unless acted upon by a force.

Once the class completed the testing, Mrs. Wilson had different groups summarize what they found. Overall, the class results supported what you had expected and your own group's findings. Mrs. Wilson wrote on the board, "The more blocks, the less distance they moved when hit by the toy car." You were pretty pleased because this seemed to support your ideas. It made sense. In the class discussion, however, Mrs. Wilson also said and then wrote on the board, "The more mass an object has, the more force that is needed to change its motion." This was confusing. You still didn't really understand "force." You wrote down both of the statements Mrs. Wilson had written. You knew that any sentence Mrs. Wilson wrote on the board would probably be on a test.

As described in Chapter 1, this kind of science teaching is called *process science teaching*. The students performing this activity did learn some new ideas, and they enjoyed themselves, but the students' observations were not connected to other ideas they were learning. Although Mrs. Wilson used the activity to answer a question—"Does mass influence how far the block will move?"—the question was tied directly to learning a topic (motion and force). Students did not see how the question was tied to their lives, except that it might appear on a test.

Scenario 3: Learning About Motion and Force Through a Driving Question

Perhaps your class was more like this: Your class was exploring the question "Why do I have to wear a helmet and knee and elbow pads when I'm rollerblading?" As part of this exploration, your class performed a number of activities. Mrs. Vasquez started each of the activities by saying, "If we are going to explore the question 'Why do I have to wear a helmet and knee and elbow pads when I'm rollerblading?' then we should know something about the laws of motion and about what causes injuries." Mrs. Vasquez selected the driving question because she knew that it would let the class explore a number of ideas related to force and motion as well as some ideas in biology related to human anatomy. She also knew that it would allow her students to do a number of related activities and also plan some investigations. Finally, she knew that a number of students in her class liked to rollerblade.

Here is how Mrs. Vasquez used the driving question. Mrs. Vasquez directed the class to work in groups to test whether mass influences how far an object will move when pushed by another object. Mrs. Vasquez handed out a sheet of directions on how to set up and carry out the activity. She directed you to set up an incline plane (a ramp raised on one end by two books). Mrs. Vasquez had the class relate this activity to the previous day's activity, which consisted of defining *force*. She asked the class why it was important to have the ramp at the same height each time. On the board in big letters she had written, "A Force Is a Push." Because of the previous day's work, your class was able to come up with the idea that it is important to have the same push on the blocks each time. She also handed out a sheet of paper with two columns on it. The columns were labeled "Number of Blocks (Mass)" and "Distance the Blocks Moved."

Once the class finished its testing, Mrs. Vasquez had various groups compare their findings and come to an agreement. All the groups posted their results on the board. Then Mrs. Vasquez asked, "How should we analyze the data?" The class had a debate on whether it was more useful to just look at it or create bar graphs. In the end, the class developed bar graphs. Mrs. Vasquez directed each group to write a conclusion based on the graphs. Your group wrote, "The more blocks (mass), the less the blocks moved when pushed by the same thing." Another group wrote, "The fewer the blocks, the farther they moved when hit by the car." Mrs. Vasquez recorded these various conclusions on the board. From the various conclusions, the class developed a consensus conclusion: "The greater the mass (more blocks), the less it will move when the same force (push) hits it; and the smaller the mass (fewer blocks), the farther it will move when the same force (push) hits it." At the end of class, Mrs. Vasquez asked, "How is this activity related to the driving question of the project: 'Why do I have to wear a helmet and knee and elbow pads when I'm rollerblading?'" Mrs. Vasquez first had each student write his or her own response. You wrote in your notebook, "I wear knee pads when I rollerblade because when I fall, my body isn't heavy enough to move the sidewalk and my knees will take the full blow. The knee pads soften the hit." Next you shared and compared responses with students at your table. The science lesson ended with various groups sharing their responses.

This third scenario illustrates what is called project-based science. The main activity is very similar to what occurred in the second scenario. However, this lesson goes far beyond that one. Rather than teaching an isolated lesson, the teacher tied all lessons to the driving question of the project. The students learned an important idea related to the motion of objects, but this important idea was connected to the driving question. The scenario illustrates how the driving question can be used to link activities in an overall project. The activity of testing whether mass influences how far an object will move was not done in isolation but rather was an essential component in the process of answering the driving question. Portfolio Activity 3.1 will give you the opportunity to think about the value of driving questions.

WHAT IS A DRIVING QUESTION?

What is a driving question? A **driving question** is a well-designed question used in project-based science that is elaborated, explored, and answered by students and the teacher. As shown in Scenario 3, the driving question is the central organizing feature of project-based science. In fact, the driving question sets the stage for all other activities and investigations of project-based science. Project-based science *requires* a question that is meaningful and important to children and serves to organize and drive activities (Blumenfeld et al., 1991; Krajcik, 1993; Krajcik et al., 1996; Krajcik et al., 2000). As students collaboratively pursue answers to the driving question, they develop understanding of key scientific concepts associated with the project.

To learn more about driving questions, let's explore further the example driving question "Why do I have to wear a helmet and knee and elbow pads when I'm rollerblading?" presented in Scenario 3. How is this question useful? First, the question serves the purpose of organizing and driving activities that take place in a science class. Second, the teacher can use the question to introduce the students to a number of important science concepts and principles—motion, force, distance, and Newton's laws of motion—that are needed to answer it. Third, the question can be used to link these various concepts together. Fourth, the question can inspire applied use of technology—students might want

> ### Key Idea
>
> Driving questions organize as well as drive and sustain activities, investigations, and instruction.

Portfolio Activity 3.1   **COMPARING THE THREE SCENARIOS**

Materials Needed:
- Paper and pencil or a computer
- *National Science Education Standards* (National Research Council, 1996)

A. Write a paragraph describing the differences among the three instructional approaches presented in Scenarios 1, 2, and 3. What are the advantages and disadvantages of each approach?

B. How does Scenario 3 compare with recommendations found in *National Science Education Standards* (National Research Council, 1996)?

C. Record your responses in your portfolio.

to use motion probes[3] in their investigations, for example, or the question might prompt exploration of the World Wide Web as students try to find out about the different types of materials used to make helmets and pads. Fifth, the question is motivating because it is meaningful to the children in the class; many children enjoy rollerblading. Sixth, the question can lead to the creation of products, such as posters or videos, that show what students have learned about why they need to wear helmets and pads and that can thus be used as assessment tools. Hence, the driving question "Why do I have to wear a helmet and knee and elbow pads when I'm rollerblading?" ties together activities, skills, concepts, and educational objectives.

Let's now look at the key features of driving questions.

Features of Driving Questions

A good driving question has several key features:

- *Feasibility:* Students should be able to design and perform investigations to answer it.
- *Worth:* It should deal with rich science content and process that match district curriculum standards.
- *Contextualization:* It should be anchored in the lives of learners and address important, real-world issues.
- *Meaning:* It should be interesting and exciting to learners.
- *Ethical:* It should not harm living organisms or the environment.
- *Sustainability:* It should sustain students' interest for weeks.

---

[3]Motion probes are sonic range detectors (like those found in Polaroid cameras), which are electronic instruments attached to a computer's USB port through an interfacing box. The probe sends out sound waves that cannot be heard by humans. The sound waves bounce off objects in front of them and are deflected back to the probe. The probe can then calculate the distance the object is from the probe. Accompanying software plots the data on a computer monitor, allowing learners to view real-time, distance-time, or velocity-time graphs.

Feasibility

A key feature of a good driving question is **feasibility**. Feasibility has several components. A driving question is feasible if (1) students can design and perform investigations to answer it, (2) resources and materials are available for teacher and students to perform the investigations necessary to answer it, (3) it is developmentally appropriate for students, and (4) it can be broken down into smaller questions that students can ask and answer. We will now explore each of these components.

CONNECTING TO
NATIONAL SCIENCE EDUCATION STANDARDS

Science Education Program Standards
Science content must be embedded in a variety of curriculum patterns that are developmentally appropriate, interesting, and relevant to students' lives (p. 212).

Good questions allow students to design and perform investigations to help find solutions to them. For instance, in the project with the driving question "What birds live in our neighborhood?" students can conduct bird watching inquiries. They can track bird types throughout the seasons. They might try to attract different birds to their playground or nature area by erecting birdhouses and hanging birdfeeders offering different types of bird seeds. A question such as "How can you cure a sick animal?" although meaningful for children, doesn't lend itself to students doing investigations because students don't have the knowledge or materials needed to cure a sick animal. Such a project also has the potential to be harmful to animals, and any project involving sick animals is potentially harmful to students as well (see Chapter 10 for more information about safety in the classroom).

Another component of feasibility is the availability of materials. Teacher and students should be able to find resources and materials to perform a variety of investigations related to the driving question. For instance, in the project with the driving question "Does our community have acid rain?" students can readily collect and measure the pH of rainwater using a variety of techniques, including pH paper, a pH meter, and a pH probe attached to a computer. Because pH paper is inexpensive, all students in the class can measure the pH of rainwater several times during the school year. Students can also take pH paper home to measure the pH of rainwater near their homes. Some questions, however, involve materials that are much more difficult to obtain. For instance, the question "How clean is my air?" does not readily allow students to design investigations. Although students can measure particulate matter earily, testing for pollutants often requires sophisticated pumps and filters that are too expensive and advanced for most school systems.

Good driving questions are also developmentally appropriate for students. For instance, the project with the driving question "What birds live in our neighborhood?" is developmentally appropriate for children of various ages because, while investigations might differ among age groups, children of many ages can investigate what birds live in their neighborhood. However, a question such as "What is the quality of my air?" although potentially very meaningful for most children, is probably not developmentally feasible for students in grades three and lower. The content and the investigations for this question, which involve understanding the particulate nature of matter, are more suitable for students in middle and high school.

A feasible driving question will also allow students to ask and answer their own **subquestions**. When a driving question is broad enough and is meaningful to students, students should be able to think of many related questions they would like to pursue. For instance, in the project with the driving question "How healthy is our stream or lake?" students might ask, "Does our stream quality change with the seasons?" or "What are some biological indicators of our stream's health?" In the project with the driving question

> ## Key Idea
>
> Feasible driving questions allow students to perform investigations and are developmentally approriate.

"What happens to all our garbage?" students might ask, "What materials decompose the fastest?" and "Does the presence of worms speed up the process of decomposition?"

Other questions don't lend themselves to students generating their own questions and pursuing solutions to those questions. For instance, it would be difficult for students to ask questions related to the driving question "Can we travel to Mars?" It's not that the curriculum content contained in the question is not important. It's that the question won't allow students to explore through investigations the questions they ask. Allowing students to ask their own questions has several benefits. First, student motivation increases with student ownership of a project. Second, by designing their own experiments, investigations, or presentations, students learn design and process skills and increase their knowledge of a topic. Finally, asking questions and pursuing solutions to these questions are essential to experiencing and "doing science."

A feasible driving question helps students realize that they can learn about the natural world by setting up and conducting their own investigations. Even the most interesting driving question will fail to generate a successful learning experience if appropriate investigations cannot be done, there is a lack of resources, or students are not developmentally ready for it. We explore further the idea of students "doing science" through investigations in Chapter 4.

Worth

Another key feature of the driving question is its **worth**. A question that is worthwhile contains rich science content that students can explore and that helps meet district, state, or national standards.

Perhaps the most important feature of a worthwhile driving question is the quality of science content and process that it can encompass. The most worthwhile driving questions cannot be answered without students gaining an understanding of the intended science content. Students should be able to see how the science content relates to the driving question, and the driving question should be used to help place all the science content into a real-world setting. For instance, in Scenario 3, students explore a number of important science concepts related to force, motion, and the human body. Students cannot answer the question "Why do I have to wear a helmet and knee and elbow pads when I'm rollerblading?" without understanding these science concepts. Also, the concepts of force, motion, and human anatomy are situated in a real-world setting with such a question because rollerblading is something students do.

Another way of looking at this component of worth is to consider that the driving question must subsume important science content that helps teachers meet district, state, or national curriculum standards. If a question cannot help a teacher meet curriculum requirements, then it lacks worth. A question such as "Does our community have acid rain?" provides students with the opportunity to explore numerous concepts related to chemistry, ecology, and geology. In exploring the question, students are exposed to much science content: They learn about acids and bases, they learn about weather, they study the effect of acid rain on the environment, and they learn about how experiments are designed. However, if these outcomes are not included in the objectives of a school's curriculum for that year, the question's worth is diminished.

Contextualization

Contextualization is a key feature of good driving questions. A contextualized question anchors the project in an important real-world situation and has important consequences. Students may not see immediately how a question relates to the real world or perceive its

---

Key Idea

Worthwhile driving questions are rich in science content and meet district, state and national standards.

consequence. However, a good driving question presents the opportunity to draw students in and *teaches* them to see how it is related to their lives. A number of instructional strategies can enhance **contextualization** of driving questions. Teachers can use investigations, observations, readings, and discussions to help students appreciate how a driving question relates to their lives. Many upper elementary and middle school students will not immediately perceive the importance of the question "What happens to all of our garbage?" Most children are not interested in what happens to their trash. Imagine that a teacher asks students to bring to class a number of items that typically get thrown out at home. Children bring in paper cups, plastic cups, newspaper, and orange peels, among other things. The teacher asks the students to put these items in some "mess stockings" (nets to hold the items), bury them in a fenced-off area of the playground, and then make predictions about what will happen to the various items they buried. As students pursue this investigation, they come to realize that some materials such as Styrofoam do not decompose at all and that some materials decompose more slowly than others. From this activity, students can make the leap to a larger context and begin to think about large landfills and the cumulative effect of garbage on the environment. At this point, the driving question, thanks to the contextualizing activity, assumes importance for the students.

In contrast, think about a question that is not contextualized such as "What are the names of rocks in my environment?" Although identification of elements of the natural world is important scientific content, unless the identification of rocks is tied to something that the children value, the question lacks the potential to motivate students and generate a successful, meaningful learning experience. Another common activity in schools is for children to make objects such as terrariums, solar cookers, or oceans in a bottle. Although these activities could easily be contextualized, they often are not, and after children make the objects, they don't do anything with them.

> **Key Idea**
>
> Contextualized driving questions are anchored in real-world situations and have important consequences.

Meaning

Driving questions should have **meaning** in students' lives. Usually, meaningful questions are those that students see as important and interesting to them. Meaningful questions intersect with their lives, reality, and culture. For instance, students might see the question "Why do I have to wear a helmet and knee and elbow pads when I'm rollerblading?" as meaningful because they (or others they know) rollerblade. The question is directly related to their lives and what they do.

> **Key Idea**
>
> Meaningful driving questions intersect with students' lives, reality, and culture.

It is important to point out, however, that learners might not immediately perceive the real-world issue involved in this question, which is the prevention of serious head injuries. In addition, students might not initially see all the ways that a driving question is related to their lives. For instance, many students might not initially care about the quality of their stream. However, through finding out about water quality and its effects on humans, students come to care about the driving question "What is the quality of our stream?"

Driving questions can also be meaningful just because they refer to phenomena that are inherently interesting to students. For instance, many early elementary students are fascinated with magnets. A good driving question for early elementary school children could be "How are magnets used around my home?" Although many upper elementary students would not find this question of interest, most early elementary students would be captivated by it. A number of phenomena have this potential to attract students' interests. Young learners are frequently interested in sinking and floating things in water, how toys work, rainbows, and animals. Such phenomena can be turned into driving questions such as "Why does a rainbow form?" that early learners can pursue. Many children also love to find out how to light a bulb with one battery, one bulb, and one wire (Elementary

School Science Program, 1970). Once they learn this, they are on to new challenges such as lighting a model house or finding out how their battery-operated toys work.

Ethical

> ### Key Idea
>
> Ethical driving questions do not harm living things or the environment.

Good driving questions are **ethical**. As students investigate their questions, they should not harm living organisms or the environment. Further, as students explore and find solutions to questions, the procedures they use should be ethical. There should be no leeway in this position.

A driving question is ethical if it holds paramount the safety, health, and welfare of living things and the environment. Students sometimes have questions that are of interest to them but, if investigated, would harm living things or the environment. For example, although students might be interested in polluting an environment to observe what happens to various organisms in it, such experiences cannot be supported in the classroom. They are unacceptable in schools and in scientific practices. As is true in professional science organizations, many school districts have written guidelines about the use of vertebrate animals and other living things in scientific research. Such guidelines provide strict rules about ethical treatment of living things. It is a teacher's responsibility to help children select driving questions that are ethical. Rather than purposely polluting an environment to observe the results, students can easily develop a driving question that investigates existing streams and ponds for levels of pollutants and observe the already existing effect on plant and animal life.

Sustainability

> ### Key Idea
>
> Sustainable driving questions engage students over a long period of time.

A final feature of a good driving question is **sustainability**—its ability to sustain student engagement over time. Teachers and students can work on a good question for weeks or even months. For instance, to develop a full understanding of the driving question "How healthy is my stream?" students not only must learn content in a variety of disciplines but also explore the content several times during the school year as the changing seasons contribute to variations in temperature, water levels, and animal life in the stream.

In addition to holding student interest over time, a sustainable driving question encourages students to study information in great detail. For instance, in pursuing solutions to the question "What birds come to my bird feeder?" students can identify, count, and keep track of various birds. The bird feeder question also encourages students to learn about the behavior of the different birds, their eating and nesting habits, and their migration patterns.

"How much water can different paper towels hold?" and "Do plants grow better in the shade or light?" are examples of questions that teach important scientific concepts and skills but are not sustainable. In one class period, students can answer the question about paper towels, and in as little as two weeks students can answer the question about the growth of plants. Both of these investigations could make worthwhile components of a project if they were subsumed under a larger driving question. For instance, the question about whether plants grow better in the shade or light could be subsumed under the broader driving question "What do plants in my environment need in order to grow?" In this case, students could plan and carry out a number of other experiments to explore the influence of fertilizer, temperature, moisture, light, soil type, and plant type that would keep the project going over time.

Table 3.1 summarizes key features of driving questions. Now that you have learned more about the driving question, revisit your ideas about the three scenarios by completing Portfolio Activity 3.2.

KEY FEATURES OF DRIVING QUESTIONS

Table 3.1

Feasibility

- Students can design an investigation to answer the question.
- Students can perform an investigation to answer the question.
- Materials for the investigations are readily available.
- The question is developmentally appropriate for the students.

Worth

- The question is related to what scientists really do.
- The question is rich in science content/concepts.
- The question helps students link science concepts.
- The question is complex enough to be broken down into smaller questions.
- The question leads to further questions.
- The question meets district, state, or national curriculum standards.

Contextualization

- The question is anchored in real world issues.
- The question has real world consequences.

Meaning

- The question is interesting and important to learners.
- The question intersects with learners' lives, reality, and culture.
- The phenomena covered by the question are of interest to students.

Ethics

- The practices used to answer the question do not harm living organisms or the environment.

Sustainability

- The question allows students to pursue solutions over time.
- Students can pursue answers to the question in great detail.

Examples of Driving Questions

In this section, we will examine the key features of three driving questions. The summary of the features of driving questions will structure our examination.

Example 1: What Kind of Insects Live on Our Playground?

Imagine that the district you are working in has a curriculum objective related to students learning about insects. Rather than covering insects as a topic, you decide to ask the driving question "What kinds of insects live on our playground?" Does this question meet the features of a good driving question? Let's explore.

First, the question is feasible because it gives children opportunities to investigate and ask new questions of their own. They might ask, "When do the various insects first appear on the playground?" "When do the insects disappear?" "What kind of food do they

---

Portfolio Activity 3.2   **COMPARING THE THREE SCENARIOS AGAIN**

Materials Needed:

- Paper and pencil or a computer

A. Now that you know more about the features of a driving question, reanalyze the first three scenarios. Write a paragraph describing the differences among the instructional approaches presented in the scenarios.

What are the advantages and disadvantages of each approach?

B. How does your analysis compare to what you wrote in Portfolio Activity 3.1?

C. Record your responses in your portfolio.

---

eat?" "Where do they live?" "What type of environment do the insects live in?" and "How do they eat?" Students can design and perform investigations to answer these questions. For example, they can keep journals about when insects appear and disappear. They can collect insects and investigate what they eat or how they react to light. They can take nature walks to investigate where insects live and how they move. Also, there isn't much sophisticated equipment—besides a hand lens, jars, and maybe a net—that is needed for this project.

Second, the question is worthwhile because it enables students to explore rich science content, including insect classification, life cycles, and behaviors. Also, the question enables students to relate to what scientists really do (ask many questions and pursue answers to these questions). This question matches up with a number of benchmarks for elementary students cited in *Benchmarks for Science Literacy* (AAAS, 1993). For instance, one of the benchmarks for grades 3–5 is "Insects and various other organisms depend on dead plant and animal material for food." By exploring the subquestion "What do insects eat?" students can attain this benchmark. The question also helps meet a number of other benchmarks (AAAS, 1993) and standards (National Research Council, 1996) for inquiry and the nature of science. For example, as students observe insect behavior and take notes, they are observing and recording information, two important benchmarks.

Third, the question is contextualized and meaningful. The type of insects found can give an indication of the quality of soil and the local environment. By observing the insects, finding out information about them, asking subquestions, and conducting investigations to answer the subquestions, students can come to understand how this is a real world question with meaning for

Children conduct investigations to find solutions to a driving question.

them: They are not just reading about insects or exploring them through classroom activities; they are exploring and learning about insects in their environment, in the backyard, on the playground, and/or in a local nature area.

Fourth, this question is ethical because it does not lead students to harm insects. By taking nature walks, for example, they are able to observe the insects without collecting or killing them. The question does not promote practices that would endanger the environment in which the insects live.

Fifth, this question is sustainable: It can take students an entire year to study all the insects in their environment, given that insects appear and disappear in different seasons. Moreover, the question might propel students to learn other information about insects.

Example 2: What Kind of Land Features Are in My Environment?

Often, school districts have curriculum objectives related to earth science. Imagine that your class is studying the question "What kind of land features are in my environment?"

The question is feasible because it allows students to ask a number of subquestions such as "What type of soil do we have?" "What kind of rocks do we have?" "How was the shape of the river formed?" and "How were the hills and valleys formed?" However, these subquestions will not come easily to upper elementary students and the teacher might need to lead walks to help focus students' observations on various geological features. Some of these questions allow students to perform investigations. For instance, students can collect a variety of rocks from around the school or at home and then try to identify what they are. Although students can't *explore* how a river was formed, they can do various explorations on a stream table (a long tray set up with sand and water to simulate erosion) to duplicate the formation of streams and rivers. They can also search the library or the World Wide Web for historical pictures of the river to see if the shape of the river has changed. Other questions such as "How were the hills and valleys formed?" cannot be explored easily through investigations. However, students can read and discuss how such phenomena occur, and they can manipulate modeling clay to simulate how a hill is formed as pressure below the earth presses up on it.

Next let's explore whether the question is worthwhile. The driving question and subquestions provide learners with opportunities to learn a number of important earth science concepts. For instance, the students can explore classifications of rocks and soil, compositions of rock and various soils, types of land formations, and reasons for various land features. Hence, by pursuing an answer to the driving question, students have the opportunity to explore important science content that meets a number of benchmarks cited in *Benchmarks for Science Literacy* (AAAS, 1993). For instance, one of the benchmarks for grades 3–5 is as follows:

> Rock is composed of different combinations of minerals. Smaller rocks come from the breaking and weathering of bedrock and larger rocks. Soil is made partly from weathered rock, partly from plant remains—and also contains many living organisms (AAAS, 1993, p. 72).

Taking students on walks to explore various local phenomena helps link the driving question and subquestions to the real world. Although some children will not immediately see the question as meaningful to them, allowing them to bring in different soil samples and various rocks from their backyards as part of their investigations will help them gain ownership of the question. For instance, students can compare various sample cores (drillings into the soil with a tube to show the soil from different layers) from their back-yards. They can explore questions such as "How are the samples different?" and "If they are different, why are they different?"

This exploration of land features is ethical because it does not involve students endangering the environment or polluting it. In fact, this particular driving question may also help students observe whether other human practices in their region, such as strip mining or blasting for stone in quarries, have destroyed land features. A study of land features could also initiate some interesting discussions of ethics among the students in the classroom.

Finally, as students begin to see the value of the driving question, the question becomes sustainable because there is much rich content associated with it. Many of the subquestions take time to explore and investigate. For example, "What type of soil do we have?" is a question that can be explored over time as students investigate what plants can grow in the soil type, whether it can be used for making things (such as bricks), and if it drains well (such as sand) or holds water (such as clay).

Example 3: How Can I Care for the Various Animals in Our Classroom?

Let's look at a third example that focuses on biological objectives. Many children will be interested in the animals that are in the classroom. Most students, as well as adults, love to watch various animals eat and play. The driving question "How can I care for the various animals in our classroom?" appears to have much potential to engage students in learning about animals.

The question appears to be very feasible. Students can ask a number of related questions and pursue answers to many of these subquestions through investigations. For instance, students could ask, "How do the eating habits of our animals differ?" "How do the various behaviors of the animals differ?" and "What kind of habitat do the various animals prefer?" All of these questions can be explored through investigations. Students can observe the eating habits of the different animals and find different feeding patterns. Note that some subquestions such as "What should I do if one of our animals gets sick?" should not be explored via hands-on investigations. Students can explore this type of question by finding literature on the topic or talking to experts, such as veterinarians. As mentioned earlier, the care of animals should always be left to the expert.

In pursuing an answer to the driving question and the various subquestions, students will need to explore a variety of different science content areas. For instance, they will study content such as nutrition and environmental needs, habitat, body systems, body function and structure, and behavior. These content areas match *Benchmarks for Science Literacy* (AAAS, 1993) and *National Science Education Standards* (NRC, 1996). Hence, with respect to students exploring important content, the driving question appears to be worthwhile. The question is also worthwhile in that students can perform a number of investigations related to it.

The question also appears to be very motivating. Observing and caring for classroom animals is meaningful. Teachers can enhance interest and ownership by assigning each student to care for a particular pet. Because the pets are in the classroom and the learners must care for them, the question is contextualized for the learners.

This question is clearly an ethical driving question as it focuses on the welfare of animals. Occasionally, students will be tempted to investigate whether animals like some types of food more than others, prefer a warmer or colder temperature, or respond to direct light. Although children might learn from such investigations, they may not be ethical. For example, if an investigation of food preferences provided an animal with food that was not nutritious, it could endanger the animal's health or shorten its lifespan. Because the driving question posed here focuses on caring for the animal, it directs children away from problematic practices such as investigating unhealthy foods or temperature.

Finally, the scope and the nature of this driving question and its subquestions appear to hold students' attention for a long period of time. Caring for and learning about the animals can be done throughout the entire school year.

HOW DOES THE DRIVING QUESTION DIFFER FROM OTHER QUESTIONS?

When you open up a traditional elementary or middle school science textbook, you are likely to see that the book is organized by topics: the solar system, phases of the moon, weather, nutrition, plants, the human body, force, and so on. Often, a chapter will also mention reasons for learning the topic. For instance, the study of genetics has led to the development of different hybrids of corn and other vegetables and so is worth study. Although knowing such reasons might increase interest, the reasons are not the driving forces behind learning, and teachers frequently find it difficult to hold students' attention when focusing on topics only because a textbook suggests they are important.

Traditional science classes, like textbooks, are also organized by topic, rather than by a driving question. Non–project-based science classes might cover the same science content as project-based science classes, but the material is not connected in the same way. By using driving questions, students can see that everything they learn has a purpose, and when they learn a new skill or concept, they can immediately apply it to help answer their questions.

Contrast the three driving questions just examined with questions that focus on topics such as "What are the six simple machines?" "What are the nine planets of the solar system?" and "What is light?" Although some students might be interested in the structure of the solar system, most children don't have a reason to be. Although these topics might encompass worthwhile content, they are not likely to engage learners because they are not directly related to children's lives. These questions lack the ability to help students develop connections between their studies and their own lives.

In addition, traditional science instruction and textbook activities lead to the development of isolated skills and understandings, without context and meaning. Typical activities that students pursue in school science are designed to demonstrate or verify concepts. For example, a traditional science textbook chapter on plants will tell students that plants need sunlight to grow. Then, the textbook activity will likely verify this information by having students grow one plant in the sun and another in a dark closet. (This kind of teaching is similar to that presented in Scenario 2.) Because such activities are tied to topics rather than to driving questions, students fail to make connections between the skills and concepts they learn. Take time now to complete Portfolio Activity 3.3.

Key Idea

Driving questions are not topic focused.

Portfolio Activity 3.3   **EVALUATING VARIOUS QUESTIONS**

Materials Needed:
- Paper and pencil or a computer

A. Listed here are several questions. Evaluate whether the questions can serve as driving questions. Are the questions feasible, worthwhile, meaningful, ethical, contextualized, and sustainable? Be sure to state your reasons.

B. Contrast your answers with those of another person in your class. Try to come to a consensus.

C. Keep this list in your portfolio.

Question	Can It Serve as a Driving Question?	Reason
What is gravity?		
Why do I need to wear a bicycle helmet?		
Why does my water taste bad?		
What is matter?		
What foods are good for me to eat?		
Do all apples have the same number of seeds?		
How can I run faster?		
How good is the soil in my playground or yard for growing plants?		
Why do only the weeds grow in the cracks of the sidewalk?		
What kind of leaves are these?		
Why is too much junk food bad for me?		
Why is it colder in the winter and warmer in the summer?		

HOW IS A DRIVING QUESTION DEVELOPED?

Key Idea

Driving questions can be teacher or student generated.

Coming up with driving questions with the features discussed earlier in this chapter is challenging work. Teachers might make a number of failed attempts before settling on a question for a project. Slowly, however, teachers can develop a repertoire of driving questions and projects.

Teacher-Generated Driving Questions

Driving questions that originate from the teacher or the curriculum have a number of advantages. Perhaps the most important is that such questions can match school district outcomes and standards with a classroom project. Another is that orchestrating a class driven by a teacher's questions is much easier than orchestrating one driven by students' questions. However, teacher-developed questions may not be meaningful to the student or provide opportunities for students to generate subquestions.

There are many ways that a teacher can develop a good driving question. Some teachers like to begin with ideas they come across in their reading. For example, a teacher might use a question found in this book. Others like to begin with ideas they have heard about or experienced in methods classes, at teacher workshops, or in working with students. Some teachers like to develop questions from the school's curriculum. Some great driving questions come from listening to students' questions and ideas. A teacher's hobbies or personal interests can provide the catalyst for driving questions. So can the local newspaper, a news event, or a television program. Finally, other teachers are great sources of ideas for new driving questions and projects. We will now discuss each of these sources for developing driving questions. We will also discuss concerns that must be addressed when using teacher-developed questions.

CONNECTING TO
NATIONAL SCIENCE EDUCATION STANDARDS

Science Teaching Standards
Teachers of science plan an inquiry-based science program for their students. In doing this, teachers select science content and adapt and design curricula to meet the interests, knowledge, understanding, abilities, and experiences of students (p. 30).

Developing Driving Questions from Personal Experiences

It is possible to glean many driving questions from your reading. This book has presented several questions that can be used to drive projects:

- What care do our classroom pets need?
- What type of trees grow in our neighborhood?
- How healthy is our stream?
- Does my community have acid rain?
- Do apples all have the same number of seeds?
- Why do I have to wear a helmet and knee and elbow pads when I'm rollerblading?
- What kind of land features are in my environment?
- What kind of insects live on our playground?

These questions can be used at a variety of grade levels. For instance, the question "Why do I have to wear a helmet and knee and elbow pads when I'm rollerblading?" could be used to drive a fourth-grade unit on motion, or it could be used to drive a seventh-grade class on the same topic. We have used the question "How healthy is my stream?" successfully at both the fifth-grade level and at the eighth-grade level. Other questions are probably best used only for lower or upper grade levels. For instance, the question "Do apples all have the same number of seeds?" is most appropriately used at the early elementary level (grades K–2).

Other personal experiences besides reading that are good sources of driving questions are methods classes, teacher workshops, and interactions with students during teaching. A typical science methods class exposes teachers to a variety of physical, life, and earth/space science topics that can be turned into driving questions. For instance, a teacher might have learned about electricity in a methods class by lighting a bulb using a wire and dry cell, constructing series and parallel circuits, and connecting small motors and switches to circuit paths. This experience could be used to develop the driving question "How is electricity used in my environment?" Teaching experience may tell a teacher that students are interested in classroom animals. This knowledge would help the teacher develop the driving question "What care do our classroom pets need?"

There are several advantages to using driving questions with which you have some experience. First, although you cannot possibly anticipate all of the rough spots in a project, knowing what students will be studying helps smooth out the rough spots. Second, with familiar questions, you can map out clearly what curriculum standards a project will meet. Third, teacher-designed familiar questions are often the most effective initial driving questions, because they allow you to start from a familiar basis instead of treading into unknown territory. Finally, with a familiar question, you can plan and prepare resources such as equipment, readings, and guest speakers.

Brainstorming Driving Questions Associated with the Curriculum

One of the authors of this book likes to start to develop a driving question by reviewing the curriculum outcomes or standards that need to be met by a project. Next, he likes to brainstorm the investigations that students might conduct. He then considers ways to contextualize the project for students. At the same time, he jots down related questions that might be meaningful to students. Figure 3.1 illustrates this process of brainstorming a driving question to meet curriculum outcomes.

One middle school teacher rejected a number of questions related to her curriculum on forces and motion before she settled on the driving question "How do I stay on a skateboard?" Science content was the teacher's first consideration in selecting a driving question for the skateboard project. Even before she began thinking about what kind of question would be meaningful and interesting to students, she clearly delineated what science content (force and motion) would need to be covered in order to meet district curriculum standards. Student motivation and interest were also a primary concern for her in the skateboard project. By using "How do I stay on a skateboard?" the teacher helped her students see tangible and interesting connections between abstract physical concepts and their own world.

The strongest advantage to brainstorming driving questions from curriculum is that the teacher can thus ensure that important curriculum outcomes are met. This is critical in most school districts, because the curricula at different grade levels are interdependent. In addition, in some areas, proficiency tests or graduation requirements are based on particular content.

Developing Driving Questions by Listening to Students

Another good way to develop a driving question is to listen to questions that students ask. Some teachers create "test banks" of student ideas. A test bank is a notebook in which teachers record student questions and ideas. For example, a student might ask, "What kind of bird is that pretty red one?" This question might later become the driving question "What birds visit our feeder?"

Another source of student questions is the dialogue journal. This is a journal of correspondence between student and teacher. Science notebooks also provide question possibilities. A teacher might notice that a student writes in her notebook, "My mom was nagging me again last night to wear that stupid helmet when I was rollerblading!" This idea might prompt the teacher to develop the driving question "Why do I have to wear a helmet and knee and elbow pads when I'm rollerblading?"

Driving questions developed from listening to students and using their experiences are potentially more meaningful to students (MacKenzie, 2001). This is a powerful reason to use these types of questions. However, because a driving question must meet district curriculum standards and other criteria, use Figure 3.1 as a guide in evaluating these types of questions.

> **Key Idea**
>
> Listen to students' ideas to develop driving questions.

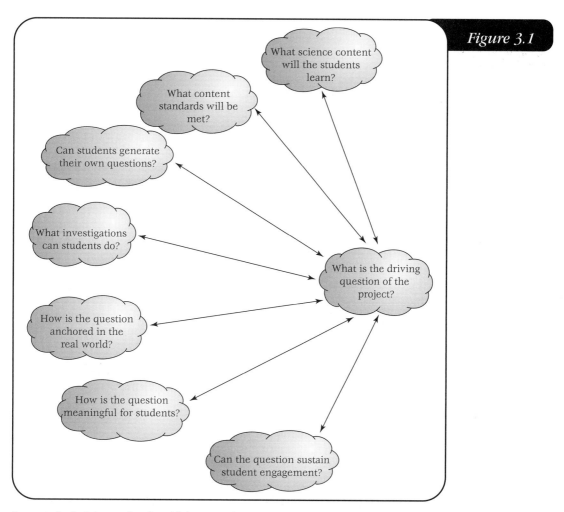

Figure 3.1

Prompts for helping to develop driving questions.

Developing Driving Questions from Hobbies and Personal Interests

Teachers can come up with ideas for driving questions from their hobbies or personal interests. Rock collecting, fishing, cooking, outdoor activities, traveling, amateur astronomy, and jewelry making can all lead to excellent driving questions.

For example, if a teacher's hobby is outdoor activities, she can take the class on various field trips to set the stage for asking questions related to environmental issues and nature. Driving questions that might arise from this are "What kind of trees and plants are in my neighborhood?" "What kind of animals are in my neighborhood?" and "What kind of land forms are in my neighborhood?"

There are several reasons for developing driving questions from hobbies and personal interests. First, teachers often show a great deal of enthusiasm for questions related to personal interests, and this enthusiasm can be contagious, making the questions meaningful to students. Second, questions related to hobbies and personal interests are frequently sustainable because the hobbies or interests themselves are sustainable. Finally, teachers know a great deal about their personal interests, enabling them to easily make connections with curriculum outcomes and standards.

Developing Driving Questions from the Media

Driving questions can also result from reading the newspaper or magazines, listening to the news, or watching documentaries and other shows on television. Newspapers and news shows present ideas that are current, usually less than a day old. Magazines and television documentaries provide information that is only a month or two old. Other ideas presented in magazines or on television shows may be interesting enough to become driving questions.

For instance, imagine that a gasoline tanker overturned a block away from a school in a large urban district. The area had to be evacuated, the sewers were pumped, the air smelled like gasoline, children and adults acquired headaches, and the expressway was closed for hours. A teacher in the district could quickly develop this driving question: "What hazards exist in my environment?" This question might lead to the study of the hazards: how chemicals become airborne, why the people got headaches, and what breathing problems exist for adults and children.

> **Key Idea**
>
> Driving questions can come from a variety of sources.

Questions that result from media sources can be very appealing to students, especially if they are familiar. Familiarity with news items helps contextualize the question for students, making the question interesting and meaningful. However, a major problem with using driving questions that come from media sources is that they are hard to plan for ahead of time. This lack of planning often prevents teachers from reaching the curriculum standards. However, a teacher who is familiar with curriculum standards ahead of time might be able to quickly capitalize on a news story. For this reason, it is a good idea to become very familiar with district, state, or national standards before the planning stage.

Developing Driving Questions by Listening to Other Teachers

The personal experiences of others are good sources of driving questions. Your colleagues have probably attended interesting classes and had varied experiences with students. They may participate in novel hobbies or watch different television shows or read different magazines than you do.

In addition to providing fresh ideas for driving questions, colleagues can provide invaluable insight into dealing with the challenges of doing a project. They may have ideas for solving a problem, meeting curriculum standards, or classroom investigations. They may also have connections to community agencies, guest speakers, or resources.

Using Driving Questions That Come from Published Curriculum

A number of projects and driving questions can result from using published curriculum. Published curriculum includes textbook series, computer programs, and CD-ROM applications, and kit-based materials. Textbook series and kit-based programs are frequently adopted by school districts to meet their science outcomes and standards. Computer and CD-ROM applications frequently augment the adopted curriculum. Often these published curriculum materials are a good place to start when doing project-based science for the first time, because they provide a structure for selecting driving questions that meet curriculum standards. In addition, they usually contain some ideas for investigations or activities, resources (such as science supplies, hands-on materials, and student hand-outs), and background information about the science content for the teacher. Many of these materials provide the structure for benchmark lessons (lessons designed to teach basic knowledge and skills necessary to investigate a driving question).

For example, most elementary science textbook series include a chapter on a topic such as land and water. Each of the topics can be turned into a number of driving questions. For instance, in a chapter on land and water, students can explore the quality of their school's water supply and investigate a number of subquestions including "What is the nitrate and chloride concentration of our school's water supply?" and "What are their sources, and how do they enter the water supply?" In answering these questions, students would deal with important science content. Students would learn about watersheds, examine where their water comes from, investigate how local topography influences their watershed, and see how sources of pollution in one component of a watershed can influence water quality in other areas. They could study pollution in terms of the context and concentration of various substances, focusing especially on the influence of nitrates in fertilizers on water pollution. Students could also engage in teacher-directed investigations. Students could, for example, measure the nitrate and chloride concentrations of their school's water supply and examine water treatment by investigating the influence of chlorine on yeast growth. Class data about nitrate levels could be shared with a research team (a team made up of representatives from other schools) via an electronic network. Students would consider how local environment, commerce, agriculture, and industry might account for the differences reported by various research teams. Students could also create a number of products that reflect their understanding. For instance, they could debate water policy, design models of sources of pollution, and create posters and videos of their debates and panel discussions. Similarly, textbook chapters on weather, geology, or pollution may also lack driving questions, but, again, it is very easy to develop some: "What makes our weather?", "What affects the landforms in my region?", or "Does our community have acid rain?"

Science Court is a motivating CD-ROM series published by Tom Snyder Productions that mixes animated courtroom drama, hands-on science activities, and humor to teach students science concepts and model scientific practices. Students use facts and hands-on science activities to predict the verdict in the simulated courtroom. For example, in the "Soil" curriculum, a character named Eddy Watt wants to use a costly and powerful machine to fix the damaged soil in the Old Dust Fields. However, another character, Nate Norton, says he can fix the soil for almost nothing. Students investigate whether he can do that and, in the process, learn about soil fertility, composition of soil, and the role of worms. From this series could emerge the driving question "How do worms help us?" Tom Snyder Productions also distributes several other excellent software programs in the *Science Seekers* series that make good sources of good driving questions: Safe Water, Endangered Species, and Hidden Rocks.

Text-based curriculum materials, such as *The Pillbug Project: A Guide to Investigation,* by Robin Burnett (1999), available through the National Science Teachers Association, also serve as sources of possible driving questions. Although there is no explicit driving question associated with *The Pillbug Project,* one easily comes to mind: "What are these critters anyway?" Teachers can show students some pillbugs, and the project work can begin. The *Great Explorations in Math and Science (GEMS)* materials, available from the Lawrence Hall of Science, can be used as a base for developing many driving questions

> ### Key Idea
> Published curricula can be a rich source of potential driving questions.

Published Curriculum Resources

and projects. There are more than fifty GEMS books, including *Ant Homes, Crime Lab Chemistry, Bubble-ology, Acid Rain, Global Warming and the Greenhouse Effect, Mystery Festival,* and *Fingerprinting.* For example, the book *Ant Homes* can be used to develop the driving question "What kinds of insects live on our playground?" Several national projects, such as the Global Learning and Observations to Benefit the Environment (GLOBE) project, provide excellent curriculum that can be the focus of driving questions.

Although topically organized, kit-based curricula, such as the *Full Option Science System (FOSS),* published by Delta (Lawrence Hall of Science, 1993, 2000), and *Science and Technology for Children (STC),* published by Carolina Biological (National Science Resource Center, 1991, 1997), are excellent project starters because they offer a wealth of resources and provide the structure for many benchmark lessons. For example, FOSS's *Trees* kit can be used to develop the driving question "What kinds of trees are in my neighborhood?" The kit entitled *Insects* can be used to study insects that live on the playground. *Earth Materials, Landforms,* or *Pebbles, Sand and Silt* can be used to study the driving question "What kinds of land features are in my environment?" STC's kit, *Food Chemistry,* can be used for benchmark lessons to study the driving question "How do we stay healthy?"

An extensive list of science curriculum materials is published in *NSTA's Science Education Suppliers,* available from the National Science Teachers Association (1840 Wilson Boulevard, Arlington, VA 22201-3000). You can also find "science suppliers and programs" on NSTA's website. We encourage you to get a copy of this book and write to companies for their catalogues. Another great resource for examining published curriculum materials is the Eisenhower National Clearinghouse for Mathematics and Science Education, available on the World Wide Web.

USING TECHNOLOGY TOOLS TO DEVELOP A DRIVING QUESTION

Technology to Create Driving Questions; LeTUS

Teachers also can use the World Wide Web as a source of driving questions and project ideas. A number of research groups are developing projects, and many of these projects can be found on the Web. The Web-based Inquiry Science Environment, the Learning Through Collaborative Visualization Project, and the Center for Highly Interactive Computing in Education all discuss their ongoing projects.

The Web-based Inquiry Science Environment (WISE) is a free online science learning environment for students in grades 4–12. In WISE, students work on exciting inquiry projects in life, earth, and physical science focused on topics such as genetically modified foods, earthquake prediction, HIV, water quality, wolves, and the deformed frogs mystery. Working in pairs, students learn about and respond to contemporary scientific controversies through designing, debating, collaborating, and critiquing solutions. Most WISE activities are completed on a computer, using a Web browser such as Netscape or Internet Explorer. Sponsored by the National Science Foundation, WISE software is free for teachers to use. The software guides students through Web pages that provide content, notes that encourage students to reflect, and other tools for data visualization, causal modeling, simulations, online discussion with classmates, and assessment. WISE also offers a project authoring environment, in which teachers can customize projects to their own needs or create their own projects.

The Learning Through Collaborative Visualization Project (CoVis) is a community of thousands of students, over 100 teachers, and dozens of researchers all working together to find new ways to think about and practice science in the classroom. CoVis students study atmospheric and environmental sciences through inquiry-based activities using state-of-the-art scientific visualization software specially modified for a learning environment. The work of the CoVis Project was completed in 1998, but this research is being continued under the auspices of the Center for Learning Technologies in Urban Schools at Northwestern University. This website now serves as an archive of CoVis curriculum materials, software, and research. The site presents curriculum materials and related software for grades 4–12 on topics such as air quality, communicable diseases, global warming, and Kids as Global Scientists. Project-based questions such as "What makes our weather?" are investigated in the Kids as Global Scientists curriculum.

Students use technology to find information related to a driving question.

The Center for Highly Interactive Computing in Education (hi-ce) features a project-based science approach to teaching, the tools of a digital library, and learner-centered software to support students' scientific inquiry into important intellectual problems. At their website students can go to the Science Laboratory to download and use a range of data collection, graphing, and modeling software tools to investigate complex problems. For example, *Artemis* is a tool that lets students access a digital library containing magazine articles, scientific journals, and a large collection of Web pages. *Model - It* allows students to build, test, and evaluate qualitative models with ease. Students can create such models of their theories about the scientific phenomena being investigated and run simulations in order to test their models. *Cooties* is a virus-transfer simulation program that students can download for use on Palm OS devices. Teachers can use hi-ce to view and download the latest in project-based science software (such as *Model-It* and *Cooties*) and curriculum (such as *Air Quality, Big Things, Communicable Diseases, Physics,* and *Water Quality*), see what other teachers are doing in their classrooms, and find out about professional development programs. Guests can go to hi-ce information to view and download research papers, access information about projects, and find contact information for members of hi-ce.

hi-ce

These sources are highly interactive. Their projects meet all of the key features of good driving questions. They are feasible (students can interact with others around the world to design and perform investigations), worthwhile (they contain rich science content that can be broken down into smaller questions), contextualized (they are grounded in the real world), meaningful to students (they offer interactivity with students around the world), ethical (they do not hurt animals or the environment), and sustainable (they can last the entire school year).

Making Sure Teacher-Generated Driving Questions Work for Students

No matter what the source of a driving question, it should provide opportunities for students to ask their own questions and explore solutions to those questions. Driving questions that are teacher-generated should not be so highly constrained that the outcomes are predetermined, leaving students with little room to develop their own approaches to them. In Portfolio Activity 3.4, you will practice generating driving questions and turning curriculum materials into good driving questions.

Portfolio Activity 3.4   **GENERATING DRIVING QUESTIONS FROM TOPICS**

Materials Needed:
- Paper and pencil or a computer
- A variety of curriculum materials (such as from GEMS, AIMS, FOSS, STC, and National Geographic)

A. Use the following topics to create teacher-developed driving questions. Write an explanation of why you think they make good driving questions.

K–4 topics from the *National Science Education Standards* (NRC, 1996):
- Changes in the earth and sky
- Light
- Electricity
- Magnetism
- Life cycles
- Organisms and environments
- Properties of earth materials
- Objects in the sky

Grades 5–8 topics from the *National Science Education Standards* (NRC, 1996):

- Changes and properties of matter
- Motions and forces
- Transfer of energy
- Heredity
- Reproduction
- Structure of the earth
- Solar system
- Environmental hazards
- Personal health

B. Examine a variety of commercially published curriculum materials. Match available materials to the topics listed from the *National Science Education Standards* (NRC, 1996). Write about how the commercially published materials could support the driving question.

C. How could the driving questions you developed provide opportunities for students to ask their own questions and explore solutions to them?

D. Record your responses in your portfolio.

Portfolio Activity 3.5 provides you with the opportunity to observe a classroom and develop and evaluate driving questions. This activity will contextualize the developing of driving questions in a real classroom.

Student-Generated Driving Questions

Initially, teachers may feel more comfortable creating questions and activities themselves. However, driving questions can also arise from students' personal interests or surface as subquestions to the main driving question of a project. With practice, students can take responsibility for creating both the questions and the investigations. One of the biggest benefits of student-generated questions is that the meaningfulness criterion is practically ensured. However, teachers must still work carefully to determine whether questions are feasible, worthwhile, ethical, and contextualized. Sometimes students select topics that have high interest but that cannot be answered through student investigations. Dinosaurs are a common topic of interest among young children, for example, but there aren't many investigations that students can perform related to this topic. For this reason, although dinosaurs might be a good topic to read about, they don't lead to feasible projects. Teachers must also worry about whether content meets district curriculum standards and whether students' questions are real world questions. For example, students might be interested in spaceships, but spaceships are not a part of students' daily lives and probably don't match any of the district's curriculum standards.

Portfolio Activity 3.5

ANALYZE CLASSROOM SCIENCE AND DEVELOP DRIVING QUESTIONS

Materials Needed:
- A classroom to visit
- A copy of the school's curriculum framework
- Paper and pencil or a computer

A. Obtain permission from appropriate school personnel to visit an elementary or middle grade classroom. Observe the teacher. Look over the classroom materials the teacher is using. Review the district's curriculum framework.

B. Analyze whether the students are exploring the solutions to questions in the science teaching that you observe. Determine if the questions meet the key features of driving questions. If they do not, how might the teacher alter the science instruction to develop questions that meet the key features?

C. Record the information from this activity in your portfolio.

To develop driving questions from students' interests, a teacher must provide students time to develop questions and establish a setting in which questions can emerge. Teachers must develop ways to support students in their asking of questions, select from among the many possible driving questions those that are worth pursuing, and sensitively handle those questions that are not selected. In this section, we explore techniques for helping students ask questions, selecting students' questions, and developing students' ideas into driving questions.

Supporting Students Asking Questions

Teachers can use various ways to encourage students to ask questions that might be turned into a driving question for a project or that might be used as subquestions in a project. One of the best ways to accomplish this is to have students make observations of their surroundings. To do this, teachers must build a classroom environment that fosters students asking questions and that exposes students to situations that they can observe. Teachers can help students recommend subquestions to the main driving question of the project. Finally, teachers also can have students brainstorm ideas they know about and help them identify hobbies and personal interests.

CONNECTING TO
NATIONAL SCIENCE EDUCATION STANDARDS

K–4 Content Standard: Science as Inquiry
Scientific investigations involve asking and answering a question and comparing the answer with what scientists already know about the world (p. 123).

5–8 Content Standard: Science as Inquiry
Students should develop the ability to refine and refocus broad and ill-defined questions (p. 145).

An Encouraging Classroom Environment. There are a number of ways that a teacher can build an environment that encourages students to ask questions. One technique involves setting up situations in the classroom that allow students to make observations and ask questions. For instance, a teacher might set up an aquarium in the classroom or plant a variety of seeds in a classroom terrarium. Imagine a series of aquariums that are missing pumps and filters but that contain sand, goldfish, snails, and duckweed. Students make careful observations, recording them on a daily basis. After several days, students notice a buildup of "black stuff" on the sand at the bottom of the aquariums. Students will likely ask questions such as "What is the black stuff on the bottom of the aquarium?" This situation forms a great learning experience for early elementary

> **Key Idea**
>
> A rich classroom environment encourages the generation of driving questions.

students in which they can test theories about where the black stuff comes from. Students might, for example, infer that the black stuff comes from "the snails and the fish going to the bathroom" or "the fish vomiting" or from the sand itself being dirty and the dirt rising to the top of the sand as it settles over time.

A second technique involves teachers exposing students to situations in which they can explore their environment. Teachers can take students on walking excursions or on field trips or bring in guest speakers. For instance, teachers can support students asking questions about the quality of the water in a stream near the school by taking the students on a stream walk. Or they can have students explore the types of trees in the neighborhood by walking around the block. On the walk around the block, students can make careful observations of the types and locations of trees. By looking at the shape of the leaves, the texture of bark, and the color variations in the leaves and the bark, students can begin to ask questions such as "Why do some trees have rough bark and others have smooth bark?" This question can naturally lead to the driving question "What trees are in my neighborhood?"

Science and Technology for Children

Helping Students Generate Subquestions.   When teachers are working with a driving question, perhaps one that comes from district or state-mandated curriculum, student-generated subquestions can increase students' interest with and ownership of the question. For example, a driving question derived from the *Science and Technology for Children* (STC) kit entitled "Food Chemistry" might be "What affects the nutrition of the food I eat?" While this driving question may not interest students at first, various techniques can help students form subquestions of their own. One tool that can help students generate their own subquestions is the brainstorming wheel pictured in Figure 3.2. Students add "spokes," or questions related to the driving question, to the wheel. Students might add questions such as, "Which snack foods have less sugar in them?" "What foods would make my hair shiny?" or "What is in potato chips that makes them high in calories?" These subquestions become projects for investigation. The question "Which snack foods have less sugar in them?" becomes the impetus to investigate glucose levels, a topic in the STC kit on "Food Chemistry."

What Students Already Know.   Another strategy that can be used to help students generate their own driving questions is to have them brainstorm about what they know. Students will come up with many ideas about animals, dinosaurs, cars, and toys. Frequently, students will come up with ideas based on interests and hobbies such as their pets, television shows, baseball card collections, doll collections, and musical instruments. Many teachers list these ideas on a chart with three columns labeled "What we know," "What we want to know," and "What we learned." The ideas that students generate can be listed under the "What we know" column. This method, called the *KWL* (for *Know, Want to Know,* and *Learned*) *method* and developed by Debra Ogle (1986), can be used in a variety of contexts.

Next, teachers help students turn these ideas into questions. For example, in the first column students might list, "Animals live outdoors," "Some animals live indoors," "Animals need food to grow," "Animals are big and little," and "Animals can be dangerous." These ideas might lead to an entry in the middle column "What animals live in our neighborhood?" One reason this is a good driving question is that it can be investigated by students. Future chapters will explore the KWL method in greater detail.

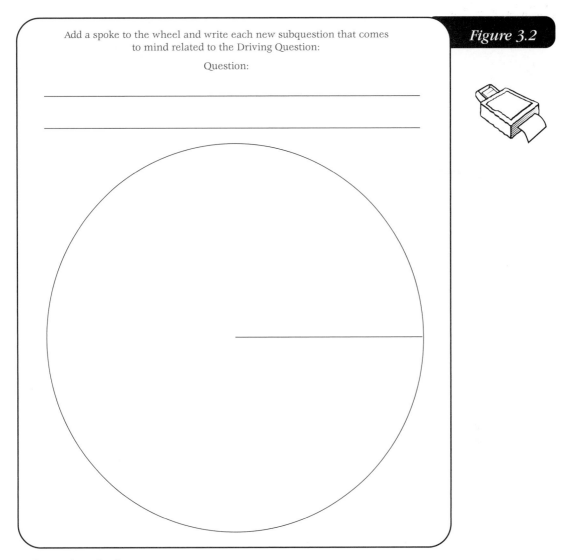

Add a spoke to the wheel and write each new subquestion that comes to mind related to the Driving Question:

Question:

_____

_____

Figure 3.2

Brainstorming wheel.

Besides having students brainstorm topics and related questions in a large group, teachers can have the class generate topics and questions in small groups. This method allows students to critique the questions as well since small-group review is much less threatening than having questions exposed to the whole class for review. Some teachers use dialogue journals to accomplish this small-group generation of topics and sharing. Dialogue journals are journals that students keep and share with peers or the teacher and that include responses from readers. Now is a good time to complete Portfolio Activity 3.6.

Portfolio Activity 3.6

DEVELOPING DRIVING QUESTIONS FROM WHAT STUDENTS KNOW

Materials Needed:

- A classroom to visit or an elementary or middle school student to interview
- Paper and pencil or a computer

A. Obtain permission from appropriate school personnel to interview an elementary or middle school student (or interview a student you know such as a son or daughter, neighbor, cousin, or student you babysit). Ask the student about his or her hobbies and personal interests. Find out what topics the child thinks he or she knows much about. Make a list of these ideas.

B. Analyze the list of ideas and decide how these could be turned into driving questions.

C. What challenges might you have meeting the key features of driving questions?

D. Record your responses in your portfolio.

Selection of Students' Questions.   After students have generated possible driving questions, teachers must help them select the questions that will be used for projects. This is not an easy task. Many students want their question selected, and their feelings can be hurt and self-esteem damaged if their questions are not selected. Several techniques can be used to sensitively select the driving questions from the pool of questions students generate.

One technique is to have students evaluate and refine their questions. In the process of evaluating and refining questions, they often discard many of them. Teachers can use the features of a driving question (see Table 3.1) and the questions in Figure 3.3 to support evaluation and refinement of questions. Most students will not know how to evaluate questions, so a critical first step is to model the process of evaluating. For example, imagine the class has generated the question "How do robots work?" The teacher can respond to this question by saying,

> My driving question is "How do robots work?" I want to know more about how to make a robot. Let's see . . . I will need to know about electricity and machines. I will also need to know about computers. I could break this question into smaller ones: How is a robot made? How expensive is a robot? Could a robot do my homework? What investigations can I do? Hmmm. I don't know. I don't have money to buy a robot, so we can't experiment on it. I have a toy robot. I could take that apart, but once I took it apart, I'd be done in a few hours. This is interesting, but I guess it's not a good driving question. I can't investigate this very much!

From the teacher's modeling of the process, students can see how the teacher eliminated the robot question because it wasn't feasible or sustainable. Once the teacher models the process, students in the class are usually ready to evaluate some of their own questions using the criteria in Figure 3.3.

Another strategy for selecting a driving question from a list of students' questions is to have two groups of students share and critique each other's driving questions. When using this technique, teachers should make sure that the groups who are having their questions critiqued also have the right to defend their questions. It also is critical that students give reasons for their comments. Just claiming that they don't like a question is not

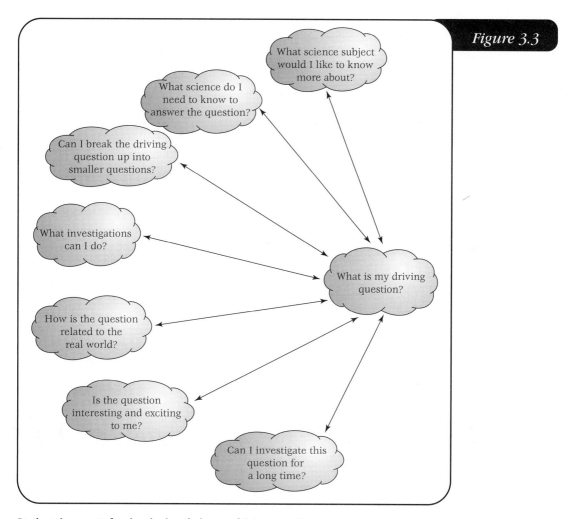

Figure 3.3

Students' prompts for developing their own driving questions.

a sufficient reason. The criteria in Figure 3.3 can be used to focus and support student evaluation of the questions posed by others. While students are evaluating and refining their questions in small groups, it is vital that the teacher give students feedback on their evaluations. This helps students stay focused. Active monitoring of group work and encouragement are critical if teachers want students to complete the task with a high level of investment.

Teachers should also help students realize that good driving questions, like most products that have value, don't emerge complete from the first round of revision. To arrive at a good product, people often must perform several revisions. Therefore, modifying questions is a critical step in developing good driving questions. To accomplish this, some teachers like to bring the separate groups back into a large group and have the groups present their questions and give justifications for selecting them. Then, the members of other groups can add their comments to the discussion of a driving question candidate. This technique helps reinforce the qualities of a good question.

Summary of Strategies to Help Students Develop Questions

Student-generated questions require a little more work on the part of the teacher, because supports need to be used to get students to develop them. Further, a teacher needs to make sure that students work through the process of determining whether all of the key criteria of driving questions are met. However, most teachers find that, with experience, children will begin to ask, refine, and develop solid projects based upon their own questions. Finally, teachers who are familiar with their school district's curriculum standards are usually able to adapt students' questions to school outcomes or have students generate subquestions related to a driving question in the school's curriculum. Table 3.2 summarizes ways that students' questions can be developed into driving questions.

WHAT IS THE VALUE OF THE DRIVING QUESTION?

A driving question has value if it (1) is meaningful for students; (2) allows teachers to link various components of a project; (3) allows students to engage in an intellectual problem over time; (4) links content and process; (5) helps students see how the science they are learning applies to their lives; and (6) connects various subject areas so that students can develop understandings about the connections.

> **Key Idea**
>
> Driving questions help students see connections between what they are learning in school and their lives.

Often in schools students see what they are learning as separate from their own interests and lives. How many times have students been told, "You will need this for life" or "You will need this for the next class"? Unfortunately, these reasons are not motivating for students of any age. Driving questions, however, help make learning meaningful (Crawford, Marx, & Krajcik, 1999). Students find the questions and, thus, the learning relevant to their lives and their world or culture, and they find the related projects exciting and interesting.

What typically happens in schools is that ideas are taught in isolation from each other. There often is no organizer that can pull together the overall ideas. For example, a common science curriculum might teach students how to classify animals, about habitats needed by animals, and about behaviors of animals. These topics are usually taught as separate ideas—perhaps even through different chapters of a book covered at different times during the year. Driving questions help teachers link the various concepts taught, which helps students develop integrated understandings. The questions become anchors for all the new information that students are learning, which results in the information making more sense.

Students frequently lack motivation to expend a great deal of energy over an extended period of time when there is no driving question to focus that energy and give them a reason for their efforts. A driving question ties the learning of concepts to the project activities and ties both to a clear, meaningful purpose. With this combination students are engaged throughout the duration of a project.

Sometimes school science is presented as though content and process were separate. Consider as an example the first scenario in this chapter. In this scenario, process was presented as separate from content. A well-written driving question gives coherence and

Table 3.2

WAYS TO HELP STUDENTS GENERATE DRIVING QUESTIONS

- Provide or create an environment in which students can make observations.
- Have students brainstorm what they know.
- Focus on students' hobbies and personal interests.
- Help students modify topics into questions of interest.
- Model the process of evaluating questions using the criteria in Figure 3.3.
- Have students share, evaluate, and refine questions in small groups.
- Have groups share questions and rationales with the whole class.

continuity to project-based science, and it links content with process. Deborah Brown, a teacher from Detroit Public Schools, illustrates this in the case report she wrote after doing the "What's in Our Water?" project (Krajcik et al., 1996):

> One of the biggest advantages to using a driving question as the focus was that it gave students a sense of purpose. As we worked together through this first unit, my students began to realize that there was a reason for everything that we did. No more questions like, "Why do we have to learn this?" No matter how different the activities seemed, the end results were the same. We were trying to find out about our tap water.
>
> This sense of purpose did not come about quickly or easily. Many times as I was teaching the first unit ("What's in Our Water?"), I would forget to emphasize our main question. The students may have understood the main concepts of that lesson and still had no idea how it was connected to the unit.
>
> When I did remember to ask the students about our main question, I would many times get blank stares. They were not used to making these kinds of connections. So, when I first asked them to go back to research they had done three weeks ago and apply it to activities they were doing today, they thought I was out of my mind. [But later] students became more adept at making connections. Students were able to draw on previous data to explain new concepts.

This quote also illustrates that a sense of purpose comes about only after the teacher does a lot of active teaching. The teacher must continually help students see how the content and process are linked to the driving question. The teacher is central to the success of project-based science, because the teacher, as an active and supportive leader and guide, orchestrates the educational environment. If the teacher does not play this role, students are not able to focus on the demanding intellectual activities of projects, and they cannot see the purposes of the activities of the project.

A common problem in science classrooms is that students learn only fragmented knowledge without ever relating school science content to the world in which they live. But when science class is centered around an interesting, real world driving question, students can more easily make connections with the content, and they can see firsthand how the study of science relates to issues and problems in their own lives.

Often students don't have experiences in school that help them attach much of what they learn in one subject area to what they learn in other subject areas. For example, students might learn how to use a ruler in mathematics class to solve math problems but not about applications to science. In science class, they might learn about various animal habitats but fail to learn about the connections to history and politics. They may learn how to write a business letter in language arts, but they never learn about the use of writing skills in math and science. As a result, students develop fragmented knowledge that they can't apply in other areas of study.

Through the driving question, project-based science explicitly links different subject areas. For example, through the driving question "How do we care for the pets in our room?" students might learn to use a ruler in mathematics class so that they can measure the amount a pet has grown. They might learn about animal habitats in order to build the best home for their classroom pet. They might learn to write a business letter in language arts so that they can write to companies that test products on animals. When learning is integrated in this way, students develop cognitive structures for processing and linking new information. In this way, learning occurs at a deeper, more permanent level. (See the Chapter 2 section on "Meaningful Understanding" and Chapter 11 where we discuss integration across the curriculum.)

HOW CAN A DRIVING QUESTION BE USED THROUGHOUT A PROJECT?

Key Idea

Linking back to the driving question helps keep students focused on the purpose of their learning.

Once a teacher has chosen a driving question and begun a project, he or she must keep referring to the driving question. The driving question gives a focus to class activities and to what the students are learning. By keeping the driving question in focus as teachers lead students through different activities, students contextualize what they are learning and help maintain continuity throughout the project. The driving question can be an excellent vehicle to maintain focus and support integration but only if the teacher takes an active role in using the driving question throughout a project.

In a project-based science classroom, investigations and activities should play a role in answering the driving question. However, making students aware of these connections can be a challenge. These connections are not always obvious to students until the teacher takes the time to help students understand the reasons behind activities. There are several techniques for applying the driving question throughout a project.

One excellent and simple technique is to refer frequently to the driving question. At the end of every class and activity, before beginning each new activity, and periodically throughout the day, the teacher can ask, "Why are we doing all this?" Soon enough, students will be able to join the teacher in responding, "To learn how to care for the pets in our room" or "To find out what birds visit our feeder." It won't be long before students begin to think about the driving question as they work, even without the teacher's prompts.

Another technique is to develop ways to link activities and investigations in class to the driving question. Teachers need to consider how to introduce a project's driving question so that the connections between the question and classroom activity start out firmly planted in students' minds. Throughout the project, teachers can reinforce this connection by asking periodically, "Why is this investigation important to our project?" and "How does it help us answer our driving question?" Students will come to expect teachers to ask these questions and will develop good responses.

Another way of linking the content and the class activities to the driving question is to have the driving question visible at all times. The teacher can point to the question every time she asks, "Why are we doing this?" Students will soon learn to look at the wall or bulletin board where the question is posted to help them stay on track. One teacher hung a large banner with the driving question on it on the wall outside her classroom. From the banner she hung various student products. The banner with the driving question and products formed a time line of project activities. The banner also generated excitement among other students in the school.

Another technique is to have students periodically write in their journals about how what they are doing is related to the driving question. Some teachers use this technique in conjunction with class discussion that encourages students to tell how what they do in class on a given day is related to their driving question. Because these projects are long term, the potential for losing focus is high, so continual reminders of the driving question can prevent fragmented learning and keep students from getting lost.

CONNECTING TO
NATIONAL SCIENCE EDUCATION STANDARDS

Science Teaching Standards

Student understanding is actively constructed through individual and social processes. In the same way the scientists develop their knowledge and understanding as they seek answers to questions about the natural world, students develop an understanding of the natural world when they are actively engaged in scientific inquiry—alone and with others (p. 29).

CHAPTER REVIEW   www.mhhe.com/krajcik2e

**ONLINE
LEARNING
CENTER**

Go to the Online Learning Center at **www.mhhe.com/krajcik2e** to review important content from the chapter and key terms, take a chapter assessment, and link to the chapter's websites.

CHAPTER SUMMARY

A driving question organizes content and drives activities that take place in a science class. The driving question is the first step in meeting all of the other key features of project-based science. The question sets the stage for planning and carrying out investigations. This chapter elaborated on the features of good driving questions: feasibility, worth, contextualization, meaning, ethics, and sustainability. It also discussed ways that driving questions can be teacher-generated from the curriculum, the World Wide Web, colleagues, personal interests, and the media and how they can be student-generated. Techniques for encouraging and selecting student questions or subquestions were explored. The chapter ended with an exploration of the value of a driving question: The question is meaningful for students; it helps teachers link lessons, process and content, and different other subject areas; and it allows students to engage in an intellectual problem over time. Developing driving questions is clearly worth the time and effort because they allow students to learn in a more educationally sound manner, and they make teaching more satisfying and rewarding.

CHAPTER HIGHLIGHTS

- Driving questions organize and drive sustained inquiry.
- Driving questions have six features. They are
  - Feasible.
  - Worthwhile.

- Contextualized.
- Meaningful.
- Ethical.
- Sustainable.
- Driving questions differ from other questions because they are not topic based, and they are related to children's lives.
- Teachers can develop driving questions from
  - Personal experience.
  - School curriculum.
  - Listening to students.
  - Hobbies and person interests.
  - Media including the World Wide Web.
  - Listening to other teachers.
  - Published curriculum materials.
- Teachers can help students develop driving questions by
  - Creating rich classroom environments.
  - Helping students generate subquestions to the main driving question.
  - Linking to students' prior experiences.
- Driving questions are valuable because they
  - Are meaningful to students.
  - Allow teachers and students to link various parts of the project.
  - Engage students in intellectual problems over time.
  - Link content and processes.
  - Help students connect school to their lives.
  - Connect subject areas.
- Throughout projects teachers continually make connections to the driving question.

KEY TERMS

Contextualization (85)   **Feasibility** (83)   **Sustainability** (86)
Driving question (81)   **Meaning** (85)   **Worth** (84)
Ethical (86)   **Subquestions** (83)

REFERENCES

American Association for the Advancement of Science. 1993. *Benchmarks for science literacy.* New York: Oxford University Press.

Atwater, M. M. 1994. Research on cultural diversity in the classroom. In *Handbook of research on science teaching and learning,* ed. D. L. Gabel. New York: Macmillan.

Blumenfeld, P., E. Soloway, R. Marx, J. Krajcik, M. Guzdial, and A. Palincsar. 1991.

Motivating project-based learning: Sustaining the doing, supporting the learning. *Educational Psychologist* 26(3 & 4):369–98.

Burnett, R. 1999. *The pillbug project: A guide to investigation.* Washington, D.C.: National Science Teachers Association.

Crawford, B., R. Marx, and J. Krajcik. 1999. Developing collaboration in a middle school project-based science classroom. *Science Education* 83(6):701–23.

Elementary Science Study. 1970. *The ESS reader.* Newton, Mass.: Education Development Center.

Haberman, M. 1991. The pedagogy of poverty versus good teaching. *Phi Delta Kappa* 73(4):290-94.

Haberman, M. 1995. *STAR teachers of children in poverty.* West Lafayette, Ind.: Kappa Delta Pi.

Krajcik, J. S. 1993. Learning science by doing science. In *What research says to the science teacher: Science, society and technology,* ed. R. Yager. Washington, D.C.: National Science Teacher Association.

Krajcik, J., P. Blumenfeld, R. W. Marx, and E. Soloway. 1994. A collaborative model for helping science teachers learn project-based instruction. *Elementary School Journal* 94(5):483-98.

Krajcik, J., B. Blumenfeld, R. Marx, and E. Soloway. 2000. Instructional, curricular, and technological supports for inquiry in science classrooms. In *Inquiry into inquiry: Science learning and teaching,* eds. J. Minstell and E. Van Zee, Washington, D.C.: American Association for the Advancement of Science Press, 283-315.

Krajcik, J., E. Soloway, P. C. Blumenfeld, R. W. Marx, B. L. Ladewski, N. D. Bos, and P. J. Hayes. 1996. The casebook of project practices—an example of an interactive multimedia system for professional development. *Journal of Computers in Mathematics and Science Teaching* 15(Vols. 1 and 2):119-35.

Lawrence Hall of Science. 1993. *Full option science system.* Nashua, N.H.: Delta Education.

Lawrence Hall of Science. 2000. *Full option science system.* Nashua, N.H.: Delta Education.

MacKenzie, A. H. 2001. The role of teacher stance when infusing inquiry questioning into middle school science classrooms. *School Science and Mathematics* 101(3):143-53.

National Geographic Kids Network. 1989. *Acid rain.* Washington, D.C.: National Geographic Society.

National Geographic Kids Network. 1991. *What's in our water?* Washington, D.C.: National Geographic Society.

National Research Council. 1996. *National science education standards.* Washington, D.C.: National Academy Press.

National Science Resource Center. 1991. *Science and technology for children.* Washington, D.C.: Smithsonian Institute, National Academy of Sciences.

National Science Resource Center. 1997. *Science and technology for children.* Washington, D.C.: Smithsonian Institute, National Academy of Sciences.

Ogle, D. 1986. A teaching model that develops active reading of expository text. *The Reading Teacher* 39(2):564-70.

Chapter 4

How Are Scientific Investigations Developed?

INTRODUCTION

INVESTIGATIONS IN ELEMENTARY AND MIDDLE
  SCHOOL SCIENCE INSTRUCTION

THE INVESTIGATION WEB

SUPPORTING STUDENTS' IMPLEMENTATION OF
  INVESTIGATIONS

CRITERIA FOR ASSESSING THE VALUE OF AN
  INVESTIGATION

CHAPTER LEARNING PERFORMANCES

- *Explain the value of elementary and middle grade students engaging in investigations.*
- *Clarify the components of the investigative web.*
- *Design and carry out investigations with students.*
- *Critique and give feedback to elementary and middle grade students on the various components of an investigation.*
- *Judge the quality of opportunities for students engaging in investigations.*

INTRODUCTION

Investigations form the essence of "doing" science. What is an investigation? How are investigations developed? How do I help students plan and design experiments? How can I help students be systematic in analyzing data? How do I help students make conclusions from data? In this chapter, we will explore how to help students engage in investigations. We will examine the various components of investigations, including asking and refining questions, planning and designing experiments, assembling and carrying out procedures, analyzing data, drawing conclusions, and sharing information with others. We will consider the various components as a web of related activities. Throughout the chapter, we will examine the various instructional supports a teacher can provide to help learners through the various components of investigations, and we will explore answers to numerous questions that might arise about investigations.

First, we will consider several types of school science activities, some of which you may have experienced yourself as a student. As you read each scenario, focus on various features of the instructional setting. What are the students doing and thinking? What is the role of the teacher? What instructional supports does the teacher provide?

Scenario 1: A Step-by-Step Activity

You may have observed a situation similar to this. Ms. Pilarski, a fifth-grade teacher, presents information on the physical and chemical properties of materials. Ms. Pilarski shows the students some white powders and tells the class they will observe what happens when they mix a small amount of each powder with some liquids the teacher calls *solutions*. Ms. Pilarski hands out a sheet of paper with step-by-step directions about the amounts of powder and liquid to use and about how to mix the materials together. Ms. Pilarski also passes out a sheet of paper with a carefully labeled table on which the students are to record their observations. The powders are labeled across the top of the table and the solutions are labeled down the side. Ms. Pilarski directs the class to describe and illustrate their observations in the table.

Ms. Pilarski allows the students to work in groups of four. Each group has thirty minutes in which to complete the activity. Ms. Pilarski directs each group to assign one member to gather the required materials—the powders and solutions—from the table at the front of the class. Students from various groups volunteer to gather the materials, but in one group none of the students wants to go get the materials. After the students return to their tables with the materials, one student, Frank, grabs some of the powders and begins mixing them with one of the liquids. In some groups, students begin by reading Ms. Pilarski's directions to decide what they need to do first. In one group, all the students begin working independently of each other. Some students become involved by reading off the directions and handing materials to the other students. Some students use magnifying glasses to make observations of the powders, and they draw pictures of what they see. The classroom is loud, but everyone appears to be on task. Students make comments like, "Hey, that was cool." A number of the groups really like it when one of the powders bubbles and fizzes when mixed with one of the solutions.

In this first scenario, the activity was selected by the teacher, the teacher gave the students directions about how to carry out the activity, and all the students performed the same activity. Although the students manipulated materials and worked in small groups to make and record observations, they spent little, if any, time planning what they were to do and little, if any, time discussing what the observations meant. Moreover, the activity the students performed was not tied to a question that the students asked or that they found meaningful.

Scenario 2: A Trial-and-Error Activity

You may have observed a situation like this. Mr. Warren, a fifth-grade teacher, passes out one light bulb, a wire, and a battery. He challenges the students to work in teams of two to find as many ways as possible to light the bulb using just the wire and the battery. Mr. Warren directs the class to work in groups of two and to sketch "all the ways you can get the bulb to light using the battery and wire." He hands out baggies that contain the various materials.

Almost all of the teams jump into the task with little or no discussion about what to do. A number of the teams try connecting the bulb, wire, and battery in a straight-line configuration, but this method fails to light the bulb. Some students comment that they have a "bad bulb" or a "battery that doesn't work." After several failed attempts, some of the teams discuss ways to get the bulb to light. As some of the groups get their light bulb to light, comments like "cool" or "wow" are heard. Some of the teams that fail to light their bulbs become frustrated and stop trying, but most of the groups persist, possibly because trying to light the bulb is more fun than answering the questions at the end of the chapter. The excitement in the room grows as various teams light the bulb. After about five minutes, most teams have lit their bulbs. Mr. Warren walks around the room, asking each team to demonstrate its strategies.

Mr. Warren challenges the teams to find out how to light the bulb in different ways. Some teams that are having difficulty finding a way to light their bulbs ask other teams for help; the successful teams seem happy to share their techniques. Mr. Warren encourages the groups that are having difficulty to think of different ways to light the bulb. Mr. Warren also challenges the teams that had success lighting the bulb in more than one way to "make two light bulbs light so that, if you disconnect one light bulb, the other goes out too." Some teams talk about how lighting the bulb is related to switching on the light in the classroom.

In Scenario 2 as in Scenario 1, the teacher selected the activity for the students. Once again, the activity was not tied to the driving question or to a question that the students asked. Unlike Scenario 1, in this case the teacher did not tell the students how to do the activity, so students conceivably could have made plans for how to light the bulb, but most just used trial-and-error methods. The activity was fun, but most of the students did not understand why the bulb would or would not light. Little, if any, discussion occurred regarding why the bulb lit in one configuration and not in others. Moreover, the class did not follow through with this activity to further explore issues related to electrical phenomena. Although some of the students were able to make a connection between lighting the bulb and lighting their school, most students did not understand how lighting the bulb related to how the lights work in a building.

Scenario 3: An Investigation

Perhaps you experienced a situation like this. In a fifth-grade science classroom, one group of four students is sitting in a circle talking with other students writing in notebooks.

Another group is standing behind a table putting soil in a pot, and another is gathered around a computer at the back of class. Ms. Tamika Brown, the teacher, is talking with a fourth group of students.

The group sitting in a circle is making a list of possible questions to explore: Do worms help decomposition? Will new worms be born in the decomposition column? What will decompose first? One student says that the group can't design an experiment to study whether worms will be born in the decomposition column because it would be hard to count all the worms. Another student responds that it doesn't matter if they count *all* the worms; they just need to see if there are *more*.

The group putting soil in a pot has already made a plan for investigating the effects of compost on the growth of bean plants. The students are planting eight bean plants. They plan to plant two plants with a 75/25 mixture of compost and soil, two plants with a 50/50 mixture, another two with a 25/75 mixture, and two with just soil. Some of the students are still discussing whether they need to plant some plants with 100 percent compost.

The group at the computer is composing a letter to another fifth-grade class. The students are explaining to the other class, which is located in another state, their plan for investigating the influence of light on decomposition. They will e-mail their letter to this class when they have finished writing it.

The fourth group is discussing with Ms. Brown how to investigate the effects of air flow on decomposition. This group's plan is to build a decomposition column with numerous holes. Ms. Brown, through a series of questions, is trying to help the group understand the need for a control and a larger sample. Ms. Brown asks, "If you use only one decomposition column, how will that help you understand how air flow influences decomposition?" The students in the group are debating this question. One student says, "You really won't know if you use only one column because there will be nothing to compare it to." Another student argues that they could investigate "how fast the various stuff decomposes" using just one column. Another student responds that "how fast" won't help them answer their question. The group continues to debate. Ms. Brown moves on to work with another group.

This scenario shows students engaging in different aspects of the process of investigation: asking and refining questions, planning and designing experiments, assembling materials and apparatus, carrying out procedures, and sharing information with others. The scenario also shows the important role that teachers play in helping students work through the various stages of investigations. Unlike the first and second scenarios, this scenario does not represent an activity that the teacher selected; what the teacher created was an educational environment in which students could learn about decomposition. Then the teacher provided instructional support by working with each of the groups, asking probing questions, and providing materials that students could use to investigate their questions.

There are times in the curriculum when step-by-step and trial-and-error activities, like those illustrated in the first two scenarios, are important. (Chapter 7 contains more information on how to develop step-by-step activities.) Such activities, however, are not investigations, because they are determined and set up by the teacher.

INVESTIGATIONS IN ELEMENTARY AND MIDDLE SCHOOL SCIENCE INSTRUCTION

The third scenario shows students involved in many aspects of investigating science questions. Students pursue solutions to questions of importance by asking and refining their own questions, debating ideas, making predictions, designing plans and/or experiments, measuring, collecting and analyzing data and/or information, drawing conclusions, making inferences, communicating their ideas and findings to others, and asking new questions. Research supports the notion that young children are capable of performing all these aspects of investigations (Krajcik, Blumenfeld, Marx, Bass, Fredricks, & Soloway, 1998; Metz, 1995; Schauble, Klopfer, & Raghavan, 1991). Metz (1995) presents a strong argument for the investigative ability of young children and for their ability to learn from investigations, although their investigations are not as sophisticated as those of adolescents and adults because of their limited prior knowledge. The teacher plays the critical role of orchestrating the investigative process and selecting curricular areas that allow students to ask questions that result in developing understanding of important concepts and principles.

Research also suggests that students should be involved throughout their school experience in the process of scientific investigation, and that children should be involved in the business of thinking scientifically:

> From their very first day in school, students should be actively engaged in learning to view the world scientifically. That means encouraging them to ask questions about nature and seek answers, collect things, count and measure things, make qualitative observations, organize collections and observations, discuss findings, etc. Getting into the spirit of science and liking science are what count the most (AAAS, *Benchmarks for Science Literacy,* p. 6).

Asking questions, designing experiments, analyzing data, and sharing what they know should be a routine part of students' science learning. However, students seldom have opportunities to ask their own questions and then define experiments to gather data related to the questions. Science textbooks seldom engage students in the process of investigation. As in Scenario 1, children are often given the purpose of activities, step-by-step directions, and procedures for how to collect data. Activities of this sort do not engage students in scientific thinking. For activities of this sort, students often are given the outcomes and not challenged to analyze the purpose or predict outcomes. Students seldom have opportunities during these activities to analyze data, yet it is the process of analysis that leads to deep understanding of a situation or phenomenon. Often, students know the expected outcome to the activity before the activity is conducted.

As clearly stated in the *National Science Education Standards* (National Research Council, 1996), students need to engage in the scientific process: They need to ask their own questions that are important to them, design their own experimental procedures, make sense of their data, analyze their data, share their plans and findings with others for feedback and criticism, and generate new ideas. In fact, congruent with recommendations of the AAAS (1993), the *National Science Education Standards* stress that there

Key Idea

Research supports the idea that children of all ages are capable of designing and performing investigations.

CONNECTING TO NATIONAL SCIENCE EDUCATION STANDARDS

Science Education Program Standards
Standard A: The program must emphasize student understanding through inquiry (p. 214).

National Science Education Standards

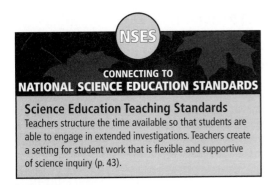

CONNECTING TO
NATIONAL SCIENCE EDUCATION STANDARDS

Science Education Teaching Standards
Teachers structure the time available so that students are
able to engage in extended investigations. Teachers create
a setting for student work that is flexible and supportive
of science inquiry (p. 43).

needs to be less emphasis on didactic instruction, which
focuses on memorizing decontextualized scientific facts,
and there needs to be new emphasis placed on **inquiry-
based learning** which focuses on developing a deep
understanding by exploring the world.

THE INVESTIGATION WEB

Engaging in the process of investigation is akin to seeking the answer to a question, for which humans seem to
have a deep need. In this section, we will examine the
investigation web, a process of carrying out an investi-
gation that includes "messing about," asking and refining questions, finding information,
planning and designing, building the apparatus and collecting data, analyzing data, making conclusions, and communicating findings.

Key Idea
Scientific investiga-tions proceed in a nonlinear fashion.

Figure 4.1 presents one visualization of the process of investigation. The term *web*
represents the **nonlinear** quality of an investigation and illustrates the way that students
revisit various components of an investigation. Science is truly a nonlinear endeavor. Each
component of an investigation provides feedback for another part.

Finding information about a topic might lead students to refine the questions that
took them to the information in the first place. In Scenario 3, students might have un-
covered information about building a compost that caused them to refine their question
regarding the impact of air flow on decomposition. Preliminary data analysis might have
suggested ways for students to modify their procedures to collect more reliable data. Students might have noticed that their decomposition column felt warm, and this observation might have encouraged them to collect data on temperature changes. Completing an
investigation should lead to other questions. For example, once students found out that
oxygen is needed to help materials decompose, they might have posed new questions regarding decomposition of materials buried in a landfill. Some investigations might have
begun with the gathering of data or with the search for a pattern. Students might have designed an investigation of decomposition only after "messing around" with different decomposing materials and noticing that air affects the rate of decomposition.

Science is a messy process. Although scientists often have good hunches about important questions based on theories and their own prior knowledge, the questions for investigation and the processes they ultimately employ often differ greatly from their
original conceptions. Some great examples of scientists' work that illustrate the investigative web in practice come from the works of Barbara McClintock, who was a famous
cytogeneticist, and Eugenie Clark, a world-renowned icthyologist and authority on sharks.

Imagine that a fourth-grade class is making observations of various crustaceans in a
nature area. One student group, which is turning over logs and rocks, notices that sowbugs can be found under the logs (messing about). Based on their observations, the students wonder if sowbugs like dark areas (wondering). In their classroom, the teacher has
students share their observations and questions with classmates (sharing ideas). The
group that has observed the sowbugs asks the question, "Do sowbugs like the dark?" (asking questions). (See Burnett, 1999.) Based on feedback from the class, the students refine
their question to "Will sowbugs choose a dark area over a lighted area?" (receiving feedback, refining questions). The students design an experimental procedure to answer their

Studying Sowbugs

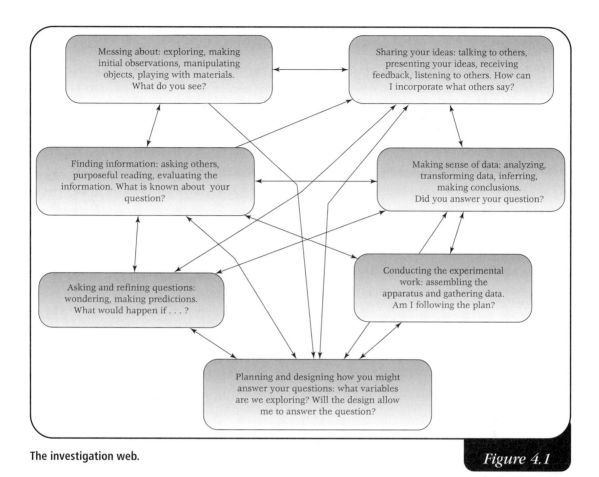

The investigation web.

Figure 4.1

question (designing). They then share their plans with the class (sharing ideas). Students in the class wonder if they are using enough sowbugs (wondering). The students incorporate the class feedback into their design (incorporating what others say). Next, the students look for information on sowbug habitats (finding information). They use the World Wide Web to obtain more information about sowbugs and pillbugs. Then they gather sowbugs from the nature area, build a habitat so the sowbugs can live, and construct their experimental chamber for testing light and dark habitats (assembling the apparatus). Next, they perform their experiment, carefully recording their data (gathering data). To make sense of their data, they create a bar chart of the number of sowbugs found in dark and light places (transforming data). They draw conclusions based on their findings and decide that sowbugs like dark areas (inferring). After some debate in the group regarding the number of trials needed, they decide to collect more data by carrying out two additional trials to see if their conclusion holds up (gathering data). They analyze their new data by comparing the old and new results and decide that they support their original conclusion (analyzing data). They then present their findings to the class (sharing ideas).

Some classmates suggest that they should have ruled out moisture to determine if the sowbugs like dark areas (receiving feedback). The students argue that moisture did not make a difference; however, after some debate, they realize that their classmates might have a point (talking to others). The students then redesign their investigation: This time, they keep some of the sowbugs in a dark dry environment, some in a dark moist environment, some in a light dry environment, and some in a light moist environment (planning and designing). The students once again analyze the data and draw a conclusion (making sense of data). The group then presents its findings and reasons to the class (sharing ideas). As students work, they ask a number of new questions about temperature and time. When the students complete their investigations, they return the sowbugs and the habitat materials to the nature area.

This example illustrates the investigative web process in its ideal form; don't expect your classroom investigations to run so smoothly from the start. As the teacher, you will need to provide instructional supports throughout the investigation process. Being good at science, like learning to play tennis, takes practice and experience. You would not expect to be a good tennis player the first time you pick up a tennis racket, and you shouldn't expect a student to be good at carrying out scientific investigations at first either. Excellent tennis players don't develop even over the course of a season, and so you cannot expect students to develop into good investigators during a single school year.

Let's play out the tennis analogy a little further: Tennis can be broken down into a variety of activities, such as forehand, backhand, serve, and volley. Skill in any one tennis activity doesn't make a good tennis player; neither does skill in all of the activities of tennis without putting them together. Practicing all the components together helps make a person a good tennis player. Similarly, conducting investigations has a number of components, such as planning, sharing, and gathering data. Skill in planning or gathering data alone does not make a good investigator. Students need to practice all of the activities of investigating, not in isolated applications but in concert.

The age of the learner will influence the type of investigations the learner can perform. Children who are in first or second grade are not developmentally ready to plan experiments in which they control variables. Children who are five to seven years old should be observing, measuring, and identifying properties of materials. For example, children in first or second grade could observe the different types of insects or birds found on their playground. Six- to nine-year-old children should be looking for evidence and identifying patterns. For example, fourth-grade students could chart throughout the day the length of a shadow cast from a stake placed in the ground to notice the pattern of the sun's "movement" across the sky. As children gain experiences and become more developmentally ready, they can perform more complex investigations. Eight- to twelve-year-old children should begin to design cause and effect experiments and develop their observations, measurements, and evidence-gathering skills; and eleven to thirteen year olds should design and conduct experiments that involve manipulating variables (AAAS, 1993). For example, middle school students could explore the influence of temperature on seed germination. A great resource for teachers to help determine the inquiry skills to teach at various grade levels is the AAAS (2001) *Atlas of Scientific Literacy.*

Messing About

How do you start students in the process of an investigation? How do you help children ask questions related to a content area? The first step in the investigative cycle is **messing**

about (Hawkins, 1965). Messing about includes exploring, manipulating materials, making initial observations, reading about phenomena, and taking things apart.

Messing about implies having fun and exploring the world. Children can learn much by checking out what is in a pond, taking apart an old flashlight, watching how various gears work in unison, or playing with a stream table. Messing about with natural phenomena creates situations that encourage children to wonder. Messing about also allows children to have essential prior experiences in exploring phenomena (Krajcik et al., 2000: Singer et al., 2000). Children cannot form ideas or ask questions about the behavior of sowbugs unless they first observe their behavior. Such experience allows students to build the prior experiences necessary to develop conceptual understanding of science concepts (Bransford, Brown, & Cocking, 1999).

> ### Key Idea
> Messing about helps students build essential knowledge and experiences related to the investigation.

Despite the implications of its name, this first step in investigation is not unstructured time. In fact, messing about needs to be carefully orchestrated by the classroom teacher. Although it may look very unplanned, the teacher selects situations that will lead children to ask questions that have important curriculum outcomes.

Students have inadequate background knowledge to ask questions about some science content areas. For example, students may not know enough about physical science concepts such as friction and momentum to ask questions about simple machines. With careful structuring, however, worthwhile investigations of even difficult and unfamiliar content can occur. For example, a teacher can structure a messing about session to help students ask good questions about skateboards (which are a type of simple machine involving wheels and axles). Teachers can use a number of techniques to create learning environments in which children can mess about and ask questions. We will consider two types: initial observations and manipulation of materials.

Initial Observations

One way to structure science lessons so that students can mess about productively and ask worthwhile questions is to encourage **initial observations.** These are introductory observations that students make of phenomena that might acquaint them with concepts, pique their curiosity, and motivate them to ask questions. Almost any type of physical object is a great catalyst for initial observations in elementary and middle grade classrooms. You might consider outdoor nature areas, playgrounds, simple machines around the school (such as pencil sharpeners), terrariums, aquariums, and classroom pets.

Imagine that you want to involve students in a biology investigation on insects. To focus early elementary students' observations, have the students map out 8-inch by 8-inch areas of the playground or of a nature area. Figure 4.2 shows how that might look. Some of the areas should be shady, some sunny, some moist, and some dry. Then have the students divide each area into a 2-inch by 2-inch grid. Ask each to select one area, or microbiome, for observation. If possible, supply students with magnifying lenses. While in the field, students might draw what they see onto 8-inch by 8-inch sheets of paper that are also marked off in 2-inch by 2-inch grids. Once in the classroom again, have students compare their grids with one another. Ask them to write down and share questions that emerge from their observations. Students might ask, for example, "Do each of the areas have the same insects?" "What is different about them?" "Why do you suppose they are different?"

Stream or pond walks are also excellent catalysts for initial observations about ecosystems. Portfolio Activity 4.1 will help you experience an initial observation activity; it places you in the role of the learner on a stream or pond walk.

Initial observations of an environment can lead to students asking questions.

If going to a nature area or a stream isn't possible for your students, you can set up some exciting observation environments for students to explore in your own classroom. For example, you and your students can create chameleon environments so that you can observe the behaviors of chameleons. Craig Berg (1994) developed some excellent techniques for using 2-liter plastic soda bottles as chameleon houses. Building such habitats will allow students numerous opportunities to observe the feeding habitats of chameleons or the life cycles of crickets. *Bottle Biology* (Ingram, 1993) offers a number of ideas on how to use 2-liter pop bottles. You can also use 2-liter plastic soda bottles to create decomposition environments or terrariums. What's wonderful about these environments is that you can easily alter conditions to make noticeable changes. For instance, you can manipulate moisture in the environment to see how it influences plant growth.

Initial observations need not be limited to biological phenomena; students can just as easily focus on physical phenomena. For example, you might have students observe the weather over an extended period. Students might keep weather journals over the course of a school year, which can lead them to ask numerous questions about how weather changes.

Manipulation of Materials

Another way to help students become involved in investigations is through the **manipulation of materials.** This may include building apparatus, taking things apart, or handling or playing with objects. For instance, you might have students set up an aquarium, take apart a flashlight, look at different objects through a magnifying glass, or plant some

GOING ON A STREAM WALK

Materials Needed:
- Writing materials
- Walking shoes

A. Where do questions come from? Questions often arise from exploring our environment. Take a thirty-minute walk around a stream or pond. As you walk, examine the bank. Look closely at the water. What do you see? You might dip a bucket into the water and draw a water sample so that you can make more thorough observations.

B. As you walk and observe your stream or pond, take notes of your observations. What do you find interesting? What catches your eye?

C. Also note any questions that come to mind. What would you like to find out more about?

D. When you have completed your walk, record your observations and questions on a chart like the following:

Observations	Questions

E. What other questions come to mind now? You might decide to order your questions from most to least interesting.

F. Compare your observations with those of other students in your class.

G. File your completed chart in your portfolio.

seeds. Many objects are good items for students to manipulate: seeds, toy cars, balls, magnets, and scientific equipment such as balances, tape measures, magnifying glasses, and measuring cups.

Imagine that you want students to learn about the relationship between streams and streambeds and banks. Have students help you set up sand or stream tables in your classroom. These are long, flat pans filled with sand that can be used to demonstrate the flow of a river or stream. Once the students have set up the tables, have them manipulate the conditions of the stream. For example, they might place clay balls, marbles, and metal objects within the stream of the water and on the banks. Ask students to make observations about what happens with each manipulation. You might want to tie this activity to a stream walk so that students can make connections between what they observed in the stream table and what happens in an actual stream. *River Cutters* (1989), developed by the Lawrence Hall of Science, describes how you can make some inexpensive stream tables for your classroom.

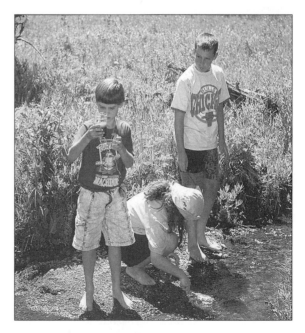

Stream walks catalyze student questions.

> ### Key Idea
>
> Teachers play essential roles in helping students focus their initial observations of worthwhile features of phenomena.

Manipulating materials and making initial observations should not be isolated activities. Manipulation should always be accompanied by observation of the effects of manipulation. Likewise, observations help students make decisions about what variables to manipulate. For example, once students have built something like a stream table or aquarium, they make observations of this environment to determine what to manipulate.

The Role of the Teacher

Making initial observations and manipulating materials can motivate students to ask questions, but it is likely that student observations at first will be scattered and unfocused. It is also likely that children's descriptions will not be detailed. For example, in describing a white powder, a child might say that it "looks like salt," but we want students to go beyond this simple labeling of the material. As the classroom teacher, your role is to provide the instructional support to help students focus their observations, write clear descriptions, and become more thorough and complete. With your support, a student might eventually be able to say about the powder, "The stuff is white. Each piece looks like a cube when I look at it with the magnifying glass. Some of the cubes look like they are scratched or chipped."

At the beginning of the school year, you might want to implement a number of **benchmark lessons** (lessons that teach a necessary concept or skill) to help students improve their observation skills. (Chapter 7 contains more information on benchmark lessons.) However, you still will need to focus students' observations throughout the school year. One benchmark lesson that many teachers have used successfully is the mystery bag activity. In this activity, a number of different kinds of materials, such as a piece of fur, a piece of a tennis ball, and odd-shaped pieces of wood are placed into opaque bags. Students stick their hands into the bags to feel the objects. Without looking, they describe what they feel. Students then can engage in interesting discussions about what they felt, comparing their observations, asking others to explain further what they mean, or disagreeing on what they felt. After discussion, give students a second chance to make observations; this way they may reach a consensus about what is in the bag.

There are a number of spin-offs from this activity. For example, you can build mystery boxes: Glue odd- or regular-shaped objects inside shoe boxes. Then seal the boxes so that students cannot open them. Have students explore what is in the boxes by inserting long wood or metal probes, such as 10-inch wood skewers, through small holes drilled into the box. Students should try to draw to scale the objects that they examine in this way.

You can also create benchmark lessons that focus on observations specific to a project. You might want to begin a project on the behavior of reptiles by having students describe what a chameleon looks like and how it behaves. Record the observations on the board. Then the class can discuss whether the observations contain sufficient detail. After the discussion, the class can create a common description of the chameleon.

Many students have a tendency to make premature **inferences** rather than observations. You need to help your students distinguish between observations and inferences. Imagine that a group of students is recording observations of the crustaceans they find in a nature area. Some students record, "Sowbugs eat wood," and others record, "I found sowbugs under a fallen tree branch." "Sowbugs eat wood" is a speculation; "I found sow-bugs under a fallen tree branch" is an observation. One way to help students make this distinction is to ask, "Did you see it?"

You should also encourage students to use tools to help them make observations. Elementary students can work with a magnifying glass, a ruler, and a scale. Older students can use a microscope, voltmeter, or light probe. By collaborating with community members, students can have access to more sophisticated equipment such as an electron microscope or a telescope.

Students need guidance to become more systematic in recording their observations. Encourage students to keep their observations in a notebook. Their observations should be specific enough and detailed enough so that they can be understood weeks or months later. Imagine that your students are exploring when various insects disappear and reappear. The student who writes, "Insects disappeared when it got cold," and months later writes, "Insects reappeared when it got warm," does not know what temperature was related to the insects' disappearance or appearance. Terms such as *cold* and *warm* are relative and tell the student very little.

One technique that you can use to help students improve their recording of observation notes is to have them read their notes out loud in class to receive feedback from other students. You can also give them written comments. Gentle reminders can also serve as strong cognitive support in helping students gain clarity and become more systematic.

Asking and Refining Questions

Once students have "messed about" and made initial observations, they need to ask questions based on those observations. The students who are observing insects in a nature area might begin to ask questions such as, "Where do different insects live?" "When do the insects first appear?" and "When do we stop seeing various insects?" Making observations and asking questions are not necessarily separate activities. Children often begin to ask questions while they are observing. Frequently, students refine these questions as they make more observations and as they find and synthesize information. Figure 4.1 illustrates how making observations and asking questions is a back-and-forth process.

> ### Key Idea
> Researchable questions can stem from children's initial observations.

Experiences may also prompt student questions. Reading the newspaper, talking to parents or other family members, or going on a family trip can all lead to questions. As students experience the world around them, questions about the environment can and will arise. For instance, if a child's family composts lawn clippings, the child might be interested in why the compost pile doesn't smell. It is the role of the teacher to support students as they move from making observations to asking questions.

The Role of the Teacher

The teacher plays a critical role in helping students develop meaningful and worthwhile questions that will help them learn important curricular content. The teacher is the curriculum leader who guides or selects the driving questions for the project and who supports

NSES

CONNECTING TO
NATIONAL SCIENCE EDUCATION STANDARDS

Science Education Content Standards
K–4—Standard A: Students should be able to ask a question about objects, organisms, and events in the environment (p. 122).

Science Education Content Standards
5–8—Standard A: Students identify questions that can be answered through scientific investigations (p. 145).

Table 4.1	OBSERVATIONS AND QUESTIONS	
	Observations	**Questions**
	Sowbugs under logs	Do sowbugs like dark places?
	Green slimy stuff on top of pond	What causes the green slimy stuff on top of the pond?
	Some leaves with different shapes	I wonder how many different kinds of leaves I can find in my neighborhood?

the selection of the phenomena that students will explore and observe. One technique for helping students generate questions is having them set up their experimental notebooks with two columns: *Initial Observations* and *Questions*. Table 4.1 shows how a student might set up his or her notebook.

Another technique to help students generate questions is to provide students with question stems. Question stems serve as cognitive supports and focus student questions. The following stems are useful in helping students generate questions: "I wonder what would happen if…?" "What if…?" "How does…?" and "What does…?"

It is also likely that students will ask more questions than they can answer; you will need to help students determine which questions are worthwhile, feasible, and ethical. Students may ask questions that are not related to the curricular goals of the project; you need to help them understand, without discouraging them, that they need to select new, worthwhile questions. Some students will ask questions that are beyond their developmental level or beyond the resources of your classroom; while emphasizing the value of the questions, you need to direct the students to ask more feasible questions. For example, let's say your class is exploring the driving question "What lives in our nature area?" One group of students asks the question "How do things move?" Although this might be an interesting question to the children, it is not directly related to the current curriculum objectives. As their teacher, you will need to redirect their question to perhaps "How do sowbugs move?" Questions also need to be ethical. For example, it is important that students not torture the insects to get them to move.

Types of Questions

There are three types of questions that students might ask as part of an investigation. **Descriptive questions** permit students to find out about observable characteristics of phenomena. **Relational questions** allow students to find out about associations among the characteristics of different phenomena. **Cause and effect questions** provide opportunities for students to make inferences about how one variable affects another variable. Table 4.2 gives examples of the different question types.

Students in early elementary school will ask many descriptive questions that will lead them to find out information about a phenomenon through making systematic observations. "What kind of foods do mealworms eat?" "How bright can I get a flashlight bulb to shine?" and "What kinds of leaves can a caterpillar eat?" are descriptive questions. Students can answer these questions by making systematic observations either in natural settings or in controlled situations. For example, students can answer the question "What kind of foods do mealworms eat?" by placing different kinds of food in a box that contains mealworms and making observations on which foods the mealworms select.

> **Key Idea**
>
> Descriptive questions provide opportunities for students to ask about observable characteristics of phenomena. Relational questions allow them to find out about associations among the characteristics of different phenomena. Cause and effect questions enable students to make inferences about how one variable affects another variable.

	TYPES OF QUESTIONS		*Table 4.2*
Descriptive Questions	**Relational Questions**	**Cause and Effect Questions**	
What materials dissolve in water?	Does salt dissolve faster than sugar?	Does the temperature of water affect the rate which salt and water dissolve?	
What macroinvertebrates are found in a stream?	Are different macro-invertebrates found in different areas of a stream?	Does water quality affect the types of macroinvertebrates found in a stream?	
How fast does my heart beat?	Who has a higher heart rate—boys or girls?	If people hear a loud sound, do their heart rates go up?	

Students in upper elementary grades should make a transition from descriptive questions to more complex relational questions. "Which dissolves faster in water—salt or sugar?" "What's a better insulator—paper, Styrofoam, or aluminum foil?" and "What conducts sound better—water, metal, air, or wood?" are relational questions. To answer these types of questions, students need to set up experimental procedures with which they can compare and contrast one or more characteristics. Such experimental situations provide opportunities for students to collect and analyze data and draw conclusions. To answer the question "What's a better insulator—paper, Styrofoam, or aluminum foil?" for example, students would need to compare and contrast the temperature of a substance when wrapped in the different materials. For instance, they could wrap soda cans in the different materials such as aluminum foil, plastic, or newspaper and collect data on how the temperature of the soda changes. To conclude which material is the best insulator, students would need to analyze the data from the different conditions.

Upper elementary and middle grade students need to make the transition to cause and effect questions that provide opportunities to explore the influence of one variable on the outcome of another. "Does water quality influence the type of macroinvertebrates found in a stream or pond?" "How does fertilizer affect the height and size of plants?" and "How does the surface of the ground affect how fast I can move on rollerblades?" are cause and effect questions. To answer these questions, students must design experiments in which they manipulate one variable (**independent variable**) to observe the effect on another variable (**dependent variable**). Such experimental situations allow students to collect data that they then can analyze to determine the reason for an outcome or result. One way to answer the rollerblade question is for students to design simulated environments in which they modify the surface of a 1-foot by 8-foot board (by adding sandpaper, rubber, oil, carpet, and vinyl flooring) and move wheels on axles across the surface. Students might choose to measure the different frictional forces with a spring scale or force probe.

Although early elementary students are more likely to ask descriptive questions and middle school students begin to make a transition to more cause and effect questions, it is not the case that middle school students should never ask descriptive questions or that elementary students should not ask cause and effect questions. Some projects might generate a natural progression through all three types of questions. For example, in a project exploring "What insects live in our playground?" students might first ask a very descriptive question: "What insects can I find?" Investigating this question may lead to a relational question: "Do I find different insects at different times of the day?" After conducting investigations, with guidance from the teacher, the students might be ready to ask a cause and effect question: "Do certain insects prefer dark or light environments?"

Although young children are unlikely to ask cause and effect questions on their own and then carry out investigations to find answers to them, you can set up an investigation in which the whole class explores the influence of one variable on another. For example, to explore if the amount of sunlight influences how green a plant is, you could set up an experiment in which one plant is kept in the sun and one in the shade. The class could make periodic comparisons between the two plants.

You will need to help students move from asking descriptive questions to asking cause and effect questions. The types of stems that you give students to help generate questions can have an effect on the types of questions they generate. "How does...?" and "What does...?" question stems are more likely to lead to descriptive questions. The "What if...?" stem tends to encourage more cause and effect questions. Another way to facilitate the transition is to list students' questions on the board or overhead, have students specify what each type of question is, and then transpose each question into another type of question. Table 4.2 shows how descriptive questions, relational questions, and cause and effect questions are related and how one type of question can be modified to another type of question. Reading across each of the rows, we see how the various questions are related to each other.

You will also find students asking basic information questions (Scardamalia & Bereiter, 1991). Students can find answers to basic information questions in reference source books or on the World Wide Web, but they can't answer them through the design of an investigation. "What is the diameter of the earth?" and "How hot is the sun?" are basic information questions. Although these questions have value and might be intellectually interesting to a student, project-based science stresses students asking questions that they can find answers to by setting up their own investigations. There is, however, a place in project-based science for basic information questions. Students might need to ask and answer basic information questions to complete the background information for an investigation. For an investigation of the influence of the amount of fertilizer on plant growth, for example, a student might need to find out what fertilizer is made of and if various brands of fertilizer differ in their composition. Benchmark lessons are a good way to answer basic information questions when a whole class needs the information. (Chapter 7 contains more information on benchmark lessons.)

Questions for Investigation and the Driving Question

If similar questions arise for a number of students, you might pick one to explore as a class. However, we find it critical that students have their own question on which to work. Working on their own questions leads students to feel ownership of a project and to be more engaged.

Conducting investigations to answer student questions should contribute to answering the driving question of the class, however. For example, students might complete a number of decomposition investigations, such as exploring what causes and promotes decomposition, to answer their own questions: "Do worms cause materials to decompose in soil?" and "Does airflow speed up decomposition?" Even though such investigations would be designed to answer the student questions, they would be related to the driving question of the project: "Where does all our garbage go?"[1] Maintaining a consistent focus ensures that what happens in the classroom is purposeful and meaningful.

Hypothesizing

Hypotheses are questions stated in testable form that relate how the independent variable affects the dependent variable. A student can design an experiment to collect data that will either give support for a question or refute a question; such a question becomes a hypothesis. "I wonder if pillbugs like cool places?" is a fine question for fourth-grade students, but it is not a testable question. It is not possible to measure if pillbugs *like* cool places. However, the question "Will pillbugs choose cool places over warm places?" can be transformed into the hypothesis "Pillbugs will move to cool places rather than warm places." Students can design an experiment to collect data that will either support or refute this hypothesis. They could count the number of pillbugs that go to the lower-temperature section of the apparatus, for example.

How might you phrase the question "Will wrapping my pop can in newspaper keep it cool?" in terms of a hypothesis? What is missing from this question is a comparison. A testable hypothesis for this question might be "A pop can wrapped in newspaper will stay cool longer than will a unwrapped pop can." A thermometer could be used to measure the temperatures of the different cans of pop. Portfolio Activity 4.2 helps you learn to identify testable questions. You might want to use this activity with your students to help them learn how to generate hypotheses from their questions.

Portfolio Activity 4.3 helps you learn how to generate hypotheses from questions. Once again, you might want to use this activity with your students.

Helping your students make hypotheses of their questions should not destroy the excitement students feel about the world around them. Making hypotheses is an intellectual skill that can be developed over time. From a developmental standpoint, you might be more concerned with helping early elementary students ask *observable* questions. You might want to have upper elementary and middle school students practice formulating *hypotheses* from their questions. What is most important is that students ask questions that are testable.

One way to help your students change questions into hypotheses is to use a table, such as Table 4.3, to show students the transformation. Display the table on the board or on an overhead. First, have students list their questions. Next, have them write tentative

KeyIdea

Hypotheses, expressed in testable form, allow students to investigate questions.

REFINING HYPOTHESES

Table 4.3

Student Questions	Tentative Hypotheses	How Might You Test Your Hypotheses?	Revised Hypotheses
_____	_____	_____	_____
_____	_____	_____	_____

[1]Thanks to Ann Novak and Chris Gleason from Greenhills School for this project idea.

Portfolio Activity 4.2   **IDENTIFYING TESTABLE QUESTIONS**

Materials Needed:
- Chart
- Writing materials

A.   Analyze which statements in the first column of the
     following chart are testable and which are not.

B.   Fill in the missing sections of the chart.

C.   File the chart in your portfolio.

WHICH QUESTIONS ARE TESTABLE?

Question	Testable?	Testable Revision of Question
Do different types of apples have different numbers of seeds?	Yes	_____
Why does my bike need to be painted?	No	What happens to metal if it is exposed to air?
How does fertilizer affect plant growth?	_____	_____
What types of objects fly?	_____	_____
Do worms like to eat garbage?	_____	_____

hypotheses and decide if these are testable by coming up with ways to test them. Finally, based on classroom feedback, including your own, have students write revised hypotheses.

Remember that the investigation web is not a linear process. As students continue in their investigative work, you should allow them to modify their questions and hypotheses. The questions and hypotheses that are published in research reports are seldom, if ever, the questions and hypotheses with which the researchers started.

Making Predictions

Key Idea

Predictions based upon previous experiences, knowledge, and observation allow students to forecast what they think might happen.

Predictions are what students think might happen. Students make predictions based on previous experiences, knowledge, and observations of the phenomena they are exploring. Having students make initial predictions on questions such as "What insects will we see on the playground?" or "How many different types of birds will we see?" is important because predictions focus students' thinking. Also, students' commitment to work increases when they make predictions. Finally, making predictions helps students become cognitively engaged in the work because it uses their prior knowledge. Making predictions also helps students synthesize their prior knowledge with the new understandings they gain from exploring their topic.

One technique you can use to help children make their own predictions and take ownership for their work is to have each child in a group make his or her own prediction. Then have group members share their predictions. Next, give group members an opportunity to comment on their predictions, giving reasons for agreeing or disagreeing with the other predictions. Once all group members have shared their predictions, ask groups to generate group predictions, while protecting each student's right to dissent

Portfolio Activity 4.3   **MAKING HYPOTHESES FROM QUESTIONS**

Materials Needed:
- Chart
- Writing materials

A. Analyze how the first question in the first column of the following chart is changed to a hypothesis in the second column.

B. Fill in the missing sections by changing the questions to hypotheses.

C. File the chart in your portfolio.

MAKING HYPOTHESES

Question	Hypothesis
Do mealworms like dry places?	Mealworms will move to dry places rather than moist places.
Do I really need to paint my bike?	_____
How does fertilizer affect plant growth?	_____
What types of objects fly?	_____
Are worms necessary for decomposition?	_____

MAKING PREDICTIONS

Table 4.4

My Predictions	Comments
My prediction: _____	Comment: _____
Member 1 prediction: _____	Comment: _____
Member 2 prediction: _____	Comment: _____
Member 3 prediction: _____	Comment: _____
	Reason for supporting or not supporting the
Group prediction: _____	group prediction: _____

from the group prediction. Table 4.4 is an example of a handout you might distribute to your class to support making predictions.

Another technique for generating student predictions is to expand Table 4.3 to include students' predictions. Table 4.5 shows this expansion.

Finding Information

Seeking information is a vital component of the investigative web. It is through the information-seeking process that students learn the background information so essential to a successful investigation. The term *information* can mean what others have *written* about a topic and it can mean data that others have *collected*.

Table 4.5

REFINING HYPOTHESES AND MAKING PREDICTIONS

Student Questions	Tentative Hypotheses	How Might You Test Your Hypotheses?	Revised Hypotheses	Predictions
_____	_____	_____	_____	_____
_____	_____	_____	_____	_____

Key Idea

For students to be successful with investigation, they need to explore relevant background information.

Artemis Digital Library

SciLinks

Students can seek out two types of data: current data and archival data. **Current data** refers to data scientists collected in the recent past; typically, it is anywhere from a few hours old to a month old. Data on today's weather is an example of current data. **Archival data** refers to data that scientists collected in the past and then stored. Data on upper atmospheric ozone readings over the past several years is an example of archival data.

Imagine that students asked the question "Does my community need to worry about lead poisoning from cars?" Students might look for basic information on lead poisoning to help them understand the problem. They might contact the Environmental Protection Agency to find out if others have collected current data on lead from cars, or they might seek archival data on lead poisoning in their community. Although current data and archival data are very different types of information, both can provide important information for a project.

Numerous resources can help students find information. To find archival data, elementary and middle grade students might consult trade books, magazines, encyclopedias, CD-ROMs, and the World Wide Web. *My Big Back Yard* is an excellent resource magazine for early elementary students, and *Ranger Rick, Science World, National Geographic,* and *Scholastic* are excellent magazines for upper elementary and middle school students. To find current information, such as a new discovery or a recent news story, students need to use a different set of resources. These include the newspaper, telephone interviews, person-to-person interviews, e-mail, and the World Wide Web. Television specials, such as Public Broadcast Station programs and NOVA programs, can provide both archival and current information. Growing access to the World Wide Web and the increasing number of resources available on the Web make it a vital source of both background and current information. Students can also use Artemis, a research engine, and its associated digital library to find and evaluate information related to their driving question. Rather than searching the Web for information, students can use Artemis, which searches a digital library. The digital library contains selected materials that are at appropriate levels of difficulty for middle grade students with respect to reading and information complexity. Supports in Artemis allow learners to sort, select, and organize documents and then easily return to them for further work. The National Science Teachers Association (NSTA) has a section at its website called *SciLinks*. *SciLinks* is a partnership between many textbook publishers and NSTA, which provides science resources that are linked to particular text programs.

The Role of the Teacher

Within an investigation it is critical for students to explore the related work of professionals. You will need to help your students develop skills in searching out information related to their questions. Young children will need several types of assistance.

First, many students will need to learn how to use a variety of resources. You may need to teach benchmark lessons on the card catalog, computerized library search systems, and the Internet.

Second, you will need to help your students learn how to determine which sources to consult for different types of information. Most children will rely on the encyclopedia for much of their information, but encyclopedias do not provide the depth of information many investigations will require. You can use a checklist like the one in Table 4.6 to guide students in their search.

Third, students need assistance in sifting through, abstracting, and outlining the information they find. Imagine a fifth-grade science class is studying acid rain. The class could seek basic information related to acid rain or archival data on acid rain to compare to the data they have collected. To help students determine what information is relevant, the teacher could use a chart like the one in Table 4.7.

> **Key Idea**
>
> Teachers play a critical role in helping students find, synthesize, and evaluate information.

Table 4.6

CHECKLIST FOR FINDING INFORMATION
Data on Car Emissions

Sources of New Information (Less Than Several Months Old)	Sources of Old Information (More Than Several Months Old)
❏ Magazine	❏ Trade book
❏ Newspaper	❏ Encyclopedia
❏ Telephone interview with an expert	❏ Compact disk
❏ Person-to-person interview	❏ Laserdisc
❏ E-mail	❏ Book
❏ World Wide Web	❏ World Wide Web
❏ Television documentary	❏ Television documentary

Table 4.7

EVALUATING INFORMATION

Information Found	Does It Add to Our Understanding Base? How?	Is the Information New or Different from What We Have Already Found?	Is the Information More Recent Than What We Have Already Found?	Does It Help Answer Our Question? How?
Acid rain is thought to be a cause of declining frog populations.	Yes. It provides biological information related to acid rain.	Yes.	Yes. It is a recent discovery.	No. We are looking for information about how acid rain erodes surfaces of buildings.

Table 4.8

ASSESSING THE VALIDITY OF INFORMATION

Information Found	What Are the Facts to Support the Claims?	Can a Claim Be Proven? Substantiated by Others? If So, How?	Is the Source Trying to Sell Something, Advocate an Opinion, or Persuade You to Believe Something?	How Reputable Is the Source?
What was said? Who said this? When did they say it?	_____	_____	_____	_____
Why did they say it?	_____	_____	_____	_____
Where did this occur?	_____	_____	_____	_____
How did it occur?	_____	_____	_____	_____

Fourth, with the explosion of available information today and the ease of its distribution due to electronic networks, you also need to help learners assess the **validity** of a source of information; that is, you need to help students decide if it is propaganda or scientific information. The World Wide Web contains a great deal of information presented by businesses or special interest groups that are trying to advocate certain positions. Such information is often not valid. Students can be taught to think critically about the validity of information by answering questions like those in Table 4.8.

Skepticism

You might want to use tabloid articles to show extreme examples of "information" that is not valid because it cannot be supported, proven, or substantiated by others. Information about a three-headed goat found in the Himalayas by one person who has no photograph of the goat or other evidence is a good example of information that is not valid. Another good source to teach skepticism about such stories can be found on the World Wide Web. Eventually, you can have your students assess the validity of more reputable information from the World Wide Web, local newspapers, and magazines.

Finally, it is important that the teacher help students synthesize information. For elementary and middle grade students, this often requires having them summarize the key ideas and related concepts. A graphic organizer like the Central Idea Diagram in Figure 4.3 helps students focus on synthesizing the information from an investigation.

Planning and Designing

Planning refers to students thinking about and working out how their investigation will take place and answering questions such as "Who will measure the data?" and "Who will get the equipment?" **Designing** refers to the structure of the experiment and answers the questions "What data do I need to answer my question?" and "How will I obtain the data?" Planning includes determining who will take which measurements and on which days, whereas designing includes determining what observations will be made (for example, observing the germination of bean plants), how often the data will be collected,

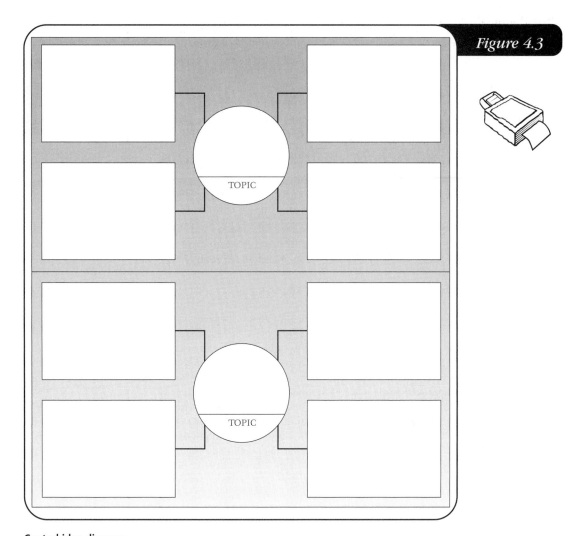

Central idea diagram.

Source: S. Park and H. Black. 1992. Organizing thinking: Graphic organizers. Pacific Grove, Calif.: Critical Thinking Press and Software.

what types of observations will be made (drawing or taking photographs of the seeds), and what variables need to be manipulated or controlled (examining the influence of temperature on germination of bean plants).

Many children find planning and designing difficult. This should not be surprising as these tasks require students to engage in difficult cognitive work. Planning and designing make students think ahead, require them to specify materials they need, force them to develop an outline of what they will do, and make them create or

CONNECTING TO
NATIONAL SCIENCE EDUCATION STANDARDS

Science Education Content Standards
5–8—Standard A: Students design and conduct a scientific investigation (p. 145).

modify materials. Many elementary and middle grade students don't have such experience, and primary grade students may not be developmentally ready to plan on their own. Don't be surprised if some students' initial designs and plans don't allow them to answer the questions adequately. Frequently, students' initial designs will be flawed, including confounded and ill-defined variables. Students will need to practice designing investigations, receiving much support from you.

Although planning and designing are difficult cognitive activities for most children (and adults too), they produce many benefits. First, students become more reflective. Focusing on planning helps students think through issues and become thorough in their thinking. Second, when students make a plan and design, they develop more ownership of an investigation. Because they make the plan and design, they also understand them. This understanding also helps them understand the science involved.

Designing Experimental Procedures

Designing an investigation requires students to develop four important capabilities. These are the ability to (1) write clear descriptions of investigations, (2) identify variables, (3) define variables operationally, and (4) control variables.

Writing Clear Procedures.   The first thing students need to learn to do when designing an investigation is communicate clearly the procedures they will follow. Portfolio Activity 4.4 demonstrates just how difficult it is for most people to write clear descriptions.

The Lego activity in Portfolio Activity 4.4 illustrates how hard it is to create clear procedures that others can follow. Because writing clear procedures that others can understand is difficult, you might encourage your students to read their plans to one another and receive feedback. Do other children understand what is intended? How can the procedures be made easier to understand?

Depending on the age and experiences of the writer, designs of investigations will range from descriptions of what observations will be made to descriptions of what variables will be manipulated. Elementary students might design an investigation to observe the life cycle of mealworms. Their data collecting might include drawings of how the mealworms look over time. Middle school students might design an investigation to examine the effects of temperature and moisture on seed germination. Their experimental designs will show more sophistication and describe ways of collecting data systematically.

> ### Key Idea
>
> In designing a procedure, students need to clearly identify, define, and control variables.

Identifying Variables.   Students need to identify variables as part of their design effort. **Variables** are the characteristics that will change in an investigation. For example, if students are studying the influence of the amount of fertilizer on the height of grass seedlings, the amount of fertilizer and the height of the seedlings are variables. The amount of fertilizer is the independent variable because it will be changed purposefully by the students. A good way to help students remember which is the independent variable is to call it the "*you* changed it" variable. The height of the plants is the dependent variable because it will change as a result of the conditions of the investigation (Cothron, Giese & Rezba, 1993). A good way to remember the dependent variable is to call it the "it changed" variable. This experiment also has a number of other variables involved in it, such as sunlight and temperature.

Defining Variables Operationally.   A critical component of an investigation design is clearly defining variables so that others can understand what is being explored. This clarity helps others replicate the experiment to see if they get the same results. For example,

Portfolio Activity 4.4   **WRITING PROCEDURES**

Materials Needed:
- Lego building blocks
- Writing materials

A. Have your students work in pairs. Give each pair ten types of Lego building blocks in different colors. Ask each pair to construct a structure using all the Lego blocks you gave them. Then ask each pair to write a detailed description of how to make the structure so that someone else, following their instructions, could make the same structure. Instruct the pairs not to look at one another's structures.

B. Have the pairs exchange their written directions. Now ask the pairs to follow the directions they have been given in building a new structure.

C. Ask the pairs to inspect the structures built from their directions. How could the directions be improved?

D. You might also have your students try to explain how to tie a shoe, make a peanut butter sandwich, or make a cube out of paper. Record your notes about this activity in your portfolio.

if students were exploring how fast students in their class could run, they would need to give an **operational definition** of *fast*. They could operationally define *fast* as "the time it takes for a student to run a particular distance" or as "how far a student can run in ten seconds." These definitions are operational definitions because they define the operation or process used to measure a variable. Defining variables operationally is a difficult cognitive activity. You will need to work with young learners to help them express variables operationally. One technique is to have students share their operational definitions with their classmates and receive feedback from classmates and from you.

Controlling Variables.   Controlling variables is holding all variables constant except for the one that is manipulated. In the fertilizer investigation, there were variables other than the dependent variable (the height of the seedlings) and the independent variable (the amount of fertilizer). These other variables, which include amount of sunlight and temperature, will have to be controlled, or held the same, for all the plants, or students will not be able to determine how the amount of fertilizer influenced the height of the seedlings.

Controlling variables is another challenging cognitive activity for students. You should expect children to have difficulty understanding how to **control variables.** With younger students, you might use the term *fair* to introduce the idea of controlling variables. Asking, "Is this a fair test?" may help students understand. Students have little trouble understanding that card games in which not all the players have the same number of cards are not fair. It is not a huge leap from that understanding to thinking about making sure that all the plants in an investigation get a "fair" chance. Portfolio Activity 4.5 is designed to help students understand what is meant by controlling variables.

The paper dragon portfolio activity demonstrates why it is critical to control variables during an investigation.

NSES

CONNECTING TO
NATIONAL SCIENCE EDUCATION STANDARDS

Science Education Content Standards
K–4—Standard A: In the earliest years, investigations are largely based on systematic observations. As students develop, they may design and conduct simple experiments to answer questions. The idea of a fair test is possible for students to consider by fourth grade (p. 122).

Portfolio Activity 4.5   **CONTROLLING VARIABLES: PAPER DRAGON RACES**

Materials Needed:
- A large file card and a small file card
- A rubber band
- Heavy cardboard
- A stapler
- Scissors
- A hole punch
- A paper clip
- Tape
- Metal washers

A. Build a Maxi-Puller/Pusher and paper dragon before doing this activity.

Building the Maxi-Puller/Pusher

The Maxi-Puller/Pusher (Berger et al., 1974) will act as a force gauge. To construct the Maxi-Puller/Pusher, fold a large file card in half lengthwise. Insert heavy cardboard between the folds of the card to add strength. Now staple together the ends of the file card. Punch a hole at one end and attach a rubber band as shown in Figure 4.4. To the free end of the rubber band add a paper clip hook. In one hand, hold the card so that the punched hole is at the top. With the other hand, gently tug down on the hook. Notice that the more you tug, the lower the hook moves along the card.

How can we measure how much an object pushes down on the Maxi-Puller/Pusher? To measure the pushes and pulls of the Maxi-Puller/Pusher, you need a way to calibrate it with equal units. Place a piece of tape down the middle of the folded file card. With nothing hanging from the paper clip hook, mark a zero on the tape beside the top of the hook. This mark shows the zero, or starting, point. Next, put one washer on the paper clip hook. Beside the top of the paper clip, mark 1W to stand for "one washer unit." Keep adding washers of the same size one at a time and mark 2W, 3W, and so on on the tape. You have now built and calibrated your Maxi-Puller/Pusher.

Figure 4.4   **Building the Maxi-Puller/Pusher.**

Building the Paper Dragon

To make a paper dragon, fold a small file card in half and cut the top on a slant so that the shorter edge is near the fold, as shown in Figure 4.5.

B. Now that you have your Maxi-Puller/Pusher and paper dragon, you're ready for some races. First, you need to practice. To use the Maxi-Puller/Pusher as a way of measuring "pushing" force, bend up the end of the paper clip hook to make a trigger. Set the end of the dragon in the cradle formed by the paper clip trigger. See Figure 4.6. Use the Maxi-Puller/ Pusher like a slingshot by holding down the Maxi-Puller/Pusher with one hand and pulling the paper clip and paper dragon back with the other hand. Let go of the paper dragon, shooting the dragon forward.

C.   Conduct several races.

Race one: Divide the class into two groups. One group should pull the Maxi-Puller/Pusher back to the 5W mark. The other group should pull the Maxi-Puller/Pusher back to the 8W spot. Each group member should have three turns to shoot the dragon. Ask students to keep track of how far the paper dragon moves. Each group should then calculate the average distance the paper dragon moves (the sum of distances divided by the number of shots made by the group).

2.5 inches

Figure 4.5   **Building the paper dragon.**

Now have the two groups discuss the results. What were the independent and dependent variables? Was the activity fair? What was wrong with how the contest was set up? How might you make it fair?

Race two: Divide the class into two groups. One group should set three paper clips into the ends of the wings of their paper dragon, and the other group should use an un-weighted paper dragon. Each group should pull the Maxi-Puller/Pusher back to the 5W mark. Make sure that each group member has three turns to shoot the dragon. Ask students to keep track of how far the paper dragon moves. Each group should calculate the average distance the paper dragon moves (the sum of distances divided by the number of shots made by the group).

Figure 4.6   **Racing the paper dragon.**

Have the two groups discuss the results. What were the independent and dependent variables? Was the activity fair? What was wrong with how the contest was set up? How might you make it fair?

D.   What other variables could you change? With older students you could try a free-throw contest or a race instead of the paper dragon activity.

E.   Record your reflections on the activity in your portfolio.

Just as adding weights affects how far the paper dragon will move, not controlling variables influences the outcomes of investigations.

The Role of the Teacher

Students will find creating plans and designs for an investigation a challenge. Planning and designing an investigation is hard intellectual work. However, if you support students in their designing, your students will show considerable improvement throughout the school year (Krajcik et al., 1998). Designs will become more complex as students include more variables, define variables with greater detail, consider more ways of measuring the variables, and use multiple samples. Students' procedures will also became more clearly defined; they will think of more ways in which to represent their data, identify necessary materials, and divide up responsibilities for conducting the investigation.

Table 4.9 lists questions to prompt and support students in creating their plans and designs. It should be modified to match the age and experiences of the children you are teaching. For example, in first grade, learners are not developmentally ready for controlled experiments and should not be concerned with independent and dependent variables. However, early elementary students are capable of thinking about the observations they will make, how they will record the data, and how data relate to their question.

There are a number of other ways to support students in learning how to plan and design. These include using goal sheets, critiquing plans and designs, modeling planning and designing, and creating class plans and designs.

> **Key Idea**
>
> Teachers play critical roles in helping students by critiquing, modeling, and creating plans and designs.

Table 4.9

PLANNING AND DESIGN CHART

Our question:

Our design:

- What variables and terms do we need to define?
- What data need to be gathered to answer our question?
- What observations should we make?
- What will I need to measure?
- What variables need to be controlled to answer the question?
- What is the independent variable?
- What is the dependent variable?
- What is my control?
- How often should I take measurements?
- How often do I need to make observations?

Our plan:

Equipment needed:

- What do we need?
- How much do we need?
- How can we obtain the material?

Procedure:

- What is it?
- How often do we do it?
- How much of each material do we need?
- Who will do it?

Using Goal Sheets.   You can help your students learn to be more thoughtful planners and follow through on decision making with goal sheets. Students can use goal sheets to track plans, determine the division of labor, develop time lines and schedules, and make decisions about resources. A goal sheet is simply a grid in which students record their steps in one column and their plans about who will take responsibility for the steps in a second column. Table 4.10 is an example of a goal sheet. You can have students record in a third column how each step will be accomplished. Table 4.11 illustrates an expanded goal sheet, including the third column and a fourth column for the time frame for completion.

Another technique that is valuable in helping students plan is to use a checklist to provoke students' thinking and expand their ideas about possible resources. In an information-based world, making decisions about what information to use is no easy task, and students will need your help. Table 4.12 shows a checklist that can help students select resources. You might even decide to work with students to develop their own checklist.

Critiquing Plans and Designs.   One way to help your students learn the initial components of planning and designing is to have them critique some good and poor plans and designs. Portfolio Activity 4.6 presents the design of an experiment you might use for student critique. Use the questions in Table 4.9 to guide your critique.

Table 4.10

GOAL SHEET

What Do We Need to Do?	Who Will Do It?
Find information about acid rain.	Bill
Contact the EPA.	Alicia
Make a design for collecting rainwater and measuring the pH of rainwater.	Precious

Table 4.11

EXPANDED GOAL SHEET

What Do We Need to Do?	Who Will Do It?	How Will It Be Done?	When Will It Be Done?
Find information about acid rain.	Bill	Go to the library.	By Friday, May 18th.
Contact the EPA.	Alicia	Go to the school office and call.	Tomorrow during class.
Make a design for collecting rainwater and measuring the pH of rainwater.	Precious	Look for information on collecting rainwater. Ask the teacher and share plans with the class.	Today. By Friday, May 18th.

Table 4.12

RESOURCES CHECKLIST

INFORMATION

What?	Can We Use It?	How?
Encyclopedia	Yes	Find out more about acid rain.
Magazines/journals	Yes	Go to library and look for information on acid rain.
CD-ROMs	Maybe	The school doesn't have any on acid rain. Check the public library.
Software	Maybe	The school doesn't have any on acid rain. Check the public library.
Guest speaker	Yes	Get from the EPA.
Telephone call	Yes	Call the EPA.
E-mail		
Interview	Yes	Talk with someone at the EPA.
World Wide Web	Yes	Do a search on acid rain.
Letter		

SUPPLIES AND MATERIALS

What?	Can We Use It?	How?
Writing materials		
Computers/probes	Yes	
Drawing materials	Yes	
Science equipment	Yes	Check with the teacher.
PH paper	Yes	
Calculator	Yes	Check with the teacher.

Although critiques of made-up plans and designs can make good benchmark lessons, it is important to remember that such critiques are artificial activities akin to practicing a serve in tennis without learning to use a serve in a real game. Within a project-based science classroom, there certainly is a place for these types of benchmark lessons because they *introduce* students to important ideas; however, the real thinking occurs when students develop their own investigations and give and receive feedback on those plans and designs.

A very useful spin-off of critiquing made-up plans and designs is to have students critique a plan and design for an investigation they will conduct in class. Some of the research conducted at the University of Michigan (Krajcik et al., 1998) indicates that giving students a plan and design and discussing (critiquing) the important features of the plan with the students is an important first step in helping students create and modify their own plans and designs. Have them ask critical questions such as, "Will the data collected help answer the question?" "How and why?" and "What are the independent and dependent variables?" Use other questions found in Table 4.9 as a guide for discussion.

Modeling Planning and Designing.   An essential step in helping students learn how to plan and design is to model the process. Model for the students how *you* might go

Portfolio Activity 4.6   SPROUTING BEAN PLANTS

Materials Needed:
- Scenario below

A. What follows is a scenario that describes an experiment that a group of students performed to study the influence of temperature on the sprouting of seeds. Read the scenario carefully.

Heather, Michael, and Jackie wonder how temperature influences the sprouting of bean plants. They decide to modify a technique they used earlier in the school year. First, they will soak some kidney beans overnight. The next day, they will place moistened paper towels into two reclosable baggies. Then they will place five soaked kidney beans and a thermometer in each of the baggies. They will set one of the baggies on top of a heating pad on the window sill and the other baggie just on the window sill.

Each day they will observe the beans in each bag, record the temperature of each bag, and moisten the paper toweling.

B. What are the independent and dependent variables in this experiment? What variables are being controlled?

C. Is the procedure complete? What is missing from the procedure? What else, if anything, might influence the sprouting of the bean seeds?

D. What are other pluses and negatives of Heather's, Michael's, and Jackie's plan and design?

E. How might you modify the design to better determine the influence of temperature on bean plants?

F. Record your ideas in your portfolio.

about planning and designing an investigation. This might include thinking aloud about what materials you would need and what procedures you would follow. For example, you could think aloud about how you might explore how shifting gears on your bike influences how fast you can go: "I wonder if the larger gear will make the bike go faster or slower." Write down the steps on the board or the overhead projector as you say them: "Shift to the gear to the largest size and determine how fast I can go." Allow students the opportunity to comment on your design and to make their own suggestions. The questions in Table 4.9 can help you think aloud about the various steps you would take.

Creating Class Plans and Designs.   The work of one of the authors of this book and colleagues (Krajcik et al., 1998) indicates that another important step in supporting students' planning and design work is to have students work on a plan and design together; this is especially true of early elementary or students new to making their own plans and designs. Again, questions in Table 4.9 can be used to guide discussion of the plans. You should freely add your own comments and suggestions.

Perhaps the best way for students to learn how to plan and design an investigation is to create in small groups a number of designs and plans. Start off your school year with some quick opportunities for planning and designing. For example, you could give students the challenge to plan and design a bridge using plastic straws and pins that could hold the most weight. The *Elementary School Studies* curriculum materials (1970) and Annenberg's *Video Case Studies* (1997) contain a number of ideas for planning and design practice.

While students are creating their plans and designs, provide feedback. Students should also share their plans and designs with the class to receive feedback. Feedback should point out the positive features of plans and designs as well as the features that students need to think about and perhaps revise. You should make sure that students record the comments on their work. Students will learn about the planning and design process not only by listening to what others have to say about their work, but also by listening to others' plans and designs and by contributing comments to others. It is critical for students to have time to revise their plans and designs based on the feedback they receive (Krajcik et al., 1998). After students have revised their designs, it is important that you give them one last round of feedback. Portfolio Activity 4.7 will give you practice on planning and designing an investigation.

Carrying Out the Procedures

Conducting the procedures of an investigation includes a wide range of activities. It might include students gathering the equipment, assembling the apparatus, following through on procedures, and making observations. Often as children carry out their procedures they will think of new ideas for modifying their work. As discussed in Chapter 5, technology tools can play a major role in assisting children in collecting data.

NSES

CONNECTING TO
NATIONAL SCIENCE EDUCATION STANDARDS

Science Education Content Standards
K–4—Standard A: Students employ simple equipment and tools to gather data and extend their senses (p. 122).
Science Education Content Standards
5–8—Standard A: Students use appropriate tools and techniques to gather, analyze, and interpret data (p. 145).

Gathering the Equipment

To perform an investigation, students need to have the necessary equipment. Equipment can be everything from a hand lens for observing insects outdoors to a thermometer for measuring the temperature of a classroom habitat or a computer-based probe for gathering data over time. Equipment is essential in extending students' abilities to make observations. Special attention should be given to obtaining equipment that will enable all students, including those who are visually impaired or have physical handicaps, to engage in investigations. *Science Activities for the Visually Impaired/Science Enrichment for Learners with Physical Handicaps* (SAVI/SELPH), available through the Lawrence Hall of Science, is a program designed for this purpose. SAVI/SELPH includes Braille, for example, on the measuring cups, test tubes, and other science equipment in its program. Much of this equipment should be standard in the elementary and middle school science classroom, but it is often a challenge to obtain the necessary materials and supplies. School budgets sometimes stand in the way. Students can find many common materials at home, but others will need to be purchased. By enlisting the participation of members of the community who might donate needed items, you can often obtain the support you need. Chapter 10 discusses how teachers can find and manage equipment and resources.

SAVI/SELPH

Using Quicktrials

The **quicktrial** is an experimental technique that should be used more frequently in schools. It involves trying out experimental procedures to see if they work. For example, students might have designs to make a rain collector in order to measure the amount of

Portfolio Activity 4.7   PLANNING AND DESIGNING

Materials Needed:
- Table 4.9
- Writing materials or a computer

A. Use Table 4.9 to create a plan and a design for an experiment to test how road surface affects the speed at which a skateboard travels. Remember to create a hypothesis and make a prediction. What are your independent and dependent variables? What variables do you need to define operationally? How many trials will you run?

B. Have a classmate critique your plan and design. What suggestions did he or she make? How will you modify your plan and design based on these suggestions?

C. Record your final plan and design in your portfolio.

precipitation. However, students might first perform a quicktrial and build a model of the apparatus to see if they left out an important design feature, such as a suitable way to anchor the rain collector during high winds.

Assembling the Apparatus

Many investigations involve building an apparatus. If students are doing a project on acid rain, they might need to build a rain collector to collect their rainwater. If students are exploring the effect of a surface on the speed of an object, they might need to build ramps with different surfaces to investigate how different types of surfaces influence the speed at which an object moves.

Another challenge you and your students will face is learning how to use the tools needed to build the apparatus. This will be the first time many of your students have ever built something from basic materials. Many students will not know how to hammer, screw, glue, or solder. Often you will need to model these techniques for students, or you will need to solicit support from volunteers in the community who can come into your classroom and supervise construction.

Following Through on Procedures

Don't be surprised if students forget a number of important experimental procedures like watering plants, adjusting temperature, or recording observations. In some circumstances, students might "overdo" their procedures—they might water plants too much or provide too much sunlight. Another common occurrence is "changing procedures on the fly," or modifying experimental procedures without recording the modification or telling anyone about it. For instance, a student might decide to add twice as much fertilizer to the plants.

To prevent these common experimental errors, you should monitor investigations carefully. You might need to remind students to make observations (record temperatures, draw diagrams, measure volumes) and to carry out procedures (add fertilizer, water plants, adjust temperature, or feed fish). You might also watch students as they carry out procedures to make sure they are doing so correctly, without overdoing anything and without making unplanned modifications.

One useful technique is to pair students. Each member of a pair can help keep the other one on track. Another technique is to have students record their observations on charts, tables, or checklists. These record-keeping systems organize data. They also serve to remind students about what data need to be collected and what procedures need to be completed.

Even though students create a table for recording data, they may not remember to use it. Take the time to discuss the importance of recording data appropriately. Again, having students work together can help them remember to record their data and complete procedures.

Making Observations

At first, students will not be very thorough and precise in making either qualitative or quantitative observations. **Qualitative observations** are detailed descriptions of what is seen. Recording qualitative observations might include making diagrams and labeling them, writing a paragraph about observations, or taking a photograph of observable results. It might be helpful to point out to students that real scientists keep careful notes and drawings. Some of the observations and notes of naturalists such as James Audubon or scientists such as Charles Darwin are useful examples for students. **Quantitative observations** are those that can be counted or recorded in a numerical format. Students can use instruments such as thermometers, rulers, and electronic pH probes to make quantitative measurements. Your students will need support collecting both qualitative and quantitative data. At first, students' descriptions will be very incomplete and measurements might not be precise.

> ### Key Idea
>
> Students need support in making qualitative and quantitative observations.

One way to support students in becoming more precise and detailed in their observations is to have all students in the class observe the same phenomenon. Then have the students in the class compare the observations they made. Typically, there will be a great deal of variation among observations. You might, for example, have all of the students in the class make observations of the sprouting of grass seeds. This is a particularly nice activity for a number of reasons. First, it can be used at a variety of grade levels. Second, both qualitative and quantitative measurements can be collected. Third, grass is easy to sprout and grows rapidly. Each group should grow its own grass, and each student should make his or her own observations. Students may make qualitative observations about the color and texture of the sprouting grass. They may make quantitative observations of the temperature and pH of the soil as well as of the height of grass seedlings. Have each member of a group share each of his or her observations with others in the group. Students should discuss how their observations are similar or different. You need to provide feedback regarding the level of detail and precision of the observations. Whole class feedback is also very valuable. Ask each group to report its observations to the class. Then have class members comment on the thoroughness and precision of the observations. Once the class has given its comments, you can give some feedback, too.

Keeping Track of Ideas

Often, as students are conducting their investigation, they will think of new ideas to modify their work. Encourage students to keep track of these ideas and to record them in their notebooks. They might use these ideas to modify a current investigation or in future experiments. For instance, a group of second grade students were observing the germination of bean seeds, one student wonders if all seeds germinate in the same amount of time. Students should record these questions in their notebooks and use them to plan additional investigations.

One of the difficult decisions you will face as a teacher is when and how to give students the time to incorporate new ideas into their current work. Although this incorporation of new ideas is time consuming, it is a valuable learning experience and it reflects the reality of scientific work. The revision process is an essential component of the investigation web. Remember, good science is not a linear process.

The Role of the Teacher

Teachers play a critical role in helping students carry out procedures. They need to help students track down and organize equipment. Teachers can save time in investigations and in helping students build routines if essential equipment such as scissors, magnifying glasses, rulers, and test tubes is accessible and always placed in the same location in the classroom. Teachers also need to help students assemble apparatus. Some students may not have the strength or manual dexterity to do the necessary cutting and fitting. Although the teacher should give students opportunities to try doing things themselves, a teacher or an adult helper might need to give assistance. This is particularly true if it looks like a student might injure herself in the process of trying.

> **Key Idea**
>
> Teachers play a critical role in helping students following through on plans and making and recording accurate observations.

Making Sense of Data

Students make sense of their data by analyzing and interpreting them. The ability or skill to analyze data is an essential aspect of scientific literacy and of doing science. Unfortunately, not many children ever take part in analysis. Frequently, what is expected of children is to answer a series of questions regarding the data they collected. Even many adults don't have good experiences with this aspect of investigative work. Observations in the classroom have demonstrated that this is perhaps the most difficult component of the investigative web (Krajcik et al., 1998). Often students think that an investigation is complete when they are finished collecting the data, yet it is only through analysis that students can learn about the phenomena they are exploring. Making sense of the data is an intellectual challenge. How can teachers support students in analyzing data? How can they find trends and patterns in their work?

> **Key Idea**
>
> Making sense of data is a critical aspect of scientific investigation because it helps students build understanding.

A couple of techniques can be used to support students in making sense of their data. One technique is to transform the data into a different form. Seeing their data in new ways gives students more opportunities to understand the data. Children can transform their data by creating tables, graphs, diagrams, or other visualizations. As students become older, they might use more descriptive statistics in the process such as means or averages. Another technique is to create models. This helps students combine the disparate aspects of their work. In general, helping students think of different ways to represent their data helps them perceive patterns and trends, which is an important element of analysis.

NSES

CONNECTING TO
NATIONAL SCIENCE EDUCATION STANDARDS

Science Education Content Standards
K–4—Standard A: Students use data to construct a reasonable explanation (p. 122).
Science Education Content Standards
5–8—Standard A: Students will develop descriptions, explanations, predictions, and models using evidence. Students think critically and logically to make the relationships between evidence and explanations (p. 145).

Transforming Data

Perhaps one of the best ways to help students make sense of their data is to have them transform, or change them, into some other form or representation. Scientists have used tables, graphs, diagrams, and maps to transform their data into other forms that might help them understand and see patterns.

Using Tables. In early elementary grades, students can create tables from tallies or counts they have made. Imagine that students made a record of the different types of insects they observed on the playground. They could then transform this data into a large table on newsprint. The table might include a column with the name of each insect, a second column with a drawing of each insect, and a third column with the number of sightings. Table 4.13 is an example of a table early elementary students might create.

Students will need practice making tables. One good way to help students learn how to make tables is to model the process for them. As you model how to develop a table, allow students the opportunity to contribute their own ideas to the process. You can also help students develop a sense of how to make tables by letting them design their own tables and by giving them feedback on their tables. Another useful technique is to have students share their tables with classmates. Allow classmates to give comments on the tables.

Once students have constructed their tables, they should write summaries of what their tables show. Such summaries are just another way to transform the data. Once again, feedback from you and classmates will be helpful.

The tables students create will vary according to grade level. Imagine that a first-grade class is carrying out a weather project. The teacher has students use a number of pictures to represent the weather. Figure 4.7 illustrates how students might do this.

Older students should record more quantitative measurements. Students might observe and record such measurements as the temperature, barometric pressure, wind speed, and precipitation. Table 4.14 illustrates a table a sixth-grade student might create to record various weather-related measurements.

Using Graphs. Graphs communicate visually the data that is collected in an investigation. Graphs show how dependent variables change with the independent variable. By convention, the dependent variables are depicted along the y-axis (the vertical axis of a graph), and the independent variables are depicted along the x-axis (the horizontal axis of the graph).

Table 4.13

A DATA TABLE

INSECT	DRAWING	NUMBER
Ant		20
Bee		3

In elementary and middle school, students can transform their data into pie charts, bar graphs, histograms, and line graphs. Software programs such as spreadsheets make this relatively easy for children to accomplish. Rather than giving a simple count, graphs offer a different visual representation of the data. Figure 4.8 shows a bar graph created by elementary students who explored the number of insects they found on their playground one afternoon. Figure 4.9 is a line graph created by seventh graders to show the differences in height over time of grass seedlings growing in different soil types.

It isn't always easy to determine when to use bar graphs and when to use line graphs. Bar graphs are typically used when the data are **discrete**; that is, when they can be divided into categories and when the intervals between the data have no meaning. Types of insects, types of trees, and color of flowers are examples of discrete data. Line graphs

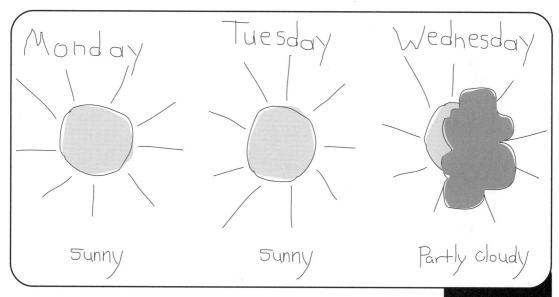

Chart created by early elementary students.

Figure 4.7

WEATHER DATA CHART								*Table 4.14*
		Monday	Tuesday	Wednesday	Thursday	Friday	Saturday	Sunday
Week 1	Temp	____	____	____	____	____	____	____
	Pressure	____	____	____	____	____	____	____
	Precipitation	____	____	____	____	____	____	____
Week 2	Temp	____	____	____	____	____	____	____
	Pressure	____	____	____	____	____	____	____
	Precipitation	____	____	____	____	____	____	____

Figure 4.8

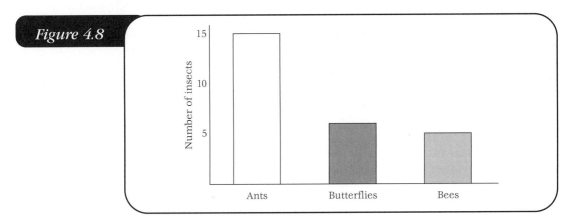

Insects on the playground.

Figure 4.9

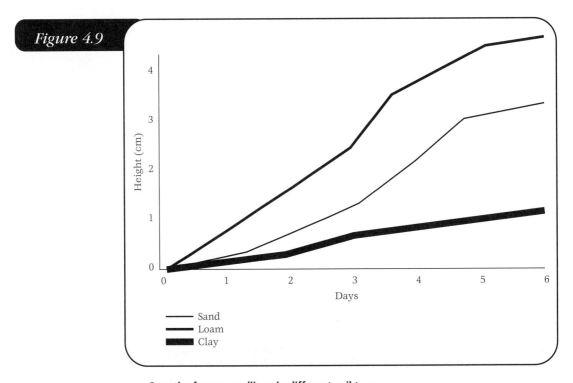

Growth of grass seedlings in different soil types.

are best used when the data are **continuous;** that is, when the intervals among the data have meaning. The concentration of fertilizer, the heights of plants, and the speed of a ball rolling down a hill are all continuous data. You should give your students practice in using the various kinds of graphs.

Once students have drawn a graph, you should have them come up with statements that describe what the graph means. A good technique is to have each student in the group make his or her statements first and then have members of the groups compare the statements. Next, have the group construct a group response and share the group statement with the class to receive additional feedback.

Classroom teachers need to support students in making graphs; this is true at both the elementary and middle school levels. Making graphs and their interpretations are cognitively challenging tasks for children, as well as adults. Modeling, sharing of graphs, and giving feedback are three techniques that you should use frequently.

Young children who do not have an understanding of number concepts should be encouraged to make concrete, physical graphs. For example, if early elementary students are counting the number of seeds in different fruits and vegetables, they can line up on a table the number of seeds from a pumpkin, a watermelon, and a cantaloupe. Then you might ask questions about which fruit has more seeds. Young learners first need to see the real seeds lined up in a row to perceive a concrete graph. Watch for conservation problems. Because the cantaloupe seeds are smaller than pumpkin seeds, for example, young children may say the pumpkin has more seeds. It is critical, therefore, to line seeds up with one another, as if there were intervals on a graph.

To make the transfer to using numbers in graphs, you first need to work with non-numerical ideas such as "Which is longer?" "Which is shorter?" "Which is bigger?" "Which is smaller?" "Which is closer?" and "Which is farther?" To make the transition to "units," use nonstandard units such as blocks, fingers, or shoes. For example, you might ask, "How many blocks high is the bean plant?" "How many fingers wide did the toy car move?" or "How many shoes long did the turtle walk?"

To help young learners make the transfer from concrete graphs to more abstract paper-and-pencil graphs, use pictures of the objects in the paper-and-pencil graphs. For example, to graph the number of seeds in a pumpkin, a watermelon, and a cantaloupe, draw the seeds on graph paper to correspond to the real seeds. Figure 4.10 shows an example of this pictograph technique using weather data. Eventually, your students will be ready to make the leap to using numbers when you match up the objects or events on the graph with numbers.

Using Visual Techniques.   Other nontraditional visualization techniques can be used by students to transform data. Imagine that some students are exploring how different soil types influence the growth of grass. The students decide to measure the height of the grass over time as an indication of growth. One excellent way to represent this data would be to transform it into a graph of the height of the different plants over time. Students could also represent this data by taking photographs of the plants over time and then link the visual pictures to the quantitative data. Students studying weather patterns may decide to create a weather map instead of a graph to organize their data.

Combining graphing techniques with other visual techniques should be encouraged strongly at all age levels. When students represent data and ideas in different forms, they are developing deep understanding of the content.

Using Descriptive Statistics.   Descriptive statistics are another way to transform data. Upper elementary students and middle school students should be encouraged to use **descriptive statistics** such as differences, averages, and ranges to make sense of their data.

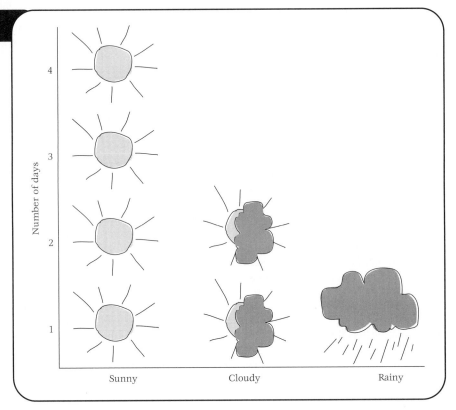

Weather pictograph.

Such basic descriptive statistics give a measure of central tendency and variation in their data. For example, a way to transform data about the influence of soil on the height of grass plants is to calculate the average heights of the grasses in each soil type. Students can then create graphs of the average heights of the grass over time. You can introduce young children to descriptive statistics by using such terms as *more, less, big, little, taller,* and *shorter.*

Modeling

A **model** is a simplified representation of a phenomenon that suggests how the phenomenon works. There are three types of models: physical, conceptual, and mathematical.

Physical models are actual devices or processes that behave like phenomena. A model airplane and a stream table are examples. Physical models are most obvious to young learners. For instance, a stream table allows students to visualize how the process of the flow of water makes a river and the land around the river change over time.

Conceptual models link the unfamiliar to the familiar through metaphors and analogies. Conceptual models depend upon the ability of students to imagine that something they do not understand is similar to something that they understand. Ping-Pong balls bouncing around (an idea that students understand) is a conceptual model for the atomic makeup of gaseous particles (an idea that students don't understand). Because conceptual models are an abstraction, the age and experience of students play a major role in determining their applicability. Direct, hands-on experiences will help students become adept at using conceptual models.

Mathematical models specify a relationship among the variables described and the behavior of phenomena. A mathematical relationship that describes how much work is necessary to move an object is "work = force × distance." The relationship specifies that the amount of work it takes to move an object is equal to the force applied to the object times the distance the object is moved. For instance, a person does work when a box is lifted vertically from the floor to a shelf. If you lift the box twice as far, you do twice the work. Mathematical models are more abstract than are physical and conceptual models. However, new computer tools allow students to build dynamic models with a natural language interface. Such modeling programs enable learners to develop an understanding of scientific concepts despite the learners' lack of mathematical sophistication.

Models, however, have their limitations. Models can be too simplified or too complex to be of value, and care must be taken to generate truly useful models. For example, round ball models of atoms have their usefulness in illustrating the particle nature of matter, but they give no insight into the structure of atoms or into how atoms combine to form molecules.

The Role of the Teacher

Students will need your support in making sense of data. A variety of instructional strategies can provide this support. Use modeling, sharing, and feedback frequently. You might start by having the class construct either a class table or a graph. Next, you might have each student write a summary of what the table or graph means. Finally, you might have students share and compare their summaries.

In addition to these supports that are designed to help students with the cognitive task of making sense of data, students sometimes need support getting along with others in their group. As students try to make sense of their data, it is likely that they will disagree in their analyses. Such disagreement is healthy because it shows that students are taking responsibility and ownership for their learning. As long as students focus their disagreement on the analysis and do not begin to demean or degrade each other, these disagreements should be encouraged. You can help students focus their disagreements by having them use evidence to support what they say and critique their evidence (Davis & Kirkpatrick, 2002). (Chapter 6 explores in detail how to manage discussions among students.)

> **Key Idea**
>
> Teachers can assist students in making sense of their data by using tables, graphs, visual techniques, statistics, and models.

Drawing Conclusions

One of the hallmarks of science is drawing conclusions from experimental data. Unfortunately, learners of many ages have difficulty doing this aspect of scientific inquiry. One of the authors of this book and his colleagues (Krajcik et al., 1998) report that, although many students in a project-based classroom clearly attempted to analyze data and determine its meaning, they tended to present data and state conclusions without explicitly linking the two. Drawing and justifying conclusions requires sophisticated thinking. In contrast to their extensive experience following procedures, most students have had limited experience drawing conclusions and justifying what they have concluded from the data. Of course, these kinds of problems are not limited to middle school students; they are typical of beginning researchers in all fields, even at the graduate level.

As in the inquiry process, there is no step-by-step procedure that a student can follow to draw a conclusion. However, there are ways to guide the process.

First, when writing conclusions, encourage students to restate their purpose. For example, imagine that a group of third graders is investigating whether objects move faster down an inclined plane that is lubricated or one that is wet. This investigation is related to their driving question "How does snow affect our daily lives?" These students should restate that the purpose of their investigation was to explore the effect of ice on students using wheelchairs to get up a school ramp when it is icy in the winter.

Second, students need to describe their findings and show how they answered the initial questions. For example, if students found that water caused less friction on the inclined plane, they would first restate that the purpose of the investigation was to explore the effect of wet ice on the wheelchair ramps at school during the winter. They would then explain that they found that ice would reduce the friction of the wheels against the ramp, which is a problem for those trying to go up the ramp. However, while findings need to be linked to the data students analyzed, the findings should not be simple restatements of the data. Rather, findings should state the *trends* or *relationships* in the data. For example, the students would state that all lubricants, including water and ice, reduced friction on the inclined plane.

Third, students need to write a general statement that relates their findings to their purpose. For example, students might write, "We found that lubricants (including oil, ice, and water) reduced friction on an inclined plane. This leads us to conclude that ice would cause problems for those using wheelchairs in the winter, because they would have a difficult time getting into the school building."

Fourth, students need to explain their findings. Often this is accomplished by making connections to background information students have found and to their data. It also includes comments on how reliable the data might be. For instance, if students performed an experiment on how ice affects friction on an inclined plane but they forgot to keep the inclined plane frozen during the entire investigation, they would need to mention this problem at this stage.

When students write conclusions, watch for several potential difficulties. Imagine that students are investigating how the amount of water influences how tall grass grows.

1. **Students only restate their data.** Students might say, "The grass that we watered a lot was 5 inches tall. The grass that we watered only a little bit was only 1 inch tall." Here students are restating their data and not making a conclusion. An appropriate conclusion might be, "If you water grass more, it will grow taller than grass that is watered less."

2. **Students make conclusions that are not linked to their findings.** Students might conclude that the amount of water doesn't make a difference in the height of grass. This finding would not be supported by the data because grass watered more was 5 inches tall and grass watered less was only 1 inch tall.

3. **Students make conclusions that don't relate to the purpose of the investigation.** Students might conclude that the amount of sun determines how tall a plant will grow when the focus of the investigation was on how *water* affects the height of the plants.

4. **Students might overgeneralize.** Students might say, "All plants grow taller with more water." If their investigation used only one type of plant (grass), it

<table>
<tr><td>

Key Idea

When writing conclusions, students need to make sure that their conclusions link to their findings.

</td></tr>
</table>

would be a mistake to assume that all plants would grow taller with more water. In fact, some plants such as cacti would die with too much watering.

5. **Students make inferences rather than conclusions.** Students might say, "You have to pay to mow the grass more frequently when it rains." Although this idea is related to the topic of investigation, it goes beyond the data the student collected and is mere supposition

The Role of the Teacher

As teachers, we need carefully to support students in the process of writing conclusions. One way to support students is to ask guiding questions that help them think about their conclusions as they relate to their data and the purpose of the investigation. Table 4.15 provides a list of questions that can be used to help students make good conclusions and justify them.

Another way to give support is to provide ample feedback in this process. First share with students a conclusion that you wrote that includes all the important features of a conclusion. You can use the questions in Table 4.15 as a guide. Of course, you shouldn't write your conclusion in a way that makes the children feel incapable of approximating it. Next, share with students a conclusion that they can critique. Include in this conclusion salient points that the children will notice. For instance, you might want the students to notice that the findings are not related to the initial purpose of the study. Next, have the students critique the conclusions of their classmates. Make sure that the students use the questions in Table 4.15 to guide their critiques. After the series of critiques, give students opportunities to revise their own work. Finally, give students thorough feedback on their written work. Once again, use the guiding questions from Table 4.15.

Sharing with Others

Sharing is an essential component of the investigation web. **Sharing** includes communicating to others your plans and progress throughout the investigation, your findings, and your final products. It also includes receiving feedback on what you have communicated. Sharing helps students gain ownership of their investigation, and students learn new science information when others share with them.

Table 4.15

GUIDING QUESTIONS TO SUPPORT STUDENTS IN WRITING CONCLUSIONS

- Did you restate the purpose?
- Did you present your major findings?
- What conclusion do your findings indicate?
- Do your findings and conclusions link to the purpose?
- Are your findings linked to your data?
- How do your findings compare to information you found on the topic?
- Do they support the information you found or are they inconsistent?
- How might you explain your findings?

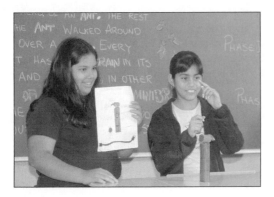

Sharing is an essential component of the investigation web.

Science Education Content Standards
K–4—Standard A: Students communicate investigations and explanations (p. 122).
Science Education Content Standards
5–8—Standard A: Students communicate scientific procedures and explanations (p. 148).

Sharing During the Investigation

Sharing should occur throughout various components of the investigation web. Sharing during the project is critical because it gives learners valuable feedback on their work. Often, this is a place where the teacher can teach students to be skeptical of findings and conclusions. This feedback often leads to revisions and new questions. Sharing is also important because students learn new science concepts when they listen to and communicate with others. At the early elementary level, sharing aspects of a project or an investigation might be part of show-and-tell. For older students, sharing can be done in science class.

Communicating the Findings

In communicating their findings, students describe in writing the trends they see in their data; they create tables, graphs, or other visualizations; and they make conclusions about how the data answer the question of the investigation.

Students can communicate their findings in a variety of formats: reports, posters, newspaper articles, hypermedia documents, videos, and e-mail documents. **Hypermedia** allows students to create links, either to other documents or to other parts of the same document. Like multimedia documents, hypermedia documents can contain various types of media (text, graphics, images, and videos). The World Wide Web is an excellent example of hypermedia. Students can now use

Figure 4.11

Procedure

- Remove all but two leaves from both plants.
- Coat one of the leaves on one of the plants with Vaseline.
- Leave all the other leaves alone.
- Give both plants equal soil, water, and sun for an equal period of time.
- Boil the chlorophyll out of all of the leaves.
- Estimate percentage of starch in leaves.

PowerPoint document—communicating procedures.

commercially available tools such as *PowerPoint* and *Claris Homepage* to create hyper-media documents easily. Figures 4.11, 4.12, and 4.13 show PowerPoint pages created by two students in a hypermedia document. No matter what form a final report takes, it should include the following typical components: title, question, background information, experimental design and procedures, data, results, conclusions, and future questions.

Data

Figure 4.12

	Day 1	Day 2	Day 3	Day 4	Day 5
Color of Vaseline plant	Healthy green	Brown line down stem but otherwise healthy	Brown along base of stem otherwise healthy	Healthy green but longer brown stem along base	No change
Color of untouched leaf	Healthy green	Healthy green	Healthy green	Healthy green	Healthy green
Color of untouched plant	Healthy green	Healthy green	Healthy green	Healthy green	Healthy green

PowerPoint document—communicating data.

Findings

Figure 4.13

- Leaves 1 are from the control plant. They had 90-95% starch.
- Leaf 2 is the leaf with Vaseline. It had 10% starch.
- Leaf 3 is the other leaf on the plant with Vaseline. It had 75% starch.

PowerPoint document—communicating findings.

The Role of the Teacher

The teacher plays a critical role in helping students learn to share information. Elementary and middle grade students don't automatically know how to share their plans, findings, and products; they will need to learn communication skills, speaking skills, and presentation skills to be able to accomplish this task. We discuss ways to teach communication and speaking skills in Chapter 6. These skills, which are frequently taught in language arts classes, create opportunities for the teacher to integrate science with language arts. We discuss integration of science across subject areas in more detail in Chapter 11.

In addition to teaching students how to share, teachers need to provide some children with support in transferring hands-on experiences to spoken and written words. Some teachers use graphic organizers to help students make this transition. For example, the KWL technique discussed in Chapter 3 is especially helpful. A teacher can lead a discussion about what was learned (the L portion of the KWL). Once a list of the concepts or skills that were learned is generated, the students can write a summary of this to communicate to others in the class. With young children, the teacher may need to write down students' findings as they dictate them. For very young students, this process itself is a form of sharing. For older students, the teacher may have to review writing skills that focus on supporting main ideas so that students can communicate clearly with others.

Moving into the Next Round of Investigation

The completion of an investigation should lead to the next round of investigation, either as a result of students coming up with new questions or as a result of students thinking of modifications to their experimental design. Students should be provided opportunities to make predictions that are based on the results of their previous investigation, formulate hypotheses based on results of their previous investigation, and apply experimental techniques to new problems. As students conduct their investigation, they should keep a record of new questions that come to mind and of questions that remain unanswered. You need to capitalize on situations in which new questions arise naturally—these are the questions students will be eager to try to answer.

Portfolio Activity 4.8 gives you the opportunity to connect all that you have read and to perform your own investigation with a partner. Remember to keep track of new questions that arise.

SUPPORTING STUDENTS' IMPLEMENTATION OF INVESTIGATIONS

Students find it difficult to implement all the components of inquiry. They also find it difficult to develop their own unique experimental designs. In fact, most scientific investigations proceed from modifications of previous designs. We can support students in doing their own independent investigations by using a similar technique in our science teaching. Teachers first conduct modeling of the process, seeking student involvement, and then teachers give feedback as students design and conduct their own *investigations*.

Ann Novak and Chris Gleason from Greenhills School in Ann Arbor, Michigan, use this technique to engage their middle school students in exploring decomposition. In a

Portfolio Activity 4.8   PERFORMING YOUR OWN INVESTIGATION

Materials Needed:
- Writing materials or a computer
- Mealworms

A. Work with at least one partner to observe mealworms (available at most pet stores). Record your observations.

B. What questions come to mind? Are your questions testable? Can you phrase your questions in terms of a hypothesis?

C. What background information do you need? Obtain that information.

D. Design an experiment to answer your question.

E. Carry out the experimental work.

F. How can you analyze your data? Complete the analysis.

G. What conclusion can you draw?

H. Share your experimental work and data with the members of your class.

I. What other questions come to mind? What would you do differently if you did your investigation over again?

J. Document your investigation in your portfolio.

project with the driving question "Where does all of our garbage go?" Novak and Gleason's goal is for students to do their own independent investigations, but they recognize that students need support in the process.

They first **model** the process. They begin by asking the question "What types of materials will decompose?" In class they discuss why this makes a good question by asking "Is it worthwhile?" "Is it feasible?" "Is it important?" Next, they demonstrate how they could investigate this question. They show students how to create decomposition environments using 2-liter pop bottles with holes to allow for the flow of oxygen. They place soil and a variety of materials into the bottles. Some of the materials, like orange peelings, will decompose, and others, like pieces of Styrofoam, will not. During the process they seek students' input. For instance, students might suggest what types of materials to place in the decomposition environment, justifying each choice. The teachers suggest a possible table format for recording data. They also model how to record the data using both qualitative descriptions (such as the smell of the decomposition column) and quantitative techniques (such as the mass or temperature). Students then create their own decomposition environments following the teachers' model.

Because it takes several days to observe the decomposition, in the meantime teachers prompt the students to ask their own subquestions of the driving question. Working in groups, students develop questions such as "Do worms affect decomposition?" "Does the amount of light influence decomposition?" and "Does the amount of water affect decomposition?" As students discuss their questions, the teachers offer *feedback*. Both in small groups and in large class discussion, the questions are critiqued for their feasibility, worth, and importance (the criteria for a good driving question are discussed in Chapter 3).

The teachers then ask their students to design investigations by modifying the techniques they used in setting up their first decomposition environments. As students develop their designs, the teachers give the students **feedback**. Some of the designs are

Key Idea

Teachers can support students in doing independent investigation by first modeling the process. Students can then perform their own investigations as teachers give feedback.

Portfolio Activity 4.9

SUPPORTING IMPLEMENTATION OF INVESTIGATIONS

Materials Needed:
- Writing materials or a computer
- Materials to complete an investigation

A. Work with a small group of students or peers to model an investigation of your choice, such as making decomposition columns.

B. After you model the investigation, ask the students to generate some of their own questions for the same question. Record their questions.

C. Have the students design an investigation of their own.

D. What did you find you needed to do to support the students in carrying out their own investigation? Record your thoughts in your portfolio.

also critiqued in whole class discussions. Based on the feedback, students can redesign their investigations and then carry them out to explore factors associated with decomposition. Using this technique of first *modeling* and then allowing students guided by *feedback* to modify the procedure, the Greenhills teachers have been successful in teaching students to do their own investigations (Krajcik et al., 1998).

Novak and Gleason have used modifications of this technique to engage their students in a number of inquiry-related projects. At the University of Michigan, Hug and colleagues (Hug & Krajcik, 2002) have further explored this strategy. In a project with the driving question "Can good friends make me sick?" teachers engage students in exploring the growth of bacteria (Hug & Krajcik, 2002). The teacher begins by asking the question "Do I have bacteria on my hands?" The teacher then teaches a benchmark lesson, demonstrating how to culture bacteria using agar plates and an incubator. The next day, the teacher demonstrates how to count the bacteria colonies (a non-contaminated plate was used as a control). Students draw conclusions from the data regarding whether bacteria are on our hands. Students then ask their own questions. Students have asked questions such as "Does washing my hands make a difference?" "Does a different type of soap make a difference?" and "Is there bacteria on my desk?" This cycle of modeling-investigation-feedback is one technique that teachers can use to support children in the inquiry process. You will try this technique yourself in Portfolio Activity 4.9.

Key Idea

Students should "do" science themselves rather than having the curriculum or the teacher do it for them.

CRITERIA FOR ASSESSING THE VALUE OF AN INVESTIGATION

Too often, teachers and textbooks "do science" for students. Students don't learn much when most of the investigative work is done for them. It is important that teachers not confuse giving students support with doing the work for students. Table 4.16 lists criteria for determining if the teacher or curriculum materials are performing the cognitive work for students.

REFLECTING ON THE STRUCTURE OF AN INVESTIGATION

Table 4.16

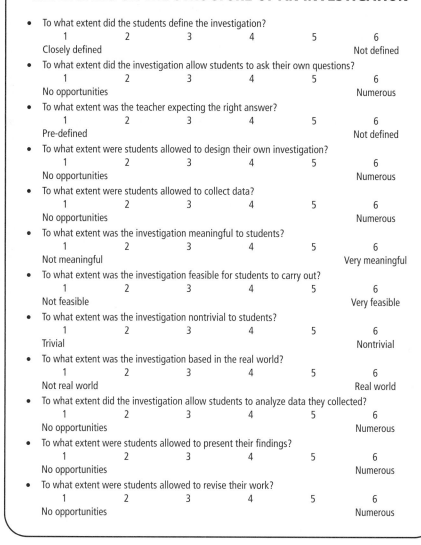

- To what extent did the students define the investigation?

  1   2   3   4   5   6

  Closely defined   Not defined

- To what extent did the investigation allow students to ask their own questions?

  1   2   3   4   5   6

  No opportunities   Numerous

- To what extent was the teacher expecting the right answer?

  1   2   3   4   5   6

  Pre-defined   Not defined

- To what extent were students allowed to design their own investigation?

  1   2   3   4   5   6

  No opportunities   Numerous

- To what extent were students allowed to collect data?

  1   2   3   4   5   6

  No opportunities   Numerous

- To what extent was the investigation meaningful to students?

  1   2   3   4   5   6

  Not meaningful   Very meaningful

- To what extent was the investigation feasible for students to carry out?

  1   2   3   4   5   6

  Not feasible   Very feasible

- To what extent was the investigation nontrivial to students?

  1   2   3   4   5   6

  Trivial   Nontrivial

- To what extent was the investigation based in the real world?

  1   2   3   4   5   6

  Not real world   Real world

- To what extent did the investigation allow students to analyze data they collected?

  1   2   3   4   5   6

  No opportunities   Numerous

- To what extent were students allowed to present their findings?

  1   2   3   4   5   6

  No opportunities   Numerous

- To what extent were students allowed to revise their work?

  1   2   3   4   5   6

  No opportunities   Numerous

Not all of the investigations your students will perform will receive high marks in Table 4.16. Indeed, there are many situations in which you would want lower scores. However, if throughout the year all your investigations are turning out low scores, you need to ask yourself if you are helping students become responsible for their learning and helping them learn to do difficult cognitive tasks on their own. Your goal should be to move students toward *doing* science. Throughout the school year, look for increasingly higher scores on the table. Portfolio Activity 4.10 provides practice in using Table 4.16.

Portfolio Activity 4.10   COMPARING TWO INVESTIGATIONS

Materials Needed:
- A partner
- Two thermometers
- Two Styrofoam cups
- Hot water
- Stirring rods

A.   Read the following investigations.

Investigation 1: Cooling It by Stirring
- Purpose: You will observe how the temperature of a hot liquid changes with stirring.
- Materials: Two thermometers, two Styrofoam cups, hot water, and stirring rods
- Procedures for collecting the data:
  1. Label one Styrofoam cup "Stirring" and one "Control."
  2. Fill the two cups with 150 ml of hot water. Caution: Hot water can burn you. Make sure both cups are secure.
  3. Place a thermometer in each cup.
  4. Gently stir one of the cups of hot water until the end of the experiment.
  5. Record the temperature of each cup every 3 minutes for 24 minutes.
- Data analysis: For each cup, make a graph of temperature versus time. Place temperature on the *y*-axis and time on the *x*-axis. Place each graph on the same grid.
- Questions:
  1. What was the starting temperature of each of the cups?

2. What was the final temperature of each of the cups?
3. Which cup changed temperature first? Why do you think this one changed first?
4. How long did it take before the temperature of the other cup began to change?
5. How does stirring affect the cooling of a hot liquid?
- Conclusions: Write a conclusion to support your data.

Investigation 2: Stirring Things Up
- Prediction: If one cup of hot liquid is allowed to cool undisturbed while another is constantly stirred for a period of time, will one cool faster than the other? Draw a graph to illustrate your prediction.
- Purpose: In this investigation, you will determine if people who constantly stir their coffee are really affecting the cooling process or just exhibiting a case of nerves.
- Challenge: Design an experimental procedure to find an answer to the question proposed.
- Questions to think about:
  1. Did your results agree with your original prediction? Why or why not?
  2. Will you continue to stir your coffee? Explain.
- Additional investigation: What other variables might have an effect on the cooling process? Set up investigations to explore these other factors.

B.   Use Table 4.16 to discuss the two investigations. How are they alike? Different? Which is most like project-based science? Why?

ONLINE LEARNING CENTER

CHAPTER REVIEW   **www.mhhe.com/krajcik2e**

Go to the Online Learning Center at **www.mhhe.com/krajcik2e** to review important content from the chapter and key terms, take a chapter assessment, and link to the chapter's websites.

CHAPTER SUMMARY

In this chapter, we discussed why investigations should be an integral part of elementary and middle school science instruction. We examined the investigation web and discussed a number of ways to help students implement the web. We considered numerous strategies for getting started, asking and refining questions, changing questions to hypotheses, using predictions, finding information, planning and designing, conducting the experimental work, making sense of data, drawing conclusions, sharing with others, and moving to the next round of investigation. Finally, we discussed supporting students' implementation of investigations and criteria for assessing the value of an investigation.

CHAPTER HIGHLIGHTS

- Investigations are an important part of elementary and middle school science instruction and meet important aspects of the National Science Education Standards.
- One way of thinking about the process of investigation is to think of a nonlinear investigation web.
- The investigation web can be thought of as consisting of several iterative processes:
  - Messing about so that students can initially explore ideas,
  - Asking and refining questions that can be investigated by students,
  - Hypothesizing,
  - Making predictions about the results,
  - Finding information that will provide direction for the investigation,
  - Planning and designing a procedure,
  - Carrying out the procedures and sometimes refining them,
  - Making sense of data by transforming it and analyzing it,
  - Drawing conclusions and making judgments about the conclusions,
  - Sharing with others, which might lead to changes and modifications, and
  - Moving into the next round of investigation based on things learned.
- It is important for teachers to support students' implementation of investigations. One way to do this is to model an investigation, have students perform their own investigation, and provide feedback.
- Teachers can assess the value of an investigation to determine if students are doing the cognitive work rather than having science done for them.

KEY TERMS

archival data (132)

benchmark lessons (124)

cause and effect
   questions (126)

conceptual models (152)

continuous data (150)

control variables (137)

current data (132)

dependent variable (127)

descriptive questions (126)

descriptive statistics (151)

designing (134)

discrete data (149)

feedback (159)

hypermedia (156)

hypotheses (129)

independent variable (127)

inferences (124)

initial observations (121)

inquiry-based
   learning (118)

investigation web (118)

manipulation of
   materials (122)

mathematical models (153)

messing about (120–21)

model (152)

nonlinear (118)

operational
   definition (137)

physical models (152)

planning (134)

predictions (130)

qualitative
   observations (146)

quantitative
   observations (146)

quicktrial (144)

relational questions (126)

seeking information (131)

sharing (155)

validity (134)

variables (136)

REFERENCES

American Association for the Advancement of Science. 1993. *Benchmarks for science literacy.* New York: Oxford University Press.

American Association for the Advancement of Science and National Science Teachers Association. 2001. *Atlas of Scientific literacy.* Washington, D.C.: Author.

Annenberg/CPB. 1997. *Case studies in science education.* Washington, D.C.: Author.

Berg, C. 1994. *Chameleon condos: Critters and critical thinking.* Shorewood, Wis.: Chameleon Publishing.

Berger, C., G. Berkheimer, L. Lewis, H. Neuberger, and E. Wood. 1974. *Pushes and pulls.* Boston: Houghton Mifflin.

Bransford, J D., A. L. Brown, and R. R. Cocking. 1999. *How people learn: Brain, mind, experience and school.* Washington, D.C., National Academy Press.

Burnett, R. 1999. *The pillbug project: A guide to investigation.* Washington, D.C: National Science Teachers Association.

Cothron, J. H., R. N Giese, and R. J. Rezba. 1993. *Students and research: Practical strategies for science classrooms and competitions.* (2nd Ed.). Dubuque, Iowa: Kendall-Hunt.

Davis, E.A., and D. Kirkpatrick. 2002. It's all about the news: Critiquing evidence and claims. *Science Scope* 25(5): 32-37.

Elementary Science Study. 1970. *The ESS reader.* Newton, Mass.: Education Development Center.

Hawkins, D. 1965. Messing about in science. *Science and Children* 2(5):5-9.

Hug, B., and J. S. Krajcik. 2002. *Scaffolded inquiry investigations: Investigating students' scientific practices.* Paper presented at the Annual Meeting of the National Association for Research in Science Teaching, New Orleans, La.

Ingram, M. 1993. *Bottle biology.* Dubuque, Iowa: Kendall/Hunt Publishing Co.

Krajcik, J. S., P. Blumenfeld, R. W. Marx, K. M. Bass, J. Fredricks, and E. Soloway. 1998. Middle school students' initial attempts at inquiry in project-based science classrooms. *Journal of the Learning Sciences* 7(3 and 4):313-50.

Krajcik, J., B. Blumenfeld, R. Marx, and E. Soloway. 2000. Instructional, curricular, and technological supports for inquiry in science classrooms. *Inquiry into inquiry: Science learning and teaching,* eds. J. Minstell and E. Van Zee. Washington, D.C.: American Association for the Advancement of Science Press, 283-315.

Lawrence Hall of Science. 1989. *River cutters.* Berkeley, Calif.: Author.

Metz, K. E. 1995. Reassessment of developmental constraints on children's science instruction. *Review of Educational Research* 65:93-128.

National Research Council. 1996. *National science education standards.* Washington, D.C.: National Academy Press.

Parks, S., and H. Black. 1992. *Organizing thinking: Graphic organizers.* Pacific Grove, Calif.: Critical Thinking Press and Software.

Scardamalia, M., and C. Bereiter. 1991. Higher levels of agency or children in knowledge building: A challenge for the design of new knowledge media. *Journal of the Learning Sciences* 1:37-68.

Schauble, L., L. E. Klopfer, and K. Raghavan. 1991. Students' transition from an engineering model to a science model of experimentation. *Journal of Research in Science Teaching* 28:859-82.

Singer, J., R. W. Marx, J. Krajcik, and J. Clay Chambers. 2000. Constructing extended inquiry projects: Curriculum materials for science education reform. *Educational Psychologist* 35(3): 165-78.

Chapter 5

How Can Learning Technologies Be Used to Support Investigations?

INTRODUCTION

ROLE OF TECHNOLOGY IN CONSTRUCTING
   SCIENCE UNDERSTANDINGS

ROLE OF THE TEACHER

INTEGRATING TECHNOLOGY INTO INSTRUCTION

CHAPTER LEARNING PERFORMANCES

- *Describe how students can use learning technologies to support them in carrying out investigations.*
- *Compare and contrast the various ways in which children can use technology to develop meaningful understandings.*
- *Use technology tools to explore scientific ideas.*
- *Explain what to take into consideration when designing instruction using learning technologies.*
- *Explain how learning technologies can extend the boundaries of the classroom.*
- *Discuss some of the pitfalls of using technology in the classroom.*

INTRODUCTION

Humans have always used tools to help them perform difficult tasks, both physical and intellectual. We use ramps to help us move objects from a lower position to a higher position, levers to move large objects, and wheels and axles to overcome friction. Humans have used graphs to see patterns in data and visual diagrams to summarize information. Teachers use concept maps as a tool to help students see and make connections between concepts. New computer-based technology tools can also serve as cognitive tools. The World Wide Web enables scientists to share information and communicate new developments rapidly and efficiently. Imagery tools enable scientists to peer at the structure of materials. Three-dimensional graphs help scientists visualize and interpret data in new ways.

As introduced in Chapter 2, computer-based technology tools can also change what we do in classrooms. Computer-based technology tools can extend learning by helping students perform cognitive tasks that otherwise might be too complex or difficult (Salomon & Perkins, 1991). In science classes, a wide variety of technology tools can support students in learning and in performing inquiry. For instance, students can use computers to access and share data on the World Wide Web, probes to gather data during investigations that otherwise might be too difficult or time intensive, graphing packages to visualize data in various ways, and multimedia development tools to create linked, multiple representations to express their ideas.

At home, in school, or around businesses, children frequently use and see technologies such as scanners, infrared devices, computers, home entertainment centers, and interactive video games. When children visit the doctor's office, they see professionals use technology to set appointments and collect information about their wellness. New technologies monitor and measure all sorts of physiological functions. Gone are the days of mercury thermometers; nurses and doctors now use digital thermometers. Grocery stores use technologies to check out groceries. Technology is used to measure the speed of pitches during baseball games and to tabulate Olympic skaters' scores. It detects moisture in dryers and records seismic events. It is even used to monitor some playgrounds. Children play with and use new technology gadgets on a daily basis. Children play with video games; download music off the Web, make CDs of their favorite music, find sports information, find pictures of music stars, and chat with friends on e-mail or with messenger programs.

The "Digital Divide"

Similarly, children should use technology in schools to help them accomplish tasks. Technology that helps students collect real data, that gives students access to numerous sources of current information, and that expands interaction and communication with others makes tasks more authentic. Using learning technologies in the classroom is also important in helping to overcome the **digital divide.** While many middle class and upper middle class students have access to technology at home, many minority children and those who come from lower income families do not. This lack of technology access increases the separation between students who typically succeed in school and those who do not. To help reduce this disparity, teachers, particularly those who work in schools with disadvantaged students, need to use technology on a regular basis.

Let's examine three scenarios that illustrate the use of technologies to teach science in elementary and middle grade classrooms.

Scenario 1: Technology as a Mindless Activity

You may have experienced a situation similar to this: Students in Ms. Williams' second-grade class are studying a unit on animals. As part of the unit, Ms. Williams has students go to the computer lab to use a computer program that enables them to click on parts of different animals to find out the names of the parts. The program also has a fill-in-the-blank component in which students type in the name of animal structures. If they are correct, colorful graphics appear on the screen to "reward" the students. The program also allows students to get background information on the animals and the various parts. Ms. Williams has students work in pairs on the program. Although students enjoy seeing the various pictures of animals and enjoy seeing the colorful graphics appear when they correctly complete the fill-in-the-blank section, they soon get bored with the program, spend time talking about other ideas, or click randomly around in the program. Although a few students select the "get more information" feature in the program, few students spend time reading the information. A number of students who become bored find the "build-an-animal" game in which they can make animals using various parts from different animals. Most of the students have fun using this part of the program, and they try to build the most ridiculous animal possible.

In this first scenario, Ms. Williams hoped students would learn from computers and accompanying software concepts that reinforced basic ideas she had taught about animals. Although the students used computers, saw interesting graphics, and had fun, they did not experience the potential that computers and software can bring to learning. As the scenario illustrated, many students can quickly become bored looking at colorful graphics and filling in blanks. Students spent little time using the technology to solve a problem or learn new ideas; rather, they used the computers simply to reinforce previously introduced ideas. This technology does not extend what students can do without the technology and, in fact, might not be as effective as other resources. For example, using technology in this manner is no different from students using a picture book. In fact, *Ranger Rick* and *National Geographic* often provide better pictures and articles than does this type of software. Moreover, the use of computers in this way is not tied to a question that students find meaningful.

Scenario 2: Going to the Computer Lab

Mr. Guzdial, a fifth-grade teacher, tries to schedule the computer room at least once a month or as frequently as he can. He often tries to think of engaging activities for his students to do in the computer room. To help his students get the most out of their day in the computer room, the day before he demonstrates how to use the program they will be using. Sometimes he has students use software tools that allow them to collect and visualize data. For instance, as part of a heat and temperature unit, he has students use temperature probes to explore who has the warmest hands in the class and to see if the wooden table-tops are the same temperature as the metal legs. The software is pretty easy to use, so most students complete the activities in the 60 minutes for which they have the computer room reserved. Some students get confused and think the program and probe aren't working correctly, because the wood tabletop and metal leg have similar temperatures, yet the leg feels much cooler to the touch. Mr. Guzdial doesn't notice this confusion. On another occasion, Mr. Guzdial has his students use the World Wide Web to find information on active volcanoes. Most students find some new information that they report to the class the next day. Although Mr. Guzdial works hard to try to monitor as many students as possible during the computer lab, some students quickly write down information about volcanoes and then spend the rest of their time looking for information on their favorite band. A few students either misspell *volcanoes* in the search window or type in the wrong URL, and so they never find any information or appropriate sites.

In this second scenario, Mr. Guzdial worked hard to ensure his students used computers for beneficial activities. He also tried to ensure that the activities the students did in the computer room were tied to the science unit they where studying in class. Finally, he attempted to monitor students' activities in the computer lab. However, because of his limited access to computers, students never really developed the idea that computers are tools for learning. Unfortunately, gaining access to computer labs on a need-to-use basis continues to challenge teachers. As a result, students see using technology as an occasional activity done in school, rather than a necessary tool to support learning in the context of daily lessons. Finally, although the use of the computers was tied to the units of study, it was not tied to questions that students found meaningful.

Scenario 3: Using Technology to Support Students Doing Investigations

Ms. Wu has students in her sixth-grade class use new technology to help them find information, gather and visualize data, and create products to share what they have learned. As part of a project on "Where does all our garbage go?" students design experiments to explore decomposition. They build decomposition environments to study the influence of a variety of variables on decomposition such as temperature, moisture, type of bedding, and material type. They use digital cameras to take pictures over time of their decomposition environments. They use probes to measure and monitor the pH and temperature of the decomposition environments. Some students use the World Wide Web to find information about other factors that influence decomposition. Other students use the Web to write to scientists to ask questions regarding landfills and rate of decomposition. Students also create multimedia documents to share what they learn with each other and with members of the school and community. With help from the school's media specialist, students convert their multimedia documents to Web pages that they post on the school's server.

In this third scenario, Ms. Wu planned for students to use technology as a tool throughout the project. Her idea was that students perceive technology the way they perceive a pair of scissors—as a tool used to accomplish a task. Ms. Wu was fortunate because she had six computers in her classroom that were connected to the Internet via cable modem. As a member of the computer planning committee, Ms. Wu advocated that computers be in the classrooms so students could have daily use of them. She showed her students how to take digital pictures and use probes to collect data in the context of a lesson. When her own background was limited, she sought the help of others to assist her. Most important, students used technology as needed to help them investigate and answer questions that they asked during a project.

CONNECTING TO
NATIONAL SCIENCE EDUCATION STANDARDS

Science Teaching Standard
Effective science teaching depends on the availability and organization of materials, equipment, media, and technology (p. 44).

Complete Portfolio Activity 5.1 to examine the ways you have used technology in your own learning. Portfolio Activity 5.2 will help you come to conclusions about the role of learning technology in children's lives.

Portfolio Activity 5.1

WAYS IN WHICH YOU HAVE USED TECHNOLOGIES FOR LEARNING

Materials Needed:
- Something to write with

A. Think of the different ways you have used technology to learn. Record them in your portfolio.

B. How do your experiences compare to the three scenarios?

C. Share your experiences with others in your class. How do your experiences compare to those of the others?

Portfolio Activity 5.2

WHY SHOULD CHILDREN USE LEARNING TECHNOLOGY?

Materials Needed:
- Paper and pencil or a computer

A. Take several minutes to brainstorm the reason(s) children should use learning technologies in science. List as many ideas as you can. Don't let any disadvantages, such as cost, get in the way of your thinking.

B. Pair with one of your classmates and compare your lists.

C. Explain the rationale for each item you listed. For example, does it improve learning concepts, change attitudes, increase skill ability, or provide a more interactive instructional strategy?

D. Record in your portfolio your conclusions about the use of technology.

ROLE OF TECHNOLOGY IN CONSTRUCTING SCIENCE UNDERSTANDINGS

One of the major global changes that has occurred since the early 1980s is the explosion in technology use. Although the capability of technology has increased since then, its cost has decreased. These two factors have made it more feasible for schools to purchase technology and to use it for instructional purposes. We refer to new technologies—in particular the use of computers, software, and various peripherals—that support students' learning as **learning technologies** (Krajcik, Blumenfeld, Marx, & Soloway, 2000). Learning technologies can support teachers and students in project-based science, because they can help students and teachers communicate, carry out investigations, and develop products. Technology can play a powerful role in enhancing student and teacher motivation by actively engaging students in the learning process. Moreover, the use of technology can help students develop understanding of complex, abstract ideas. For instance, Marcia Linn and colleagues (Linn & Hsi, 2000) found that students using software that enables them to make predictions and explanations were able to understand difficult science concepts such as temperature and heat energy.

> ### Key Idea
> Learning technologies can help students carry out investigations, communicate, and develop products.

CONNECTING TO
NATIONAL SCIENCE EDUCATION STANDARDS

Content Standards

A variety of technologies, such as hand tools, measuring instruments, and calculators, should be an integral component of scientific investigations. The use of computers for collection, analysis, and display of data is also part of this standard (p. 175).

CONNECTING TO
BENCHMARKS FOR SCIENTIFIC LITERACY

The Design World

Grades 3–5: Students are now beginning to encounter challenging information-processing problems in their school work. These problems have one or more procedures (software) for processing data, and these procedures often can be performed more efficiently with the aid of technology (hardware). Students should be encouraged to identify the data presented in the problem, develop a procedure for processing the data, implement the procedure with the aid of technology, and evaluate the reasonableness of their results. As students encounter more sophisticated problems with more complicated data sets, the procedures and tools that they use should also become more sophisticated. Eventually, students should be gathering data, processing information, and presenting results of their data-analysis activities (p. 201).

CONNECTING TO
BENCHMARKS FOR SCIENTIFIC LITERACY

The Design World

Grades 6–8: Students should use simple electronic devices for sensing, making logical decisions, counting, and storing information (p. 202).

Dwyer (1994) found that technology transformed the way teachers taught. With technology, the classroom changed from one in which the teacher was the center of attention and mostly lectured to one in which children became the center of learning and children interacted with each other, the teacher, and the computer. The teacher's role changed from "expert" to "collaborator." These changes in a classroom can contribute to student learning. The teacher becomes not a provider of information but a guide who helps students develop understanding through active engagement with phenomena by asking "What if" questions.

Technology enables students to explore phenomena otherwise inaccessible to them. Creating multimedia artifacts and products helps students share information and develop meaningful understandings. Throughout this chapter, we will show ways in which students can use technology tools to develop understandings. Table 5.1 summarizes the potential of learning technologies in science classrooms.

Learning Technologies to Support Active Engagement with Phenomena

A number of learning technologies can support students in actively engaging with phenomena. These applications enable students to use technologies much as scientists do—as tools to explore phenomena. This active engagement can help students develop rich ideas from the science content and become proficient in science **procedural knowledge.**

Microcomputer-based laboratories (MBLs) allow students to use microcomputers as laboratory tools. Interfaced electronic probes can detect temperature, voltage, light intensity, sound, distance, dissolved oxygen, or pH while the microcomputer digitally records and graphs the data. Using **microcomputer-based laboratories (MBLs),** students can observe graphs being produced while an experiment is being conducted and thus obtain immediate graphical results of their data. Immediate graphical results help students understand concepts such as temperature, see trends in their data that allow them to focus on the concepts they are exploring, and ask new questions related to an experiment.

Using **probes** and accompanying software, students are able to direct the computer to collect, record, and

POTENTIAL OF LEARNING TECHNOLOGIES

Table 5.1

- Help teachers and students communicate, carry out investigations, and develop products.
- Change the nature of classroom instruction so students can construct understanding.
- Actively engage students in the learning process.
- Allow for exploration not possible in the science classroom.
- Provide dynamic visuals to represent abstract concepts.
- Provide opportunities to ask "What if?" questions.
- Provide opportunities to plan, synthesize, question, predict, and apply.
- Facilitate student creation of multimedia artifacts and products.
- Support students in communicating and collaborating with other students and community members.
- Help students create models of complex systems.

graph data just as scientists do. A temperature probe interfaced to the computer or hand-held device enables students to collect data related to temperature as it occurs rather than at intervals after temperature has changed.

Probes used as laboratory tools may support students' development of science concepts (Mokros & Tinker, 1987) as well as their procedural knowledge in a fundamentally new way. For instance, temperature probes allow students to explore the concept of evaporative cooling. Many of us feel cool after we come out of a swimming pool, and we might be able to explain that this phenomenon is an example of evaporative cooling, but few us have explored this concept. If you place a probe in water, withdraw it, and allow it to dry in the air, you can observe a graph of temperature versus time. What you observe is that the temperature of the probe dipped in water drops below room temperature! This type of experience helps students develop deeper understanding of science concepts. Portfolio Activity 5.3 asks you to use probes to explore the concept of evaporative cooling.

With probes students can collect and visualize data much more quickly than before, giving them the opportunity to ask "What if?" questions. Moreover, probes enable students to perform investigations that were difficult to impossible to perform before (Krajcik & Layman, 1992). In addition, this use of probes may strengthen students' graphing, science process, and problem solving skills (Linn, Layman, & Nachmias, 1986).

A variety of studies have illustrated the value of students using probes to collect and visualize data (Linn, 1998). The microcomputer's capability of providing **real-time graphs** of temperature versus time as students carry out experiments may be one of the key elements in helping students develop science concepts and graphing skills. One possible explanation is that, with probes, students have more time to spend interpreting and evaluating the data because they spend less time gathering and recording it. Brasell (1987) showed that the simultaneous linking of real time data collection with the production of graphs results in substantial learning gains.

A variety of different types of probes exist, including temperature, motion, pH, dissolved oxygen, conductivity, force, and pressure. One type of probe, the motion detector, works by sending out a sound signal that reflects off an object back toward the detector. The motion detector contains a device that can detect the reflected sound sources. Because the speed of sound is known in air, accompanying software can calculate the distance an object is from the sensor. Figure 5.1 shows a graph of a student walking away

PASCO and
Vernier Probes

Portfolio Activity 5.3

USING MICROCOMPUTER-BASED LABORATORIES TO VISUALIZE EVAPORATIVE COOLING

Materials Needed:
- Paper and something to write with
- Beakers
- Computers and temperature probes and accompanying software
- Hot water
- Rubbing alcohol

A. Predict the shape of a curve that a temperature probe would produce if initialiy dipped in water at 50°C, then withdrawn, and then allowed to dry in a room.

B. Use a probe and accompanying software to collect data and create a graph of room temperature.

C. Place a probe in a 100 ml beaker filled with water that is about 50°C. Start the probe software. Let the software collect data for about 30 seconds and then take the temperature probe out of the water and allow it to cool. Let the software collect data until there is no longer a change in the temperature for at least one minute.

D. Describe how the wet probe cooled. What is the lowest temperature reached? How does this temperature compare to the room temperature recorded earlier? What is the final temperature reached? How does it compare to room temperature?

E. How does your final graph compare with your prediction?

F. How can you explain your graph?

G. Try this activity with rubbing alcohol. What are the results? How do they compare with the results found with water?

H. What other question might you ask and investigate related to this concept?

I. Record your conclusions in your portfolio.

from a motion detector at various speeds. Probes and accompanying software can be purchased from a number of manufacturers, including PASCO and Vernier.

Probe Manufacturers

Probes are now available for various hand-held devices, such as the Palm, through ImagiWorks, and the PASPORT System, through PASCO. Figure 5.2 shows both the Palm and PASPORT. With probes, these hand-held devices become portable laboratories for collecting data outside of the classroom. For instance, students can use temperature probes to explore how the temperature of the soil changes during the spring. Novak and Gleason (2001) present a wonderful description of how to use portable probes in middle school classrooms to study water quality. They have students explore the quality of water in a stream behind their school by collecting pH, temperature, dissolved oxygen, and conductivity with hand-held technologies during the fall, winter, and spring. They ask students to use their data to explain why the quality of their stream might change during the different seasons.

Some teachers have students use Texas Instruments' graphing calculators to investigate phenomena in real world contexts (Christmann, 2002). This learning technology lets students explore science and mathematics by connecting Texas Instruments' CBL kit and Vernier probes (for temperature, voltage, light, and so on) to the graphing calculator. With Texas Instruments' CBR, which can be used alone or connected to the CBL, students can collect and analyze distance, velocity, and acceleration. Connectivity software for these technologies enables teachers and students to download data and graphs to the computer. In addition, a peripheral connects the graphing calculator to an overhead projector

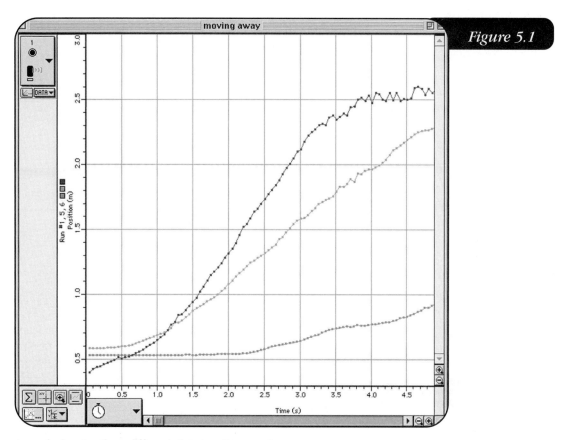

A graph showing three different distance–time graphs.

so an entire classroom of students can view it. To learn more about this technology, visit the Texas Instruments website.

Microcomputer-based laboratories have many applications for elementary and middle school science. In a pond project, students can use temperature probes to monitor the temperature, use a pH probe to measure the pH, or use a dissolved oxygen probe to test how dissolved oxygen varies at different locations. Although many of these measurements can be taken with traditional laboratory equipment, using probes and accompanying software offers a number of advantages. Probes are often time-efficient. They are also more reliable instruments. Because they can display the results both graphically and numerically, children can more easily interpret the results. One of the biggest advantages is the simultaneous collecting and graphing of data. Research (Brasell, 1986; Morkos & Tinker, 1987) supports the importance of simultaneous data gathering and graphing to help students form understanding. Although the exact mechanism is not known, the simultaneous creating of a graph and seeing it supports students in learning. The final advantage is that probes allow students to do explorations not typically possible in the science classroom. For instance, with the motion probe students can explore if mass

Texas Instruments

Key Idea

The use of probes can help students collect and visualize data.

Figure 5.2

| ImagiWorks Probe with Palm m100 | PS-2000 PASPORT Xplorer datalogger |

Hand-held devices using probes.

influences the speed at which objects fall. Most students, because of everyday experiences, believe that heavier object fall faster than lighter objects. Using the motion detectors, students can explore and visualize what happens. Such explorations were difficult, if not impossible, in classrooms before the use of probes. Portfolio Activity 5.4 will help you think more about the use of MBLs in the classroom.

NSES

CONNECTING TO NATIONAL SCIENCE EDUCATION STANDARDS

Content Standards

The use of tools and techniques, including mathematics, will be used guided by the question asked and the investigations students design. The use of computers for the collection, summary, and display of evidence is part of this standard. Students should be able to access, gather, store, retrieve, and organize data, using hardware and software deigned for these purposes (p. 145).

Visualization Tools

Various technology tools enable students to explore and analyze scientific data. **Visualization tools** are software programs that enable students to "see" phenomena and abstract concepts they are trying to understand (Edelson, Gordin, & Pea, 1999). The Kids as Global Scientists project enables upper elementary and middle

Visualization Tools

school students to use the Internet to research weather and climate and to *see* weather fronts the way meteorologists do. Figure 5.3 shows a graph from the Kids as Global Scientists program. The program includes visualization software, activities, and an interactive message board that allows students to talk with each other. Using the Kids as Global Scientists program, elementary students can use child-appropriate visualization tools to track a variety of weather data including temperature, humidity, precipitation, barometric pressure, cloud cover, and wind speed. Songer and her research group (Songer, 1996 & 1998) have demonstrated the positive learning gains achieved when students use the program.

The Worldwatcher program lets middle school students visualize climate patterns. With the FeederWatch program, students can enter data on birds they are tracking and

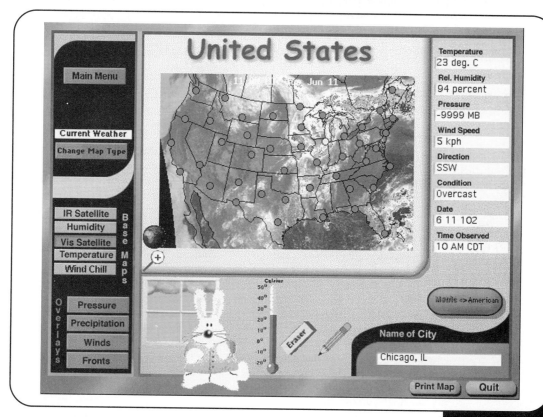

Portfolio Activity 5.4

THE VALUE OF USING MICROCOMPUTER-BASED LABORATORIES IN THE CLASSROOM

Materials Needed:
- Paper and something to write with

A. Describe the value of using microcomputer-based laboratories (MBLs) in the classroom.

B. Observe a classroom of students using MBLs.

C. From these observations, how would you modify your original thoughts? Are there features you would add, delete, or modify? Explain. Record in your portfolio.

Sample from Kids as Global Scientist program.

Figure 5.3

visualize the distribution of different bird populations throughout North America. For instance, students can use the FeederWatch program to track the migration of different bird species. Visualization software creates opportunities for students to use tools similar to those used by scientists to explore and manipulate data and to perceive trends. Such

Portfolio Activity 5.5

USING THE WORLD WIDE WEB TO ACCESS AND VISUALIZE DATA: EXPLORING THE FEEDERWATCH PROGRAM

Materials Needed:
- Computer with high-speed Internet connection
- A World Wide Web browser such as Internet Explorer or Netscape Communicator

A.   Use a browser program to go to the FeederWatch program (http://birds.cornell.edu.pfw/). Please visit the text's Online Learning Center at www.mhhe.com/krajcik2e to link directly to these websites and for updates to these URLs.

B.   Explore the various parts of the program.

C.   How might you make use of the program in your teaching?

D.   Record your thoughts in your portfolio.

Key Idea

Visualization tools allow students to explore and manipulate data and to see trends they couldn't otherwise see.

exploration and manipulation of data help make science learning more like doing real science and help students to develop meaningful understandings (Cohen, 1997). Portfolio Activity 5.5 challenges you to explore a visualization tool.

Simulations, Microworlds, and Interactive Multimedia

Simulations, microworlds, and interactive multimedia combine video, pictures, computer graphics, text, and interactivity to present to students phenomena that otherwise would be inaccessible, too hazardous, too time-consuming, or too expensive for students to observe. Some of this technology enables students to explore difficult questions through simulation that they would otherwise be unable to explore ethically.

In the artificial environments of **microworlds,** students explore and manipulate environments that are otherwise inaccessible. Extraneous details are minimized, making it easier for students to note interactions among variables. For example, students can explore the galaxies or the structure of the atom. Another example is a microworld created by White and Frederiksen (2000) that allows students to explore Newton's Laws of Motion. Most students have difficulty with these physics concepts because their everyday experiences seem to contradict them. When asked, most students believe that a force needs to be applied to an object to keep it moving. However, in a microworld without friction students can see that objects do keep moving unless a force is applied to change or stop the motion. The microworld challenges students to ask many "What if" questions, make predictions, and test predictions.

Technology lets students explore phenomena that would otherwise be too hazardous. Using **interactive multimedia,** students can observe the colorful but violent and noxious reaction between liquid bromine and aluminum foil, they can explore the inside of the eye of a hurricane, or they can get close looks at tornadoes.

Activities that would normally be too time-consuming or expensive are possible with technology. Interactive multimedia technologies simulate trips through the human body, voyages through outerspace, and adventures into the ocean. Chariot Corporation offers two programs entitled *Eco-Adventures in the Oceans* and *Eco-Adventures in the Rainforest* that simulate these unique environments. Similarly, the Sunburst/WINGS for Learning

Interactive Multimedia

programs *Earthquest Explores Ecology, The Voyage of the Mimi, A Field Trip to the Sea,* and *A Field Trip to the Rainforest* ask students to explore ecological issues, participate in a whale research expedition, explore ocean life, and visit the rainforest. The *Great Ocean Rescue* and *Great Solar System Rescue* by Tom Snyder Productions actively engage students in solving problems. In the *Great Ocean Rescue,* students participate in challenging rescue missions that require them to apply what they know about marine ecosystems, earth science, and environmental science and to conduct research in these areas to learn more. We have observed numerous teachers implementing these programs, and each time students engaged in lively conversation and debate. All of these programs take students on an electronic adventure, complete with full color pictures and authentic sounds, to places they may not visit in person.

Using **simulations,** students explore what it might be like to manipulate variables that would otherwise be just too unethical, difficult, or impossible to do. For instance, Genscope (Horwitz & Christie, 2000) allows middle school students to breed various types of dragons to see the effect of selective breeding on observable characteristics, or phenotypes, in the offspring. Learners can also view what happens as a result of the mating at the chromosome and DNA levels (genotypes). Although selective breeding is done routinely, it is impractical and perhaps unethical to do so in middle school classrooms. *Genscope* allows students to ask "What if" questions and do exploration that would otherwise not be feasible. Moreover, the linking between the visual characteristics of the offspring and the invisible world of chromosomes and DNA provides for unprecedented learning outcomes.

In Chapter 2, we introduced you to Dale's Cone of Experience. As Dale's Cone illustrates, direct purposeful experiences provide the best opportunity for students to develop understanding. Simulations, interactive multimedia, and microworlds are the *next best thing* to direct, purposeful experiences with phenomena. These technologies, as a type of contrived experience, also provide beneficial experience for students. They allow students to ask "What if" questions, make predictions, and test out their ideas. Many of these technologies ask students to record their observations or explain what they see. Linking concrete phenomena with writing about the phenomena can help students develop deep understandings. Simulation programs that combine interactive multimedia technologies also give learners opportunities to actively explore phenomena that would be otherwise too small or too big to explore. Such active student engagement can help students develop meaningful science concepts. Portfolio Activity 5.6 will help you explore the value of simulations in the science classroom.

Learning Technologies to Support Using and Applying Knowledge

Some learning technologies help students apply their knowledge by supporting them in planning, explaining, and reflecting. Whereas in simulations, students manipulate phenomena according to an underlying model, in developing **models** students must begin by creating the concepts, principles, and rules that govern the phenomena.

Model-It (Metcalf-Jackson, Krajcik, & Soloway, 2000) is a program that helps students plan models, supports them in building dynamic models using qualitative relationships, and helps them test and evaluate their models. This program supports students in an essential component of learning science—making models—that previously was extremely difficult to accomplish in most middle school audiences. With *Model-It*, students represent,

Genscope simulation program

Portfolio Activity 5.6

THE VALUE OF USING SIMULATIONS TO HELP STUDENTS LEARN SCIENCE CONCEPTS

Materials Needed:

- Genscope (downloadable at http://genscope.concord.org). Please visit the text's Online Learning Center at www.mhhe.com/krajcik2e to link directly to these websites and for updates to these URLs.
- Computer lab
- Paper and something to write with

A. Use the Genscope program to create some imaginary dragons.

B. What is the benefit of using this program to help students learn about how traits are passed on from one generation to another?

C. Make a list of the ways using simulations in science classrooms is valuable.

D. Record your ideas in your portfolio.

interpret, and refine their thinking so that they develop more robust understanding. By building models, students also make their thinking visible.

To create a model of a specific phenomenon, students create *Objects*, which are real-world entities related to the phenomenon. For example, to create a model of pollution, students might create a stream and a golf course. Then the students define quantifiable *Factors*, which are characteristics related to the *Objects*. In the pollution example, one *Factor* might be the amount of pollution given off by a factory. Students connect related factors with *Relationships*, which they create with qualitative rather than quantitative or formulaic representations. For example, a direct causal relationship represented mathematically by the function $y = x$ may be expressed qualitatively in *Model-It* with the phrase "as x increases, y increases by about the same." These verbal representations are visually linked with graphical representations. The model as a whole may be viewed as an abstract representation similar to a concept map. Finally, *Model-It* provides graphs, meters, and sliders for interactive testing of the model.

Model-It

Figure 5.4 shows a screen shot from the *Model-It* Testing Window. In this example, students built a model of water quality to explore how the number of people can impact the number of fish in a stream. The left side of the screen shows the tools available for students in the Testing Window. The screen also shows that the students have tested their model. The graphs across the bottom indicate that, as the number of people increases, the number of fish decreases; and as the number of people decreases, the number of fish increases.

Marcia Linn's *Knowledge Integration Environment* also helps students explain and reflect on a range of scientific phenomena including light and temperature. Linn and her colleagues (Linn, 1992; Linn, Songer, Lewis, & Stern, 1993) have also used built-in questions in a microcomputer-based laboratory environment to encourage students to make predictions and then to compare their results to their predictions.

Computer Programs That Help Students Create Concept Maps

Do Portfolio Activity 5.7 now to explore the value to students of building models.

Other learning technologies help students use and apply metacognitive knowledge. As discussed more thoroughly in Chapter 2, **metacognitive knowledge** refers to

Screen shot from *Model-It* Testing Window.

Figure 5.4

knowledge about cognition in general as well as awareness and knowledge about one's own cognition (Anderson & Krathwohl, 2001). Computer programs such as *Inspiration* (Helfgott & Westhaver, 2000), *Kidspiration* (Inspiration Software, 2000), and *Pic Map* (a free Palm application downloadable from the hi-ce website) help students create concept maps. Concept maps help students with **content knowledge,** but they are also useful tools to help students examine their own thinking about concepts. Groups of students can discuss their understandings of a topic. Such conversations help students become aware of their own thinking and their own knowledge.

Learning Technologies as a Source of Information

Technology expansion, especially of the World Wide Web, has made information so accessible that students can easily find out about key ideas, concepts, and subject matter

> ### Key Idea
>
> The World Wide Web can serve as an excellent source of the latest scientific information and data.

Portfolio Activity 5.7

THE VALUE OF BUILDING MODELS FOR HELPING STUDENTS LEARN SCIENCE CONCEPTS

Materials Needed:
- *Model-It* (downloadable at http://www.hi-ce.org). Please visit the text's Online Learning Center at www.mhhe.com/krajcik2e to link directly to these websites and for updates to these URLs.
- A computer lab
- Paper and something to write with

A. Use *Model-It* to create a model of water quality, air quality, or some other dynamic system of your choice.

B. What is the benefit of using this program to help students build meaningful understandings?

C. Record your ideas in your portfolio.

topics that arise as they explore solutions to questions. Many of the sources of information on the Web are **primary data sources,** meaning they often contain the same data sets that scientists use. The Web provides access to instruments such as telescopes, modeling tools, and remote sensing devices that can help students carry out their investigations. Finally, the Web makes it possible for students to publish their works—on their own websites or on other sites. Many such websites enable students to collaborate with scientists and other students about science topics. Table 5.2 summarizes the advantages of using the World Wide Web for supporting inquiry in the classroom.

One example of a website that incorporates many of these ideas is the Windows to the Universe Project. This site provides a host of information and images regarding space science and earth science topics. Figure 5.5 shows one page from the Windows to the Universe Project.

Windows to the Universe Project

Wallace and her colleagues (Wallace, Kupperman, Krajcik, & Soloway, 2000) warn that, although the World Wide Web does offer these many advantages, it also presents difficulties, particularly for young learners:

- Students may have difficulty locating and taking advantage of information. Often when students do a search, they get back hundreds of hits. Most middle school and high school students (and adult learners) don't have the skills to sift through this many hits. Moreover, most of these hits have little to do with the learner's intended search.
- Students often become lost and disoriented while navigating.
- Students require a substantial amount of support to frame their activities.
- Students often do not evaluate the resources they find.
- Students have difficulty using Web tools to the extent they are designed to be used and instead stick to basic operations.

Digital libraries

Thus, simply providing access to information does not guarantee that it will be useful to learners. Unlike a library, the Web contains many documents that have not been screened for content and validity of information. **Digital libraries,** such as The University

ADVANTAGES OF THE WORLD WIDE WEB FOR SUPPORTING INQUIRY

Table 5.2

- *Broad range of information:* Learners need access to information to help them refine their questions and find solutions. On-line information will bring learners the most current information available.
- *Primary data sources:* Learners need access to demographic data, remote sensing data, and other types of data to support their inquiry. In many circumstances, students will use the same data and information sources as scientists do.
- *Instruments:* On-line instruments such as telescopes and remote sensing devices serve as sources of direct data as learners carry out inquiry.
- *Computational instruments:* Modeling, simulations, and visualization tools help students analyze and examine on-line data in new ways.
- *Publishing tools:* Learners need tools that will help them translate information and publish their information for others. This translation is a critical step in helping learners construct their own understanding.
- *Collaboration tools:* Inquiry will be supported if learners have access to synchronous (live) and asynchronous (not simultaneous or live) communication tools that support interaction between students and scientific mentors.

of Michigan's Middle Years Digital Library Project (Wallace, Kupperman, Krajcik, & Soloway, 2000) and NSTA's SciLinks, overcome many of these problems by screening documents available on the Web for content, validity, and developmental level of the learner. After students become proficient in the use of the Web, they can be taught to navigate on their own and evaluate the merit of information (see Chapter 4, particularly Tables 4.7 and 4.8, for more information about teaching students to evaluate the quality and validity of information).

The Middle Years Digital Library Project uses an interface and searching device designed for learners called Artemis. When using Artemis, students receive in response to search requests only a small number (ten or twenty) of documents that are related to their search, rather than the large lists that include many unrelated documents that other search engines produce.

CONNECTING TO
BENCHMARKS FOR SCIENTIFIC LITERACY

The Design World
Grades 3–5: Children should have the opportunity to use and investigate a range of information-handling devices such as electronic mail, audio and video recorders, and reference books. They should gather, organize, and present information in several ways, using reference books, paper files, and computers (p. 201).

SciLinks, developed by the National Science Teachers Association, also provides access to preselected and preapproved online materials. NSTA and textbook publishers have provided an alternative to random searches of the Web. NSTA's teacher-Web watchers have preselected and preapproved Internet science sites for a variety of textbooks. Using SciLinks, students can access websites that can provide richer and deeper representations of what they are studying, access the latest news in science, and ask scientists their questions. You can take a tour of SciLinks by going to the online learning center. Portfolio Activity 5.8 will help you explore the value of digital libraries.

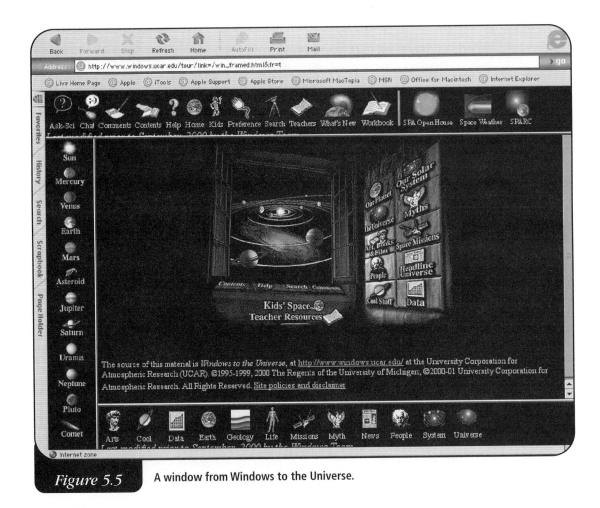

Figure 5.5   A window from Windows to the Universe.

Learning Technologies to Support the Creation of Multiple Representations

There has been an explosive growth in the use of media (sound, graphs, color pictures, and video). The variety of media provides for representation of concepts in multiple, simultaneous ways. For example, when studying tornadoes, students can use media to observe tornadoes, hear sounds associated with a real tornado, examine graphs of wind speed, read text explaining how a tornado works, and interpret graphical illustrations of tornadoes. Much has been written about the value of helping students develop deep understanding through the use of **multiple representations** (Spitulnik, Stratford, Krajcik, & Soloway, 1997). Exploring these linked multiple representations can enhance student understanding of concepts.

Technology also allows students to manipulate and construct their own representations in several media. Software tools such as Roger Wagner Publishing's *HyperStudio,* Microsoft

Creating Hypermedia

Portfolio Activity 5.8

THE VALUE OF SEARCHING FOR MATERIALS ON THE WORLD WIDE WEB USING DIGITAL LIBRARIES

Materials Needed:
- A Web browser
- Computer lab
- Paper and something to write with

A. Using a Web browser, go to a search engine such as Google to search for information on the topic of biodiversity (http://home.netscape.com/escapes/search/netsearch_E.html). Please visit the text's Online Learning Center at www.mhhe.com/krajcik2e to link directly to these websites and for updates to these URLs.

B. How many sites were returned? How long did it take you to find some information that might be of value to young learners? What was the scientific accuracy of the material presented on the sites?

C. Now use a digital library such as Artemis (http://webartemis.org) to search for the same information. Note: You can sign on to Artemis as a guest.

D. How many sites were returned? How long did it take you to find some information that might be of value to young learners? What was the scientific accuracy of the material presented on the sites?

E. What are the advantages and disadvantages of using a search engine like Google in the classroom? What are the advantages and disadvantages of using a digital library, such as Artemis, in the classroom?

F. Record your ideas in your portfolio.

Office's *PowerPoint,* or ClarisWorks' *Homepage* allow students to create hypermedia documents of their investigations. For instance, students can take pictures of plants germinating and growing, scan them (if they were taken with conventional cameras rather than digital cameras), and import them into their documents. They can also record their observations around their pictures and include graphical information such as how the heights of their plants changed over time. The incorporation of multiple representations of concepts within documents is especially important in helping students develop conceptual understanding of scientific concepts (Kozma, 1991). By building thoughtful connections and constructing meaningful relationships among representations, students form more integrated understandings (Linn, 1998). For instance, Harel and Papert (1990) have noted substantial gains in mathematics learning among students who devised various graphical and textual representations of fractions in Logo programs.

Figure 5.6 depicts one page of a *PowerPoint* presentation from an eighth-grade project on photosynthesis. The class explored the question "How do plants get their energy?" The students asked their own subquestion "How does the color of light affect the amount of starch produced?" The figure shows a page from the multimedia document describing their procedure.

Learning technologies and application software minimize the physical work that students need to do to create products, freeing them to learn more and develop deeper understandings. Application software such as word processors, spreadsheets, desktop publishing programs, and drawing programs can help students create a variety of products to represent what they know in a variety of forms. Students can now use new tools such as *HyperStudio,* Microsoft's *PowerPoint,* and ClarisWorks' *Homepage* to manipulate video, text, and graphics to develop multimedia products and presentations. Using these tools, upper elementary students can easily incorporate diagrams, drawings, graphs, and

Key Idea

Technology tools allow children to create their own multimedia documents.

Figure 5.6

Our Procedure

- What we need:

- 3 Bean Plants
- 3 Different colored lights
- Methanol test for starch amounts

A slide from a student's *PowerPoint* presentation.

video into computer-generated products. Moreover, students can link products together in unique ways to represent their understandings.

Using technology tools to create products also allows students the opportunity to more readily revise their work and develop understanding over time (Spitulnik, Zembal & Krajcik, 1998). Because of the digital nature of multimedia documents, students can revisit their productions over time by continuing to construct new versions as they gather more information and develop their ideas further. For instance, a student could continue to add digital images of plant growth over time to a hypermedia document. The student could also link these images to observations of plant growth and to background information.

Finally, with technology tools that support the creation of multiple representations, students can increase the quantity and quality of their writing. Word processing and hypermedia programs help students expand and elaborate on what they have already written.

Teachers need to be cognizant of students who want to create "beautiful" multimedia documents that look, at times, professionally done but that lack substance. Some students will put irrelevant pictures and/or sounds into their documents, not because it helps to present the information but because the students enjoy doing so. This phenomenon not only happens with multimedia documents, but also when teachers ask students to develop a report or a poster. We certainly want to encourage students' creative tendencies to make nice-looking documents but not at the expense of the time needed to conduct research, investigate, or understand the topic in depth.

One way to prevent students from spending all their time on beautifying their documents at the expense of the purpose of the lesson is to give them clear criteria about how you will evaluate their product. Clearly point out that presenting information in a clear manner is the most important criterion. Stress to the students that you will look for

Portfolio Activity 5.9

THE VALUE OF CREATING MULTIMEDIA DOCUMENTS

Materials Needed:
- *PowerPoint, HyperStudio,* or *ClarisWorks*
- Computer lab

A. Using a multimedia program, such as *Hyperstudio,* create a multimedia document. Create a document about a topic of interest to you (such as a science topic, a hobby, or a sport) or a document that records your development as a teacher. If you choose to document your development as a teacher, you could include your philosophy of teaching, video clips of your teaching, commentary on your teaching (critiques), reflections on becoming a teacher, examples of your planning documents, commentary on your teaching plans, and perhaps some comments from your cooperating teachers or students you are teaching. You might want to focus on just one area of teaching (a theme), such as how you created an environment that fosters inquiry or how you promote student collaboration; however, you might choose to document and comment on several areas of your teaching.

B. Your multimedia document should include the following components:
- an introduction that describes your multimedia document,
- written or oral commentary about your video clips,
- sound (a recording, a purposefully selected sound effect or music),
- a picture (scanned from a conventional photo or a digital photo), and
- a graph or table.

depth and accuracy of information. Stress also that the images, videos, and sounds that are used in the document should help viewers understand the presentation and not serve as extraneous special effects. You can certainly include appearance and ease of use in your evaluation, but these should not be the major criteria in a science class. See Chapter 9 for further information on how to use rubrics.

To help students learn how to make presentations look good without sacrificing content, you might enlist the help of a peer. The technology teacher could teach about Web design, for example, model how to make a professional-looking page, and grade students on the design of their projects.

The art teacher could teach about color and aesthetics. Do Portfolio Activity 5.9 now to explore the value of having students create multimedia documents.

Digital Cameras

Students can use **digital cameras** as data collection tools. For instance, if students are investigating the growth of bean plants, they can take digital images in addition to taking written descriptions and measurements of their plants. Students can take their digital cameras on stream walks to make visual records of what they see. One of the advantages of using digital photography instead of conventional cameras is the great ease of integrating the images into multimedia documents (Rivet & Schneider, 2001).

Hi-ce's *Go and Tell* application for the Palm allows students to use the Palm and the Palm's digital camera as a camera and an annotation tool to create multimedia products. Students can take a picture and then annotate their image on the Palm. Back in the classroom, students can easily upload their files to a computer, and the *Go and Tell* application will create a Web page with the students' images and annotations.

Go and Tell
software

Video

Students can also use **video cameras** as data collection tools. For instance, students might use a video camera to collect information about the quality of their stream. If students use *digital* video cameras, they can easily incorporate a short segment of video into a multimedia document. Apple Computers' iMovie tools have made it simple for even very young learners to edit movies and incorporate them into multimedia documents.

Learning Technologies to Support the Creation of Learning Communities

Telecommunication, including e-mail, threaded discussions, and chat rooms, gives students access to a wider community across the world. Students can use e-mail to communicate with other schools, community members, and even members of the scientific community. Threaded discussions allow students to follow up on questions and sets of responses that build on each other. One student might submit a question to which several students or scientists might reply, sometimes with new questions. One advantage of this technology is the rapid rate of response that the medium encourages. Another advantage is the breadth of response that can occur.

Chat rooms allow a number of individuals from a variety of locations to communicate in real time. Through chat room technology, live conferences can be set up involving students from one school, scientists, and students from other schools. These conferences encourage and support students in finding solutions to questions of interest and in debating ideas and evidence.

For instance, the *One Sky Many Voices* (Songer, 1996, 1998) project involves middle school science students investigating meteorological phenomena. This project links Internet resources, real-time and near-time data, and visualization resources with peers across the globe and practicing scientists to promote authentic science teaching. Students can communicate directly with individuals who have firsthand experiences with phenomena they are studying and work directly with professional-quality, real-time data in much the same manner as professional scientists do. Through message boards, students talk with other students and meteorologists to share data and information. You can learn more about the *One Sky Many Voices* project at OLC link.

GLOBE, Global Learning and Observations to Benefit the Environment (Rock, Blackwell, Miller, & Hardison, 1997), provides opportunities for children to communicate and collaborate with scientists and other GLOBE students around the world. Students can take part in threaded discussions with scientists on a variety of topics related to various investigations. GLOBE also supports students in the collection and analysis of data. In GLOBE, students take scientifically valid measurements in the fields of atmosphere, hydrology, soils, and land cover. After collecting data, they report their data through the Internet. Students compare their data to archived data collected in previous years. Over a million primary and secondary students in more than 10,000 schools have taken part in the program.

ROLE OF THE TEACHER

The use of the computer as a laboratory tool to support data collection and visualization changes the science classroom into a science laboratory. Achieving this goal takes much support from the teacher. Teachers must encourage students and provide opportunities

---

Key Idea

The World Wide Web, in conjunction with various programs, allows the teacher to create a learning community that extends beyond the classroom.

Online Projects That Encourage Telecommunication

for them to use the various tools to ask new questions. Many students will not feel comfortable asking their own "What if" questions unless you give them permission. For instance, let's suppose that students are exploring whether stirring helps to cool a hot cup of chocolate. In the process, students might also wonder if blowing over the surface of the cup or the type of cup makes a difference. As a teacher, you need to encourage these types of further explorations using technology tools. One way to do this is to ask the class to keep track of additional questions that come to mind during their initial exploration. As a whole class activity, students can share the variety of questions that they developed and discuss which might be explored using technology tools. Another way to promote the exploring of additional questions is to have students share the questions with you in their small groups. Because technology tools have been designed to promote easy explorations as well as the acquisition and visualization of data, give students permission to carry out these additional explorations using the appropriate technology tools.

> ### Key Idea
>
> Teachers play a key role in helping students to use technology effectively for exploring science.

Although technology tools have features that allow students to explore and take part in a variety of scientific practices, too often technology is used in a way that is as unimaginative and boring as a dry lecture. If the technology tools are used as fill-in worksheets, children will do just that. They will fill in the worksheet rather than cognitively engage in exploring the science phenomena. As a teacher, you need to create an environment that will encourage students to explore. As you have done in other aspects of inquiry, you will need to support children in the process. (See the section "Supporting Students' Implementation of Investigations" in Chapter 4 for some ideas.) You can do this by modeling how to use the technology to engage in inquiry-based investigations. For example, you could show students how motion detectors can be used to calculate the speed of a moving object.

Teachers also need to make sure that students understand the mechanics and concepts behind the technology. For example, a student should not use a temperature probe unless he understands how to use the probe and what he is measuring. You should first teach students how to use the probe accurately and safely. To teach students what they are measuring, you might first have students use the probe to explore who has the coldest hands in the class. This can be done without the use of technology by having students determine a ranking based on their sense of touch. Next, contrast their sense-of-touch rankings with the recordings from the temperature probe.

Just as you will need to support students in interpreting graphs that result from their investigations, you will need to support students in interpreting the visualizations created by technology visualization programs. The FeederWatch project allows students to see a distribution of a bird population on a color-coded chart of North America. Although this type of visualization is becoming commonplace in newspapers, many students might still not know how to interpret it. One way to help students learn how to interpret distribution maps is to allow them to create a distribution map of a bird population across North America using their own bodies. First download a data chart of a population of birds from the FeederWatch site. Select a bird, such as the American Robin, with which all of the children are familiar. Next, using chalk or masking tape, trace a map of North America or a map of a state on the classroom floor. Let's imagine that you trace the State of Illinois. For every five robins found in a particular location of the state, have one student stand on the map in that location. If there were sixty robins seen in southeastern Illinois in November, you would have twelve students stand in southeastern Illinois. Another fifty birds were spotted in southwestern Illinois, so you would have ten students stand there. However, only ten birds were spotted in northeastern and five in northwestern Illinois in November. You would have two students go stand in the northeastern part of the state and only one stand in the northwestern part of the state. You would then have students look around to observe the pattern. You could ask students where more robins were spotted in Illinois in November of last year. Using such graphic techniques, you can help your students learn how to interpret distribution maps.

INTEGRATING TECHNOLOGY INTO INSTRUCTION

Frequently, teachers, administrators, and parents mistakenly believe that just because technology is used, students will learn from it. Our work and that of others shows that this statement doesn't even come close to representing what needs to happen in classrooms to promote learning. Technology is rarely an effective standalone teaching tool. Using technology effectively in the classroom generally requires that teachers spend substantial time creating a learning environment to support it. As depicted in Scenario 2, technology cannot be used only once in a while. If it is going to benefit students, they need to use it frequently so that they perceive it as a tool. Perhaps more importantly, technology should not be used just for the sake of using it. Technology tools should only be used if they help the teacher meet instructional objectives.

Before using technology for instruction, we encourage teachers to do the following:

- Work extensively with the tool so that students fully understand its capabilities and limitations.
- Consider carefully the understandings that students might gain from working with the tool and how those understandings fit in with the rest of the curriculum.
- Plan and create a learning environment that will help students develop an understanding of the tool and its relevance to learning that goes beyond the superficial procedural level of knowing what buttons to push or what commands to type.

When used over time as a tool, technologies like those discussed in this chapter can help students learn. The tools, however, cannot be used as a once-in-a-while activity. To impact student learning, students need to use technology tools in a sustained manner over time. Just as it is too time consuming and complex to learn how to use a table saw to cut just one board, learning to use new technology tools is too time consuming and complex just to use for one day. To benefit from the time and effort it takes to learn the tool, students need repeated opportunities to use new technology tools throughout the school year.

Issues to Consider When Incorporating Technological Tools into Your Curriculum

When designing lessons to use technologies, we encourage you to consider the following ideas:

- What science ideas will the technology tool help students explore? Is technology the best instructional method for teaching these ideas?

- Does the tool allow students to be active participants in creating their own understandings, rather than passive recipients of factual material? What support materials or activities can you design to encourage active student participation?
- What aspects of the tool do you expect to be difficult for students to understand and/or use? How can you structure initial explorations with the tool to address these difficulties?
- Do you expect gender or cultural differences in how interested students will be in the tool? If so, what support materials or activities can you design to address this issue?
- Are there potential misunderstandings that the tool might encourage? If so, what support materials or activities can you design to address these potential misunderstandings?

If the technology tool cannot help you address some important learning outcome, then we encourage you not to use it. Instructional time is too precious to use on activities that don't directly address what you want students to learn. Like hands-on activities, technology should not be used just for the sake of using it. You need to think about whether the technology helps students explore phenomena that they otherwise could not explore. You need to consider whether the technology supports students carrying out investigations.

Like other instructional interventions, technology-based activities need to engage children in the learning process and help them create their own understandings. The learning technologies that we presented in this chapter have the potential to do this. If the technology presents information in a manner that students must simply receive passively, then you should probably not use the technology. If books or other media can present the information or teach a concept more effectively, use them. As experienced teachers, we always look for powerful instructional activities to use with our students. However, it is the role of a professional teacher to determine the simplest, most effective instructional strategy to use to teach a concept.

Although many children find technology interesting and many of them have less difficulty using it than many adults do, as a teacher you need to consider all the potential difficulties students might have using technology tools. For instance, in using the World Wide Web, it isn't unusual for students to navigate away from a website that they find valuable to a point from which they can't find their way back. Having students bookmark electronically the URL or write down each useful URL on a piece of paper is one way to prevent this.

Many studies have documented that boys will dominate in the use of computers over girls and other at-risk students who traditionally do not succeed at science. For example, the American Association of University Women (AAUW) website reports research that indicates that girls are not well represented in the area of technology. This research reveals that it isn't that girls aren't interested in technology, but that girls find many computer programming classes dull and tedious and computer games redundant and violent. Equity issues come into play when boys in classes are given more attention by teachers during technology use or allowed to dominate the computer and other technology tools. The AAUW research suggests that teachers need to emphasize the computer as a productivity tool. Further, teachers need to watch for unequal use and ensure that students have equal access to using the computer and keyboard. One easy technique is to tell students to change who is using the keyboard or the equipment every fifteen minutes. You could even use a timer. We also recommend that you have no more than two students share a

Technology Research from the American Association of University Women

Portfolio Activity 5.10

USING LEARNING TECHNOLOGIES TO HELP STUDENTS LEARN SCIENCE

Materials Needed:
- Various computer tools discussed in the chapter
- Paper and a pencil

A. Select a content area that students have difficult learning. What technology tools might be appropriate for helping students learning this idea? Explain.

B. As a teacher, what problems might you encounter? What difficulties would students have using the tool?

C. Record your ideas in your portfolio.

D. After reading this chapter, return to Portfolio Activity 5.1. Record in your portfolio any new thoughts you have.

computer or other learning technologies. We have observed, as have others, that once there are more than two students at a computer, one of the students tends to daydream and not be engaged in the activities.

Some programs might unintentionally give students misunderstandings about the world. Although simulation programs are valuable in helping students take part in experiences that they otherwise might not have, some of the generalizations that occur in these programs might give an overly simple view of how a process works. For instance, a program that represents the microscopic world of atoms as small spheres could lead students to think that atoms actually look like spheres. Stress to students that they are only seeing a representation of atoms.

Although we have tried to show throughout this chapter that new learning technologies can help students learn important ideas in science and that they can also help students perform investigations, they should not be used indiscriminately. We encourage the use of learning technologies when they are the most effective instructional strategy for teaching a concept or skill, and we encourage you to be aware of the possible pitfalls when using technology with children. Take the time to plan carefully how technology will be used and how to help your students use it safely and effectively. Portfolio Activity 5.10 will help you explore the use of learning technologies in your classroom.

Key Idea

The use of technologies in elementary and middle schools can be a very powerful instructional intervention; however, technology should not be used indiscriminately.

ONLINE LEARNING CENTER

CHAPTER REVIEW   www.mhhe.com/krajcik2e

Go to the Online Learning Center at **www.mhhe.com/krajcik2e** to review important content from the chapter and key terms, take a chapter assessment, and link to the chapter's websites.

CHAPTER SUMMARY

In this chapter, we discussed the use of learning technologies to support students in developing meaningful understandings of science concepts and in doing investigations. We defined *learning technologies* as the computers, software, and various peripherals that support students' learning. We discussed how learning technologies can help students actively engage with phenomena, use and apply knowledge, find new sources of information, create multiple representations of learning, and create learning communities. We explored how technology tools such as microcomputer-based laboratories are particularly powerful because they allow students to collect, visualize, and analyze data. The simultaneous linking of real-time data collection with graphs that help students visualize data seems to support student learning. Simulations, microworlds, and interactive multimedia allow students to explore phenomena when it is unsafe, too expensive, impractical, or perhaps even unethical for students to have firsthand experiences. Such environments allow students to ask "What if?" questions, make predictions, and test their ideas.

The World Wide Web brings many benefits to the classroom. Through the Web, students have unprecedented access to the newest information and data. In many cases, students can use the same data as scientists. However, using the Web also brings challenges, particularly the high number of sites that are returned when students conduct a search. Many of these sites are irrelevant or contain inaccurate information. We recommend that, because of these issues and the limited time available in classrooms, for research students use digital libraries that contain preselected and preapproved sites. As students become more proficient in using the Web, they can learn to navigate on their own and evaluate the sites they find.

Learning technologies also allow students to create their own multimedia documents. Students can thus document their understandings using different types of media. Learning technologies also open up the classroom to sharing and debating with other students and scientists to create an extended learning community.

Although we strongly believe that learning technologies present many advantages for instruction in science, we do not support using technology just for the sake of using it. We encourage teachers to make use of technology when it can help students meet important instructional learning outcomes or develop meaningful understandings. It is the responsibility of the teacher to make decisions regarding when and how to best use learning technologies in the science classroom.

CHAPTER HIGHLIGHTS

- Humans have always used tools to help them perform difficult tasks, both physical and intellectual.
- Technologies include computers, software, and various peripherals.
- Learning technologies can support teachers and students in project-based science, because they can help students and teachers communicate, carry out investigations, and develop products.
- Using learning technologies in the classroom is important in helping to overcome the digital divide.
- Technology can play a powerful role in enhancing student and teacher motivation by actively engaging students in the learning process.
- Technology can help students develop understandings of complex, abstract ideas.
- Technology transforms the way teachers teach.
- When students become actively engaged with phenomena using technology, they are able to explore phenomena they would otherwise not be able to access.
- The creation of multimedia artifacts and products helps students share information and develop meaningful understandings.
- Technology can generate dynamic visuals to represent abstract concepts.

- Technology supports students in communicating and collaborating with other students and community members.
- Microcomputer-based laboratories (MBLs) allow students to use microcomputers as laboratory tools.
- Visualization tools allow students to explore and manipulate data to see trends they would otherwise be unable to see.
- Simulations, microworlds, and interactive multimedia combine
  - Video.
  - Pictures.
  - Computer graphics.
  - Text.
  - Interactivity.
- Simulations, microworlds, and interactive multimedia present to students phenomena that otherwise would be inaccessible, too hazardous, too time-consuming, or too expensive.
- Some learning technologies help students apply their knowledge by supporting them in planning, explaining, and reflecting.
- Models differ from simulations in that, by developing models, students describe the concepts, principles, and rules that govern the phenomena being modeled.
- The expansion of technology, especially of the World Wide Web, has enabled students easily to obtain information about key ideas, concepts, and subject matter topics that arise as they explore solutions to questions.
- The Web provides several advantages
  - A broad range of information.
  - Primary data sources.
  - Instruments.
  - Computational instruments.
  - Publishing tools.
  - Collaboration tools.
- There are difficulties with the Web, particularly for young learners
  - Students have difficulty locating and taking advantage of information.
  - Students often become lost and disoriented while navigating.
  - Students require a substantial amount of support to frame their activities.
  - Students do not evaluate the resources they find.
  - Students have difficulty using Web tools to the extent they are designed to be used.
- Digital libraries can help overcome many of these problems by screening documents available on the Web for
  - Content.
  - Validity.
  - Developmental level of the learner.
- There has been an explosive growth in the use of media (sound, graphics, color pictures, and video) that provides for representation of concepts in multiple, simultaneous ways.
- Multiple representations can enhance students' understanding of concepts.
- Application software such as word processors, spreadsheets, desktop publishing programs, and drawing programs helps students create a variety of products to represent what they know in a variety of forms.
- Students can use digital cameras as data collection tools.

- Telecommunications, including e-mail, threaded discussions, and chat rooms, allow students access to a wider community.
- Using technology in the classroom takes much support from the teacher.
- Frequently, teachers, administrators, and parents mistakenly believe that, just because technology is used, students will learn.
- Technology tools should only be used if they help the teacher meet instructional objectives.
- The use of technologies in elementary and middle schools can be a very powerful instructional intervention; however, technology should not be used indiscriminately.

KEY TERMS

content knowledge (181)

digital cameras (187)

digital divide (168)

digital libraries (182)

interactive multimedia (178)

learning technologies (171)

metacognitive knowledge (180)

microcomputer-based laboratories (MBLs) (172)

microworlds (178)

models (179)

multiple representations (184)

primary data sources (182)

probes (172)

procedural knowledge (172)

real-time graphs (173)

simulations (179)

telecommunication (188)

video cameras (188)

visualization tools (176)

REFERENCES

American Association for the Advancement of Science. 1993. *Benchmarks for science literacy.* New York: Oxford University Press.

Anderson, L. W., and D. R. Krathwohl, eds. 2001. *A taxonomy for learning, teaching and assessing: A revision of Bloom's taxonomy of educational objectives.* New York: Longman.

Brasell, H. 1987. The effect of real-time laboratory graphing on learning graphic representation of distance and velocity. *Journal of Research in Science Teaching* 24 (4): 385–95.

Christmann, E. P. (2002). Graphing calculators. *Science Scope* 25(5):46–48.

Cohen, K. C., ed. 1997. *Internet links for science education: Student-scientist partnerships.* New York: Plenum.

Dwyer, D. C. 1994. Apple classrooms of tomorrow: What we've learned. *Educational Leadership* 51:4–10.

Edelson, D. C., D. N. Gordin, and R. D. Pea. 1999. Addressing the challenges of inquiry-based learning through technology and curriculum design. *Journal of the Learning Sciences* 8(3&4): 391–450.

Harel, I., and S. Papert. 1990. Software design as a learning environment. *Interactive Learning Environments* 1:1–32.

Helfgott, D., and M. Westhaver. 2000. *Inspiration 6.0.* Portland, Ore.: Inspiration Software, Inc.

Horwitz, P., and M. Christie. 2000. Computer-based manipulation for teaching scientific reasoning: An example. In *Innovations in science and mathematics education: Advanced designs for technologies and learning,* eds. M. Jacobson and R. B. Kozma. New York: Lawrence Erlbaum Associates.

Inspiration Software, Inc. 2000. *Kidspiration.* Portland, Ore.: Author.

Kozma, R. 1991. Learning with media. *Review of Educational Research* 61(2): 179–211.

Krajcik, J., B. Blumenfeld, R. Marx, and E. Soloway. 2000. Instructional, curricular, and technological supports for inquiry in science classrooms. In *Inquiry into inquiry: Science learning and teaching,* eds. J. Minstell and E. Van Zee. Washington, D.C.: American Association for the Advancement of Science Press, 283–315.

Krajcik, J. S., and J. W. Layman. 1992. Microcomputer-based laboratories in the science classroom. In *Research matters to the science teacher,* eds. F. Lawrenz, K. Cochran, J. Krajcik, and P. Simpson. Manhattan, Kans.: National Association of Research in Science Teaching.

Linn, M. C. 1998. The impact of technology on science instruction: Historical trends and current opportunities. In *International handbook of science education,* ed. M. C. Linn. Netherlands: Kluwer Publishers.

Linn, M. C. 1992. The computer as a learning partner: Can computer tools teach science? In *This year in school science 1991: Technology for teaching and learning,* eds. K. Sheingold, L. G. Roberts, and S. M. Malcolm. Washington, D.C.: American Association for the Advancement of Science, 31–69.

Linn, M. C., and S. Hsi. 2000. *Computers, teachers, peers: Science learning partners.* Mahwah, N.J.: Lawrence Erlbaum Associates, Inc.

Linn, M. C., J. W. Layman, and R. Nachmias. 1987. Cognitive consequences of microcomputer-based laboratories: Graphing skills development. *Contemporary Educational Psychology* 12, 244–53.

Linn, M. C., N. B. Songer, E. L. Lewis, and J. Stern. 1993. Using technology to teach thermodynamics: Achieving integrated understandings. In *Advanced educational technology for mathematics and science,* vol. 107, ed. D. L. Ferguson. Berlin, Germany: Springer-Verlag.

Metcalf-Jackson, S., J. S. Krajcik, and E. Soloway. 2000. Model-It: A design retrospective. In *Innovations in science and mathematics education: Advanced designs for technologies and learning,* eds. M. Jacobson and R. B. Kozma. New York: Lawrence Erlbaum Associates.

Mokros, J. R., and R. F. Tinker. 1987. The impact of microcomputer-based labs on children's ability to interpret graphs. *Journal of Research in Science Teaching* 24(4):369–83.

National Research Council. 1996. *National science education standards.* Washington, D.C.: National Academy Press.

Novak, A., and C. Gleason. 2001. Incorporating portable technology to enhance an inquiry: Project-based middle school science classroom. In *Portable technologies: Science learning in context,* eds. R. Tinker and J. S. Krajcik. Netherlands: Kluwer Publishers.

Rivet, A., and R. Schneider. 2001. Ubiquitous images: Digital cameras to support student inquiry. Paper presented at the Annual Meeting of the National Association for Research in Science Teaching, St. Louis, Mo.

Rock, B. N., T. R. Blackwell, D. Miller, and A. Hardison. 1997. The GLOBE Program: A model for international environmental education. In *Internet links for science education: Student-scientist partnerships,* ed. K. C. Cohen. New York: Plenum.

Salomon, G., T. Globerson, and D. Perkins. 1991. Partners in cognition: Extending human intelligence with intelligent technologies. *Educational Researcher* 20, 2–9.

Songer, N. 1998. Can technology bring students closer to science? In *International handbook of science education,* eds. B. J. Fraser and K. G. Tobin. Dordrecht, The Netherlands: Kluwer.

Songer, N. 1996. Exploring learning opportunities in coordinated network-enhanced classroom: A case of kids as global scientists. *The Journal of Learning Sciences* 5.

Spitulnik, M. W., S. Stratford, J. Krajcik, and E. Soloway. 1997. Using technology to support students' artifact construction in science. In *International handbook of science education,* ed. K. Tobin. Netherlands: Kluwer Publishers.

Spitulnik, M. W., C. Zembal, and J. Krajcik. 1998. Using hypermedia to represent student understanding: Science learners and preservice teachers. In *Teaching science for understanding: A human constructivist view,* ed. G. D. Phye. San Diego, Calif.: Academic Press.

Wallace, R., J. Kupperman, J. Krajcik, and E. Soloway. 2000. Science on the Web: Students on-line in a sixth grade classroom. *Journal of Learning Sciences* 9(1): 75–104

White, B. Y., and J. R. Frederiksen. 2000. Technology tools and instructional approaches for making scientific inquiry accessible to all. In *Innovations in science and mathematics education: Advanced designs for technologies and learning,* eds. M. Jacobson and R. B. Kozma. New York: Lawrence Erlbaum Associates.

Chapter 6

How Do I Develop Collaboration in the Science Classroom?

INTRODUCTION

THE NATURE OF COLLABORATION

TYPES OF COLLABORATIVE LEARNING

CREATING A COLLABORATIVE ENVIRONMENT

USING TECHNOLOGY TOOLS TO CREATE A
    COLLABORATIVE ENVIRONMENT

CHALLENGES THAT ARISE WHEN STUDENTS
    COLLABORATE IN SMALL GROUPS

WHY COLLABORATION ALMOST ALWAYS WORKS
    BETTER THAN INDIVIDUAL LEARNING

CHAPTER LEARNING PERFORMANCES

- *Describe various types of collaboration.*
- *Explain the role a teacher can play in supporting collaboration.*
- *Clarify challenges that a teacher might need to overcome to implement collaborative learning groups.*
- *Describe how to help children learn skills needed to work in collaborative groups.*
- *Critique learning environments to determine their ability to foster collaborative learning.*
- *Design and implement different types of collaborative learning environments.*
- *Explain why collaborative learning is almost always better than individual learning and explain how it particularly helps female and minority students pursue science study.*

INTRODUCTION

This chapter explores the nature of collaboration and why it almost always works better than individual learning. The topic of collaboration raises a number of questions: *How do I get students to work together on intellectually challenging tasks? How do I get members of the community to work with students to find answers to their questions? What are the benefits of such a classroom environment? What is the role of the teacher in a classroom characterized by collaboration?* This chapter will address these and other questions. Scenarios will illustrate the various types of collaboration among students, teachers, and members of the community. Because collaborative learning doesn't just happen in a classroom, the chapter focuses on creating a collaborative environment over a long period of time. You will learn about the social skills students need to work in groups with others and how to hold students accountable during collaboration. The chapter concludes with a discussion of ways to overcome challenges that might arise in the implementing of collaborative groups. We'll begin with scenarios of several types of group situations that you may have experienced in elementary or middle school. As you read each scenario, focus on what the teacher is doing or thinking, what the students are doing or thinking, and how students are working together to complete an assignment.

Scenario 1: Group Work with Little Guidance

Your fourth-grade teacher, Mrs. Weinstein, has covered the topic of dinosaurs for several weeks. Now she explains to your class that you are going to work in teams to complete a project on dinosaurs. Mrs. Weinstein divides your class into teams of four students. She tells you that you and your teammates are to write a report on a certain type of dinosaur, draw a picture of the dinosaur, and give a class presentation about the dinosaur. Shelly, who is really bossy, tells everyone else in the group what to do, and she dominates the entire project. She decides which dinosaur you will research and how the report will be written. She instructs Marcus to search through some encyclopedias from the library, but he doesn't read them as Shelly has asked. Frustrated, Shelly takes the books home, reads them, and writes the report for everyone else. Sarah, who has good handwriting, recopies the report Shelly wrote. You can draw well, so you are left to draw the picture of the dinosaur for the cover. Although you and the others find Shelly's bossy behavior frustrating, you all know you will receive a good grade because she is smart, so you happily let her do all the work. Shelly makes the presentation to the class while you and the others stand behind her. One classmate asks a question; you don't know the answer because you didn't learn much about dinosaurs anyway, but, luckily, Shelly is able to answer it.

In this first scenario, the topic was selected by the teacher. The teacher placed the students in groups but gave very little guidance or assistance that would ensure that students worked together in a joint intellectual effort. Although the students did cooperate with each other enough to complete the project, they did not have the skills to work together effectively. As a result, students were not motivated. Although all the students received the same grade, not all learned about dinosaurs.

Scenario 2: Individual Jobs in Group Work

As a whole class, you read the textbook section on cells. Then the teacher, Ms. Potter, places you into groups of five to learn about cells. Your teacher instructs your group to learn all you can from reference books. Another group learns how to use a microscope to view cheek (animal) and onion (plant) cells. A third group learns how to use a software program on cells. A fourth group watches a video that compares and contrasts plant and animal cells. Ms. Potter assigns each student in each group a job: a runner to get the materials, a recorder of the findings, a timer to keep the group on time, the manager to keep everyone on task, and a cheerleader to keep everyone involved. You are assigned to be the runner. You retrieve the encyclopedias from the shelf for your group and then proceed to watch others in the class. You wish you had been in the computer group because you find reading the encyclopedia boring. When it comes time to share your group's work, you wonder where the information came from, because you hadn't really been paying attention. The other groups share their information about microscopes, the computer, and the video. Their projects seem really interesting, and you learn a lot from them.

In this scenario, the teacher assigned each student a "job" so that the work was shared by members of the group. The teacher provided each group some guidance to complete the activity. However, because the teacher had selected the problems and learning approaches for each group, the technique did not motivate all students to learn. Some team projects seemed more fun than others, and some students' attention wandered. They didn't learn the intended material. In addition, not every "job" was equally important, and not every job was critical to completing the task.

Scenario 3: Using Expert Groups

Mr. Earl Jackson tells you that you are going to investigate the topic of sound and that the goal of this lesson is for you to become an expert on one subtopic or concept and teach it to others. Mr. Jackson divides the class into teams of four and assigns each team member a job. One person serves as a runner who gathers the materials, one is a recorder who writes down the results, one acts as a manager who gets to do the experiment, and one is the timer who makes sure the group completes the project in the time allotted. Mr. Jackson also provides you with a sheet of questions to answer to help you determine if you are "expert" enough to teach the concept to other students. Your assignment is to find out what material (air, water, or solids) sound travels through best. Sarah, assigned to be the runner, collects the supplies (a bucket of water, a tuning fork, and a paper tube) for the activity. John, the manager, gets to experiment with the tuning forks to see when they seem the loudest. You record the results after everyone agrees upon the answers. Marcus watches the clock the whole time and announces the time at ten-minute intervals. Once each of you has become an "expert" and knows that sound travels best in solids, you are put into "learning teams" where you teach this idea to three students who had not been in your group. You engage the three new students in the same activity with the tuning fork, water, and tube of paper to demonstrate that sound travels best through the solid table, next best through the water, and least well through the air. You feel happy that you did the experiment that only John had been permitted to do when you were in your first group. Each of the three other students has become an expert in another topic and teaches you what he or she has learned. You have a great time and really understand which material sound travels through best. Although you learn some interesting ideas from what the other students taught you, you are still a bit fuzzy on others. On the test Mr. Jackson gives, you do well on questions about the type of materials sound travels through, and you do okay on the items about frequency, pitch, amplitude, and sound insulation that the other expert teams taught you.

In this example, the teacher structured the lesson by choosing the activities and providing all the directions for the students. The teacher provided students with guidance on the criteria for being an expert. In this way, each student was cognitively engaged because she needed to teach the concepts to others. This strategy seemed to work well.

Scenario 4: A Learning Community

Your class has been exploring the driving question "What causes living things to become endangered?" Ms. Nadarajah leads the class in a discussion of possible threats to plant and animal survival. After you all decide on some causes of endangerment, Ms. Nadarajah lets you choose your teammates. One group decides to investigate how pollution affects animals and plants. They conduct experiments on plants with various amounts of acids and other substances, and they research the decline of frog populations throughout the world. Another group studies the gorilla and the effect of past wars in Rwanda on the gorilla population. A third group investigates how the sea turtle in Florida has been affected by humans building along the coastline where they reproduce. Your group decides to learn more about the rainforest and causes of endangerment in the rainforests of the world. In your group, each member discusses his or her interests and ideas for investigating the rainforest. Juanita says, "I read the story called *The Great Kapok Tree* by Lynn Cherry, and I think the animals are dying because they're cutting down all the trees." Monika adds, "Yeah, but my Dad says it's because we eat a lot of hamburgers. The ranchers cut down trees to raise cows." "I don't know," Brian says. "I think it has more to do with pollution. Pollution is killing the animals." "Yeah, I saw something on TV about frogs dying because of pollution, and there's frogs in the rainforest," says Kameel. "Yeah, but I don't think frogs are the only animals dying in the rainforest," replies Monika. "And what would cutting down trees have to do with frogs dying? They live in water!" says Kameel. Ms. Nadarajah comes over to work with your group to help you figure out how you would finish the task. Ms. Nadarajah also asks you questions to get you thinking about what types of artifacts, or products to share, you might create to show what you learn.

Through collaborative planning and some guidance from Ms. Nadarajah, your group decides to divide this topic into types of endangered animals in the rainforest, causes of endangerment, and solutions to endangerment. As a team, you decide to learn about these three topics by reading books, visiting the zoo, watching a video on rainforests that you noticed in the school library, and e-mailing students in South America to talk with them. You divide into smaller working pairs to answer questions about endangered animals, causes, and solutions. Over the course of a few days, you find out that deforestation is a major cause of endangerment, so you decided to conduct a small experiment to see what would happen to insect populations in a section of the schoolyard when you slowly changed their habitat by removing sticks and leaves, cutting the grass, and pulling out the grass. Ms. Nadarajah helps you understand what types of insects might live in the area by teaching a lesson about insect classification and helping you locate some resources for insect identification.

At each stage, you keep data and develop artifacts to show what you are learning. You decide to take closeup photos of the schoolyard insect population. Soon after Ms. Nadarajah asks you to give a presentation, you and others in the group analyze and synthesize what you have learned and decide to present your information to classmates in the form of a poster labeled *Cause* and *Effect*. Finally, the big day comes. Your group gives its presentation to the class, and everyone applauds. The other students in the class are very interested in your project, but one team comments that you might have left out variables when comparing insect populations to the rainforest. They wonder if you could really compare the two situations because the rainforest is much more complex than a 3-foot by 3-foot area on the playground. You decide that this is a valid point and begin to wonder how to address it. The other teams present the results of their projects, and you learn that there might be other factors that you did not think about such as acid rain, economic factors, and social factors. These ideas give you some direction for further exploring the rainforest.

In this scenario, the teacher served as an instructional planner and guide. The teacher helped students design questions, provided learning materials, and organized discussions. The driving question "What causes living things to become endangered?" was a meaningful and important question that served to organize the activities. The students in the group formed a learning community. Each negotiated with others in the group to select an investigation. Students shared the work, discussed ideas, and completed portions of the entire project. Differences in opinion were resolved amicably. Members of the community were included in the project. The Internet provided e-mail access to students in South America. The project's direction and outcome were determined by members of the group. The students were involved in "hands-on" investigations of habitats. Students developed "artifacts" that they shared with others. Students critiqued these artifacts and the presentation in a positive manner, thereby providing the group with ideas for future exploration. In this sample scenario, students had a voice in their learning, were motivated, and were cognitively involved. Students worked together to create meaning and understanding. There weren't some "jobs" that were less attractive than others.

This fourth scenario describes a project-based science classroom in which collaborative learning is one of the major instructional features; it involves students, teachers, and members of society in trying to work through an important problem in which people are interested. Collaborative learning requires students to work with others to solve a problem or conduct an investigation.

These four scenarios illustrated different types of collaborative learning. Portfolio Activity 6.1 will further clarify the characteristics of different approaches.

THE NATURE OF COLLABORATION

Understanding the nature of collaboration will help you comprehend its importance in project-based science classrooms. In this section, we will explore two questions about collaboration: *What is collaboration?* and *What are the characteristics of collaboration?*

What Is Collaboration?

Think of **collaboration** as a joint intellectual effort of students, peers, teachers, and community members to investigate a question or problem. When students work with others on a joint intellectual effort to explore a problem and to build understanding, they form a community of learners. For example, a community of learners who are collaborating to answer the question "Why does algae grow in the fish tank?" might debate the cause of

> **Key Idea**
>
> Collaboration is a joint intellectual effort of students, peers, teachers, and community members to investigate a question or problem as a community of learners.

Portfolio Activity 6.1

HOW DOES COLLABORATION CHANGE THE NATURE OF THE CLASSROOM?

Materials Needed:
- Two classrooms to observe

A. With the help of your instructor, a school principal, or a school curriculum director, identify two teachers and classrooms for observation. Obtain permission to observe each of these teachers. Make sure you observe at least one collaborative group setting.

B. As you observe both classrooms, analyze how collaboration changes the nature of the classroom. Try to answer the following questions:
   - How are students working together in these classrooms?
   - How does the teacher structure the group work?
   - Are students given jobs or roles to play? Are the roles or jobs meaningful intellectually, or are they only procedural tasks?
   - Are the jobs or roles necessary to complete the overall task?
   - What is the role of the teacher in the classroom?
   - What are the teacher's objectives in the lesson?
   - What instructional strategies does the teacher use?
   - How does the teacher help students work in groups (by developing interpersonal skills, encouraging students to talk with each other, resolving conflicts)?

C. What do you see as the advantages and challenges of a collaborative classroom? Discuss with peers how these challenges might be overcome.

D. Record your thoughts and observations in your portfolio.

algae in an aquarium. This process encourages students to challenge and support their conceptions and ideas. They work with others in the class to test their ideas and build understanding. They might set up several aquariums under different conditions such as in the window of the classroom with sunlight, in a dark room without sunlight, in a cool place, and in a warm place. The teacher might present a lesson about algae being an aquatic organism that has some characteristics of plants (it makes its own food through the process of photosynthesis) but that lacks true roots, stems, leaves, and embryos. In the lesson, the teacher has students observe algae under a microscope so that they can see these characteristics. The students might ask the owner of a local pet store how to control algae in an aquarium. In this learning community, the students, teachers, and other community members work together to find resolutions to questions or problems.

In Chapter 2, we examined Vygotsky's ideas about child development and learning. Teachers can use Vygotsky's (1986) ideas to create learning environments in which students have contact with others with different levels of expertise; that is, with multiple zones of proximal development. Vygotsky's **zone of proximal development** is described as the difference in performance between what a learner can accomplish unassisted and what he could accomplish with the assistance of a more knowledgeable or capable other. Think of the zone of proximal development as a range of cognitive tasks that you can learn with the assistance of someone who knows more. There are some tasks that you could not master even with assistance, but there are also tasks you could complete with just a little help. For example, a ten-year-old can, over a short period of time with adult guidance, master the process of using a simple single-focus microscope (the zone of proximal development has then shifted, and the ten-year-old might next work on using a microscope with multiple magnification lenses). The same ten-year-old, however, cannot manage using an electron microscope, no matter how many times or how much her teacher or a scientist assists her. So, from Vygotsky's notion of zone of proximal development, we can use the idea that providing timely and relevant support and guidance to learners can be of great assistance in their development of science knowledge and skills.

CONNECTING TO NATIONAL SCIENCE EDUCATION STANDARDS

Science Education Teaching Standards
Student understanding is actively constructed through individual and social processes (p. 29).

Such a learning environment can be created by benchmark lessons, lessons where more knowledgeable others provide students with basic knowledge or skills that are just beyond their level of intellectual attainment and that will enable them to expand and continue their learning. (See Chapter 7 for more information or benchmark lessons.) Students learning about the cause of algae in an aquarium, for example, are exposed to new concepts when the teacher gives a benchmark lesson on how to observe algae under the microscope, a skill they did not possess earlier. When the teacher supports their learning by teaching them how to use a microscope, the teacher provides that little bit of help needed to help students be able to conduct their own investigation—something they were unable to complete before learning this skill. The students can now learn that algae make their own food through the process of photosynthesis. This concept helps the students understand that an aquarium in the sunlight will grow algae more quickly than will an aquarium placed away from a window. This same type of learning environment is created when a student explains how his family keeps algae from growing in the swimming pool or when the pet store owner explains how she keeps algae from forming on the aquariums in her store.

What Are the Characteristics of Collaboration?

Collaborative learning, unlike other types of group arrangements, encourages high levels of *equality* and *mutuality* (Damon & Phelps, 1989) as students work with others to create meaning. **Equality** refers similarity in the *level* of knowledge or ability that members bring to a group. In a collaborative classroom, each member should contribute equally (Cohen, 1998). This does not mean that each member of the group possesses the same knowledge or abilities—in fact, it is desirable that members have had different experiences and contribute varied prior knowledge and varied abilities. This is different from other group arrangements that encourage only cooperation—getting along or being compliant with others in a group to finish a task. It also differs from task sharing in which each person in a group completes one part of a presentation thrown together with little or no shared effort. For example, of the students studying algae growth, one has a swimming pool at home and is familiar with the techniques used to control algae; one has a fish tank in her bedroom, and she has noticed that it has less algae when she keeps it away from the window; and one thinks he has algae growing in his shower at home (where it is warm and moist), so he has theories about the cause of algae growth. All three share different, but equal, ideas with the group.

Mutuality refers to the common goals of the students. In collaborative classrooms, mutuality should be high—the students in a group should be working to answer the same question, complete the same task, reach the same goal, or find solutions to the same problem. The students studying algae growth are all investigating why algae grows on the fish aquarium in the classroom. They have a driving question that they are investigating together. They all work together to find ways to prevent algae growth.

Other group arrangements sometimes involve each student having a separate "job." The students have different goals—each task corresponds to a different goal. Look back to the first scenario in this chapter. Although the students did cooperate to present a dinosaur report to the class, the goal of one student was to make sure the report was illustrated. The goal of another student was to make sure the report was legible. Mutuality was low.

Another characteristic of collaboration is that it creates **meaning**. Think back to the four scenarios that started this chapter. In the first two scenarios, students in the groups did not work together to understand the topics. Some students did all of the work; others did not play important roles that would enable them to develop any understanding. Some students' attention wandered, and most did not cognitively engage in the learning process. In contrast, the third and fourth scenarios illustrated students collaborating. In the third scenario, students shared their expertise on various aspects of sound. In the fourth scenario, students worked together and with others (the teacher and members of a broader learning community) to create understanding about the rainforest.

The students studying the question "Why does algae grow in the fish tank?" were collaborating because they created meaning, and they experienced high levels of equality and mutuality. They all contributed knowledge and skills to the group's effort and they worked to answer the same question. Without creating understanding and establishing high levels of equality and mutuality, group work consists solely of students *being* in groups.

> ### Key Idea
> Collaborative learning differs from other group learning arrangements in that students each bring a similar level of knowledge and skills to the group (equality), students work together to answer the same question (mutuality), and together they create meaning.

TYPES OF COLLABORATIVE LEARNING

Collaboration can occur among all members of a community. In this section we will explore three types of collaborative learning: among students, between students and teacher, and between students and community.

Among Students

CONNECTING TO
NATIONAL SCIENCE EDUCATION STANDARDS

Science Education Teaching Standards
Science often is a collaborative endeavor, and all science depends on the ultimate sharing and debate of ideas. When carefully guided by teachers to ensure full participation by all, interactions among individuals and groups in the classroom can be vital in deepening the understanding of science concepts and the nature of scientific endeavors. The size of a group depends on age, resources, and the nature of inquiry (p. 31–32).

Student-to-student collaboration is a powerful method of instruction. It can occur at several different levels, ranging from one-on-one collaboration to various group configurations. In one-on-one situations, one student can tutor another. A pair of students can also work together to investigate science questions. This one-on-one collaboration can occur within a classroom or even across a geographical distance via e-mail or regular mail. Collaboration among groups of students can involve students of a single class working together on a project, students from two or more classes within a school building or district exchanging ideas, or students from one class communicating with other classes via e-mail or regular mail.

Imagine groups of fourth-grade students trying to answer the driving question "How do things with wheels help us move?" As students begin experimenting with skateboards, rollerblades, bicycles, and other everyday objects with wheels to find out how they help us move, they find that they need to multiply distance by force to figure out how much work is accomplished. One student in the group does not know how to multiply. Rather than hold the entire group back while the student learns multiplication, the teacher could set up a peer tutoring situation. While the one student worked with another to learn multiplication, the entire group could move ahead with the project.

To encourage student-to-student collaboration, some teachers start by pairing students during group activities. Pairs of students can be given specific prompts to discuss ideas and make meaning from science activities. For example, teachers can ask students to compare and contrast their own ideas with those of their partners. One such open-ended prompt is "My idea is like _____'s because _____, but my idea is different from _____'s idea because _____." Over the course of a school year, teachers can begin to put students in larger groups. As students become comfortable working in groups, some teachers have them share information, debate ideas, and brainstorm solutions with students from other classes within a school building or a district. Teachers of the same grade level can encourage this level of collaboration by having their students all study the same driving question and by providing their students time to meet with members of the other classes. If meeting with other classes is not possible, e-mail or regular correspondence can facilitate collaboration. Finally, once students are skilled collaborators, a teacher can encourage collaboration with other students around the world. For example, one sixth-grade teacher's students studied the question "What's in our water?" and collaborated with students in another class via the World Wide Web.

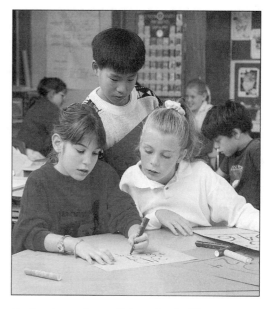

Student-to-student collaboration facilitates science learning.

NSES

**CONNECTING TO
NATIONAL SCIENCE EDUCATION STANDARDS**

**Science Education Teaching Standards—
Standard B**
Teachers of science guide and facilitate learning. In doing this, teachers orchestrate discourse among students about scientific ideas (p. 32).

There are several reasons for using student-to-student collaboration. First, peers are not authority figures, so students tend not to feel threatened in these situations. Second, students come to school with many different prior experiences that give them different levels of knowledge about subjects. Each student has different interests, personalities, learning styles, and attention spans. As students explore solutions to driving questions, they can use these varied interests, abilities, knowledge levels, personalities, and attention spans to help their fellow students learn new ideas. Finally, deeper learning takes place when students challenge others' ideas. Alfie Kohn (1996) writes, "To create a classroom where students feel safe enough to challenge each other—and us—is to give them an enormous gift" (p. 77). This idea is consistent with Vygotsky's zone of proximal development, because students with a little bit more knowledge or skill than their peers are providing a scaffold to help the others learn new ideas.

Scaffolding, discussed in Chapter 2, is a process in which a more knowledgeable other uses various techniques, such as modeling or coaching, to direct those aspects of the intellectual task that are initially beyond the capacity of the learner.

Between Students and Teacher

A cornerstone of collaboration is equal participation among members of a learning community. Collaboration between teachers and students is a situation in which students and teachers participate equally. Although students do not have the same level of expertise as the teacher, there are some areas in which students have more experiences or different understandings. Such experiences and understandings can become a valuable resource for the classroom.

Imagine a sixth-grade teacher whose class is studying the driving question "Are there poisons in our environment?" The teacher can generate her own questions such as "Is insecticide a poison in our environment?" She also can suggest to students that they are experts when it comes to their own experiences and investigations. The student whose parents purchase only organically grown foods might ask, "Are food preservatives a poison?" The student who reads information on the Internet about harmful products around the home might ask, "Are cleaning products poisonous?" The student whose family just purchased a radon detector might ask, "Is radon a poison?" In such a classroom, the teacher can participate equally with the students by asking them to generate questions rather than being the sole director of the lesson.

To enter into a teacher-student collaboration, a teacher must show students that she finds their ideas important and that she is a learner in the classroom as well. When a teacher encourages students to contribute questions and ideas to classroom projects, students become empowered. They begin to feel that they have important knowledge, and they no longer perceive the teacher as the sole source of information in the classroom. Students begin to take responsibility for their own learning and help teach the class. Once the imbalance between roles is reduced, students and teachers can begin to collaborate equally.

In establishing a collaborative relationship with students, a teacher must take on two roles—that of the collaborator who shares and debates ideas, negotiates meaning, and takes risks as well as that of the instructor who orchestrates instructional events and keeps the class focused on learning goals. Adequately taking on both roles can be difficult. The teacher needs to establish trust among students so that students feel comfortable discussing ideas, asking questions, seeking information, and posing probable solutions. This can be accomplished by letting students know that they won't be punished or ridiculed for their ideas. The teacher can also admit to students that he doesn't know everything—that he's a learner in the classroom, too. However, the teacher also needs to maintain control of certain classroom events, maintain appropriate behavior, and keep students on task. This can be accomplished by establishing guidelines for acceptable classroom behavior, timelines for lessons and projects, limits on use of resources, and overall learning goals. (Classroom management is discussed more fully in Chapter 10.)

Collaboration between students and teachers offers several benefits. First, it helps students see classroom projects as real world problems rather than as "cookbook" lab work with a single right answer. They come to view learning as more meaningful because they begin to see that the solutions to their questions extend beyond the teacher. They come to understand that no one—not even the teacher—has all the answers, and every person must learn how to answer the questions posed. They learn that adults continue to learn and that learning is an ongoing process. Second, students gain self-esteem because they see that their ideas are valued. Third, they tend to be more motivated to learn because they are excited to find answers to their questions—especially answers that the teacher may not even know!

Between Students and the Community

In collaboration between students and the community, students work with parents, neighbors, friends, relatives, and other community members either by meeting or by communicating over the telephone, via e-mail, or through the mail to share information, investigate ideas, or develop artifacts.

Collaboration with community members can take many forms. A student might call a person at a governmental office to request information about a given topic. A guest speaker might visit the classroom to demonstrate a concept, discuss an idea, or answer students' questions. Community members might provide resources; schools with limited budgets sometimes cannot afford materials that community members and businesses can provide. Students might correspond with community members, sharing their ideas, questions, and investigations over an extended period. Finally, community members may become mentors for students, working collaboratively with students to answer a driving question and modeling for the students specific strategies or behaviors.

To extend collaboration beyond the four walls of the classroom, a conduit for communication must first be established. There are many ways to establish this communication. A teacher might encourage students to invite to the classroom parents, neighbors, friends, and relatives who have expertise in an area being studied. A teacher might invite community resource people such as doctors, water quality experts, chemists, and veterinarians to the classroom. As students become comfortable working with adults in the community, they can contact and interview community members on their own. Another conduit is technology. Telephones, fax machines, e-mail, and Web pages are tools that can connect students to the community. For example, in the acid rain project, students could link via the Internet to experts in the field.

NSES

CONNECTING TO
NATIONAL SCIENCE EDUCATION STANDARDS

Science Education Teaching Standards
An important stage of inquiry and of student science learning is the oral and written discourse that focuses the attention of students on how they know what they know and how their knowledge connects to larger ideas, other domains, and the world beyond the classroom (p. 36).

NSES

CONNECTING TO
NATIONAL SCIENCE EDUCATION STANDARDS

Science Education Teaching Standards
Teachers directly support and guide discourse in two ways: They require students to record their work—teaching the necessary skills as appropriate—and they promote many different forms of communication (for example, spoken, written, pictorial, graphic, mathematical, and electronic) (p. 36).

Teachers also need to establish a classroom environment that encourages collaboration with community members. To accomplish this, the teacher needs first to help students understand that she and the science textbook aren't the only sources of information in a classroom—that students can learn from each other and from people in the community. Second, the teacher needs to allot class time for community members to visit and for students to communicate with others outside school. Third, the teacher should help students understand the different roles community members can play in teaching them science.

Individuals in the larger community represent a wealth of information for learners; they can provide resources and ideas otherwise unavailable to students. Through collaboration with the community, students see that science learned in school relates to real world problems. They learn about people and their careers. They learn to communicate with adults in a collaborative fashion. Upper elementary and middle school students especially seem to appreciate working with adults in the community because the adults treat them as young adults capable of understanding science in the real world.

> **Key Idea**
>
> Collaboration between students and members of the community helps students engage in real world problems, access a wealth of relevant information, and learn to communicate with adults and others.

CREATING A COLLABORATIVE ENVIRONMENT

Collaboration doesn't just happen. Teachers must work to create a collaborative environment in their classrooms. Collaboration is new to many students; it does not resemble the typical interactions that most students have experienced. To understand what real collaboration is, students need experiences and guidance in collaborating. Some students will be frustrated by collaboration at first if they are not used to taking initiative and responsibility for their own education.

For these reasons, it is important to introduce students gradually to collaboration. Over the course of an entire school year, a teacher can create a foundation for collaborative learning. In this section, we will explore some considerations when designing collaborative classrooms: how to form groups, how to develop collaborative skills, and how to get all students equitably involved.

Forming Groups

CONNECTING TO
NATIONAL SCIENCE EDUCATION STANDARDS

Science Teaching Standards
Effective teachers design many of the activities for learning science to require group work, not simply as an exercise, but as essential to the inquiry. The teacher's role is to structure the groups and to teach the skills that are needed to work together (p. 50).

Before students can collaborate in small groups, the groups must be established. Many factors need to be considered when forming groups: Should groups represent mixed academic ability or similar abilities, mixed personalities or like personalities (all shy students in the same group and domineering students in another group), and one or both genders? How many students should there be in a group? Should the teacher create the groups or allow students to select their own group members? Should groups be randomly assigned? Should friends be allowed to be in a group together? Should groups stay together throughout the entire project or should new groups be formed for each activity? As you think about forming groups in your own classroom, on what basis will you determine group composition to facilitate the best collaboration? Next we discuss some of the most important factors to consider.

One of the most important steps a teacher can take when designing a collaborative classroom is to think carefully about group composition before placing students into groups. This placement can affect students' interactions in groups (Blumenfeld, Marx, Soloway, & Krajcik, 1996; Leonard & McElroy, 2000). Collaboration works most effectively in heterogeneous groups with moderate differences in ability, personality, and prior experience and to which each student brings different strengths and weaknesses. Vygotsky's (1986) theory supports the need for situations in which discrepancies among children's views exist to promote cognitive development. Students are exposed to more zones of proximal development when they are grouped with students who may be a little more knowledgeable or have slightly different viewpoints. If differences among students are too drastic, however, problems can arise. For example, a highly competent reader in the fourth grade may become frustrated working with a peer who cannot read beyond a second-grade level. This student may even come to reject or mistreat the student who has difficulties reading. Students with extremely incompatible personalities may not work well together either. For example, an extremely extroverted student may totally dominate an extremely introverted student. Drastically different prior experiences may also inhibit students' abilities to complete a task. For example, a student who has never worked with a computer may not be a good choice for working with students who are computer fanatics. However, a student who knows a little about working with computers might make a good partner for someone who is very comfortable working with computers.

Although heterogeneous groups tend to foster collaboration, there are exceptions to this with regard to gender. Researchers studying equity issues in education have found that girls sometimes feel intimidated in groups dominated by boys (Baker, 1988; Kahle & Rennie, 1993). Boys tend to take control of conversations, activities, and decisions. Girls are often relegated to serve as scribes, taking the notes for the group or writing out the results of investigations. These educational researchers have found that girls, particularly upper elementary and middle school girls, tend to participate more in science when they work only with other girls (Baker, 1988; Kahle & Rennie, 1993). To avoid these potential problems, teachers can help make girls feel more comfortable with science by sometimes creating girl-only and boy-only groups. Then, as the girls' confidence increases, the teacher can gradually introduce mixed-gender groups.

The size of collaborative groups is also important. With younger elementary students who are in the self-centered stage of development, smaller groups—such as pairs—work best because such children have not yet learned to share attention with a large number of other people at once (Edwards & Stout, 1990). There is only one line of communication in pairs (between the two students), and no one is left out. Groups of three can be effective if there are three tasks, roles, or parts for students to take. However, there is the risk that two students will pair up, excluding the third. Groups of four seem to work better than groups of three because, even with pairing up, no one is left out. Groups of four are also physically easy to arrange—four student desks can be put together to form one larger table area for student work. When more than four students are grouped, behavior management sometimes becomes a problem, and it is more likely that students will be left out of the group dynamics.

Teachers need to decide whether students will be allowed to choose their own groups or whether the teachers will assign group membership. This decision is not always an easy one. Most teachers find that students who are not used to working in

> ### Key Idea
> Group size and composition are important in forming collaborative groups.

collaborative groups will select team partners who diminish effective collaboration. They tend to select their friends, and this type of group composition can sometimes cause off-task behavior and cliques that dominate activities. Some teachers randomly select members of a group because students see this as a "fair" group selection technique. Some research suggests that random selection among friends (rather than totally random assignment) leads to greater results (Mahenthiran & Rouse, 2000), and other research has found that girls have greater shared goals among friends—an important consideration for better task performance (Strough & Cheng, 2000). Other teachers make groups based on the physical arrangement of the classroom, such as by dividing the class into quadrants. Another option is to form interest groups. For example, all students who want to explore the same question can be grouped together.

Students who have learned to work in collaborative groups have skills that help them overcome the problems inherent in grouping. In fact, older elementary and middle grade students who are comfortable with collaboration will appreciate being given the responsibility of selecting their own groups.

Regardless of who selects groups, it is important to build team identity. Team identity creates team rapport and camaraderie. Young adolescents have a need for peer approval and for feeling that they belong to a group, so it is important to build team identity with upper elementary and middle school students. Some teachers have students select group names, make team banners, write team cheers, or create team slogans. The identity of a team can be related to characteristics of members of the team or to the problem it is solving. For example, a team investigating wetlands might create the team name "The Swamp Things."

The decision to keep groups together throughout a project or to form new groups presents a challenge for teachers. Some teachers find that, once the momentum has built up in a project, students want to stay together. Further, students in a group build mutual understandings and interpretations that must be built all over again each time new groupings are formed. Other teachers find that students need change to keep them interested in a project. Students may become bored working with the same group members, ideas may become stale in the group, and students eventually may learn all they can from each other. Regardless of what their final decision is, teachers find that it is only through continual monitoring of the dynamics within a group that they can make this decision.

To overcome the problem of switching groups frequently, some teachers form different levels of groups. Informal groups are used for short-term activities such as quick brainstorming sessions. Such groups may exist for only a few minutes. Other groups may stay together for months during a project. **Home groups**, groups that are used for critiquing work and supporting each other, may be used the entire school year. One option is to form base groups and sharing groups. **Base groups** are groups of students who work together on a project. They become experts in their topic area, on their driving question, or on their problem. After they have finished their project, the students move to new groups— the **sharing groups**—in which they share information about their respective projects.

Table 6.1 lists the factors teachers need to consider when forming groups.

> ### Key Idea
>
> For collaboration to be successful, teachers must give careful consideration to forming groups.

Developing Collaborative Skills

To foster collaboration, teachers need to help students develop collaborative skills. Most students have not experienced collaborating, talking to each other about ideas, and working independently in small groups and may need to learn how to do so. Also, collaboration requires students to take risks. By sharing their ideas, students open themselves to criticism from their peers. Teachers need to provide a safe environment so that students are willing to take such risks, by teaching students how to sensitively give feedback. Collaborative skills are essential in this type of situation as well as in many other real world interactions such as completing projects with others at work or getting along as a member of a family. For effective collaboration, students need to learn the skills of decision making, task completion, trust building, communication, and conflict management.

Groups will quickly fail unless the teacher analyzes the collaborative skills needed by students and discusses, models, practices, and evaluates them. In other words, collaborative skills must be taught just as purposefully as academic skills. Before starting a lesson, many teachers discuss the skills that are necessary for collaboration. Portfolio Activity 6.2 explores ways to purposefully approach collaborative skills.

FACTORS TO CONSIDER WHEN FORMING GROUPS

Table 6.1

- Are students with different ability levels placed in the same group?
- Are the personalities of the students in the group compatible?
- Have you avoided placing students with extremely incompatible abilities in the same group?
- Have you formed heterogeneous groups?
- Has attention been paid to making sure girls are not dominated by boys in the group?
- Is the size of the group appropriate for the age of students and the task?
- For this task, do you think it better to select the students for the groups or allow students to select their groups?
- For this task, will it be important for you to select students for the groups from among friends or select them totally randomly?
- Does the physical arrangement of your room affect how you need to select groups?
- Have groups created a team identity (team name, cheer, etc.)?
- Will you need to keep the group together or break it up throughout the project?
- Have you considered creating different functional groups such as home groups, base groups, or sharing groups?

SAMPLE T-CHART
Negotiating

Table 6.2

Looks Like	Sounds Like
• Heads nodding in agreement or disagreement • Students making eye contact with each other • Students brainstorming more than one alternative • Students not putting down any ideas	• "What is your idea?" • "Can we come up with a compromise?" • "That's an interesting alternative!" • "How can we use both ideas?"

Portfolio Activity 6.2

HOW DO I INTRODUCE COLLABORATIVE SKILLS TO STUDENTS?

Materials Needed:
- Something to write with

A. Elementary and middle grade students need to be introduced to collaborative skills, and these skills need to be developed over time. Children don't naturally collaborate. For each of the following skills, think of questions you might ask children as a means of introduction. For example, imagine you are introducing the skill "agreeing with others." You might ask students, "What does it mean to agree with others?" (to compromise or reach the same opinion on something), "Why should members of a group agree with each other?" (so that arguments and fights are avoided), and "How will the group's ability to complete science projects improve if students are in agreement?" (it can proceed with a project without being sidetracked by disagreements).

Skills
- Talking in appropriate voices in small groups.
- Taking turns using science equipment.
- Sharing science materials.
- Acknowledging others' contributions in a group.
- Staying on task during a project

- Completing work on time
- Helping others understand science ideas
- Using "I" messages (saying what one thinks rather than blaming others, such as "I wish you would re-design that artifact" rather than "You didn't design that artifact correctly")
- Criticizing in a positive way
- Listening actively
- Rephrasing others' science ideas
- Being patient
- Compromising
- Negotiating
- Asking for justification for science answers/responses
- Probing or redirecting questions in a group

B. Discussing collaborative skills is only a first step in introducing collaborative skills. Develop a collaborative lesson. Decide what you would do to reinforce these skills. How would you develop the skills?

C. Try the lesson. Evaluate how well the introduction worked with students. What else do you need to do?

D. Record your ideas in your portfolio.

Another technique that teachers use to develop collaborative skills is to ask students questions such as "What is *negotiating?*" "Why is it important to negotiate?" "Why will your groups work better if you negotiate with each other?" "How do you know if people are negotiating?" A teacher might use a T-chart to teach about this skill (Johnson & Johnson, 1990). The T-chart is simply a chart in the shape of a T. Write the name of a skill above the T, descriptions of what the skill looks like to the left of the T, and descriptions of what the skill sounds like to the right of the T. Table 6.2 is a sample T-chart of the skill *negotiating*. The teacher would have students generate examples of what they would see each other doing and hear each other saying if they were negotiating. The teacher could model these behaviors or ask students in the class to model them. Next, students would practice the skill. Finally, at the end of the class period, the teacher would have students discuss and evaluate how well they negotiated with each other. In some cases, teachers even make a video of the classroom activities and have students watch and analyze themselves to determine how well they worked together. The students would conclude by determining what areas still needed refinement.

In Portfolio Activity 6.3, you will create your own T-charts to teach students skills that will be helpful in collaborative groups.

Portfolio Activity 6.3   **MAKING T-CHARTS**

Materials Needed:
- Something to write with

A. Practice developing a T-chart. Make two columns and develop your own ideas for the following:
- Resolving conflicts
- Criticizing ideas, not people
- Respecting others
- Disagreeing politely
- Maintaining self-control
- Showing appreciation
- Taking turns
- Encouraging others

- Praising
- Respecting others
- Accepting differences

B. Try making a T-chart of these skills with others in your group (or with children). How are their ideas different from and similar to yours? How did developing a T-chart help you communicate with the other people in your group? With children?

C. Keep these T-charts in your portfolio so that you can use them at a later time.

Decision-Making Skills

In a project-based science classroom, students take responsibility for making many decisions. Students must make decisions about division of labor (who will do what and how the work load can be equitably distributed), timelines and scheduling (when people will complete things and in what sequence), activities (what are the solutions to problems, which activities need to be completed, and what artifacts need to be made), and resources (information, supplies, and materials).

As discussed in Chapter 4, a teacher can help students learn decision-making skills by providing students with goal sheets to track division of labor, timelines and schedules to plan and sequence their time, and checklists to make decisions about resources. A goal sheet is simply a chart on which students can record their goals for the week and their plans for who will take responsibility for each goal. Table 6.3 is a sample goal sheet. After students have completed their goal sheets, they can move to developing timelines and schedules. This can be accomplished with the use of a weekly or monthly calendar, or the goal sheet can be expanded to include a plan and timeline. Table 6.4 is an example. You can use a checklist to provoke students' thinking and expand their ideas about resources needed to complete their project. A checklist option is shown in Table 6.5. Another option is to work with students to develop their own resource list.

> **Key Idea**
>
> When students collaborate, they need to make decisions about who will perform particular tasks.

Task-Completion Skills

Task-completion skills are necessary to teach students to stay focused on the driving question and complete projects within a reasonable time frame. Once students understand the task at hand, they need to learn how to actually complete the task. To complete a task, students must *know how* to complete it, *remember* to complete each step of the task, *stay focused,* and *monitor* their time. (Remember that it usually takes more time to cover the same objectives in a collaborative learning environment than in a traditional classroom. Students need time to discuss ideas, work together, build understanding, and complete projects.)

> **Key Idea**
>
> To complete a task, students must learn how to manage their time and stay focused.

Table 6.3

GOAL SHEET

What Do We Need to Do?	Who Will Do It?
Find information about air pollution.	Liz
Contact the EPA.	Jeff
Figure out an experiment we can do to test for particulate matter.	Rosario

Table 6.4

GOAL SHEET WITH PLAN AND TIMELINE

What Do We Need to Do?	Who Will Do It?	How Will It Be Done?	When Will It Be Done?
Find information about air pollution.	Liz	Use World Wide Web.	By Friday, Sept. 12th
Contact the EPA.	Jeff	Call from home.	At home
Figure out an experiment we can do to test for particulate matter.	Rosario	Look in resource books.	Today, by Friday, Sept. 12th

Table 6.5

RESOURCES CHECKLIST

What?	Can We Use It?	How?
INFORMATION		
Encyclopedia	Yes	Find out more about air pollution.
Magazines		
Journals		
Books		
CD-ROMs	Yes	Use in library.
Software	No	The school doesn't have any on air pollution.
Guest speaker	Yes	from the EPA
Telephone call	Yes	to the EPA
E-mail		
Interview	Yes	Of someone at the EPA
World Wide Web	Yes	Do a search
Letter		
SUPPLIES AND MATERIALS		
Writing materials		
Computers		
Drawing materials		
Science equipment	Yes	Check with the teacher.
Calculator		

To help students complete tasks, some teachers use a progress report. A progress report is a modification of Tables 6.2, 6.3, and 6.4 in which students review how much they have accomplished at the end of a day or a week. You might have students turn the progress report in to you, share it with classmates, put it in a science journal, or include it in an evaluation portfolio. The main point is to engage students in the reflective practice of examining how much they have completed. This will keep students conscious of starting in a timely manner and avoiding off-task behavior.

Trust-Building Skills

Trust-building skills form a critical aspect of collaboration. Trust building makes all students feel comfortable working in small groups. Each student should be at ease giving suggestions or opinions, participating in discussions, and helping answer the driving question. Although students must feel safe when sharing their ideas, an important part of science is the critiquing of ideas, and students must be willing to have their ideas critiqued. In addition, students need to learn how to critique ideas without offending others. Students can learn to build trust within a group by including everyone in discussions. When all students feel that their ideas are wanted and considered, they will be more likely to trust their peers.

Getting to Know Others.   If students in the classroom do not know each other or if the school's population is highly transient, an important first step for building trust is helping students get to know each other. Many people lack the confidence to share ideas with or take risks among strangers. Students need to introduce themselves to each other and discuss hobbies or interests. They need time to develop some common lines of communication. Teachers who neglect to facilitate students' getting to know each other will find students frequently not on task because they are taking the time themselves to build trust by talking about their lives and their interests.

> ### Key Idea
> Trust-building is critical to establishing collaboration.

To help students get to know each other, engage them in icebreaker activities. In one icebreaker, children complete a worksheet with the names of their classmates: "Who knows how to play a piano?" "Who has a chemistry kit?" In another icebreaker, students simply interview each other. Portfolio Activity 6.4 introduces ways to help students get to know each other.

Feeling Needed.   In building trust, it is not only important for students to know each other, but also for them to feel needed by the group. One way to accomplish this is to identify situations in which not all students are participating and to encourage the non-participating students. You might draw quieter students into group discussions by inviting them to share their thoughts or ideas. To encourage sharing, you might make it a requirement for each student to share a given number of ideas during a lesson. You might use a "round-robin" approach in which each student must contribute one idea. Some teachers use children's literature to teach about sharing and other collaborative skills. For example, the story *The Rainbow Fish* by Marcus Pfister (1996) can teach children about making friends through sharing. *Seven Blind Mice* by Ed Young (1992) teaches children about collaborating to solve a problem and using observation skills. (See Sapon-Shevin, 1999, pp. 205–7, for a comprehensive set of children's literature suggestions.) To encourage equal participation, you might give each student a limited number of tokens. Each time a student contributes an idea, she "pays" a token. When she runs out of tokens, she cannot contribute more ideas until all the other students have also used up their tokens. Another approach is to have groups of students break into pairs temporarily to talk or

Portfolio Activity 6.4   HOW DO CHILDREN BUILD TRUST IN A GROUP?

Materials Needed:
- Something to write with
- Index cards
- Scissors

A. What follows are techniques for developing trust among members of a group. Try them out with a group of peers or a group of children.

Name Cards

Each participant should write his or her name in the center of a 5 × 8 index card. In each corner, the person should write some type of information about him- or herself. For example, children might list where they were

born, personality characteristics, favorite hobbies, favorite science topics, the names of people they admire, accomplishments they are proud of, or favorite school subjects. Participants should gather in groups of four to share their cards. Participants should take on different roles—probers, recorders—to elicit more information about what is written on the cards. Each person in each group should introduce another group member to the whole class.

People Search

Each participant should complete the following chart by circulating among the entire group to find people who meet the criteria.

Someone who likes comedy shows:	Someone who plays basketball after school:	Someone who likes science:	Someone who has visited a science museum:	Someone who took a vacation last summer:
Someone who collects stamps, coins, stickers, or baseball cards:	Someone who likes pizza:	Someone who has a chemistry kit:	Someone who likes: _____ (fill in the name of a restaurant)	Someone who loves cats:
Someone who loves dogs:	Someone who dances:	Someone who likes: _____ (fill in the name of a TV star)	Someone who has the middle name Marie:	Someone who has lived on a farm (or in the city):
Someone who walks to school (or takes a bus):	Someone who owns a computer:	Someone who is shy:	Someone with a science software program:	Someone who likes: _____ (fill in the name of a particular song)
Someone who likes to read science fiction for enjoyment:	Someone who has used a telescope:	Someone who likes to swim:	Some who likes to sleep late:	Someone who likes to get up early:

work together before returning to the large group. While students are working in pairs, they will all participate equally. When back in the large group, they may continue to participate at a high level. Portfolio Activity 6.5 introduces a strategy for teaching students that they must depend on others in their group.

Offering Constructive Criticism.   After students have learned about one another and have begun to feel needed by the group, they must learn how to critique others' ideas without offending. This is probably the most difficult component of trust building to teach as students often speak before thinking. You can use a number of strategies to

Partner Interview

All participants should pair up. Each member of a pair should interview the other by asking the following questions:

What is your favorite science fiction movie?

What is your favorite hobby?

What is your favorite sport?

What science magazine have you read?

What's your favorite book? Why?

What do you like to do after school?

What is your favorite science topic?

What sports do you play?

What is your favorite computer program?

Who's your favorite actor or actress?

What is your favorite school subject?

What is your least favorite science topic?

What is your favorite song?

What would embarrass you?

What's your favorite science experiment? Why?

Where have you gone on vacation?

What is your favorite restaurant?

What is your middle name?

What do you think you want to be when you grow up?

What science topic have you noticed in the newspaper this week?

What science museums have you visited?

Do you have any pets? Which kind?

Where do you live?

What makes you laugh?

What science topic would you like to know more about?

Interview Cube

Make paper cubes (or cover some other types of cubes). On each side of each cube write the name of a topic such as *favorite science fiction movie, favorite science topic, science-related hobby,* or *best experiment ever conducted.* Participants should form groups of four or five. Each member should "roll" the cube and respond to the topic that rolls face up. For example, if the cube lands on *science fiction movie,* the roller must tell the others the title of her favorite science fiction movie. Then members of the group must ask probing questions about the topic. For example, they might ask, "When did this become your favorite movie?" At the end of the activity, each participant should share something interesting about the person next to him or her.

Finding Common Ground

Participants should form groups of four or five and then select a topic such as *sports, science class, TV shows,* or *school.* Each group should discuss its topic until members

find an interest, dislike, or quality that *every* member of the group shares.

Finding Qualities

Participants should circulate around the room to find one positive quality about each other person. Participants should list each person's name with at least one positive quality such as "Is always friendly toward others" or "Helps others understand science ideas."

B.   After you have completed some of these activities, analyze how each contributed to building trust among members of a group.

C.   Why would it be important for children to build trust before working in collaborative groups?

D.   Record your ideas in your portfolio.

support students in thinking about their classmates' feelings and to foster mutual respect. A T-chart, like the one in Table 6.6, can be used to help teach students how to show respect for the ideas of others.

Many children find it difficult to avoid putdowns. You might have students make lists of insulting words they should not use in a group, such as *stupid* or *dumb.* Then, students practice accepting others' ideas and avoiding the prohibited words. Another strategy involves having students create lists of acceptable words. For example, students might be tempted to say, "That's a dumb idea." The teacher can have the class brainstorm a list of respectful ways to point out the problems with an idea. Students might list, "You seem to be having trouble with this idea" or "You need to think about this again."

Portfolio Activity 6.5

WHAT SKILLS ARE HELPFUL IN COOPERATIVE GROUPS?

Materials Needed:
- Five squares cut up as shown and sealed in envelopes[1]

A.   Cut up five squares (all of the same dimensions) as shown in Figure 6.1 for each group of five people. Distribute the five squares among envelopes as shown.

B.   Each member of the group should get an envelope. The goal is for each person in the group, *without communicating in any way* (without talking, gesturing, or writing notes), to form a square that is the same size as all the other members' squares. Members of the group may hand their own pieces to others in the group, but

they may *not* take pieces from another person or point to pieces they want. They can only wait for a person to hand them a piece. They cannot gesture that they do not want a piece; they must accept it and give it to someone else if they do not want it. When a member gives a piece to another member of the group, she must simply hand the piece to the member and not place the piece so as to help complete a square. The activity is not timed, and it may take anywhere from a few minutes to over a half hour to complete.

C.   When all the members of the group are finished, discuss what happened. What skills does it take to complete this task? Was it frustrating? Why? Was there collaboration among the members of the group? What skills would facilitate collaboration in elementary and middle grades classrooms?

1. Adapted from Abruscato, J., and J. Hassard. 1976. *Loving and beyond: Science teaching for the humanistic classroom.* Glenview, Ill.: Scott, Foresman.

Figure 6.1
The five square activity.

Students also need to be taught to avoid a tone of voice that suggests ridicule. Rules regarding making faces might need to be established. Students will probably need to practice critiquing others' work without being offensive or abusive. Finally, when students disagree with other people's ideas, they need to learn to criticize the *ideas*—not the people. To learn to criticize ideas rather than people, students can practice using "I"

RESPECT-BUILDING T-CHART
Showing appreciation

Looks like ...	Sounds like ...
Smiling	"Thanks, I appreciate your help with this."

Table 6.6

messages instead of "you" messages. For example, saying, "I think this might be a better way to solve this problem" is less threatening than saying, "You cannot solve this problem this way."

Communication Skills

For students to be successful at collaboration, they need communication skills. Communication skills can be broken down into three components. One, students need to learn to talk about learning. Two, they need to learn to speak clearly. Three, they need to listen carefully to what others are saying so that miscommunication doesn't arise. These three components help students communicate clearly with others, and effective communication helps prevent arguments, frustrations, and disagreements among group members.

Talking About Science Learning.   Children don't automatically know how to talk about science. They need to be taught how to ask questions and generate alternative solutions to questions. One way to teach children how to generate questions and alternative solutions is to hold a whole group brainstorming session, during which you record questions and plausible answers on the board.

Children also need to learn how to probe for more information and request justification for ideas and evidence for conclusions. If a student says, "I think the aquarium is dirty because the fish go to the bathroom in it," other students might learn to ask probing questions like, "Why do you think that? Fish go to the bathroom in lakes and oceans too." However, when students are challenged to elaborate, they often resort to nonanswers like, "Because." To overcome this problem, teachers can have students practice responding in complete sentences and providing evidence. Evidence might be in the form of observations; data collected; or things read in books, in articles, or on the World Wide Web. Students can also create T-charts for skills such as summarizing information, paraphrasing others' ideas, checking for scientific accuracy, elaborating, probing for more information, advocating a position, and justifying a science answer. Table 6.7 shows a sample T-chart on elaborating.

Children also need to learn how to advocate a position. Teachers can foster this skill by engaging students in role-playing situations (such as role-playing whether to report to the authorities a person who litters), mock trials (during which students have to argue for the prosecution or defense), letter-writing campaigns (such as to newspaper editors about a local issue), making posters (such as those advocating conservation of energy), or participation in news groups on the World Wide Web (such as those advocating bans on types of tuna fishing that endanger dolphins).

Key Idea

Students find offering and accepting criticism one of the most difficult aspects of collaborating with others. To foster the ability to give and receive criticism, teachers need to help students get to know and respect each other.

NSES

CONNECTING TO
NATIONAL SCIENCE EDUCATION STANDARDS

Science Teaching Standards
A fundamental aspect of a community of learners is communication. Effective communication requires a foundation of respect and trust among individuals (p. 50).

Key Idea

Most students are not used to talking about science. To foster the ability to do so, teachers need to teach students how to ask questions, generate alternative solutions, probe for more information, and justify ideas.

Table 6.7

ELABORATING T-CHART
Elaborating

Looks like ...	Sounds like ...
Pointing to an investigation in progress Holding up an artifact	"Please tell me more about your project." "I think ... because. ...."

Speaking Clearly.   Speaking clearly means enunciating words, using appropriate voice levels, and facing others when talking to them. Young children, of course, are still developing a repertoire of words, and they often mispronounce them. They also lose teeth and sometimes find it difficult to say certain words. In addition, children sometimes get very excited about science and so speak too quickly. Although these are normal characteristics of children's speech, teachers can help their students practice more effective speech by enunciating and talking more slowly so that others can understand, talking at appropriate voice levels so that people want to listen, and talking face-to-face so that others can hear them better.

Listening Carefully.   Listening carefully is as important as speaking in good communication. Children like to talk but frequently don't listen carefully to what others say. They need to be taught active listening, which includes using names and making eye contact when speaking to each other, paraphrasing what others say, asking for explanations, and summarizing conversations. Standards can be set about raising hands, taking notes when others talk, and not interrupting others in midspeech.

> **Key Idea**
>
> Teachers need to help students learn to speak clearly and listen carefully.

For example, while working on a display board for an artifact, one student might say, "I think we should do something different." A second student could interpret this to mean that they should have made a different type of display. In fact, the first student meant that they should complete their experiment before making the display board. Without understanding what the first student meant, the second student might suggest a different format for the display. This, of course, could lead to confusion and anger. To avoid misunderstanding, the second student could have said, "You said we should do something different. Do you mean that we need to have a different type of display?" The first student could then clarify his intent without causing problems.

Conflict-Management Skills

Even after students have learned decision-making, task-completion, trust-building, and communication skills, conflicts can arise among members of a group. For this reason, students also need to develop conflict-management skills. These skills include the ability to clarify disagreements, negotiate, and compromise.

> **Key Idea**
>
> Students don't always get along at first in collaborative situations. They need skills in clarifying disagreements, negotiating, and making compromises.

Clarifying Disagreements.   To clarify disagreements within a group, students need to learn to understand the points of view of others. Children frequently have difficulty understanding others' opinions. This is partly developmental (with young elementary children) and partly due to inexperience.

With young elementary students, teachers can help foster understanding others' points of view by using literature, stuffed animals, and pets. A teacher might read a

Table 6.8

WIN-WIN CHART
Who Gets to Call the Guest Speaker

Table 6.8

Matt	Luther
I can call since my dad knows the speaker.	You can mention that I suggested this.

story and ask children to express how the character in the story feels. The *Story of the Three Bears* is a good story to use in this way. A teacher might have students pretend that a favorite stuffed animal or pet can talk and tell stories about how the animal thinks and feels.

With older elementary and middle grade students, teachers can have students pretend (role-play) that they are other people. Students can ask themselves, "What would I think if I were the other person?" Older students respond well to courtroom dramas. Teachers can read a courtroom drama or set up a courtroom simulation in which each student plays a different role. Students can discuss the thinking, feelings, beliefs, values, attitudes, desires, wants, and problems of each person in the drama. Imagine that students disagree about who should contact a guest speaker. One student wants to contact the guest speaker because he thought of the idea; another student wants to contact the guest speaker because his father works with her. By switching roles (pretending each is the other person), the students can try to understand why each believes he is the best person to call the speaker.

Negotiating.   Next, students need to learn to negotiate. Negotiation does not mean that one person wins and the other loses. Negotiation results in both parties feeling as if they had won.

To teach negotiation, many teachers use T-charts or a hybrid of the T-chart, a win-win chart. On each side of the T in a win-win chart, students write the names of the disagreeing parties. The students list under each name how the person or group will win in the situation. Table 6.8 is an example of a win-win T-chart. The chart illustrates that both Matt and Luther want to feel like they contributed to the project. Matt wants the students to know that his father knows the speaker. Luther wants the speaker to know that inviting her was his idea. In order for both students to win, Luther will help Matt make arrangements for the speaker's visit. Matt will call the speaker. He will tell the speaker that inviting her was Luther's idea and he will introduce her to Luther when she arrives.

Another way to teach negotiation is to use Venn diagrams for finding common ground. Students list differences in the outer circle and common ideas in the area of intersection of the two circles. The Venn diagram in Figure 6.2 indicates that students originally wanted to include different types of pictures in their project but agreed upon a photograph.

Students can also send an e-mail about the problem to another school or student requesting new ideas for resolving the differences. A group of students having difficulty reaching a consensus on how to build a machine to test for friction, for example, could e-mail their ideas to another school in their district and ask the students at the other school to vote on the best idea.

Figure 6.2

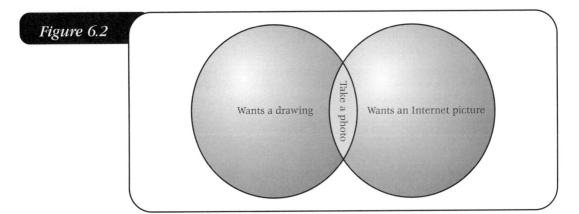

Venn diagram.

Table 6.9

COMPROMISE
How Should We Build a Machine to Test Friction?

Yolanda's Ideas	Anchee's Ideas
Make a skateboard. Test it on different surfaces. See if you fall off the skateboard on rough surfaces. See if the wheels get hotter going across some surfaces.	Build a pulley system to measure accurately. Drag objects across different surfaces. Chart how hard it is to move the objects.

Key Idea

Students need to be taught skills that will be needed in collaborative situations. These include skills in decision making, task completion, trust building, communication, and conflict-management.

Compromising.   If negotiation fails to produce a win-win situation, students need to learn to compromise. In a compromise, students settle differences and reach an agreement in which each "side" or person makes concessions. The resulting decision may combine the best qualities or elements of different ideas.

To teach the skill of compromise, a teacher might have students list all of the major points in their arguments. Then, the teacher instructs each side in the disagreement to give up one or two of its ideas in an exchange. Slowly, the two sides should come to an agreement that is a fair compromise. For example, students trying to decide how to best measure friction might use ideas from Table 6.9 to compromise. The compromise might turn out to be building a skateboard and measuring the friction of the skateboard across different surfaces using a pulley.

Involving All Students Equitably

One of the essential features of collaboration involves equal participation by all members. However, frequently students feel reluctant to collaborate for one reason or another—lack of self-confidence, unfamiliarity with collaboration, and not knowing others.

Students need to understand that the products and ideas developed through collaboration must represent everyone, including them. Each student should feel that his or her contribution to the collaborative task is essential. A collaborative environment keeps all members of a group equitably involved and needed by others in the group. Some educators call this condition **positive interdependence**—the linking of all group members so that one cannot succeed unless the other group members succeed.

You probably noticed in the first two scenarios at the beginning of the chapter that some students' "jobs" weren't really critical to the success of the group as a whole. Students whose efforts were not critical to the project's success quickly lost interest, got bored, or failed to participate intimately with others in the group. Positive interdependence may be built through establishing common goals or rewards, building common understanding, dividing up labor, and assigning roles.

Establishing Common Goals

Teachers can establish common goals by teaching students to move from individual ideas to group ideas. During all stages of collaborative learning (designing a driving question, investigating, developing artifacts, and sharing artifacts), students can first write down their own ideas. Open-ended prompts such as "My idea is . . . ," "My plan is . . . ," and "My goal is . . ." are helpful. After students have recorded their own ideas, they can work in small groups to share ideas. Then students can record the ideas and goals of others in the group. Finally, by comparing and contrasting goals, they can develop a common goal. Table 6.10 shows examples of charts that can be used to help students build common goals.

Building Common Understanding

To build common understanding, teachers need to have students discuss intellectual ideas. The first step involves getting students to really listen to each other. When one student gives her idea and another student recites it back to her, two other students can add modifications to the idea, and once all of the ideas are out, students can discuss the similarities and differences among the ideas. Understanding the similarities and differences among ideas helps students listen to each other, and it helps clarify ideas and build understanding among the members of the group.

One technique for facilitating discussion of intellectual ideas involves asking students to think about the validity of their responses. Students can be asked to justify the positions they take, and no one's idea can be included or excluded without a reason. Students can use sentences such as "We think X is better than Y because. . . ," "We think it is. . . because. . . ," "We don't think it is . . . because. . . ," and "I think we should . . . because. . ." At first, charts like the one in Table 6.11 are useful to encourage discussions. The charts can be photocopied and distributed to other groups for discussion. Groups can discuss how their ideas are different from those of other groups. For example, the teacher can ask, "Which other group had a prediction similar to your group?" Over the course of the year, students will gain the skills to discuss ideas without the prompts in the charts. Portfolio Activity 6.6 illustrates how a group of students can build common understandings.

Dividing up Labor

Division of labor occurs when students collaborate, negotiate, compromise, and interface with others to investigate a driving question. **Division of labor** does not mean *divide and conquer.* Divide and conquer strategies rarely lead to equitable distribution of

Table 6.10

CHARTS FOR BUILDING COMMON GOALS
Driving Question

Ideas	How the idea is like mine	How the idea is different from mine	Our group idea for a driving question
My idea	_____	_____	_____
Sara's idea	_____	_____	_____
Richard's idea	_____	_____	_____
Rahel's idea	_____	_____	_____

Investigation

Ideas	How the idea is like mine	How the idea is different from mine	Our group idea for an investigation
My idea	_____	_____	_____
Sara's idea	_____	_____	_____
Richard's idea	_____	_____	_____
Rahel's idea	_____	_____	_____

Artifacts

Ideas	How the idea is like mine	How the idea is different from mine	Our group idea for artifacts
My idea	_____	_____	_____
Sara's idea	_____	_____	_____
Richard's idea	_____	_____	_____
Rahel's idea	_____	_____	_____

Table 6.11

DEFENDING YOUR IDEAS

Idea	Why?
We think _____	Because _____
We think it is not _____	Because _____
We think _____ is better	Because _____

knowledge, skills, or effort. Someone always seems to carry a larger workload, have a more interesting task, or contribute more information to the group. Students need to learn that true division of labor can only occur when members of the group participate equally in a task. All students need to take an active role and no one can dominate. In a collaborative environment, it is in the division of labor that the teacher serves the role of guide—making sure students are cued to listen to one another's ideas rather than only to work individually.

Portfolio Activity 6.6

HOW CAN YOU HELP STUDENTS BUILD UNDERSTANDING?

Materials Needed:
- Materials to conduct a short science investigation
- A science activity book

A. With the help of your instructor, obtain a science activity book and select from it an investigation that you can complete with a group of students or a group of your peers. Keep the investigation simple. For example, you might investigate how to light a flashlight bulb using only one wire, one flashlight bulb, and one dry cell.

B. Members of the group should predict the results of the activity. For example, members can complete the sentence "I predict that the bulb will . . ." Each

member of the group should provide a prediction and recite the previous person's prediction. Have other students add modifications. Once all of the ideas are out, students can discuss the similarities and differences among their predictions.

C. Conduct the investigation.

D. Members of the group should discuss the results and justify the reasons for their beliefs. For example, students can use sentences such as "We think the bulb lit up because . . . ," "We think it did not light because . . . ," "We don't think it is . . . because . . . ," and "I think we should . . . because . . ."

A teacher can help facilitate a true division of labor by putting students in situations in which they depend upon one another's resources. Resources include skills, abilities, knowledge, prior experiences, access to information, and friends and acquaintances. Students who have slightly different prior experiences may nonetheless contribute equally in a significant way to answering a driving question—thus dividing the labor. Imagine that students are trying to find out what factors affect plant growth. A student who has grown houseplants in an apartment complex has prior knowledge about window locations, the size of pots, and the amount of water. Another student who lives in a rural

CONNECTING TO NATIONAL SCIENCE EDUCATION STANDARDS

Science Education Teaching Standards
Using collaborative group structure, teachers encourage interdependency among group members, assisting students to work together in small groups so that all participate in sharing data and in developing group reports (p. 36).

area grows food crops. This student brings to the group knowledge about farm machinery, commercial fertilizers, pesticides, herbicides, and crop yields. A third student who lives in a subdivision has a garden in her backyard. This student has experience using a compost pile as a source of fertilizer and organic gardening methods. These students can work together to divide the labor in an equitable fashion based upon their prior experiences. The first student could help the others set up an experiment to grow plants in pots of different sizes under various lighting conditions (in north, south, east, and west windows). The second student could help the others investigate how commercial fertilizers and pesticides help plants grow by setting up conditions in which some plants are treated with fertilizers and pesticides and others are not. The last student could contrast this investigation with one on organic gardening methods.

Assigning Roles

If students have difficulty working together, assigning roles can alleviate the problem. The assignment of roles ensures that all students participate and that no one dominates. It also teaches responsibility by making each student responsible for a part of the task.

It is critical that each role be important and contribute in a substantial way to solving the problem or reaching understanding. **Interpersonal roles** help ensure that members of a group work well together. Interpersonal roles include a facilitator (who makes sure everyone is participating), an encourager (who makes sure all students are participating or provides positive feedback to members of the group), a checker (who keeps notes about how well the group is doing on skills or tasks), and a noise monitor (who makes sure the group isn't too loud). **Managerial roles** include a reader (who reads directions to the group), a timekeeper (who makes sure the group finishes the task in a given amount of time), a recorder (who writes down the team's answers), and a runner (who gets materials that the group needs). **Cognitive roles**, or roles that require a specific type of thinking or specialized knowledge, include an executive, a skeptic or critic, an educator, and a conciliator. Cognitive roles can also correspond to scientific fields; such roles include a veterinarian, a botanist, a paleontologist, a geologist, an ecologist, a meteorologist, a zoologist, an oceanographer, an astronomer, and a chemist. Portfolio Activity 6.7 will enable you to experience cognitive roles in collaborative learning.

Interpersonal and managerial roles, more than cognitive ones, tend to focus on separate jobs to get a task finished. Interpersonal and managerial roles are also less likely to be significant for the completion of a task. For example, the job of a student who is a runner is over as soon as supplies are acquired, and the student who is the encourager is likely to lose interest in the role and feel that it is phony or silly. For this reason, interpersonal and managerial roles are best used only with young children or students who lack even extremely basic skills for working together. For older elementary or middle school students (or students with more developed collaborative skills), cognitive roles are more effective. If students are studying acid rain, for example, they might take the roles of chemist, botanist, geologist, and ecologist. The chemist studies how the chemicals determine acidity. The botanist learns about how plants are affected by acid levels. The geologist researches the effect of acid rain on rocks, minerals, and soil. The ecologist looks at the overall picture, determining how acid rain interacts with the environment. With these cognitive roles, each person is needed throughout the project and each contributes equally to the task.

USING TECHNOLOGY TOOLS TO CREATE A COLLABORATIVE ENVIRONMENT

Technology tools can help teachers create a collaborative climate and enhance the quality of collaboration. Teachers can use telephones, fax machines, e-mail, and the World Wide Web to connect students with others and with the community. These technology tools create collaborative environments not otherwise possible. These applications allow students to share data, discuss and explore ideas, and talk about trends in data from various sites. E-mail, chat rooms, and listservs encourage discourse among large groups of people. Using the World Wide Web, students can create, share, and critique multimedia documents.

The quality of the collaboration is enhanced through technology because it enables students to collaborate with a large number of peers outside of their classroom, people in their community, scientists, and others around the world. By sharing ideas and data

Portfolio Activity 6.7

HOW DO ROLES FACILITATE COLLABORATIVE LEARNING?

Materials Needed:

- *The Great Solar System Rescue* or *The Great Ocean Rescue,* by Tom Snyder Productions
- A laserdisc player with a monitor or a computer with a CD-ROM player (depending upon the version of *The Great Solar System Rescue* or *The Great Ocean Rescue*—both are available in either laserdisc or CD format)
- A computer with a cable connection to a laserdisc player (optional with the laserdisc version)

A. Complete one lesson from either *The Great Solar System Rescue* or *The Great Ocean Rescue.*

B. After you have completed the lesson, analyze how each person's role contributed to the group's success in solving the mystery presented in the activity. Could the mystery have been solved effectively without one of the roles? Explain your views.

C. How did having a particular role contribute to your achievement, social skills, and self-esteem? How do you think the role would affect students engaging in the activity?

D. Record your ideas in your portfolio.

with this larger community, students and teachers take part in practices similar to those of scientists. New ideas can be quickly introduced and discussed. This extended network of collaborative partners also builds multiple zones of proximal development, because the wide range of people adds different levels of knowledge and expertise. Learning scaffolds are created when many different individuals help others explore a topic. Further, some teachers have found that many students are more comfortable asking questions or discussing topics electronically than they are in person.

A number of programs allow students to share data and ideas on the World Wide Web. Project FeederWatch allows students throughout the winter months to collect and share data about birds that visit feeders in the school playground, nature area, or garden. In the project, students periodically count the highest numbers of each bird species they see at their feeders from November through April. After each count, students report their bird counts to scientists at the Cornell University Lab of Ornithology. Students can view their results and the results of other FeederWatchers by viewing different maps. They can look at maps that summarize their data, or they can look at maps that present movements of bird populations. Scientists at the lab will use the data to conduct bird population research. The FeederWatch program helps scientists track movements of winter bird populations and long-term trends in bird distribution and abundance. They can also track the movement of the most common birds found at bird feeders. As members of the project, students learn more about winter birds, their movement, and how the birds fare during the winter months. By being part of the FeederWatch program, students take part in ongoing scientific investigation.

In the *Kids as Global Scientists* project, students can share and discuss ideas with other students and scientists to learn about weather phenomena. Students use the World Wide Web to telecommunicate with others via an electronic message board. Using the electronic tools available, students can share ideas and data as well as discuss questions. Students in the *Kids as Global Scientists* program learn about weather and weather patterns. As in the FeederWatch program, students in *Kids as Global Scientists* take part in scientific practices of communicating and sharing their ideas with others.

Key Idea

Technology tools help teachers develop collaborative environments by allowing students to share data as well as present and debate ideas.

Online Programs That Encourage Collaboration

Students can also use various applications on the World Wide Web to create, share, and critique multimedia documents. The *Collaborative Software Laboratory* (CSL) is an example of a Web environment that is designed specifically to allow teachers and students of various ages to create, share, and critique multimedia documents with other students. CSL is designed with supports that enable students to create and collaborate on multimedia documents.

We have shared only three of the many projects that are available on the World Wide Web. Many of these programs allow students to share and discuss ideas as well as share data. By taking part in such activities, students are participating in scientific practices and joining a much larger collaborative community to promote learning. Recent research (Tao & Gunstone, 1999) has found that collaborative learning at the computer fosters conceptual change. Computer-supported collaborative learning helped students co-construct an understanding that enhanced learning.

CHALLENGES THAT ARISE WHEN STUDENTS COLLABORATE IN SMALL GROUPS

Students don't automatically collaborate with others, and groups do not always work well together. Students may argue, fail to communicate, or resist compromise. Students' personalities may lead to situations in which some students do all the work and others contribute virtually nothing. Sometimes higher-ability students feel they are being taken advantage of by others, or they dominate. Status among members of a group can cause problems—high-status members (those with higher academic status, peer status, or social status) may take control of a group. Sometimes, members of a group may make a pact to do the least amount of work possible. Differences in diversity among students (gender, culture, physical ability, or academic ability) can also cause problems in small groups. Some students even become socialized to believe they cannot work well in a group. Students can also become socialized to believe that there is a "right answer" for everything and thus find it difficult to work in project-based science classrooms where students find solutions among many possibilities. Finally, parents, colleagues, or administrators may not understand the nature of collaboration and cause problems by questioning a teacher's techniques.

A Lack of Collaborative Skills

As discussed earlier, students need to learn collaborative skills to be able to work effectively in small groups (Johnson, Johnson, & Holubec, 1986). Children do not learn these skills overnight; it can take months or years for students to learn to work well in groups. However, without these skills, students may experience unresolved conflicts, aggression, failure to challenge the viewpoints of others, and failure to make meanings explicit.

When problems arise during collaboration, try two approaches: (1) carefully examine the types of collaborative skills students seem to be lacking and work on these specific skills and (2) get students to try to work out their own problems. Use these two approaches before moving problem students to another group or forming new groups. If you are too quick to move students to a new team, you will only reinforce negative behaviors—students will learn that complaining results in getting to be on a team with the people they want to be with.

If students seem to argue excessively, work with them so that they learn to summarize ideas in a positive fashion, request help, agree with each other, and support others' ideas. Try to get students to understand that they do not need to have arguments, give negative criticism, or overlook the positive contributions of members of the group. Have students work out their own problems, if possible. You might ask some of the following questions:

- What have you done to try to resolve the argument?
- What could you try next?
- What are some other ways to solve this?

Some teachers find that when students realize that they will work as a team for a length of time and that they must work together to be successful, they will often work out their problems and get along.

Students may still refuse to work together, however. When this happens, you may need to remove a student from the group and let him or her work alone until ready to work with others. Sometimes, isolation while seeing team members enjoying themselves may motivate students to want to join the team. A private meeting with an uncooperative student might also reveal reasons for negative behavior. Some teachers ask team members to think of ways to help an uncooperative student participate as a productive member of the team. Similarly, some teachers call class meetings to discuss ways to improve teamwork.

Sound levels can also become a problem in collaborative classrooms—especially if the school is not built with acoustical tiles, carpeting, and more modern ways to absorb sound. Although talking is expected and desired in a project-based science classroom (students, after all, must debate ideas, construct understanding, carry out investigations, and make artifacts), unproductive noise can be distracting. If the teacher must say, "Shhhhh," every few minutes, something is wrong. Either the teacher's expectations for noise level are too strict, or students are too noisy. To determine which is the case, observe the classroom for a moment. Students should not be yelling at each other. Students should be able to talk and hear each other within a group. If you can see that students are struggling to hear one another, reinforce (or establish) ground rules for talking. Turn off the lights, for example, to get the room quiet and then establish appropriate noise levels.

Finally, students may not use collaborative time effectively. During a project, some talk will be off-task. If much of the conversation focuses on off-task ideas, try to find out why. Is it that the students do not know each other and so are talking about common interests to become acquainted? Are they finished too early and trying to amuse themselves in the remaining time? Are they failing to focus on the driving question? Did they fail to make sure everyone understood the material? It is only through working *with* the groups that you will get to the heart of the problem. You may need to give them time to get to know each other (Kohn, 1996). Perhaps students need more challenging work. You may need to refocus students' attention on the driving question and create new zones of proximal development so that they can sustain collaboration. You may need to show students strategies

CONNECTING TO
NATIONAL SCIENCE EDUCATION STANDARDS

Science Education Teaching Standards
Teachers also give groups opportunities to make presentations of their work and to engage with their classmates in explaining, clarifying, and justifying what they have learned (p. 36).

for making sure all members of the group understand the concepts. For example, students may need to create quizzes for each other or practice giving group presentations to see if each member really understands what has been learned.

Loafing

The **loafer effect** happens when one or more group members allow others to do all the work. Constant monitoring of group members' contributions to the group goal will help you determine if loafers exist. If you keep groups small (three to four students), you will notice these free riders more easily. As you move about the classroom, you can momentarily conference with each group to discuss what each student is doing. You can try to engage the loafers by directing them to tasks they can complete, ideas they can contribute, or ways they can enhance the group's work. You can also provide support mechanisms that will ensure that all students contribute to completing a project. For example, students can complete daily journals in which they record their contributions to the project. You can collect daily charts in which students document their day's accomplishments and record each group member's contribution. These types of support focus on individual and group accountability and help eliminate the loafer effect.

The Fear of Being Duped and the Dominating of Others

Sometimes a higher-ability member of a group fears being "used" or **duped** by the other members and so doesn't want to collaborate. Sometimes a member of a group uses others to his or her advantage, thereby gaining more than he or she would have alone. By requiring individual accountability and self-assessment, teachers can eliminate either of these effects. For example, a teacher may require each student to complete a daily journal to chronicle individual contributions and learning and to account for the accomplishments of the entire group. In this fashion, students have the opportunity to show the teacher their own work as well as that of the group.

Status Differential

The **status differential effect** occurs when a high-status member of a group takes control. Higher status can be caused by many things—membership in a clique, socioeconomic status, race, age, or academic achievement (Cohen, 1994). You can approach this type of problem from several directions. First, you can continue to stress collaborative skills so that all members of the group are contributing equally and learning to accept their individual differences. Second, you can form groups carefully in an effort to avoid status differentials. Third, you can give low-status students prior training on a topic or skill so that they can teach it to high-status students. Finally, you can require individual accountability within a group so that all members are recognized for their efforts.

For example, a teacher may purposefully avoid placing a group of students who all play on the basketball team with a student who is not on the team. The collegiality formed among members of the basketball team may cause a clique to form that excludes the one student who is not on the team. Similarly, a teacher may teach a lower socioeconomic student who she believes will be shunned by others how to use a new computer program. This student, armed with prior knowledge that the others do not have, can teach the rest of the group how to use the computer program.

NSES

CONNECTING TO NATIONAL SCIENCE EDUCATION STANDARDS

Science Teaching Standards

Teachers monitor the participation of all students, carefully determining, for instance, if all members of a collaborative group are working with materials or if one student is making all the decisions. This monitoring can be particularly important in classes of diverse students, where social issues of status and authority can be a factor (pp. 36–37).

Pacts

When all members of a group make a **pact** to avoid work and contribute the least amount of effort to complete a task, a poor quality product or inadequate completion of the goal results. A teacher who knows the abilities of the students in his classroom will quickly recognize this type of behavior.

When you spot evidence of a pact, stress high standards. You might demonstrate or model what is expected at the end of the lesson by showing a sample finished product. You might establish minimum competencies so that students complete an acceptable level of work. For example, you could require each student to have at least two complete artifacts to document science learning or a certain number of entries in a portfolio. Another strategy involves having students complete **learning contracts** in which they establish standards for completion of their work before they begin it. Some teachers promote peer reviews among collaborative groups. Most elementary and middle grade students are motivated to do their best when they know they are going to be required to share their work and be evaluated by other groups. Some teachers believe that friendly competition among groups helps establish high standards. While the members of a group are collaborating, the groups are competing with each other for recognition of high-quality work. However, Kohn (1996) believes that teams should never be set against each other in competition, because this practice does not build a community atmosphere in a classroom. Sapon-Shevin (1996) suggests that exclusion of certain groups of people and competition are barriers to collaboration.

> ### Key Idea
> Teachers need to carefully plan lessons so that students learn collaborative skills that will limit problems such as loafing, status differentials, or pacts. This will help insure that collaborative environments are successful.

Diversity

Research findings on collaborative learning show that, over time, students working in groups learn to appreciate each other's differences, including gender, racial, cultural, and physical or mental ability differences (Cohen, 1994; Manning & Lucking, 1992). With collaborative learning, students tend to accept others different from themselves, make friends with diverse members of their class, and raise the self-esteem of isolated students. However, these same differences in gender, culture, physical ability, and academic ability can cause problems in some group learning situations. For example, research in education has shown that male students frequently dominate science activities, and female students are left behind (Baker, 1988).

You may need to directly address the differences in gender, culture, race, and physical and academic ability. For example, you can point out situations in which male students dominate group situations, or you can subtly encourage female students to participate. Sometimes, making gender-specific teams can eliminate this problem.

Problems certainly can arise when students see some group members as *different,* but they also can arise when students see some group members as *better.* The student who is interested and gifted in science and mathematics may be labeled a "nerd" in a traditional classroom environment because she is always the one raising her hand, getting called upon by the teacher, giving the right answers, and being praised by the teacher. Other students may come to resent her because her success makes them look bad. In contrast, members of a sports team do not resent a talented athlete on their team, because the talent of the star athlete is shared with the team—everyone becomes a winner when one person does well. By fostering such a team mentality with your students, diversity can come to be celebrated and students with special abilities can come to be members of the group.

Socially Induced Incompetence

Socially induced incompetence occurs when members of a group ostracize or disparage a student to the point that he or she feels unable to contribute to the group's work. Children and adults are not always aware of how their behavior can affect others, how talking in a certain tone of voice intimidates, or how making faces or laughing at fellow students can create feelings of inadequacy. You should discuss these problems, model appropriate behavior, and evaluate group work so that students are not socialized to believe they are incompetent. For example, a teacher can purposefully display as a representation of good work an artifact created by a student who has low self-esteem.

A Belief in the "Right Answer"

Even as early as the elementary grades, students become socialized to believe that "right answers" exist for problems or exercises. In project-based science classrooms, teachers frequently find that students rely too heavily on the notion of correct answers. You need to work with students so that they come to understand that many problems or situations in real life have many possible solutions and answers. Reliance on correct answers can cause students continually to seek you out for approval, information, or reassurance. You may need to "wean" students from you, slowly teaching them that they themselves are sources of information, that they can help themselves find answers, and that they have the ability to find resources and information. You need to help them learn that reassurance comes from completing a project as a group rather than from getting minute-to-minute approval from you.

Portfolio Activity 6.8 will help you think about what to do if collaboration fails to work well in your classroom.

Lack of Support from Parents, Colleagues, or Administrators

Key Idea

Students don't automatically collaborate with each other, and teachers can face many challenges when implementing collaborative learning. Awareness of potential challenges can help teachers overcome them.

Parents, colleagues, or principals may not understand the benefits of collaborative learning. Colleagues or administrators with differing beliefs about learning may view a collaborative classroom as unstructured, noisy, or time-consuming. These people think that teaching is not taking place when the teacher does not lecture, write on the chalkboard, or ask questions of the whole class. Principals, in particular, can become problematic if they are not supportive of the instructional techniques being used in a teacher's classroom. Pressure to conform to traditional classroom methods such as having students sit in rows or keeping students quiet can destroy a teacher's efforts to develop and sustain collaboration.

One of the major erroneous beliefs that parents or guardians may have is that higher-ability students are harmed in mixed-ability groups or inclusive classrooms. Research does not support this belief (Manning & Lucking, 1992; Sapon-Shevin, 1999). Findings suggest that higher-ability students do just as well or better in mixed-ability or heterogeneous groups as they do in homogeneous groups. On the other hand, lower-ability students tend to fall further behind when they are placed in same-ability groups. Parents may also believe that students are not learning when they are talking in small groups. Another erroneous belief is that collaborative learning is incompatible with the demands of

Portfolio Activity 6.8 — TROUBLESHOOTING

Materials Needed:
- Something to write with
- Peers to work with
- A teacher experienced with having students work in collaborative groups

A. Think about each of the following situations. As the teacher of an elementary or middle grade classroom, what would you do in each situation? List your ideas.
   - Team members are not working well together and one student is begging you to let her out of the group.
   - Two students monopolize the activities and discussions.
   - The groups are too noisy.
   - One shy student doesn't want to work with others.
   - You have an ESL student (a student for whom English is a second language).

- Parents complain that their children are being cheated by having to work with others. One father says his child is gifted and is being held behind by working with lesser-ability students.
- A student is habitually absent and so doesn't contribute to her group's work.
- A student in a group complains that he has done all the work.
- A student in a peer tutoring situation complains that the tutor is mean.

B. Now discuss each situation with a group of peers. How do your ideas compare?

C. Discuss these issues with a teacher experienced in using collaborative strategies. How would the teacher handle each situation?

D. Record your findings in your portfolio.

---

standardized tests and the kinds of individual projects students must learn to complete in schools. Research has demonstrated that collaborative learning, in fact, increases student achievement, higher-order thinking skills, and problem-solving skills (Bowen, 2000; Schulte, 1999; Wenglinsky, 2000).

Changing people's beliefs can be difficult. A teacher can circumvent problems by explaining to parents, colleagues, and administrators early in the school year what the class is doing and why they are doing it. For example, a teacher might write a letter to parents or to the principal explaining reasons for using collaborative learning. Another strategy is to invite parents, colleagues, or principals into the classroom to engage them in collaborative learning situations. Make them active members of the learning community, not just observers. You can put parents' careers, colleagues' hobbies, and a principal's expertise to work in your learning community. These community members can become sources of information and potential guest speakers. Very often, such a positive experience will convince them of the benefits of collaborative learning. Over time, parents and guardians will see the positive effects of collaborative learning on their son's or daughter's attitudes toward school. Portfolio Activity 6.9 will help you practice what you might tell a parent, principal, or peer.

NSES
CONNECTING TO NATIONAL SCIENCE EDUCATION STANDARDS

Science Teaching Standards
Working collaboratively with others not only enhances the understanding of science, it also fosters the practice of many of the skills, attitudes, and values that characterize science (p. 50).

Portfolio Activity 6.9

HOW DO I EXPLAIN COLLABORATIVE LEARNING TO COLLEAGUES AND PARENTS?

Materials Needed:
- Pen and paper or a computer

A. Imagine that you are planning to use collaborative learning in your science classroom. Think about how you will explain your teaching strategies so that others will understand your goals, expectations, and management strategies.

B. Write a letter to each of the following groups to explain why you are using collaborative learning and how your classroom will function:
- The principal of the school.
- Parents or guardians.
- A substitute teacher (in case you are absent).

C. File your letters in your portfolio.

WHY COLLABORATION ALMOST ALWAYS WORKS BETTER THAN INDIVIDUAL LEARNING

Collaboration is an essential component of project-based science. It almost always works better than individual learning for seven main reasons:

1. Collaborative learning environments create multiple, overlapping zones of proximal development so that students help one another. The students also interact with the teacher and members of the community, forming additional zones of proximal development.
2. Collaborative learning has been found to be more effective than other teaching techniques for raising achievement, enhancing problem-solving abilities, and developing understanding.
3. Collaborative learning helps spread among members of a group the cognitive load that a task or project might demand.
4. Collaborative learning encourages students to become autonomous, self-motivated learners.
5. Collaborative learning tends to lessen anxiety about learning.
6. Girls and minorities—groups traditionally left behind in science classrooms—tend to become essential, active members in a collaborative classroom.
7. In collaborative classrooms, students develop skills necessary for real life situations.

Using Multiple Zones of Proximal Development to Provide Cognitive Support for a Variety of Learners

Trying to learn a new concept or skill without the assistance of others is often very difficult. Have you ever taken a correspondence course or tried to learn something new solely from reading a book or watching a video? Have you ever tried to learn a foreign language from an audiotape? If you have, you probably know that learning is more likely to occur in a social situation, a situation in which you can see a new skill modeled by a teacher, before you try it out on your own or you can receive the assistance of someone more knowledgeable.

In collaborative classrooms, as students interact with others, they introduce new strategies for solving problems. Additional, new, or conflicting ideas crop up. Group members create learning scaffolds for one another. For example, one student might model for another how she used a motion detector to gather data about the speed that a skateboard went down a ramp. Modeling is one example of a scaffold. These collaborative interactions foster joint formation of ideas, construction of shared meaning, development of new skills, and the creation of different ways of solving problems. Collaboratively, students advance from a state of uncertainty, frustration, or confusion toward understanding.

In a traditional classroom, students compete with each other instead of helping each other learn. Low-achieving or quiet students frequently try to avoid attention and so don't participate or interact with others.

Yolanda, an elementary teacher, has her class answer a driving question about the effects of acid rain on the environment. Groups of students work on different subquestions. One group of students has decided to collect water samples from nearby lakes, rivers, streams, ponds, and puddles. They have measured the pH of each water sample. Now students are contemplating the reasons why the pH in the puddles, created by a fresh rainfall, had a much higher acid level than did the lake, river, stream, and pond. After all, they think, a puddle is fresh, and standing bodies of water should accumulate higher levels of acid over time. Yolanda has the group members write down what they believe are the reasons for this surprising finding. Then she has each student share his or her reason by completing the sentence "My idea is . . . ." One student says, "My idea is the air is very polluted and the rain picked up additional acidity when it fell." Another says, "My idea is there was something on the asphalt that was acidic—the rain was simply absorbing acid from the pavement it was sitting on." Another says, "My idea is that cars sitting on the asphalt put acid into the puddle with their exhaust." Still another student says, "My idea is that the puddle is the closest of all the water sources to a factory." Each student, with a different prior level of knowledge about acid, provides a zone of proximal development for others in the class. After students thoroughly discuss the possible causes of this phenomenon, Yolanda suggests that they test each of the ideas. She provides suggestions for testing the ideas and of people with whom they can talk. Students call the factory and find out that factory officials monitor the air and ground surface around the factory for pollution. Now they know they can obtain information about the acid level of both the air and the ground. One student contacts a local automobile dealership owner to get information about car exhaust and the environment. As the students interact with Yolanda and with other knowledgeable adults in the community, they continue to be exposed to new zones of proximal development. Each zone provides students with links to higher learning, links that would not have occurred if students had been working alone or in traditional classrooms.

> ### Key Idea
> Collaborative learning almost always works better than individual learning.

Effects on Achievement, Problem Solving, and Understanding

Several research studies have shown that when students work in groups, their academic achievement improves (Bowen, 2000; Manning & Lucking, 1992; Slavin, 1992; Wenglinsky, 2000). Recent research has found that collaborative learning improves problem-solving skills and higher-order thinking skills and helps students learn concepts—two important

A community member shares her expertise with the class.

goals of the *National Science Education Standards* (National Research Council, 1996). As students interact with others, disagreements usually arise over ideas, methods to test ideas, and answers. The disagreements and their resolutions help students solve problems. In the process of resolving disagreements, students construct understanding, improve their reasoning skills, and enhance their problem-solving skills. They are also likely to form richer conceptual understandings. Attempts by students to validate their views help bring about cognitive change. Arguments that require students to defend their views help some students become dissatisfied with their own views and abandon them. Further, students are more likely to retain material learned in collaborative groups because ideas and relationships are formed and modified via communication with others. When students express ideas, they must represent ideas in new ways so stronger connections are formed. Students use cognitive elaboration—strategies that enable them to form more detailed, thorough mental understanding—when they discuss concepts, debate ideas, and explain concepts to others in their group.

In the acid rain project, as students discuss reasons that fresh rain puddles contain more acid rain than other bodies of water, they begin to disagree and argue. Some students insist that the factory caused the acid rain, and others argue that it had something to do with the asphalt. Because the students disagreed, they decided to test out all their ideas. As a result of this exploration, students learn that the factory exceeds all EPA air quality regulations, enabling them to rule out proximity to the factory as a cause.

Spread of Cognitive Load Among Learners

Rarely in today's world is there a science topic that is simple. Most topics are complex and interdisciplinary—they overlap various science subjects, social issues, mathematics, and technology. The study of acid rain, for example, involves many disciplines. Understanding the formation of acid in the environment relies on understanding chemistry. Examining the effects of acid rain on the environment includes areas of biology, geology, meteorology, and physical science. Measuring and monitoring acid rain involves mathematics. Evaluating the sources of pollutants in the air that cause acid rain is a social concern.

Many scientific questions and problems have more than one plausible solution. For example, numerous ways exist to limit acid rain in the environment (limit sulfur-burning coal factories, add scrubbers to factory smokestacks, find ways to neutralize acid, and so on). New knowledge in science and technology is increasing at such a rapid pace that journals and textbooks, unless they are electronic, cannot keep up with it. It is nearly impossible for people to acquire, synthesize, and assimilate all the information available to answer a question that they find important.

Most children cannot on their own answer many science questions that arise. In collaborative learning situations, however, the **cognitive load** is spread among members of the group. Not every student in the class has to answer every question, grapple with every idea, obtain information from all community members, or test all possible hypotheses. The cognitive load of acquiring, synthesizing, and assimilating information is spread among members of the class who have different learning styles and intelligences.

For example, the student with strong interpersonal skills may want to interview business leaders about efforts to control acid rain, whereas the student with visual/spatial skills might build a model to demonstrate the effect of acid rain on the environment. Some students may read journals and books, while others search the World Wide Web for information. A few students can conduct a scientific experiment, while others interview people in various careers.

Promotion of Autonomous, Motivated Learning

Collaborative learning shifts the responsibility for learning from the teacher to the students. Students learn from each other as well as from the teacher and others in the community. A collaborative environment promotes students taking active roles in their own learning as well as in the learning of others, determining what is learned, how it is learned, and when it is learned. When students take an active role in their learning, the subject matter content becomes interesting to them, and they are motivated to learn. This type of responsibility helps students become autonomous learners who know how to ask questions and find solutions to questions.

Collaborative learning reinforces the idea that effort, not solely innate ability, begets rewards. For example, in a traditional classroom, if a student fails a test, she may conclude, "I'm just not smart enough to understand molecules!" In a collaborative environment, students are more likely to conclude that, with effort, time, and cooperation, every member of the group can learn to understand basic chemistry. This type of success is motivating.

> ### Key Idea
> Collaborative learning shifts responsibility to the students.

The collaborative classroom environment is particularly powerful for preadolescents and young adolescents because it matches their developmental needs (Barnes, Shaw, & Spector, 1989). They desire peer interaction, want to be accepted by others, need to be trusted to make their own decisions, and crave meaningful learning. A collaborative environment also develops students who are intrinsically motivated to learn, thereby reducing or eliminating the need to enforce punishments or give artificial rewards.

In the acid rain project, Yolanda explores ways to make her relationship with her students more collaborative. She wants to move away from the traditional role of the teacher as holder of knowledge to one in which she is a co-investigator with her students. She accomplishes this by becoming a learner along with her students—asking questions and exploring with students without ever being certain of the solutions that will arise. She empowers her students' status by behaving as if they have important knowledge and experiences that are useful in their exploration of the problem. The students respond by selecting resources to help them investigate the problem. They read local newspapers, consult reference books, and talk with individuals who work in related fields. Some students choose to investigate the topic on the World Wide Web. Others set up experiments to measure acid rain levels and the effect on plant life. The students become responsible for their own learning. The classroom is a democratic one—both the students and the teacher share in the decision making. In Portfolio Activity 6.10, you will explore how the role of the teacher changes in a collaborative classroom.

Reduction of Anxiety about Learning

In collaborative classrooms, **anxiety**, or uneasiness and apprehension, about learning science is reduced for several reasons (Sheridan, Byrne, & Quina, 1989). First, students share ideas without fear of being put down or ridiculed. Peers typically will not feel

---

Portfolio Activity 6.10

HOW DO TEACHERS' ROLES CHANGE IN A COLLABORATIVE CLASSROOM?

Materials Needed:
- Two teachers

A. With the help of your instructor, a school principal, or a school curriculum director, identify two teachers—one who does not use much group work and one who uses many collaborative techniques in his or her classroom. Obtain permission to observe and interview each of these teachers.

B. Observe each teacher. Analyze the likenesses and differences between the teachers in terms of

- The academic goals for students.
- The structure of daily lessons.
- The style of classroom management.
- The reactions of students during lessons.
- The level of interaction among students in the class and between the teacher and students.
- The methods of evaluation in each class.

C. What do you see as the advantages and disadvantages of collaborative learning? How do teachers' roles change in collaborative classrooms? Record your ideas in your portfolio.

---

threatened by one another, so they can engage in quality discussions, share thoughts, and debate ideas without anxiety. Second, collaborative work tends to be supportive rather than competitive. Collaborative learning classrooms form caring environments in which students show kindness, fairness, and responsibility. Third, in collaborative classrooms, the teacher and the students become allies in the learning process. The teacher isn't an authority but rather a guide in the learning process. In addition, the teacher is not the sole disseminator of information; students play an important role in asking questions, finding information, and sharing what they have learned. Fourth, the collaborative classroom stresses that there aren't only short, correct answers but possibly many answers, interpretations, or solutions to questions. In this atmosphere, students know that there are often many ways to answer a question or solve a problem and that their ideas are as valid as those of others.

The students learning about acid rain feel very comfortable asking questions. Neither the other students in the class nor their teacher, Yolanda, will make them feel intimidated for asking questions. In fact, students are encouraged to ask as many questions as possible since it is part of the learning process to answer questions. As students take control of their own learning and become more comfortable in the project-based classroom, their self-esteem increases. Their attitudes toward learning about the effects of acid rain are very positive. Yolanda finds that, over the course of a school year, she is able to get students more involved. All students participate equally, and they don't seem anxious about learning science. Students seem to like school, enjoy science class, and are concerned for others in their group. This caring environment reduces or eliminates the anxiety frequently observed in a traditional, competitive classroom.

Inclusion of Groups Traditionally Left Behind in Science

Research indicates that girls and minorities lag behind others in their pursuit of learning about science, developing science-related interests, selecting science electives in high school, and embarking on careers in science (Kahle, 1985; Pollina, 1995; Rosser, 1990;

Seymour, 1995). Collaborative learning has been demonstrated to be a positive teaching strategy for including girls and minorities in science (Baker, 1988; Harwell, 2000; Manning & Lucking, 1992; Mayberry, 1998; Strough & Cheng, 2000). There are several explanations for why collaborative learning helps girls and minorities. First, collaborative learning removes the competitive atmosphere that prevails in some science classrooms in which some girls and minorities feel intimidated. Second, because collaborative learning demands that all students participate equally in investigating a question, students who may not perceive science as a strength do not "fall through the cracks." They must participate in discussions, investigations, and decisions. Third, collaborative learning develops the social and interpersonal skills of all students, making them better able to work with students from backgrounds different from their own and making them more accepting of others and their opinions or ideas.

> ### Key Idea
> Collaborative learning engages girls and minorities in science.

American Indians, for example, are underrepresented in science, typically drop out of high school, and often do not attend college. Although differences exist among Native American tribes, Native Americans hold certain core values. For example, Native Americans respect all life and encourage respect for individual people (Soldier, 1989). They teach their children to solve their own problems and look to their elders for wisdom. Many Native American children are part of extended families in which they learn to cooperate, share, and live in harmony with others. Traditional classroom environments that stress competition for grades, individual work rather than group work, and the authority of the teacher conflict with basic Native American values. Collaborative classrooms, on the contrary, promote cooperation, group work, sharing, and respect for all individuals in a group. Further, collaboration in a project-based science classroom encourages student-directed learning; the teacher is not the authority but rather the guide who might be sought out for his or her wisdom—a concept of teacher that is consistent with American Indian culture.

In the acid rain project, a quiet girl named Maria is confident enough to share her ideas with three other classmates, but she tends to fail to participate in whole-class situations. Maria's family, originally from West Virginia where coal mining is a major industry, believes very strongly in the benefits of burning coal to produce energy. As a result of sharing her experiences with classmates about the economy in West Virginia, others in the group learn to accept her and have greater tolerance for her ideas. They begin to explore ways that factories might still use sulfur-burning coal and not damage the environment.

Development of Real Life Skills

Collaborative learning helps develop the abilities and skills students need in real life. The Labor Secretary's Commission on Achieving Necessary Skills (Brock, 1991) identified five minimum competencies (called the *new basics*) necessary for all adult citizens. These are the abilities to work with others; acquire and use information; identify, organize, and allocate resources; understand complex interrelationships; and work with a variety of technologies. To work with others, for example, a person must be able to participate as a member of a team, contribute to a team's efforts, negotiate with others, resolve differences, and work with people of diverse backgrounds. These types of skills are developed in collaborative learning situations.

As students in the acid rain project investigate the driving question, they develop skills they will use throughout their lives. They need to work effectively with other students in their group. This project requires them to communicate with others,

Portfolio Activity 6.11

HOW DOES COLLABORATION CHANGE THE NATURE OF THE CLASSROOM?

Materials Needed:
- Two classrooms to observe

A. Reexamine your answers to these questions from Portfolio Activity 6.1:
   - How are students working together in these classrooms?
   - How does the teacher structure the group work?
   - Are students given jobs or roles to play? Are the roles or jobs meaningful intellectually, or are they only procedural tasks?
   - Are the jobs or roles necessary to complete the task?
   - What is the role of the teacher in the classroom?
   - What are the teacher's objectives in the lesson?
   - What instructional strategies does the teacher use?
   - How does the teacher help students work in groups (by developing interpersonal skills, encouraging students to talk with each other, resolving conflicts)?

B. What do you see as the advantages and challenges of a collaborative classroom? Discuss with peers how these challenges might be overcome.

C. How have your thoughts changed (if at all) about collaborative strategies?

D. Record your thoughts and observations in your portfolio.

compromise, develop new ideas together, and resolve differences. Although they come from diverse backgrounds and have different opinions, they must learn to work together. To acquire and use information, the groups of students need to read the local newspapers, identify appropriate journals and books to read, and synthesize information from these readings. They figure out how to obtain related information from the World Wide Web. To conduct their plant experiments, they need to identify, organize, and allocate such resources as pH meters, plants, sources of acid rain, and locations for taking samples. To understand the effect of acid rain on the environment, they have to make sense of complicated interrelationships such as the effects of biological factors on plants, the physical effects of acid rain on buildings and other surfaces, the chemical relationship between sulfur-burning coal and the formation of acid rain, and the geological processes that take place in the atmosphere and hydrosphere. They use scientific equipment and technological tools that include pH meters, microscopes, computers, fax machines, and telephones.

Portfolio Activities 6.11 and 6.12 ask you to revisit the activity you completed at the beginning of this chapter, reassess the nature of collaborative classrooms now that you know more about it, and learn about available curriculum resources that use collaborative strategies.

ONLINE LEARNING CENTER

CHAPTER REVIEW   www.mhhe.com/krajcik2e

Go to the Online Learning Center at **www.mhhe.com/krajcik2e** to review important content from the chapter and key terms, take a chapter assessment, and link to the chapter's websites.

Portfolio Activity 6.12

WHAT CURRICULUM RESOURCES USE COLLABORATIVE STRATEGIES?

Materials Needed:
- A variety of curriculum resources listed in the following activities

A. In recent years, a variety of curriculum materials that use various collaborative strategies have emerged on the market. Obtain several of the following curriculum materials and investigate them. If possible, use the materials with a class of students:
- *Science for Life and Living: Integrating Science, Technology, and Health.* 1992. BSCS, 830 N. Tejon, Suite 405, Colorado Springs, CO 80903, or Kendall/Hunt Publishing Company, 4050 Westmark Drive, P.O. Box 1840, Dubuque, IA 52004-1840. An elementary science textbook series.
- *Decisions, Decisions Series.* 1990, 1991, 1993. Tom Snyder Productions, 80 Coolidge Hill Rd., Watertown, MA 02172-2817, 1-800-342-0236. Different simulation programs about colonization, immigration, revolutionary wars, environmental issues, and more.
- *The Great Solar System Rescue.* 1992. Tom Snyder Productions. Simulation in which students work to find space probes lost in the solar system.
- *The Great Ocean Rescue.* 1993. Tom Snyder Productions. Simulation in which students work to solve environmental problems about the oceans.
- *Fizz and Martina.* 1991. Tom Snyder Productions. Cooperative learning activities for mathematics.
- *The Geometric Supposer.* 1987. Education Development Center, Sunburst Communications Inc., 39 Washington Ave., Pleasantville, NY 10570, 1-800-431-1934. Cooperative learning activities to teach about geometry.

B. How are these materials different from other curriculum materials you've seen for teaching science to children?

C. How well do the materials utilize the following philosophical framework for project-based science?:
- *Focus on a driving question.* Students investigate meaningful and important questions that orchestrate activities and organize concepts and principles.
- *Investigations.* Students investigate the driving question by asking and refining questions, making plans, designing experiments, debating ideas, collecting and analyzing information and data, drawing conclusions, and communicating ideas and findings to others.
- *Generation of products or artifacts.* As a result of performing inquiries, students develop a series of artifacts or products that represent their knowledge in a variety of ways.
- *Learning communities and collaboration.* Students, teachers, and individuals outside the classroom collaborate to investigate the driving question.
- *Use of cognitive tools.* Learners represent and share ideas and support their research efforts with cognitive tools such as computers.

CHAPTER SUMMARY

In this chapter we discussed the nature of collaboration among students, teachers, and members of the community. Because collaborative learning doesn't just happen in a classroom, the chapter focused on ways to create a collaborative *environment,* including forming groups, developing collaborative skills (such as decision-making, task-completion, trust-building, communication, and conflict-management skills), and getting all students equitably involved (through establishing common goals, building common understanding, and allocating labor and roles equitably). We discussed ways teachers can overcome challenges that arise during the implementing of collaborative groups. Specifically, we discussed what to do when students lack collaborative skills and how to deal with particular problem situations such as students failing to work in groups or not being accepted by peers. We discussed how to work with parents, colleagues, and administrators who may not be familiar with collaborative group work. Finally, we discussed reasons collaboration is almost always better than individual learning, such as the development of zones of proximal development; improvements in achievement, problem solving, and understanding; the spread of cognitive load; the promotion of motivated learning; the reduction of anxiety about learning; the inclusion of groups traditionally left behind in science; and the development of real life skills.

CHAPTER HIGHLIGHTS

- Collaborative learning is a key feature of project-based science.
- There are three types of collaborative arrangements
  - Among students.
  - Between students and teacher.
  - Between students and the community.
- Teachers are responsible for creating a collaborative environment.
- Collaboration must be planned. Planning includes
  - Forming groups.
  - Developing collaborative skills among students in the class.
  - Involving all students equitably.
- Students' collaborative skills need to be developed. These include
  - Decision making.
  - Task completion.
  - Trust building.
  - Communication.
  - Conflict management.
- Teachers face many challenges when implementing collaborative groups. These include
  - A lack of collaborative skills.
  - Loafing.
  - The fear of being duped and the dominating of others.
  - Status differential.
  - Pacts.
  - Diversity.
  - Socially induced incompetence.
  - A belief in the "right answer."
  - Lack of support from parents, colleagues, or administrators.
- Collaboration almost always works better than individual learning. There are numerous reasons
  - Multiple zones of proximal development are created among students that help scaffold learning.
  - It positively affects achievement, problem solving, and understanding.
  - The cognitive load is spread among students.
  - It promotes autonomous, motivated learning.
  - Anxiety about learning is reduced.

- Groups traditionally left behind in science are more likely to be included.
- Real life skills are developed.

KEY TERMS

anxiety (239)	interpersonal roles (228)	scaffolding (208)
base groups (212)	learning contracts (233)	sharing groups (212)
cognitive load (238)	loafer effect (232)	socially induced
cognitive roles (228)	managerial roles (228)	incompetence (234)
collaboration (203	meaning (206)	status differential
division of labor (225)	mutuality (205)	effect (232)
duped (232)	pact (233)	trust-building skills (217)
equality (205)	positive	zone of proximal
home groups (212)	interdependence (225)	development (204)

REFERENCES

Baker, D. April 1988. Teaching for gender differences. *Research Matters to the Science Teacher* (30):3. National Association for Research in Science Teaching (NARST).

Barnes, M. B., T. J. Shaw, and B. S. Spector. 1989. *How science is learned by adolescents and young adults*. Dubuque, Iowa: Kendall/Hunt.

Blumenfeld, P. C., R. W. Marx, E. Soloway, and J. S. Krajcik. 1996. Learning with peers: From small group cooperation to collaborative communities. *Educational Researcher* 25(8):37–40.

Bowen, C. W. 2000. A quantitative literature review of cooperative learning effects on high school and college chemistry achievement. *Journal of Chemical Education* 77(1):116–19.

Brock, W. E. 1991. Continuous training for the high-skilled work force. *Community, Technical, and Junior College Journal* (61):4, 21–25.

Cohen, E. G. 1994. *Designing groupwork: Strategies for the heterogeneous classroom*. New York: Teachers College Press.

Cohen, E. G. 1998. Making cooperative learning equitable. *Educational Leadership* 56(1):18–21.

Damon, W., and E. Phelps. 1989. Critical distinctions among three approaches to peer education. *International Journal of Educational Research* 13:9–19.

Edwards, C., and J. Stout. 1990. Cooperative learning: The first year. *Educational Leadership* 47(4):38–41.

Harwell, S. H. 2000. In their own voices: Middle level girls' perceptions of teaching and learning science. *Journal of Science Teacher Education* 11(3): 221–42.

Johnson, D. W., and R. T. Johnson. 1990. Social skills for successful group work. *Educational Leadership* 47(4):29–33.

Johnson, D. W., R. T. Johnson, and E. J. Holubec. 1986. *Circles of learning: Cooperation in the classroom*. Edina, Minn.: Interaction Book Company.

Kahle, J. B. 1985. *Research matters to the science teacher: Encouraging girls in science courses and careers*. Cincinnati, Ohio: National Association for Research in Science Teaching.

Kahle, J. B., and L. J. Rennie. 1993. Ameliorating gender differences in attitudes about science: A cross-national study. *Journal of Science Education and Technology* (2):1, 321–34.

Kohn, A. 1996. *Beyond discipline: From compliance to community.* Alexandria, Va.: Association for Supervision and Curriculum Development.

Leonard, J., and K. McElroy. 2000. What one middle school teacher learned about cooperative learning. *Journal of Research in Childhood Education* 14(2):239–45.

Mahenthiran, S., and P. J. Rouse. 2000. The impact of group selection on student performance and satisfaction. *International Journal of Educational Management* 14(6):255–64.

Manning, M. L., and R. Lucking. 1992. The what, why, and how of cooperative learning. In *Relevant research,* ed. Marcia K. Pearsall. Washington, D.C.: National Science Teachers Association.

Mayberry, M. 1998. Reproductive and resistant pedagogies: The comparative roles of collaborative learning and feminist pedagogy in science education. *Journal of Research in Science Teaching* 35(4):443–59.

National Research Council. 1996. *National science education standards.* Washington, D.C.: National Academy of Science.

Pfister, M. 1996. *Rainbow fish.* New York: North South Books.

Pollina, A. 1995. Gender balance: Lessons from girls in science and mathematics. *Educational Leadership* 53(1):30–33.

Rosser, S. V. 1990. *Female-friendly science.* New York: Pergamon Press.

Sapon-Shevin, M. 1999. *Because we can change the world: A practical guide to building cooperative, inclusive classroom communities.* Boston: Allyn and Bacon.

Schulte, P. 1999. Lessons in cooperative learning. *Science and Children* 36(7): 44–47.

Seymour, E. 1995. The loss of women from science, mathematics, and engineering undergraduate majors: An explanatory account. *Science Education* 79(4): 437–73.

Sheridan, J., A. C. Bryne, and K. Quina. 1989. Collaborative learning: Notes from the field. *College Teaching* 37(2):49–53.

Slavin, R. E. 1992. Achievement effects of ability grouping in secondary schools: A best evidence synthesis. In *Relevant research,* ed. Marcia K. Pearsall. Washington, D.C.: National Science Teachers Association.

Soldier, L. L. 1989. Cooperative learning and the Native American student. *Phi Delta Kappan* 71(2):161–63.

Strough, J., and S. Cheng. 2000. Dyad gender and friendship differences in shared goals for mutual participation on a collaborative task. *Child Study Journal* 30(2):103–26.

Tao, P. K., and R. F. Gunstone. 1999. Conceptual change in science through collaborative learning and the computer. *International Journal of Science Education* 21(1): 39–57.

Vygotsky, L. 1986. *Thought and language.* Cambridge, Mass.: MIT Press.

Wenglinsky, H. 2000. *How teaching matters: Bringing the classroom back into discussions of teacher quality.* Princeton, N.J.: Milken Family Foundation and Educational Testing Service.

Young, E. 1993. *Seven Blind Mice.* New York: Scholastic.

Chapter 7

How Do I Develop and Use Benchmark Lessons?

INTRODUCTION

THE ROLE OF BENCHMARK LESSONS IN PROJECT-BASED SCIENCE

PLANNING A BENCHMARK LESSON

USING DEMONSTRATIONS

USING LARGE GROUP DISCUSSION

PRESENTING INFORMATION

USING LITERATURE

USING CONCEPT MAPS

USING QUESTIONS

CHAPTER LEARNING PERFORMANCES

- *Explain why benchmark lessons are a critical component of project-based science.*
- *Describe how a teacher can determine when to plan a benchmark lesson.*
- *Create a lesson plan for and teach a benchmark lesson.*
- *Compare and contrast the reasons for using various types of strategies (demonstrations, large group discussion, etc.) for benchmark lessons.*
- *Explain the value of using children's literature in science and suggest literature that can be used to teach a science concept.*
- *Justify why concept maps are useful and create a concept map for several related science concepts to be taught.*
- *Distinguish among various types of questions.*

INTRODUCTION

This chapter focuses on the various ways teachers can represent science content and concepts in benchmark lessons to help students develop meaningful understandings in a project-based science environment. The topic of benchmark lessons raises a number of questions: *What is a benchmark lesson? How do I use benchmark lessons? How do I plan benchmark lessons?* This chapter will address these and other questions. The chapter will also discuss the use of student-developed concept maps as a way to express ideas. Because good questioning techniques are an essential component of conducting benchmark lessons, we will also focus on questioning techniques to promote student thinking. Finally, we will discuss how teachers can prepare benchmark lessons.

Benchmark lessons are teacher-directed classroom activities that present concepts, principles, or skills that students need in order to understand the work of a project. Benchmark lessons may involve giving demonstrations, facilitating discussions, role-playing, presenting information, making concept maps, going on field trips, and using literature. Before beginning our discussion of benchmark lessons, consider the following three scenarios on the presentation of scientific ideas. These scenarios will illustrate the importance of a project approach and how to use benchmark lessons in your teaching.

> **Key Idea**
>
> Benchmark lessons are teacher-directed activities used to teach important concepts, principles, or skills.

Scenario 1: Reading About Insects

Mrs. Patterson, your fifth-grade teacher, starts class like this: "Okay, let's open our science textbook and turn to page twenty-eight. Today, we are going to read about the variety of insects that live in our world. Karen, would you please read the first paragraph?" At the end of each paragraph, Mrs. Patterson asks a different student to read the next section and writes new vocabulary words on the board. After about twenty minutes of reading and summarizing, Mrs. Patterson says, "Now turn to page forty-one and answer the first four questions about insects. Make sure to use complete sentences and check your spelling." You turn to page forty-one, take out a piece of paper, and start to answer the questions.

You follow most of the reading, but occasionally you drift off and think about playing soccer after school. You are happy that you answered the questions in the amount of time Mrs. Patterson gave you. You aren't sure why you were reading about the insects. Some of the pictures of the insects are pretty cool and you wonder if you have insects like that in the school yard or in your backyard.

Sound familiar? Chapter 1 referred to this method of science instruction as *reading about science*. Although important new terms were introduced to students with this method, students experienced science as a reading activity. The concepts of science were not linked to everyday life. Reading is an important component of science learning, but when reading about science is not tied to a larger picture that has meaning for students, it can become a routine and uninteresting way of learning.

Scenario 2: Using a Microscope

Mr. Morales, your fifth grade science teacher, starts class by saying, "Today we're going to find out about how to use a microscope." Mr. Morales gives a number of cautions about handling a microscope and then gives a demonstration. For the remainder of the class period and the next day, you and your partner practice using a microscope and look at some "neat" stuff under the microscope. Mr. Morales wants you to draw what the objects look like when viewed through a microscope. You examine and draw pictures of onion skin, human hair, and a fly wing. You hear "oohs" and "aahs" during class as students look at the various objects under the microscope. You and your partner do not fully understand why you learned to use the microscope, but you remember Mr. Morales mentioning that scientists use it to make discoveries.

In Chapter 1, you learned that this kind of science teaching is called *process science teaching*. Although it was awesome to see things under the microscope and the activity generated excitement in the classroom, learning to use the microscope wasn't tied to a larger purpose. Mr. Morales used the activity to meet one of the district's curriculum objectives: use scientific tools to make more precise observations. Although you learned how to make observations using a microscope, the observations were not connected to new ideas or to answering questions. Although at the elementary and middle school level it is important to develop students' skills, skills learned in isolation are often not transferred to new situations. As we discussed in Chapter 4, you don't learn to play tennis by learning a backhand return; the skills must be practiced in context.

Scenario 3: Observing Insects

Your class is exploring the question "When do various insects appear on our playground?" As part of your project activities, you are observing when various insects appear on the playground and in the small wooded area behind the school. As part of your work, you decide to draw the various insects and to write down the date when you first see them. A number of the children in the class ask your teacher, Ms. Cheng, how they could better observe the insects. Ms. Cheng, noticing your activities, decides that it would be beneficial for the class to learn how to make more careful observations with either a microscope or a magnifying glass. She also realizes that a benchmark lesson on microscopes and magnifying glasses would help meet several of the district's objectives: using scientific tools to make more precise observations and teaching students about the taxonomy, structure, and function of parts of insects. She decides to plan a lesson on how to use a magnifying glass and a microscope to observe and identify insects and learn about their taxonomy, structure, and function. Ms. Cheng starts the next science class by explaining what she observed about the students and what questions students asked. She then says, "How can we better observe the insects we see on the playground?" After several students' responses, Ms. Cheng summarizes and elaborates on what the students said: "Scientists often use various tools to help them in their work. Tools that can help people better see the insects are magnifying glasses and microscopes." She demonstrates how to use a microscope, shows the class how to make slides to observe various parts of the insects, and gives a number of cautions about how to handle a microscope. She also demonstrates how to use a magnifying glass. For the remainder of the class period and the next day, you and your partner practice using a microscope and look at some "neat" stuff under the microscope. You look at onion skin, human hair, and a fly wing. You hear "oohs" and "aahs" throughout the class as students look at the various objects under the microscope. Once you know how to use the microscope and understand the cautions about using it, Ms. Cheng allows you and your partner to use your new tool to continue your observations of insects and to learn more about insects' body parts and the structure and function of the parts. Science is fun, you do some new activities, and you learn how to use a tool to help you answer questions you have about insects.

This third scenario illustrates a project-based science environment and how a teacher might use a benchmark lesson to help students further their work in the project as well as meet some curriculum objectives. The students learned how to make observations with a microscope, but their learning was connected to new information that would help them answer their questions. The students learned about the taxonomy, structure, and function of insects' body parts through active observation of them. The project and the benchmark lessons exposed the students to new ideas, allowed them to interact with materials, held their interest, and were meaningful.

THE ROLE OF BENCHMARK LESSONS IN PROJECT-BASED SCIENCE

Practicing and preservice teachers frequently ask if activities traditionally performed in school science, such as demonstrations or hands-on activities, have a place in a project-based science environment. As Scenario 3 illustrates, teacher-led activities do have an important place in project-based science. During a project, the teacher frequently must trigger students' thinking about a phenomenon, present particular concepts so that students will develop deeper understandings of the concepts in the project, or illustrate procedures necessary to carry out the experimental work of the project. Often, these benchmark lessons are related to the curriculum objectives of the district or state. Or they may match up with curriculum objectives advocated by national organizations such as the Association for the Advancement of Science (1993) or the National Research Council (1996, 2000). When activities or lessons are tied to projects, they are known as benchmark lessons (Hunt & Minstrell, 1994). Teachers help students learn the principles and concepts involved in a project by interspersing throughout the project benchmark lessons related to content and skills that students need to further their project work. Students can also use these concepts and skills in subsequent discussions and project work.

> ### Key Idea
> Benchmark lessons use a variety of strategies such as demonstrations, teacher-led activities, discussions, field trips, or presentations involving visual aids, analogies, and children's literature.

Benchmark lessons can take many forms: demonstrations, field trips, teacher-led discussions, teacher-led activities, or presentations of new information involving a variety of visual aids, powerful analogies, and even children's literature. They can be as short as fifteen minutes or as long as several class periods, depending on their purpose.

Benchmark Lessons: A Critical Component of Project-Based Science

Benchmark lessons are a critical component of project-based science. Benchmark lessons can help students learn difficult concepts during project activities, illustrate important laboratory techniques, develop investigation strategies that they will need to complete a project, model thinking, or stimulate curiosity.

Help Students Learn Difficult Concepts

One of the most appropriate uses of benchmark lessons is helping students learn key scientific concepts and principles associated with a project. Imagine that a fourth-grade class is exploring the question "What chemicals are found in the home?" The teacher might use a benchmark lesson to help students develop ideas about chemical properties, chemical change, or chemical reactions. Such lessons might focus on the chemical properties of simple cooking items such as flour, salt, sugar, and baking soda. The teacher might explore chemical reactions by showing the students how a gas is formed when vinegar is mixed with baking soda. Finally, the teacher might decide to show a video that explains what chemical changes occur in the mixing of vinegar and baking soda.

Imagine a class explores the question "Is my water safe to drink?" The teacher might use benchmark lessons to introduce students to concepts such as groundwater, aquifer, runoff, point pollution, or nonbiodegradable. These are all concepts that students must understand to be able to explore the question effectively.

Young children learning about plant growth need to learn some basic concepts as well. The teacher might give benchmark lessons on parts of a plant (stems, roots, and leaves) and functions of plants (plants make their own food, take in water, and give off oxygen).

A benchmark lesson differs from a traditional lesson in that in benchmark lessons students are not just learning the concepts for the sake of learning them. Rather, they learn the concepts and principles to help them understand and find solutions to the driving question of the project. Hence, the concepts and principles are tied to a meaningful and important question. This connection will make the concepts and principles more memorable to learners (Singer et al., 2000).

During a benchmark lesson, it is important to refer often to the driving question of the project so that students see how the lesson connects to their project. If a class explores the question "When do various insects appear on our playground?" the teacher might give a benchmark lesson about the life cycle of insects. Students need to understand that insects go through several stages during metamorphosis. Otherwise, they may think they are observing different insects instead of different stages of the same insects. Although insect life cycle might be a sophisticated concept for some students to learn, it will be easier for them to understand if connected to the driving question.

> ### Key Idea
> Benchmark lessons differ from other traditional lessons in that they help students learn important concepts, principles, laboratory techniques, and skills needed to help them understand and find solutions to the driving question of the project.

**CONNECTING TO
NATIONAL SCIENCE EDUCATION STANDARDS**

Principles and Definitions

Understanding science requires that an individual integrate a complex structure of many types of knowledge, including the ideas of science, relationships between ideas, reasons for these relationships, ways to use the ideas to explain and predict other natural phenomena, and ways to apply them to many events (p. 23).

Illustrate a Laboratory Technique

Benchmark lessons also help in illustrating how to perform a laboratory technique. Again depending on what a teacher needs to illustrate, lesson time will vary. Imagine a third-grade class explores the driving question "How can I get large pumpkins to grow in my garden?" As part of the project activities, students compare the growth of different kinds of pumpkin seeds. The teacher knows that the students will need to understand how to use a ruler to measure the height and length of the plants, so once students have planted their seeds, the teacher gives a benchmark lesson on how to read a ruler. First, he explains that to measure the height of a plant, everyone will need to know how to read a ruler. Next, he demonstrates how to read a ruler and has students practice the skill. Finally, he has the class measure a number of objects and compare their readings. The teacher ties the skill of reading the ruler to the students' work in the project.

Imagine a first-grade class explores the question "What is alive?" As part of this project, students might explore whether various seeds are alive and what it means "to grow." As part of the project activities, the students need to observe seeds germinating, so the teacher illustrates how students might do this. In a benchmark lesson, she shows them how to use resealable plastic bags, seeds, and moist paper towels to sprout seeds and watch them grow. Again, the teacher ties this benchmark lesson to the driving question of the project.

The science activities routinely performed in elementary and middle school are seldom tied to large projects or students' questions and, as a result, often fail to be meaningful. Tied to projects, benchmark lessons that illustrate laboratory skills have meaning for students and become more memorable.

Build New Inquiry Abilities

Teachers can also use benchmark lessons to help students learn important inquiry strategies such as asking and refining questions, evaluating information, justifying and building arguments, analyzing data, and drawing conclusions. Again, the time for such lessons will vary. For instance, in the project on the growth of various types of pumpkin seeds, a teacher might observe that not all students record their results in a systematic manner. She decides to review with the class the importance of systematically recording observations. Because the class had explored this idea earlier, the teacher feels that only a short discussion with the class is necessary. During the project, the teacher realizes that students will need a way to compare their results. Because the students have not been introduced previously to bar graphing, she decides that a lesson on bar graphing would be appropriate, and she knows it will take several days to teach it since it is an unfamiliar concept. See Chapter 4 to learn about more ideas for developing lessons to help teach investigation strategies.

Model Thinking

Key Idea

Through the use of benchmark lessons, teachers can model thinking including asking questions, reflecting aloud, deciding how to compare experimental data, and wondering what might be done differently.

Through benchmark lessons, teachers can **model thinking**. This type of benchmark lesson overlaps with the other types described so far; however, because it is so critical for teachers to model thinking, it deserves special consideration. During various parts of projects, many opportunities will surface to model thinking. Model thinking includes asking yourself questions, reflecting aloud, and wondering what might be done differently.

Imagine that you want to illustrate to students the importance of questioning information found on the World Wide Web. During a project exploring the driving question "Does my environment influence my health?" students might find information about the effects of smog on the health of young children. One way to help students evaluate this material is to model the thinking process that you would use to evaluate it. For instance, you could model questioning the source of the materials: "Does it matter if the source is the manufacturer of cars, an environmental advocacy group, or a university group?" or "How can I determine if this is a reputable source of information?"

In the project on growing pumpkins a teacher could think aloud about how she came to the decision to use bar graphing to compare results. One technique would be to introduce the bar graph lesson by saying, "Today we are going to learn bar graphing so we can compare the heights of the pumpkin plants." Although this tells the children why the teacher is introducing bar graphing, it isn't the most powerful technique because it doesn't capture student curiosity and it doesn't model thinking. Another technique is to model coming to the decision to use bar graphs. The teacher might, for instance, start by asking, "How are we going to compare the data we have on the heights of plants grown from different kinds of pumpkin seeds?" Next, the teacher could ask the students for their ideas or she could continue to think aloud. She might say, "Let's see. Putting the data in a table might help, but it won't allow me to see trends easily. What kind of visual representation might I use? Aha! A bar graph would let people see the trends."

Stimulate Curiosity

Although projects should be propelled by driving questions that students find important and interesting (and also contain worthwhile information), children are children. Their curiosity may need to be stimulated throughout a project, and benchmark lessons can help accomplish this task. It might be important at the beginning of a project to illustrate to students the importance of the topic. For instance, a teacher could give a benchmark lesson about the largest pumpkin recorded in the *Guinness Book of Records*. The lesson could point out to students that it is important to investigate how to grow large pumpkins, because students might want to grow a garden themselves, and they might want to eat the largest produce or sell it to customers at a roadside produce stand.

Sometimes in the middle of the project a teacher will sense that students are losing interest in the topic. When this happens, it is beneficial to use a benchmark lesson to refocus the students' attention on the goal and value of the project. For example, imagine that students are losing interest in exploring when insects first appear on the playground. To refocus their attention and get them motivated, the teacher might introduce a benchmark lesson on some fascinating feature of insects (such as the behavior of the praying mantis or the camouflage features of the walking stick). The teacher might also have students share interesting aspects of their explorations with others in the class. This sharing sometimes stimulates students to become more interested in the topic.

Chapter 3 and Chapter 4 offered additional suggestions for stimulating curiosity in a project. For example, a benchmark lesson in which students go on a walk to observe their surroundings can stimulate curiosity. To raise curiosity in a project with the driving question "How many different birds live in my neighborhood?" a teacher might take students on a walk around the school grounds to look for different birds. Discrepant events, discussed later in this chapter, also help stimulate curiosity.

When to Plan a Benchmark Lesson

Since benchmark lessons can occur at different times, how do teachers know when to use a benchmark lesson? We suggest three ways to identify the need for a benchmark lesson: the use of concept maps (Novak & Gowin, 1984), observing and listening to students during a project, and the KWL strategy (Ogle, 1986).

Concept maps are visual representations of the relationships among concepts. As such, concepts maps are an external representation of ideas an individual holds. Concept maps (Novak & Gowin, 1984) enable learners (students and teachers) to link ideas and concepts, helping them construct integrated understanding. By developing concept maps of a project, a teacher can identify the major concepts students will need to understand to complete the project and can plan benchmark lessons accordingly. Later in this chapter, we will explore how students can use concepts maps as external representations of their understanding and how teachers can use them to guide the flow of a project and ensure that students are exploring worthwhile science content.

Teachers also identify when to use benchmark lessons by observing and listening to children during a project. As teachers observe students during project work, they notice what concepts and skills students need to complete the project. They also become acutely aware of students' interests so that they can make instruction relevant to their lives (Haberman, 1995). For example, the teacher described in Scenario 3 noticed that students needed to know how to use a microscope and a magnifying glass to better observe insects. That's when she planned a related benchmark lesson.

> ### Key Idea
>
> Concept maps are visual representations of the relationships among concepts. Teachers can use concept maps to determine what understandings students need to develop during a project and when to introduce benchmark lessons.

Portfolio Activity 7.1   **WHAT IS A CONCEPT?**

Materials Needed:
- Something to write with

A. Think of the word *dog*. What comes to your mind? What images do you see? Close your eyes and think about the word *dog*. Open your eyes. Write down all the words that describe what you see.

B. Share the list with members of your group. How do your ideas differ?

C. Now do the same thing with either *oxidation, photon, stomata,* or *xerophytes*. Close your eyes and write down all the words that describe what you see.

D. Share the list with members of your group. How do your ideas differ? Note: Just about any word can be used, but the idea of *dog* seems to work well.

E. Record this in your portfolio.

A third technique is a strategy frequently used in reading instruction, the **KWL strategy** (Ogle, 1986). In this technique, the *K* stands for "what you already know," the *W* stands for "what you want to know," and the *L* stands for "what you learned." *K* and *W* are typically determined prior to beginning a topic, investigation, or lesson. *L* is determined after instruction or the investigation. Frequently, *L* is used as an assessment technique.

Using Concept Maps

Before we can discuss how to use concept maps to identify benchmark lessons, we need to further examine what we mean by *concept map*. A concept map is an educational tool used to tap into a learner's cognitive understanding and to externalize that understanding. On a typical concept map, each word representing a **concept** is enclosed by an oval, circle, or rectangle. The concepts are connected by **lines** and **linking words** to represent relationships among concepts. Together, the linked relationships form a **network**.

A very simple concept map would consist of just two concepts connected by a linking verb to form a **proposition** or single relationship. For instance, the concept *chemical reactions* could be linked with the concept *products* by the verb *form* to make the proposition *chemical reactions form products*. However, most concept maps are much more complex. Figure 7.1 shows an example of a concept map drawn with a computer program. Although there are some advantages to using software programs to draw concept maps, teachers and students can quite easily make concept maps with paper and pencil, index cards and tape, or even poster board and yarn.

Computer Programs That Help Students Create Concept Maps

In a concept map, the relationships among concepts are **hierarchical**. The more general (**superordinate**) concepts—*chemical change, chemical reaction*, and *physical change*—are located toward the top of the hierarchy, and the more specific (**subordinate**) concepts—iron oxide and salt in water—are located below, to reflect the degree of their generality. Linking words connect the various concepts. **Cross-links** show the **interrelationships** among the concepts included on the map. Portfolio Activity 7.1 will help you develop an understanding of what a concept is.

The mental images you see when you think about *dog* are your concepts of *dog*. You might picture a golden retriever or a French poodle or a mutt. You probably picture other associated concepts as well, such as a dog snuggling up to you on a chair or a dog barking

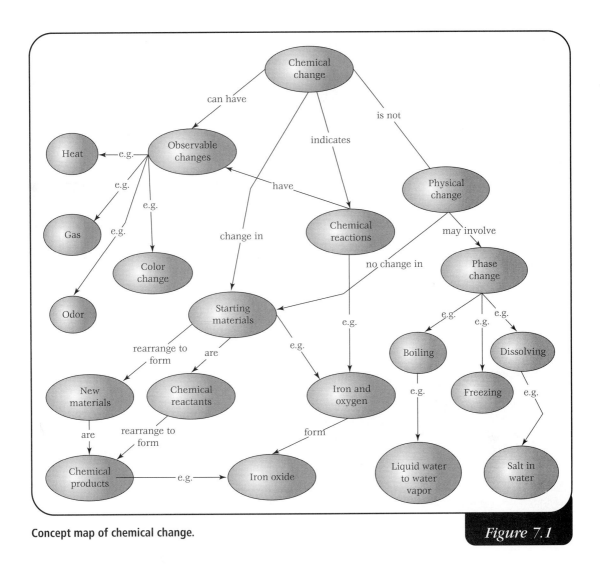

Concept map of chemical change.

Figure 7.1

and chasing you down the road. All affiliated images form your conceptual map (framework) of *dog*. When you hear the terms *oxidation* and *stomata,* the images that come to your mind probably are not as rich. In science teaching, we want to create understandings that are as rich and detailed as those that occur when you think of *dog.* One goal of science teaching is to develop concepts that have numerous associated concepts and that can grow and change as students learn more information.

A good way to start developing a concept map is to brainstorm all the concepts related to a topic of the project. You can leaf through books to help you identify concepts. Once you have developed your list of concepts, identify which concepts are superordinate (the most general) and which are subordinate (the most specific). Identify the most superordinate concept and link it to subordinate concepts. Remember

Table 7.1

LINKING WORDS

Types of Linking Words	Examples
Common linking words	Are, where, the, is then, with, such as, as in the, by the, has
Illustration linking words	Is for example, is needed by, is made of, can be, is in a, comes from, is in, determines, depends on, is the same as
Relational linking words	Is bigger than, is faster than, contains, live in, is part of, leads to, helps, divides into, is based on, is done to, occurs when, is essential for, involves, depends on, describes, is a kind of
Process linking words	Causes an increase, produces, consumes, changes, uses, results in, aids in, employs, is formed from, comes from, goes into, washes away

that, on a typical concept map, each concept word is enclosed by an oval, circle, or rectangle and that the concepts are connected by lines and linking words. If you are like most learners, you will find it difficult to determine the exact hierarchy on your first attempt. When first developing a concept map, you might write your ideas on sticky notes, small index cards, or scraps of cardboard so that you can make changes easily. Place one concept on each index card, sticky note, or piece of cardboard. The sticky notes, index cards, or pieces of cardboard can easily be moved around. You also can easily use computer programs such as *Inspiration* (Helfgott & Westhaver, 2000), *Kidspiration* (Inspiration Software, 2000), or *Pico Map*, which is a Palm application program downloadable for free from the hi-ce website to make concept maps and modify them.

Linking words are used with concept words to construct sentences with meaning. Table 7.1 shows a number of different types of linking words. The first row in Table 7.1 shows general linking words. The second row shows linking words that signal an illustration. The third row contains linking words that show a relationship among concepts. The fourth row shows process linking words, which are used to show how one concept affects another concept.

CONNECTING TO NATIONAL SCIENCE EDUCATION STANDARDS

Science Content Standards

Students need opportunities to present their abilities and understanding and to use the knowledge and language of science to communicate scientific explanations and ideas. Writing, labeling drawings, completing concept maps, developing spreadsheets, and designing computer graphics should be a part of science education (p. 144).

Portfolio Activity 7.2 will give you the opportunity to practice building a concept map for a project of your choice. We illustrate the procedure using a project with the driving question "What happens to all our garbage?"

The various concepts drawn on a concept map can help you identify potential benchmark lessons. For instance, in Figure 7.2, *food chain* is the uppermost concept. A teacher might want to have an ongoing benchmark lesson in which the children in the class create a drawing of a food chain, showing what animals eat what other animals and plants. Other benchmark lessons might teach students about producers, consumers, and decomposers.

Portfolio Activity 7.2 — BUILDING A CONCEPT MAP

Materials Needed:
- Paper and pencil (with a good eraser!)
- Sticky notes, index cards, or scraps of cardboard (or a computer program like *Inspiration*)

A. Brainstorm a list of concepts related to a project you might want to do. You might consider the following:
    producers
    cow
    consumers
    sunflower
    decomposers
    fungus
    plants
    food chain
    animals
    herbivore
    carnivore
    omnivore
    lion
    algae
    bacteria

B. Order the concepts from the most inclusive (superordinate) to the most specific (subordinate):
    food chain
    producer
    consumers
    decomposers

herbivores
carnivores
omnivores
plants
animals
sunflower
cow
lion
algae
fungus
bacteria

Don't worry if you don't get the order right the first time. It usually takes a number of trials to develop a concept map; use sticky notes or index cards to help you determine the hierarchy.

C. Show the relationships among the superordinate and subordinate concepts. Link the superordinate concept with subordinate concepts by using arrows and linking words. If there is a directionality to the relationship, use an arrow to show the direction of the directionality. Make sure to include cross-links. Figure 7.2 is an example.

D. Review the concept map you have developed. Share it with a classmate and discuss the connections. After this discussion, make revisions if necessary. Put this in your portfolio.

You may need to redo or expand a concept map during a project. Like the children in a class, a teacher will develop understanding as a project progresses. When you revise a concept map, you may identify additional benchmark lessons. For example, students might become interested in the nutritional value of being a vegetarian. This might lead to new benchmark lessons on various aspects of health such as cholesterol, vitamins, and fiber. Portfolio Activity 7.3 will give you additional opportunities to practice making concept maps and identifying benchmark lessons.

Using Observations and Listening

Teachers can also identify necessary benchmark lessons by **observing** and **listening** to students. During a project, you might notice that students are having particular trouble understanding or applying a concept, employing a laboratory technique (like using

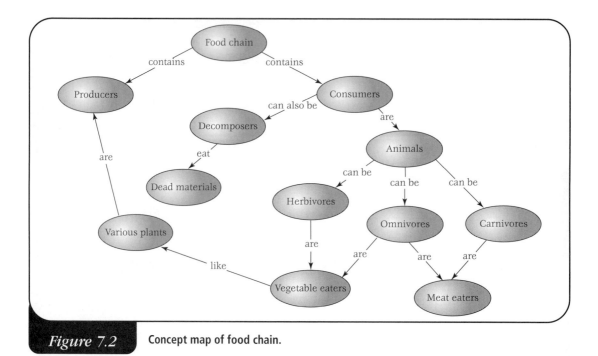

Figure 7.2   **Concept map of food chain.**

NSES

**CONNECTING TO
NATIONAL SCIENCE EDUCATION STANDARDS**

Science Teaching Standards
At all stages of inquiry, teachers guide, focus, challenge, and encourage student learning. Successful teachers are skilled observers of students, as well as knowledgeable about science and how it is learned (p. 33).

Key Idea

Teachers know when a benchmark lesson is needed because they monitor students' progress by making concept maps, observing and listening to students, and using the KWL strategy.

a microscope), or perhaps following a procedure (like calculating the mean of a list of numbers). Based on your observations, you could plan a benchmark lesson for the next day. Or you might change the plans for the day and carry out an impromptu lesson. You might hold an immediate discussion to help clarify a concept that students are having difficulty with at the moment. Chapter 10 contains a more in-depth discussion of listening to and observing students during project work.

Using KWL

The KWL strategy (Ogle, 1986) is another good strategy for determining what benchmark lessons to use during project activities. As already mentioned, the *K* stands for "what you already know," the *W* for "what you want to know," and the *L* for "what you learned."

Asking students what they already know and what they want to learn helps teachers get to better know their students and determine what benchmark lessons to use. The *K* assesses students' prior knowledge and so helps teachers better understand what concepts and skills will be needed in the project. The *W* helps teachers develop lessons based upon students' interests. The *L* can be used to develop new investigations—once you have an understanding of what students have learned, you also have an idea of what they still need to learn. Some teachers like to add a "how," or *H*, section to the KWL strategy—KWHL—so that students focus on how they will acquire knowledge before they report what they learned.

Portfolio Activity 7.3

DEVELOPING A CONCEPT MAP TO IDENTIFY BENCHMARK LESSONS

Materials Needed:
- Pencil and paper (or a computer program like *Inspiration*)

A. Imagine that you are teaching second grade and your class is pursuing the driving question "How do we take care of our class pets?" Follow the procedure for developing a concept map to develop a map for this project.

B. Brainstorm a list of concepts or use various resources to identify concepts.

C. Order the concepts from the most inclusive (superordinate) to the most specific (subordinate).

D. Show the relationships among the superordinate and subordinate concepts. Make sure to include cross-links.

E. Show the concept map to a classmate. Discuss it. How would you revamp your map based on your discussion?

F. Identify benchmark lessons that might be used to help students learn important concepts or skills. How did the concept map help you identify benchmark lessons?

KWL CHART 1

Table 7.2

Know	Want to Know	Learned
Insects are dangerous.	_____	_____
Insects come from eggs.	_____	_____
Insects come out in the spring.	_____	_____

Imagine that students are exploring the project question "When do various insects appear on our playground?" A teacher might start this project by creating three columns on the board: *Know, Want to know,* and *Learned.* The teacher asks the students, "What do you *know* about insects?" The teacher uncritically accepts the students' answers; she allows students to generate as many ideas as possible. Some of the students' responses are not accurate, but the teacher doesn't try to correct them at this point. Students might say, "Insects are dangerous," "Insects come from eggs," and "Insects come out in the spring." These responses inform the teacher that students need benchmark lessons on insect characteristics, metamorphosis, insect defense mechanisms, and seasons. The KWL chart the teacher is creating so far looks like the one in Table 7.2.

NSES

**CONNECTING TO
NATIONAL SCIENCE EDUCATION STANDARDS**

Science Teaching Standards
The actions of teachers are deeply influenced by their understanding of and relationships with students (p. 29).

Next, the teacher asks, "What do you *want* to know about the insects?" and records responses. The teacher lets students brainstorm questions for the list. Students might generate questions like "How are insects born?" "What insects are dangerous?" and "Where do insects live in the winter?" These questions help the teacher plan benchmark lessons on metamorphosis and insect behavior. The chart now looks like the one in Table 7.3.

CONNECTING TO
NATIONAL SCIENCE EDUCATION STANDARDS

Science Teaching Standards
In determining the specific science content and activities that make up a curriculum, teachers consider the students who will be learning the science. Whether working with mandated content and activities, selecting from extant activities, or creating original activities, teachers plan to meet the particular interests, knowledge, and skills of their students and build on their questions and ideas (pp. 30-31).

To further explore insects, the teacher has students observe insects on different 3-foot by 3-foot plots on the playground. Once this activity is completed, the teacher has the students list their observations. Throughout the project, the teacher has students update this list and the two columns of the chart, correcting what they thought they knew or adding to what they want to learn.

At the end of the project, the teacher refers again to the chart and asks the students, "What did you learn?" Students might say, "We learned that insects go through several stages called *metamorphosis*," "Insects lay eggs that stay dormant during the winter and hatch in the spring," and "Insects can camouflage themselves to hide from predators." Answers like these help the teacher develop new benchmark lessons such as one on defense mechanisms other than camouflage. The final KWL chart looks like the one in Table 7.4.

Table 7.3

KWL CHART 2

Know	Want to Know	Learned
Insects are dangerous.	I want to know how insects are born.	_____
Insects come from eggs.	I want to know what insects are dangerous.	_____
Insects come out in the spring.	I want to know where insects live in the winter.	_____

Table 7.4

KWL CHART 3

Know	Want to Know	Learned
Insects are dangerous.	I want to know how insects are born.	We learned that insects go through several stages called *metamorphosis*.
Insects come from eggs.	I want to know what insects are dangerous.	Insects lay eggs that stay dormant during the winter and hatch in the spring.
Insects come out in the spring.	I want to know where insects live in the winter	Insects can camouflage themselves to hide from predators.

PLANNING A BENCHMARK LESSON

Although the best planned lessons don't always succeed, unplanned lessons rarely succeed. Planning is critical for a successful lesson. As a beginning teacher (or even an experienced teacher trying project-based science for the first time), you will spend much time planning your benchmark lessons and thinking through each step. You will need to ask and answer a series of questions: *What am I teaching? What are the learning and performance outcomes? How is what I am teaching related to the driving question? What materials are needed for the lesson? How will I proceed with the lesson? How will I evaluate students?* With practice, you will find that you are asking yourself many of these questions automatically. However, it will still be essential for you to make plans to structure your benchmark lessons so that you can help students learn what you are trying to teach them.

CONNECTING TO NATIONAL SCIENCE EDUCATION STANDARDS

Science Teaching Standards
Teachers plan activities that they and the students will use to assess the understanding and abilities that students hold when they begin a learning activity (p. 32).

Developing Learning Performances

To plan a benchmark lesson, teachers need to first specify what students will learn. We prefer the term **learning performances** to the commonly used *objectives* for specifying student learning outcomes. The term *learning performances* specifies what achievement we expect of the students (Perkins, Crismond, Simmons, & Unger, 1992; Wiggins & McTighe, 1998). *Objectives*, on the other hand, usually are vague and only specify what students will know at the conclusion of an activity, project, or lesson. They don't tell us *how* we will know that students have learned or *how* we will know what they have learned. They don't tell us what students will *do* to demonstrate understanding. Without identifying the learning performances we expect, it is difficult to design a lesson and assess deeper conceptual understanding. Do we want students to recall information or do we want them to apply principles to explain what might happen? A range of learning performances can be identified that require different cognition from students. For instance, we might want to have students define the term *ecosystem* or we might want them to explain the relationship among different species in an ecosystem. Either performance will make a different cognitive demand of students. The first asks for simple recall of a definition, whereas the second requires students to understand connections among principles.

> **Key Idea**
>
> Learning performances specify what achievement we expect of the students.

The cells in Table 7.5, which was modified from Anderson and Krathwohl (2001), illustrate various learning performances. Each row shows different knowledge dimensions: factual knowledge, conceptual knowledge, procedural knowledge, and metacognitive knowledge. **Factual knowledge** is knowledge of facts and details. For example, a student uses factual knowledge to recall the definition of *photosynthesis*. **Conceptual knowledge** is knowledge of interrelationships, principles, theories, and models. For instance, a student uses conceptual knowledge to explain the relationships between geologic time and the theory of evolution. **Procedural knowledge** is knowledge of how to do something, conduct inquiry, or use a skill. A student uses procedural knowledge of technological probes when she uses a light probe to measure the amount of light a plant receives. **Metacognitive knowledge** is self-knowledge or knowledge of one's own cognition.

Students use metacognitive knowledge when they think about their own learning and record them in a science journal.

In Table 7.5, each column shows categories and cognitive processes: remember, understand, apply, analyze, evaluate, and create. Students **remember** when they simply recall something from memory. For example, students might remember the names and symbols on a periodic table of elements. When students **understand**, they are able to comprehend and explain. For example, a student understands how to use a light probe if she can explain to a fellow student how to use it to measure the light reaching a plant. An elementary student will **apply** knowledge when he uses it to solve problems or develop solutions. A young student who uses her knowledge of magnets to create a way to pick up paper clips scattered on the floor is applying her knowledge to solve a problem. Students **analyze** when they examine a concept or process in detail to learn more about it. If a student breaks down a table of data to determine which factors are affecting plant growth and which are not, he is analyzing the data. Students **evaluate** when they use their knowledge to make judgments about the value, quality, importance, or condition of something. A student who critically examines the town's policy on recycling and writes a letter to the mayor pointing out problems is evaluating the recycling process. Finally, students **create** when they produce something. A young student creates when she devises a new procedure for observing changes in the weather.

Creating a Lesson Plan for a Benchmark Lesson

Key Idea

Careful and thorough planning are the essential ingredients for developing successful benchmark lessons.

Think of a lesson plan for a benchmark lesson as a road map. You wouldn't plan a trip to an unknown region without consulting a map. Similarly, you shouldn't perform a benchmark lesson without constructing a **lesson plan**. When planning a benchmark lesson, it is a good idea to use a lesson plan format. Lesson plan formats vary—the following format is useful for science teachers in a project-based classroom. (Later we will discuss two additional strategies that can be used in the instructional sequence stage: the learning cycle model and the 5-E model. In Chapter 11, we also discuss these topics in more detail.)

Lesson Plan Format

- *Student learning performances*: What do I hope to accomplish in the benchmark lesson? What concepts or inquiry skills will students develop? Will students develop background experiences for the project? What is it that I want students to be able to do?
- *Relationship to the driving question*: How is the lesson related to the driving question of the project?
- *Materials*: What materials will I or the students need?
- *Instructional strategies*: What strategies or learning activities will I use to help students reach the learning performance? Will I use demonstration or discussion, for example?
- *Time required*: How much time will it take to complete the benchmark lesson?
- *Cautions*: Are there any dangerous or hazardous components of the activities associated with the lesson? What precautions need to be taken? (We discuss safety more thoroughly in Chapter 10.)
- *Instructional sequence*: How will I proceed through this lesson?

Table 7.5

LEARNING PERFORMANCES*
The Cognitive Process Dimension

THE KNOWLEDGE DOMAIN	REMEMBER	UNDERSTAND	APPLY	ANALYZE	EVALUATE	CREATE
	Definition: To recall something from memory	*Definition:* To comprehend and be able to explain the meaning of a concept or process	*Definition:* To develop solutions to familiar or new problems	*Definition:* To examine a concept or process in detail to learn more about it	*Definition:* To make judgments about value, quality, importance, or condition	*Definition:* To produce something
Factual Knowledge *Definition:* Knowledge of details and facts	*Example:* State that matter is made up of atoms	*Example:* Use the idea of conservation of atoms to explain how the mass after a chemical reaction compares to before the reaction	*Example:* Carry out an experiment to illustrate the conservation of mass	*Example:* Given a table of data, be able to discriminate the relevant from irrelevant data needed to answer a question related to conservation of mass in a chemical reaction	*Example:* Judge if appropriate conclusions were drawn regarding a set of data collected from a series of chemical reactions	*Example:* Design an experiment to illustrate the conservation of mass
Conceptual Knowledge *Definition:* Knowledge of interrelationships, principles, theories, and models	*Example:* Define "flow of energy" in an ecosystem	*Example:* Explain how sunlight is transformed through photosynthesis to provide food for plants, herbivores, and carnivores	*Example:* Implement an experiment to show the influence of sunlight on the growth of plants	*Example:* Analyze an ecosystem to show how extinction of a small omnivore might influence the population of a herbivore	*Example:* Evaluate how a new government policy might influence various species in an ecosystem	*Example:* Create an alternative EPA policy to improve the ecosystem of the Great Lakes
Procedural Knowledge *Definition:* Knowledge about how to do something, conduct inquiry, or use a skill	*Example:* Recognize the parts of a microscope	*Example:* Clarify to a fellow student how to focus a microscope	*Example:* Use a microscope to observe single-celled pond organisms	*Example:* From observations of single-celled organisms, organize a data chart to distinguish the organisms	*Example:* Determine whether conclusions drawn from observations of single-celled organisms are appropriate	*Example:* Devise a procedure to determine if the number of single-celled organisms in a pond sample changes over time
Meta-cognitive Knowledge *Definition:* Self-knowledge, knowledge of one's own cognition	*Example:* Recall that you find writing in a science journal challenging	*Example:* Summarize which tasks you find most difficult in science classes and why they are difficult for you	*Example:* Implement a procedure to help yourself study for a science test	*Example:* Break down the components of a science test that you will need to focus on to be successful	*Example:* Critique whether you have improved your own test taking skills	*Example:* Construct a portfolio and organize it in a manner that would be most compatible with your own learning style to show what you have learned

Modified from Anderson, L. W., and D. R. Krathwohl, 2001.

1. *Introducing the lesson*: How will I introduce the lesson to the students? How will I motivate and capture students' attention? How will I find out about students' prior knowledge?

2. *Representing the content*: How am I representing the content students will learn? What explanations or learning activities am I using? How will I connect the ideas to students' prior knowledge?

3. *Establish links to the driving question*: How is the activity related to the driving question? How will I point out to students how what they are learning is related to the driving question of the project?

4. *Evaluating learning*: How will I determine if students met the learning objectives? What is the relationship between this benchmark lesson and student products or artifacts?

Sample Benchmark Lesson Plan

Let's look at a specific plan for a benchmark lesson that helps middle grades students develop the idea that, when chemicals react, they often give observable evidence. The benchmark lesson is situated in a project with the driving question "What chemicals are in my home?" When developing a benchmark lesson, you need to ask yourself a series of questions based on the lesson plan format. The answers given here pertain to the chemical reaction lesson:

- *Student learning performances*:
  Based on the concept map you developed for the project (see Figure 7.1), you decide that students need to explain and give an example of what is meant by a chemical reaction.
- *Relationship to the driving question*:
  The driving question was selected so that the study of basic chemical ideas could be introduced to students. This is necessary to help them identify chemical changes that occur in their homes.
- *Materials*:
  You will need about 10 tablespoons of sulfur (this can be purchased through any science catalog); steel wool; a magnet; a Pyrex test tube; and a propane torch, Bunsen burner, or Sterno can.
- *Instructional strategies*:
  You will use a teacher demonstration.
- *Time required*:
  At least forty minutes will be required.
- *Cautions*:
  Good safety precautions should be followed throughout the demonstration. You and the students should wear safety goggles. This will both protect your eyes and model good laboratory practice. Do not point the mouth of the test tube toward the children. Finally, the test tube will get hot. Do not let the children touch it. Wear heat-resistant gloves or use hot pads. Break the test tube open by wrapping it in an old cloth that you can then discard. After wrapping the test tube, gently tap it with a heavy object like a hammer. Always practice the demonstration before doing it in class. Make sure the room is well ventilated.

- *Instructional sequence:*
  1. Students should sit in groups of four. At each table there should be a sample of steel wool and sulfur.
  2. Ask students to describe what the steel wool and sulfur look and feel like.
  3. Ask the students to test the magnetic properties of steel wool with the magnet (the magnet will attract to the steel wool).
  4. Have groups share their observations.
  5. Ask students to come to a class consensus about the descriptions.
  6. Ask students to predict what will happen if you heat the sulfur and steel wool together. Also ask them to give justifications for their predictions.
  7. Next, have students share their predictions and justifications with the class. Write predictions and justifications on the board or newsprint paper.
  8. Now place about two tablespoons of sulfur and a small amount of steel wool in a beaker. Heat the two materials using a propane torch, a Bunsen burner, or a Sterno can. Caution: Wear safety glasses and don't point the mouth of the test tube toward the children. Children should also wear safety glasses for this demonstration. The room should be ventilated.
  9. Once all of the sulfur has burned off or reacted with the steel wool, walk around the classroom, showing the students the material in the test tube. Ask them to describe what they see. Caution: The test tube will be very hot. Wait a few minutes to let it cool down and pick it up using an insulated test tube holder or hot pad.
  10. Once the test tube has cooled, pass out a small sample to each group. Note: You may have to break the test tube to get the sample out of it. Caution: To break the test tube, first wrap it in an old cloth that can be discarded. Again ask students to describe what the material looks and feels like.
  11. Have them test the magnetic properties of this material (it is no longer magnetic).
  12. Ask them to compare what they observed with their predictions.
  13. Have them try to explain why their predictions differ from their observations.
  14. Have the students share their observations with the class.
  15. Ask students to discuss in their groups what occurred.
  16. Ask them if the material that was in the tube is the same as the sulfur and steel wool (iron).
  17. Ask them to justify their reasons.
  18. Have the groups share their ideas with the class.
  19. Share with the class a verbal explanation of *chemical reaction.* The material sulfur and the material iron reacted (came together) to form a new substance called *iron sulfide.* This new substance has different properties than the original substances. It looks different. It is not magnetic.
  20. Tell students that this is an example of a chemical reaction: Starting materials come together to form a new material. Ask them how they know a new material was formed.

This demonstration could be followed by another showing that chemical reactions usually give evidence. For instance, you could break water up into hydrogen and oxygen through electrolysis (running electricity through it with a 9- or 12-volt battery). With a little practice, this demonstration is not difficult to do. Another idea is to follow up this demonstration with a student activity. For instance, you could have students mix baking soda and vinegar and then starch and iodine together.

This sample benchmark lesson used a demonstration to introduce students to the idea of chemical change. The instructional sequence provided in the lesson plan format worked well for this activity. However, at other times you will want to provide students with the opportunity to explore concepts on their own. These situations call for the use of two different models during the instructional sequence stage: the learning cycle model and the 5-E model. Both models are supported by constructivist theory, because they take into consideration children's prior experiences, and they enable students to construct understanding from activities in which they are actively engaged. Recent research on the learning cycle model suggests that it is significantly better than expository methods for teaching concepts (Odom & Kelly, 2001).

Learning Cycle Model

The **learning cycle model** is a three-phase model for teaching developed by Robert Karplus (1977), who was a professor of physics at the University of California at Berkeley (Renner & Marek, 1988). It is based upon the belief that students need first to **explore** a concept using concrete materials. After children explore a concept, the teacher can introduce or **invent** the concept by relating what the children explored to the concept that is to be learned. Finally, the teacher can provide opportunities for children to apply the concept to a new situation or further explore the concept. Let's look at each stage more closely.

> ### Key Idea
>
> The learning cycle is a three-phase model including exploration, concept invention, and concept application.

Exploration.   In the exploration stage, students have initial experiences with phenomena that are essential to developing understanding of a concept. Most students have at one time or another memorized information with little meaning, such as the words to a song in a school play or vocabulary words for a test. For example, a little boy who knew his baby-sitter was studying to become a teacher asked her on several occasions who Richard Stands was. Each time she said that she did not know. One day in frustration the child yelled, "You're going to be a teacher, so you better find out who Richard Stands is!" When she asked him where he had learned about "this Richard Stands guy," the boy said that they pledged to him every day—"I pledge allegiance to the flag of the United States of America and to the Republic for Richard Stands, one Nation, under God, invisible [as opposed to indivisible] with liberty and justice for all." This type of confusion also happens in science. Students sometimes encounter concepts that are totally foreign to them. Unless they have the opportunity to explore the concepts, develop understanding of them, put words to them, and expand upon them, the concepts have little real meaning. For instance, many of us may have memorized the names of various types of rocks without first observing and classifying the rocks in our environment. The purpose of the exploration stage in the learning cycle model provides children with the opportunity to create meaning from phenomena.

Imagine a child about the age of seven who is learning about magnets. She places the magnet near a paper clip, and it is picked up. She places it near a pile of paper clips, and they are all picked up. She slowly moves the magnet across the top of a table, and, to her surprise, a paper clip jumps over to the magnet before the magnet actually touches it. She tries this again. She holds the magnet about an inch above the paper clips, and several jump into the air to reach it. She places the magnet below the table and moves it around under the pile of paper clips. They follow the magnet across the table. She thinks about the refrigerator magnets used to hold up her schoolwork, so she places a sheet of paper over the paper clips and places the magnet over the paper. Sure enough, the magnet lifts both the paper and the paper clips.

What has this child discovered? She knows that the paper clips are attracted to the magnets, and she knows that the magnet can "go through" air, paper, and desk "to attract" the paper clips. Does she know that this phenomenon is called the *magnetic field*? Does she know that the magnetic field can pass through nonmagnetic materials? Does she know that magnets attract to materials such as iron and nickel? Conceptually, she understands the answers to many of these questions, but she simply hasn't yet put the words to them.

Contrast her situation with that of the child whose teacher gives him the definitions of *magnetic field* and *magnetic attraction.* Does the child have any real understanding of the concepts this way? Maybe, but it is unlikely that a seven-year-old really understands these concepts very well after having only been given definitions. Most children will not really understand such concepts unless they have had prior experiences with them. The central purpose of the exploration phase of the learning cycle is to enable children to explore phenomena so that they will be ready to develop new understandings of important science concepts. The child who thought about the refrigerator magnet holding up her work was developing new understandings (of the magnet being able to attract paper clips through air) with those she already had (about magnets going through paper) and is now in a position to learn more formal ideas about magnets.

> ### Key Idea
>
> Benchmark lessons can serve the same role as exploration or concept invention in the learning cycle.

Concept Invention.   In the concept invention stage, the teacher discusses and provides formal instruction of a concept by helping students relate science concepts to experiences in the concept exploration stage. In the magnet lesson, the teacher might gather the children to discuss what they observed. Students would share their findings about the magnet being able to "pass through" air, paper, and desk to pick up a paper clip. The teacher would introduce related concepts to the students, explaining that these findings showed that the magnet's *magnetic field* can pass through *nonmagnetic* materials. Because the students had experience with these phenomena, they are able to use the related scientific terminology with much less confusion. The scientific words most likely merely substitute for the words they have been seeking. A child who has been searching for a word to explain the magnet's ability to "go through" things can accommodate the term *magnetic field* easily into his or her mental structure or schema. Benchmark lessons can serve the same role as exploration or concept invention in the learning cycle.

Concept Application.   Once a child has been introduced to new ideas about magnetic fields and magnetic materials, she is ready to integrate these new ideas with other experiences. In the concept application phase of the learning cycle, the teacher expands upon the ideas learned, and students use their newly learned concepts and vocabulary. The teacher might engage students in another investigation in which they explore whether the magnet will attract through plastic, glass, aluminum, metal, and other materials. Students expand their current understanding to encompass the idea that magnetic fields will pass through nonmagnetic materials but not other magnetic fields. The teacher might also show a video or an educational television program or read related text passages.

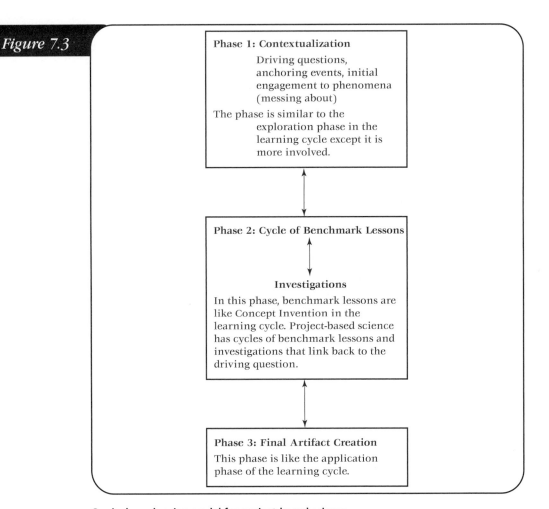

Figure 7.3

Phase 1: Contextualization

Driving questions, anchoring events, initial engagement to phenomena (messing about)

The phase is similar to the exploration phase in the learning cycle except it is more involved.

Phase 2: Cycle of Benchmark Lessons

Investigations

In this phase, benchmark lessons are like Concept Invention in the learning cycle. Project-based science has cycles of benchmark lessons and investigations that link back to the driving question.

Phase 3: Final Artifact Creation

This phase is like the application phase of the learning cycle.

Curriculum planning model for project-based science.

The learning cycle stages support a constructivist approach. Students explore phenomena, tie experiences to concepts, and reinforce their ideas. Students' understandings are rooted in experience with the phenomena, and they are provided more than one experience with each concept. The learning cycle, however, must not be viewed as a rigid three-step model for teaching. Although we have examined a three-step learning cycle in this section of the chapter, a teacher might expand the three steps into four or more. For example, the teacher might have several application activities, and the learning cycle might be presented as exploration, invention, application, and application. The teacher might also take three or four separate lessons to accomplish the cycle.

Curriculum Planning Model

The learning cycle model is a subset of project-based science. Figure 7.3 shows an overview. In project-based science, the first phase is contextualization. The driving

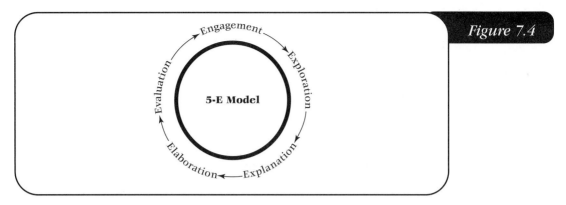

The 5-E model.

question is anchored in the daily life experiences of students as they mess about and explore phenomena. The second phase is a cycle of benchmark lessons and investigations. In this phase, the benchmark lessons provide opportunities for students to develop concepts that are linked back to the driving question. Finally, the third phase is the production of an artifact. In this phase, students apply what they have learned about their driving question to create products that demonstrate their learning.

5-E Model

The learning cycle has been expanded in recent years by the Biological Science Curriculum Study (BSCS) organization into a five-stage model. The **5-E model** shown in Figure 7.4 includes the stages of **engagement**, **exploration**, **explanation**, **elaboration**, and **evaluation**.

Engagement.   In the engagement stage, the teacher tries to make some type of connection between students' past experiences and the present lesson. The purpose is to focus students' thinking on the current concept or skill to be learned. There are many ways to accomplish this. The teacher might provide the students with an advance mental organizer (such as telling them they are about to read about electricity), tell a story, create an analogy, recall a previous experience, ask about students' experiences, or remind students of a lesson or investigation done earlier in the year.

In a benchmark lesson used to teach about electrical circuits, conductors, and insulators, a teacher might read a passage from the story *Dear Mr. Henshaw* by Beverly Cleary. The passage is about a boy named Leigh Botts who keeps having his dessert stolen out of his lunch. He decides he wants to build a burglar alarm so that he can catch the dessert thief. The teacher asks students how they think Leigh might build this burglar alarm. This sets the stage for learning about circuits, conductors, and insulators, and it enables the teacher to find out about students' prior knowledge about electricity.

Exploration.   As in the learning cycle, in the exploration stage students develop understanding about a concept by engaging in concrete experiences with materials. They develop an understanding by exploring on their own; the teacher does not tell them what concepts they need to learn.

In the electricity benchmark lesson, the students use dry cells, wires, and bulbs to try to construct their own circuits to light the bulbs. They test various materials in the circuit pathway, such as rubber bands, pop can tabs, coins, erasers, wires, and paper clips, to see if they will light the bulb.

Explanation.   In this stage, the teacher introduces formal vocabulary or students verbalize understanding about the explorations in which they have been engaged. The intention is to focus the students mentally on the concepts they are exploring. This stage is similar to the concept invention stage in the learning cycle.

In the electricity lesson, the teacher directs students at this stage to notice that there are two types of circuits: series and parallel. She formally introduces the word *conductor* for the items that let the bulb light when they are in the circuit pathway and the word *nonconductor* to those items that do not let the bulb light when they are in the circuit pathway.

Elaboration.   This stage is similar to the concept application stage in the learning cycle model. During elaboration, students can gain a deeper understanding of the concept by engaging in additional activities related to the concept.

In the electricity benchmark lesson, students make a simple switch that, when connected, will set off a buzzer. This extends students' learning about circuits (the circuit is closed when the switch is on and it is open when the switch is off) and conductors (the metal in the switch conducts electricity when the switch is on).

Evaluation.   The last stage in the 5-E instructional model is evaluation. In the electricity benchmark lesson, students are evaluated on their knowledge of circuits, conductors, and insulators when they complete the following task: Figure out a way to "alarm" a lunch box so that when it opens, the buzzer goes off. Students must have working knowledge of circuits, conductors, and insulators to be able to figure out how to make the buzzer come on when the lunch box opens. Some students construct the lunch boxes so that the electrical circuit is connected when a piece of metal (a conductor) touches a loose metal end of the buzzer when the lid of the lunch box is pulled up (thus closing the circuit). Note: To learn more about this electricity lesson and ways to integrate science with other disciplines (mathematics, reading, and social studies), see Sandmann, Weber, Czerniak, and Ahern (1999).

The BSCS instructional model, while essentially the same as the learning cycle, clarifies the constructivist theories by stressing two additional items: engagement and evaluation. The engagement stage is consistent with the constructivist model because it provides the teacher a chance to activate students' prior understandings and experiences before starting the exploration stage. The evaluation stage is in accord with the constructivist theory that advocates embedded assessment.

Portfolio Activity 7.4 will help you synthesize what you have learned about the lesson plan format, learning cycle model, and 5-E model.

At this point in the chapter, you have learned why benchmark lessons are a critical component of a project-based classroom, you have learned some techniques for knowing when to plan a benchmark lesson, and you have learned some strategies for planning a benchmark lesson. The remainder of this chapter will explore in more detail techniques and strategies that can be used in benchmark lessons. Regardless of the

---

Key Idea

The learning cycle and 5-E model are lesson planning strategies that are consistent with constructivist theories.

Portfolio Activity 7.4   **PLANNING AND TEACHING A BENCHMARK LESSON**

Materials Needed:
- Paper and pencil or computer
- A video camera
- Teaching supplies and equipment as planned

A. Using the lesson plan format presented earlier, prepare a short benchmark lesson, no more than ten or fifteen minutes long, on a topic of your choice. Even short lessons need to be planned. You may use the instructional sequence provided in the first example, or you may use the learning cycle or 5-E model during the instructional sequence.

B. Situate the benchmark lesson in a project. What is the driving question of the project?

C. Teach the benchmark lesson to a small group of your peers. Arrange to have a video made of your lesson.

D. Watch yourself on video and analyze your lesson:
   1. How did you help students understand the concepts or skills?
   2. What kinds of questions did you ask?
   3. What did your classmates think of the benchmark lesson?

strategy selected, it is critical, especially for urban, minority, and children living in poverty, that teachers capitalize on students' strengths and interests (Haberman, 1995). Creating an environment where all learners are valued is critical for the success of any teaching strategy.

USING DEMONSTRATIONS

Think of a **demonstration** as showing something to someone. In a project-based science classroom, the purpose for showing something to students is to prepare them to find solutions to the driving question or to conduct their own investigations. Imagine that a fifth-grade class is exploring a stream that runs next to the school. One of the questions that the students want to explore is how the temperature and clarity of the stream change throughout the school year. Before sending students to the stream, the teacher needs to demonstrate how to use a thermometer to measure the temperature and how to use a secchi disk to measure water turbidity.

The Purpose for Demonstrations

Demonstrations can be a particularly effective strategy for benchmark lessons. They can be used to teach a difficult concept, model a new skill, show something that would be too difficult or too dangerous for students to do on their own, or encourage children to question and wonder.

A teacher can use a demonstration to illustrate a difficult concept associated with a project. For instance, during a weather project exploring "When are skies blue?" a teacher might demonstrate a number of properties associated with weather, including air pressure. Also, a teacher might demonstrate a laboratory technique or skill or show how to use an apparatus. For instance, if students wanted to measure pH, a teacher would need to demonstrate how to use a pH probe or pH paper.

> ### Key Idea
> Teachers can use benchmark lessons to teach a difficult concept, model a new skill, show something that would be too difficult or too dangerous for students to do on their own, or encourage children to question and wonder.

Although students need to experience science for themselves, depending on their age and maturity, some activities may be too dangerous for children to do on their own. Sometimes, the teacher needs to perform a demonstration for safety purposes. For instance, in a project on "What chemicals are found in my home?" the teacher might demonstrate how some household substances like vinegar (acetic acid) and "Drano" (sodium hydroxide) can generate very high temperatures if mixed together. Such a demonstration would illustrate to students how dangerous some chemical reactions can be, demonstrate safety techniques (such as the use of a safety shield) for some investigations, and teach students about the properties of certain chemicals.

A final purpose for demonstrations is to have students begin to question and wonder. In a project about "How safe is our water to drink?" a teacher might demonstrate what happens when various substances, such as cooking oil, car oil, and lemon juice, are added to water and how some substances mix and others don't. Such a demonstration could provoke some students to ask, "How do we know what is dissolved in water?" or "How do we remove materials that sink to the bottom but don't dissolve?"

Presenting Demonstrations to Learners

What techniques should a teacher use to present a demonstration and how can teachers engage students during demonstrations? Teachers can conduct demonstrations in an interactive manner that stresses inquiry and engages students. In any demonstration, teachers can ask students to make predictions about what will happen and list the predictions on the board. For instance, the teacher can start by asking students what they think will happen when cooking oil is added to water. Next, he can ask students to describe what they see and to compare their observations with their predictions. Again, the teacher can list their observations on the board. Do all students agree? Finally, the teacher can engage students in a discussion to explain their observations. Predicting, observing, and explaining should be central features of all demonstrations because they help students practice important inquiry skills and they keep students cognitively engaged.

CONNECTING TO
NATIONAL SCIENCE EDUCATION STANDARDS

Science Content Standards
In partial inquires, [students] develop abilities and understanding of selected aspects of the inquiry process. Students might, for instance, describe how they would design an investigation, develop explanations based on scientific information and evidence provided through a classroom activity, or recognize and analyze several alternative explanations for a natural phenomenon presented in a teacher-led demonstration (p. 143).

Besides engaging students in demonstrations, teachers need to make sure that all students in the class can see what occurs during the demonstration. Nothing is worse than sitting in the back of the room and not seeing what is going on. Make sure demonstrations are visible to all by standing in an appropriate place in the room, moving students' desks to help them see, or removing obstructions. You may want to refer to Chapter 10 for more information about classroom arrangements.

Make certain that demonstrations do not become dry, boring information sessions. Students typically find demonstrations more interesting and motivating when the teacher is exciting. This can be your chance to ham it up. Some teachers tell jokes, act silly, or dress up for demonstrations.

Cautions in Giving Demonstrations

Demonstrations can be exciting as well as informative, but they can also be dangerous. Fire comes out of a test tube, we hear a loud bang, a top blows off a can, a can is crushed when placed in water. Because of potential hazards, a demonstration is sometimes preferred to student activity. However, there are safety precautions that you, too, must follow when leading a demonstration:

- Practice good laboratory technique by always wearing safety goggles. At times, you might need a safety shield. Protect your eyes and the eyes of students.
- Students frequently want to crowd around the teacher during a demonstration. Although this is never good practice, it is especially poor practice during a demonstration that involves safety hazards. Teachers should make sure students are at all times at a safe distance from the demonstration area. Make sure students are not standing in the way of objects that might project toward them.
- Whenever a flame of any type is used in a classroom, whether from a candle or a propane torch, make sure that a fire extinguisher is at hand. Also, before using a flame in a classroom think if an electrical form of heat would work as well. Remember when handling hot objects to use heat-resistant gloves or hot pads.
- As with any instructional technique, teachers should practice demonstrations before doing them in front of the class. Practice will help you understand what precautions to take and make you aware of what can go wrong. Practice will also help ensure that the demonstration will work when it is performed in front of the class.

Discrepant Events

Discrepant events comprise a special class of demonstrations. A **discrepant event** consists of a grabber—an event that goes against what students expect and thus sparks an open-ended question to stimulate student thought. The unexpected event captures the attention of the class, and the open-ended question engages students intellectually. Demonstrations featuring discrepant events can be used as benchmark lessons to contextualize a project, stimulate curiosity and interest, and provide focus on central concepts.

Discrepant events can be used to grab student attention at the start of an investigation or a new project. For instance, in a project with the driving question "How can I stay on a skateboard?" a teacher can start off the project by demonstrating the center of mass of an odd-shaped object (that appears to defy gravity by balancing in an awkward position). A discrepant event can also be used as the central focus of a lesson to help students learn important concepts linked to the project. For instance, in a project on weather forecasting with the driving question "Will we have blue skies?" the teacher might demonstrate the force that air pressure can exert by crushing a pop can with air pressure.

Two excellent sources of discrepant event ideas are *Invitations to Science Inquiry* by Tik Leim (1981) and *Teaching Science to Children: An Inquiry Approach* by Alfred E. Friedl and Trish Yourst Koontz (2000). Portfolio Activity 7.5 will familiarize you with some discrepant events.

In Portfolio Activity 7.5, you probably did not expect the result you observed; you probably thought that the paper cup would catch fire, and you were probably very surprised

> ### Key Idea
>
> A **discrepant event** goes against what students expect and thus sparks an open-ended question to stimulate student thought.

Portfolio Activity 7.5   HEATING WATER IN A PAPER CUP

Materials Needed:
- A paper cup
- Water
- A Sterno can
- A thermometer
- Matches

A. Fill a paper cup with water. Measure the temperature of the water. Light a Sterno can and heat the cup of water over the Sterno. If you have a ring and ring stand, you might want to suspend the paper cup filled with water on the ring.

B. Predict what will happen. How hot can the water become? Will the cup start on fire? Why or why not?

C. What do you observe happening? Record your observations. Explain the observations.

D. As an alternative to this activity, prepare the demonstration and present it to some of your classmates. How do they react to the demonstration? What issues arise?

E. How do your predictions compare to your observations? Record your ideas in your portfolio.

that you could boil water in a paper cup. This discrepant event probably caused some dissonance between what you observed and what you thought should occur. As a result, you are probably curious about the reasons behind what you observed. Your interest is raised and you are more likely to want to learn more. Just like you, after students have seen a discrepant event, they invariably ask, "Why?" and they are motivated to find an answer. Students are very likely to remember discrepant events for a long time because they engage them intellectually. Portfolio Activity 7.6 presents another discrepant event.

Student Demonstrations

Demonstrations don't always have to be performed by teachers. Students can also perform demonstrations. Several positive results occur when children lead demonstrations. First, when children make a presentation, most other children find it extremely motivating. Presenting a demonstration is a good time for students to "show off" in a productive manner. Second, when students have to present and explain the material to others, they themselves develop a better understanding of the concepts involved. Many experienced teachers recognize the value of explaining a concept for the first time and have experienced the "ah ha!" phenomenon when teaching a concept for the first time. In the process of teaching the concept, they come to finally understand it. Third, by making a presentation, students practice presentation skills. Fourth, presenting to a live audience can be a very motivating experience—presenters want to do well so they work hard to prepare. Fifth, by presenting a demonstration students build ownership of their project. A word of caution is in order; a teacher should never let a student give a demonstration without first reviewing the content and format. This lets the teacher clear the demonstration for safety issues.

NSES

CONNECTING TO
NATIONAL SCIENCE EDUCATION STANDARDS

Science Content Standards
Students should present their results to students, teachers, and others in a variety of ways, such as orally, in writing, and in other forms – including models, diagrams, and demonstrations (p. 192).

Portfolio Activity 7.6   **THE INVERTED JAR**

Materials Needed:
- A glass jar
- Water
- A note card
- A group of elementary or middle school students to work with

A. Slowly pour water into a jar. Fill the jar to the edge. Place a note card over the mouth of the jar. Now hold the card in place and turn the jar and card over. Ask students to predict what will happen if you let the card go. Let the card go. What happens?
- *Variation 1*: Stretch two layers of cheesecloth over the mouth of a jar and hold them in place with a rubber band. Pour water into the jar slowly. What do students think will happen if you quickly turn the jar over? Try it. What happens?

- *Variation 2*: To add some excitement, have a student sit in a chair and turn the jar and card over the student's head (do this only after you have practiced a few times).

B. What concepts are covered in this discrepant event that serve as a central focus in a benchmark lesson? For what driving question might this discrepant event provide a benchmark lesson?

C. Interview the students. What are their questions? What do they want to learn more about after having seen the discrepant event?

D. Record your observations and thoughts in your portfolio.

An example of a student demonstration that serves as a benchmark lesson to help answer the driving question "When do various insects appear on our playground?" is a demonstration of how to use a magnifying glass. Early elementary students can demonstrate how to hold the magnifying glass, focus it on an insect, and clean it without scratching the lens.

USING LARGE GROUP DISCUSSIONS

Large group discussions are a key component of a project-based science classroom. Large group discussions help students pull together ideas and arrive at shared understanding of a project. Imagine that a third-grade class is completing a project on the behavior of pillbugs. Students have just finished making observations of pillbugs, estimating their size, and looking for behavior patterns. The teacher now wants to synthesize these various observations and determine how many of the children agree to them. A classroom discussion is an appropriate strategy for accomplishing this synthesis.

Value of Discussions

Throughout a project, a teacher may want to hold numerous large group discussions. These benchmark lessons do not have to be long; they can last for as few as ten minutes and still provide valuable information to both the teacher and the students. First, discussions can provide teachers with **feedback** regarding how the project is going and let them know if they need to provide any additional benchmark lessons. Second, a discussion

> **Key Idea**
>
> Large group discussions help students pull together ideas and arrive at shared understanding of the project, but discussions must be carefully planned and thoughtfully carried out to ensure success.

Science Teaching Standards

Teachers encourage informal discussion and structured science activities so that students are required to explain and justify their understanding, argue from data and defend their conclusions, and critically assess and challenge the scientific explanations of one another (p. 50).

can help students synthesize ideas. For instance, during a project with the driving question "Is our water safe to drink?" a discussion about the various water quality indices (such as the effect of turbity on the amount of dissolving oxygen and animal life) will serve not only as a review of the indices, but also as a way to synthesize the ideas.

Discussions offer additional advantages. Students will find discussions engaging because they enable them to share their ideas and findings. Discussion is also an excellent instruction technique for building *student-to-student interaction*. Students can also hear *different viewpoints* during discussions, which can help scaffold the learning of new ideas.

Leading a Discussion

Good discussions don't just happen. Engaging students and helping them to express themselves is a difficult task. Leading a discussion that fosters thinking and student interaction will take much thought on your part. Discussions must be carefully planned out beforehand. Beginning teachers often mistakenly blaze into class and lead a discussion without preparation. Learning how to lead an excellent discussion will come about only with much practice, preparation, and thought.

How do you start the discussion? How do you help students discuss ideas among themselves and not just with you? How can you help students to express their ideas more clearly? One way to plan a discussion is to prepare beforehand a set of guiding questions. Asking open-ended questions is critical. Such questions promote in-depth responses and foster student-student interaction. "What" and "how" questions tend to be effective: "What observations did you make?" "What other observations were made?" "Who doesn't agree with this and why?"

Techniques for Improving Classroom Discussions

Several techniques can help teachers improve discussion techniques. Techniques such as wait-time, probing, and redirecting encourage better dialogue among students, engage more students in discussions, facilitate the flow of discussions, and increase student interaction.

Wait-Time

Wait-time refers to the amount of time teachers wait to call on specific students after asking a question and to the amount of time that elapses between a student answer and the teacher response. Mary Budd Rowe, a former professor at Stanford University, and Pat Blosser, a former professor at Ohio State University, researched questioning in classrooms and found that, with increased wait-time, students' responses improved in duration, quantity, and quality; students' confidence increased; the number of questions among students increased; responses from students who typically didn't respond increased; and more students became involved in answering questions. These results were evident when teachers waited for between three and five seconds (Blosser, 1990; Rowe, 1996; Swift, 1983; Wilen, 1987). This amount of time allows the students to think about, reflect on, improve, and elaborate on answers. Therefore, one way to improve your class discussions is simply to wait after asking a question.

When you first try to wait three to five seconds, it may seem as though an eternity is passing and as if you are wasting time. At first, you may feel a bit nervous about the "empty time." Science education researchers have found that teachers fear wait-time for three reasons: (1) they feel as if they have too much material to cover to slow down, (2) they think fast-paced questions keep students motivated, and (3) they fear that discipline problems will occur if they wait too long between questions (Swift, Gooding, & Swift, 1996). Research does not, however, support these teacher fears. When too much material is covered, students aren't really learning it; fewer students participate in fast-paced drills; and because fewer students are engaged, it is more likely that classroom discipline problems will erupt with fast-paced questioning. Don't worry that wait-time will cause problems or waste time. Try it. To make sure you really wait a few seconds after asking a question, silently count to ten before calling on someone. Most teachers find that with longer wait-times, more students get involved in class discussions and give more thoughtful responses.

Probing

Teachers also find probing a useful technique for improving classroom discussions. **Probing** involves asking students to elaborate on their answers. This technique is especially useful for identifying students' prior conceptions and possible misunderstandings. It is also useful to help students clarify understandings and form new conceptions. Imagine a teacher has just dropped a toothpick into a gallon of water and asked, "Why did the toothpick float on top of the water?" If an elementary child answered, "Because it is lighter," a teacher might assume that the child understood that the toothpick was less dense than the water and move on to the next question. However, the child could mean that the toothpick is lighter than air, not water. The teacher probes the response by asking the child, "What do you mean, it is lighter?" The child answers, "Well, it's lighter. It floats because it is small compared with the gallon of water." This response tells the teacher that the child is comparing the tiny toothpick to a gallon of water and concluding that, because of their relative sizes, the toothpick must be lighter. The child is not comparing the density of the material—the amount of mass in a given area. The teacher probes the child's answer further and, through questioning and further explorations, directs the child's thinking to the idea that the toothpick would float on a much smaller amount of water. The teacher could also use counterexamples, asking the students to predict if a thin nail would float. Teachers also can probe by asking for more information: "Tell me a little more about what you mean by that?" or "How did you come to that answer?"

> ### Key Idea
>
> Teachers can improve the quality of classroom discussion by using wait-time, probing, and redirecting techniques.

Redirecting

Many teachers do all the talking in a classroom. They ask all the questions and provide feedback to all student answers. Sometimes, in the rush for an answer, teachers even answer their own questions. In fact, many students have been conditioned to wait to answer the teacher's questions and *not* to respond to their neighbors' questions or comments. In a project-based science classroom, teachers strive to have students evaluate themselves and their peers. They make every effort to have students discuss with other students, not just with the teacher.

How do teachers accomplish this? If students are not talking to each other, asking each other questions, or critiquing each other's responses and ideas in classes, teachers might start by **redirecting** students' answers to other students in the class. For example,

Portfolio Activity 7.7   **LEADING A DISCUSSION**

Materials Needed:
- Paper and pencil or a computer
- A video camera

A. Prepare a short discussion, no more than ten or fifteen minutes long, on a topic of your choice. Situate the discussion in a project. What is the driving question of the project?

B. Lead the discussion with a small group of your peers. Make sure to create a video of the session.

C. Watch yourself on videotape and analyze the discussion. Use the categories in Table 7.2 to track your verbal behavior:
   1. What was the average number of questions you asked per minute?
   2. What kind of questions did you ask?
   3. What is your pattern of asking questions?
   4. Did you use wait-time, probing, and redirecting?

D. How would you like to change your questioning? What other issues might come up in a science class? Record your ideas in your portfolio.

if a child cannot elaborate on her answer or express why she thinks the toothpick is lighter, the teacher might redirect the question to another student in the class: "Anissa, could you provide more information to Jessica's answer?" "Is there anyone else who could help provide information?" This redirecting is not meant to ridicule Jessica for her inability to elaborate on her answer. Care should be taken to make sure that there is a sense of trust in the classroom and that students feel free to give answers without worrying about being wrong or being perceived as failures (see Chapter 10 for more information about class climate). The teacher could ask Jessica to respond to Anissa's answer. This type of redirecting encourages students to talk with each other. It stimulates student-to-student discussions.

Keeping Track of Your Comments

During a discussion, keep track of your comments so that you can evaluate how well you are using discussions. The scheme in Table 7.6 was developed by Vincent Lunetta, a professor from the Pennsylvania State University, to track teachers' verbal commentary. This table will help you complete Portfolio Activity 7.7.

In Portfolio Activity 7.7, you will lead a discussion. Try to make responding (student-centered) and initiatory (questioning) comments. Try to ask extended-answer questions that foster an environment suitable for project-based science.

PRESENTING INFORMATION

At times, you will find it necessary to present information to students to further the work of a project. We all learn by listening to what others say. However, there is strong evidence that merely presenting facts will not help children develop understandings that they can apply and build upon. We have already discussed presentation techniques such as demonstrations and discrepant events. Other techniques exist that can be used to present

Table 7.6

TRACKING TEACHER'S VERBAL COMMENTS DURING DISCUSSIONS

INITIATORY (TALKING)
- Lectures (presents information) or gives directions (for example, tells the students to get out a pencil, paper, and magnifying glass).
- Makes statements or asks rhetorical questions (for example, says, "The magnifying glass is a good way to observe the insect in your jar").

INITIATORY (QUESTIONING)
- Asks short-answer questions (for example, says, "What kind of insect do you think you have in your jar?").
- Asks extended-answer questions (for example, says, "How are the insects in your jar alike or different from those found by other students in the class?").

RESPONDING (TEACHER-CENTERED)
- Rejects students' comments, answers, or questions (for example, says, "No, that isn't quite correct").
- Accepts students' comments or answers (for example, says, "Yes. That's correct!").
- Confirms students' comments or answers (for example, says, "John's ideas regarding how insects are alike and different are right on target!").
- Repeats students' answers or comments (for example, says, "Did you hear Lesley's ideas about insect behavior? She said she thinks insects behave this way to protect themselves").
- Clarifies or interprets what students said (for example, says, "Do you mean to say that insects are protecting themselves against predators that might eat them?").
- Answers students' questions (for example, student asks, "Do all insects have six legs?" and teacher responds, "Yes, that is true").

RESPONDING (STUDENT-CENTERED)
- Asks students to clarify or elaborate (for example, says, "Could you please explain what you mean by 'protect themselves'?").
- Models questions he or she wants students to ask each other (for example, says, "You will want to ask your partner a question that makes him or her use observations of the insects, such as 'What color is your insect?'"
- Uses students' questions or ideas (for example, says, "That idea of protection is a good one. How could we test this idea further?").
- Asks for other ideas (for example, says, "Does anyone else in the class have an idea as to why this insect is holding up its tail in the air?").

Source: Modified from Vince Lunetta. 1977.

information in powerful ways. Analogies and metaphors, graphs, movies or videos, educational television programs, and diagrams or pictures represent other ways to powerfully present information. Guest speakers often can present information in interesting ways that tie to a project, and community resources provide great sources of information.

Teachers can also present information in more active ways. For instance, teachers can present information to students by setting up short activities for them. Other ways to actively present information include role-playing, investigation centers, and field trips.

Metaphors, Similes, and Analogies

Metaphors, similes, and analogies actively involve students in constructing meaningful knowledge by linking new ideas or concepts to prior knowledge or previous experiences. Educational researchers (Vosniadou & Brewer, 1987) suggest that metaphors, similes, and analogies can help students develop understandings by making connections between students' prior knowledge and the target understandings.

A **metaphor** is an implicit comparison between two things that helps you understand something about one of them. For example, a teacher might say, "The heart is a pump" or "Don't eat garbage food." The first metaphor helps students picture the heart (an unfamiliar object) as a pump (a familiar object). In the second metaphor, the use of the word *garbage* compares something with negative connotations (garbage) to unhealthy snack foods.

A **simile**, a type of metaphor, makes a comparison between two things using the words *like* or *as*. For example, a teacher might say, "An exoskeleton of an insect is like a shield of armor," "The iris in the eye is like a shutter in a camera," "Dots and dashes in Morse code are like DNA in genes," or "The arteries of the body are like the plumbing of a house." Each of these similes compares a familiar object to an unfamiliar object. The similes also help students understand relationships between ideas. For example, understanding that a camera shutter opens and closes helps students understand that the iris in the eye opens and closes.

An **analogy**, a comparison between seemingly unlike things, points out a similarity between them and thus implies that they might be alike in other ways as well. For example, "the circulatory system is to the body what a transportation system is to a country" helps people envision that the circulatory system transports things for the body. Once a person has begun to think of the body as a country, it is a small leap to think about the nervous system as analogous to a country's information system. The skeletal system might then be compared to the economy of a country, and the immune system in the body can be compared to a country's military. Such analogies help students make connections among all the things they are learning, they improve their retention of new information, and they encourage them to anticipate new information, which increases motivation.

Diagrams, Graphs, and Pictures

A picture says more than a thousand words. This old adage is perhaps more pertinent in today's media-driven society. Showing students diagrams, graphs, and pictures that represent key ideas helps students understand the ideas and form links between them, helping learners build deeper understandings.

Imagine a class exploring why the land around the school has the form that it does. Water that cut through the school's neighborhood made a meandering stream. A teacher could describe to students what a meandering stream looks like; however, showing them aerial views of meandering streams or perhaps even an aerial view of the particular stream would do much more for understanding than a description. After showing the students the meandering stream, a teacher could have them describe what they saw.

New technologies such as CD-ROMs and the World Wide Web are excellent sources of a variety of diagrams, graphs, and pictures. The images available on the Web can bring real meaning into the classroom. A CD-ROM might be the better source for high-quality illustrations of a meandering stream; however, the World Wide Web might offer pictures and diagrams not yet available on CD-ROM. Imagine that a class is completing an activity

---

Portfolio Activity 7.8   **FINDING IMAGES ON THE WORLD WIDE WEB**

Materials Needed:
- A computer connected to the WWW

- Live information (such as minute-to-minute weather maps or global atmospheric maps).

A. Complete a search of the World Wide Web to find some educationally important images that would not be available through other media. Topics that often meet this criterion include
  - Current news events.
  - Recent scientific discoveries.

B. How can these images help students answer a driving question?

C. Keep the addresses of interesting and important websites in your portfolio.

---

on "Can life exist on Mars?" As of this writing, some excellent, current pictures of Mars that are available on the World Wide Web at the NASA site are not available elsewhere.

In Portfolio Activity 7.8, you will search for images on the Web.

Movies, Videos, and Educational Television

If a picture says more than a thousand words, then a video says more than a book. Although videos certainly can be overused, when used judiciously, they provide numerous beneficial educational experiences.

Teachers can use videos to set the context of a project, and they can use them to enhance the context. A teacher completing a project on air pollution could use a video to show children the influence of acid rain on the environment. Time-lapsed photography would give students the chance to watch the changes that occur on a rock as a result of acid rain. Showing and discussing a video would help contextualize the project for students. The *Jasper Woodbury* series developed by Vanderbilt University (Cognition and Technology Group at Vanderbilt, 1992), the *Scientist in Action* series developed by Vanderbilt University, and *The Great Ocean Rescue* (1992, 1994) and the *Rainforest Researchers* (1996) developed by Tom Snyder productions are excellent examples of video-based material available on compact disc that contextualizes an instructional unit.

Videos also enable children to experience phenomena that would be too dangerous or costly to experience firsthand. Imagine that students are doing a project on weather and exploring the driving question "What will it be like outside tomorrow?" Videos about tornadoes can represent for children the power of this natural phenomenon without requiring their actual involvement. Similarly, videos of earthquakes and volcanoes show children the power of natural phenomena in a safe but dramatic manner.

Videos can also be used to raise issues or help pull together a number of issues raised throughout a project. Imagine students are exploring the driving question "Why do we need to recycle?" A number of excellent videos could be used in this project. One of the best is the Dr. Seuss video *The Lorax* (Geisel & Geisel, 1971), which raises a number of issues regarding conservation and recycling in a style that both young and old children (and adults) find entertaining. The *Twentieth Earth Day Special* produced by Time-Warner also raises a number of conservation issues.

Guest Lectures

Teachers want their students to see them as people who like to learn, who are knowledgeable, and who care about their learning, but it would be unreasonable to expect teachers to be experts on all subjects. Guest lecturers can easily fill in gaps in expertise. Guest lecturers offer informed perspectives, share in-depth information, create excitement, and present ideas in new ways. Guest lecturers also share careers, serve as role models, bring in resources not normally found in schools, and build community ties. Don't be shy when it comes to asking community members to come into the classroom; many of them will respond to the request enthusiastically.

Imagine that students are completing a project exploring the question "How do we care for our classroom pets?" This is a perfect opportunity to invite in a local veterinarian to explain to the class how to care for pets. The veterinarian will further explain some of the concepts discussed already in class and introduce many new ideas that will help the children develop better understandings of nutrition, health needs, and anatomy.

Community Resources

> ### Key Idea
>
> Teachers can take advantage of guest lecturers and community resources to enhance a project.

Teachers also have opportunities during a project to make use of community resources. Research has shown that connecting learning to students' lives is critically important for children living in urban environments and children of poverty (Haberman, 1995). Community resources provide valuable sites for field trips and sources of educational materials and experiences. During a project exploring the driving question "Will we have blue skies?" a class could take a trip to a local weather station. The local meteorologist could explain how to predict the weather using a variety of different scientific instruments. Although the meteorologist might explain some concepts the class has already explored, he or she would also introduce new ideas, such as the influence of weather on crop growth and local economies, that will help the students understand their topic in greater detail. The review will also help the students develop further understandings of how weather affects daily life. Students will also be able to see how new technologies and new visualization tools are used to predict the weather.

Science museums provide students with hands-on displays, interactive experiences, and special programs. Many science museums have wonderful interactive exhibits of the principles of motion such as large, swinging pendulums. During a project related to motion that addresses the question "Why do I need to wear seat belts?" a trip to a science museum could give students opportunities to interact with various exhibits on force and motion. Other community resources are local zoos, parks, hospitals, police stations, courts, radio stations, universities, and businesses. In Portfolio Activity 7.9, you will explore the educational benefits of various educational resources.

Active Strategies

To enhance the learning that takes place during a project, teachers need to create opportunities for students to develop understanding of the key ideas of the project. Information can be presented to students with active strategies, including role-playing, teacher-planned activities, investigation centers, field trips, and literature.

Portfolio Activity 7.9

WHAT EDUCATIONAL VALUE DO COMMUNITY RESOURCES HAVE?

Materials Needed:
- Pencil and paper or a computer
- Auto dealership
- Mechanics shop

A. On a sheet of paper or on a computer, make two columns—one marked *Community Resource* and the other marked *Scientific Educational Value*. For each of the following community resources, identify a scientific educational value. For example, a radio station can teach students about sound production and broadcast and expose them to a science-related career.

Community Resource	Scientific Educational Value
Radio station	• Teach students about careers • Teach students about sound production and broadcast
Zoo	
Park	
Hospital	
Police station	
Fire station	
Library	
Water treatment plant	
Sewage treatment plant	
Court	
Universities	

Retail businesses:
- Photocopy store
- Grocery store
- Pet store
- Bookstore
- Welding business
- Furnace and air-conditioning business
- Restaurant
- Gas station

B. Select one community resource and an elementary or middle school in your geographic area. Pretend you are teaching at the school. How would you answer the following questions?
1. What is educational about a field trip to this location? Is there a clear purpose for going there?
2. What travel arrangements could you make?
3. Who would handle the arrangements?
4. Is there any legal liability? Do you need parents' permission? Does the community resource have any particular rules concerning student age, safety, or behavior?
5. What is the cost?
6. How long would the trip take?
7. What is the area of expertise of the people at the community resource?
8. Do these people know how to handle and talk to children?
9. What arrangements will you make to visit the location yourself in advance so that you know what the students will encounter?
10. What is the phone number of the resource person to contact?
11. How much lead time is required to arrange a trip to this resource?
12. How will you keep track of the students when you are there? Will you need parent assistance?

C. If possible, contact this community resource and find out the answers to the questions you were unable to answer on your own. What have you learned about community resources? Record this in your portfolio.

Role-Playing

Role-playing can raise excitement as well as help students develop deep understanding of the issues, concepts, and principles of a project. Through role-playing, students may explore subject matter and their attitudes and values, which are brought out in these simulated situations. Role-playing can also help students develop greater comfort in expressing their feelings. Role-playing allows learners to put themselves in the roles of experts—scientists, doctors, local politicians, or teachers. Role-playing can also help children imagine themselves in situations that they can't actually experience. For example, students cannot see digestion as it occurs, but they can role-play the human digestive system digesting a hamburger.

Placing children in these role-playing situations, allows them to "act out" or represent their understanding. Howard Gardner has written a number of books about **multiple intelligences** (1983, 1993, 1999) in which he asserts that people have many types of intelligences (verbal/linguistic, logical/mathematical, visual/spatial, bodily/kinesthetic, musical/rhythmic, interpersonal, intrapersonal, and naturalist). Role-playing is a powerful method of reaching students with strong visual/spatial and bodily/kinesthetic skills, enabling them to learn in a way that is consistent with their forms of intelligence. Because children act out their understandings during role-playing, it can be considered another form of embedded assessment. Chapters 7 and 8 addresses this issue in greater detail, and Chapter 11 provides an in-depth discussion of Gardner's theory of multiple intelligences.

> ### Key Idea
> To enhance the learning that takes place during a project, teachers need to use active strategies including role-playing, teacher-planned activities, investigation centers, field trips, and literature.

Imagine a class is exploring the driving question "Why do I need to wear a seat belt?" Students could engage in a role-playing activity about revoking the law that mandates the wearing of seat belts. During a mock court debate, one or several students could take on the role of physicians explaining why seat belts can *prevent* injuries. Others might role-play scientists explaining how seat belts can *cause* injuries. Students can also play the parts of lawyers, judges, community members, and insurance agents.

Teacher-Planned Activities

Teacher-directed activities can help students learn important concepts or skills associated with a project. For instance, during a project focused on exploring whether the community has acid rain, a class could explore the concept of acidity by first investigating the acidity of various household materials. Next, students might explore how acids affect different materials. Such activities would need to be teacher-directed since they would involve potentially dangerous chemicals and since students would not necessarily be able to envision how to carry them out on their own.

Teacher-directed activities can also show children how to use various scientific instruments such as microscopes, graduated cylinders, and rulers. The teacher might lead a classroom activity in which students learn how to use a pH meter by measuring the pH of various household chemicals such as bleach, ammonia, shampoo, and detergent.

For a teacher-led activity to have meaning for the learner, it must be connected to the project's driving question. Students must understand that learning how to use a pH meter, for example, is related to their driving question about acid rain.

Investigation Centers

Investigation centers, self-instructional science learning activities, help small groups of students learn particular science concepts, principles, or laboratory skills associated with a project. Investigation centers typically provide a set of detailed instructions for students to follow on their own without need for further direction and science materials needed to complete the activity. An investigation center need not be elaborate—it can be as simple as a shoe box containing the materials, instructions, and maybe a list of understanding performances, a glossary of scientific terms, and a posttest for assessing learning. Usually, the center requires the learner to submit a product (such as observations, a posttest, or a self-evaluation checklist) to the teacher.

Imagine a class investigating how many birds visit the classroom bird feeder. One possible instructional objective is for students to notice subtle differences among birds so that they can identify them. The teacher might set up an investigation center where students examine subtle differences among several everyday objects such as sea shells, buttons, nuts, bolts, and screws. By investigating differences (such as size, shape, color, and luster), young students improve their observation skills (Bredekamp, 1987). After this activity, the teacher might set up an investigation center near the window with the bird feeder where students use a bird guide to identify the types of birds coming to the feeder. After completing the independent activities, students might turn in observation sheets describing the different types of buttons they found and a checklist of birds they saw at the feeder.

Field Trips

During a project, many opportunities to make connections with the community will arise. Making connections to the community is particularly important for children living in urban and poor communities, because it helps teachers build on students' interests (Haberman, 1995). One project-related opportunity for investigating the question "What birds live near school?" is a visit to a zoo to learn about birds that live in different environments. Students might take a field trip to a local nature preserve or wildlife refuge to see what other types of birds live there. Field trips, like other strategies for presenting information, should be related to project activities. Such related activities help students build a deeper understanding of the concepts and principles being explored in the project.

Field trips in the community do not need to be elaborate. Often the best trips are those around the school to streams, ponds, fields, woods, or playgrounds. Have students mark off a 1-meter by 1-meter area of the playground and record everything they see and hear in the area during a five- or ten-minute period. They will learn a great deal from this simple field trip about the animals and plants that live in the area, and they will learn about people from the litter they find.

Make sure children know the purpose of the field trip. To prepare students for a trip to a community resource, use the KWL strategy (Ogle, 1986). Ask students what they know (K) about the location you are visiting. List their ideas on the board or have students record them. Next, have students tell what they want to learn (W). Again, record these questions or ideas. After the trip, summarize what was learned (L). Record these ideas, too. Another technique is to give students a list of questions they need to answer during the trip or on the bus home from the trip. Providing students the questions ahead of time gives them an advanced organizer for focusing their attention during the trip.

Portfolio Activity 7.10 asks you to prepare another benchmark lesson. The purpose is for you to continue to synthesize what you have learned about benchmark lessons.

USING LITERATURE

Reading is a critical aspect of project-based science. Through reading, students can learn valuable background information, they can find information related to their projects, and they can learn new ideas associated with the project work. Reading, abstracting information, and evaluating what is read play central roles in project work.

Many teachers new to project-based science think that students don't need to read in a project environment. How wrong they are. It is true that in project-based science students don't read from a single textbook, but they do read from a variety of sources to

> **Key Idea**
>
> Students can gather valuable information from textbooks, magazines, and trade books that they can use to find solutions to their driving questions.

Portfolio Activity 7.10

PLANNING AND TEACHING ANOTHER BENCHMARK LESSON

Materials Needed:
- Paper and pencil or a computer
- A video camera
- Teaching supplies and equipment

A. Prepare a short benchmark lesson, no more than twenty to thirty minutes long, on a topic of your choice. Situate the benchmark lesson in a project. What is the driving question of the project? Make sure you use some of the strategies already discussed, such as demonstrations, discussion, activity centers, and role-playing.

B. Teach the lesson to a small group of your peers. Make a video of the lesson.

C. Watch yourself on video and analyze your lesson:
1. What strategies did you use?
2. How did you help students understand the concepts?
3. What kind of questions did you ask?
4. What would you do differently next time? What would you keep the same?

D. Record your answers in your portfolio.

obtain information related to the project. As they explore their question, they read from textbooks, magazines, trade books, newspapers, and World Wide Web postings. For example, during a project related to air quality, sixth-grade students might search the Web for related articles, read the local paper, and read trade books about pollution. In a project about insects in the neighborhood, first graders might look through insect picture books to identify insects they found.

Children's Literature

Children's literature and trade books can serve as powerful resources in a project-based science environment. With its illustrations and high accessibility, children's literature tends to capture the attention of students in a way that textbooks don't. Children's literature prompts children to *imagine* science concepts, and the writing often relates these concepts to their lives. In addition, this literature enables the teacher to match children with appropriate reading levels.

Imagine that a class explores the driving question "Will humans always be on earth?" As part of the project, the teacher needs to teach a benchmark lesson on dinosaurs. Dinosaurs are one of those topics that are difficult to teach since dinosaurs are not around for students to observe. However, children's literature provides an excellent resource for teaching about these magnificent creatures. *Dinosaur Dreams* (1990) by Dennis Nolan (New York: Macmillan Publishing) helps children imagine what life would be like if dinosaurs still lived today. *My Visit to the Dinosaurs* (1969) by Aliki Brandenburg (New York: Harper & Row) tells children about characteristics of dinosaurs. *Dinosaur Babies* (1991) by Lucille Recht Penner (New York: Random House) explains how dinosaurs hatched from eggs and how they survived. *Digging up Dinosaurs* (1981) by Aliki Brandenburg (New York: Harper & Row) teaches children how archaeologists find dinosaur fossils and learn about dinosaurs from the fossil remains. *The Day of the Dinosaur* (1987) by Stan and Jan Berenstain (New York: Random House) tells children all about dinosaurs. *How Big Is a Brachiosaurus?* (1986) by Frederic Marvin (New York: Platt &

Munk Publishers, a division of Grosset & Dunlap, Inc.) helps children conceptualize the size of a Brachiosaurus by relating it to the size of more familiar objects. Give children's literature a try; many teachers find that it is a great resource for the science classroom.

If you are not familiar with children's literature, your first stop should be the children's section of a local library or bookstore. Children's librarians are usually very eager to assist you in locating books on a given topic. The National Science Teachers Association's journals, *Science and Children* and *Science Scope,* publish annual lists of recommended children's literature that can be used to teach science. These journals also often feature reviews of new books. The number of children's stories and trade books available today is enormous, so these reviews are excellent ways to keep up on what is being published. Other good sources of ideas for using children's literature in science include the following:

Brainard, A., and D. H. Wrubel. 1993. *Literature-based science activities: An integrated approach.* New York: Scholastic.

Butzow, C. M., and J. W. Butzow. 1989. *Science through children's literature: An integrated approach.* Englewood, Colo.: Teacher Ideas Press.

Cerbus, D. P. 1991. *Connecting science and literature.* Huntington Beach, Calif.: Teacher Created Materials, Inc.

Gertz, S. E., D. J. Portman, and M. Sarquis. 1996. *Teaching physical science through children's literature.* New York: Learning Triangle Press.

Mayberry, S. C. 1994. *Linking science with literature.* Greensboro, N.C.: Carson-Dellosa Publishing Company, Inc.

Staton, H. N., and T. McCarthy. 1994. *Science and stories: Integrating science and literature—Grades K–3.* Glenview, Ill.: Goodyear Books.

Staton, H. N., and T. McCarthy. 1994. *Science and stories: Integrating science and literature—Grades 4–6.* Glenview, Ill.: Goodyear Books.

Magazines and Periodicals for Children

Many magazines and periodicals written especially for children make great resources in a project-based science environment. Teachers can use these resources to broaden the context of a project, present new information, or review ideas explored previously in project work. Just like literature books, children's magazines and periodicals are written to capture children's attention, and they are filled with wonderful illustrations and photographs. Because magazines and periodicals are printed monthly or quarterly, they contain more up-to-date information than do books. Portfolio Activity 7.11 will familiarize you with some of these resources and help you identify ways to use them in the classroom.

Using Technology Tools to Acquire Written Information

New technology-based resources, such as those found on the World Wide Web, are a rich source of information for students as they explore their driving question. Resources found on the World Wide Web have several advantages over text-based materials. First, the content is more current. On the Web students can obtain information that may be just minutes old. For example, weather data are continuously updated on the Web. Second, the Web offers a great deal of **primary-source material**, or firsthand information, For example, weather data is provided by the U.S. National Oceanic and Atmospheric Administration (NOAA); the primary source of these data are NOAA's website. Scientists, too, use NOAA's databases for this reason. Third, Web content is comprehensive. Typical libraries used by children offer only subsets of popular and scholarly material on a given subject.

Portfolio Activity 7.11

HOW CAN I USE A CHILDREN'S SCIENCE MAGAZINE?

Materials Needed:
- Pencil and paper or a computer
- One or more of the following children's magazines (visit your local library, if necessary): *Ranger Rick, My Big Back Yard, Science World, The Curious Naturalist, World, Zoo Books*

A. Read through as many magazines as you can. Identify ways you could use these resources in a project-based science environment. What would be the driving question of the project? How could you use the magazine in a benchmark lesson?

B. If possible, have an elementary or middle school student look through each of the magazines. Interview the student about his or her opinion of the magazines. What do students like and dislike about them?

C. Record the ideas in your journal.

NOAA

The Web expands the range of content enormously, thereby giving students access to an unprecedented range of information sources. For example, although students will find plenty of information about weather in library books, the WWW offers real-time weather maps, satellite images of hurricanes, and historical data on weather patterns. Fourth, Web resources are represented in various formats, including digital form, which students can then easily manipulate. Information can also be conveyed through video and sound—imagine dynamic views of the ozone holes and the sounds of a tornado. These new ways of conveying information are particularly helpful for students who are visual/spatial learners. Fifth, students can publish their own work online, sharing it with a wide audience. Many students find this sharing valuable and motivating, because immediate contact with others makes their work more meaningful. Sixth, Web content is readily accessible. Information on the Web is gathered in a single source, with a single point of access (the computer).

Clearly, the World Wide Web offers a wide range of learning opportunities. However, some of the Web's advantages have the potential to become disadvantages. Although advanced learners might find it valuable to read from the same sources that scientists do, such material may confuse young learners. The materials available on the Web are sometimes too comprehensive and dense for a young student to sift through. The University of Michigan's Artemis Digital Library project, discussed more extensively in Chapters 3, 4, and 5 and other similar projects provide a structured environment in which sixth-, seventh-, and eighth-grade students can have positive and productive Web experiences.

Artemis Digital Library

Making Sense of Written Material

Many readers, including many adults, find making sense of written text very difficult. Students can use a number of strategies to help them construct meaning from text. One strategy is to ask a variety of questions before, during, and after reading. Before a student starts to read, he might ask himself, "What do I want to learn from reading this text?" During reading, he might ask, "What are the author's goals and purposes?" After reading, he might ask, "How can I summarize what I just read?" Table 7.7 lists a variety of questions that students can ask to make meaning of text.

CONSTRUCTING MEANING FROM TEXT

Table 7.7

BEFORE READING
- What are my goals for reading this text? What do I want to learn?
- How can I use the text structure to help me learn? (headers, side bar questions, key words)
- Which parts of this text will most likely contain relevant information (for my goal)?
- What are my initial ideas about what the text is about?
- How might this text or reading relate to what I already know?

DURING READING
- What is the important information?
- Where are the key words?
- Where are the topic sentences?
- What are the writer's goals and purposes?
- What was the last sentence or section about?
- What do I think will happen next?
- What were my initial ideas about the materials? Were they correct? If not, what are some new ideas?

AFTER READING
- Am I rereading sections that were unclear?
- What important information is in the text?
- How did my ideas work out? Why?
- How can I summarize the material?
- Do I understand what I read?

MONITORING AND EVALUATING TEXT MATERIALS

Table 7.8

MONITORING
- Am I finding appropriate information for my goal?
- Do I reread sections when I need to?
- Do I agree with what the author said?
- Am I finding definitions to unfamiliar terms?

EVALUATING
- Do I agree with arguments made in the text?
- Are the examples clear?
- Is the writing clear?
- Is the content trustworthy? Can I believe the material?
- What are my reactions to the text?

Key Idea

Monitoring what they read helps students make sense of text material.

Another strategy to help reading is to monitor what is read. A learner might ask, "Do I understand what I just learned?" Evaluation is another critical habit that good readers employ consistently. A learner might ask, "Do I agree with arguments made in the text?" Table 7.8 lists questions that learners can ask themselves to help monitor and evaluate the materials they are reading.

USING CONCEPT MAPS

Key Idea

Concept maps can be used in a variety of ways to help students learn how to learn.

As described at the beginning of this chapter, concept maps provide visual external representations of the relationships among concepts. Concept mapping empowers learners by making them aware of their own thinking. By connecting or linking new ideas and experiences with existing ones, concept maps help structure information into long-term memory, developing meaningful understanding (Eggen & Kauchak, 1992). Each link in the network increases the meaningfulness of the concept, because it represents a connection to another related topic. Through this networking, the learner develops a working schema. Once information is stored, mapping aids in the retrieval of the information from long-term memory and facilitates through a greater number of associations the transfer of a new idea to another setting. Through mapping, learners can take charge of their learning—in essence, they can learn how to learn.

Joseph Novak, a professor at Cornell, created the concept map as a tool to assess the changes in conceptual learning that were occurring in the science students he was studying over a twelve-year span of schooling (Novak & Gowin, 1984). Since then, concepts maps have been be used in a variety of ways to help children learn science. Using concept maps before a project starts elicits students' initial understandings, providing a baseline. During a project, students can use concept maps to track the concepts they are learning and to integrate them with prior understandings. As the project continues, students make new concept maps, helping them form links among concepts. By comparing earlier versions of their concept maps with later versions, students see how their conceptual understandings are developing. Additionally, students can compare their concept maps with those of other students in order to see the connections formed by other students, sparking new connections for themselves. Concept maps developed at the end of a project help students tie together all the concepts explored and serve as a form of assessment (see Chapters 8 and 9 for more assessment information). For additional ideas on how to use concept mapping with young children see Novak and Gowin, 1984.

Issues to Consider When Using Concept Maps

You need to consider a number of issues when introducing students to concept maps:

- Most learners, including many adults, find making concept maps a very difficult cognitive activity. Don't be surprised to find that students dislike making concept maps at first. One way to help students learn about concept maps and see their value is to have them start by creating concept maps of familiar things— the grocery store, movies, songs, or sports. The maps they create about what is familiar will flow easily and show students how rich their ideas are. This activity also isolates learning about concept maps from learning about a particular concept, focusing students' attention and energy on one learning task at a time. If students don't know how to create a concept map and they are trying to map new ideas related to decomposition, for example, they will struggle with both making the map and understanding the links among the new concepts.
- Students don't always recognize all of the concepts that can go in a concept map. You need to help students identify additional concepts. One way to do this is to have students brainstorm concepts and ideas. For example, for a concept map of *home*, you might have students first brainstorm rooms in a home,

such as bedroom, bathroom, garage, kitchen, den, and basement. Then, they might brainstorm as many things as they can that might go in a garage. By brainstorming as a class, students usually exhaust most concepts that should be included on a map. Some teachers keep a running list of concepts and ideas that they have taught. Students can be encouraged to add to the list when they find new concepts. This makes them aware on a daily basis of the new concepts they are learning, and it provides them with a prompt of ideas for mapping. Finally, some teachers help students identify concepts that should be included in a map by having them refer to field trips, guest speakers, textbooks, books, activities, the Web, and other project materials and experiences. The act of remembering all that has been experienced during the course of the project often will help students remember additional concepts.

- Students will show reluctance to creating concept maps with a hierarchy. You need to encourage students to search for inclusive concepts and order less-inclusive concepts under more-inclusive ones. A useful strategy to help students learn how to develop hierarchy is to pick a familiar concept, like a home, and elaborate on all the subconcepts associated with it. First, have students identify rooms in a home. Second, have students list what is found in these various rooms. Students will be able to understand that the items in a room (such as tissue paper, soap, shampoo, and toothpaste) are subordinate to the rooms in a home (such as a bathroom). Record each concept on sticky notes, index cards, or scraps of cardboard so that students can easily move the concepts around. Finally, have students share their ideas with partners to generate a hierarchy. By working with others, students usually see new and more detailed ways to link ideas.

- Students sometimes fail to use linking words to connect concepts in a concept map. Linking words are critical in clearly communicating hierarchical relationships. Stress to students the importance of selecting linking words. At first, you will need to help students choose good linking words. Posting a chart similar to the one in Table 7.1 will give students a resource of potential linking words to use. You might pair students and have them discuss the relationships among the concepts. As one student tells the other about the relationships among the concepts, the other writes down the linking words on the lines connecting the ideas. A conversation between students in a pair might sound like this:

> "I connected the rooms like *bathroom, garage, mom and dad's bedroom, my sister's bedroom, kitchen,* and *family room* all to the word *house* because they are all in the house."
> "So these rooms are all in a house?"
> "Yeah."
> "So, we could say the link is *contains a*—the house *contains a* bedroom and a bathroom."
> "Yeah, that's right. Write down 'contains a' on each of those lines."

- Students frequently don't use arrows on their links. You need to encourage them to do so, however, because arrows show the direction of relationships, and it is crucial for students to indicate the direction in the relationship. Pairing students, as described, can help students use arrows. Another way to stress the value of arrows is by asking questions of students as they work on their maps. For example, you could ask, "So, are you saying that a bathroom is made of toothpaste?" Children will laugh and say, "No. Toothpaste is found in a bathroom!" You might then say, "Oh, so what direction should the arrow go so that I don't get confused about that?"

- Students are unlikely to produce good maps on the first attempt. To encourage better maps, have students revisit and redraw their maps whenever possible throughout a project. Students very often will be surprised to compare their initial maps to their final project maps. Filing maps in portfolios is an excellent way to track how students' understandings change throughout a project. Show that you value the process of revision by giving students time to work on their maps. Show that you value the revisions themselves by having students compare, in class discussions, how their maps have changed or by acknowledging improvement on maps (either with verbal praise, points, or grades).

USING QUESTIONS

Key Idea

When teachers ask questions, it helps engage students cognitively.

Questioning is a central aspect of project-based science teaching. Why is this so? Children need to manipulate real materials and experience phenomena, but manipulating materials and experiencing phenomena is not an end in itself. Hands-on science is a means to an end. Project-based science seeks to cognitively engage students in hands-on activities. By using probing and open-ended questioning, teachers can cognitively engage children.

Project-based science teachers seek out and use students' questions and ideas to guide lessons and projects. They encourage students to discuss, elaborate upon their responses, and challenge others' ideas. Questioning techniques help the teacher identify prior conceptions, understandings, and possible misconceptions. These techniques also help students create, refine, and elaborate upon their understandings.

NSES

CONNECTING TO
NATIONAL SCIENCE EDUCATION STANDARDS

Science Teaching Standards
In the science classroom envisioned by the *Standards*, effective teachers continually create opportunities that challenge students and promotes inquiry by asking questions (p. 33).

Types of Questions

Over the last few decades, many researchers have examined questioning strategies used in classrooms. Researchers have found that teachers ask many questions. Unfortunately, most questions are too low level and factually oriented (Gall, 1984; Wilen, 1987). This means that teachers ask questions that only require students to *tell about, define, recite, list,* or *identify.* Few questions ask students to *analyze, differentiate, contrast, imagine, create, prove,* or *evaluate.* In other words, most teachers are simply stressing rote memorization of factual material. In a project-based science classroom, higher-level questions need to be stressed.

The types of questions teachers ask will greatly affect the quality of the answers they receive from students and the character of classroom discourse. Educators classify questions as **divergent** and **convergent** or **higher order** and **lower order**. Here we will put questions into three general classifications: higher-level, medium-level, and lower-level. Higher-level questions require complicated thinking, such as evaluation, synthesis, or application. Medium-level questions require understanding of concepts. Lower-level questions require recall and can often be answered without understanding of ideas.

Consider this question: "What is the best way to clean up an oil spill?" The question has more than one answer, requiring students to think about multiple possibilities and evaluate the best one. The question takes more intellectual thought than just, for example, recalling an explanation given in a textbook. Now consider this question: "What is a vertebrate?" This question is a lower-level question that narrows the thinking of the learner to one scientifically acceptable answer. A student could also simply memorize a definition for the word *vertebrate* without having a true understanding of the concept.

Teachers want to plan the major questions they will ask in a benchmark lesson. Although a lesson should always be flexible—lessons would probably resemble drills if teachers did not allow for deviation from planned questions—few effective teachers let all questions surface serendipitously during a lesson. They usually plan in advance a list of higher-level questions to cover during the lesson.

Table 7.9 presents a classification scheme for lower-level, medium-level, and higher-level questions. You will notice that this table uses the same classification scheme that we presented earlier when we discussed learning performances. These clue words in Table 7.9 will help you plan lessons, form questions, and facilitate higher-level thinking. Although at times you will want to ask lower-level questions, the most effective questioning you do will be questioning that sparks higher-order thinking.

In Portfolio Activity 7.12, you will determine the levels of questions and practice writing your own higher-level questions.

Teachers should be very concerned with developing their questioning skills. Many of us went through school experiencing the bombardment of low-level questions, focusing on giving "correct responses" to questions in a designated textbook or a teacher's lecture. This recitation method of questioning was short and fast paced. It went something like this:

> Teacher: "What is a molecule?"
> Student: "A building block."
> Teacher: "A building block of what?"
> Student: "Of everything."
> Teacher: "Good. What are all molecules made of?"
> Student: "Atoms."
> Teacher: "Right. What are atoms made of?"
> Student: "Protons, neutrons, and electrons."
> Teacher: "Right."

This type of recitation leads students to believe that science questions always have one "correct answer." Such questioning does not demand much thinking, and it does not lead to discussion. Because of teachers' prior experiences and beliefs about teaching, multiple answers, uncertain responses, tentative answers, opinions and judgments, and divergent answers may seem frightening. Because many teachers have limited science preparation, they fear open-ended and divergent questions, questions to which there are no answers written in the textbook. Consider this type of questioning:

> Teacher: "What did you find out about landfills from your research?"
> Student 1: "I found out that landfills are filling up, and the state has laws prohibiting the opening of new ones unless you go through a lot of regulations and red tape."

Key Idea

It is important for teachers to plan questions that they will use in a lesson, because the kinds of questions asked greatly affect the quality of the answers received from students and the character of classroom discourse.

Table 7.9

QUESTION CLASSIFICATION SCHEME

Level of Question	Clue Words
LOWER-LEVEL QUESTIONS REMEMBER (recognizing, identifying, recalling, and retrieving)	Give me the *definition* of . . . *Locate* the word for . . . *List* examples of . . . *Name* as many . . .
MEDIUM-LEVEL QUESTIONS UNDERSTAND (interpreting, clarifying, translating, exemplifying, classifying, summarizing, generalizing, inferring, concluding, comparing, contrasting, explaining)	*Describe* what happens when . . . *Retell* what happened when . . . *Explain* what . . . *What are* some . . .
HIGHER-LEVEL QUESTIONS APPLY (executing, carrying out, implementing, using)	*Make use of* the information . . . *Implement* an experiment to show . . . *Carry out* a procedure to show how you could . . . *Apply* what you learned to . . .
ANALYZE (differentiating, distinguishing, organizing, attributing, deconstructing)	*Differentiate* between . . . *Break down* details in this situation to . . . *Compare and contrast* the . . . Give an *alternative way* to . . .
EVALUATE (checking, monitoring, critiquing, judging)	*Decide* if you would . . . *Critique* the design of . . . *Judge* the circumstances in . . . *Evaluate* the situation and . . .
CREATE (generating, planning, producing, designing, constructing)	*Invent* an alternative way to . . . *Design* an experiment to . . . *Produce* a way to . . . *Construct* an argument to show . . .

Source: Modified from Anderson, L. W., and D. R. Krathwohl. 2001.

Student 2: "We also found out that our city doesn't allow grass clippings or tree branches in the garbage."

Student 3: "Yeah, and my subdivision doesn't allow composting, so what are we supposed to do?"

Student 1: "What do you think we should do?"

Student 3: "I don't know. Maybe write to the city."

Teacher: "What do others in the class think?"

Student 4: "I think we should make posters and hang them up in town to tell about this problem."

Portfolio Activity 7.12   IDENTIFYING LEVELS OF QUESTIONS

Materials Needed:
- Pencil and paper
- An interesting newspaper article

A. Using the information you have learned about questioning as well as Table 7.9, identify each of the following questions as either lower level, medium level, or higher level.
1. What are the causes of animal extinction?
2. Explain what happened in your investigation.
3. What is a *molecule?*
4. Why would or wouldn't you want a low-level toxic waste site in your town?
5. What causes oil to float on top of the water?
6. What might life be like on Mars?
7. How are frogs different from toads?
8. How effective is your state at handling solid waste problems?
9. Do you think that the spotted owl should be protected? Why or why not?
10. What is *evaporation?*
11. What causes evaporation?
12. How might you stop water from evaporating from a swimming pool?
13. How might you increase water evaporation from a wet towel?
14. What are the characteristics of a reptile?
15. Who invented the light bulb?
16. How is sedimentary rock formed?
17. What is a fossil?

B. After you have identified each of these questions as higher level, medium level, or lower level, meet with a small number of classmates to discuss your answers. Come to a consensus on the level of each of the questions.

C. Form teams. In your team, locate an interesting article in the local newspaper that covers an important current event that might be discussed in an elementary or middle school classroom. Try to find a different article from the other teams. Write three lower-level questions, three medium-level questions, and three higher-level questions for your article. After you have accomplished this task, pair up teams and trade articles. Then ask your paired team your three higher-level or medium-level questions and take notes about their responses. Do not ask them the lower-level questions.

D. Analyze the answers to the higher-level questions. What did you notice? What types of thinking occurred? Did team members demonstrate knowledge of the lower-level questions when they answered the higher-level questions or even the medium-level questions? If so, what does this tell you about the lower-level questions? Record your ideas in your portfolio.

Teacher: "Do you think this would be beneficial?"

Student 4: "Yeah, it would make people aware of the problem, and maybe they'd do something about it."

Teacher: "Is there anything else we could do and is there any 'red tape' that we'd encounter?"

As you can see in this example, the teacher asks very open-ended questions. Students can respond in a variety of ways, and the teacher may not know the answers to the questions asked. Remember: Science is a process and a way of thinking. Use community resources, guest speakers, the Web, and other resources to find the answers you don't know. You don't need to be afraid. In a project-based classroom, everyone participates in finding solutions.

Does asking higher-order questions increase student achievement? When asking higher-order questions, remember to use techniques such as wait-time, probing, and redirecting to allow all students to participate. Using such techniques can result in greater student achievement (Wilen, 1987). Portfolio Activity 7.13 will help you analyze your own questioning style.

Portfolio Activity 7.13   ANALYZING YOUR QUESTIONING STYLE

Materials Needed:
- A video camera
- A video
- A prepared lesson

A. Prepare a short benchmark lesson, no more than ten or fifteen minutes long, on a topic of your choice. Teach it to a small group of your peers. Make a video of yourself teaching.

B. Watch yourself on video and analyze your lesson:

1. What was the average number of questions you asked per minute?
2. What percentage of your questions were lower level? Medium level? Higher level? Procedural (just part of organizing the lesson)?

C. After analyzing your lesson, list in your portfolio ways that you could improve your questioning strategies. What are you doing well?

ONLINE LEARNING CENTER

CHAPTER REVIEW   www.mhhe.com/krajcik2e

Go to the Online Learning Center at **www.mhhe.com/krajcik2e** to review important content from the chapter and key terms, take a chapter assessment, and link to the chapter's websites.

CHAPTER SUMMARY

In this chapter, we explored the role of benchmark lessons in a project-based environment and discussed their importance. Benchmark lessons serve several purposes. They help students learn difficult concepts, they illustrate laboratory techniques, they build new inquiry abilities, they model thinking, and they stimulate curiosity. The chapter introduced strategies for identifying when to plan benchmark lessons, including using concept maps, observations, and the KWL strategy. Several lesson plan formats and models for structuring lessons were presented, including the learning cycle model and the 5-E model. We explored many strategies and techniques that teachers can use in benchmark lessons, including demonstrations, large group discussions, presentations (metaphors, diagrams, graphs, videos, guest lectures), and community resources. We considered strategies to make benchmark lessons more active, such as role-playing, teacher-planned activities, investigation centers, and field trips. We discussed ways that teachers can use literature, including chiidren's books, magazines, and the World Wide Web. We also discussed ways that teachers can help students make sense of textual material. Finally, we discussed the use of concept maps and questioning. In project-based teaching, information should never be presented in an isolated manner, not even in benchmark lessons. Ideas and principles must be related to a driving question that is meaningful to students.

CHAPTER HIGHLIGHTS

- Benchmark lessons play a critical role in project-based science.
- Benchmark lessons
  - Help students learn difficult concepts during project activities.
  - Illustrate important laboratory techniques.
  - Develop investigation strategies that students will need to complete a project.
  - Model thinking.
  - Stimulate curiosity.
- Teachers decide when to plan a benchmark lesson by
  - Using concept maps to evaluate what students understand.
  - Observing and listening to students.
  - Using the KWL strategy to probe what students know, want to know, and have learned.
- Benchmark lessons must be carefully planned to be successful.
- Lesson plans are a road map to teaching.
- The learning cycle model and the 5-E model are constructivist models for planning lessons.
- Several tools enhance benchmark lessons
  - Demonstrations.
  - Discrepant events.
  - Student demonstrations.
  - Large group discussions.
- Discussions must be planned to ensure success.
- Wait-time, probing, and redirecting are techniques that can be used to improve the quality of discussions.
- Sometimes information must be presented to students.
- Several tools are useful in presenting information
  - Metaphors, similes, and analogies.
  - Diagrams, graphs, and pictures.
  - Movies, videos, and educational television.
  - Guest lectures.
  - Community resources.
- Reading is an important aspect of project-based science.
- Teachers use many reading resources in project-based science
  - Children's literature.
  - Magazines and periodicals for children.
  - The World Wide Web.
- Teachers must help students make sense of written material. This can be accomplished through questioning, monitoring of reading, and student evaluation of reading materials.
- Questioning is critical in project-based science.
- Different types of questions affect the quality of responses from students and classroom discourse.

KEY TERMS

analogy (282)

analyze (264)

apply (264)

benchmark lessons (250)

children's
   literature (288)

concept (256)

concept maps (255)

conceptual
   knowledge (263)

convergent (294)

create (264)

cross-links (256)

demonstration (273)

discrepant event (275)

divergent (294)

elaboration (271)

engagement (271)

evaluate (264)

evaluation (271)

explanation (271)

exploration (271)

explore (268)

factual knowledge (263)

feedback (277)

5-E model (271)

hierarchical (256)

higher order (294)

interrelationships (256)

invent (268)

investigation
   centers (286)

KWL strategy (256)

learning cycle
   model (268)

learning
   performances (263)

lesson plan (264)

lines (256)

linking words (256)

listening (259)

lower order (294)

metacognitive
   knowledge (263)

metaphor (282)

model thinking (254)

multiple
   intelligences (286)

network (256)

observing (259)

primary-source
   material (289)

probing (279)

procedural
   knowledge (263)

proposition (256)

questioning (294)

redirecting (279)

remember (264)

role-playing (285)

simile (282)

subordinate (256)

superordinate (256)

understand (264)

wait-time (278)

REFERENCES

American Association for the Advancement of Science. 1993. *Benchmarks for science literacy.* New York: Oxford University Press.

Anderson, L. W., and D. R. Krathwohl, eds. 2001. *A taxonomy for learning, teaching, and assessing: A revision of Bloom's taxonomy of educational objectives.* New York: Longman.

Berenstain, S., and J. Berenstain. 1987. *The day of the dinosaur.* New York: Random House.

Bloom, B. 1956. *Taxonomy of educational objectives: The classification of educational goals.* New York: D. McKay.

Blosser, P. March 1, 1990. Using questions in science classrooms. Research matters to the science teacher. *NARST*, 9001.

Bradekamp, S. 1987. *Developmentally appropriate practice in early childhood programs serving children from birth through age 8.* Washington, D. C.: National Association for the Education of Young Children.

Brandenburg, A. 1969. *My visit to the dinosaurs.* New York: Harper & Row.

Brandenburg, A. 1981. *Digging up dinosaurs.* New York: Harper & Row.

Cleary, B. 1983. *Dear Mr. Henshaw.* New York: William Morrow.

Cognition and Technology Group at Vanderbilt. 1992. The Jasper series as an example of anchored instruction: Theory, program description, and assessment data. *Educational Psychologist* 27:291–315.

Eggen, P., and D. Kauchak. 1992. *Educational psychology: Classroom connections.* New York: Macmillan.

Friedl, A. E., and T. Y. Koontz. 2000. *Teaching science to children: an inquiry approach.* Boston: McGraw-Hill.

Gall, M. 1984. Synthesis of research on teachers' questioning. *Educational Leadership* 42:40–47.

Gardner, H. 1983. *Frames of mind: The theory of multiple intelligence.* New York: Basic Books.

Gardner, H. 1993. *Multiple intelligence: The theory into practice.* New York: Basic Books.

Gardner, H. 1999. *The disciplined mind.* New York: Simon & Schuster.

Haberman, M. 1995. *STAR teachers of children in poverty.* West Lafayette, Ind.: Kappa Delta Pi.

Helfgott, D., and M. Westhaver. 2000. *Inspiration 6.0.* Portland, Ore.: Inspiration Software, Inc.

Hunt, E., and J. Minstrell. 1994. A cognitive approach to the teaching of physics. In *Classroom lessons: Integrating cognitive theory and classroom practice,* ed. K. McGilly. Cambridge, Mass.: The MIT Press, pp. 51-74.

Inspiration Software, Inc. 2000. *Kidspiration.* Portland, Ore.: Author.

Karplus, R. 1977. Science teaching and the development of reasoning. *Journal of Research in Science Teaching* 14: 169-75.

Leim, T. 1981. *Invitations to science inquiry.* Lexington, Mass.: Ginn Custom Publishing.

Lunetta, V. N. 1997. The role of the laboratory in school science. In *International handbook of science education,* eds. D. Tobin and B. J. Fraser. The Netherlands: Kluwer.

Marvin, F. 1986. *How big is a brachiosaurus?* New York: Platt & Munk Publishers.

National Research Council. 1996. *National science education standards.* Washington, D.C.: National Academy Press.

National Research Council. 2000. *Inquiry and the national science education standards.* Washington, D.C.: National Academy Press.

Nolan, D. 1990. *Dinosaur dreams.* New York: Macmillan Publishing.

Novak, J. D., and D. B. Gowin. 1984. *Learning how to learn.* Cambridge, England: Cambridge University Press.

Odom, A. L., and P. V. Kelly. 2001. Integrating concept mapping and the learning cycle to teach diffusion and osmosis concepts to high school biology students. *Science Education* 85(6):615-35.

Ogle, D. 1986. A teaching model that develops active reading of expository text. *The Reading Teacher* 39 (2):564-70.

Penner, L. R. 1991. *Dinosaur babies.* New York: Random House.

Perkins, D., D. Crismond, R. Simmons, and C. Unger. 1992. Inside understanding. In *Software goes to school: Teaching for understanding with new technologies,* eds. D. Perkins, J. Schwartz, M. West, and M. Wiske. New York: Oxford University Press, pp. 70-87.

Renner, J. W., and E. A. Marek. 1988. *The learning cycle and elementary school science teaching.* Portsmouth, N.H.: Heinemann.

Rowe, M. B. September 1996. Science, silence, and sanctions. *Science and Children* 34:35-37. Reprinted from March 1969 issue.

Sandmann, A., W. Weber, C. Czerniak, and J. Ahern. 1999. Coming full circuit: An integrated unit plan for intermediate and middle grade students. *Science Activities* 36 (3):13-20.

Seuss, Dr. (T. S. Geisel and A. S. Geisel). 1971. *The Lorax.* New York: Random House.

Singer, J., R. W. Marx, J. Krajcik, and J. Clay Chambers. 2000. Constructing extended inquiry projects: Curriculum materials for science education reform. *Educational Psychologist* 35(3): 165–78.

Swift, J. N. November 1983. Interaction of wait time and questioning instruction on middle school science teaching. *Journal of Research in Science Teaching* 20:721–30.

Swift, J. N., C. T. Gooding, and P. R. Swift. October 23, 1996. Using research to improve the quality of classroom discussions. Research Matters to the Science Teacher. *NARST* 9601.

Tom Snyder Productions. 1996. *Rainforest researchers.* Watertown, Mass.: Author.

Tom Snyder Productions. 1992, 1994. *The great ocean rescue.* Watertown, Mass.: Author.

Vosniadou, S., and W. F. Brewer. 1987. Theories and knowledge restructuring in development. *Review of Educational Research* 57(1):51–67.

Wiggins, G., and J. McTighe. 1998. *Understanding by design.* Alexandria, Va: Association for Supervision and Curriculum Development.

Wilen, W. W. 1987. *Questioning skills for teachers.* Washington, D.C.: National Education Association.

Chapter 8

Why Do We Assess Students in Science?

INTRODUCTION

THE PURPOSE OF ASSESSMENT

THE NATURE OF CLASSROOM ASSESSMENT

WHAT TO ASSESS

WHEN TO ASSESS

USING TECHNOLOGY TOOLS TO EXAMINE
   ASSESSMENT

CHAPTER LEARNING PERFORMANCES

- *Explain why assessment is a critical component of project-based science.*
- *Distinguish between classroom assessment and large-scale assessment.*
- *Explain the value of using various assessment techniques to promote learning for populations of students traditionally at risk in science learning.*
- *Compare traditional assessment techniques to current assessment techniques.*
- *Create learning performances and corresponding assessments for content, procedural, and metacognitive knowledge across different cognitive dimensions.*
- *Justify why a variety of different assessment approaches should be used during different time frames in science classrooms.*
- *Identify ways that teachers can network with colleagues to improve their assessment practices.*

INTRODUCTION

This chapter focuses on the purpose of assessment in a project-based science class and in other school settings. You may have many questions about assessment: *Why is assessment such an important topic today? How do I assess science understanding? When should students be assessed? What kinds of learning should be assessed? Are some ways to assess better than others? How do I know that all students are learning?* This chapter answers these and other questions about assessment. We start by discussing the purpose of assessment in science classes and the ways today's assessment differs from traditional forms of assessment. Large-scale assessments are reviewed, and we explain why assessment is such an important topic for educators today. We cover many topics related to making assessment fair and consistent with today's educational goals. We consider what to assess in science classrooms and when to assess student learning. Finally, we introduce the idea of using technology tools to network with colleagues to improve assessment practices. Before we begin deliberating the purpose of assessment, let's examine three classroom scenarios that focus on assessment.

Scenario 1: Traditional Paper-and-Pencil Tests

Mr. Isarov says, "Now that we've finished grading the pop quiz in science, I have a few reminders for you. Remember, boys and girls, next Friday is the last day of the quarter, so you will be taking tests each day next week that will be included in this grading period. On Monday, you will have a test on Chapter 3 of the social studies book, which covers the Revolutionary War. Tuesday's test in math will cover division of decimals. Wednesday, we will have a test on Chapter 4 of the science book on simple machines. On Thursday, you will take a test on possessive nouns, and Friday's test will be the regular week's spelling list. Oh, I almost forgot. Make sure you take home the letter I gave you this morning about the Iowa Test of Basic Skills that you'll be taking in two weeks. Study hard and have a nice weekend; we'll be starting to learn all new topics next quarter!"

Do these words bring back memories of school testing? In the past, teachers commonly administered paper-and-pencil tests as the sole form of assessment. Students were expected to pass these tests, which for the most part determined their letter grades in each school subject. These tests were usually multiple choice, true/false, matching, or essay, and they were administered to the whole class after the class covered a chapter or some other unit of study. After completing the designated chapter or unit, the teacher rarely brought up the topic again for the rest of the year. *Assessment* was synonymous with *test*, and *test* meant *grades*. The whole idea of testing caused nervousness, anxiety, and perhaps sweaty palms.

Scenario 2: Tests Used in a Project-Based Environment

Mr. Corry, a science teacher who teaches a combined fourth- and fifth-grade science class, hopes his students will develop understandings of two National Science Education Standards:

Science Content Strand K–4; Physical Science; Motion and Force.
The position and motion of objects can be changed by pushing or pulling. The size of the change is related to the strength of the push or pull.

Science Content Standard 5–8; Physical Science, Motion and Forces.
If more than one force acts on an object along a straight line, then the forces will reinforce or cancel one another, depending on their direction and magnitude. Unbalanced forces will cause changes in the speed or direction of an object's motion.

To help his students develop these ideas, he plans a project on simple machines. Mr. Corry decides that the driving question "How can I move big things?" will allow his students to engage in a number of activities to help them develop understandings identified in the standards. In his planning, he realizes that the project will also allow him to meet a number of National Science Education Inquiry Standards, such as *develop descriptions, use explanations, make predictions,* and *use models for evidence.*

Mr. Corry is pleased with how the project proceeds. His students seem engaged during the activities, and the work students turn in is of high quality. As students design experiments to explore ideas such as "Why do you use ramps to move heavy objects onto a truck?" he walks around asking the students questions. Although he is pleased with most of the responses, he wonders if all students would respond appropriately to basic questions that focuses on the main ideas of the project. He decides to give his students a short test that focuses on the main ideas explored in the project. He tells the class that they will have a test on Friday that will ask them to use ideas they explored in the project. He spends part of the day reviewing with the students what they learned through their investigations.

Mr. Corry writes a test consisting of short answer responses that match the content objectives of the project. Some of the questions ask students to recall basic definitions, but others have students consider ideas in everyday life situations. Some of the questions follow:

- How would you define *force*?
- When a book is sitting on a desk, what forces are acting on the book?
- What do you need to do to slide a box of bricks along the floor? Explain what is happening using scientific ideas.

Over the weekend, Mr. Corry scores the test using a rubric he created. He is surprised that some of the students who did well in class and wrote strong reports did not do so well on the test. Some of the students simply did not explain their ideas clearly enough. Mr. Corry writes notes on the tests asking the students to explain their ideas further. He uses the results of the test to reinforce some of the major ideas he intended students to learn in a class discussion on Monday when he goes over the test and helps students build even further understanding. He contrasts various responses to help students in the class develop a better idea of what constitutes a complete response on a short answer test.

When used and designed appropriately, tests can serve as important vehicles for giving both the teacher and the students feedback. Both Mr. Corry and his students obtained important information about the understanding that was developed. Perhaps even more importantly, Mr. Corry used the results of the test to further help his students develop understanding, both of the content he wanted students to learn and also on how to write complete thoughts to explains one's ideas. Using paper-and-pencil tests in this manner is consistent with a project-based environment.

Scenario 3: Embedded Assessment

Students in a third-grade class ask, "Why do pumpkins decay after Halloween?" To answer this question, they plan several investigations. Some students think that pumpkins rot when they freeze outside because they noticed that fresh fruit is mushy after being frozen. That group investigates how fast a pumpkin decays when it is frozen and when it is left inside the building. Another group of students investigates whether "germs" have anything to do with the decay. They wash one pumpkin with an antibacterial soap and leave another one alone to investigate which decays first. Another group buries pumpkins in some leaves and soil to see what effect this has. Some students compare carved and uncarved pumpkins, while another group leaves its pumpkins in the sun and in the shade. Between team investigations, the teacher, Mrs. Molina, teaches several lessons on bacteria, decay, and mold growth. The class also visits a compost site where the city dumps leaves to generate fertilizer for sale. Some students write to grocery store managers to see how they keep fruit and vegetables from decaying.

Next, Mrs. Molina has students design a poster (an artifact) depicting what they learned as they completed their investigation. The poster is divided into two sections labeled "Things that cause a pumpkin to rot" and "Things that stop a pumpkin from rotting." Students draw pictures and take photographs of the things listed on each side of the poster to illustrate it. Students include with the poster a short essay on the benefits of decomposition in their daily lives.

> This third scenario is also characteristic of project-based science. What did the students learn in this investigation? They learned to ask questions and devise investigations. In the process, they learned about the effect of freezing on plant cells, about bacteria and using soap to kill bacteria, and about composting and the relationship of sunlight and oxygen to decomposition. They used communication skills to write letters, and they learned about community efforts to compost leaves. Their learning did not occur in a single, discrete step but unfolded gradually through a variety of activities in a learning community. Not all students were required to do the same activities at the same time.

As you can imagine, assessment for this project environment would need to differ from the traditional assessment described in the first scenario to accurately measure what students had learned. Students could take a single multiple choice test at the end of the unit with questions like "What is decomposition?" and answers like "a. dead plants and animals, b. rotting, c. separation of matter into its basic components, d. breaking up of elements, e. none of the above." However, one test at the end of the entire unit with questions like these would fail to assess the multitude of ideas students learned. Such a test wouldn't measure students' ability to work as a team. Tests serve an important role in assessing student learning, but they often fail to identify the most important ideas students learned. They would not show how students could apply their knowledge and skills to everyday life. They would not show that they could plan investigations or interpret data. The use of paper-and-pencil tests as the sole measure of understanding is not consistent with the philosophy of project-based science. It does not measure the kinds of understandings students gain while in the process of pursuing answers to driving questions, and it is not used as a tool to give students information that will help them gain further understandings.

Assessment techniques in a project-based science environment differ considerably from the technique depicted in the first scenario. First, various forms of assessment (not just tests) are used so that a wide variety of understandings, skills, and attitudes are measured. Second, assessment takes place during instruction as well as after. Third, higher-level cognitive skills such as asking questions, designing investigations, interpreting data, and drawing conclusions are assessed, as are affective outcomes such as curiosity, skepticism, and open-mindedness. Fourth, students are involved in assessment decisions along with their teachers. Fifth, assessment is a continuous process, embedded in learning, not an end in itself.

Although some teachers stubbornly refuse to move beyond end-of-term paper-and-pencil assessment practices, most teachers have learned to use a variety of techniques to assess their students throughout a unit of study. After reading this chapter, you should understand why the opening scenario does not exemplify assessment practices recommended today. Before we move to the next section, Portfolio Activity 8.1 will help you think about the purpose of assessment.

THE PURPOSE OF ASSESSMENT

Assessment can be thought of as any method used to judge or evaluate an outcome or help make a decision. We use assessment data for a variety of purposes in educational settings today: to gather evidence of student learning, assist learning, guide teaching, measure individual achievement, give grades, allocate resources, evaluate programs, and inform local, state, and national policy. Used for these purposes, assessments tell us how students are learning, improve education, and give feedback to students, educators, parents, policymakers, and the general public about how students are doing in science (Pellegrino, Chudowsky, and Glaser, 2001). In fact, the National Science Education Standards state, "Research shows that regular and high-quality assessment in the classroom can have a positive effect on student achievement."

Assessment may be classified into two categories: classroom assessment and large-scale assessment (sometimes called **high-stakes assessment** because of the importance placed on the tests). Assessment in the context of a classroom and large-scale assessment differ in their purpose.

Classroom assessments are used to help teachers evaluate students' progress during a unit of study and make day-to-day decisions regarding curriculum and instruction. These types of day-to-day assessments, sometimes called **formative assessments**, are found in many formats such as short quizzes and tests, observations of students, and artifacts. Teachers use these assessments to provide immediate feedback to students with the goal of helping them learn.

Large-scale assessments are used to evaluate school curriculum, school district progress, and programs. Large-scale assessments to measure students' achievement include familiar tests such as the Advanced Placement Test, Scholastic Achievement Test (SAT), and American College Testing Program (ACT). An example of a large-scale assessment often used to evaluate programs is the National Assessment of Educational Progress (NAEP) in which student achievement can be compared across states and with previous generations of students (NAEP testing began in 1969). Sometimes, large-scale assessments are used to compare a student's individual

NSES

CONNECTING TO
NATIONAL SCIENCE EDUCATION STANDARDS

Classroom Assessment and Inquiry
Assessment data can be used to plan a lesson, guide a student's learning, calculate grades, determine access to special programs, inform policy, allocate resources, or evaluate the quality of curriculum or instruction. In the breadth of its application, assessment merges seamlessly into considerations of the curriculum and teaching (NRC, 2000, p. 76).

Portfolio Activity 8.1   **WHAT IS THE PURPOSE OF ASSESSMENT?**

Materials Needed:
- Pencil and paper or a computer

A. Think about why we assess students. What do you think is the purpose of assessment? On a sheet of paper or on a computer, make three columns. Label the first column *Know*, label the second column *Want to know*, and label the third column *Learned* (Ogle, 1986). Take a few moments to list in the first column as many things as you know about why we assess students.

B. Interview a classmate to see why he or she thinks we assess students. How does his or her viewpoint compare with yours? Find another classmate (or a teacher) with a different viewpoint. Compare and contrast these two colleagues' ideas about assessment.

C. Interview an elementary or middle grade student (preferably a student in grade four, five, six, or higher in which testing becomes more frequent) and ask the student why he or she is assessed or tested in school. How does the student's view of assessment compare with the teacher's? With yours?

D. After conducting these interviews, list as many things in the second column that you can think of that you want to know about assessment. At the end of the next chapter, you will assess your own learning by filling in the third column with what you have learned about assessment (see Portfolio Activity 9.9).

E. Place your ideas in your portfolio.

---

achievement with that of peers. Assessment of individual achievement in the form of end-of-unit tests, letter grades, and large-scale assessments is called **summative assessment**; some happen in the context of the classroom and some are delivered as large-scale assessments. More and more, high-stakes assessments are used to make important decisions regarding student advancement to the next grade level and graduation from high school. They are also used to determine which students or schools receive special services (such as gifted programs, special education programs, and tutoring services), evaluate teachers and administrators (and sometimes determine how they are paid), determine how resources are allocated to schools, and determine whether schools get rewards or sanctions from the state (Pellegrino, Chudowsky, & Glaser, 2001).

Assessment used to improve curriculum and instruction determines what knowledge and skills children bring to science lessons and identifies what students know and can do following instruction. Scenarios 2 and 3 both used assessment to help guide and improve instruction. Assessment for this purpose is matched to instruction and conveys expectations to students and their parents in a way that motivates and helps students to learn. Assessment used in this manner also assists teachers in making decisions about what instruction has not been effective and how it should be modified. This type of assessment is an ongoing process that occurs during as well as after project-based science instruction and helps students, teachers, and parents monitor individual students' learning. Portfolio Activity 8.2 examines teachers' views of and beliefs about instruction and assessment.

> **Key Idea**
>
> Assessment is a key component of project-based science because it helps measure whether students learned, and it helps teachers make decisions about instruction.

Large-Scale and High-Stakes Assessment

Assessment is a fervent topic in education today, and it is scrutinized at the public level and within our educational system. At the public level, it seems that we face almost daily

Portfolio Activity 8.2

HOW DO TEACHERS' BELIEFS ABOUT INSTRUCTION AFFECT THEIR METHODS OF ASSESSMENT?

Materials Needed:
- Materials to conduct an interview

A. Interview several teachers about their beliefs on teaching and assessment. Try to determine whether each teacher believes teaching is "telling students information" or "helping students construct their own understandings." Ask each teacher how he or she typically assesses students. What types of assessment do they use? What do the assessments measure? How do the teachers determine grades?

B. Analyze the difference between the "teller" teachers and the "constructivist" teachers. How does the curriculum vary? What about instruction? Assessment?

C. Record these ideas in your portfolio.

issues pertaining to assessment. This increase in attention paid to educational assessment is due primarily to the focus in the last two decades on high standards and measuring students' progress toward standards. Journalists have written articles about how our nation's students compare on standardized tests with previous generations (National Assessment of Educational Progress) or with students in other countries (TIMMS). Policymakers, community leaders, parents, and school administrators are demanding that students be held to certain levels of performance and understanding. As a result, most states have debated and implemented new educational standards that include large-scale or high-stakes testing such as proficiency testing or high school graduation qualification testing. Many people believe that these externally mandated tests inform the public about how our schools are doing. They are intended to measure the nation's educational achievement.

The increase in focus on large-scale and high-stakes assessment has sparked debates about what should be tested and how it should be tested. Within our educational system, many people are debating the relevance of using only traditional paper-and-pencil tests commonplace in schools and used for most large-scale assessments and are looking for alternative means of assessment. For example, Mislevy (1993, p. 19) writes, "It is only a slight exaggeration to describe test theory that dominates educational measurement today as the application of twentieth century statistics to nineteenth century psychology." Advances in cognitive science (how people learn) and psychometrics (how we measure learning) have taught us a great deal in the last several decades about how people learn, and this has led to recommendations for changes to assessment to include measuring different types of knowledge: content, procedures, and metacognition. New types of measurement instruments and statistical procedures make it easier to examine data in different ways. However, some testing techniques, such as looking at students' products after they conduct an investigation, limit widespread use of these instruments and procedures because of cost, feasibility, and concerns about subjective interpretation of students' answers.

Societal, economic, and technical changes have also prompted demands for changes in assessment by illustrating the need to focus on a wider range of knowledge and competencies such as applying knowledge in a meaningful way (McAfee & Leong, 2002; Pellegrino, Chudowsky, & Glaser, 2001). For example, a student who can repeat a memorized definition of *density* may possess little to no understanding of density, whereas a student who can use scientific equipment to figure out the density of an object has in-depth

CONNECTING TO
NATIONAL SCIENCE EDUCATION STANDARDS

Executive Summary
It is necessary to align assessment in the classroom with externally developed examinations, if the goals of science education are to be consistent and not confuse both teachers and students (NRC, 2001, p. 2).

knowledge of the concept. It is this in-depth knowledge that societal, economic, and technical changes demand. In scenario 2, the teacher not only asked students for the definition of a concept on a paper-and-pencil test but also asked them to apply the concept to something in everyday life. However, use of an item such as this on a large-scale assessment would require large numbers of people to read and score students' answers—a process too time-consuming and costly for widespread use.

Many educators argue that large-scale assessments are only one-shot methods (they don't show progression or growth) that may not measure what is taught in the local school's curriculum. Since our state and local district curriculum can vary dramatically, a "one size fits all" testing policy may not be fair. Thus, policymakers who see these large-scale assessments as a way to measure achievement and change what is going on in schools, may be using the assessment data inappropriately. It is more fair to view large-scale assessments as targets for educators to pursue than as perfect measurements of students' learning and growth. All assessments are flawed and only estimates of student learning.

Some educational leaders view large-scale assessments as an insufficient means of meeting the assessment standards found in the *National Science Education Standards* (NRC, 1996). Most of the large-scale assessments do a reasonable job of measuring knowledge of facts and procedures, but they fail to capture the breadth and richness of knowledge. For example, Pellegrino, Chudowsky, & Glaser (2001) point out that current tests don't measure students' organization of knowledge, problem representation, use of strategies, self-monitoring skills, and individual contributions to group problem solving. As a result of pressure on schools to do well on high-stakes tests, many teachers are "teaching to the test" or teaching to the low-level questions on the test rather than focusing on the intent of educational reforms. To meet the assessment standards found in the *National Science Education Standards* (NRC, 1996; p. 100), there needs to be a greater emphasis on "assessing what is most highly valued" (as opposed to what is easily measured); "assessing rich, well-structured knowledge" (as opposed to discrete knowledge); "assessing scientific understanding and reasoning" (as opposed to only knowledge); "assessing to learn what students do understand" (as opposed to what they do not know); "assessing achievement and opportunity to learn" (instead of only achievement); and "engaging students in ongoing assessment of their work and that of others" as opposed to end-of-term assessments given by teachers.

Finally, many criticize the fact that, although teachers and those who work in schools are judged by the results of high-stakes assessments, the assessments do little to inform teachers' day-to-day decisions, modify instruction, or change the curriculum. Frequent testing doesn't necessarily improve instruction. An analogy we once heard compared this phenomenon to the frequent weighing of a cow to ensure its growth. To grow, a cow needs proper nutrition, medical care, and habitat. Weighing it alone won't make it grow. Similarly, frequent testing without changes in curriculum or instruction won't improve students' learning. However, many states' standards and, as a result, the high-stakes tests used to measure attainment of the standards vary in their focus and are often too vague to serve as a useful blueprint for curriculum, instruction, and assessment. The results of tests reported to the schools and teachers are often limited—providing only general

Portfolio Activity 8.3 — HIGH-STAKES TESTING

Materials Needed:
- Reference materials

A. High-stakes testing is testing that has a significant consequence for students—testing that is required for high school graduation, placement in "remedial" or "advanced" classes, or for national and international comparisons. Find out more about this type of testing by researching your state's testing policies; national tests such as NAEP, SAT, and ACT; and international tests such as the International Science Study. Report your findings.

B. Why do some people feel these tests are important? Why do others dislike them? What are the advantages and disadvantages of this type of assessment? Why do you think it has become more popular in recent years? Will high-stakes testing improve our educational system? Include in your report your opinion of high-stakes testing.

C. Find out what other countries do in terms of assessment. Are there high-stakes testing programs? How do teachers assess within classrooms? Countries you might want to investigate include Japan, Germany, England, Singapore, and Australia. Good sources of information on this topic are the TIMSS Web pages at http://nces.ed.gov/ and http://wwwcsteep.bc.edu/timss. Please visit the text's Online Learning Center at www.mhhe.com/krajcik2e to link directly to these websites and for updates to these URLs.

D. File your report in your portfolio.

---

information about how students did relative to their peers. Furthermore, these scale assessments are usually given only once a year. There is a large lag until the results of the tests come back and, therefore, they are seldom used to help students or teachers in day-to-day curricular or instructional decisions that affect learning. Pellegrino, Chudowsky, & Glaser (2001) point out the need to create a better match between classroom practices and large-scale assessments: "A vision for the future is that assessments at all levels—from classroom to state—will work together in a system that is comprehensive, coherent, and continuous" (p. 9).

At this time, complete Portfolio Activity 8.3 on high-stakes assessment to explore this topic more thoroughly.

THE NATURE OF CLASSROOM ASSESSMENT

Although there are many reasons we assess students in schools today, in this book we focus primarily on the nature of *classroom* assessment. Just as instruction in project-based science has certain characteristics that distinguish it from traditional science teaching, assessment best suited for a project environment has special characteristics that distinguish it from traditional assessment as described in the first scenario. Assessment that is appropriate for project-based science has many different labels: *active assessment, direct assessment, performance assessment, alternative assessment,* and many others. Let's examine one label, **authentic assessment**. The word *authentic* means "genuine or justifiable." This suggests that assessments that most closely measure what happens during instruction and inform instruction are more genuine and justifiable.

Key Idea

Teachers in project-based science classrooms use a variety of assessment techniques embedded in instruction to continuously monitor growth in individual students' knowledge, skills, and attitudes and to help plan instruction accordingly.

Assessment Resources

Assessment appropriate for today's science classrooms has the following features:

1. It is responsive to context.
2. It is a continuous process embedded in instruction.
3. It is multidimensional.
4. It engages students in the assessment process.
5. It is valid and reliable.
6. It matches today's educational goals.
7. It accommodates cultural diversity.
8. It is consistent with learning theory.
9. It measures meaningful understanding.

Current Assessment Is Responsive to Context

As depicted in the opening scenario, assessment traditionally has been thought of as mainly a measure of students' understanding of content knowledge at the end of a unit of study. It does not help students reflect on their own learning. It is not used to determine what should be taught. It does not influence teachers' day-to-day lessons or provide a means for revising lessons and teaching techniques. On the other hand, assessment in a project-based science environment is context-responsive. It is used to help plan instruction, guide day-to-day interactions with students, and, if necessary, revise instruction on a moment-to-moment basis.

Teachers in a project-based environment use assessment techniques to diagnose students' prior knowledge of science and any problems they may have with science learning. Teachers also examine students' interests. These diagnoses assist teachers in planning and carrying out lessons. For example, if students are having difficulty making meaning of the effects of seasonal change on the behavior of animals and the growth of plants, a teacher would revisit the concepts in a different way and plan new experiences to help students better understand the concepts. If students are extremely interested in the Venus flytrap, the teacher might use this interest as an avenue for teaching about types of plants, including carnivorous ones.

Assessment techniques also provide teachers with information that may alter their moment-to-moment and day-to-day decisions. Teachers using assessment to monitor understanding, skills, and attitudes are less likely to blindly continue lessons without regard to how students are progressing. In other words, teachers using this type of assessment are **reflective practitioners**. They think about, analyze, and mentally debate what should be done to most effectively teach particular students at any given moment. Such teachers continually ask themselves questions such as "Are the students interested in the lesson?" "Was the student misbehavior a result of my management and questioning?" "Did I choose the best instructional strategy to get across the concept?" "Was my pacing okay?" "Did I call on the same students or many different students?" "Did I wait long enough after I asked questions?" "Did I give good examples?" "Were my transitions good?" "Did I end the lesson in a way that summarized what was learned today?" Such ongoing reflection frequently results in teachers changing the direction of their questioning, instructional strategies, choice of curriculum, and classroom environment.

Key Idea

Teachers who use assessment to plan, monitor, and improve teaching are reflective practitioners.

Current Assessment Is a Continuous Process Embedded in Instruction

In the opening scenario, traditional assessment was portrayed as something that always happens at the *end* of instruction. Such assessment is a discrete event separate from instruction. Assessment in a project-based science classroom is consistent with the instruction. It is a *continuous process* that is **embedded** in instruction. Treagust, Jacobowitz, Gallagher, and Parker (2001) and Wenglinsky (2000) conclude that assessment embedded in teaching does lead to improved science learning. It is contextualized and realistic rather than contrived or staged. It does not occur under artificial testing conditions; rather, it matches classroom instruction and real life. Teaching, learning, and assessment are thought of as reciprocal. Assessment continuously monitors student learning; it is not solely an end product of learning. Assessment with these characteristics looks more like the assessment discussed in Scenarios 2 and 3.

> ### *Key Idea*
> Assessment is embedded in instruction and is difficult to distinguish from instruction.

Imagine that you are on a month-long vacation to Australia, you have only brought black and white film, you only have enough to take one photograph per week, and your camera has only one setting. How well will your photographs portray your vacation experiences? How could you have improved the documentation of your vacation? First, you might have brought more film so that you would not be limited to one picture per week. You might also have purchased color film, and you might have used a 35 mm camera so that you could change the focus. If you had a wide angle lens and a zoom lens, you could take panoramic pictures and closeup photographs. You might even have brought a video camera so that you could document continuous sights as well as sounds, and you might have carried a diary so that you could write down your impressions of Australia. Finally, you might have gathered souvenirs to take back home with you.

CONNECTING TO NATIONAL SCIENCE EDUCATION STANDARDS

An Overview

Ideas about assessments have undergone important changes in recent years. In the new view, assessment and learning are two sides of the same coin. When students engage in assessments, they should learn from those assessments (pp. 5–6).

This analogy is very similar to a teacher's efforts to document students' progress in school using assessment techniques. Traditional forms of assessment, when used appropriately, supply the teacher with only quick monochrome snapshots of what students know, can do, and are like. Today's forms of assessment are more analogous to the use of a digital video camera, a 35 mm camera, and a journal and the gathering of souvenirs—strategies that gather a wide range and depth of information. In a project-based classroom, teachers and students will continually collect information during the instructional process. The "souvenirs" of science, which are the artifacts of a project, are especially important because they are often the most remembered and therefore the most meaningful for students and teachers. Students will create many different types of "science souvenirs" or artifacts that can be used to assess their knowledge, skills, and attitudes.

Current Assessment Is Multidimensional

Assessment in a project-based science classroom aims to make fair and accurate judgments about student progress, and the most legitimate judgments come from diverse sources of information to document student learning. Traditional paper-and-pencil assessment techniques can provide teachers with important information but, if used alone, can ignore differences in students' learning styles, interests, attention spans, or types of intelligences. For example, on traditional tests, a student might not correctly identify the definition of *metamorphosis* from five choices provided. However, the student might be able to demonstrate understanding of *metamorphosis* by drawing a diagram illustrating stages of growth or choreographing a performance depicting changes occurring in an animal's life cycle. A student who demonstrates understanding of *metamorphosis* in one of these ways has exhibited understanding of the concept as much as if not more than the student who identified the term from a list of choices.

For teachers who work in schools that require letter grades, the alternative assessment techniques used in project-based science can be of great assistance. Using diverse forms of assessment helps teachers make more valid decisions about students' grades. Students also tend to learn concepts in a more in-depth manner, so they are more likely to score well in other types of assessments. We address different assessment techniques and grading in more detail in Chapter 9.

> **Key Idea**
>
> Effective teachers use many different assessment techniques.

Current Assessment Engages Students in the Assessment Process

In a project environment, teachers and students engage collaboratively in assessment. At each stage of the assessment process, teachers and students work together to collect data, make decisions about individual progress, document progress, and set goals. This collaborative process helps students become self-reflective, self-monitoring learners who regulate and take responsibility for their own learning. This is supported by the National Science Education Standards (NRC, 2001).

Imagine that students are engaging in an investigation. During the investigation, they make numerous observations and record this information in their science notebooks. While students engage in this process, the teacher makes notations in his journal about the students who are having trouble making observations and recording information. Later, while students work in collaborative groups to make decisions about the artifacts they will present to the class, the teacher assembles information from the students' notebooks to file in their portfolios. The teacher judges each student's depth of understanding from the items contained in his or her portfolio. After the artifacts are presented to the class, the entire class engages in a critical dialogue. Later, the teacher discusses with each student the items contained in his or her portfolio. The teacher reviews individual progress with each student, and together they devise strategies to improve the student's academic growth. Students are involved in every step of the assessment process, which has been designed to help them become motivated, self-regulated learners.

> **Key Idea**
>
> Assessment engages students in the process to help them become reflective learners who regulate their own learning.

> **NSES**
>
> **CONNECTING TO**
> **NATIONAL SCIENCE EDUCATION STANDARDS**
>
> **Executive Summary**
> Student participation is a key component of successful assessment strategies at every step. If students are to participate effectively in the process, they need to be clear about the target and the criteria for good work, to assess their own efforts in light of the criteria, and to share responsibility in taking action in light of the feedback (NRC, 2001, p. 1).

Current Assessment Is Valid and Reliable

Good assessment is both valid and reliable. **Valid assessment** is appropriate and allows the teacher to make accurate generalizations from it about a student's understanding. Invalid assessment does not permit a teacher to make accurate decisions about what students know and what they are ready to learn. Each one of us can provide examples of tests or assessments from our own educational experience that we felt weren't fair. We agonized over the results because we knew that they didn't represent what we really knew or what we were capable of doing. Therefore, any generalizations made about us were incorrect or at best only partially correct. When assessment focuses on more than simply the attainment of content knowledge, uses diverse sources of information, and involves the student in the assessment process, it is less likely that it will result in biased conclusions or errors.

Reliable assessment provides consistent results across different trials. In other words, a reliable assessment tool will yield similar results on different occasions or will result in different assessors coming to similar conclusions about the student being assessed. Think about your car. If it starts one day but not another under similar weather conditions, you would say that the car isn't reliable. The results are not consistent, so the car isn't trustworthy. Of course, if this happened only once, you could not blame your car for being unreliable. If, however, your car repeatedly starts one day and not the other, you could assuredly conclude that it isn't reliable. With traditional end-of-term paper-and-pencil assessment techniques, a single "snapshot" of students' abilities is taken at the "conclusion of learning." Many factors such as testing conditions, the assessment items themselves, and a student's frame of mind can influence the reliability of these snapshots, and so the results are not always trustworthy. Assessment techniques are more reliable because they give students many opportunities and ways to demonstrate their abilities, thus eliminating variables that may alter results.

> **Key Idea**
>
> Assessment should consistently and accurately measure students' learning.

Current Assessment Matches Today's Educational Goals

It is widely recognized today that learning should be active and integrated; the knowledge explosion has made it futile to ask students to memorize large quantities of facts as they will quickly become outdated. In our information age, labor force experts are calling for students who can solve problems, make decisions, learn, collaborate with others, and manage themselves (*SCANS Report,* 1991, in Packer, 1992). Educators think it is important for students to be able to understand how they have arrived at an answer, transfer knowledge to real life situations, think critically, document and communicate information, and analyze and synthesize information.

These new educational goals have required changes in the way we teach. Active and integrated strategies such as collaborative learning, which is used in project-based science, are stressed. Therefore, assessment practices need to be holistic and complex. If a teacher were trying to measure content knowledge, or knowledge that is concerned only with what central concepts, principles, and theories students have acquired, selected response assessments such as true/false and multiple choice tests would measure a small part of students' understandings. However, as we discussed in Chapter 2, teachers today are trying to measure much more: **content knowledge, procedural knowledge,** and **metacognitive knowledge** as related to out-of-school experiences. Students are assessed on their abilities to solve problems, make decisions, and collaborate. Not only do assessment techniques *match* today's goals, but they also help to meet them. By engaging students in the assessment process, assessment pushes students to become independent learners responsible for their own learning.

> **Key Idea**
>
> Teachers today are trying to monitor knowledge, skills, and attitudes relevant to out-of-school life.

Portfolio Activity 8.4 asks you to compare assessment practices with several reform documents that have established today's educational goals.

Portfolio Activity 8.4

HOW DOES SCIENCE REFORM AFFECT ASSESSMENT PRACTICES?

Materials Needed:
- Reference materials including *Benchmarks for Science Literacy* (AAAS, 1993); *Project 2061: Science for All Americans* (Rutherford & Ahlgren, 1990); *National Science Education Standards* (National Research Council, 1996); and *Classroom Assessment and the National Science Education Standards (2001)*

A. On a sheet of paper, list as many answers as you can to the question "What is a scientifically literate person?" You completed a similar list in Portfolio Activity 1.5 in Chapter 1. You might refer to your notes in your portfolio.

B. How could you assess whether a person had met this criteria? List ways to assess each criterion.

C. How many of the items did you choose to assess with traditional multiple choice, true/false, and essay questions? How many required different approaches to assessment? Why is this so?

D. Compare your list of characteristics of scientific literacy to those in major national reform reports such as *Benchmarks for Science Literacy, Project 2061: Science for All Americans, National Science Education Standards*, and *Classroom Assessment and the National Science Education Standards*. How do your criteria for scientific literacy compare with the criteria in these policy reports? What effect do you think these reports will have on curriculum, instruction, and assessment?

E. Record your ideas in your portfolio.

Current Assessment Accommodates Cultural Diversity

Key Idea

Assessment techniques need to pay attention to meeting the needs of diverse students.

Recent policy reports in science education have called for changes that will attract all students to science learning (National Research Council, 1996; Rutherford & Ahlgren, 1990). When considering the diverse needs, interests, and abilities of students in our country—particularly girls, minorities, students with disabilities, and those with limited English proficiency—it becomes clear that traditional or narrow assessment techniques sometimes discriminate against some populations of students. They overlook the prior experiences, learning styles, multiple intelligences, and interests of our diverse population. Use of a variety of assessment techniques, on the contrary, allows for students' unique differences.

For example, a student with limited English proficiency might have difficulty answering essay questions about the process of metamorphosis. This test, however, would more likely be assessing her ability to write English sentences than her understanding of metamorphosis. An assessment that asked her to draw pictures of the stages of life that an insect goes through from egg stage to adult stage would more likely measure her understanding of the concept.

A recent study (Lawrenz, Huffman, & Welch, 2001) found significant differences among ethnic groups (Caucasians, Asian Americans, Hispanic/Latino Americans, and African Americans) for different test formats. For example, Caucasians performed better on multiple-choice and open-ended tests, while Asian Americans fared best at hands-on stations. Atwater (2000) points out that many test items fail to measure the content taught in African-American classrooms, don't match the language used by African-American children, and are incongruent with many minority children's life experiences. Solano-Flores and Barber (2000) note that sociocultural differences can affect the validity of assessment items. Sociocultural influences include students' values, beliefs, experiences, communication patterns, teaching and learning styles, and socioeconomic status. Similarly, Fusco and Calabrese-Barton (2001) point out the need to assess science understanding of diverse students. McAfee and Leong (2002) have outlined several guidelines for teachers to be more sensitive to cultural and social differences among students:

CONNECTING TO
NATIONAL SCIENCE EDUCATION STANDARDS

Assessment in the Classroom
Assessments should be equitable and fair, supporting all students in their quest for high standards (NRC, 2001, p. 58).

- Assume that there are cultural differences in every classroom that will affect assessment.
- Learn the difference between social, cultural, ethnic, language differences, and disabilities that require special services.
- Use multiple assessment measures.
- Involve parents and the community in the assessment process.
- Design assessment measures so that they match students' interests, experiences, and prior knowledge.

Current Assessment Is Consistent with Learning Theory

In Chapter 2, we examined how students construct understanding, the social nature of learning, and the need for science to be anchored in students' daily lives. Social constructivist theory has several implications for assessment. One major tenet is that learners actively construct knowledge and connect new learning to prior knowledge that enables them to integrate knowledge in new ways and to solve problems. Cognitive theories focus on how people develop structures of knowledge, including concepts associated with subject matter expertise and procedures for reasoning and problem solving (Pellegrino, Chudowsky, & Glaser, 2001). One implication for assessment, for example, is that assessment techniques that measure only content knowledge in short-term, working memory (and sometimes only inert knowledge) are inadequate. What follows are a number of learning principles and the assessment practices that derive from them (adapted from Herman, Ashbacher, & Winters, 1992, and Pellegrino, Chudowsky, & Glaser, 2001).

> *Key Idea*
>
> Assessment techniques are consistent with how children learn.

People generate knowledge through an active process of creating personal meaning by integrating new information with prior knowledge. This principle implies that students must actively generate meaning for themselves. For example, in project-based science, some students might create posters to demonstrate what they have learned, while others might create a video documentary. This principle also implies that assessment should measure how students relate new learning to personal experiences and prior knowledge. Finally, assessment should measure how well students apply what they have learned. For example, students investigating why the water in the classroom faucet doesn't flow well might present their data to the city water department, creating a perfect opportunity for assessment.

Students of all ages and abilities can think and solve problems. This principle implies that assessment techniques should engage students in problem-solving activities and investigation. Because learning does not happen in discrete, small steps, assessment should measure holistic knowledge and abilities. When students present artifacts, they are demonstrating a wide variety of knowledge, skills, and attitudes learned—not isolated facts. More than one right answer should be encouraged.

Children differ in learning styles, attention spans, memory, and developmental rates. This principle implies that assessment techniques should be varied and multidimensional. Students should be given more than one chance to demonstrate their competence, and they should have time to complete tasks. Students should be allowed to revise work and show improvement over time. Finally, students should be able to demonstrate their various abilities, whether they be academic, artistic, verbal, or social. Student production of artifacts presents an opportunity for appropriate assessment because students can construct the products over time and present information in whatever format best matches their learning styles. After presenting their artifacts to a public audience, students receive feedback, which can then be used for revision or further development of the artifacts.

People need to know when to use knowledge and how to adapt it. They also need to learn how to manage their own learning. This principle suggests that students should be able to participate in their assessment, consulting with the teacher, reflecting upon their own work and progress, and helping set their own learning goals.

Motivation and effort affect learning and performance. This principle implies that students should play a part in identifying what they will do, how they will do it, and how it will be evaluated, because motivation and effort are enhanced when learners are able to set their own goals and when the criteria for assessment are demystified. Learners also need clear guidelines about expectations, and they need to see the connection between their efforts and their results. When students determine what artifacts to include in their portfolios for assessment, their motivation increases. They play active roles in selecting, developing, and giving presentations that will be assessed. They participate in assessing the presentations and artifacts of their classmates.

Learning occurs within a social context. This principle implies that assessment of group work should be included in evaluation. As students work together, they construct understanding and find solutions to questions and problems. As a result, it is critical to assess the products that emerge from students working together.

Current Assessment Measures Meaningful Understanding

Do you remember memorizing answers for a test and not understanding what you were memorizing? What is Avogadro's Number? What is the equation that represents the process of photosynthesis? What type of lens focuses light to a single focal point and then inverts it to enlarge the image? What are the names of the three bones in the ear? What is a vacuole? What are the six simple machines? If you cannot answer these questions, it's probably because you learned them by rote memorization in order to regurgitate them on a test at the end of a chapter or quarter. It is likely that you have never used or applied these concepts since and that you lack a meaningful understanding of them.

Paper-and-pencil tests are typically true/false, multiple choice, matching, short essay, fill-in-the-blank, or circle the correct picture. Although these types of tests can be structured to measure meaningful understanding of concepts, they frequently are not (NRC, 2000). Students can easily memorize terms and guess at correct answers based on shallow and disconnected understanding of material. Sometimes ambiguous words, unclear questions, or vague sentences make it difficult for students even to respond during these types of tests. Imagine a question that instructs children to look at pictures of plants to identify which plant needs the least amount of water. Two of the plants pictured are a cactus and a head of cabbage. The "correct" answer is supposed to be the cactus. However, students could reason that since the head of cabbage is dead (since it has been cut from its roots), it no longer needs *any* water to live. Choosing the head of cabbage actually demonstrates a deeper, more meaningful understanding of the concept in question. Such questions fail to measure what students know; instead, they measure what students do not know.

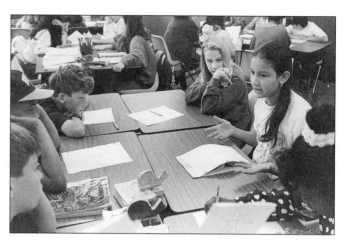

Today's educational goals require a variety of techniques.

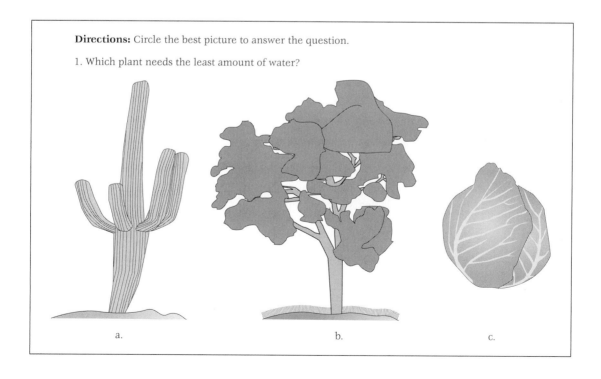

Directions: Circle the best picture to answer the question.

1. Which plant needs the least amount of water?

a.

b.

c.

Teachers need to write paper-and-pencil tests so they measure higher-level thinking rather than low-level, factual answers. True/false, sequencing, and multiple choice tests can limit student answers but can be expanded to let students answer open-ended follow-up questions as well. Students often take paper-and-pencil tests on statewide assessments. For this reason, some teachers like to use paper-and-pencil tests in their classrooms. For more information regarding the construction of good paper-and-pencil tests, see Chapter 9.

Authentic assessment measures meaningful understanding by stressing open-ended answers rather than a single "correct" one. Students engage in higher-level reasoning through discourse with others (teachers, peers, members of the community). Creating artifacts is more complex and engaging than is selecting answers from a multiple choice list. Artifacts can demonstrate higher-level thinking skills such as planning, inventing, and making conclusions. Students construct knowledge rather than simply repeat memorized information. Finally, students engage in self-reflection, which develops self-regulation and personal responsibility.

Imagine that your students have spent considerable time investigating the driving question "Why does flooding cause so much damage?" You could try to measure students' understanding of water pressure on levees by asking a multiple choice question such as "What is water pressure? a. the amount of force a given amount of water gives on an object, b. the amount of water that presses down upon the earth, c. the amount of pressure on water from the air above it." Or you could assess understanding of water pressure on levees by using a performance-based assessment technique. You could provide students with 2-liter soda bottles, each with three holes about 2 inches apart—one near the top, one in the middle, and one near the bottom. Instruct students to tape the holes and then pour water into their bottles. Ask students to explore what happens as they remove the tape from each hole. Ask them to explain the results of the activity and then to compare the results of this activity to the breaking of levees during Mississippi River floods of many towns in the Midwest or during wet El Niño weather in the winters. Question them about their opinions on building levees along a river.

Which of these examples of assessment measures meaningful understanding? Although paper-and-pencil tests can measure meaningful understanding, in the aforementioned example a student could memorize a definition of *water pressure* from a textbook and really not understand the concept. Although not all performance assessments are necessarily well constructed to measure meaningful understanding, in the aforementioned example a student must have a meaningful understanding of water pressure to explain the results of an investigation. The student must construct meaning to explain why the water in the bottom hole flows out faster and at a different angle. The student must also have a deep, meaningful conceptual framework to discuss how the results of the investigation resemble the river flooding and whether levees are ultimately helpful or harmful.

In Portfolio Activity 8.5, you will compare traditional assessment techniques with contemporary assessment techniques and examine the pitfalls of traditional testing in order to better understand the merits of today's assessments.

Key Idea

Assessment should measure meaningful understanding rather than focusing on single, correct answers.

WHAT TO ASSESS

When you were in school, your teacher probably focused almost solely on measuring your attainment of scientific facts. You may remember asking the teacher, "Is this going to be on the test?" You and your classmates were probably keenly aware that tests

Portfolio Activity 8.5

WHAT ARE THE PITFALLS OF TRADITIONAL TESTING?

Materials Needed:

- Traditional textbooks and accompanying commercial tests

A. Reread Scenario 1 at the beginning of this chapter. Make a list with two columns labeled *Traditional assessments* and *Contemporary assessments*. Under each of these headings, make two additional columns labeled *Advantages* and *Disadvantages*. Identify as many advantages and disadvantages as you can for each type of assessment.

B. With a few classmates, compare and discuss the advantages and disadvantages. Make a list of what you all agree are the most important advantages and disadvantages. How do the advantages of each category help students learn, help teachers administer assessment, help parents understand student progress, and help students understand their own progress?

C. Discuss whether the advantages of today's assessment techniques outweigh the disadvantages. How can the disadvantages be overcome?

D. Examine the commercial tests that accompany a traditional elementary or middle grade textbook. How many of the following can you find in the tests or assessments?

1. A variety of testing formats including whole class, small group, and individual
2. A variety of formats including artifacts, teacher observations, essays, student-produced products, student self-evaluation, and concept maps
3. Assessment throughout the learning process
4. Measurement of higher-level cognitive outcomes
5. Measurement of skills
6. Monitoring of affective outcomes
7. Student monitoring of his or her own progress and time to continue to learn content until it is mastered
8. Measurement of relationships, the nature of science, critical thinking, problem solving, and interrelationships between school science and life outside of school
9. Measurement of student understanding of the subconcepts within the test
10. Feedback beyond a letter grade or percentage score

E. As a classroom teacher, what steps would you need to take to make a traditional test accompanying a textbook series more valid in its assessment method?

F. Record your thoughts in your portfolio.

---

measured certain content, and you wanted to make sure you memorized the particular answers that you would be asked to give. It is unlikely that your teacher paid much attention to whether you had misunderstandings about scientific ideas. The teacher probably did not focus on procedural knowledge—whether you were able to ask and refine questions, plan and design investigations, collect data, make sense of data, or report your findings. It is even less likely that your teacher was concerned with examining your metacognitive knowledge, your attitudes and dispositions toward learning science, or your motivation to learn. Teachers using project-based methods might still use paper-and-pencil tests from time to time, but the focus of their tests is different. These tests measure what students learned by doing investigations. The focus is not mastery of inert knowledge such as vocabulary terms for the sake of learning the terms. Rather, understandings that can be measured on a test are the outcome of investigations. The test, as shown in the second scenario, may be used to help students monitor their own progress or to help the teacher adjust his or her teaching.

CONNECTING TO
NATIONAL SCIENCE EDUCATION STANDARDS

The Relationship Between Formative and Summative Assessment

Tests that are given before the end of a unit can provide both teacher and student with useful information on which to act while there is still opportunity to revisit areas where students were not able to perform well. Opportunities for revisions on tests or any other type of assessment give students another chance to work through, think about, and come to understand an area they did not fully understand or clearly articulate the previous time (NRC, 2001, p. 62).

CONNECTING TO
NATIONAL SCIENCE EDUCATION STANDARDS

Classroom Assessment and Inquiry

In the context of inquiry, assessments need to gauge the progress of students in achieving the three major learning outcomes of inquiry-based science teaching: conceptual understandings of science, abilities to perform scientific inquiry, and understandings about inquiry (NRC, 2000, p. 75).

Key Idea

Assessments should measure content, science process, and understandings about inquiry.

Traditionally, students were expected to know vocabulary words such as *vertebrate, invertebrate, crustacean, mollusk,* and *reptile.* For almost all students, this type of knowledge didn't have much relevance outside of school. It was thought that knowing such vocabulary words would build a foundation for understanding science. Today, science educators see the teaching of such concepts as a much more complex process than simply requiring students to memorize definitions and recognize examples. Today, teachers are concerned with examining students' prior beliefs about the scientific world and their understanding of its major concepts. Science educators also see knowledge as something that helps students analyze a question, solve a problem, or conduct an investigation in a way that is meaningful to them. This type of knowledge is not superficial. For example, rather than focusing on the definition of *invertebrate, crustacean,* and *reptile,* a teacher might have students analyze how a crustacean (with a hard outer covering) and a reptile (with a hard shell) are alike and different. This knowledge of similarities and differences would help students set up a functioning aquarium to investigate a driving question about how some crustaceans and reptiles can coexist in a saltwater tank with poisonous invertebrates. If a group of students actually assembled a functioning aquarium, they would be applying their knowledge and skills. As a result, the assessment of such an activity would extend beyond measuring inert knowledge. This assessment is more consistent with today's assessment goals (NRC, 1996; NRC, 2000; NRC, 2001; NSTA, 2002). In Portfolio Activity 8.6, you will develop your own assessment procedure for measuring understanding.

The National Science Teachers Association (NSTA, 2002) recently released a position statement about assessment in science. The NSTA stressed assessment of understanding of science content and process; ability to think critically and solve problems; ability to design scientific experiments, analyze data, and draw conclusions; ability to recognize relationships between science topics and real world issues; and skill in using mathematics as a tool to learn science. Similarly, the National Research Council (2000) stressed that we need to assess science content, science process, and understandings about inquiry.

Current assessment also monitors the affective side of learning. Students are encouraged to ask questions, become excited about an investigation, remain open-minded about new ideas, be thorough in their investigation, stay fair in their conclusions, and be honest in their presentation of evidence. Imagine that a group of students is investigating the driving question "Where does all the garbage go?" The students could become aware of landfill problems, discuss their attitudes about the situation, and create artifacts that depict the problem without exhibiting positive dispositions or taking action, two other objectives of the project. It would be better if students responded to the landfill problem by

Portfolio Activity 8.6

HOW CAN I CHOOSE A GOOD ASSESSMENT TECHNIQUE TO MEASURE UNDERSTANDING?

Materials Needed:
- Paper and pencil or a computer

A. What follows are several learning performances that might be contained in a typical elementary or middle school curriculum. Form a team of three students. Read each learning performance and decide what would be the most beneficial ways to measure whether students have gained understanding of the topic. Keep in mind that good assessment should:
    1. Be responsive to context.
    2. Be a continuous process embedded in instruction.
    3. Be multidimensional.
    4. Engage students in the assessment process.
    5. Be valid and reliable.
    6. Match today's educational goals.
    7. Accommodate cultural diversity.
    8. Be consistent with cognitive learning theory.
    9. Measure meaningful understanding.

Learning Performances
- After investigating simple machines, each student will show how machines help us do work.

- After investigating what animals need to eat, each student will be able to distinguish between a consumer and a producer.
- After investigating what types of trees are in our environment, each student will be able to identify two types of trees.
- After investigating where garbage goes, each student will be able to tell why it is important to recycle.

B. As a team, develop a lesson to teach one of the learning performances. Develop two different ways of assessing the objective after you have taught it. Teach the lesson to another team in your class and try the two different methods of assessment.

C. Ask the team you taught which method of assessment best measured what they learned. How do that team's beliefs about good assessment techniques compare to yours?

D. Record your ideas in your portfolio.

---

recycling aluminum cans and encouraging others to recycle. It would be even better if students organized a schoolwide recycling program for all possible school products—glass, aluminum, steel cans, paper, cardboard, and plastic. By focusing assessment on the different types of knowledge (content, procedural, and metacognitive), skills, and attitudes of students, it broadens the purpose of assessment and treats it as a process that matches instructional goals and life outside of school.

Table 8.1 illustrates how we can assess different knowledge domains. It expands the table of learning performances in Chapter 7 to illustrate how a teacher could assess the learning performances. Portfolio Activity 8.7 will challenge you to complete Table 8.1 on your own for a project of your choosing.

Studying the Environment

WHEN TO ASSESS

Research shows that assessment can help students learn science (Black & Wiliam, 1998). For assessments to help students learn, however, they need to inform practices in the classroom. If used effectively, both formative and summative assessments can inform classroom practices and help students learn. Formative assessments are those that help teachers make day-to-day decisions about instruction or help students learn. These

> **Key Idea**
>
> Teachers should use formative and summative assessments to improve teaching and learning.

Table 8.1

ASSESSING LEARNING PERFORMANCES
The Cognitive Process Dimension

	Remember	Understand	Apply	Analyze	Evaluate	Create
THE KNOWLEDGE DOMAIN	*Definition:* to recall something from memory	*Definition:* to comprehend and be able to explain the meaning of a concept or process	*Definition:* to develop solutions to familiar or new problems	*Definition:* to examine a concept or process in detail to learn more about it	*Definition:* to make judgments about value, quality, importance, or condition	*Definition:* to produce something
Factual Knowledge *Definition:* Knowledge of details and facts	*Learning Performance:* State that matter is made up of atoms *Assessment:* Have students select the correct definition of *matter* on a multiple choice test item	*Learning Performance:* Use the idea of conservation of atoms to explain how the mass after a chemical reaction compares to the mass before the reaction *Assessment:* Have students complete a short answer test item asking how the mass after a chemical reaction compares to the mass before the reaction	*Learning Performance:* Carry out an experiment to illustrate the conservation of mass *Assessment:* Examine a student's science journal to see how he or she carried out an experiment	*Learning Performance:* Given a table of data, be able to discriminate the relevant from irrelevant data needed to answer a question related to conservation of mass in a chemical reaction *Assessment:* Interview a student to probe what he or she means by *relevant* and *irrelevant data*; ask what the relevant data are	*Learning Performance:* Judge if appropriate conclusions were drawn regarding a set of data collected from a series of chemical reactions *Assessment:* Examine student's daily journals for evidence of appropriate conclusions	*Learning Performance:* Design an experiment to illustrate the conservation of mass *Assessment:* Examine student's notes from a science journal to determine how the experiment was designed
Conceptual Knowledge *Definition:* Knowledge of interrelationships, principles, theories, and models	*Learning Performance:* Define *flow of energy* in an ecosystem *Assessment:* Have students write a poem that illustrates flow of energy in an ecosystem	*Learning Performance:* Explain how sunlight is transformed through photosynthesis to provide food for plants, herbivores, and carnivores *Assessment:* Have students write a song that explains how sunlight is transformed through photosynthesis to provide food for plants, herbivores, and carnivores	*Learning Performance:* Implement an experiment to show the influence of sunlight on the growth of plants *Assessment:* Have students make a video of their experiment and evaluate the ability to implement the experiment from watching the video	*Learning Performance:* Analyze an ecosystem to show how extinction of a small omnivore might influence the population of a herbivore *Assessment:* Have students draw a diagram that illustrates how extinction of a small omnivore might influence the population of an herbivore	*Learning Performance:* Evaluate how a new government policy might influence various species in an ecosystem *Assessment:* Have students write a position statement regarding how a new government policy might influence various species in an ecosystem	*Learning Performance:* Create an alternative EPA policy to improve the ecosystem of the Great Lakes *Assessment:* Have students write to their local newspaper to suggest an alternative EPA policy to improve the ecosystem of the Great Lakes

	Remember	Understand	Apply	Analyze	Evaluate	Create
Procedural Knowledge *Definition:* Knowledge about how to do something, conduct inquiry, or use a skill	*Learning Performance:* Recognize the parts of a microscope *Assessment:* Have students label the parts of a microscope from a drawing	*Learning Performance:* Clarify to a fellow student how to focus a microscope *Assessment:* Have a student teach a peer how to focus a microscope	*Learning Performance:* Use a microscope to observe single-celled pond organisms *Assessment:* Observe students while they are focusing a microscope to determine if they can focus it to see a pond organism	*Learning Performance:* From observations of single-celled organisms, organize a data chart to distinguish the organisms *Assessment:* Have students create a chart (with appropriate labels) of single-celled organisms	*Learning Performance:* Determine whether conclusions drawn from observations of single-celled organisms are appropriate *Assessment:* Have students record their conclusions in a science journal and defend how the conclusion logically follows the observations	*Learning Performance:* Devise a procedure to determine if the number of single-celled organisms in a pond sample changes over time *Assessment:* Have students present their procedures to the class for determining if the number of single-celled organisms in a pond sample changes over time; rate the quality of the procedure
Metacognitive Knowledge *Definition:* Self-knowledge, knowledge of one's own cognition	*Learning Performance:* Recall that you find writing in a science journal challenging *Assessment:* Interview a student about his or her strengths or weaknesses recalled from past science experiences	*Learning Performance:* Summarize which tasks you find most difficult in science classes and why they are difficult for you *Assessment:* Have students summarize in a portfolio which tasks they find most difficult in science classes and why	*Learning Performance:* Implement a procedure to help yourself study for a science test *Assessment:* Have a student reflect in a journal entry on his or her learning and design a way to study	*Learning Performance:* Break down the components of a science test that you will need to focus on to be successful *Assessment:* Have students send you an e-mail message stating how they will change their study habits to better understand the material	*Learning Performance:* Critique whether you have improved your own test-taking skills *Assessment:* Have students summarize their improvement on test-taking skills by making an entry in a portfolio	*Learning Performance:* Construct a portfolio and organize it in a manner that would be most compatible with your own learning style to show what you have learned *Assessment:* Discuss with a student why his or her portfolio is arranged as it is

Source: Modified from L. W. Anderson and D. R. Krathwohl (2001).

Portfolio Activity 8.7   **ASSESSING LEARNING PERFORMANCES**

Materials Needed:
- Something to write with
- Table 8.1

A. Select a driving question for a project such as "What plants grow in my environment?"

B. Develop a list of learning performances that might be associated with learning about your topic. Try to fill in as many of the knowledge domains as you can in Table 8.1.

C. Think about ways you might assess each learning performance and share your ideas with others in your class. How do your ideas compare to those of others in your class?

D. Record your ideas in your portfolio.

assessments are used in the context of instruction to assess prior knowledge and are also embedded into instruction to guide teaching and learning. Summative assessments occur at the end of a unit of instruction or time period (such as upon completing a grade level) to determine achievement, issue grades, promote students, or demonstrate accountability (NRC, 2001). As discussed earlier, summative assessments are often external tests used to determine placement, promotion, achievement, or program success (accountability of the schools). Summative assessments can also inform instruction and learning if used as illustrated in the second scenario. When used in this fashion, the distinction between formative and summative can become somewhat blurred—the assessment can help students revise and redo their work or help teachers revise their subsequent teaching.

The National Science Education Standards assert that effective formative assessment has a framework of three guiding questions:

1. Where are you trying to go? (identify and communicate the learning and performance goals).
2. Where are you now? (assess or help the student self-assess current levels of understanding).
3. How can you get there? (help the student with strategies and skills to reach the goals) (NRC, 2001, p. 14).

Using this framework, a teacher clearly communicates expected learning or performance goals to students. For example, the teacher might explain to the students that they will understand the concept of *friction* after they finish investigating their subquestion "How can we make rollerblades go faster?" The teacher uses a variety of techniques to help students assess their current level of understanding. For example, the teacher might have students keep a science journal where they record their investigations involving rollerblades rolling across different surfaces (rough, smooth, wet, dry, etc.). The teacher would provide students with timely **feedback**. For example, a teacher might sit down with a student to discuss his or her journal and provide suggestions for testing additional ideas related to friction against the rollerblades. If the students in the class are having a difficult time understanding the concept of friction, the teacher might modify his or her teaching to introduce a new benchmark lesson to teach about friction.

Regardless of technique used (such as written remark or conferences with students), it is the teacher's responsibility to implement the science standards and provide students with regular feedback regarding how they are progressing toward desired learning performances. It is also the teacher's responsibility to keep good records so that he or she can give each student feedback and report progress to parents. Teachers should give students opportunities to revise their work and improve it based on feedback. It is the student's responsibility to use feedback to take action to learn the desired knowledge or skill. Many techniques can be used to give students feedback, such as journals, and to help students take responsibility to learn, such as self-evaluations. We devote Chapter 9 to discussing numerous assessment techniques.

USING TECHNOLOGY TOOLS TO EXAMINE ASSESSMENT

One way that teachers can improve assessment is to network with other teachers. By networking, teachers make time to discuss their teaching and assessment practices with others. Often this discussion focuses on students' work to determine whether the students understand the expected learning performances. Technology tools can help you become part of a community of learners who are interested in this type of discourse. For example, teachers who have little time to meet together might exchange ideas with each other over e-mail, discuss particular assessment concerns in an online chat room, or share assessment ideas in a threaded discussion.

The National Science Teachers Association (NSTA) has a section at its website entitled *NSTA Community*. This section of the NSTA website includes a discussion board where you can talk with others. The NSTA *Building a Presence for Science* section is a networking initiative designed to improve the teaching and learning of science. The specific goal of this initiative is to break down the isolation some teachers face and develop a professional network of colleagues. In this project, NSTA connects key leaders around the country to school districts to provide electronic communication and support for teachers. Similarly, many state science professional organizations have websites where teachers can interact with others to discuss curriculum and assessment. These websites often enable teachers to talk with others about their state's standards and high-stakes assessment. Finally, the Eisenhower National Clearinghouse website contains a number of links to places where teachers can communicate and collaborate with others.

CONNECTING TO NATIONAL SCIENCE EDUCATION STANDARDS

Assessment in the Classroom

Formative assessment refers to assessments that provide information to students and teachers that are used to improve teaching and learning. These are often informal and ongoing, though they need not be. Data from summative assessments can be used in a formative way. *Summative assessment* refers to the cumulative assessments, usually occurring at the end of a unit or topic coverage, that intend to capture what a student has learned, or the quality of the learning, and judge performance against some standards. Although we often think of summative assessments as traditional objective tests, this need not be the case. For example, summative assessments could follow from an accumulation of evidence collected over time, as in a collection of student work (NRC, 2001, p. 25).

Key Idea

Technology tools can help teachers network with others for the purpose of improving assessment practices.

CONNECTING TO NATIONAL SCIENCE EDUCATION STANDARDS

An Introduction to Assessment in the Science Classroom

Teachers need time and assistance in developing accurate and dependable assessments. Much of this assistance can be provided by creating settings in which teachers have opportunities to talk with one another about the quality of student work (NRC, 2001, p. 9).

CHAPTER REVIEW   www.mhhe.com/krajcik2e

Go to the Online Learning Center at **www.mhhe.com/krajcik2e** to review important content from the chapter and key terms, take a chapter assessment, and link to the chapter's websites.

CHAPTER SUMMARY

In this chapter, we discussed the purpose and nature of assessment and explored the advantages and disadvantages of large-scale assessments. We considered features of high-quality assessments that are responsive to context, embedded in instruction, and multidimensional. Current assessments also engage students in the assessment process, are valid and reliable, match today's educational goals, accommodate cultural diversity, are consistent with learning theory, and measure meaningful understanding. The chapter examined what to assess by focusing on measurement of learning performances across a variety of knowledge domains. We discussed both formative and summative assessments. Finally, we discussed how technology tools can help teachers network with others to examine their assessment practices.

CHAPTER HIGHLIGHTS

- Assessment is any method used to judge or evaluate an outcome or help make a decision.
- Assessment data are used for a variety of purposes in educational settings today:
  - Assisting learning.
  - Guiding teaching.
  - Measuring individual achievement.
  - Giving grades.
  - Allocating resources.
  - Evaluating programs.
  - Informing local, state, and national policy.
- Research shows that regular, high-quality assessment can have a positive effect on student achievement.
- Large-scale assessments are used to evaluate students' achievement, school curriculum, school district progress, and programs.
- Many educators argue that large-scale assessments are only one-shot methods and may not measure what is taught in a local school's curriculum.
- Some educational leaders view large-scale assessments as insufficient for meeting the assessment standards found in the *National Science Education Standards.*
- Assessment appropriate for today's science classrooms has several features:
  - It is responsive to context.
  - It is a continuous process embedded in instruction.
  - It is multidimensional.
  - It engages students in the assessment process.
  - It is valid and reliable.

- It matches today's educational goals.
- It accommodates cultural diversity.
- It is consistent with cognitive learning theory.
- It measures meaningful understanding.
- Assessments measure science content, science process, and understandings about inquiry.
- Assessment also monitors the affective side of learning.
- The cognitive process domain can be used as a framework to assess student understanding.
- Formative assessment helps teachers evaluate students' progress during a unit of study and make day-to-day decisions regarding curriculum and instruction.
- Effective formative assessment has a framework of three guiding questions:
  - Where are you trying to go?
  - Where are you now?
  - How can you get there?
- Summative assessment occurs at the end of a unit of instruction or time period to determine achievement, issue grades, promote students, or demonstrate accountability.
- Both formative and summative assessments can inform classroom practices and help students learn.
- Technology tools can help teachers become part of a community of learners who are interested in improving assessment practices.

KEY TERMS

assessment (309)

authentic
   assessment (313)

classroom
   assessments (309)

content knowledge (317)

embedded (315)

feedback (328)

formative
   assessments (309)

high-stakes
   assessment (309)

large-scale
   assessments (309)

metacognitive
   knowledge (317)

procedural
   knowledge (317)

reflective
   practitioners (314)

reliable
   assessment (317)

summative
   assessment (310)

valid assessment (316)

REFERENCES

American Association for the Advancement of Science. 1993. *Benchmarks for science literacy.* New York: Oxford University Press.

Anderson, L. W., and D. R. Krathwohl, eds. 2001. *A taxonomy for learning, teaching, and assessing: A revision of Bloom's taxonomy of educational objectives.* New York: Longman.

Atwater, M. M. 2000. Equity for black Americans in precollege science. *Science Education* 84(2):155–79.

Black, P., and D. Wiliam. 1998. Assessment and classroom learning. *Assessment in Education* 5(1):7–74.

Fusco, D., and A. Calabrese-Barton. 2001. Representing student achievements in science. *Journal of Research in Science Teaching* 38(3): 337–54.

Herman, J. L., P. R. Ashbacher, and L. Winters. 1992. *A practical guide to alternative assessment.* Alexandria, Va.: Association for Supervision and Curriculum Development.

Lawrenz, F., D. Huffman, and W. Welch. 2001. The science achievement of various subgroups on alternative assessment formats. *Science Education* 85(3):279–90.

McAfee, O., and D. J. Leong, 2002. *Assessing and guiding young children's development and learning.* Boston: Allyn and Bacon.

Mislevy, R. J. 1993. Foundations of a new test theory. In *Test theory for a new generation of tests,* eds. N. Frederiksen, R. J. Mislevy, and I. I. Bejar. Hillsdale, N.J.: Erlbaum.

National Research Council. 1996. *National science education standards.* Washington, D.C.: National Academy Press.

National Research Council. 2000. *Inquiry and the national science education standards.* Washington, D.C.: National Academy Press.

National Research Council. 2001. *Classroom assessment and the national science education standards.* Washington, D.C.: National Academy Press.

National Science Teachers Association. 2002. NSTA position statement on assessment. *NSTA Reports* 13(3):14–15.

Ogle, D. 1986. A teaching model that develops active reading of expository text. *The Reading Teacher* 39(2):564–70.

Packer, A. H. 1992. Taking action on the SCANS report. *Educational Leadership* 49:27–31.

Pellegrino, J. W., N. Chudowsky, and R. Glaser. 2001. *Knowing what students know: The science and design of educational assessment.* Washington, D.C.: National Academy Press.

Rutherford, F. J., and A. Ahlgren. 1990. *Science for all Americans.* New York: Oxford University Press.

Solano-Flores, G., and S. Nelson-Barber. 2001. On the cultural validity of science assessments. *Journal of Research in Science Teaching* 38(5):553–573.

Treagust, D. F., R. Jacobowitz, J. L. Gallagher, and J. Parker. 2001. Using assessment as a guide in teaching for understanding: A case study of a middle school science class learning about sound. *Science Education* 85(2):137–57.

Wenglinsky, H. 2000. *How teaching matters: Bringing the classroom back into discussions of teacher quality.* Princeton, N.J.: Educational Testing Service.

Chapter 9

How Is Student Understanding Assessed?

INTRODUCTION

ASSESSMENT OF STUDENT UNDERSTANDING

ANOTHER LOOK AT THE ADVANTAGES OF
EDUCATIONAL ASSESSMENT

CHAPTER LEARNING PERFORMANCES

- *Explain the steps a teacher can use to assess student growth and achievement.*
- *Create assessments using different strategies to measure content, procedural, and metacognitive knowledge.*
- *Compare and contrast the reasons for using various types of assessment.*
- *Describe how a teacher can determine if a test or quiz is well constructed.*
- *Justify why artifacts and portfolios should be consistent with goals in a project-based environment.*
- *Design a scoring rubric to evaluate a performance.*
- *Explain the value of assessment for teachers, students, and parents.*

INTRODUCTION

This chapter focuses on ways that we can assess student understanding in a project-based science class. You may have many questions about assessment: *How do I assess science understanding? Are some ways to assess better than others? What are portfolios and how do I use them in science classes? How do I know that all students are learning?* This chapter answers these and other questions about assessment. In this chapter we consider numerous strategies for gathering assessment information, such as conducting observations, using concept maps, writing test items, and implementing performance-based assessments. We discuss artifacts as ways to form lasting memories in students' minds, strategies for assembling information into artifacts, and ways that students can present information. We consider information about using scoring rubrics to evaluate assessment information. We discuss how to use assessments for determining grades. Before we begin, let's examine three classroom scenarios that focus on stages of assessment: gathering, assembling, and making judgments.

Scenario 1: Gathering Assessment Information

Mrs. Miller tells her fourth-grade class, "Please pass your papers to the front of the row. I will be grading these tonight and putting them down in the grade book for this quarter. Also, remember to study tonight for the test tomorrow on animal classification. This will be the last test that will go toward determining your science grade for this quarter." You tense up a bit with the thought of tomorrow's test on animal classification, because you really don't have time to study tonight—it is the big soccer game night. Oh well, you know that Mrs. Miller will put down the test and homework score and average it with the rest from the semester. You think you did well on the other tests this quarter, but there are a few that Mrs. Miller hasn't passed back to the class yet. If you are correct, your average (and thus, your grade for the quarter) shouldn't be affected much even if you don't do as well on the test tomorrow.

In this scenario, Mrs. Miller viewed assessment as solely for the purpose of summative evaluation (determining achievement from end-of-unit tests and homework). She used the average of scores on homework and tests to issue a letter grade at the end of the quarter. She did not always hand back homework or tests in a timely manner, and she did not use tests or homework to help students improve their learning, set goals, or monitor their own progress.

Scenario 2: Assembling Assessment Information

Ms. Mominee, a second-grade teacher, sits down with one of her students, Rachael, to discuss her drawings of her plant in the plant portfolio she turned in at the end of the previous week. Ms. Mominee says, "Rachael, I see that you have five drawings here in your portfolio that show how your plant has looked in the last few weeks. Tell me something that you learned about plants." Rachael responds, "I learned that they need water or they will wilt like this one did." Ms. Mominee probes, "How do you know that this one wilted because of lack of water?" Rachael says, "Because I know the bell rang to go to lunch that day when I was watering my plants, and I stopped to go to lunch. I forgot to water that one." "Oh," responds Ms. Mominee, "are there any other things you learned about what plants need to grow?" Rachael says, "Dirt!" Ms. Mominee probes further to determine Rachael's understanding of the need for sunlight, and she helps Rachael come to understand that some plants grow without dirt. She finishes the discussion by asking Rachael how well she thinks she did on the plant project. After she finishes talking with Rachael and other students about their plant portfolios, she makes some written comments on the portfolios, records a grade in her grade book for this project, and sends the portfolios home for the students' parents to see.

In this scenario, Ms. Mominee used summative assessments to help determine progress and grades. She provided the students with feedback but only at the end of the project. The teacher did not meet with students to provide them with feedback while they were growing their plants, a benchmark activity in the project "How do plants grow in our environment?" She used more than one method of assessment (self-evaluation, portfolios, and a formal clinical interview). Thus, the students could not use the feedback to modify their project, and the teacher could not use the feedback to reflect on her teaching and possibly change her instructional plans.

Scenario 3: Making Judgments About Assessment Information

Students in Mr. Iwamoto's sixth-grade class are investigating the question "How do plants grow in our environment?" Several students have set up an investigation to examine the effect of organic insect-control methods (as opposed to using pesticides) on plant growth. As students plan their investigations, Mr. Iwamoto asks them to keep a journal about their plans. The students set up a few quicktrials to test out some homemade greenhouses. Mr. Iwamoto sits down with the group to discuss their plan and quicktrials and give the students feedback. He says, "Tell me why you decided to construct a small greenhouse for your investigation." Lei responds, "Well, we think that we need to make sure that the temperature is controlled so that it doesn't affect our results. The insects need to be in the same temperature so that it doesn't affect if they live or die." Mr. Iwamoto says, "Will one greenhouse let you compare the organic and pesticide-sprayed plants?" Lei and her classmates say, "Yes." Mr. Iwamoto realizes that he hasn't clearly taught about controlling variables and students may need a benchmark lesson on pesticides. His students don't seem to realize that they have two separate variables involved (organic and chemical uses to control for insects), and they aren't aware that pesticides placed in close proximity to the organically controlled plants could run off to the organic plants and contaminate the investigation. Thus, Mr. Iwamoto adapts his instruction and teaches about controlling variables and pesticides in several subsequent lessons.

The next week, Mr. Iwamoto gives a small quiz to his class about topics they are studying. The quiz covers concepts of photosynthesis, plant form and function, and environmental factors that affect plant growth. He returns the quiz to students and discusses the results. He asks the students whether they need to modify anything in their investigations based on what they have learned so far. One group of students decides that they need to be able to measure the temperature of the soil where their plants are growing in order to have accurate data regarding use of organic compost soil.

When students are finished with their study of plants, Mr. Iwamoto has the groups of students present their artifacts to their classmates. Some students have photographs of their investigations. One group gives a PowerPoint presentation to the class. Students in the class are encouraged to critique each other's presentations and offer suggestions for further study. Finally, Mr. Iwamoto uses a scoring rubric to provide students with summative feedback and give them a grade (score).

In this scenario, Mr. Iwamoto used both formative and summative assessment procedures. He used formative assessments to provide students with feedback that helped them learn and to modify his teaching. Mr. Iwamoto also used a variety of assessment techniques and did not rely only on the quiz he administered. He used summative assessment to judge students' achievement and issue a grade.

ASSESSMENT OF STUDENT UNDERSTANDING

In the previous chapter, we defined **assessment**, and we discussed the nature and benefits of assessment. In this chapter, we will discuss how teachers assess student understanding in a project-based science environment.

The process of assessing student understanding might be thought of as a three-step procedure. First, you and your students gather information that will help in forming generalizations about students' learning. Second, after securing information, you and your students assemble and present the information in some fashion so that it is recorded. Third, you and your students evaluate the assessment information. The purpose of evaluation is to make judgments about student growth, to set goals, and to report information to students and their parents.

Imagine a group of third-grade students investigating how insects grow and change. Students could record in their notebooks information about the length, mass, and appearance of the insects at different stages of growth. During inquiry, the teacher could observe the students and keep information about their progress on a checklist. To assemble and present information, students might draw pictures or take photographs of the insects at each stage and share them with classmates. The teacher could place copies of these items into each student's portfolio. Finally, to evaluate progress, the students might keep a journal in which to enter their personal reflections. The teacher could use a scoring rubric (described later in this chapter) to determine levels of understanding or skill attainment on a performance-based assessment. Assessment that can provide feedback to students and to the teacher requires multiple sources of information and methods of evaluating. The following sections will discuss specific methods of collecting, assembling, and evaluating assessment information.

CONNECTING TO
NATIONAL SCIENCE EDUCATION STANDARDS

Assessment in Science Education

Assessment is a systematic, multistep process involving the collection and interpretation of educational data (p. 76).

CONNECTING TO
NATIONAL SCIENCE EDUCATION STANDARDS

A Case for Strengthening Assessment in the Science Classroom

Portfolios (collections of student work, regular self-reflection and peer assessment, assessment conversations, journals, projects, class discussions, performances, well-planned quizzes, and tests)—any combination of these assessment activities—can support improved science learning (NRC, 2001, pp. 18-19).

Gathering Assessment Information

Classroom teachers have many assessment options. No matter which options they choose, teachers need to be able to collect sufficient information so that they can make generalizations about students' learning and make good planning decisions. The information needs to be relevant to teaching and the goals desired in the classroom. Therefore, the information-gathering techniques presented in this section are only options, not recommendations. It is up to you, the expert on your classroom, to continually reflect upon your curriculum, your teaching methods, your students' performance, and your goals in order to select and develop methods for gathering information that meet the particular needs of your classroom.

Observation-Based Assessment

Observation is a great technique for gathering data. Observations can help teachers make valid decisions about curriculum and instruction and determine how much progress students are making. Observations play a key role in a teacher's minute-to-minute decision making during a project.

Teachers often make informal observations of students. For example, you might notice that a particular student raises her hand often during social studies but very rarely during science, indicating that she understands social studies topics but is having difficulty with science concepts. A puzzled look on a student's face might provide you with the evidence that a student is having difficulty with a concept or task. Off-task behavior by students might indicate problems with methods of instruction. These types of observations can help you make "in-flight" curricular or instructional decisions that refocus a lesson.

However, observations can also be planned and formal. For example, you may intentionally ask groups of students questions about the driving question and their investigative plans. You can also purposefully listen to and watch a particular student while he solves a problem, reads aloud, or creates a project to identify problem areas as well as areas of mastery.

Observations are inevitably subjective to some degree. When you observe a particular behavior, you interpret what you see. For example, a college student wore a Walkman with headphones during his science methods class. During the first week of class, the professor interpreted his behavior as rude and inattentive, and she decided that he was a mediocre student. However, after talking with him about the headset, she discovered that he was taking sixteen quarter hours and working two jobs to pay for his tuition. The science methods class was his last class of the day, and he was listening to music to stay awake during class. Incidents like this demonstrate why it is preferable to use a variety of observation techniques that provide varied information than to rely on a single technique. There are several observation techniques that you can use to ensure that you gather varied information. These include discussion-based observations, anecdotal records, checklists, and clinical interviews.

> ### Key Idea
>
> Observations made through discussions, anecdotal records, checklists, and clinical interviews can help teachers make decisions about curriculum and instruction and determine how much progress students are making.

Discussions.   During the instructional process, discussions can provide a rich array of information about students' understanding of important science concepts. **Discussions** can also be used to identify students' process skills and thinking patterns during investigations. Finally, discussions can be used to check students' attitudes. Using discussions to extract information about students' knowledge, skills, and attitudes is also less threatening to most students than are traditional forms of testing and, consequently, invites broader student participation.

Unfortunately, teachers' lack of discussion skills often limits the information they glean from students during a discussion. They sometimes ask too many superficial questions, give students too little time to formulate answers to their questions, or call on the same students all the time. To obtain better answers from more students during a discussion, teachers should learn the techniques of **wait-time**, **probing**, and **redirecting**. These techniques were discussed more thoroughly in Chapter 7. With good questioning technique, teachers can find out from students how well they really understand science concepts.

Teachers can also engage students in discussions about their thought processes and their investigative procedures. For students to discuss their thought processes, teachers sometimes have them "think aloud"—that is, talk about what they are thinking during an investigation. Ensuing discussions can then focus on their reasoning, beliefs, and misconceptions.

Discussions in project-based classrooms can also be used to detect students' attitudes. For example, students investigating why frogs are disappearing in their state might discover that sulfur-burning factories in the area have increased the acid in the air to a level that is toxic to frogs. Students can then discuss whether they would vote for stricter air pollution laws. This type of value-oriented discussion is good for making students confront their own beliefs and encouraging them to apply those beliefs in the area of social policy.

Anecdotal Records.   In elementary and middle grade classrooms with twenty to thirty students, teacher observations can easily be forgotten or associated with the wrong students. For these reasons, many teachers choose to keep anecdotal records of their observations. **Anecdotal records** include written notes that describe student behaviors made at or near the time that the behaviors occurred. These records can be kept in a teacher's notebook, in folders, on index cards, on sticky notes or labels, or on the computer. After a class period, you might make notations about students' understandings, types of questions they asked, and possible misunderstandings demonstrated. Some teachers have all students jot down their responses on paper before calling on anyone to give an answer. This technique gives each child the time to think about and compose his or her response before the question is discussed, and it gives the teacher a written record of students' thinking. Hand-held computers or Personal Digital Assistants (PDAs) permit teachers to easily make observations *during* instruction instead of after.

We find keeping a file with an index card on each student to be a valuable technique. At the end of each day, take a moment to write down any significant observations about students on their cards. You will find these cards very beneficial when you write up a student's progress report or have discussions with parents at parent-teacher conferences.

Checklists.   To keep track of students' observations, teachers often keep **checklists**. These checklists can be used to evaluate knowledge, skills, or attitudes. When used for assessment, checklists can count or tally the frequency of something. For example, on a class roster you can easily tally the frequency of students' participation in classroom discussions. Or you might maintain a checklist of important concepts and check off students who demonstrate understanding of the concepts. For example, such a list might include "understands why machines make work easier," "sees why we lubricate machines to reduce friction," and "knows how energy is transferred in a system."

You can assess skills by observing students and recording on a checklist which skills they use. During a lesson, walk around the room with your checklist while students are working. Choose a few students to observe and mark on the checklist the skills in which they seem to be proficient. Imagine your students working on a project that explores the kinds of trees in the neighborhood. As part of the project, they observe leaves, classify them into groups, and graph the numbers of trees in each classification. You might use the checklist in Table 9.1 for this type of classification project.

Portfolio Activity 9.1   **DEVELOPING A SKILLS CHECKLIST**

Materials Needed:
- Materials to teach a lesson developed in this investigation

A. Design a lesson that requires a great number of skills such as observing, measuring, classifying, inferring, and concluding. Teach this lesson to a team of classmates after you design a checklist of all the skills you might observe while your classmates are engaging in

the investigation. Try to keep track of your classmates' performance while they participate in your lesson.

B. Share the checklist with your classmates. Discuss whether it was an accurate measure of the skills they used. How might it be improved?

C. Put the checklist in your portfolio.

PROJECT-SPECIFIC CHECKLIST   *Table 9.1*

1. OBSERVATION
_____ 1.1 Can identify major characteristics of the leaves
_____ 1.2 Notices similarities among the leaves
_____ 1.3 Notices differences among the leaves

2. CLASSIFICATION
_____ 2.1 Can determine a method of grouping leaves into two groups
_____ 2.2 Can determine a way to group leaves within groups
_____ 2.3 Can explain why leaves are classified
_____ 2.4 Can classify a new leaf into the existing classification scheme

Checklists save teachers time. Teachers can rapidly mark off on a checklist evidence of a skill or the meeting of an objective. You might keep an observation sheet for each student in a three-ring binder, making a functional grade book for tracking student progress. This method of observation has the added benefit of keeping you focused on your lesson objectives. It also helps you make sure that no one falls between the cracks and goes unnoticed. Finally, it provides documented evidence of progress for grade cards or progress reports or for discussions with students and their parents.

Checklists can be either project specific, as was the leaf-classification checklist, or generic. Table 9.2 shows a generic checklist designed to gather information about general skill development. In Portfolio Activity 9.1, you will try your hand at developing a skills checklist.

Checklists can also provide you with a list of affective attributes to look for in a project-based science classroom. Table 9.3 is an inventory of dispositions to be used as a guide when observing students. In Portfolio Activity 9.2, you will develop an assessment for monitoring affective attributes.

Table 9.2

GENERIC CHECKLIST

Questioning

The student can
____ Explore ideas
____ Form a question
____ Remain curious
____ Design an investigation
____ Formulate a hypothesis
____ Note discrepant events
____ Notice problems
____ Challenge ideas
____ Remain skeptical

Gathering Data to Explore Questions

The student can
____ Observe properties
____ Identify ways to measure data
____ Seek additional information
____ Use science equipment
____ Measure accurately
____ Estimate answers
____ Examine more than one variable
____ Select variables
____ Name an object

Examining Data to Answer Questions

The student can
____ Classify objects into groups
____ Make predictions
____ Analyze results
____ Describe observations
____ Make comparisons
____ Graph information
____ Order or sequence data
____ Search for patterns
____ Tabulate information
____ Identify errors
____ Interpret data
____ Control variables
____ Calculate
____ Make drawings or diagrams

Answering Questions

The student can
____ Communicate results
____ Summarize information
____ Make revisions
____ Make decisions
____ Demonstrate knowledge
____ Identify limitations
____ Make inferences
____ Describe discrepancies
____ Establish criteria
____ Offer evidence
____ Verify results
____ Solve problems
____ Generate new questions
____ Establish relationships

Clinical Interviews. Interviews with people seeking jobs can tell an employer a great deal that résumés, grade transcripts, or applications cannot. For example, an interview can provide insight into a candidate's motivation and rapport with people. Also, during an interview, a candidate has time to elaborate on specific items in his or her résumé, transcript, or application. Interviews are also common for candidates seeking master's or doctoral degrees. During these one- or two-hour interviews, university committee members can ask candidates unanticipated questions, and candidates can demonstrate in greater depth what they know.

Classroom interviews, or **clinical interviews**, with your students can serve similar purposes. In an interview, students can explain in greater detail what they understand, how they're progressing, what problems they're having, and what steps they or you might take to improve learning. In an interview, you can get to know students, work on individual student goals, and clarify misunderstandings and concerns. Interviews provide

Portfolio Activity 9.2   ASSESSING AFFECTIVE ATTRIBUTES

Materials Needed:
- Pencil and paper

A. Evaluate a science lesson (one you participated in during this course or one you taught to children). What affective attributes (attitudes or dispositions) do you think would be important to the lesson? List them.

B. Create a method to monitor the dispositions. Would it be a formal attitude inventory, an interview, a journal?

C. Some educators do not believe that monitoring attitudes or dispositions is an important teacher activity. Write an essay presenting your opinion on the matter or debate the idea with others in your class.

D. Put your essay or notes about your discussion in your portfolio.

Table 9.3

AFFECTIVE ATTRIBUTES OF STUDENTS IN PROJECT-BASED SCIENCE

Abilty to compromise with others	Flexibility with ideas	Responsibility to project
Ambition to investigate	Honesty in artifacts	Satisfaction with artifacts
Cooperation with others	Independence	Self-confidence
Curiosity about the world	Objectivity	Self-discipline
Dependability	Open-mindedness	Self-reliance
Disciplined thinking	Patience with others	Sensitivity to others
Enthusiasm to continue	Persistence with a task	Skepticism about results
Excitement about science	Precision	Thoroughness
Fascination with findings	Questioning attitude	Tolerance for change
	Respect for evidence	Willingness to change

a depth of information that other forms of assessment cannot. They also provide opportunity for clarification of classroom observations (Southerland, Smith, & Cummins, 1999). For example, you might observe that a student never raises her hand during class and conclude that she's having difficulty with the topic. However, an interview with the student may reveal that she is simply bored, tired, or shy.

Interviews with students can be either informal or formal. Students find **informal interviews**, which resemble teacher-student discussions (written notes can be made after the discussion), less stressful than other forms of assessment. Imagine that in an informal interview about a water quality project you ask, "Why did you use the balance to measure the amount of water?" and the student answers, "I wanted to see which weighed more." To probe for more in-depth understanding and to ascertain why the student is only interested in a general level of measurement ("more water" versus "less water") rather than an exact measurement in milliliters, the teacher might say "Tell me what you mean by 'more.'"

Formal interviews may seem more stressful, but they don't have to be. What differentiates formal and informal interviews is the greater structure of formal interviews. You might set up formal interviews, for example, to elicit the same information from each student. A list of guiding questions will keep you focused on your objectives. Some guiding questions you might ask are "What is your driving question?" "What makes that an appropriate driving question?" "What is the design of your investigation?" "How does the design help you answer your questions? "What materials or equipment are you using?" "What have you accomplished so far?" "Are you having any problems?" "What kinds of results have you obtained?" "What are your conclusions so far?" and "What do you intend to do next?" However, guiding questions only provide the foundation to a formal interview. You will need to ask additional questions to clarify student answers and elicit in-depth answers.

Open-ended questions are a great way to start either formal or informal interviews. These are discussed in Chapter 7 as well, where we call them divergent and convergent questions or open and closed questions. An open-ended question gives a child a cue to explain what she thinks. Compare the following starting questions: "Lisa, how many stages did the butterfly go through?" "Lisa, what can you tell me about butterfly stages?" and "Lisa, what have you learned about butterflies this week?" The first question squelches conversation and limits the child's response. She will have answered the question if she only says, "Five." The teacher could just as easily have obtained this amount of information with a written test. The second question, while still focusing on butterfly stages, permits a richer explanation. However, the third question gives Lisa the greatest opportunity to elaborate on what she knows and doesn't know about butterflies, and it may lead to some unexpected responses. The teacher can then ask additional probing questions to see if Lisa has any misunderstandings and to find out how much she knows about butterflies and their stages of growth.

Another effective technique for either informal or formal interviews is the "What if?" question. For example, a teacher might ask, "What if the balance were used to measure the helium balloon? What would you see?" This type of question probes students' understanding even further by forcing them to think about new variables and different situations.

Keeping records of both informal and formal interviews provides a rich source of information for portfolios, parent-teacher conferences, and future discussions with students. *After* an interview, jot down your thoughts about students' understandings and misunderstandings. If you take notes *during* interviews, some children will become intimidated and stop talking. Also, jotting down a note about each question makes the interview process too time-consuming.

Assessment Based on Concept Maps

In Chapter 7, we learned that concept mapping can be used to link new ideas or experiences with earlier ones. **Concept mapping** can also be a powerful method of assessing individual students' conceptual understandings or the understandings being formulated among groups of students (Edmondson, 1999).

Examine the concept maps shown in Figures 9.1 and 9.2. If a fourth-grade student had completed the first map to show prior understanding about magnets, what would you be able to say about the student's misunderstanding? What major concepts are missing? First, magnets are not attracted to all types of metal, so the map demonstrates an incomplete understanding. Second, opposite poles attract and like poles repel, but the student depicts both the north and south poles attracting to the north pole. Third, the map fails to include some major concepts such as temporary and permanent magnets, natural and human-made magnets, and magnetic fields. In short, you could use this concept map to diagnose the student's knowledge of magnets and adapt instruction accordingly. If the same fourth-grade student later completed the second concept map following a project that investigated magnets, you could conclude that the student's conceptual understanding of magnets had improved dramatically.

Some teachers use concept maps with groups of students during discussions, interviews, and group projects. A concept map drawn on the board or projected on an overhead transparency or with a computer projector can form the basis for a class discussion about the relationship among ideas that surface while investigating a driving question. Concept maps can be used to probe student interpretation of investigation findings. Finally, students can collaborate on their own concept maps to illustrate the relationships among their findings.

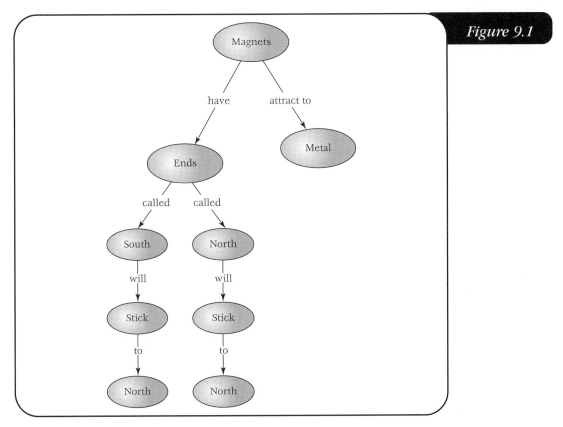

Figure 9.1

Limited concept map.

Figure 9.2

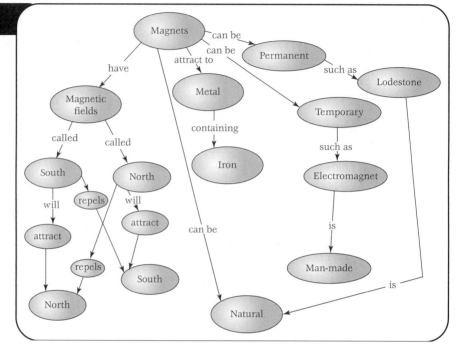

Complex concept map.

Concept maps can also be evaluated. Students' concept maps are commonly scored according to the complexity of the conceptual relationships they illustrate (Novak & Gowin, 1984). For example, students might be awarded one point for every hierarchical level in a concept map, quantifying the complexity of their thinking. A point could also be given each time a concept was branched into new categories. For example, in the second concept map, the student has branched the idea of magnetic fields into two subcategories, north and south. Likewise, students may be awarded points for cross-links such as those between human-made magnets and electromagnets and between natural magnets and lodestone. You might award more points for branches and cross-links that occur at higher hierarchical levels.

Assessment Based on Classroom Tests

Because assessment should be integrated throughout the teaching and learning process, at times you might want to write some classroom tests or quizzes to assess the progress of your students. Quizzes and tests can give both you and your students information regarding their basic understanding of concepts and use of process ideas. Tests and quizzes provide another opportunity for students to demonstrate what they understand. Tests provide students and teachers with feedback. You can also use the results of the tests and quizzes to modify your classroom instruction. Their effectiveness depends on how you use them. Tests that provide students and teachers with feedback and that are used to enhance instruction are a positive example of test use.

> ### Key Idea
>
> Classroom tests can provide both teachers and students with important feedback. Classroom tests also provide students with another opportunity to demonstrate what they understand.

Creating Tests and Quiz Items.   You can construct test items to measure both content and process understanding. Consider the following problem:

> *Test/Quiz Item 1:* While riding your bike, you drop a quarter out of your hand. Someone watching you would see the quarter hit the ground _____
>   A. in front of you.
>   B. beside you.
>   C. behind you.
>   D. there's no way to tell.

This item would measure a student's understanding of **content knowledge** related to Newton's First Law of Motion. You might recall that Newton's First Law states that an object will stay in motion unless acted upon by an outside force.

Now, consider the following item:

> *Test/Quiz Item 2:* Which of the following distance-time graphs shows an object with the greatest speed?

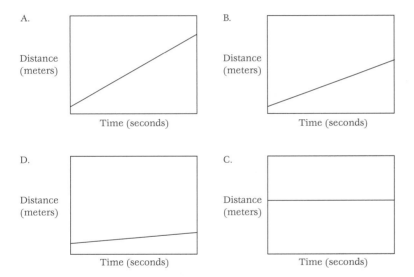

This item would measure a student's understanding of interpreting graphs, a process skill.

Test and quiz items can also be constructed across several cognitive levels—low, medium, and high. Low cognitive items would measure a child's understanding to recall, recognize, identify, or retrieve information. We discussed levels of cognitive items in Chapter 7. The following item would be an example of a low-level cognitive domain item:

> *Test/Quiz Item 3:* The movement of soil from the side of a river bank is an example of which process?
>   A. Runoff
>   B. Deposition
>   C. Erosion
>   D. Absorption

To respond to this item, a student needs only to recall the definition of *erosion,* so we classify it as a low-level cognitive item. In contrast, medium-level cognitive items require students to interpret, clarify, translate, exemplify, classify, summarize, generalize, infer, conclude, compare, contrast, or explain. Test/quiz items 1 and 2 are examples of medium-level cognitive demand items. To answer test item 1, a learner needs to clarify a situation by applying understanding of Newton's First Law of Motion.

High-level cognitive demand items require a student to apply, analyze, create or evaluate. Item 4 illustrates a high-level cognitive demand item:

> *Test/Quiz Item 4:* Design an experiment to show the relationship between plant growth and the amount of sunlight a plant receives.

To answer item 4, a student would need to design an experimental procedure to show how sunlight influences plant growth. The student would need to define and control variables, discuss the importance of trials, and describe how to measure plant growth. Such an item is very open-ended with several possible solutions. Therefore, we would classify it a high-level cognitive item.

Types of Paper-and-Pencil Items.   In the previous examples, we used primarily two types of techniques: selection and supply (Airasian, 2001). **Selection** techniques require students to select a response from choices provided on the test. **Supply** techniques require a student to construct a response to a question or problem.

Items 1, 2, and 3 are examples of multiple choice selection items that require a student to select the best answer. **Multiple choice** items include a stem and various options. The *stem* presents the problem or question to the student and the *options* present the various choices from which a student can select a response.

True and false, matching, and short answer items are other types of selection items. **True and false** items require a student to classify an item as true or false, correct or incorrect, or yes or no. As such, true and false items are typically classified as low-level or medium-level cognitive demand items. Test/quiz item 5 is an example of a true and false item.

> *Test/Quiz Item 5:* As the amount of nitrates increases in a lake, the lake becomes less likely to support a variety of different kinds of living organisms. a. True b. False

To respond to test/quiz item 5, a student needs to recall basic information (what nitrates are) and then make a decision if the statement (regarding the effect on living organisms) is true or false. As such, we classify the item as a medium-level cognitive demand question.

Matching requires students to connect premises made in one column with responses in another column. Typically, matching items are low-level cognitive demand items. An example would be a list of words in one column to be matched to their definitions in the second column.

Supply techniques require students to construct a response to a problem. **Short answer** items typically require students to respond with only one or two words. Most often, short response items are low level and require a student merely to recall information. Test/quiz item 6 illustrates a short answer item:

> *Test/Quiz Item 6:* As water flows in a river, soil may be transported downstream where it is "laid down." The process of the soil being "laid down" can be described as _____.

Item 4 is another example of a supply item. **Essay** items such as this require students to construct a response that typically measures high-level understanding. Essay tests can be more cognitively challenging for students than other types of supply items because often they require students to explain and interpret. For example, students might be asked on an essay test to explain weather data (date, temperatures, barometer readings, wind speed, and location of high and low fronts) found on a map and predict (with explanations and justifications for their predictions) the weather one might expect the next day.

Each type of test/quiz item offers advantages and disadvantages over the others. For instance, true-false, matching, short answer, and multiple choice formats are easy to score and are considered more impartial (not open to interpretation by the person grading the item). However, many teachers find it very difficult to write good, high-level cognitive items for such tests. Students can also guess correctly on these types of items. Essay items, on the other hand, are very time-consuming to score and are open to interpretation. Moreover, teachers are more easily able to write challenging essay items. However, very verbal students might be able to bluff their way through an answer. Essay and performance items are also more time-consuming for students to complete and, as a result, teachers may not be able to use them to test all of the intended learning performances.

Issues to Consider When Writing Test/Quiz Items.   Constructing good test items can be challenging. Although you might be able to write low-level cognitive items fairly easily, you may find it very difficult to write medium-level and high-level items. We will discuss several issues that need to considered when writing good test and quiz items.

When writing tests, make sure items match and measure the learning performances you expect of the students. The items you write should test the content you hope students will learn and allow students to perform at the level you expect. For instance, if you ask students to recall the definition of *force,* the item might match the content of the unit, but because it only requires low-level cognitive demands it doesn't match the level at which you expect students to perform.

Although the items you write might correlate to the learning performances you designed for the unit, you need to make sure you actually stressed these learning performances in your teaching. Often, what we hoped we would get accomplished in our teaching did not really occur. Be careful not to write items that measure learning performances not included in your instruction. Even if you have covered an idea in class, you might not have had students engage in the level of difficulty intended. For example, you may have had students describe an idea rather than use it in an everyday life application. Hence, make sure the level of difficulty of the item matches what happened during instruction.

Teachers also take into consideration students' reading levels and language. A science test isn't fair if it measures the student's ability to read rather than understand science concepts. Make sure that vocabulary words on the test are ones students recognize and are able to read. Be careful that language, especially for students whose first language isn't English, doesn't limit their ability to express what they know in science.

CONNECTING TO
NATIONAL SCIENCE EDUCATION STANDARDS

Assessment in Science Education
Assessment tasks must be appropriately modified to accommodate the needs of students with physical disabilities, learning disabilities, or limited English proficiency (p. 85).

CONNECTING TO
NATIONAL SCIENCE EDUCATION STANDARDS

Assessment in Science Education
Assessment practices must be fair. Assessment tasks must be reviewed for the use of stereotypes, for assumptions that reflect the perspectives or experiences of a particular group, for language that might be offensive to a particular group, and for other features that might distract students from the intended task (p. 85).

Finally, teachers need to consider students' cultural backgrounds. They need to think about students' beliefs, values, prior experiences, and other factors that may influence how students respond on assessments. For example, urban students may not respond well to a test item asking about the acidity of soil for growing soy beans. Even if they might be able to reason through such a question, they might not even try because they believe they don't know anything about growing soy beans. The same item could be more culturally sensitive if rephrased to ask about the acidity needed to grow house plants.

In summary, ask yourself these questions when writing a test:

- Does the item match the content I hoped students would learn?
- Did I really help students develop these ideas in class?
- Is the item written at a level of difficulty that matches how students were encouraged to perform in class?
- Is the test written at a reading level that my students can understand? Is language a barrier to answering items?
- Is the test fair to students from differing cultural backgrounds?
- Are a variety of difficulties and formats used?

If you can answer "yes" to each of these questions, you will have written a fair test. A fair test is valid. A **valid** test measures what the students have been prepared to understand and makes accurate generalizations about students' learning.

A second concern you need to consider is reliability. **Reliability** refers to how consistently a test measures a student's performance. To illustrate the idea of reliability, Airasian (2001) uses the example of weighing yourself. If you step on the scale and it reads 121 lbs. and then you step on it again one minute later and it reads 126 lbs., you probably won't trust either reading. Now let's say you step on it a third time after another minute, and it reads 119 lbs.

CONNECTING TO
NATIONAL SCIENCE EDUCATION STANDARDS

Assessment in Science Education
Assessment tasks and the methods of presenting them provide data that are sufficiently stable to lead to the same decisions if used at different times (p. 84).

Key Idea

A valid test measures what students have been prepared to understand and allows teachers to make accurate generalizations about students' learning. A reliable test consistently measures a student's performance, yielding similar results.

You would conclude that something is wrong with your bathroom scale because it isn't measuring your weight consistently. This is an example of an instrument that is valid (it is measuring what it is suppose to be measuring—your weight), but it isn't doing so consistently (it isn't reliable). A reliable bathroom scale would read the same weight consistently if you stepped on and off it during a particular time period. As classroom teachers, we strive to build classroom tests on which a student could achieve a similar result if she took the test again within a short time period.

Writing clear items that do not include vague or ambiguous terms helps to improve the reliability of test items. Clearly written items help ensure that each time the student reads them, he interprets them in a similar manner. You can also improve the reliability of classroom tests by including on them two or more items that measure the idea you are trying to assess. If a student misses one of the items, you can look at how he or she responded to the other item that measures the same concept or skill to determine the student's understanding.

Although you might try very hard to write items that reflect what your instruction stressed, a student's score on the test doesn't necessarily reflect what he or she really knows. Some students experience **test anxiety**. Most of us have experienced some test anxiety, particularly before a very important examination, such as the Scholastic Aptitude Test (SAT) for admission to college. Some students, however, consistently experience high-test anxiety, which affects how they perform on a test. In severe cases, students

Portfolio Activity 9.3   WRITING A CLASSROOM TEST

Materials Needed:
- The list of guidelines for writing test items

A. Write a classroom test. Make sure the test includes items that measure both content and process that are written at different cognitive levels. Also make sure that you include a variety of formats.

B. Classify each of the items as content or process and also state the cognitive level of the item.

C. File the test in your portfolio.

freeze and simply cannot respond. In other cases, students cannot recall even easy answers. Test anxiety represents one threat to the validity of a test.

Sometimes even well-intentioned teachers promote test anxiety by stressing the importance of a test. We saw this in the opening scenario of Chapter 8. Although we want students to take assessment seriously, we don't want to overemphasize the importance of a classroom test. As a classroom teacher, you can help students with test anxiety by creating multiple ways to assess students in a classroom. If a student realizes that her evaluations on other classroom assessments are acceptable, she might not be as nervous when it comes time to take a test. Multiple assessment techniques help students build positive self-images. You can also reduce test anxiety by teaching effectively, bringing closure to lessons so that students understand what they were to have learned, giving students ample opportunities to prepare for a test, and practicing sample test items. Including items at different cognitive levels on tests also helps reduce anxiety. Some teachers like to start the test out with relatively low-level items so that students can gain some confidence before facing more stressful items.

CONNECTING TO
NATIONAL SCIENCE EDUCATION STANDARDS

Assessment in Science Education
An individual student's performance is similar on two or more tasks that claim to measure the same aspect of student achievement (p. 84).

The following guidelines can help a teacher write test items that are valid and reliable (modified from Airasian, 2001):

- Write items clearly at the level of the students' reading level.
- Try to avoid statements that are vague.
- Use language that students in your class will understand.
- Use appropriate vocabulary. Be mindful of your students and their reading level.
- Make sure there is only one correct answer for each item (unless it is intended to be an open-ended response item with more than one possible answer).
- Make sure you develop rubrics for open-ended items (rubrics are covered more thoroughly later in this chapter).
- Make sure the items match the instruction students experienced.
- Make sure that the items match the level of difficulty for which students were prepared.
- Make sure that several items attempt to measure the same understanding.

Try writing one of your own tests now by completing Portfolio Activity 9.3.

Performance-Based Assessment

Performance-based assessment refers to methods of directly examining students' knowledge, skills, and dispositions. Through these methods, teachers collect assessment information while students perform a targeted activity. The activity can be a natural part of a lesson (observing students as they look under a microscope), or it can be a prompt given to provoke an observable action (providing equipment and a set of directions asking students to assemble a slide and focus a microscope).

In project-based science environments, students must integrate knowledge and skills to carry out their investigations, create artifacts, and present their projects to others. Performance-based assessments involve similar integration and, consequently, are a good fit with project-based science. For example, students who have been investigating how to set up and maintain an aquarium may have learned about acids and bases (pH), nitrogen cycles, life cycles of fish, salt- and freshwater, and classifications of animals. They may also have used a variety of science skills such as *observing* the behavior of fish, *measuring* the pH or temperature of the water, *classifying* the types of fish that can get along together, *making inferences* about fish that die, and *forming conclusions* about appropriate conditions for the fish. A performance-based assessment might consist of giving students a pH test kit and five water samples. A prompt tells the students that certain tropical fish can only survive in pH levels ranging between 7 and 8. Students are then asked to determine which of the water samples would be safe for the fish. This question could be extended to measure problem-solving skills by asking students what they could do to make the inappropriate water samples livable for the fish. This performance-based assessment item integrates students' abilities to measure water accurately, interpret a chart, understand pH, and draw a conclusion.

To summarize, good performance-based assessment seeks to put students in realistic situations in which they must integrate relevant knowledge and skills in order to perform a target activity. A good performance-based test item usually includes the following characteristics:

- It reflects important curriculum targets. Good performance-based assessment reflects those curriculum goals that have been the objects of classroom instruction. For example, if students have been investigating the weather, they needed to learn how to use a thermometer. It is, thus, more *realistic* in an assessment to have students use a real thermometer to measure and record the temperature of air than it is to have them identify the temperature on a picture of a thermometer.

- It asks students to create a product (artifact). For example, students who make their own barometer to measure air pressure show their understanding of the purpose of a barometer, of how it works, and of the effect of barometric changes on the weather.

- It supports students in collaboration and use of resources. The performance-based test asks students to work with others and with equipment, materials, or resources to solve a problem and create a product. For example, students might work in a team to solve a problem about what types of ground cover collect the most heat in the summer. The team might decide to use a thermometer to measure and a computer spreadsheet to record the temperature of four different materials—stone, grass, asphalt, and sand.

- It encourages active investigation by students. Students engage in exploration of ideas and questions rather than in passive activities such as listening to the teacher, watching a movie, reading about a concept, or watching a demonstration.

- It permits students to apply multiple approaches to solving a problem. For example, students might be asked to construct an "ear" that would be a good sound collecting device.[1] There is no one answer to this task. Students could design a cone-shaped ear that looks like a megaphone. They could make a long, narrow ear like a rabbit's. They could draw pictures of their ears and explain the design of the human ear in accompanying text.

- It requires students to integrate ideas. If students create an "ear" that is cone shaped and has "hairs" in it, they have combined the idea that funnel shapes gather sound waves with the idea that hairs (which are solids) carry sound waves better than does air. They also have used their artistic skills to design the ear and their literacy skills to explain the design.

- It requires students to apply higher-order thinking and to understand concepts rather than memorize individual facts. For example, students are asked to demonstrate how air pressure affects the weather or how well sound travels through various objects as opposed to regurgitate definitions memorized of *air pressure* or *frequency* and select the "correct answer" from among a list of possible answers.

- It promotes students' interest. Good performance-based assessment is inherently more interesting to students than traditional paper-and-pencil tests. Making a barometer or an "ear" is more challenging and motivating than selecting from a list of definitions. When students enjoy the learning process involved in assessment, they feel less anxiety, yielding more reliable assessment results.

- It is developmentally appropriate. Performance-based assessment emphasizes the characteristics promoted as developmentally appropriate for both early childhood and young adolescent students (NAEYC, 1986; NMSA, 1995). These characteristics include the use of concrete materials. Performance-based assessment stresses problem-solving processes over memorization of abstract ideas. It doesn't punish students who are nonreaders or poor readers. It engages students in direct, purposeful experiences rather than in contrived assessment tasks. It integrates subject areas. By encompassing multiple approaches, it builds self-esteem and allows for differences in learning types, ability, and development. Finally, it is interesting and motivating.

How do you go about designing a performance-based assessment? You follow these five steps:

1. Decide what science content to include in the performance. For example, the learning performance might be "Students will demonstrate how energy is transferred in an electrical system."

2. Determine what skills or complex processes to observe while students engage in the activity. For example, students assembling an electrical system will classify objects according to whether they conduct electricity or not, make inferences about the type of energy used in a dry cell, and make conclusions about the transfer of energy from the dry cell to the wires and the light bulb to give off light.

---

[1] Credit for this idea goes to our colleagues in science education, Dr. Jodi Haney at Bowling Green State University and Dr. Andrew Lumpe at Southern Illinois University.

3.   Generate the activity for the performance assessment. For example, you might decide to set up an activity in which students are given light bulbs, dry cells, wire, and a small motor and asked to make the motor work using only the items provided.

4.   Test the assessment item by letting students try out the activity.

5.   Revise the performance-based task based upon trial runs.

In recent years, implementing performance-based tasks has become such a popular technique for collecting assessment information that large assessment companies, such as the Educational Testing Service (ETS), are now developing and adopting these types of tests. This should not be surprising. In all other aspects of our lives we make evaluations on the basis of actual performance. We want our automobiles to run, our doctors to rid us of our ailments, our dentists to fix our cavities, and our plumbers to fix our sinks. We expect artists to generate emotions, entertain, and challenge and athletes to amaze us with their physical abilities. Why, then, do we expect our students only to regurgitate answers and not also to do what it is that they should be able to do? Portfolio Activity 9.4 asks you to develop a performance-based assessment.

Assembling and Presenting Assessment Information

> ### Key Idea
>
> Artifacts and portfolios can be used to assemble assessment data into a presentable form for others to view.

After teachers and students have collected assessment information, they must assemble it into a presentable form for others to see. In project-based science, there are two main ways to assemble and present information: artifacts and portfolios.

Artifacts are the products that result from an investigation: writing samples, journals, physical or computer models, drawings, videos, or multimedia documents. Artifacts, which represent students' work and emerging understandings, are a concrete product that can be assessed. They have long been a natural part of assessment in the arts, but they are now being recognized for their potential contribution to science education.

What do you think of when you look at the shells you collected at the ocean, the turquoise jewelry purchased in the Southwest, the miniature lighthouse you bought in Maine, the alligator-shaped mug you collected in Florida? What do your parents think of when they look at your baby pictures, that Mother's Day card you drew in first grade, or that graduation tassel? Like souvenirs and keepsakes, artifacts that have been assembled for the purpose of assessment form lasting memories in our minds. Students are more likely to remember what they learned in science if it culminates in some type of public presentation: a presentation about landfills given to younger students, a poster about recycling displayed at the mall, or a video about weather that becomes a tool for future instruction.

Why would students more likely remember artifacts than abstract knowledge? There are six good reasons:

1.   Through the creation of artifacts, understanding is constructed in students' minds. As students reflect upon what they have learned and develop artifacts, they actively manipulate science ideas and thereby generate understanding.

2.   The fact that learning does not occur in linear, discrete steps argues against assessment items that are constructed around small, discrete bits of information. Artifacts, on the other hand, enable students to display their learning in a fashion consistent with real-life learning, which unfolds as a continuous process.

Portfolio Activity 9.4

DEVELOPING A PERFORMANCE-BASED ASSESSMENT

Materials Needed:
- Materials to teach a lesson developed in this investigation

A. Following are two ideas an elementary or middle grade teacher might want a student to develop in a project-based environment. These require a complex combination of knowledge and skills. Form a team of three. Read each idea and decide what would be the most genuine ways to measure whether students have gained the pertinent knowledge and skills.
- Each student will be able to observe the differences between two types of soils and determine which one is the best in which to plant a cactus.
- Each student will be able to read a weather map and determine what the weather will be like tomorrow.

During your decision making, consider the following criteria of good performance-based assessment:
1. It reflects important curriculum targets.
2. It is consistent with instruction.
3. It asks students to collaborate and use resources.
4. It encourages active investigation.
5. It permits multiple approaches.
6. It integrates ideas.
7. It requires higher-order thinking.
8. It is interesting.
9. It is developmentally appropriate.

B. As a team, develop a lesson to teach one of the two learning performances. Develop two different ways of assessing the performance after you have taught it. Teach the lesson to another team in your class and try the two different methods of assessment.

C. Ask the team you taught which method of assessment best measured what they learned. How did their beliefs match yours about good techniques for assessing complex combinations of knowledge and skills?

D. How do these findings fit with your state science proficiency model? Record your lesson, assessment methods, and conclusions in your portfolio.

3. All students learn differently; students can display their learning in ways that are compatible with their learning styles. Students who are interested in drama might role-play their understanding. Those interested in music might write songs to describe what they learned. Artistically inclined students can create models, posters, and murals. Talented writers can compose reports and papers.

4. Students remember what is meaningful to them. Do you remember an obscure lesson from fifth grade that involved calculating the area of a 4-inch by 3-inch square? Probably not. However, if you ever had to measure a floor or wall to purchase carpeting or wallpaper, you might remember making those calculations because there was a real

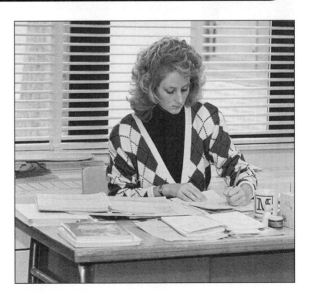

Teachers provide thoughtful feedback to students.

purpose to them. Likewise, when students develop artifacts to share with an audience, they are more likely to remember the experience since it has social meaning.

5. Artifacts developed as part of a collaborative process provide social experiences students will remember.

CONNECTING TO
NATIONAL SCIENCE EDUCATION STANDARDS

The Relationship Between Formative and Summative Assessment

... many aspects of the portfolio and the portfolio process provide assessment opportunities that contributed to improved work through feedback, conversations about content and quality, and other assessment-relevant discussions. The collection also can serve to demonstrate progress and inform and support summative evaluations (NRC, 2001, p. 61).

When you think back to your own education, you probably have vivid memories of friends you played with or collaborating on a school play. Do you have similar memories of routine classroom lessons? Social experiences form lasting memories that we tend to cherish. Because project-based science stresses development of student artifacts in collaborative settings, students are far more likely to have lasting memories of these group experiences than they are of typical school lessons that involve little social interaction.

Portfolios, collections of student artifacts, can be thought of as both objects and methods of assessment. As objects, they are a place for holding materials such as papers, photographs, or drawings that are representative of students' work and progress. As methods of assessment, portfolios provide ways for teachers to continuously collect and assess student work. Haberman (1995) points out that exemplary teachers of children in poverty (star teachers) spend little time on tests and grading. They focus more on students' effort and accomplishments, and portfolios are much more in line with the proclivities and predispositions of students who live in poverty.

Assembling Artifacts

Students can assemble information to place into artifacts in a variety of ways. We will focus on writing samples, daily journals, physical products, drawings, music, videos, and multimedia documents.

> ### Key Idea
>
> Artifacts can take many forms: writing samples, daily journal entries, physical products, drawings, music, videos, and multimedia documents. The artifacts students create during a project give evidence of what they understand.

Writing Samples.   Students can demonstrate understanding in a number of ways using writing samples, and there are several good reasons for using this technique to assemble information (Champagne & Kouba, 1999). First, **writing samples** provide a creative and accurate measure of student understanding. Second, writing is a curriculum-based task; it matches goals of instruction and integrates the language arts into science. Third, writing engages students in an active rather than a passive activity. Fourth, writing allows students to provide rich interpretations of their investigations. Fifth, writing targets students with verbal/linguistic abilities, enabling them to show what they know in a way that will enable them to succeed. Finally, students consider writing a worthwhile task.

As a teacher you will need to show students how to write a report because, when children write reports, several benefits accrue. Having children write reports assesses their ability to obtain and synthesize information and to communicate through reading and writing. Also, students can learn a great deal from writing independent reports on given topics.

Students can create many other types of writing samples that can be used for evaluating understanding. Students can write stories, create poetry, make television commercials, produce plays or puppet shows, create newspaper articles, write documentaries, draft letters, compose essays, keep diaries, write computer presentations, or create comic strips. Students also can write reactions to guest speakers, films, videos, or software programs;

they can develop biographies or autobiographies; and they can create annotated bibliographies. Each of these samples can be a powerful way to assess science understanding.

Imagine that fifth-grade students write stories about parasitic and symbiotic relationships. One boy writes a clever story about a flea named Billy. Billy wanted a new world away from the familiar scene he had on the back of an old, outdoor dog. The story tells of the flea's adventures in the big city—almost getting run over by a car, being fumigated by a pest control sprayer, and being stepped upon by a pedestrian. The flea, hungry, scared, and tired, decided that there was no place like home and returned to the back of the dog where he was safe and ate well. Of course, the dog wasn't too happy about Billy the Flea's return![2] Using a story format, this student explained most of what he knows about this particular parasitic relationship. This same student might have failed a test item that asked him to identify the correct definition of *parasite*. Would the teacher accurately have measured the boy's understanding with a test item? Would he have been able to elaborate on the parasitic relationship with the depth and richness that he displayed in this story?

Here are some other writing ideas that can be used in science classes. Have students take the viewpoints of other people to illustrate their understandings of particular concepts. For example, a student might present a lesson on evolution from the point of view of Charles Darwin—how would Darwin argue about evolution? Or imagine that students have launched an investigation into the changes over the last century in Lake Erie, Lake Okeechobee, or the Great Salt Lake. After learning about the history of the lake, they might create a travel brochure telling about the lake's geological and environmental features and the impact of humans. Students could draw maps, diagrams, or illustrations of the area for the travel brochure.

Daily Journals.   Daily **journals** record the personal events, experiences, and reflections of children. They offer several advantages over other forms of assessment. First, they enable students to assemble some of their own assessment information. Second, they permit the teacher to conduct assessment at the most convenient time. Third, journal writing encourages students to connect science to their daily lives. Fourth, journals encourage candid teacher-to-student or student-to-student communication.

The typical elementary or middle grade teacher's day is very busy and hectic. Teachers are usually responsible for teaching all subjects to twenty-five to thirty students of varying ability levels and cultural backgrounds. When students make their own observations in a journal about what they have learned from a particular activity and about what continues to present difficulty, the teacher is relieved of some of the assessment burden. Because teachers can read journals after school hours when things aren't so hectic, journal assessment helps ease the assessment burden even further.

Journal writing also encourages students to associate science with their everyday lives. For example, a teacher might ask students to keep track in their journals of the science-related literature stories they read, of science-related news items, and of science-related shows they see on television. They could also comment in their journals on what they learn in science class and how it is related to their lives.

Journal writing enhances communication between students and teachers because students often open up in journals and write things that they would not say publicly. Students are often more willing to write than talk about what they learn, and they commonly describe their feelings, attitudes, and fears in a journal. When teachers respond to what students have written, what results is an ongoing dialogue that helps guide instruction. For

[2] Credit for this story goes to one of Charlene's former fifth grade students, Robert Coggin.

example, if a student were to share in her journal that she is nervous about presenting in front of her classmates, the teacher could take steps to alleviate this fear— perhaps by having the student present with a partner.

Some teachers encourage students to communicate with each other by trading journals. By writing back and forth with a friend, students can discuss what they did in science class, construct understandings in a social context, and compare what they are learning to what others are learning. Other teachers ask students to keep electronic journals on the computer and send e-mails to others about their learning.

Physical Products

If you wanted to buy a new automobile, would you rather read about and see the car in a catalog or see the real product? What's the difference? The real product provides you with a *realistic* assessment of the car's riding comfort, sound quality, road handling, acceleration rate, turning ratio, workmanship, and design. Reading about it might only give you the opinions of others. Similarly, to see what students really know and can do, teachers need to make evaluative judgments of actual student products. The finished work of students provides excellent evidence of the knowledge and skills applied to create the product.

A **product** can be a book, a physical model of some kind, or a working apparatus that a student makes to demonstrate what she has learned. For example, imagine that students were interested in the human lung. They could develop a project in which they researched how human lungs worked; write a report about lungs; develop a physical 3-D model of the lung using ordinary household objects such as straws, balloons, sponges, and cups; and give a presentation on how smoking is harmful to lungs. When finished, students would have demonstrated their ability to collect and synthesize information, to communicate and to solve problems, and to create a product.

Teachers should always inform students about their expectations for a project and how they will be evaluated on it. Expectations and evaluation criteria can be communicated verbally or in the form of checklists. Checklists are particularly effective because they can be shared with parents and because teachers easily can convert them into scoring rubrics to evaluate products. Figure 9.3 shows an example of a parent letter and checklist for the human lung project.

Drawings.   Drawings give students a chance to represent scientific understanding in diverse forms such as murals, bulletin boards, posters, and bumper stickers. For example, students investigating the types of animals and plants in their neighborhood might create a mural of the neighborhood. Students might create posters of what they found in their school trash that would end up in a landfill. Finally, they might create bumper stickers using permanent markers on strips of contact paper to communicate their opinion of local recycling policies.

Drawing, as a form of assessment, offers the following advantages to students. First, it lets visual/spatial learners demonstrate their knowledge in a way that is comfortable for them. Second, drawings are sometimes a more accurate reflection of understanding because children can depict concepts such as the water cycle more completely through illustration than they can through exposition. Third, drawings can be used to express attitudes or feelings about science. Fourth, drawings are particularly effective for assessing science understanding in early elementary grades when student aren't able to read and write well. The following examples illustrate some of the benefits of assessments based on drawings.

Imagine that you are teaching seventh-grade students how to use a microscope to observe animal cells (a common activity in which students observe prepared animal cells

Figure 9.3

Dear Parents,

Your son/daughter has been learning about the human body in science. So far, we have learned about the skeletal system and the circulatory system. The students have become interested in how the lungs work and are now investigating this topic. The project they are working on will show what they learned from their investigations and will be shared with classmates on November 15th.

The project is designed so that your son/daughter will work as part of a collaborative team investigating this topic. However, you can help by taking him/her to the library or helping obtain materials that could be used to develop a project. The project may require some common household materials such as straws, balloons, sponges, paper, cups, and glue, but you should not spend any significant amount of money on these materials.

When your son/daughter shares the project on November 15th, it will be evaluated on the following criteria:

1. The report must answer the question "How do our lungs work?"
2. The report should be thorough enough to answer the question completely.
3. Teams are expected to use at least two references in the report, with only one of the references being an encyclopedia.
4. Pictures or diagrams should be used to help communicate this information.
5. Teams should construct a physical model that demonstrates how the lungs work.
6. Each team member should be able to explain how the model represents a real lung.
7. Each team member should be able to explain why smoking harms the lungs.

If you have any questions about this project, please contact me at school.

Sincerely,

Mrs. Czerniak

Parent Letter.

on a slide) and onion cells (an activity in which students place a single layer of onion skin on a slide) because they are investigating how plants and animals differ. Your learning preformances for the students might include learning to use a microscope correctly (a skill) and learning the differences between animal and plant cells (knowledge). While an elementary student could probably describe to you the differences between cells, if you want students to notice that animals cells are rounded with a cell membrane and plant cells are stiff and rectangular with a cell wall, then having the students draw what they observe will give you a good way to measure achievement of your objectives.

Imagine a third-grade classroom in which students are learning about how animals see. The teacher has taught students how the eye works, and students have participated in a teacher-led activity in which they used flashlights to observe how classmates' pupils expanded or contracted in the presence or absence of light. To assess students' understanding, the teacher asks them to draw pictures that explain how their eyes work. One child draws a picture of rays shooting out of the eyes toward an object and then returning to the eye. This drawing tells the teacher that the child has an inaccurate conception of sight and thinks that we see because of rays that come from our eyes. Drawings help teachers identify when children are having difficulty understanding science concepts.

Imagine a classroom in which students are drawing pictures of scientists. This technique, called *draw a scientist,* examines students' beliefs and attitudes about science (Barman, 1996; Bodzin & Gehringer, 2001; Boylan, Hill, Wallace, & Wheeler, 1992; Finson, Beaver, & Cramond, 1995; Huber & Burton, 1995; Rampal, 1992; Sumrall, 1995). Researchers have found that students commonly depict scientists very stereotypically, as white, balding men wearing glasses and white lab coats. Of course, the scientist is usually surrounded by glassware out of which vapors are rising. Frequently, he has a disheveled or evil appearance. This activity can be used to monitor students' beliefs about who can become scientists and about what scientists can do in their careers.

Science-Related Music Websites

Music.   Students who possess strong musical/rhythmic intelligence can demonstrate their understanding of science by creating songs, raps, jingles, or cheers. They can engage in choral readings or set plays to **music**. A number of commercial science songs provide students with stimuli for their own writing. Songwriter Raffi, Linda Penn's Sing-Along-Science series (available through singer Kerry Clark), the Banana Slug String Band, and other bands have created science-related songs, such as "Baby Beluga" and the "Water Cycle Boogie," that are popular among elementary students.

Videos.   Students can record the images and sounds of their investigations on **video**. Videos are useful forms of assessment for several reasons:

1.   Creating a video is easy. The technology has advanced to the point at which even young elementary students are able to use it.
2.   The videos can be edited to reflect changing understandings.
3.   They permit subsequent playback or broadcasting to public audiences. Since videos can be played back for broadcast, they are records that can be used for assessment and for instruction.
4.   They conveniently document long-term projects, because video can be filmed in segments, edited, and stored until additional filming is done. An investigation about why leaves drop from trees in the fall might span an entire school year. Video footage could be collected over a long period of time to document this year-long process. Moreover, it is very easy for students to create iMovies using digital video to illustrate their long-term projects.
5.   Videos form vivid memories in students' minds. Videorecording a vacation, for example, provides continuous sight and sound documentation. In a fifth-grade classroom, one of the authors of this book made an 8 mm movie of William Tell. To this day, many years later, the author remembers more about Swiss history than about the history of any other European country.

6. The act of creating a video can force students to focus on the main ideas learned. If, for example, students are required to present their science project to classmates in a fifteen-minute video, they must focus on only the most important concepts and best examples. As a teacher, you will need to help students focus on ideas and not on just the way the product looks. This editing process can help students sift out the most important information from a mass of facts or unrelated data.

7. Videos can be used to generate unique and complex presentations, vividly capturing what students know. For example, older elementary students can connect video cameras to microscopes and computers to add new dimensions and edit video and audio footage. New digital video cameras can document images and scenes that can be added to electronic documents such as PowerPoint presentations, Web pages, and electronic portfolios.

Almost all schools now have access to video cameras and VCRs. Many are now purchasing digital video cameras.

Presenting Artifacts

Any of the artifacts (writing, journals, products, drawings, music, videos, and multimedia documents) already discussed can be used in presentations to groups of younger students, peers, parents, or community members. Presentations don't necessarily have to involve artifacts, however. For example, students who possess a strong bodily/kinesthetic ability may enjoy engaging in debates, simulations, plays, and role-plays. Whatever the format, presentations can motivate students and enhance their self-esteem.

Students are more motivated to complete investigations and put forth their best effort to develop artifacts when they see a purpose to the activity. Too often in elementary and middle grade classrooms, students complete work that is only seen by the teacher. Presenting an artifact to a real audience provides an investigation with a real, meaningful purpose and gives students the experience of dialoguing with others about their work.

> **Key Idea**
>
> Artifacts can be presented to a real audience (peers, parents, community members) to help make project work meaningful.

Developing Portfolios

Portfolio assessment is a process of collecting representative samples of students' work over time for purposes of documenting and assessing their learning. Typically, four types of documentation are contained in portfolios: artifacts, reproductions, attestations, and productions (Collins, 1992). As already discussed, artifacts include writing samples, journals, physical products, drawings, music, videotapes, and multimedia documents produced in the normal course of a science investigation.

Reproductions are documents attesting to the learning process—not the actual items produced. They include photographs of projects, videos of projects, or audiotapes of presentations. The difference between artifacts and reproductions is that artifacts are created during the investigative process, whereas reproductions are created afterward to document a project. A student's photographs of trees taken during the year to track seasonal changes are artifacts. A teacher's photographs of students' leaf collections is a reproduction.

Attestations are testimonials about a student's work prepared by someone other than the student, such as the teacher, a parent, or a peer. Some examples are a critique by a peer, a letter from a parent, and a report card from the teacher.

> **Key Idea**
>
> Portfolios typically contain four types of documentation: artifacts, reproductions, attestations, and productions.

Productions are documents that help explain the contents of a portfolio. They include such items as goal statements, personal reflections, captions, and descriptions of what the items in the portfolio represent.

While studying neighborhood trees, students might take photographs of trees throughout the seasons, write reports about trees, collect samples of leaves or needles, map the locations of the trees, and draw pictures of the seeds of trees. Some or all of these artifacts could be placed in a portfolio. Since the actual leaf collection would not hold up well in a portfolio, a photograph of the set (a reproduction) could be added to document the learning. The portfolio might also include a testimonial (an attestation) from a parent about a child's trip to a local park to identify different types of trees. Students could reflect on their experiences and add to the portfolio a letter to the teacher (a production) telling the most important idea they learned about trees in the neighborhood.

Portfolios as Containers of Artifacts

A portfolio can be contained in a file folder, a box, or any other suitable container for student work. However, a portfolio is not just a random collection of student work carelessly thrown together. It is a carefully planned collection that includes representative samples of student artifacts, reproductions, attestations, and productions collected over the entire school year organized so as to clearly represent learning for the viewer. Like documentation of a vacation that includes photographs, diaries, videos, and personal mementos, a good portfolio contains a carefully assembled sample of student work that encourages reflection.

There are many questions and issues to think about when implementing portfolios in a project-based science classroom. First, the purpose of the assessment should be established before starting the portfolio. Working together, the teacher and student should decide what kinds of documents best demonstrate the student's knowledge and abilities. Will the portfolio contain only the "best" samples of work or samples of varied quality? Must the evidence be individual student products or should the work be completed and documented through a collaborative effort of several students? How much evidence should be in the portfolio? What criteria will be used to judge each piece of work? Teachers frequently construct their criteria, scoring rubrics, checklists, or other methods of judgment prior to selecting the student work to be included in the portfolio. Teachers must also decide if all students will be evaluated by the same criteria; determine how often and by whom the portfolio will be evaluated; decide where the portfolio will be kept and what access students will have to it; help students select samples of their work that accurately represent their abilities; and periodically critique the portfolio for its effectiveness in helping make decisions and in determining what students know, can do, and are like.

A portfolio can be useful for teachers as well. Portfolio Activity 9.5 will help you develop a teaching portfolio.

Making Judgments from Assessment Information

The purpose of evaluation is to make judgments about student growth, set goals, and report information to students and their parents. In the past, teachers used assessment mostly for reporting grades, and only the teacher had a voice in determining how well students were doing. Today, assessment techniques give students a voice in the assessment process. In this section, we will discuss how scoring rubrics can be used to assess artifacts, performances, and portfolios. We address the processes of self-assessment and peer assessment. Finally, we discuss grading.

Portfolio Activity 9.5

CREATING YOUR OWN PORTFOLIO

Materials Needed:
- Paper and something to write with

A. Think about the major concepts, skills, and techniques you've learned in your science teaching methods course. List them on a sheet of paper. You might refer to your instructor's syllabus for help on this or talk to your instructor about it.

B. Now think about things you've done in class that could provide evidence that you've met the learning performance. What artifacts could you include in the portfolio? Are there reproductions or attestations from the instructor, cooperating teachers, peers, and children that you can include? What productions will you add?

List as many things as you can that will provide evidence of your learning. You might include photos of your teaching; videos; assignments from class; your philosophy of teaching science; lesson plans; unit plans; samples of student work; letters from students, parents, cooperating teachers, and instructors; samples of your own writing; reflections on your teaching; evaluations from instructors and cooperating teachers; letters of recommendation; and lists of your educational activities.

C. Begin a teaching portfolio. Think about items that a prospective employer might want to see. What items would add value to your portfolio and help you obtain a job or get a good evaluation from a principal?

Scoring Rubrics

One helpful technique for evaluating an artifact, performance, or portfolio is to use a scoring rubric. A **scoring rubric** is a brief, written description of different levels of quality for student performance that can be used to rank or rate a level of performance. It often uses the same set of observable criteria that go into a checklist. Typically, rubrics are classified as either holistic or analytic.

Holistic rubrics measure the overall quality of an artifact, performance, or portfolio (Arter & McTighe, 2001). They evaluate criteria such as creativity, relevance to real life, impact, clarity, completeness, content accuracy, and organization. For example, the following holistic rubric contains four general criteria. Although the rubric provides a general framework for scoring students, it does not provide *specific* criteria such as the focus of the scientific content or the characteristics that would make the project creative, complete, and clearly presented:

> **Key Idea**
>
> A scoring rubric (either holistic or analytic) is a brief, written description of different levels of student performance that helps guide teachers as they evaluate students' work.

- *3 points:* The student makes logical inferences supported by data collected in the investigations, gives rationales for the inferences, and supports the inferences with diagrams and drawings.
- *2 points:* The student makes inferences supported by data collected in the investigations but does not support them with rationales.
- *1 point:* The student makes a logical inference, but it is not supported by the data collected in the investigations.
- *0 points:* The student fails to make a logical inference.

Analytic rubrics measure artifacts, performances, or portfolios in a quantitative manner by assigning or taking away points for specific traits, dimensions or criteria that are present or missing (Arter & McTighe, 2001). For example, a teacher who is evaluating the

Table 9.4

ANALYTIC SCORING RUBRIC

	Excellent	Good	Satisfactory	Poor
Uses logical inferences	4	3	2	1
Is scientifically accurate	4	3	2	1
Has supporting data	4	3	2	1
Has supporting rationale	4	3	2	1
Has supporting diagrams and drawings	4	3	2	1

investigative process and students' abilities to make inferences might use the analytic scoring rubric shown in Table 9.4. It contains five observable criteria: logical inferences, scientific accuracy, supporting data, supporting rationale, and supporting diagrams and drawings.

Imagine that students have been investigating how sound travels and how animals use their ears to collect sounds. They have learned that sound travels best through solids, next best through liquids, and least well through air. They have discovered that sound can be collected or projected in a cone-shaped object. Students create a model of an animal ear to demonstrate what they have learned. How will the teacher assess this model ear? The following rubric might be used to accomplish this task:

- *5 points:* The students designed an ear that clearly demonstrates all four sound concepts learned from the investigations—sound travels best through solids; sound travels better through liquids than air; sound travels least well through air; and a funnel/tunnel shape can be used to collect and amplify sound waves so that they sound louder. The students can explain why the ear would help an animal obtain food and avoid predators, and they provide evidence from their investigations to support their design.
- *4 points:* The students designed an ear that demonstrates at least three of the four sound concepts learned from the investigations—sound travels best through solids; sound travels better through liquids than air; sound travels least well through air; and a funnel/tunnel shape can be used to collect and amplify sound waves so that they sound louder. The students can explain why the ear would help the animal obtain food and avoid predators, but they fail to support their design with data from their investigations.
- *3 points:* The students designed an ear that demonstrates at least two of the concepts learned from the investigations—sound travels best through solids; sound travels better through liquids than air; sound travels least well through air; and a funnel/tunnel shape can be used to collect and amplify sound waves so that they sound louder. The students can explain why the ear would help an animal obtain food and avoid predators, but the explanation is not linked directly to their investigations.
- *2 points:* The students designed an ear that demonstrates at least one of the concepts learned from the investigations—sound travels best through solids; sound travels better through liquids than air; sound travels least well through

air; and a funnel/tunnel shape can be used to collect and amplify sound waves so that they sound louder. The students can explain why the ear would help an animal obtain food and avoid predators.

- *1 point:* The students designed an ear and can give a logical explanation about how it would help an animal obtain food and avoid predators. However, the students do not demonstrate any of the four sound concepts covered in the investigations.

- *0 points:* The students designed an ear but are unable to explain how it would help an animal obtain food and avoid predators, and the design is not logical or consistent with concepts learned about sound.

By including evaluative criteria in the scoring rubric, the teacher establishes an objective basis for judging the artifact, performance, or portfolio. Scoring rubrics also provide students with feedback or data supporting grades and evaluations. When students know the criteria on which they were judged, they can take steps to expand their knowledge and improve their skills. Additional reasons for using scoring rubrics are outlined by Andrade (2000): Rubrics make it easy to explain students' progress to others, make teachers' expectations clear, support learning and the development of skills, and support the development of understanding and good thinking.

The criteria used in scoring rubrics depend upon the teacher's goals and learning performances for the lesson. Some criteria will be mandated by state and local school districts' curricula guidelines, while others are likely to follow national trends or curriculum frameworks such as the *National Science Education Standards* (National Research Council, 1996, 2000, 2001) or *Benchmarks for Science Literacy* (AAAS, 1993). In project-based science classrooms, the following criteria may be used to design scoring rubrics:

- *Understanding of concepts:* Determine whether students developed shallow, inert knowledge or deep, meaningful understanding by examining the level of detail in the artifact, performance, or portfolio. Note missing links and levels of differentiation or completeness in the explanations.

- *Use of higher-order thinking:* Determine whether students used higher-order thinking by examining such factors as their ability to formulate and answer questions, interpret or explain decisions, and discuss assumptions that underlie the artifact, performance, or portfolio. Also assess their ability to explain relationships and formulate new problems or questions and apply information to new situations or problems.

- *Ability to answer driving questions:* Judge how well students answered the driving question. Was there a weak or strong relationship to the driving question? Did students specify the relationship in clear, specific terms?

- *Relatedness to the world:* Determine if students made strong connections between the artifact, performance, or portfolio and the real world. Did students apply information to a real life example in a strong convincing manner?

- *Level of collaboration:* Does the artifact, performance, or portfolio show interaction with others? Is the sharing of ideas and the use of other resources, especially community resources, evident?

- *Level of creativity:* Does the artifact, performance, or portfolio reveal a high level of creativity? Does it construct new ideas or connect existing ideas with new ones? Does it use ideas in novel ways or translate ideas from other subject areas?

**CONNECTING TO
NATIONAL SCIENCE EDUCATION STANDARDS**

Assessment in Science Education

The process of scoring student-generated explanations requires the development of a scoring rubric. The rubric is a standard of performance for a defined population (p. 93).

- *Presentation:* Did students thoroughly explain the key ideas that answered the driving question? Were their classmates engaged? Did they answer classmates' questions? Did they use enough detail to support their conclusions?
- *Use of cognitive tools:* Did students use cognitive tools such as print media, computers, peripherals, software applications, and telecommunication? Determine the level of use of these types of tools.

After you have determined the criteria for your scoring rubric, you need to create the rubric using a series of general steps (Andrade, 2000; Arter & McTighe, 2001):

1. Gather samples of student work and performances and sort them into groups by quality. Examine samples of related student work to get a feeling for the range of possible answers and responses.
2. Determine how an "expert" would perform in the situation. List the knowledge, skills, or dispositions an "expert" might display.
3. Identify the observable differences between "excellent" and "poor" performance. For example, a student who has mastered an understanding of sound waves is able to explain the related science concepts, how the ear is designed to collect and amplify sound, and how the ear helps an animal obtain food and avoid predators. In contrast, the student who has a poor understanding of sound may be able to create an "animal ear" and explain how it helps an animal avoid predators but is unable to explain the science concepts related to the design of the ear.
4. Turn the "good" and "poor" performance into a range of possible performances that exemplify the traits for a variety of levels. You should use no more than three to six levels or ranges that will become *points* on a rubric (Arter & McTighe, 2001). For example, students are able to identify all four concepts, three of the concepts, two of the concepts, one concept, or none of the concepts.
5. Try to assess students with the range of performances you identified.
6. Revise the criteria as needed.

Creating Rubrics

There are also a number of useful Web sites for creating rubrics. Go to the Online Learning Center for links to rubric websites. In Portfolio Activity 9.6, you will develop your own scoring rubric.

Assessment of Portfolios

After students have collected a wide range of items for their portfolios, they need to reflect upon each item and sort out those that best represent what they have learned. Some teachers have students think about "added value." What evidence will an item add to the portfolio? They ask open-ended question stems such as, "Looking at everything in my portfolio, I like this piece most because ...." or "This artifact shows that I ....". If nothing is gained by including an item, it should be left out. For example, while investigating why pumpkins rot, students might produce a short report on decomposition, photographs of

Portfolio Activity 9.6

DEVELOPING A SCORING RUBRIC

Materials Needed:
- Paper and pencil
- The results of Portfolio Activity 9.4

A. After completing Portfolio Activity 9.4 (or another performance-based activity), develop a scoring rubric to evaluate the performance. Use the following steps:
  1. Collect samples of student work.
  2. Determine how an "expert" would perform in the situation. List the knowledge, skills, or dispositions an "expert" might have.
  3. If possible, examine work that students have completed to see the range of possible answers and responses.
  4. Identify the observable differences between "excellent" and "poor" performance.

5. Turn the "good" and "poor" performance into a range of possible performances.
6. Try to assess students with the range of performances you identified.
7. Revise the criteria as needed.

B. Work in teams to try to score the performance using the rubrics created. Did the rubrics seem accurate and fair? How might they be revised? If you need more information, see Arter, J., & J. McTighe, 2001. *Scoring rubrics in the classroom: Using performance criteria for assessing and improving student performance.* Thousand Oaks, Calif: Corwin Press, Inc.

C. Record your observations in your portfolio.

---

their investigation, notes, audiotapes of interviews with a grocery store manager, transcripts of the audiotaped interview, drawings of the various stages of pumpkin rot, graphs of decomposition over time, and journal entries. After reflecting upon their accumulated evidence, they would probably decide that the journal entries and the audiotape of interviews did not depict what they had learned and omit these items from the portfolio.

After they have selected items to include in the portfolio, students need to reflect upon their progress and overall growth. This reflection can occur in different ways. Teachers frequently have students write captions for each artifact to explain what learning it depicts. Some teachers have students write letters describing all the items in their portfolios and explaining why each artifact is evidence of learning. Others have students create tables of contents to organize their portfolios in a meaningful way. A table of contents might be arranged in a linear fashion to show progression, or it might be arranged around themes to show the relationships among concepts learned.

Students find "portfolio reviews" with the teacher, parents, or peers meaningful. The portfolio review gives students and teacher an opportunity to discuss progress, achievement, and goals. Students can share their portfolios with parents or peers, either in small groups or before the whole class. This final step encourages positive critiques from significant others, and it helps students celebrate with others their progress and success.

Self-Assessment

Self-assessment can encourage students to think about such things as learning styles, what was learned, the quality of that learning, and personal goal setting. When students think about their own learning styles and preferences, they reflect on how they best learn (metacognitive knowledge)—whether through reading, hands-on manipulation of physical objects, or working collaboratively with others, for example. When students

> ### Key Idea
>
> Portfolios help students reflect on their growth. Many students find it meaningful to share their achievements with others.

Key Idea

Self-assessment can encourage students to think about their own learning and help them set goals.

**CONNECTING TO
NATIONAL SCIENCE EDUCATION STANDARDS**

Introduction

Student participation is a key component of successful assessment strategies at every step. If students are to participate effectively in the process, they need to be clear about the target and the criteria for good work, to assess their own efforts in light of the criteria, and to share responsibility in taking action in light of the feedback (NRC, 2001, p. 9).

reflect on what they learned, they also think about how they feel about their learning. When they think about the quality of their learning, they examine how well they are doing and how much they have improved and their strengths and weaknesses. Using such self-assessment information, students can then decide what steps to take to improve. Many teachers use self-assessment as one step in a process that encourages students to rethink and revise their work. The teacher has the students reflect on their progress, provides feedback to the students, and gives the students an opportunity to redo their work. As students progress further down the path of self-regulated learning, their intrinsic motivation to learn also grows, and this, of course, is what teaching and learning are all about—the production of highly motivated, self-regulated learners.

Several useful techniques can be used to encourage self-evaluation. You might have students keep journals detailing what they learn in their investigations. However, some students fail to open up in journals, and they make useless entries such as "I did my math homework after school. Then I worked on my science investigation." This type of information doesn't reveal much a student's thinking, learning, or problems. To encourage true self-assessment, you might provide students with guiding questions. Students can answer these questions directly, or they can answer them as part of a journal, portfolio, or interview. Guiding questions might include "Look back over your science report—what did you find easy about writing the report?" "What was difficult for you?" "What was the most important idea you learned?" "Why?" "How does this relate to the driving question?" "What do you like about your artifact?" "What do you feel are its strengths and weaknesses?" "What would you like to improve or change?" "What skills would you like to work on?" "Are you satisfied with your progress in answering the driving question?" "What else do you need to investigate?" and "In what areas of science do you think you have improved the most?"

You might choose to base self-assessment on open-ended statements. For example, you could have students complete the following statements:

- The things I am still wondering about are . . .
- I discovered . . .
- I'm beginning to wonder why . . .
- I learned . . .
- I could improve by . . .
- I never realized that . . .
- I was surprised that . . .

You might assess curiosity by determining how many things a student is wondering about. You might use "attitude inventories" that ask students open-ended questions about their interests and beliefs:

- The thing I like best about science is . . .
- My favorite topic to study is . . .
- My favorite subject is . . .

These open-ended self-assessment techniques also encourage students to continue wondering or questioning —affective attitudes in a project-based science classroom.

Finally, students can assess their own attitudes about science with a formal assessment instrument. For example, if you are interested in measuring how excited the students are about studying natural disasters, you could ask them the following questions:

CONNECTING TO
NATIONAL SCIENCE EDUCATION STANDARDS

Assessment in Science Education
Students need the opportunity to evaluate and reflect on their own scientific understanding and ability. Before students can do this, they need to understand the goals for learning science. The ability to self-assess understanding is an essential tool for self-directed learning. Through self-reflection, students clarify ideas of what they are supposed to learn (p. 88).

a. How excited are you about learning about hurricanes, floods, tornadoes, and earthquakes? (1) very, (2) somewhat, (3) not at all.

b. How important was your investigation in terms of answering the driving question? (1) very, (2) somewhat, (3) not at all.

Whatever self-assessment method you choose, it will foster **metacognitive knowledge** that makes students more aware of what they are learning, how they are investigating, and how they are feeling about science.

Peer Assessment

In **peer assessment**, students give feedback to other students in the class. Most students respect the opinions of their peers and value their input. Peer assessment, therefore, can be an effective motivator for many students. In addition, when students know that they will be presenting artifacts to a real audience, they are more likely to see a purpose for their work.

In collaborative learning groups, students can assess the contribution each member made to successfully completing a task (Strom, Strom & Moore, 1999). Teachers frequently have students evaluate such outcomes as how well their group members were able to work together, carry out assigned tasks, stay on task, share materials, monitor their own time, listen to each other, ask questions, generate alternative answers, contribute ideas, take different perspectives, summarize information, encourage each other, show respect for one another's ideas, and challenge ideas.

Be careful, however, when you first start to use peer assessment in a project-based science environment. Students need to trust each other before they can function well in such an environment. Before trying this method of assessment, build a trusting classroom environment. As discussed in Chapters 6 and 10, you can create this trusting environment by developing interpersonal skills and encouraging collaborative group work. Also be careful to protect the privacy of students' grades. A recent court case challenged the practice of having students grade their peers' papers and seeing peers' grades as a violation of the Family Educational Right to Privacy Act (Buckley Amendment), but the court did not uphold this challenge.

Figure 9.4 summarizes what you have learned about the assessment process.

> ### Key Idea
>
> Most students respect the opinions of their peers and value their input, so peer assessment can be a useful technique for feedback in a project-based environment.

Grading

We have discussed assessment in this chapter as a process of collecting information about students' progress, assembling the information, and making judgments about progress or achievement. **Grading** is an interpretation or judgment made from data collected and recorded and thus is an extension of evaluation. To issue grades, a teacher

Figure 9.4

STAGE	TECHNIQUES	ADVANTAGES
Gathering Information	• Observations of students during instruction —e.g., watching students while they conduct an investigation	• Helps in minute-to-minute and day-to-day decisions • Can be formal or informal
	• Focused questioning of students—e.g., asking students why they completed an investigation in the manner they did	• Provides teachers with in-depth information about students' understanding • Can be formal or informal
	• Anecdotal records—e.g., notes about student performance jotted on index cards	• Is helpful for determining progress at end of a term • Is useful for parent conferences • Helps teachers remember information
	• Checklists—e.g., lists of concepts (understand causes of weather), skill (can record data accurately), and dispositions (appreciate usefulness of weather predictions)	• Can be used while students are working • Cuts down time charting assessments information • Keeps teacher focused on obtaining data from all students
	• Clinical interviews with students—e.g., sitting down with each student and asking, "What is the design of your investigation?" and "What have you accomplished so far?"	• Provides teachers more detailed information • Enables teachers and students to know each other • Can clarify any misinterpretations made of students while observing them
	• Concept maps—e.g.,: 	• Lets students demonstrate complex understanding of concepts • Can diagnose misunderstandings
	• Test items—e.g., Explain why it isn't a good idea to build a house on the bank of a river that flows quickly.	• Easy to grade • Can measure a variety of levels of understanding
	• Performance-based assessment—e.g., providing students a prompt to complete a skill-based activity	• Is based on actual classroom activity • Measures complex skills and depth of knowledge • Is linked to instruction • Is concrete and active

The assessment process.

Portfolio Activity 9.7   CREATING A REPORT CARD

Materials Needed:
- Pencil and paper or a computer

A. Think about a report card you received as an elementary or middle grade student. What kinds of things did it tell about your performance in science? What do you wish it had included?

B. Imagine you are on a committee to design a new report card. It is your task to design the section for reporting science learning in a project-based classroom. Design a report card that you think best reflects what students and parents should know. Share the report card with others in your class.

C. Would your report card have letter grades? Debate with others whether letter grades should be obsolete.

D. What are the major implications of constructivist theory that would influence your report card?

E. How would you explain to parents that your assessment procedures and report card are effective?

F. File a copy of your newly developed report card in your portfolio.

must think about all of the various techniques used to gather and assemble assessment data. For example, do you want to include only written products? Do you want to include observations? Self-assessments? Once you make these decisions, you need to develop a logic or set of operating rules for converting this information to a grade.

Assigning grades is no easy task if the school uses letter grades. All assessments are flawed in some ways and only an estimation of student learning. A single letter grade can be problematic, because it reduces students' achievement in a variety of areas such as content knowledge, process skills, decision-making skills, motivation, and team and collaborative skills to a single evaluative statement. You need to determine what you think is most valued, whether some things will be weighted more than others, and whether you will give grades based on progress and effort or only end products or final achievements. After you make a decision on the logic or rule you will use, you need to look for patterns and changes and compare them with your intended learning outcomes. From this, a teacher makes his or her best professional judgment about a grade.

Not all schools use a single letter grade for grade reports, and some allow teachers to add additional materials to the grade card such as narrative reports in which statements about progress or achievement can be included. Other school district grade cards look more like scoring rubrics. In these districts, procedures resembling those described earlier for creating rubrics can be used for determining grades. If you find yourself in a situation in which single letter grades are the only method of reporting to parents at the end of a term, we encourage you to supplement the grades with written narratives or other more detailed explanations of students' progress and achievement.

Now that you know more about student assessment in a project-based science classroom, what type of report card would you develop? Portfolio Activity 9.7 helps you answer this question.

USING TECHNOLOGY TOOLS TO ENHANCE ASSESSMENT

Earlier, we discussed how artifacts can be meaningful for students and result in thorough and useful assessment. Technology tools can be used to create **multimedia documents** that combine writing, illustrations, photographs, videotapes, audiotapes, computer applications, and other media to enrich conceptual understanding and assessment even further. Multimedia documents give students an opportunity to present their understandings more fully than words alone ever could. In addition, they give students the opportunity to depict learning in ways that are most consistent with their learning styles.

For example, student photographers in your classroom might enjoy documenting their learning with photographs. Computers enable students to combine images and edit them into their written documents. Students can take photographs with digital cameras, and these digital pictures easily can be added to documents. Students can readily collect data and create graphs using computer programs. Using a digital video camera and Quick-Time or Macintosh's iMovie, students can add short clips of footage to their writing or Web pages. PowerPoint and Web design programs such as Front Page or Page Mill enable students to combine writing, audio, and visual images into a single document.

Technology tools have also begun to improve the assessment process. Assessments no longer need to consist solely of pencil-and-paper tests, and they don't need to be done only by the teacher. Many school districts offer computerized exams, quizzes, and performance items on which students simply input answers into the computer. These assessments are then scored by computer. Technology can also provide rapid feedback to teachers and students, thereby improving the teaching and learning process.

Grading Software; SciLinks

Technology can enrich the nature of science instruction by providing multimedia, probes, simulations, and interactive programs for examining and measuring students' problem-solving skills, actions, and decisions. Such technology allows teachers to measure in-depth, meaningful learning rather than discrete facts and inert knowledge. For more information about assessment, see NSTA's SciLinks website.

ANOTHER LOOK AT THE ADVANTAGES OF EDUCATIONAL ASSESSMENT

Assessment in a project-based science classroom, regardless of the method used, should be designed to help the teaching and learning process—not humiliate, demean, or trick students. Good assessment matches instruction and helps diagnose, monitor, and evaluate students' acquisition of concepts, skills, and attitudes. Assessment is both formative and summative. It is an ongoing process that guides curriculum selection and instruction. Teachers in project-based science think of assessment as a responsibility shared between teacher and student for the purpose of informing students, parents, and teachers.

A college student who took an ornithology class learned about different types of birds and how to identify them by color, plumage, shape, size, and song. He learned where they live, what they eat, and whether they are endangered. The final exam consisted of fifty pictures of birds' legs. It asked students to identify the birds only by their feet. The student, frustrated and exasperated, told the professor that the test was unfair as it did not measure what had been taught in the course and that he wasn't going to take it. The professor replied, "That is fine. I will just record a zero in my grade book for this test. Now, what is your name, young man?" The student pulled up his pant leg and said, "I'm not going to tell you. See if you can identify me by my legs!"

This story makes a point very well. In project-based science classrooms, teachers purposefully, carefully, and thoughtfully design and implement assessment procedures to provide information to help students grow and also to learn about students' progress. When assessment is carefully crafted and executed, there are numerous advantages for teachers, students, and parents.

Advantages for Teachers

The assessment techniques used in project-based science classrooms encourage teachers to become more **reflective** in their practice. They force them to think about the design of their curriculum and instruction and about ways to revise and adapt their lessons so that all students learn. They also encourage teachers to take students' comments into account when planning their instruction. Teachers and students thus become allies in the learning process. Assessment is not an end in itself but a means to a mutually sought end —student learning.

> **Key Idea**
>
> Assessment helps teachers become reflective practitioners who help all students learn to the best of their ability.

Teachers come to know their students better when using assessment consistent with project-based science. All students become important, and it is less likely for students to fall between the cracks. Because each student works with the teacher, the teacher can discern each child's capacity, style of learning, and rate of learning. Teachers use more active learning techniques in their practices because they arrive at a deeper understanding of what students know and how they have come to know it. If a school requires letter grades, a variety of assessment strategies provide teachers with a more honest and valid appraisal of students' learning on which they can base letter grades.

Advantages for Students

Most educators feel that assessment in a project-based environment encourages students to become involved in their own learning and helps them become reflective, self-regulated learners. Teachers and students work together to determine which pieces of work represent students' abilities and how the work will be evaluated. Students can analyze the strengths and weaknesses of their own work and establish their own goals for improvement. This **self-monitoring** behavior and metacognitive knowledge helps students develop intrinsic motivation to learn and strengthens their relationship with their teachers.

> **Key Idea**
>
> Assessment helps students become reflective, self-regulated learners who focus on improvement and growth.

Assessment in project-based science also allows for individual differences in student abilities, since the focus is on student improvement rather than on comparison with others. Students are encouraged to chart their own improvement over time. Unlike **criterion-referenced tests**, which grade all students according to a single set of preestablished standards, assessment that focuses on individual student improvement tends to promote self-esteem.

Effective assessment techniques also promote collaboration with peers. Students work with classmates to develop and share artifacts and portfolios, and they learn to seek suggestions for improvement. During this process, students develop important social skills. They learn to support and coach others and to work collaboratively and cooperatively. Finally, assessment techniques provide a less-threatening environment for evaluation since evaluation is an ongoing part of instruction rather than an occasional, anxiety-producing situation.

Advantages for Parents

Parents and guardians play a crucial role in the education of their children. Many people believe that the assessment techniques used in project-based classrooms accomplish for parents what traditional forms of assessment alone cannot.

Standardized (normed) test scores, while important for standardized comparisons of all the other children who have taken the test, do not provide the depth of understanding stressed in the *National Science Education Standards* (NRC, 1996, 2000, 2001). A 50th percentile score on mathematics, for example, means only that half of the students who took the test did better and half of the students who took the test did worse. This tells the parents how their child compared to other children taking the test. However, this kind of information tells parents little about children's capability, progress, strengths, and weaknesses. It tells nothing about children's motivation to improve.

Traditionally, letter grades did not offer much more information than standardized test scores because most were based on memory-oriented, criterion-referenced tests. These tests were often administered at the end of a chapter or other unit of study, and a child's single score would determine his or her letter grade. For example, a C grade would tell the parent only that the child answered approximately 75 percent of the questions correctly. Was the test valid and reliable? Did the child learn more things about science than the test measured? Is the child interested in science? Has the child developed scientific thinking and problem-solving skills? Formal criterion-referenced tests provide only a partial answer to such questions in parent-teacher conferences.

Contemporary assessment techniques offer to parents a strong, multidimensional approach to understanding their children's learning. By viewing samples of work over time, they gain a better understanding of the entire learning process and of a child's improvement. Since many schools require criterion-referenced letter grades, these alternative assessments are often used in conjunction with other methods.

It is the job of teachers in project-based classrooms to communicate with parents about their children's progress and explain why project-based science requires different forms of assessment. Parents may need to be won over to these new ideas through involvement in the assessment process.

To involve parents in the assessment process, teachers can, for example, have parents help select some of their children's work to be included in a portfolio. Parents might also play the role of teacher by holding their own conferences with their children about their work, progress, strengths, weaknesses, and future goals. Parents can also supply valuable observations of their children's learning at home. For example, a parent might supply information about a child's trip to a science museum and resulting interest in building paper airplanes and rockets or Lego structures. Parents might even help fill out checklists of science skills, attitudes, or abilities that they have observed at home. Most teachers who have used alternative assessment techniques and kept in close communication with parents find that the parents appreciate the depth of understanding the teacher has about their children. In short, assessment in project-based classrooms brings together all the stakeholders (students, teachers, and parents) in the learning process.

> ### Key Idea
>
> Assessment helps parents understand in detail their sons' or daughters' academic growth.

CONNECTING TO
NATIONAL SCIENCE EDUCATION STANDARDS

Science Teaching Standards

Teachers of science engage in ongoing assessment of their teaching and of student learning. In doing this, teachers use multiple methods and systematically gather data about student understanding and ability (p. 37).

Portfolio Activity 9.8 — EFFICIENCY OF ASSESSMENT

Materials Needed:
- Pencil and paper or a computer

A. Some educators have argued that today's assessment techniques, while more valid and reliable, cost a considerable amount of money to implement and uses an exorbitant amount of teacher time. Interview several classroom teachers about this issue.

B. Write a short essay explaining your own beliefs on this issue.

C. If time allows, have a debate in your classroom about the "costs" and "benefits" of today's assessment techniques.

D. Investigate how computers, hand-held computers, and CD-ROMs are making assessment easier and saving time. Examine specific products such as *Learner Profile* by Sunburst/WINGS company, *Grady Profile* by Aurbach and Associates, and *Performance Plus* by National Computer Systems (NCS).

E. Record your findings in your portfolio.

Portfolio Activity 9.9 — WHAT HAVE YOU LEARNED ABOUT ASSESSMENT?

Materials Needed:
- The KWL list from Portfolio Activity 8.1

A. In Portfolio Activity 8.1, you made three columns on a piece of paper or with a computer word processing program. You listed in the first column as many things as you knew about assessment, and in the second column you listed what you wanted to know. Reread your second column. Think about what you learned about assessment in Chapters 8 and 9, both of which were devoted to assessment. In the last column, list everything you learned in these chapters that answered the questions you had before you read the chapters.

B. How did your beliefs about teaching elementary and middle grades change after reading these chapters?

C. Record your ideas in your portfolio.

Although today's assessment techniques offer many advantages, some educators are concerned about the cost and time it takes to use these techniques. You will explore the efficiency of contemporary assessment in Portfolio Activity 9.8. To assess your own learning about assessment from Chapters 8 and 9, complete Portfolio Activity 9.9.

CHAPTER REVIEW   www.mhhe.com/krajcik2e

Go to the Online Learning Center at **www.mhhe.com/krajcik2e** to review important content from the chapter and key terms, take a chapter assessment, and link to the chapter's websites.

ONLINE LEARNING CENTER

CHAPTER SUMMARY

In this chapter, we discussed the purpose of assessment, and we explored a three-phase method of assessing student understanding: gathering information, assembling and presenting assessment information, and evaluating assessment information. We explored numerous techniques for gathering information, including administering tests/quizzes, making observations, keeping anecdotal records, using checklists, using interviews, using concept maps, and conducting performance-based assessment. We considered techniques for improving observations and discussions and examined types of tests and testing methods. We discussed how to construct valid and reliable test and quiz items. We also considered a number of methods for assembling and presenting information, including student writing samples, daily journals, physical products, drawings, music, videos, and multimedia documents. We explored the use of portfolios and artifacts to present information, including different methods to document work in portfolios—artifacts, reproductions, attestations, and productions. The chapter introduced four techniques that teachers can use to evaluate assessment information: scoring rubrics, portfolios, self-assessment, and peer assessment. We considered the difference between holistic and analytic scoring rubrics, and we discussed procedures for creating rubrics. We examined how assessment information is used to give grades and make decisions, and we examined how technology tools can enhance the assessment process. Finally, we looked again at the advantages of assessment for teachers, students, and parents.

CHAPTER HIGHLIGHTS

- The purpose of evaluation is to make judgments about student growth, to set goals, and to report information to students and their parents.
- The process of assessing student understanding might be thought of as a three-step procedure:
  - Gathering information that will help in forming generalizations about students' learning.
  - Assembling and presenting the information so that it is recorded.
  - Evaluating the assessment information.
- Teachers can make formal or informal observations of student progress.
- Discussions can be improved by practicing wait-time, probing, and redirecting.
- Concept maps can be used to assess students' conceptual understandings or the understandings being formulated among groups of students.
- Tests and quizzes can be used to measure students' understanding of content knowledge and process skills.
- Tests and quizzes can be written at low-, medium-, and high-cognitive levels.
- Paper-and-pencil items can use two techniques: selection and supply.
- Selection formats include
  - Multiple choice.
  - True and false.
  - Matching.
- Supply formats include
  - Essay.
  - Short answer.

- Some formats (such as multiple choice and matching) are easy to score and more objective. Other formats (such as essay) take time to answer and grade, and they are open to interpretation.
- Teachers need to take care to write good test/quiz items.
- Good teachers help alleviate text anxiety by teaching well, bringing closure to lessons, reviewing lessons, and practicing sample test items.
- *Performance-based assessment* refers to methods of directly examining students' knowledge, skills, and dispositions.
- After teachers and students have collected assessment information, they must assemble it into a presentable form for others to see.
- In project-based science, there are two main ways to assemble and present information: artifacts and portfolios.
- Portfolios, collections of student artifacts, can be thought of as both objects and methods of assessment.
- Artifacts include writing samples, daily journals, physical products, drawings, music, videos, and multimedia documents.
- Artifacts can be can be used in presentations to groups of younger students, peers, parents, or community members.
- Portfolio assessment is a process of collecting representative samples of students' work over time for purposes of documenting and assessing their learning.
- Typically, four types of documentation are contained in portfolios:
  - Artifacts.
  - Reproductions.
  - Attestations.
  - Productions.
- The purpose of evaluation is to make judgments about student growth, set goals, and report information to students and their parents.
- A scoring rubric is a brief, written description of different levels of quality for student performance that allow a teacher to rank or rate a level of performance.
- Scoring rubrics can be holistic or analytic.
- There are six steps for creating a rubric:

  1. Gather and sort student work by quality;
  2. List the knowledge, skills, or dispositions of an "expert";
  3. Identify differences between "excellent" and "poor" performance;
  4. Identify performance levels;
  5. Assess students according to performance levels; and
  6. Revise criteria as needed.

- After students have selected items to include in the portfolio, it is essential that they reflect upon their progress and overall growth.
- Self-assessment can encourage thinking about learning styles, what was learned, the quality of that learning, and personal goal setting.
- In peer assessment, students give feedback to other students in the class. Most students respect the opinions of their peers and value their input.
- Grading is an interpretation or judgment made from data collected and recorded.
- Technology tools have begun to improve the assessment process.
- When assessment is carefully crafted and executed, there are numerous advantages for teachers, students, and parents.

KEY TERMS

analytic rubrics (363)

anecdotal records (340)

artifacts (354)

assessment (338)

attestations (361)

checklists (340)

clinical interviews (342)

concept mapping (344)

content

    knowledge (347)

criterion-referenced

    tests (373)

discussions (339)

drawing (358)

essay (348)

formal interviews (344)

grading (369)

holistic rubrics (363)

informal

    interviews (343)

journals (357)

metacognitive

    knowledge (369)

matching (348)

multimedia

    documents (372)

multiple choice (348)

music (360)

observation (339)

open-ended

    questions (344)

peer assessment (369)

performance-based

    assessment (352)

portfolio

    assessment (361)

portfolios (356)

probing (339)

product (358)

productions (362)

redirecting (339)

reflective (373)

reliability (350)

reproductions (361)

selection (348)

scoring rubric (363)

self-assessment (367)

self-monitoring (373)

short answer (348)

supply (348)

test anxiety (350)

true and false (348)

validity (350)

videotape (360)

wait-time (339)

writing samples (356)

REFERENCES

Airasian, P. W. 2001. *Classroom assessment: Concepts and applications.* New York: McGraw-Hill.

American Association for the Advancement of Science. 1993. *Benchmarks for science literacy.* New York: Oxford University Press.

Andrade, H. G. February, 2000. Using rubrics to promote thinking and learning. *Educational Leadership* 57(5):13–18.

Arter, J., and J. McTighe. 2001. *Scoring rubrics in the classroom: Using performance criteria for assessing and improving student performance.* Thousand Oaks, Calif: Corwin Press, Inc.

Barman, C. 1996. How do students really view science and scientists? *Science and Children* 34(1):30–33.

Bodzin, A., and M. Gehringer. 2001. Breaking science stereotypes. *Science and Children* (1):36–41.

Boylan, C. R., D. M. Hill, A. R. Wallace, and A. E. Wheeler. 1992. Beyond stereotypes. *Science Education* 76(5):465–76.

Champagne, A. B, and V. L. Kouba. 1999. Writing to inquire: Written products as performance measures. In *Assessing science understanding*, eds. J. J. Mintzes, J. H. Wandersee, and J. D. Novak. San Diego, Calif: Academic Press.

Collins, A. 1992. Portfolios for science education: Issues in purpose, structure, and authenticity. *Science Education* 76(4):451–63.

Edmondson, K. M. 1999. Assessing science understanding through concept maps. In *Assessing science understanding*, eds. J. J. Mintzes, J. H. Wandersee, and J. D. Novak. San Diego, Calif: Academic Press.

Finson, K., J. B. Beaver, and B. L. Cramond. 1995. Development of and field-test of a checklist for the draw-a-scientist test. *School Science and Mathematics* 95(4):195–205.

Haberman, M. 1995. *STAR teachers of children in poverty.* West Lafayette, Ind: Kappa Delta Pi.

Huber, R. A., and G. M. Burton. 1995. What do students think scientists look like? *School Science and Mathematics* 95(7):371–76.

McAfee, O., and D. J. Leong. 2002. *Assessing and guiding young children's development and learning.* Boston: Allyn and Bacon.

National Association for the Education of Young Children. 1986. *Developmentally appropriate practice in early childhood programs serving children from birth through age 8.* Washington, D.C.: Author.

National Middle School Association. 1995. *This we believe: Developmentally responsive middle level schools.* Columbus, Ohio: Author.

National Research Council. 1996. *National science education standards.* Washington, D.C.: National Academy Press.

National Research Council. 2000. *Inquiry and the national science education standards.* Washington, D.C.: National Academy Press.

National Research Council. 2001. *Classroom assessment and the National Science Education Standards.* Washington, D.C.: National Academy Press.

Novak, J. D., and D. B. Gowin. 1984. *Learning how to learn.* Cambridge, England: Cambridge University Press.

Pellegrino, J. W., N. Chudowsky, and R. Glaser. 2001. *Knowing what students know: The science and design of educational assessment.* Washington, D.C.: National Academy Press.

Rampal, A. 1992. Images of science and scientists: A study of school teachers' views. I. Characteristics of scientists. *Science Education* 76(4):415–36.

Southerland, S. A., M. U. Smith, and C. L. Cummins. 1999. "What do you mean by that?" Using structured interviews to assess science understanding. In *Assessing science understanding,* eds. J. J. Mintzes, J. H. Wandersee, & J. D. Novak. San Diego, Calif: Academic Press.

Strom, P. S., R. D. Strom and E. G. Moore. 1999. Peer and self-evaluation of teamwork skills. *Journal of Adolescence* 22:539–553.

Sumrall, W. J. 1995. Reasons for the perceived images of scientists by race and gender of students in grades 1–7. *School Science and Mathematics* 95(2):83–90.

Chapter 10

How Do I Manage the Project-Based Science Classroom?

INTRODUCTION

CLASSROOM CLIMATE

CLASSROOM ORGANIZATION

MANAGEMENT STRATEGIES

USING TECHNOLOGY TOOLS TO FACILITATE
CLASSROOM MANAGEMENT

CHAPTER LEARNING PERFORMANCES

- *Explain how the constructivist framework is useful for thinking about classroom management in project-based science.*
- *Describe how a teacher can create an effective classroom climate.*
- *Evaluate classrooms to determine their atmosphere.*
- *Compare and contrast the reasons for using various types of classroom management strategies.*
- *Explain the value of planning classroom management before, during, and after instruction.*
- *Justify why equitable classroom practices are necessary for managing project-based science.*
- *Distinguish among various types of safety precautions.*

INTRODUCTION

Project-based science creates many unique management challenges in the elementary or middle grade classroom. To be successful, teachers need to create a learning environment of trust and self-responsibility, a task that may raise numerous questions: *What does a teacher need to do to establish a positive classroom climate? How do I organize a classroom? How do I structure the school day? What can be done to make sure students are safe? How do I manage student behavior?* In this chapter, we will explore how teachers can create learning environments that support project-based science. We will focus on classroom climate, classroom organization, and management strategies.

In the classroom climate section, we will consider ways to establish a positive learning environment and examine a framework for thinking about classroom climate in the context of constructivism. We will discuss the roles of teacher and student, the relationship between teacher and student, and classroom interactions.

In the classroom organization section, we will review how to arrange a science classroom, structure the school day, and maintain a safe classroom. We will explore how to prepare for a lesson and what to do when off schedule.

In the section on management strategies, we will examine ways to foster positive student behavior, anticipate problems, distribute materials, make transitions between classes, deal with disturbances, and reinforce good behavior. We also will consider ways that teachers can handle multiple groups of students working on the same activities as well as groups of students working on different activities at the same time. The chapter outlines techniques for dealing with students with diverse abilities and students who finish activities at different rates.

Although this chapter offers realistic management strategies, these strategies are not panaceas for problems in the classroom. Building a classroom learning environment that supports project-based science takes a great deal of hard work. The trade-offs for the hard work are the positive results seen in student learning and motivation.

What follows are several scenarios of lessons about pesticides in a food chain. As you read each scenario, focus on various features of the instructional setting. What are the students doing? What does the classroom climate seem to be like? What is the role of the teacher? What is the relationship between the teacher and the students? What instructional supports does the teacher provide? How has the teacher managed the instruction? How is the room arranged?

Scenario 1: Reading About Science

Sixth-grade students are sitting at individual desks. They are about to read a section of their science textbook on pollution in a food chain. Ms. Jung decides to use the KWL method to focus the students' reading (see Chapter 7 for more information on KWL). Before students begin reading, Ms. Jung asks the students what they already know about food chains. She lists this information under the *K* column, representing what students know. Next, she asks students what they want to know more about. She lists these responses under the *W* column, representing what students want to learn. Ms. Jung then selects one student at a time to read a paragraph in the book. When the section is completed, she asks the students to answer in writing the two questions at the end of the chapter. The two questions will be used to focus a discussion about what students learned—the *L* on the KWL chart. A few students seem eager to begin reading the assignment, because they want to complete an investigation tomorrow that focuses on pesticides in a food chain. Most of the students begin to answer the two questions: "What is pollution?" and "How does pollution affect the animals at the top of a food chain?" Ms. Jung walks around as students are answering the questions to check that each student is on task and quiet. April, who is sitting at the front of the class, is playing with something in her desk and laughing with another student. Ms. Jung reminds April that the classroom rules require students to be quiet when they are reading or writing. After five minutes, Ms. Jung notices that Robbie has not started his assignment. She asks him if he has any questions, and she helps him focus on the topic of the paragraph—pesticides. Dr. Sylvia Brown, the principal, walks in to ask Ms. Jung a question and smiles as she sees the students working diligently. Ten minutes later, Ms. Jung collects the students' answers so that she can give them feedback. She also holds a discussion with the class about what they learned from the reading. She lists these items under the *L* column on the chart at the front of the room. She informs the students that they will begin to design an investigation the next day that is about pollution found in a food chain. The students seem excited about this and begin to talk about some ideas that they have. After a few ideas have been shared, Ms. Jung instructs the students to take out their mathematics books.

Scenario 2: Direct Science Instruction

In a sixth-grade classroom down the hall, Mrs. Lochbihler is teaching the same topic. She has ten students wear signs made of envelopes labeled *mice*, ten students wear signs made of envelopes labeled *snakes*, and five students wear signs made of envelopes labeled *hawks*. The twenty-five students are told that mice eat grains, snakes eat mice, and hawks eat snakes or mice. Next, Mrs. Lochbihler says, "We will be going outside to play a game. We will be running around on the playground during this game. How can we make sure that everyone learns and that no one gets hurt during this activity?" The students decide that they need to stay away from playground equipment, and they should have a discussion after the game is over to see what people learned from it. Mrs. Lochbihler and the students go outside. The game begins by the mice eating grain represented by an assortment of white and colored bits of paper. The mice put the bits of paper into their envelopes as they "eat" it. Then the snakes are allowed to tag or "eat" the mice, and the hawks are allowed to tag mice or snakes. As the students tag each other, they collect the envelopes of their "prey." They put these envelopes inside their own. Students are laughing and enjoying the game of tag. Mrs. Lochbihler cautions a few students that they are near the playground equipment.

After a number of mice and snakes are "eaten," Mrs. Lochbihler asks the students to return to the classroom. The students are excited by this outdoor activity, and they arrive at their classroom in a noisy fashion. Mrs. Lochbihler models for the students how they should get quiet as they reenter the school, and the students seem to do this quickly. Dr. Sylvia Brown, the principal, is waiting for Mrs. Lochbihler as she returns to the room with her students. The principal is happy to see that the students are enjoying science, and she joins the class so she can see what all of the excitement is about. The students begin to count how much "food" they "ate" and how many white and colored bits of paper are contained in the envelopes they collected. Mrs. Lochbihler informs the students that the colored bits of paper represent food that is contaminated with a pollutant called DDT. If an animal ate any food that included any colored bits of paper, the animal will become sick and its offspring might be deformed. If an animal's food supply consisted of at least as many colored bits of paper as white, the animal will die from the pollution. Students complete the task of counting their bits of paper, and Mrs. Lochbihler engages the students in a discussion about the effects of DDT pollution. She asks them to think about the effect that DDT may have on other animals, particularly humans if they eat animals that have been exposed to it. Finally, she instructs the students to compare how the mice, snakes, and hawks were affected by DDT. The students notice that the animals at the top of the food chain, the hawks, collected a lot more DDT than did the other animals. Mrs. Lochbihler finishes the lesson by having students draw a picture of how the pollution was passed through the food chain. A few students finish early, so Mrs. Lochbihler asks them to go to the computers to see if they can learn more about DDT. When students finish their pictures, they file them in their portfolios. The students who finished early share the information they found on the World Wide Web about DDT. Students in the class are so interested in this topic that they keep talking about the fact that DDT is still found in our environment even though it was banned in the United States years ago. Mrs. Lochbihler is surprised that this lesson has run a half hour longer than she planned. At the end of the lesson, Mrs. Lochbihler helps the students determine how they will structure their investigation tomorrow.

Scenario 3: Process Science

A few students in Mr. Morales's class bring to class an article about the level of PCBs found in fish from a local lake. In the article, students find that PCBs are reported to be in the fish caught in the lake. The article refers to *ppm*, and students wonder what *ppm* means. Mr. Morales approaches the topic of PCBs in food chains by using a laboratory activity as a benchmark lesson. Following directions, the students fill small plastic cups with red food coloring. The red food coloring is a 1 part per 10 solution. Next, the students take one drop of this red food coloring and transfer it to a clean plastic cup, and they add 9 drops of clear water. The solution becomes a 1 part per 100 solution of red food coloring. After they have done this, they take one drop from this cup and transfer it to a clean plastic cup and add 9 drops of clear water. This becomes a 1 part per 1000 solution of red food coloring. The students continue this procedure until they have mixed up a 1 part per million (1 ppm) solution. Mr. Morales notices that Martin is not following directions, and he reminds him about the contract they made for him to complete assignments in class. Next, Mr. Morales tells the students that pollution is frequently measured in parts per million (ppm) or parts per billion (ppb), and he tells the students that these tiny amounts of pollution can enter the food chain through many different sources (through plants that we eat, animals that we eat, or plants that animals we eat have eaten). The students in the class seem excited to learn this information; they now understand what the term *ppm* means. Tomorrow they will conduct an investigation in which they will measure pollutants from a local stream and report them in ppm.

Scenario 4: Multiple Investigations

Mrs. Kimble is teaching her sixth-grade class about food chains. Students in her class are investigating the question "How do chemicals affect an animal's food supply?" Several groups of students have decided to investigate different topics, so Mrs. Kimble sits down at her desk to grade some papers.

One group of students is studying the effect of pollution on the bald eagles in the Great Lakes region of the United States. Today these students are working on the computer, and they are communicating with a group of students in California who are studying a similar question: the effects of pollution on the condor. The students from both schools are comparing the pollutants found in their regions.

A second group of students is reading an article from the local paper about consumption of fish caught in the Great Lakes. They learn that there are recommended limits for consumption of fish from some of the lakes because of pollutants called *PCBs* and *mercury*, which are found in the fish. These students are discussing whether they could set up an experiment to test the effects of pollution on fish in an aquarium in their classroom. The discussion is getting very loud and is disturbing other groups. Mrs. Kimble gets up from grading papers and walks over to this group to question the students about their plan and helps the students understand procedures and regulations governing research conducted on vertebrate animals. She also points out that they need to keep their voices down.

A third group of students is studying the topic of biotechnology, investigating whether there are any known effects on humans who drink milk from cows given chemicals to increase their milk production. These students have decided to invite a guest speaker to come to their classroom to talk about research findings on dairy production, and they are excited at the prospect of calling the speaker.

Another group of students is studying the effects of pesticides and herbicides on fruits and vegetables. These students are trying to find out whether these chemicals are harmful to humans who eat the foods. They want to locate two farmers with different opinions about the use of pesticides and herbicides: one who uses organic farming practices and one who uses the chemicals. They are asking other students in the class if they know any local farmers who use these methods.

Like the scenarios you read in Chapter 1, the first three scenarios you just read represent what is called *read about science*, *direct instruction*, and *process science teaching*. Each type of science instruction can be used in a project-based environment as long as it supports student investigations. In these scenarios, the *read about science*, *direct instruction*, and *process science teaching* lessons are used as benchmark lessons to give students basic information about food chains and pesticides that will enable them to conduct investigations later. The last scenario illustrates students working on separate activities. Each scenario demonstrates different classroom management characteristics. The *climate* (prevailing feeling or state of mind of members of the class), *organization* (how the teacher structures classroom activities and space), and *management style* (how the teacher sets, models, and reinforces classroom behavioral expectations) of these four classrooms vary, but the management objective is the same in all of them. In this chapter you will be learning about managing a project-based science classroom. You'll start by analyzing in Portfolio Activity 10.1 the opening scenarios to glean from them some basic aspects of managing a project-based science classroom.

As you completed Portfolio Activity 10.1, you probably discovered that the objective of each lesson in the scenarios was the same—students will be able to define pollution, and they will understand the effect that pollution has on a food chain. During your comparison, you probably grappled with many questions: *What should a classroom look like? How noisy or quiet should it be? Should students be moving around or sitting down? Should they be laughing and talking, or should they be quiet and attentive?*

Portfolio Activity 10.1   **MANAGING A SCIENCE CLASSROOM**

Materials Needed:
- Pencil and paper or a computer

A. Compare and contrast the four classrooms described in the opening scenarios. How are they alike and different with respect to climate, organization, and management? What are the advantages and disadvantages of the management of each classroom? Use the following list of questions in your comparison.

Climate
- What are the classroom goals and expectations? Do students have a role in making the rules? What happens when someone doesn't follow the rules?
- Does the teacher smile a lot or frown? Do students seem to be enjoying themselves—or do they seem unhappy?
- Are students encouraged to take initiative and be autonomous, or are they expected to follow the directions of the teacher?
- Do students talk with each other and with the teacher, or is the classroom discourse only between students and teacher?

- Do students' ideas and responses help drive instruction and behavior in the classroom, or does the teacher determine the topics, activities, and behavioral expectations?
- Do students share responsibility for classroom decisions with the teacher, or does the teacher make all decisions?
- Does the teacher focus on "correct answers" to science questions, or are students encouraged to come up with many different answers?
- Are students encouraged to critique the teacher and give suggestions for improving instruction that will help them learn?
- How does the teacher assure that each student's self-esteem is improved?
- Does the teacher believe that all students can learn science? How does the teacher show this? What does the teacher do to ensure that all students are successful?
- How are girls and minorities treated in science classes? What does the teacher do to encourage all students in science?

Should they read from the textbook? Can they learn if they are playing a game? What kind of classroom environment best facilitates learning? Will they learn more if they are having fun? It is not always easy to answer these questions. Numerous factors influence how teachers organize their classrooms and affect classroom climate.

In the next sections, we will discuss three basic aspects of managing a project-based science learning environment: classroom climate, classroom organization, and management strategies. Although some of the topics and techniques introduced here are applicable to any subject area, each of these sections is designed to help teachers deal with some of the unique concerns and challenges associated with a project-based science environment.

CLASSROOM CLIMATE

The opening scenarios in this chapter depicted very different classrooms. One way they differed was in terms of **climate,** or prevailing conditions and environment in the classroom. What factors determine classroom climate? Why is it important to facilitate a good classroom climate? In this section, we will examine a constructivist rationale and frame-

Organization
- How are students' desks arranged? How is the furniture in the classroom organized?
- Are students free to move about the classroom? Do they sit at their desks?
- Where are materials stored? How are they set up for student use?
- How does the teacher structure the day?
- How many minutes are given to each subject?
- How does the teacher structure a lesson? How are materials introduced and used? What comes first and last?
- What does the teacher do to make a transition between subject areas?
- Is the classroom set up to enhance students' safety? How?

Management Strategies
- What is acceptable student behavior? Who establishes this—the teacher or the students and teacher working together?
- Does the teacher use contracts to establish and reinforce good behavior?
- How does the teacher create a climate for good behavior?
- Does the teacher anticipate problems that might occur and plan for them?

- How are materials distributed?
- How does the teacher deal with disturbances?

B. What do you think an elementary or middle grade classroom should look like? What should be going on in the room? What should the teacher and the students be doing? Imagine looking through a window or a door into a project-based science classroom. Describe your view of a classroom with respect to organization and climate.

C. Compare your views with those of others. How are each of your views similar and different? How might you work with colleagues with differing viewpoints on classroom management? How would you work with a principal or administrator who had different ideas of management?

D. If possible, visit an elementary or middle grade science classroom. Make a video of the classroom and take detailed notes about the climate, organization, and management of the room. How would you characterize the teacher's management style? What is your opinion of the classroom environment?

E. Record your observations in your portfolio.

work for thinking about classroom climate. We consider ideas about establishing a climate in which students solve classroom problems. We also discuss some basic concerns and challenges associated with classroom climate and the responsibilities of the teacher to create an effective classroom climate. We will consider how the teacher must be a role model, select good curriculum, promote a positive attitude toward science, enhance positive affective factors, balance the relationship between student and teacher, and ensure equality. Before we begin to discuss these topics, use Portfolio Activity 10.2 to explore classroom climate.

Your descriptions in Portfolio Activity 10.2 of positive classroom experiences probably included classrooms in which teachers boosted your self-esteem and made you feel important and capable. Your ideas were valued, and you were pushed to try harder, take risks, and think for yourself. The teachers probably had senses of humor and cared about students. They did not favor some students over others and did not discriminate against students based on gender, socioeconomic status, or race. The classroom was a safe haven, and students enjoyed being there. There was a sense of belonging. Lessons were interesting and motivating. The teachers seemed to enjoy teaching the subjects. There were few classroom management and student behavior problems. You probably still think of those teachers as role models.

> **Key Idea**
>
> Climate is affected by a number of factors.

WHAT MAKES A POSITIVE PROJECT-BASED SCIENCE CLASSROOM CLIMATE?

Materials Needed:
- Pencil and paper or a computer

A. Although it may not be comfortable or fun, reflecting on negative classroom experiences in your educational career is an important activity. If you have not had any, good for you. However, it is likely that sometime in your thirteen or more years of formal education you have had some negative experiences—miserable or boring classroom situations that made you uncomfortable; circumstances in which teachers seemed to favor others; and practices that seemed unfair. Think for a while about these negative experiences. What specifically made the classroom climate so unpleasant?

B. Now think about your favorite classes. What specifically made the educational experience pleasant?

C. What would you conclude about developing a positive classroom climate?

D. Record your ideas in your portfolio.

A Constructivist Rationale and Framework for Thinking About Classroom Climate

Key Idea

Teachers in constructivist classrooms focus on helping students reflect on behavior and solve problems together rather than on getting them to comply with specific behaviors.

The work of Alfie Kohn (1996), *Beyond Discipline: From Compliance to Community*, provides a rationale and framework for thinking about climate in a constructivist classroom. Kohn asserts that most unwelcome classroom behaviors can often be traced to the larger classroom context and the curriculum. Kohn argues that many discipline plans try to do things *to* children rather than *with* them and are, therefore, not constructivist in nature. He argues that making students act "appropriately" is not consistent with constructivist classrooms:

> My argument is that the quest to get students to act "appropriately" is curiously reminiscent of the quest to get them to produce the right answers in academic lessons. Thus, the constructivist critique, which says that a right-answer focus doesn't help children become good thinkers, also suggests that a right-behavior focus doesn't help children become good people (p. xv).

Kohn compares a right-behavior focus to a traditional model of teaching:

> This approach is strikingly similar to the traditional model of academic instruction, where information or skills are transmitted to students so they will be able to produce correct answers on demand. For anyone who understands the limits of the "right answer" approach to learning, it can be illuminating to see that classroom management is basically about eliciting the "right behavior." This analogy also may help us to think about what we could be accomplishing instead (p. 66).

Kohn argues that a constructivist classroom with a positive climate is not one characterized by forcing or coercing children to comply with the teacher's demands. Rather, it is one in which students are asked to reflect on what they should do and to solve problems together.

If you asked a group of teachers to think about the long-term goals they have for their students (what they would want students to know, be like, or act like long after they had been their teachers), what would they say? Probably, they would hope that the students would be responsible, caring problem solvers. Most classroom management programs, however, are totally inconsistent with this long-term goal. Kohn (1996) writes, "It is unsettling because it exposes a yawning chasm between what we want and what we are doing, between how we would like students to turn out and how our classrooms and schools actually work" (p. 61). He adds, "No one says, I want my kids to obey authority without question, to be compliant and docile" (p. 61). He argues that there is conflict among our ultimate goals, short-term goals (classroom management), and methods (coercion, threats, punishment, bribes, and so on). In order for there to be cohesion between the goals of a project-based curriculum, which stresses inquiry and collaboration, and classroom management, the management system too must stress inquiry and collaboration.

Creating an Effective Classroom Climate

It takes hard work to establish a positive classroom climate. Creating an effective classroom climate requires a comprehensive effort on the part of the teacher. The teacher must give real choices, be a role model, select curriculum carefully, promote a positive attitude toward science, promote positive affective factors, maintain a balanced teacher-student relationship, and ensure equality.

> **Key Idea**
>
> Children learn to control their behavior when they have real choices.

Giving Real Choices

Real choices help teachers create positive learning communities in which students respect and care about each other (Horsch, Chen, & Nelson, 1999). Kohn (1996) gives several other reasons that students should have real choices:

- People of any age ought to have a say in what happens to them.
- If they have a say, it is more likely that they will do essentially what we want.
- Misbehavior will diminish when children feel less controlled.
- Children are more respectful when their need to make decisions is respected.
- Children become more self-disciplined when given choices.
- Choices help children grow into ethical and compassionate people.

What are **real choices?** Real choices are ones that are not contrived by the teacher. A good way to have students make real decisions in a classroom is to ask them, "What do you think we could do to solve this problem?" The teacher depicted in Scenario 2 asked the students to work out how to play a game on the playground. With this question, students were given a chance to reason through a real problem related to their behavior, analyze possibilities, and negotiate solutions. Asking, "How do you want to line up to come in from recess?" however, does not present a real choice. A real choice would be "Should we line up?" or "How can we best come into the room from the playground?" The question "Do you want to raise your hands during the discussion or do you want to take turns?" does not offer a real choice. Asking, "What do you think would be the best way for us to share our results with minimal problems?" does offer a real choice.

NSES

CONNECTING TO
NATIONAL SCIENCE EDUCATION STANDARDS

Science Education Teaching Standards
Teachers of science design and manage learning environments that provide students with the time, space, and resources needed for learning science. In doing this, teachers engage students in designing the learning environment (p. 43).

Children may not be used to making real choices, however, and a teacher may have to work with them throughout the year to get them ready. For example, at the beginning of the year, students might be asked to select one method from a list of ways to control noise during investigations. Later, the teacher should move students toward making their own list of possibilities. Or a teacher might have students vote on the best way to take turns at the computer. Later, the teacher should move students toward coming to a consensus. Or a teacher might hold a class meeting to discuss ways for students to critique classmates' artifacts without insulting them. Class meetings have been found to be an effective technique for fostering a positive school climate (McEwan-Landau & Gathercoal, 2000). Later, the teacher should move students toward making their own decisions about behavior continually throughout the day.

Being a Role Model

Teachers who are **role models** in a project-based science class exemplify the behavior appropriate for inquiry science. Such teachers seek answers to questions and model how to find these answers. For example, a teacher might say, "Class, I read in the newspaper last night about some people over on Waterford Street who were getting sick from their drinking water. I was wondering if I could find out what was causing the problem. I think I could probably investigate this." The teacher models curiosity and questioning and shows the students how to find answers through reading, conducting investigations, or contacting members of the community. The teacher might say, "You know, I think I could find out what is causing the water problem by reading about water pollution on the Web." The teacher models using technology by logging on to the Internet. Teachers show students that they themselves are members of a learning community. The teacher might say, "I found a lot on the Web, but I don't know where to start to solve this problem. Maybe I need to call someone from the Environmental Protection Agency." Finally, teachers model the sharing of artifacts. The teacher might share with the students a synthesis of articles she found on the Web, notes from her inquiry, and the conclusions she formulated.

Selecting Good Curriculum to Promote Positive Classroom Climate

An essential contributing factor to classroom climate (and the way students behave) is instructional planning. One critical component of instructional planning is the curriculum. Kohn (1996) writes, *"When students are 'off task,' our first response should be to ask, 'What's the task?'"* (p. 19; italics Kohn's). He adds, "If discipline programs studiously refrain from exploring whether an adult's request was reasonable and, more generally, how the environment created by the adult might have contributed to a student's response, their most salient omission must surely be the curriculum. A huge proportion of unwelcome behaviors can be traced to a problem with what students are being asked to learn" (p. 18). The curriculum is often too simple, boring, or too difficult. Students need rich curriculum that extends thinking, elicits curiosity, and helps students answer questions that are important to them (Kohn, 1996,

Key Idea

Good curriculum helps eliminate misbehavior in a classroom.

NSES

**CONNECTING TO
NATIONAL SCIENCE EDUCATION STANDARDS**

Science Education Teaching Standards
Teachers of science plan an inquiry-based science program for their students. In doing this, teachers develop a framework of yearlong and short-term goals for students (p. 30).

p. x). Kohn suggests that we should ask if the curriculum is worth doing, meaningful, and relevant (p. 19). Similarly, Haberman (1995) stresses the importance of using project work with urban children in poverty because project-based work is meaningful and important to their daily lives.

Promoting a Positive Attitude Toward Science

Attitudes are one of the strongest predictors of behavior (Ajzen & Fishbein, 1980; Bandura, 1986; Pajares, 1992), and a teacher's attitude can influence the learning environment (Rutherford & Ahlgren, 1990). It is critical that elementary and middle grade teachers exude a positive attitude toward science. They should enjoy teaching science, give it a substantial amount of time in the curriculum, and encourage students to explore science topics.

A teacher needs to display genuine interest and enjoyment in science by talking about science topics and being excited about teaching the subject. A teacher's enthusiasm about science will rub off on the students. The *National Science Education Standards* (NRC, 1996) stresses that enthusiastic teachers who demonstrate the wonders of science help students develop positive attitudes. Imagine that a third grader is excited about his new pet guinea pig and wants to bring it to school the next day. A teacher who wants to promote a positive attitude toward science will build upon this interest and show excitement about the topic. This could result in a visit from the guinea pig to the classroom or some other type of investigation about pets.

A teacher who wants to promote a positive attitude toward science will also spend time teaching science. Research findings (Nelson, Weiss, & Capper, 1990; Nelson, Weiss, & Conaway, 1992; Weiss, 1978; Weiss, 1987) indicate that science is often the subject that gets the least attention in the elementary curriculum. Elementary teachers must give science equal priority with other subjects. Science cannot be considered a subject that "we'll get to if we have time after everything else has been taught." In the next chapter, we discuss ways that science can be integrated throughout the curriculum and be given sufficient time in the school day.

Finally, a teacher who promotes a positive attitude toward science will encourage students to explore science topics. The third grader who comes to school excited about his new guinea pig might, for example, be encouraged to investigate the types of foods his guinea pig needs and likes. Teachers in a project-based science classroom listen to students, ask questions, and seek information about students' interests so they can encourage science inquiry. Students' ideas and responses help drive instruction in the classroom; the teacher is not the only person who determines the topics and activities.

CONNECTING TO
NATIONAL SCIENCE EDUCATION STANDARDS

Science Education Teaching Standards
Teachers who are enthusiastic, interested, and who speak of the power and beauty of scientific understanding instill in their students some of those same attitudes (p. 37).

Promoting Positive Affective Factors

Affective factors include curiosity, excitement, persistence, enthusiasm, flexibility, skepticism, and open-mindedness. Teachers promote positive affective factors when they themselves display them and when they encourage them in students. Rather than discouraging multiple answers in science and emphasizing a single right answer, a teacher who is fostering open-mindedness will seek more than one solution to a question and encourage students to do the same. Table 10.1 provides a few illustrations of ways to promote positive affective factors. In Portfolio Activity 10.3, you will add to the chart.

Key Idea

Teachers play a critical role in helping build positive attitudes in a science classroom.

Table 10.1

WAYS TO PROMOTE POSITIVE AFFECTIVE FACTORS

Affective Factor	Teacher Strategy
Curiosity about the world	• The teacher shows her own curiosity about what she reads in the paper by talking about it with the students.
Excitement about science	• The teacher brings in science books to read.
Enthusiasm to continue	• The teacher encourages students to keep trying to find an answer by pushing them to find other sources of information.
Ambition to investigate	• The teacher encourages students to ask "Why?" "What if?" and "Could we?" questions.
Sensitivity to others	• The teacher asks, "How could I help you with this problem?"
Disciplined thinking	• The teacher encourages students to analyze potential flaws in their thinking.
Respect for evidence	• The teacher says, "Do you think your conclusion is supported by your data?"
Willingness to change	• The teacher shows that the schedule can change if students are really interested in a topic.
Questioning attitude	• The teacher says, "I wonder if we could find an answer to this question."
Fascination with findings	• The teacher says, "Wow! I didn't realize that. Isn't that interesting!"
Responsibility to project	• The teacher asks students how they should play a role in completing the project.
Skepticism about results	• The teacher says, "You know, I am wondering if this is correct. Do you think we should try it again to see if we get the same results?"
Tolerance for change	• The teacher shows a willingness to change a classroom rule if it isn't working.
Confidence in self	• The teacher encourages a student by saying, "I know you can do this. You are really good at asking questions."
Open-mindedness	• The teacher shows a willingness to accept students' ideas.
Dependability	• The teacher demonstrates that he can be depended upon—for example, he brings something to school that he promised the students.
Independence	• The teacher encourages students to think for themselves.
Self-reliance	• The teacher says, "I think you can do this by yourself."
Willingness to compromise	• The teacher models compromise by saying, "I see your point. Let's compromise."
Willingness to cooperate	• The teacher encourages students to get along with others in the group.
Honesty in artifact	• The teacher stresses that students should be honest—it is not acceptable to lie about data just to create a good artifact.
Objectivity	• The teacher says, "Well, let's wait until we get some more evidence."
Flexibility with ideas	• The teacher encourages students to try different ideas.
Patience with others	• The teacher doesn't get frustrated when a student is having difficulty understanding something.
Precision	• The teacher encourages students to measure things accurately.
Thoroughness	• The teacher stresses thoroughness by asking students to take meticulous notes.
Satisfaction with artifacts	• The teacher tells students they should be proud of their product.
Self-discipline	• The teacher says, "I'm going to put mind over matter and finish this."
Methodicalness	• The teacher models being organized.
Persistence with a task	• The teacher says, "I think you could answer this if you just stick with it a little longer."

Maintaining a Balanced Teacher-Student Relationship

Teachers in a project environment need to maintain a delicate balance between being the ones in charge and being members of the collaborative group. The teacher cannot be too authoritative or the collaboration will be squelched, because students will tend to

Portfolio Activity 10.3   **PROMOTING POSITIVE AFFECTIVE FACTORS**

Materials Needed:
- Pencil and paper or a computer
- Table 10.1

A. Fill in additional ideas in the second column of Table 10.1

B. Meet with members of your class to discuss the ideas that you all came up with. What new ones did classmates think of?

C. How do these affective factors contribute to a positive classroom climate? How do they compare with your memories of positive and negative classroom experiences?

D. Keep these ideas in your portfolio.

look to the teacher for answers rather than collaborating with peers. However, if the teacher is too relaxed, she may fail to achieve basic curricular outcomes required by the school district or state. Teachers in project-based science classrooms need to continually reflect on desired goals and outcomes, daily lessons, students' academic progress, students' skills, and classroom climate. Through this reflection, teachers can analyze where collaboration is succeeding or failing and take steps to sustain it.

A second factor to consider in maintaining a balanced teacher-student relationship is whether students are encouraged to critique the teacher and give suggestions for improving instruction to enhance their learning. Many educators using constructivist theories (Brooks & Brooks, 1993; Taylor, Fraser, & White, 1994) believe that students should have a "voice" in establishing classroom practices. This means sharing some decisions that are made in the class. Sharing decision making with students (such as about class rules, norms, topics to be studied, group arrangements, and methods of assessment) requires a delicate balance between teacher as adult with authority and student autonomy. When this balance is achieved, students are encouraged to take initiative and be autonomous, and the classroom learning environment fosters inquiry.

Teachers also balance teacher-student relationships by using various questioning strategies that encourage students to talk to one another (see Chapter 7 for more information). Not all classroom discourse should be between the students and the teacher. When students interact with each other, the classroom becomes a community of learners. Teachers can also create a positive classroom climate by asking questions that promote creativity, critical thinking, and many different answers. For example, a teacher can ask, "How might we look at this differently?" or "Do you think there might be another way to solve this problem?" This type of climate invites students to take risks without fear of failure.

> **Key Idea**
>
> A safe classroom environment can be created when teachers maintain a balance between teacher and student control.

Ensuring Equality

One essential component of the current national reform efforts in the United States is the premise that *all* students need to be scientifically literate (Rutherford & Ahlgren, 1990; NRC, 1996). Teachers need to believe that all students can learn, and they must treat all

Key Idea

An important factor in creating a positive classroom climate is using equitable classroom practices that help girls, minorities, and special needs children feel comfortable and encouraged in science.

TIMSS

students equitably. Research on equity issues finds, however, that girls and minorities still lag behind their white male counterparts in achievement and interest in science (National Council for Research on Women, 2001).

One way to measure your students' self-images when it comes to science is to have them draw pictures of scientists. The draw-a-scientist activity has been done with many populations of people, and the typical drawing is very stereotyped (Barman, 1996; Boylan, Hill, Wallace, & Wheeler, 1992; Huber & Burton, 1995; Rampal, 1992; Sumrall, 1995). The scientist is usually depicted as a white man who is either bald or has wild, unkempt hair. He is usually wearing a lab coat while working in a laboratory with chemicals and glassware. Often, he is pictured with a sinister look on his face. He wears eyeglasses, and he usually has a pocket protector filled with pens and pencils. Portfolio Activity 10.4 gives you the opportunity to test for yourself science-related self-images.

Although girls start elementary school with similar interests and abilities as boys and overall gender differences in science achievement are decreasing, the gap between high-achieving girls and boys is increasing. Girls do less well. Between 1978 and 1990, boys were the top-scoring students in school (National Council for Research on Women, 2001; Wilson, 1992), and the TIMSS study shows that boys continue to have significantly higher achievement in science literacy than do girls (Schmidt, et. al., 2001; TIMSS, 1998).

Middle class girls now take about the same number of high school math and science courses as do middle class boys. However, in college, these girls are much less apt to major in math, science, or engineering fields than are similarly talented boys. They also drop out at faster rates. Low-income girls have had access to far fewer programs than have middle class girls (National Council for Research on Women, 2001). The end result is that women are still greatly underrepresented in fields like physical science, engineering, and technology (Pollina, 1995). White women and minorities continue to be underrepresented in science and engineering employment (National Council for Research on Women, 2001). Current workforce projections indicate that unless more women and minorities are attracted to science, the United States will not have the trained personnel necessary to meet its needs (National Council for Research on Women, 2001).

A number of different factors have been associated with the gender and racial differences in science. Some studies indicate that girls and women and minorities are socialized to believe that science is for white boys and men (Hardin & Dede, 1992). Television shows and movies that depict scientists as weird "geeks" continue to reinforce this stereotype. Patricia Campbell (1996) suggests that even the news reinforces the stereotype that boys are better than girls in science and mathematics. She writes,

> Research that supports math and science stereotypes gets much more attention in the media than does work that challenges them. For example, when one researcher says boys' higher SAT scores mean that boys are biologically superior to girls in math, she gets invited to the "Today Show" and is written up in *The New York Times*. But when another researcher says that society and test bias cause boys' higher SAT scores, she gets to go home and make dinner. Her results aren't considered news (Campbell, 1996).

Parents may contribute to biases against science. It is not uncommon for parents to expect different behaviors from boys than from girls. Boys often are expected to be tough, play basketball, and be active in outdoor activities, while girls are expected to be soft, play with dolls, and stay neat and clean while playing indoors. Gender-biased toys

Portfolio Activity 10.4 **DRAW A SCIENTIST**

Materials Needed:
- Paper and drawing materials
- The following chart
- A group of students

A. Give children drawing paper and drawing materials and ask them to draw pictures of scientists. Do not give them any other directions.

B. Analyze the students' pictures according to the following list. How many students draw their pictures with these characteristics?

Gender
Male _____
Female _____
Race or Ethnic Background
White _____
Hispanic _____
Asian _____
African American _____
Other _____
Work Environment
Laboratory _____
Office _____
Outdoors _____
Other _____
Personal Characteristics
Frizzy/wild hair _____
Eyeglasses _____
Pocket protector with pens/pencils _____
Bald head _____
Mean or sinister look _____
Other _____

C. Ponder this: In 1957, Margaret Mead and Rhoda Metraux published a report entitled "Image of the Scientist Among High-School Students" in Science (vol. 126, p. 387). They found that

The scientist is a man who wears a white coat and works in a laboratory. He is elderly or middle aged and wears glasses. He is small. He may be bald or may be unshaven or unkempt. He may be stooped or tired. He is surrounded by equipment: test tubes, Bunsen burners, flasks and bottles, a jungle gym of blown glass tubes and weird machines with dials. The sparkling white laboratory is full of sounds: the bubbling of liquids in test tubes and flasks, the squeaks and squeals of laboratory animals, the muttering voice of the scientist. He spends his days doing experiments. He pours chemicals from one test tube into another. He peers aptly through microscopes. He scans the heavens through a telescope (or a microscope!). He experiments with plants and animals, cutting them apart, injecting serum into animals. He writes neatly in black notebooks.

D. Has the image of a scientist changed since 1957? Why do you suppose it has or has not? Why are these images so hard to displace?

E. Where do you suppose these images come from?

F. Who benefits or suffers from the maintenance of these images? What effect do you think these images have on girls' and minorities' career aspirations? What might a classroom teacher do to counter these images?

G. Record your ideas in your portfolio.

still permeate television ads—boys are more likely to be shown playing with erector sets, microscopes, and chemistry sets, while girls are more commonly shown playing with dolls, makeup, and stuffed animals (Hardin & Dede, 1992).

School practices also tend to contribute to gender and racial differences in science. Kahle and Lakes (1983) found that teachers give boys more opportunity to engage in science and math tasks. Teachers speak to boys more often, ask boys more high-level questions, and favor boys' responses (Baker, 1988). They have boys elaborate more on their answers than they do girls and they let boys dominate classroom conversations

Table 10.2	EQUITABLE CLASSROOM PRACTICES

- The teacher helps girls and minorities by making sure that they are provided with challenging activities and that they succeed in the activities.
- Girls and minorities are active participants in the lesson rather than passive observers or recorders of information.
- The teacher has high expectations of all students (for example, he or she doesn't give the girls the answers and expects that they can complete the work in science).
- Girls use manipulative materials in science classes.
- The teacher fosters collaboration so in science girls have equal roles to boys.
- The teacher chooses language carefully (doesn't use male pronouns only to refer to doctors, engineers, or scientists).
- If students are in mixed-gender groups, rules are established to make sure girls have a chance to participate equally with boys.
- The teacher exposes students to women and minority role models in science so that students of both genders and all backgrounds can think of science as a possible career area.
- Girls and minorities are encouraged to do well in science and mathematics (and to take these subjects in school).
- Girls use computers in the classroom as much as their male counterparts do.
- Girls and minorities are involved in science and mathematics competitions (such as MathCounts and Science Olympiad) and extracurricular science and math activities (visiting science museums, participating in science clubs, and reading science journals).
- Girls are called on in class as much as their male counterparts are.
- Girls' answers are elaborated upon (teachers don't simply say, "Okay," and move on).
- The teacher uses interdisciplinary curriculum materials.

(Baker, 1988; Sadker & Sadker, 1992). Finally, Guzzetti and Williams (1996) found that boys dominate laboratory experiences by manipulating lab equipment, and girls are given the job of recording information in journals.

Textbook publishers have made concerted efforts to depict girls and women and minorities doing science, but Bazler and Simonis (1992) found that illustrations, photos, and text of boys and men far outnumber those of girls and women. Further, textbooks portray life science as a female interest and physical science as a male domain (Kahle & Lakes, 1983).

To help develop a project-based science classroom in which girls and minorities feel comfortable with science and are encouraged in science as much as their white male counterparts, teachers need to be cognizant of their curriculum and instructional practices (Lynch, 2000). Table 10.2 illustrates some of these practices (King, Hollins, & Hayman, 1997; Rosser, 1990; Sanders, 1994; Tobias, 1992; Wilson, 1992). In addition, teachers need to be aware of cultural influences on classroom behavior. Garrick-Duhaney (2000) points out that teachers can help prevent discipline problems and promote equitable learning by teaching children about cultural differences and being sensitive to cultural orientations and nuances. In addition, teachers need to create a responsive classroom with a strong sense of classroom community where *all* students are made to feel competent and connected to others in the class.

Portfolio Activity 10.5 will help you think about equitable classroom practices.

Portfolio Activity 10.5 **EQUITABLE CLASSROOM PRACTICES**

Materials Needed:
- A classroom to visit or teach in
- Video recording equipment if you teach the lesson

A. Obtain permission to watch a teacher teaching a science lesson or film yourself teaching a science lesson. Interview the teacher about his or her views about equitable practices in schools or watch the video of your lesson.

B. Analyze the classroom interactions and interview for the following:
- How did the teacher help girls and minorities be successful?
- Were girls and minorities active participants in the lesson rather than passive observers or recorders of information?
- Did the teacher have high expectations of girls and minorities (didn't give them the answers and did expect that they could complete the work in science)?
- Did girls and minorities use manipulative materials?
- Did the teacher foster collaboration so that girls and minorities had equal roles to the boys?
- Did the teacher choose language carefully (didn't use male pronouns exclusively to refer to doctors, engineers, or scientists)?
- If students were in mixed-gender groups, were rules established to make sure girls had a chance to participate equally with boys?
- Did the teacher expose students to women and minority role models in science so that students of both genders and all backgrounds could think of science as a possible career area?
- Were the girls and minorities encouraged to do well in science and mathematics (and to take these subjects in school)?
- Did girls and minorities use computers in the classroom as much as their male counterparts did?
- Were girls and minorities involved in science and mathematics competitions (such as MathCounts and Science Olympiad) and extracurricular science and math activities (visiting science museums, participating in science clubs, reading science journals)?
- Were girls called on in class as much as their male counterparts?
- Were girls' answers elaborated upon (teachers didn't simply say, "Okay," and move on)?
- Did the teacher integrate science throughout the curriculum?

C. Record your ideas in your portfolio.

CLASSROOM ORGANIZATION

Classroom organization is the second major topic of classroom management that we will examine. In this section, we discuss three aspects of **classroom organization**: planning the physical arrangement of a project-based science classroom, structuring the school schedule, and maintaining a safe classroom. In each area, we will consider some practical strategies for dealing with student behavior and maintaining a productive and safe classroom environment. Finally, we will review in each section management tools that can help teachers organize and maintain a project-based science environment.

Arranging the Classroom

In a project-based science environment, the **physical arrangements** of the classroom need to be carefully planned to facilitate student investigation and collaboration and to minimize behavioral problems. To stimulate and encourage students to investigate the world around them, the classroom should offer science attractions for students to observe and manipulate, stimulating materials to read, and computers with telecommunication access. To facilitate investigation, science equipment should be readily available, and there should be areas where students can easily work on different aspects of projects.

Depending on the project, the physical environment will change. For instance, the classroom might be overflowing for several months with plants while students are investigating the effect of fertilizers on plants, but when they are studying pollution, the room might be filled with air and water quality testing equipment. Even though the physical organization of the room continually changes in a project-based science classroom, there are fundamental features that must be maintained.

Most teachers don't have the luxury of determining the size and shape of their classrooms, but teachers usually have a great deal of flexibility to move desks and tables, decorate, and arrange materials. A smoothly running classroom doesn't just happen. Teachers who have effective, productive, stimulating classrooms are very aware of how they have organized students' desks, equipment, and supplies (Haberman, 1995). Evertson and colleagues (1984; 2000) have identified four keys to good physical arrangement of a classroom: (1) keep high traffic areas free of congestion, (2) be sure students can easily be seen by the teacher, (3) keep frequently used teaching materials and student supplies readily accessible, and (4) be certain students can easily see instructional presentations and displays (pp. 4–5).

> ## Key Idea
>
> Classroom organization involves planning the physical arrangement of a project-based science classroom, structuring the school schedule, and maintaining a safe classroom.

Keep High Traffic Areas Free of Congestion

What are **high traffic areas**? These can include but are not limited to doorways, the area around the trash can, the teacher's desk, the area around the pencil sharpener, sinks, bookshelves with literature or encyclopedias, investigation centers, and the drinking fountain. It is best to keep high traffic areas away from each other. Keep aisles wide and clear around these areas so that they are easy to get to. Be aware of maintaining accessibility for wheelchair users or students with mobility problems. All students should be able to reach necessary items during the course of the school day. It is also a good idea to keep quiet areas like reading centers away from the high traffic areas. Classroom pets and aquariums should also be kept away from high traffic areas, because animals can easily become stressed from too much noise or movement around their cages.

When people first start teaching, they often give little attention to the logistics of their rooms and instead arrange things so that they look good, designing and putting up fancy bulletin boards. Although an attractive classroom is certainly part of classroom organization and climate, attractiveness is not the primary consideration; a well-conceived classroom can facilitate learning and help minimize behavior problems. One beginning teacher mistakenly placed a set of encyclopedias near a science learning center where students were supposed to work with magnets. While individual students were working in the science center, other students had to walk past to get encyclopedias from the shelf. Students at the center were continually distracted, often by passersby looking at what they were doing with magnets.

In a project-based classroom, different areas will become high traffic areas at different times, depending on the project. For example, when students are investigating plants, the window area might become a high traffic area, but when students are investigating wheels, they might never go near the windows. Areas that are typically high traffic, regardless of the project, are areas with resources (reference materials, children's literature, and children's magazines), computer areas, areas where laboratory equipment is housed, and office supply areas (where students might obtain construction paper, tape, and glue to construct artifacts). Since students often work at their desks or at tables in collaborative groups in a project-based environment, it is wise to try to arrange sets of desks away from other sets of desks. In this way, one collaborative group will not interfere with another.

Be Sure Students Can Be Seen Easily by the Teacher

Good instruction and good behavior management depend a great deal on teachers' abilities to see all of their students. This is especially true in a project-based science classroom in which students are moving about and collaborating with each other. There is nothing more annoying to a teacher than hearing students talking or misbehaving but not being able to see who they are. To help solve this problem, teachers arrange their classrooms so that they have a clear line of sight to all student desks, bookshelves, learning centers, table areas, and science storage facilities.

One beginning teacher arranged a free-standing literature bookshelf so that the shelf created a private study area where there was a bean bag chair. The bookshelf obstructed the teacher's view of any student sitting in the bean bag chair, making it a prime site for misbehavior.

Project-based science teachers need to be able to see students in order to facilitate discussions, diagnose learning problems, and help students as needed. If teachers cannot see students, they cannot engage them in conversation or notice if they are struggling with reading material, a question, or an activity. In Scenario 4, the teacher sat down to grade papers while the students worked on multiple activities. This is when students became loud and disruptive. Moving about the room to help students, facilitating discussions, or keeping students engaged with prompts and questions will minimize misbehavior. Just being able to see students and the fact that students know they can be seen will go a long way to keeping the classroom running smoothly.

Another important reason for making sure that all areas of the room are visible is that even simple science materials, such as a glass jar, can become dangerous if dropped and broken. Teachers need to be able to keep an eye on students while they are using equipment to make sure they are not in danger of hurting themselves and to respond quickly when accidents happen.

Keep Frequently Used Teaching Materials and Student Supplies Readily Accessible

Keeping often used materials and supplies readily accessible saves time for the teacher and students. When off-task time between activities and lessons is thus curtailed, invitations for students to misbehave are minimized. Frequently used teaching materials include student textbooks, science equipment, and office supplies (rulers, tape, glue, and paper).

Clear shoe boxes and zipper-closure bags make good storage containers for science equipment and supplies. They can be handled easily by students distributing materials, and they make collecting materials easy and fast. Because such storage containers are clear, the teacher and the students can easily see what is inside. They can be stored on shelves or in larger boxes. Rolling carts (the type that libraries use for returned books) make great locations for storing frequently used textbooks, reference materials, and magazines. The movable carts let teachers rearrange their classrooms as needed, and the carts can be moved out of the way when not in use.

In a project-based science classroom, it is useful to have materials for investigations and for making artifacts readily accessible. Keep magnifying lenses and simple

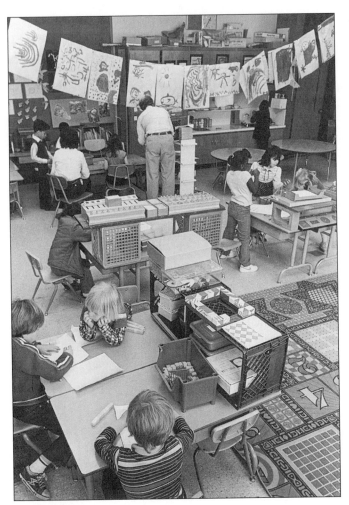

Careful attention to classroom arrangement will facilitate project-based science.

microscopes accessible at all times. This accessibility promotes curiosity and inquiry since it enables students to examine objects at any time of the day. Other objects to keep readily available are measuring cups, measuring spoons, bowls or containers, bug cages, eye droppers or dropper bottles, balance scales, rulers, flashlights, mirrors, and tweezers. Materials that are commonly used to create artifacts include rulers, tape, glue, cardboard, tagboard, paper, stencils, crayons, markers, and construction paper.

Be Certain Students Can See Displays and See and Hear Instructional Presentations

The obvious reason for making presentations and displays accessible and visible is that students need to be able to see them in order to learn. The less obvious reason is that students become bored or frustrated when they can't see what you and the other students are talking about, and boredom and frustration often lead to misbehavior.

Teachers sometimes erroneously blame students for misbehaving during presentations. In one classroom, a teacher was demonstrating a science technique (how to focus a microscope accurately) to approximately twenty-five students. The sole microscope was sitting on a desk in the front of the room where the teacher was demonstrating the techniques for adjusting the stage, adjusting the mirror, moving the knobs, and fine-tuning the view. Since the microscope was placed at the eye level of the students in the first row, the rest of the class could not see what was being demonstrated. Some students in the back began to misbehave, and the teacher became frustrated and angry with them. When students were given the microscopes to use, most did not know how to use them, and the teacher again became angry and frustrated. It did not occur to her that the primary cause of the problem was the position of the microscope.

In Chapter 7, we discussed benchmark lessons. These lessons are designed to teach students basic information or skills they need in order to investigate and answer driving questions. We discussed how benchmark lessons might include demonstrations, discrepant events, presentations (diagrams, pictures, graphs, movies, videos, and television

ARRANGING A CLASSROOM

Table 10.3

KEEP HIGH TRAFFIC AREAS FREE OF CONGESTION
- Arrange high traffic areas away from each other.
- Keep aisles wide and clear.
- Pay attention to accessibility for wheelchair users.
- Make sure students can easily get to and reach necessary items.
- Keep quiet areas away from the high traffic areas.
- Keep classroom pets and aquariums away from high traffic areas.
- Try to arrange sets of desks away from other sets of desks.

BE SURE YOU CAN EASILY SEE STUDENTS
- Arrange the classroom so that you have a clear line of sight to all student desks, bookshelves, learning centers, table areas, and science storage facilities.
- Watch for potential safety problems.

KEEP FREQUENTLY USED TEACHING MATERIALS AND STUDENT SUPPLIES READILY ACCESSIBLE
- Keep student textbooks, science equipment, and office supplies in readily accessible areas.
- Use clear shoe boxes and zipper-closure bags as storage containers.
- Use rolling carts.
- Keep materials used in investigations readily accessible.
- Keep materials used for making artifacts readily accessible.

BE CERTAIN STUDENTS CAN SEE DISPLAYS AND SEE AND HEAR INSTRUCTIONAL PRESENTATIONS
- Make sure that students can easily see and hear presentations and guest speakers, discrepant events, or demonstrations.
- Keep displays where students can see them.
- Position televisions, screens, and monitors so that all students have a clear view.
- Consider height, angle, distance, and glare.
- Make sure hearing impaired students have a clear view of the sign language interpreter.

shows), and guest lectures. Make sure that students can easily see and hear all such presentations and guest speakers. Keep displays such as diagrams, pictures, or graphs in locations where students can see them. Position televisions, screens, and monitors so that all students in the class have a clear view of them. Make sure that students have a clear view and that other students' heads or classroom objects aren't in the way. Make sure that objects to be viewed are positioned at proper distances and heights. Check that glare from overhead lights or the sun doesn't interfere with viewing. In addition, make sure all students can hear the presentation. Particular attention needs to be given to making sure that students who are hearing impaired have a clear view of the teacher or person using sign language.

Table 10.3 presents a summary of key considerations to think about with regard to the physical arrangement of elementary and middle grade science classrooms. In Portfolio Activity 10.6, you will imagine that you are setting up a classroom. Try to think about the aspects of classroom organization just discussed as you design a classroom setting.

Portfolio Activity 10.6

ARRANGING A PROJECT-BASED SCIENCE CLASSROOM

Materials Needed:
- Drawing materials such as pencils, rulers, and compass
- Paper or a computer with a drawing program
- A classroom to observe

A. Using the four principles of good classroom organization you just read about, design a 20-foot by 40-foot classroom so that it contains all of the following items:
- 25 flat-topped (not slanted) student desks
- 25 student chairs
- A 12-foot by 3-foot table
- 10 extra chairs
- A freestanding bookshelf
- A teacher's desk and chair
- A round table with a 5-foot diameter
- A file cabinet
- An overhead projector
- Two computers on carts
- An aquarium with fish
- A cage with gerbils
- Four plants in pots
- A pencil sharpener
- Textbooks

- Student belongings
- The teacher's supplies

Permanent features of the classroom are shown in Figure 10.1.

B. Describe how your classroom organization will facilitate project-based science learning. You may want to review chapters that discussed benchmark lessons, collaborative learning, and other techniques that facilitate learning science.

C. What specific types of learning centers, bulletin boards, and visual displays would you design to interest students in science and promote the development of driving questions and investigations?

D. Visit an elementary or middle grade classroom to determine whether the classroom follows the four guidelines for good organization. If not, what would you do to change it?

E. Record your ideas and file your design in your portfolio.

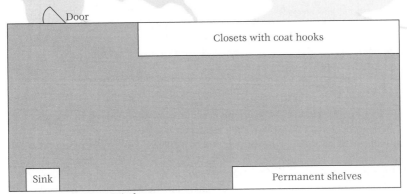

Figure 10.1
Permanent features of classroom.

Structuring the School Day

Although a teacher may not be able to structure the entire school day, given that there are often fixed schedules for art, music, physical education, meetings, and assemblies, a teacher generally has a great deal of flexibility to structure the day within the classroom. The structure of the school day includes the number of minutes a teacher allocates to various subject areas, the delivery of science as a subject (discontinuous and presented as a separate subject or integrated and continuous), and the day's schedule of activities ("set in stone" or flexible). In this section, we will discuss each of these aspects of structuring the school day.

The Number of Minutes Allocated to Subjects

The number of minutes allocated to a subject area is determined by many different factors: the students' knowledge, skills, and abilities; state and local curriculum guidelines; and the driving question being investigated. These factors can sometimes dramatically alter a teacher's preplanned lesson. You might prepare a forty-minute lesson and take only five minutes to teach it. You might prepare a forty-minute lesson and take three days to teach it. The teacher in Scenario 2, for example, was surprised that her lesson took longer than planned. However, while plans always change, it is important to plan, including determining the number of minutes a lesson should last. Without a plan, the day will likely become disorganized and chaotic.

Imagine that a group of first-grade students is investigating the driving question "What animals live in my neighborhood?" Because first graders are only beginning to learn to read, a teacher may spend more minutes teaching reading than teaching science. However, children can practice their reading skills by reading science tradebooks. Because first graders are unlikely to know how to use a magnifying glass or a simple microscope, the teacher will need to spend a great deal of time developing these skills before students can investigate what animals are in a pond, for example.

With experience, allocating amounts of time for particular benchmark lessons becomes easier for teachers. However, because sometimes even the most experienced teacher is fooled about the amount of time needed to cover a topic, develop a skill, or conduct an investigation, good teachers always think ahead to have contingency plans ready. Otherwise, classroom management problems can arise. In anticipation of lessons that go more quickly than expected, it is a good idea to have extra specimens for students to observe, science tradebooks available for students to look at, and computer-based activities or other activity centers set up to which students can move when they are finished with work. The teacher in Scenario 2 had students learn more about the topic of DDT through computer research when they were finished with their work. Table 10.4 lists activities for students to engage in when there is extra time.

Some state and local curriculum guidelines predetermine the number of minutes a teacher must allocate to a given subject area. For example, some schools may tell teachers that they need to spend forty-five minutes a day on reading and writing and thirty minutes a day on science at the first-grade level. Good teachers understand their curriculum thoroughly enough that they can often blend science throughout the curriculum. They do not worry, as a result, about the exact number of minutes they spend on a subject. Martin Haberman (1995), in fact, points out that exemplary teachers working with children in poverty become masters at knowing how to work around "rules" such

Key Idea

The structure of the school day includes the number of minutes a teacher allocates to various subject areas, the delivery of science as a subject (discontinuous and presented as a separate subject or integrated and continuous), and the day's schedule of activities ("set in stone" or flexible).

Table 10.4

WHAT TO DO WHEN THERE'S TIME LEFT OVER

Students might
- Look up related topics in tradebooks;
- Consult the encyclopedia for more information;
- Engage in silent reading for personal enjoyment;
- Use the World Wide Web to find more information on the topic;
- Explore additional examples of the same topic;
- Brainstorm related topics to investigate;
- Design an activity that classmates could participate in;
- Make an entry in a journal or portfolio;
- Make a drawing or model to explain what they learned today;
- Create a quiz for classmates;
- Explore the same topic through a different subject (art, music, mathematics, social studies, language arts, reading, or physical education);
- "Peer tutor" other students in the room;
- Play an educational game; or
- Go to activity centers to explore new topics or ideas.

as time allotments so that their children learn. They realize that a smoothly flowing school day facilitates good classroom management, and a smoothly flowing school day is not always characterized by a specific number of minutes and a schedule set in concrete. Good teachers plan their days so that, ultimately, all subjects are covered and outcomes are reached. For example, on one day a teacher had students read about animals for an hour and plan an investigation for fifteen minutes. The next day, students spent forty-five minutes completing the investigation. Then students spent fifteen minutes working with the teacher to write stories about their investigation. Next, the students *read* their investigation "stories" to others in the class for fifteen minutes. On this second day, then, the class spent forty-five minutes on science and thirty minutes on reading and writing. Over the course of two days, the students spent a total of ninety minutes on reading and writing and sixty minutes on science. This is equivalent to the recommended number of minutes of reading/writing (forty-five minutes per day) and science (thirty minutes per day).

The driving question that is being investigated can dramatically influence the number of minutes allocated to science. The type of project, where the students are in the project, and the level of student motivation are all factors influenced by the driving question. For example, a project that investigates "What animals live in my neighborhood?" may take more time to prepare and finish than a project investigating "What do our classroom pets need to be healthy?" simply because it takes more time to get children ready to go outside, walk outside, investigate, and return to the school to resume other work than it takes to observe a pet eating in a cage in the classroom.

Where the students are in the project will also influence the time spent on different subjects. When students are beginning an investigation, the teacher may need to teach many benchmark science lessons to provide students with the knowledge and skills needed for their investigations. The science investigations themselves take time. As students finish their investigations and begin to make artifacts, the teacher may spend more time teaching writing skills.

Portfolio Activity 10.7

PREPLANNING THE NUMBER OF MINUTES ALLOCATED TO SUBJECTS

Materials Needed:
- Pencil and paper or a computer

A.   Imagine that students in your third-grade class have decided (with your guidance) to investigate the driving question "How can magnets be used around school and home?" Think about the knowledge and skills that third graders would need in order to begin investigating this driving question and make a list of them. Then, think about lessons that might meet these needs and make a list of these as well.

B.   Using these parameters, plan a week's worth of lessons focusing on the amount of time that you think it will take to cover various topics (make sure you include all subject areas: science, mathematics, social studies, and language arts/reading). Use Table 10.5 as your planning grid.

C.   If possible, meet with a practicing classroom teacher to discuss your plans. Are they feasible? Where does the experienced teacher think you need more time and less time?

D.   Find out what guidelines the teacher must follow with regard to the number of minutes per subject area. Does the state or local school district stipulate the number of minutes to allocate to various subjects? What is the teacher's experience with this in his or her classroom?

E.   Record your findings and file your plan in your portfolio.

PLANNING GRID

Table 10.5

Monday	Tuesday	Wednesday	Thursday	Friday
9:00 School starts 11:00–12:00 Art class with art teacher	9:00 School starts	9:00 School starts	9:00 School starts	9:00 School starts
12:00–12:45 Lunch	12:00–12:45 Lunch	12:00–12:45 Lunch 1:00–2:00 Physical education class with PE teacher	12:00–12:45 Lunch	12:00–12:45 Lunch
			2:00–3:00 Music class with music teacher	
3:00 End of day	3:00 End of day	3:00 End of day	3:00 End of day	3:00 End of day

Finally, student motivation will influence the amount of time spent on a topic. One driving question may motivate students so much that it is difficult to get them to stop their investigations. For other driving questions it may be difficult to get students to finish their investigations.

Portfolio Activity 10.7 will work you through planning times for subjects during the school day.

The Delivery of Science as a Subject

You probably discovered in Portfolio Activity 10.7 that the structure of the school day is influenced by how the teacher presents science and other subject areas. If the teacher presents each subject area separately, the school week might look like what is shown in Table 10.6.

In Table 10.6, each subject area is treated separately, and seldom is there a connection among the subject areas. If a teacher presents science as a continuous subject integrated with other subjects, the week will look very different. Imagine a teacher starts out the week by reading a fifteen-minute story about how magnets are used in everyday life. Next, the teacher explains to students that they will need to know something about magnets to explore the driving question "How can magnets be used around school and home?" In a benchmark lesson, the students spend about an hour learning that magnets have a north and a south pole, and they test the poles of the magnet to learn that opposite poles attract and like poles repel. The teacher explains that maps are used in everyday life and that maps have directional arrows on them to indicate north, south, east, and west. The teacher introduces the idea that the earth has a magnetic north that can be identified with a compass. The teacher spends about an hour showing the students how to use a compass. After lunch, the class discusses situations in which maps are used, and they identify objects on a map (such as cities, states, roads, streams, and lakes) using the compass. Finally, the students are given a home assignment requiring them to investigate how magnets are used in their homes.

The next day, students discuss the findings of their home assignment. They begin a portfolio where they gather pictures that illustrate how magnets are used in everyday life. To accompany the pictures, they create descriptions of how the magnets are used. The teacher notices that many of the descriptions in the students' portfolios contain incomplete sentences and lack end punctuation, so he includes a lesson that will teach students about complete sentences and end punctuation. Next, the teacher explains to students that they will be graphing information about magnets and that they may develop artifacts that display information in graph form. The teacher introduces graphing by having students sort objects that stick to a magnet and objects that don't stick to a magnet. Students make a bar graph to display data about the number of objects that attracted or did not attract the magnet. Students make two pie graphs to show what types of items (such as metal, paper, and plastic) attracted or did not attract the magnet.

On the third day, the teacher reviews how to use a compass for finding directions and contrasts this method with using the grids and coordinates on a map. Students practice finding various geographical features and sites on a map of their state. Next, the teacher holds a discussion about how students could use a compass if they were lost and did not have a map. The class goes outside and practices finding various things on the playground using a compass. After lunch, the teacher returns to the driving question "How can magnets be used around school and home?" The students discuss investigations that they might develop to answer this question. One group decides to investigate how a magnet could be used to keep things open or closed. Another group decides to investigate how magnets are used to keep things together. A third group decides to investigate how magnets are used in machines and other technology. A fourth group decides to investigate how magnets are used in hobbies and crafts.

The next day, each group works to come up with subquestions and a preliminary investigation plan. They write down the plans. Table 10.7 shows the groups' plans.

After lunch, the teacher helps students locate resources, supplies, and materials needed to conduct the investigations, and students begin their investigations.

Table 10.6

SAMPLE SCHEDULE

Monday	Tuesday	Wednesday	Thursday	Friday
9:00 School starts 9:00–10:00 *Reading/writing:* Read first chapter of *How to Eat Fried Worms* and discuss.	9:00 School starts 9:00–10:00 *Reading/writing:* Read second chapter of *How to Eat Fried Worms* and discuss.	9:00 School starts 9:00–10:00 *Reading/writing:* Write an opinion piece about whether you would be willing to eat fried worms.	9:00 School starts 9:00–10:00 *Reading/writing:* Read third chapter of *How to Eat Fried Worms* and discuss.	9:00 School starts 9:00–10:00 *Reading/writing:* Read fourth chapter of *How to Eat Fried Worms* and discuss.
10:00–11:00 *Science:* Test whether opposite ends of a magnet attract or repel.	10:00–11:00 *Science:* Use iron filings to see evidence of magnetic fields at the end of a magnet.	10:00–11:00 *Science:* Test what magnets stick to and don't stick to.	10:00–11:00 *Science:* Plan an investigation to see how we use magnets in our daily lives.	10:00–11:00 *Science:* Carry out science investigation.
11:00–12:00 *Art class with art teacher*	11:00–12:00 *Mathematics:* Introduce graphing.	11:00–12:00 *Mathematics:* Make a graph Showing how many students in the class have blue, brown, and green eyes.	11:00–12:00 *Mathematics:* Teach about types of graphs (bar, circle, and line).	11:00–12:00 *Mathematics:* Practice making one of each type of map using student eye color.
12:00–12:45 Lunch 12:45–1:00 Silent reading	12:00–12:45 Lunch 12:45–1:00 Silent reading	12:00–12:45 Lunch 12:45–1:00 Silent reading	12:00–12:45 Lunch 12:45–1:00 Silent reading	12:00–12:45 Lunch 12:45–1:00 Silent reading
1:00–2:00 *Mathematics:* Finish lesson on adding two-digit numbers and give end-of-chapter test.	1:00–2:00 *Social studies:* Introduce symbols on a map (keys, north, south, east, west).	1:00–2:00 *Physical education class with PE teacher*	1:00–2:00 *Social studies:* Learn about geographical features on maps and identify key features in state.	1:00–2:00 *Social studies:* Make a map of the neighborhood, including directional key and geographical features.
2:00–3:00 *Social studies:* Discuss how maps are used in everyday life. Examine a map.	2:00–3:00 *Health:* Introduce lesson on nutrition and food pyramid.	2:00–3:00 *Social studies:* Look at a map of the United States and locate regions based on directional keys.	2:00–3:00 *Music class with music teacher*	2:00–3:00 *Reading:* Write a summary of chapters read in *How to Eat Fried Worms*
3:00 End of day	3:00 End of day	3:00 End of day	3:00 End of day	3:00 End of day

Table 10.7

PRELIMINARY INVESTIGATION PLANS

GROUP 1: HOW CAN MAGNETS OPEN OR CLOSE THINGS?
Plan: Using magnets of various sizes and shapes, investigate how magnets can open and close things (such as doors, boxes, bags, and folders). Find out if magnets are used this way in real life.

GROUP 2: HOW CAN MAGNETS KEEP THINGS TOGETHER?
Plan: Using one magnet, test things that can be kept together (such as papers, books, bags, and clothing). Find out if magnets are used this way in real life.

GROUP 3: HOW ARE MAGNETS USED IN MACHINES OR OTHER TECHNOLOGY?
Plan: Get on the Internet and find out more about uses of magnets. Call an expert who uses machines. Take apart old, broken machines and computers.

GROUP 4: HOW ARE MAGNETS USED IN HOBBIES OR CRAFTS?
Plan: Visit a hobby or crafts store. Invite to class a parent who makes crafts. Try making a useful object out of magnets.

On Friday, the morning begins with students continuing their investigations. The teacher notices that one group is having difficulty adding up a list of numbers of machines found that use magnets. This prompts him to take some time to teach a lesson about adding two-digit numbers. After the lesson, students are ready to continue with their investigation.

After lunch, the teacher shows the students how to summarize information using a chart. At the tops of the charts, students write down statements that reflect the topics of their investigations. In the charts, they list all the things they found. Students use the topics at the tops of the charts to form the topic sentences of their summaries, and they use the items in the charts to make supporting sentences. The teacher has students summarize in writing what they have done so far in their investigations. Students share their summaries with classmates and discuss what else they will need to do to answer the driving question.

In a project-based science classroom, teachers are more likely to structure the school day in the integrated manner discussed in this second example. The delivery of science content in this example is continuous and integrated across the other subject areas. Connections are made for students to show them how benchmark lessons fit with the driving question. For example, when students learn to graph, they understand that they need this skill in order to present information in their artifacts. When they learn about compasses, they know that they need this information to understand how some machines use magnets. Teachers who present science (and other subject areas) as separate entities run the risk that students won't see the relationships between knowledge and skills or transfer understanding and skills to new situations.

NSES

CONNECTING TO
NATIONAL SCIENCE EDUCATION STANDARDS

Science Education Teaching Standards
Teachers of science actively participate in the ongoing planning and development of the school science program. In doing this, teachers participate in decisions concerning the allocation of time and other resources to the science program (p. 51).

The Day's Schedule of Activities

Although planned, the daily schedule in an elementary project-based science classroom is **flexible**. In *some* middle schools organized around large blocks of time, the teacher has a great deal of flexibility, but in other middle schools, students switch classes every fifty minutes, and so the day is much less flexible. Regardless of the flexibility of school organizational structure, good teachers understand that they must be flexible, that some activities take more time or less time than anticipated, and that they must be willing to alter the day's schedule accordingly.

For example, the teacher may never get to the benchmark lesson on reading a compass on Monday because students' investigations take a different focus. These types of changes are expected and welcomed in a project environment. If it is necessary to teach the lesson on reading a compass, the teacher will introduce it on another day.

Because project-based science does not focus on correct answers, frequently there are multiple answers to a question. Therefore, lessons and activities evolve and flow with students' findings. Because learning is student directed, not all activities and lessons can be planned exactly as they will be executed. Imagine that students discover that magnets can be used to hold things (such as holding the lid of a can on a can opener) as well as close things (such as the door of a refrigerator). This discovery motivates students to invent a lunch box that can be opened and closed with a magnet. Although the hours needed to test this idea were not in the original plans, the teacher lets students complete the activity. It may even lead to a new benchmark lesson that she did not originally consider. For example, she may need to introduce a benchmark lesson on magnetic poles in magnets of different shapes—the poles of a bar magnet are on the ends, whereas the poles of a circular magnet are on opposite sides. Students may need this information if they opt to use a round magnet to open or close the lunch box.

Table 10.8 presents some key ideas to remember about structuring the school day. Portfolio Activity 10.8 asks you to study a teacher's schedule and plans and observe how much they change.

Maintaining a Safe Classroom

Because students in a project-based science classroom are self-directed, they share a role in developing activities, locating resources, and conducting investigations. They frequently move about the room to collaborate with others, work on a computer, or engage in an activity. Often, different groups of students investigate different subquestions. All of this activity raises unique **safety** concerns.

In general, teachers need to be aware of school district policies on all safety-related issues. For example, does the school have a policy about having animals in the classroom or the use of chemicals in a science class? Is there a policy on administering first aid? Who is supposed to be notified in case of an accident or injury? How are field trips arranged, and what are the legal liabilities?

In this section, we will discuss several issues related to maintaining a safe classroom. These include working with animals and plants in the classroom; planning for

Key Idea

To create a safe classroom, teachers pay careful attention to working with animals and plants in the classroom; plan for safe use of equipment and materials; deal with fire and glassware; plan safe field trips; and are ready to administer first aid.

NSES

CONNECTING TO
NATIONAL SCIENCE EDUCATION STANDARDS

Science Education Teaching Standards
Teachers of science design and manage learning environments that provide students with the time, space, and resources needed for learning science. In doing this, teachers ensure a safe working environment (p. 43).

Portfolio Activity 10.8   SCHEDULING

Materials Needed:
- Pencil and paper or a tape recorder
- One to three teachers to interview

A. Find a teacher to interview on a Monday of a week. Discuss with the teacher his or her lesson plans for the week. Interview the teacher again on Friday of the week. How did the teacher's schedule change? Why? What implications does this have for teaching in a project-based environment?

B. If possible locate two more teachers—one who integrates science across the curriculum and one who teaches each subject area separately. How does the delivery of science (integrated versus separate) affect the schedule?

C. Record your findings in your portfolio.

Table 10.8   STRUCTURING THE SCHOOL DAY

NUMBER OF MINUTES ALLOCATED TO SUBJECTS
- Preplan the number of minutes needed for a subject.
- Preplan the number of minutes a lesson will last.
- Have activities ready for situations in which too much time is left over.
- Become thoroughly aware of the curriculum so you know how to blend science throughout it.
- Don't worry about the exact number of minutes actually spent on a subject or lesson.
- Be concerned with meeting curriculum goals and lesson objectives.

---

safe use of equipment and materials; dealing with fire and glassware; planning safe field trips; and being prepared to administer first aid. At the end of the section is a checklist to assist you in planning for a safe classroom.

Animals and Plants in the Classroom

Many teachers like to have animals and plants in the classroom. Not only are living things motivating for students (they might lead to driving questions), but they are needed in some investigations. However, there are a number of considerations involved in bringing plants and animals into the classroom.

It is essential that animals be healthy and well cared for and that they not harm the students in the class by biting, scratching, or passing on a disease. The National Science Teachers Association handbook on safety in the elementary classroom (Dean, Dean, Gerlovich, & Spiglanin, 1993) suggests that several rules be adopted regarding animals in the classroom:

- Don't let students bring in live or deceased wild animals, snapping turtles, snakes, insects, or arachnids that might be carrying a disease.
- Make sure animals are housed properly: in clean and securely closed cages.

- Purchase animals from reputable stores or supply houses. Carolina Biological Supply Company (2700 York Road, Burlington, NC 27215; 1-800-334-5551) is one of the most-used suppliers of live animals and specimens for science classes. Other suppliers and resources can be found on the National Science Teachers Association Web page.

Animal Supply Companies

- If students bring personal pets to school as part of a class activity, make sure that the pets have proper housing during the day and that strangers don't handle them because they may become frightened and bite or scratch and because it may injure them.
- Don't let students pick up or touch unfamiliar animals—even if they are other students' pets.
- Don't allow students to tease or poke at an animal in a cage, even if their intention is only to wake up a sleeping animal and not to hurt it.
- Teach students how to properly pick up different animals. For example, a rabbit should be picked up by the scruff of the neck. Make sure students wear gloves when picking up most animals and always wash their hands after handling animals.
- Familiarize yourself with the necessary care for and best way to handle the animals in your classroom. Check local libraries for books or call a local zoo or veterinarian for more information.

Some plants can be toxic (even fatal) to students. The National Science Teachers Association (Dean, Dean, Gerlovich, & Spiglanin, 1993) provides several guidelines for using plants safely in the classroom:

- Teach students not to put plants in their mouth.
- If students are handling plants, have them wash their hands after the investigation so that sap or juice doesn't remain on their skin. Make sure they wash their hands before eating any food.
- Don't let students inhale smoke from any burning plant or pick any unknown flowers, seeds, or plants, because some fumes or toxins can be very dangerous. For example, poison sumac and poison oak are poisonous to the skin, and foxglove or jimson weed are poisonous when eaten.

Equipment and Materials

Teachers should wear and require students to wear goggles to protect their eyes against impact or contact with liquids or fumes. Even simple activities such as burning a candle, working with a mild acid like vinegar, or melting sugar in a test tube have the potential to cause eye damage or irritation. Classrooms should have sets of safety goggles, and teachers need to teach students how to use them. Goggles should always be cleaned after each use, because eye diseases, such as conjunctivitis, are very contagious. Some activities involve blindfolding students. Once a blindfold has been used, it should not be used on another student.

Safety Precautions

Safety shields can protect students during demonstrations. For example, if you are conducting a benchmark lesson in which you demonstrate that hot air expands by heating a test tube with a cork in it, you should use a safety shield since the cork will pop out (and sometimes fly out) of the test tube.

Students in a project-based classroom are active participants in designing and carrying out investigations. This means that they may gather their own materials and supplies. Improperly stored materials are invitations for accidents. Make sure that the area where materials and supplies are stored has plenty of space, or limit the number of students allowed into the area. Make sure that the place where you store equipment and supplies has adequate shelving that is sturdy, deep enough so items don't easily fall off, and secured to a wall or floor so that it cannot tip over on students. Chemicals and glassware should be stored only on lower shelves so they are easy to get to. Keep supplies in small jars so that students can handle them easily. For example, rather than having students pour vinegar from a gallon jug, keep small dropper bottles of vinegar available for student use. Although the typical elementary classroom does not have many (if any) volatile liquids and acids, some middle school or junior high classrooms have these items. A popular middle grade life science book on the market uses nitric acid in one of its protein activities. Do not store volatile items together, near heat sources, or near electricity, and keep these items in locked storage areas. Finally, make sure all items are labeled, and keep handy a quick reference on precautions, antidotes, and proper disposal.

Always be vigilant when students are using electricity. During one teacher's first year of teaching, students were investigating batteries and bulbs (using size D dry cells, bell wire, and flashlight bulbs). She asked the students to figure out a way to make the bulb brighter (intended to be done by adding more batteries or using a different wattage flashlight bulb), and a student headed toward a wall outlet to plug in his little electrical setup. Fortunately, she caught the student before he got there and injured himself. Many elementary teachers let students connect too many batteries in a series circuit. The uninsulated wire in the overloaded circuit gets very hot, burning the students. Instruct children how to use electrical devices. Teach them not to touch items (such as hot plates) right after they have been turned off, because they will usually still be hot. Teach them to unplug electrical objects by pulling on the plug rather than the wire. Avoid using electrical extension cords because they can be overloaded or students can easily trip over them in the classroom. Be very careful when using any small electrical device such as a hot plate, small motor, fish aquarium pump, or fan so that students' hands or clothing don't come in contact with a hot surface or fast-moving part.

Fire

Many elementary teachers do not let students use fire in the classroom, but some middle schools and junior high schools use Bunsen burners, Sterno cans, matches, or other sources of flame. Teachers and students should know where fire alarms are positioned in a building and be aware of the quickest fire escape from the room. Accidental fires in a classroom often happen when clothing or hair come too close to an open flame. All classrooms should be equipped with fire extinguishers and fire blankets. There are different types of fire extinguishers (for electrical fire, flammable liquids, and so on), so most schools like to use multipurpose ABC fire extinguishers.

Glassware

Glassware presents particular problems in any classroom, but it is of great concern in an elementary classroom. Teachers need to think carefully about using glass jars, mirrors, thermometers, and prisms. Many teachers use glass only if it is absolutely necessary and a plastic alternative will not work. If glass is used, make sure that any sharp edges (such

> ### Key Idea
>
> Be careful when using an open fire and glassware in a classroom.

as on mirrors or prisms) are taped, painted, or ground smooth. If students are going to put glass tubing into a rubber or cork stopper, make sure that they use a lubricant and that they do not put the glass tubing into the palms of their hands to press into the stoppers (Dean, Dean, Gerlovich, & Spiglanin, 1993).

Field Trips

Field trips are valuable in a project-based environment because they link the driving question and investigation to a broader community and the world outside of school. In fact, Haberman (1995) points out that exemplary teachers working with urban children and children of poverty use field trips and community resources much more frequently than unsuccessful teachers do. However, there are a number of precautions that should be taken when going on field trips. The National Science Teachers Association (Dean, Dean, Gerlovich, & Spiglanin, 1993) provides several tips:

- Don't take anything for granted on the trip.
- Bring along a second adult approved by the school administration.
- Obtain parent permission before taking students away from school.
- Alert parents about proper clothing or supplies needed for the trip. For example, ask students to wear long-sleeve clothing if they will be outside and could come in contact with ticks or be scratched by branches.
- Always bring along a first aid kit on a field trip in case something happens to a student while away from the school building. Many teachers also bring along cell phones in case they need to make an emergency phone call for help.
- Take special precautions for any field trip near a body of water, a stream, or a river. Become familiar with animals or plants near or in the water. Use a "buddy system" if students are actually in the water. Learn CPR.
- If taking a field trip to a factory, laboratory, or business, make sure that the trip is well supervised and that someone from the site conducts the field trip. On-site guides will be the most familiar with potential danger areas for students and can alert participants to situations in which more caution is needed.

Additional information about field trips and community connections can be found in Robertson, W. C. 2001. *Community connections for science education*. Arlington, Va.: NSTA Press.

First Aid

First aid is meant primarily to protect, not treat. The American National Red Cross is the best source of information for first aid procedures for staying calm, restoring breathing, stopping bleeding, and preventing shock, so we won't go into first aid procedures here. Become familiar with first aid procedures in case anything happens in the classroom or on field trips.

American Red Cross

Safe Lessons

As a regular part of any lesson, teachers should think about potential safety precautions before beginning to teach. The checklist in Table 10.9 (modified from Dean, Dean, Gerlovich, & Spiglanin, 1993) summarizes safety considerations and provides some guidelines for planning and teaching on a daily basis with safety in mind. Portfolio Activity 10.9 will work you through a safety audit of a classroom.

Table 10.9

PLANNING SAFE LESSONS

Questions to Ask Regarding General Safety Concerns	Answers
1. Do you have a copy of the federal, state, and local regulations that relate to school safety as well as a copy of your school district's policies and procedures?	_____
2. Check your classroom. Are equipment and materials properly stored (in the right types of cabinets for chemicals, on sturdy shelving that won't tip over, and on deep shelving so that items won't fall off of easily)?	_____
3. Are you familiar with possible hazards involved in using the equipment and materials in your room?	_____
4. Do you know your school's policies and procedures in case of accidents?	_____
5. At the start of each science activity, do you instruct students regarding potential hazards and precautions?	_____
6. Is the number of students working together on an experiment limited to a number that can safely perform the experiment without causing confusion and accidents?	_____
7. Do students have sufficient time to perform the experiments and clean up and properly store the equipment and materials after use?	_____
8. Do you instruct students not to taste substances? Do you instruct students not to touch substances without first obtaining specific instructions from you?	_____
9. Are your students aware that all accidents or injuries—no matter how small—should be reported to you immediately?	_____
10. Do you instruct your students that it is unsafe to touch the face, mouth, eyes, and other parts of the body while they are working with plants, animals, or chemical substances and afterwards, until they have washed their hands and cleaned their nails?	_____
11. Does your classroom have safety goggles and a first aid kit? Do you know how to use these items? Do students use the safety goggles? Are the goggles cleaned and disinfected after each use?	_____
12. Are materials and supplies that students use stored in an area with plenty of space to avoid accidental collisions among students?	_____

Questions to Ask Regarding Safe Use of Chemicals	Answers
1. Have you taught students that they must not mix chemicals "just to see what happens"?	_____
2. Have you taught students to never taste chemicals and to wash their hands after use?	_____
3. Do you forbid students from mixing acid and water?	_____
4. Do you keep combustible materials in a metal cabinet equipped with a lock?	_____
5. Do you store chemicals under separate lock in a cool, dry place but not in a refrigerator?	_____
6. Do you store only a minimum amount of chemicals in the classroom? Do you give students only small amounts of materials to work with (such as a dropper bottle of vinegar rather than a gallon jug)?	_____
7. Do you properly discard chemicals not used in a given period?	_____
8. Are all chemicals labeled?	_____
9. Do you keep handy a quick reference for precautions, antidotes, and proper disposal of all chemicals?	_____

Questions to Ask Regarding Glassware	Answers
1. Do you use plastic instead of glass when possible?	_____
2. Do students know how to use glassware? (For example, do they know how to insert glass tubing into a rubber stopper and how to heat hard glass test tubes—not from the bottom but tipped slightly and not in the direction of another student?)	_____

Table 10.9

(CONCLUDED)

Questions to Ask Regarding Glassware *(continued)*	Answers
3. Are a whisk broom and dust pan available for sweeping up pieces of broken glass?	_____
4. Are students aware that they should not drink from glassware used for science experiments?	_____
5. Are thermometers for use in the classroom filled with alcohol, not mercury?	_____

Questions to Ask Regarding Electricity	Answers
1. Are your students taught safety precautions for the use of electricity in all situations (not to touch an item recently turned off, not to pull out an electrical appliance using the cord, to keep fingers and clothing away from moving parts)?	_____
2. Have you told students not to experiment with the electric current of home circuits?	_____
3. Are you allowed to use extension cords in your building? Are they in good condition and plugged into the nearest outlet (so they won't cause a short circuit)?	_____
4. Are students' hands dry when they touch electrical cords, switches, or appliances?	_____

Questions to Ask Regarding Fire	Answers
1. Do you know your school's fire regulations and evacuation procedures and the location of and use of fire-fighting equipment?	_____
2. Does your room have an ABC fire extinguisher and a fire blanket? Do you know how to use them?	_____
3. What extra cautions do you take when dealing with fire? What special instructions do you give students? Could you use a hot plate instead of fire?	_____

Questions to Ask Regarding Plants and Animals	Answers
1. Are the animals healthy, well cared for, and in a suitable habitat?	_____
2. Are your students aware that they are not allowed to bring live or deceased wild animals into the classroom?	_____
3. Do you buy animals only from reputable stores or supply houses?	_____
4. Do you instruct students not to pick up unfamiliar animals? Do they know not to poke at an animal in a cage?	_____
5. Do you and your students know how to properly care for an animal and how to pick it up?	_____
6. Are your students aware that they should never put a plant into their mouths?	_____
7. Do students wash their hands after touching plants and animals?	_____
8. Do you forbid students from inhaling smoke from a plant or picking up an unknown plant, flower, or seed?	_____

Questions to Ask Regarding Field Trips	Answers
1. Are you thoroughly familiar with a field trip location before you take students there?	_____
2. Do you have extra adult supervision for a trip?	_____
3. Are your field trips approved by the proper school administration?	_____
4. Do you secure written parent permission for taking students on a trip?	_____
5. Are the students aware of proper clothing or supplies needed for a trip?	_____
6. Do you have a first aid kit to take with you? Is a cellular telephone available to take with you?	_____
7. Do you have a "buddy system" set up for students?	_____
8. Do you have students' home phone numbers, medical records, and medications before leaving school?	_____

Portfolio Activity 10.9   **CONDUCTING A SAFETY AUDIT**

Materials Needed:
- A copy of Table 10.9
- Permission to conduct a safety audit of a classroom

A. Obtain permission from proper school personnel (such as the principal and teacher) to conduct a safety audit of a classroom.

B. Study the features of the classroom. Observe a science lesson.

C. Audit the school and classroom for the safety concerns listed in Table 10.9. What recommendations would you make to the teacher or school to improve safety?

D. Record your recommendations in your portfolio.

MANAGEMENT STRATEGIES

Management strategies are the third major management concern and challenge that we will discuss. In this section, we will focus on three stages of **classroom management**: before instruction, during instruction, and after instruction. All management strategies are used to help develop welcoming classroom learning communities where students can learn effectively.

Before Instruction

Key Idea
Before instruction starts, it is important to establish norms for the classroom, create an atmosphere for fostering positive behavior, set up contracts, and anticipate possible problems before they occur.

Teachers need to take several steps before starting any classroom lesson in order to ensure a smoothly running classroom. First, teachers must establish classroom norms about what is acceptable behavior. Second, they must establish an atmosphere that fosters "good" behavior. Third, they must set up agreements, or contracts, with students to define objectives, choices, and consequences of behavior. Fourth, they must anticipate problems before they happen.

Establishing Norms for Acceptable Student Behavior

In order to establish acceptable student behavior, many teachers begin a school year by setting general class rules and ground rules for behavior during different types of lessons (such as investigations, reading time, or computer sessions). As discussed earlier in this chapter, an important question to ponder when setting rules is whether the teacher should determine acceptable classroom norms or whether the teacher should involve students in the development of those **norms**.

Kamii (1984, 1991) and Kamii, Clark, and Dominick (1994) argue that children need to invent ethical meanings. Katz (1984) suggests that getting children to comply with rules does not develop the primary goal of generating good children. What does is giving children choices and helping children learn for themselves in a caring classroom community. Haberman (1995) stresses that children in poverty quickly learn to rebel against mandates for compliance. In other words, teachers need to move beyond simply enforcing rules. Kohn (1996) writes that it is far better to ask children to create rules—but even this strategy is not constructivist as students might come up with only the rules they think the teacher wants to hear or that they recall from previous years. He argues that it is better to get students to solve problems and engage them in discussion about what they want their class to be like. Kohn writes, "The construction of meaning is an active process. It can't be done unless the learner has substantial power to make decisions. . . . If we are talking about learning to be a responsible, caring person, then the decisions include how to solve problems and get along with others" (p. 78).

Although the answer to the question of who should determine the rules may, in part, be determined by the age level of the students, rules tend to be easier to enforce if students in the class helped create them. When students have some ownership over the classroom environment, they are invested in making it work. In addition, when students help generate rules, they understand them better because they put them in the language that they use and that has meaning for them. For example, a word like *vom*, while meaningless to the teacher, may be considered offensive by students and need to be put on the unacceptable language list.

To set general **classroom rules**, many teachers engage students in discussion about what their classroom should be like and what classroom rules might be established to make the classroom this way. Even very young students have experiences that help them accomplish this task. Frequently, students will come up with rules such as "treat others with respect," "be fair to others," "no hitting," and "no cheating." Many teachers post these rules on a chart in a prominent place in the classroom.

A well-managed classroom is planned and designed in advance.

Having students create classroom rules may sound easy, but it is not always. Children may not be used to making decisions about their behavior, and they may act out during the transition period. They might "test" you to see if you are really going to let them have choices. You might experience outright resistance. Some children might be silent and not attempt to solve classroom problems. Children may just "parrot" what they think you want to hear. To solve some of these transition problems, you can try several strategies:

- Try going slower; children may be overwhelmed with choices.
- Let students make some "bad" decisions and rules (as long as they are not emotionally or physically dangerous) and let them analyze and reflect on whether they are working. For example, if students say there is no reason to write their names on their papers, you might go along with this for a while. If students don't quickly decide to change this rule, then approach them to help you solve the problem of not knowing who to give what grades to for written work.
- If students refuse to participate, saying it is your job to make the rules, reassure them that you will still make some rules, but that you can make some rules together.

Portfolio Activity 10.10   **ESTABLISHING GROUND RULES**

Materials Needed:
- Table 10.10

A. Table 10.10 shows at least one ground rule that might be established during each phase of a project. Think about additional ground rules that might be established during each phase. List them in the third column.

B. Discuss your ideas with classmates or a practicing teacher. How did your ground rules differ from the ideas of others?

C. If possible, visit an elementary or middle grade classroom and discuss these ideas with students. What types of ground rules do students devise to answer the questions about project-based activities?

D. Record your findings in your portfolio.

- Find out why students are silent when it comes to making rules. Are they shy? Do they feel safe? The reason will determine your approach.
- If students are only parroting answers, push them to defend the answers they give. Ask, "Why is it important?" "What does it mean?" "Does everyone agree?" (Kohn, 1996, pp. 96–97).

Although these general rules are important for any classroom, there are some **ground rules** specific to a project-based science classroom. These ground rules establish acceptable student behavior during various aspects of project activities. For example, teachers might want students to be quiet when they are reading but lively when critiquing each other's ideas. Table 10.10 illustrates some aspects of project-based science instruction for which specific rules might be needed. You can use the table with students to establish ground rules. It can also be used to communicate with parents about your expectations. Many teachers find the table most helpful before the start of a specific activity.

The teacher in Scenario 2 established rules before taking students outdoors to play a game. Another important time for establishing ground rules is when students are brainstorming ideas for a driving question. Before brainstorming, the teacher draws three columns on the board: *Activity, Questions,* and *Ground Rules.* Then the teacher might engage students in a discussion about the ground rules that need to be in place during the brainstorming activity. The resulting ground rules can be posted in the classroom and referred to at a later time.

Portfolio Activity 10.10 will work you through the process of establishing ground rules.

Another useful technique for establishing acceptable student behavior is filling in a behavior tree. A **behavior tree** is a diagram in which the teacher and students establish the goals that need to be met during a specific activity and set ground rules that need to be followed to meet the goals. The behavior tree focuses students' attention on behavior needed for a specific task or activity. The behavior tree in Figure 10.2 illustrates acceptable behavior during an acid rain activity. The teacher might say to the class, "Boys and girls, this afternoon we are going to be testing different samples of acid rain. You will be

Table 10.10

ACTIVITIES AND RELATED GROUND RULES

Project-Based Activity	Questions to Ponder	Resulting Ground Rules
Brainstorming ideas for driving questions	How can we brainstorm ideas without getting off track?	Keep to the topic.
	How can we brainstorm and not hinder good ideas?	Don't put down people's ideas.
	How can we value all students' ideas?	
Collaboration with others	How can we make sure all people participate?	Make sure everyone has a job to do in the group.
	How can we keep one person from taking over?	
	How can we make sure there aren't "loafers" in the group?	
	What voice level is acceptable?	
Critiquing each other's ideas	How can we make sure we don't insult someone?	Say good things about the project first.
	How can we nicely help someone make his or her project better?	
Investigations	How can we safely use science equipment?	Don't run with science equipment.
	How can we make sure we are exploring an idea fully?	
	How can we make sure all students help with the investigation?	
	Can we move around the classroom?	
	Can we get our own equipment or must the teacher get it for us?	
Working on the computer	How do we find only information that is related to our topic?	Let everyone in our group conduct one search on a topic.
	How do we use the computer safely?	
	How does everyone get a chance to use the computer?	
Demonstrations or guest speaker visits	How do we treat a guest speaker?	Don't talk when someone else is talking to the class.
	What is important to do during a demonstration?	
	How do we sit and listen respectfully?	
Field trips	How do we behave in public?	Make our community proud of kids at our school.
Making artifacts	How can we make sure that all students' ideas are used in the artifact?	Keep a list of each person's contribution or idea.
	What amount of noise is acceptable?	We should use talking voices.
Sharing artifacts	How do we give people new ideas without insulting them?	Say, "I like your idea, but did your group consider . . . ?

working in groups. What are some goals we have been working on as a class that might apply to group work during an investigation?" Students might respond, "Recording information accurately, completing the task, and giving everyone a chance to work." The

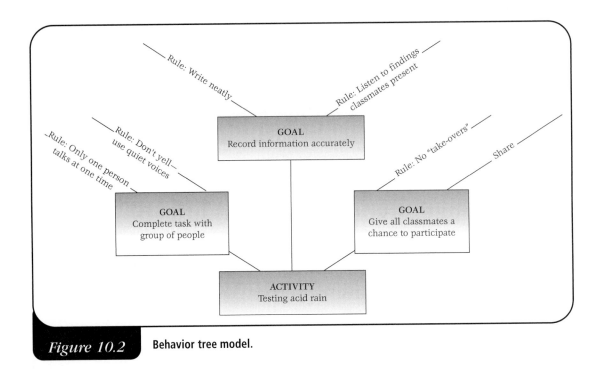

Figure 10.2   Behavior tree model.

teacher would record these three goals on the behavior tree, and students would generate the rules they believe applied to the desired goals.

Establishing an Atmosphere That Fosters "Good" Behavior

After classroom rules and ground rules for behavior during different situations have been
set, an **atmosphere** that encourages the desired behaviors must be established. Helping
students learn the required behaviors and norms often requires support. Also, many successful teachers encourage proper behavior by modeling it themselves. The teacher in
Scenario 2 at the beginning of this chapter modeled for students how to come into the
building quietly after being outdoors. Students are quick to notice when teachers say one
thing but do another. For example, when a teacher sits in a corner grading papers while
students are working on their investigations, as in Scenario 4 at the beginning of this
chapter, the message to students is that the teacher is not interested in what they are
doing. In addition, when teachers are grading papers, they cannot help students think
through questions, design investigations, and find resources; facilitate collaboration
among students; and help students develop artifacts. Some teachers give lectures about
wearing goggles during investigations and fail to wear them themselves or insist that students be quiet when working but talk loudly with a colleague who walks by the room.

In addition to supporting learning about behavior and modeling classroom behaviors, teachers must reinforce good behavior. This **reinforcement** does not consist of
tangible rewards like stickers, points for free time, or certificates to local fast-food restau-
rants. Kohn (1996) argues that tangible rewards only accomplish temporary compliance,
and they do nothing to help a child become kind or caring. He says that **rewards** also

warp the relationship between student and teacher, because they don't create a caring alliance based on warmth and respect. Successful reinforcement consists instead of praise and especially recognition. Haberman (1995) notes that exemplary teachers working with children in poverty consistently reward and recognize *effort* more than right answers or achievement. Similarly, Campbell (1999) notes that teachers should promote collaboration over competition and improvement over ability. Students appreciate and respond well to the recognition of teachers, peers, and community members. A personalized note (that goes beyond a one-word comment like "good") by the teacher in a student's portfolio or a positive letter home to a student's parent(s) is very rewarding for most students. Having the results of a project published in the school or town newspaper, receiving a personal letter from a member of the community complimenting students' work, or hearing comments from peers about how a student's ideas helped the group complete a project are all effective forms of recognition that reinforce positive behavior. So are simple comments from the teacher that indicate that she is noticing a student's efforts. It is very easy to say to a student, "I noticed that today you seemed really interested in the discussion." Comments like this go a long way. Remember that *all* students need to feel seen and appreciated.

Finally, a teacher can set an atmosphere for good behavior by focusing on what is positive rather than what is negative. An enthusiastic teacher who shows a positive interest in students is much more successful than a teacher who is constantly correcting students or who does not seem to care about them as people. For example, rather than reprimanding the student who is talking out of place, recognize the student who is working well (ignoring the other one). However, make sure the recognition is genuine and not contrived to make other students in the class jealous. A teacher can sincerely recognize a student for her unique idea or question, creative way of solving a problem, multifaceted conclusions to an investigation, or insightful way to display the results of a project. Haberman (1995) stresses the importance of making all children feel important. Therefore, if a child misbehaves it is important to focus less on the misbehavior than on the fact that the child is a vital and necessary member of the class or contributor to a project.

Setting Up Contracts with Students

Some teachers find that using learning contracts effectively promotes self-responsibility. The teacher in Scenario 3 used a contract with his students. **Learning contracts**, a written agreement made between a teacher and members of a group, accomplish several things. First, they force students to think about the expectations people have of them. They require them to delineate what type of project they will complete and what quality they expect to produce. Second, they outline specific ways students will meet objectives. Students can, for example, set parameters for work to be completed, artifacts to be created, or types of presentations to be given to the class. Third, contracts can specify how projects will be evaluated. Will the teacher evaluate it? Will peers judge its quality? What will be evaluated? Fourth, learning contracts can also establish procedures for group collaboration such as making decisions equitably, getting all members of the group involved, and coming to decisions in a fair manner.

Essential features of contracts include, but are not limited to, the following:

- A description of the project (students list the driving question, the subquestions they are investigating, and the names of the students on their team);

Names of team members: _____

Date: _____

Description of project:

We are trying to answer questions about acid rain. We are trying to find out if there is acid rain in our environment. Our group's driving question is "Can acid rain hurt plants in our neighborhood?"

How we're going to accomplish this project:

We are going to set up four geranium plants in pots. We are going to put all of them in the window in the room and give them the same amount of water. But to the water for one plant, we will add 1/2 teaspoon of vinegar. For the second plant, we will add 1 teaspoon of vinegar to the water, and for the third plant we will add 2 teaspoons of vinegar. The fourth plant will get plain water. We will measure the pH of the water with pieces of universal indicator paper that the teacher showed us how to use when we learned about acids and bases. We might call a nursery or a farmer to interview him or her about the effects of acid rain on plants.

Evaluation plan:

We will take photographs of our plants as they grow for 2 weeks. We will look up *acid rain* in the encyclopedia or on the Web to see what we can find out. We will measure the plants and see if they look healthy. The height and color of the plants will be recorded each day. The pictures, a graph of height versus time, and descriptions of how they look will be our artifacts. The teacher can grade this, but we will tell how well we think we did in our portfolio. We expect to get along with everyone in our group so we can answer this question.

Signatures: _____

| *Figure 10.3* | Learning contract. |

• An outline of how students expect to accomplish tasks (students list what they will investigate, what materials they plan to obtain, who they intend to contact in the community, and what artifacts they expect to create); and

• An evaluation plan (students describe the quality of work they expect of themselves, how they want to be evaluated, such as with a rubric or with an interview by the teacher, and what aspects they want to be the assessment criteria, such as concepts learned and ability to collaborate together).

Figure 10.3 is an example contract that a group of fifth graders might complete for an acid rain project. Portfolio Activity 10.11 will guide you through developing student contracts.

Anticipating Problems

Effective classroom teachers think about problems that might occur in their classroom, and they plan accordingly. In a project-based science classroom, teachers must consider the fact that different groups of students might be working on different tasks at the same time, compounding potential problems. In general, potential problems fall into several general categories:

Portfolio Activity 10.11   **MAKING A CONTRACT**

Materials Needed:
- A group of elementary or middle grade students

A. Visit an elementary or middle grade classroom and discuss the "essential features of a contract." From the discussion, develop a contract with the students. Find out if the students think the contract is fair. Would they sign it?

B. Based on this discussion, what features would you want to include in student contracts?

C. If you have the opportunity to teach, try implementing student contracts. Evaluate how successful they are in your classroom.

D. Record your contract ideas in your portfolio.

- Giving directions.
- Materials and supplies.
- Student behavior.
- Timing.
- Complexity of task.
- Sustaining interest over time.

Some teachers find it useful to think through potential problems using a fish-bone model. A **fish-bone model** is a diagram that lists tasks leading to a goal. On each "bone," teachers list possible problems. Figure 10.4 is a fish-bone model representing potential problems during four different tasks related to learning about acids and bases. Portfolio Activity 10.12 will work you through the creation of a fish-bone model.

During Instruction

We will discuss five factors to consider during instruction. These are the distributing of materials and supplies, making transitions, dealing with disturbances, handling multiple instances of the same activities, and handling multiple instances of different activities at the same time. On first sight, project-based science classrooms may seem chaotic. However, effective project-based classrooms are actually organized and efficient—and the reason is that the teachers have very clear management strategies for instruction.

Distributing Materials and Supplies

Whether it is the teacher or students who distribute materials and supplies in a science class, the distribution portion of a lesson is often the time when students misbehave or accidents occur. In part, this is because distribution represents **downtime**—a time when students are not actively participating in instruction or investigation. It is a time when students are simply waiting for something to happen, and so it often does. For this reason, it is important to distribute materials and supplies in an efficient manner to limit the amount of downtime between tasks. There are several efficient ways to distribute materials and supplies.

One way is to keep all materials and supplies in handy clear plastic boxes, plastic tubs, or zipper-closure bags that can be located quickly and easily passed around a table area to students.

Key Idea

During instruction, teachers pay careful attention to distributing materials and supplies, making transitions, dealing with disturbances, and handling various activities.

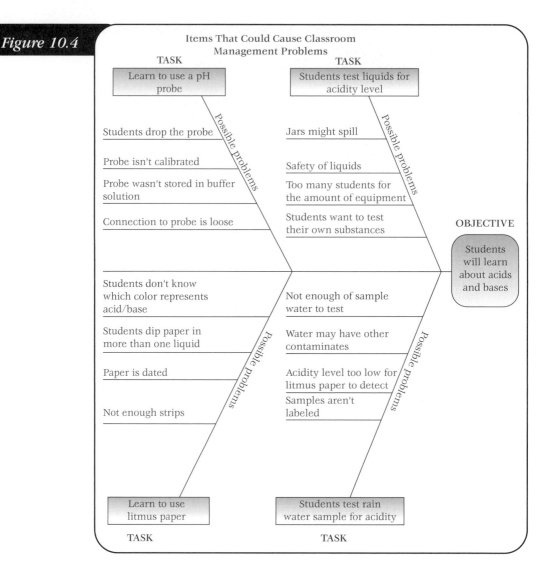

Figure 10.4

Fish-bone model.

Some teachers like to place all of the needed materials for an investigation or lesson in a single box or bag. For example, to investigate circuits (a benchmark lesson), students need a dry cell, wires, bulb holders, a flashlight bulb, and a dry cell holder. Rather than pass around five different boxes with these different items, the teacher could put one of each of the items into a zipper-closure bag before class and hand each table area one bag with all of the materials the students at that table would need for the lesson. This method is especially useful for young children with short attention spans who don't tolerate downtime well.

Portfolio Activity 10.12   ANTICIPATING PROBLEMS

Materials Needed:
- Figure 10.4
- Something to write with

A. Using the fish-bone diagram in Figure 10.4, determine what the teacher would need to do to avoid the potential problems.

B. Plan to teach a benchmark lesson. Complete a fish-bone diagram of the potential problems in the lesson.

C. How could the potential problems be resolved?

D. File your diagram in your portfolio.

It takes teachers a considerable amount of time to set up and organize materials in advance. Many teachers consider this part of their professional lives and spend time gathering materials and setting up before school, during lunch, and after school. Other teachers solicit help from parents, grandparents, and retirees in the community, older students in the school, or students in the class who volunteer to be lab assistants.

Many teachers find that once students have materials and supplies in their possession, they are eager to begin the activity or investigation. At this point, it is usually very difficult to give directions to students. For this reason, it is most often a good idea to give clear and complete directions *before* materials are distributed for a benchmark lesson or other whole class activity.

In a project-based science classroom, students will frequently obtain their own supplies and materials because they are investigating different subquestions related to the driving question, and they are making different artifacts. For example, students using pillbugs to study ecosystems might investigate separate subquestions about the habitats of the crustaceans, the desired temperature preferred by the crustaceans, and the amount of light preferred by the crustaceans. Although these are related activities, they require different materials: bug cages, different soils, thermometers, sources of light, and light probes. For this reason, teachers in a project-based science classroom face some unique problems regarding distribution of materials and supplies. Students need to know where to obtain necessary supplies, and they need to have some parameters for doing this. Some teachers require students to submit to them lists of needed materials, materials that the teacher then gathers and distributes. Others teach students where materials and supplies are stored and allow them to get items for themselves. With this approach, it is important to make sure the supplies and materials are stored in an area that is safe for students. It is also important to teach students how to use materials. For example, students need to learn how to carry expensive microscopes and focus the lenses without scratching them.

Making Transitions

Transitions are the few minutes that elapse between investigations, discussions, readings, and other activities. Transitions, like distribution of materials, are points of departure for students. Teachers handle transitions in different ways but always try to limit the amount of time between activities. Some teachers like to establish a standing rule for transitions, such as requiring students to read silently or make entries in their journals during transitions. Some teachers like to make transitions fun and interesting. For instance, they might pose an interesting science question for students to ponder during this time. Some like to engage students in quick games or songs during transitions. Finally, teachers can engage students in discussions about what they think can be done during transitions; students may have good ideas for handling downtime.

Dealing with Disturbances

Many potential disturbances are eliminated in a project-based environment because students are genuinely interested in what is happening. Haberman (1995) asserts that projects are the most effective way to capture the attention of children living in poverty and thus eliminate many behavior problems. In addition, if there is a positive classroom climate, if there are established ground rules for behavior, if good behavior is modeled, and if downtime is minimized, the potential for disturbance is already lessened. Nevertheless, disturbances will still occur. For example, one group of students might be working at the computer while another group is conducting an investigation. These multiple instances of classroom activity create opportunities for one group of students to disturb another group, often unintentionally.

It is impossible within the scope of this book to discuss all potential disturbances and all possible teacher responses. However, there are several general strategies that are recommended in most cases that we can discuss.

First, it is usually best to *have students try to solve their own problems*. For example, when a disturbance occurs, you might ask the student involved to think about how he or she could solve the problem, or you might ask all the students in the class to come up with solutions. This technique fits with constructivist theories discussed earlier.

Second, *establish consequences* in advance for disturbances that are severe. Established consequences are *not* threats or punishments. Threats and punishments are usually only temporarily effective. They don't teach students to solve their problems, and they frequently cause more problems. Kohn (1996) argues that bribes and threats do three things: disrupt a lesson, warp the relationship between punisher and punished, and impede moral or ethical development. Threats and punishments teach children not to think about how the behavior affects others but rather about what might happen if they get caught. **Consequences**, on the other hand, are the predetermined outcomes of student choice. For example, if a student chooses to disrupt work in her group, she knows that the consequence is that she will have to take a time out. Consequences can be established when class rules are set, or if absolutely necessary, students can be informed of consequences by the teacher.

Third, *be consistent* in reacting to disturbances. Don't let students get away with a certain behavior sometimes but enforce consequences on other instances. For example, if calling a classmate a bad name is considered inappropriate during science class, it should also be considered inappropriate on the playground.

Fourth, *be fair*. Some teachers treat girls less harshly than boys. For example, they might let girls talk in class but scold boys for doing the same thing. Similarly, teachers sometimes let more academically oriented students get away with behaviors that they would not tolerate from other students in the class. For example, they might let the brightest student in the class turn in a late paper but insist on deadlines for the other students. Students will be quick to spot unfair treatment, and perceiving that they are being treated unfairly may induce them to further misbehave.

Fifth, *be a good role model*. It is important that teachers not display the very behaviors they are trying to eliminate. Hardin and Harris (2000) point out that teachers must be good role models by not having tantrums, making insults, raising their voices, berating children, or being rude toward children. These authors stress that crisis prevention begins with treating all students with respect.

For more information about classroom management and different viewpoints on discipline (sometimes conflicting viewpoints), see Figure 10.5.

Handling Multiple Instances of the Same Activities

Even in project-based classrooms, teachers frequently facilitate the same activity for all students. This occurs frequently in a benchmark lesson on a concept or skill that all students will need in order to complete a project. The teacher described in Scenario 3 was handling multiple instances of the same activity to teach about parts per million. Several problems can occur when all students are participating in the same activity. Some students will finish earlier than others. Some students will "drop out."

Figure 10.5

Albert, L. 1992. *An introduction to cooperative discipline.* Videotape. Circle Pines, Minn.: American Guidance Service.

Albert, L. 1989. *A teacher's guide to cooperative discipline: How to manage your classroom and promote self-esteem.* Circle Pines, Minn.: American Guidance Service.

Canter, L., and M. Canter. 1992. *Lee Canter's assertive discipline: Positive behavior management for today's classroom.* Santa Monica, Calif.: Lee Canter & Associates.

Child Development Project. 1996. *Ways we want our class to be: Class meetings that build commitment to kindness and learning.* Oakland, Calif.: Developmental Studies Center.

DeVries, R., and B. Zan. 1994. *Moral classrooms, moral children: Creating a constructivist atmosphere in early education.* New York: Teachers College Press.

Dreikurs, R., B. Grunwald, and F. C. Pepper. 1982. *Maintaining sanity in the classroom: Classroom management techniques,* 2nd ed. New York: HarperCollins.

Emmer, E. T., and C. M. Evertson. 1981. Synthesis of research on classroom management. *Educational Leadership* 38:342–47.

Evertson, C. M., E. T. Emmer, B. S. Clements, J. P. Sanford, and M. E. Worsham. 1984. *Classroom management for elementary teachers.* Englewood Cliffs, N.J.: Prentice Hall.

Evertson, C. M., E. T. Emmer, B. S. Clements, and M. E. Worsham. 2000. *Classroom management for elementary teachers.* Boston: Allyn and Bacon.

Freiberg, J. H., ed. 1999. *Beyond behaviorism: Changing the classroom management paradigm.* Boston: Allyn and Bacon.

Kamii, C. 1984. Obedience is not enough. *Young children* 39:11–14.

Kamii, C. 1991. Toward autonomy: The importance of critical thinking and choice making. *School Psychology Review* 20:382–88.

Kohn, A. 1996. *Beyond discipline: From compliance to community.* Alexandria, Va.: Association for Supervision and Curriculum Development.

National Association for the Education of Young Children. 1986. *Helping children learn self-control: A guide to discipline.* Pamphlet. Washington, D.C.: Author.

Purkey, W. W., and D. B. Strahan. 1986. *Positive discipline: A pocketful of ideas.* Columbus, Ohio: National Middle School Association.

Wolfgang, C. H., B. J. Bennett, and J. L. Irvin 1999. *Strategies for teaching self-discipline in the middle grades.* Boston: Allyn and Bacon.

Classroom management resources.

The problem of early and late finishers can be caused by a diversity of abilities among students. More academically advanced or skilled students frequently finish activities much sooner than do their less academically able peers. Students with learning problems can have related behavioral problems. Gifted and talented students might become disruptive because they are unchallenged and bored. When there are differences among early and later finishers, it is a good idea to set classroom rules for finishing early, such as "Always take out a book to read silently when finished before others." Some teachers have students who finish early provide peer tutoring for classmates who are still struggling with an activity. Some teachers set up learning centers (locations in the room with enrichment activities) where students can go to work if they finish early. If learning centers are used, teachers need to be careful that the activities in these locations aren't more motivating than the primary classroom activity, or students may rush through their primary work to get to the enrichment activities.

"Dropping out" can become a problem when all students in the class are completing the same activity. **Dropouts** are students who lack interest in an activity or who fail to be motivated to complete it. Teachers need to monitor carefully students' interests and plan activities that are motivating. One way to monitor students' interests is to take time to talk with each student periodically. Ask questions to find out what the student is interested in, if he or she is unchallenged, frustrated, or bored. Another way is to have students keep dialogue journals (in which they write to each other or in which you and students correspond). These journals provide you with powerful insight into concerns students have about classroom activities.

Handling Multiple Instances of Different Activities at the Same Time

The apparent chaos found in a project-based science class is compounded when there are different activities going on at the same time. Scenario 4 illustrates a classroom with different activities going on at the same time. In such situations, teachers must be able to orchestrate students working on different activities. They must be able to make different materials, supplies, and equipment available for different activities and keep different groups of students focused on the main project.

Having materials, supplies, and equipment available for different activities at the same time is no easy task. In fact, because of the evolving nature of projects, students don't even always know what they will need before the start of an investigation. To make this job easier, teach students how to get many of their own science supplies, materials, and equipment. In addition, rely on parent and community volunteers to help with materials distribution. Structure your lessons so that students submit supply lists to you before a break, lunch period, or classes taught by other teachers so that you have time to gather materials.

To keep different groups of students focused on the project, a teacher must show students the relationships among their separate activities and to the driving question. Although one group of students may be on the computer looking up information about current weather conditions throughout the state and another group may be measuring current weather conditions outside the classroom, these two activities may be tied together by the driving question "How does weather affect our environment?" The activities are also related to each other since both are looking at current weather conditions. Students don't always see these connections, but knowing that everyone's work is connected can keep students focused and eliminate some of the management problems associated with working on different activities at the same time.

Table 10.11

PROJECTS ARE LINKED

Group 1 Activity	Group 2 Activity	Relationship to Driving Question "How Does Weather Affect Our Environment?"
We're using the Web to find current weather conditions in Ohio. We're doing an investigation to see if more molds grow in our environment when weather conditions are wet. We're growing mold in wet and dry conditions.	We're taking the temperature outside of the school. We're growing different grass seeds under different conditions (wet, dry, hot, and cold) to see if the weather will affect plaints in our area.	We're both trying to find out what the weather is right now. We're both investigating how weather conditions affect the growth of things.

One way to emphasize this connection is to have students share ideas and discoveries with each other throughout a project. Groups can share their ongoing investigations with the whole class, or small groups can be paired to discuss their projects with each other. Another strategy is to have students draw Venn diagrams or complete charts like the one shown in Table 10.11.

After Instruction

Just because ground rules and procedures have been established in a classroom does not mean they will be followed. The teacher needs to continually reinforce classroom norms, revisit classroom norms, and evaluate progress *before*, *throughout*, and *after* the project. In addition, after instruction students and teachers should *reflect* on classroom norms, on the effectiveness of instruction, and on student behavior. *The National Science Education Standards* (NRC, 1996) promotes such reflective practices in science education: "Teachers of science engage in ongoing assessment of their teaching and of student learning. In doing this, teachers use student data, observations of teaching, and interactions with colleagues to reflect on and improve teaching practice" (p. 37). It adds, "They use self-reflection and discussion with peers to understand more fully what is happening in the classroom and to explore strategies for improvement" (NRC, 1996, p. 42).

Reinforcing Classroom Norms

Teachers need continually to ask students to *reflect* on their objectives and encourage behaviors that help students meet these objectives. In a project-based environment, this is frequently accomplished by reminding students of the driving question they are trying to answer. This type of reminder focuses their attention on the purpose of their activities, and it can guide them in thinking about appropriate behaviors needed to accomplish their goals.

Teachers also need to *reinforce* established classroom rules. The teacher in Scenario 1 reminded students about classroom rules regarding talking when a reading assignment was given. Some teachers like to have students complete self-evaluation checklists or

T-charts (like those discussed in Chapter 6) at the end of a lesson to assess whether they are following established classroom norms. Some teachers like to have debriefing sessions or class meetings in which students discuss their progress toward following classroom norms. Finally, some teachers like to send home "progress reports" or letters to report on students' behavior and progress in school.

Revisiting Classroom Norms

Classroom rules or norms are not established only once during a school year. Good teachers continually revisit and reexamine the established rules and norms. They have students analyze whether the rules make sense and if new rules should be made to replace those no longer appropriate. Not only does revisiting classroom norms limit problems that might occur throughout the school year, it teaches students many of the problem-solving skills that project-based science seeks to foster. Students analyze whether rules are effective and solve the resulting problems if they are not working.

Evaluating Progress

One way to evaluate progress is to hold students accountable for their work. In a project-based environment, however, students must be accountable not only to the teacher, but also to one another. Each individual becomes accountable for his or her own learning, and the group is held accountable for learning and working well together.

Individual Accountability.   Individual **accountability** is the responsibility that individuals in a group have for their own learning. Teachers make it clear to students that individual members of a group cannot coast along on the work of others and cannot disturb the learning of others. Each person must learn the assigned material with the support of the group. For example, while completing a project, all students in a group contribute to the creation of an artifact and to the group's presentation. This individual accountability must be assessed. Students might keep journals or complete scoring rubrics to reflect their personal contributions to the project investigation, ideas, or artifacts. A rubric can also measure each person's collaborative skills such as accepting ideas from others, listening carefully to others, interacting constructively with others, and following classroom rules. Individual students might be required to pass a test on certain material, or each student might keep a portfolio to demonstrate his or her own personal progress toward mastering learning concepts. A sample rubric that students could use to evaluate their collaborative skills is pictured in Table 10.12.

Group Accountability.   We often think of accountability as the ability to demonstrate one's skill and knowledge to the teacher. In project-based classrooms, groups also have accountability. Group accountability most often falls into one of two types—collaboration and acquisition of certain knowledge or mastery of skills. In order for a group to demonstrate its ability to work well, many teachers have students complete questionnaires designed to ascertain whether interpersonal skills are being acquired and maintained, whether the classroom environment fosters sharing and respect, and whether students feel comfortable sharing and critiquing each other's work. Students can also complete a group scoring rubric that evaluates whether everyone participated, solved problems without arguing, talked in appropriate voices, treated one another with respect, stayed on task, and negotiated solutions. Another option is to assign to one student the task of evaluating with a rubric his or her group's collaborative skills. A sample group

Table 10.12

HOW DID I DO?

Name: _____

Rate yourself on how well you think you collaborated with your teammates on this activity.

Criteria	5 Very well	4 Somewhat well	3 Somewhat	2 Somewhat poorly	1 Poorly
I accepted ideas from my classmates.	_____	_____	_____	_____	_____
I listened carefully to the people on my team.	_____	_____	_____	_____	_____
I provided constructive criticism to help my team.	_____	_____	_____	_____	_____
I followed the rules our class generated.	_____	_____	_____	_____	_____

Table 10.13

HOW DID OUR TEAM DO?

Name: _____

Names of members of my team: _____

Rate how well you think you worked together on this activity.

Criteria	5 Very well	4 Somewhat well	3 Somewhat	2 Somewhat poorly	1 Poorly
Everyone participated.	_____	_____	_____	_____	_____
We solved problems without arguing.	_____	_____	_____	_____	_____
We talked in appropriate voices.	_____	_____	_____	_____	_____
We treated each other with respect.	_____	_____	_____	_____	_____
We stayed on task.	_____	_____	_____	_____	_____
We negotiated to solve problems.	_____	_____	_____	_____	_____

scoring rubric is shown in Table 10.13. The teacher may also assess the group's progress and have a conference with each team about its collaborative skill development.

To evaluate group members' acquisition of knowledge or mastery of skills, a teacher may have students ask one another questions about what they learned. Some teachers issue a final grade on a project based on a student's individual achievement and his or her accomplishment as part of a group. The grade could be the student's individual score plus bonus points from a group score. Teachers must decide what weights individual achievement and group accomplishment have in determining grades. Some teachers give all students in a group the same grade, the average of all students' work. Other teachers

Portfolio Activity 10.13

RETHINKING YOUR VIEWS ABOUT MANAGING A PROJECT-BASED SCIENCE CLASS

Materials Needed:
- A classroom to visit
- Portfolio Activity 10.1

A. If possible, observe several elementary or middle grade classrooms. How would you characterize the climate, organization, and management of each? How does the classroom teacher view his or her classroom?

B. Has your view of a science classroom been reconceptualized since you completed Portfolio Activity 10.1? If so, how? If not, why not?

C. Record your ideas in your journal.

Key Idea

Technology tools can help teachers collaborate with others to improve classroom management.

collect only one paper (sometimes randomly) from a group and assign the grade from that paper to all members of the group. Whatever method is used, it is important to establish assessment guidelines before the start of a project. Before a collaborative project is assigned, students should understand what weight will be given to individual and group progress. They should also understand how grades will be determined. If students recognize that collaboration is important and that they will not be harmed in the assessment process, there will be group cohesion and potential problems will be eliminated.

In Portfolio Activity 10.13, you will revisit your views on classroom climate, organization, and management.

USING TECHNOLOGY TOOLS TO FACILITATE CLASSROOM MANAGEMENT

Sometimes teachers benefit from the help of others to improve their classroom management strategies. Other teachers may have encountered similar problems and have ideas for handling specific situations. The process of collaborating with peers to discuss problems faced in the classroom can also be a great mentoring experience for new teachers. Even veteran teachers sometimes need a "shoulder to cry on," and peers can provide them needed support to help them cope with the stresses related to teaching.

Communicating Electronically with Peers

Electronic communication with peers through sites such as the one maintained by the National Science Teachers Association (NSTA) can be the tool needed to obtain and share classroom management ideas. Teachers can talk with colleagues who have used project-based science through the Web-based Inquiry Science Environment (WISE).

ONLINE LEARNING CENTER

CHAPTER REVIEW   www.mhhe.com/krajcik2e

Go to the Online Learning Center at **www.mhhe.com/krajcik2e** to review important content from the chapter and key terms, take a chapter assessment, and link to the chapter's websites.

CHAPTER SUMMARY

This chapter introduced three key components of the basic management of a project-based science classroom: classroom climate, organization, and management strategies. In the classroom climate section, we considered a constructivist framework for establishing a positive classroom environment. In this framework, teachers try to have students participate fully in helping solve classroom problems and forming norms or ground rules. The teacher serves as a role model who promotes a positive attitude toward science and a positive classroom climate. The teacher develops affective factors such as curiosity about the world, excitement about science, and enthusiasm to continue activities and generates worthwhile curriculum materials that are of interest to students. To develop a positive classroom climate in which students help solve problems, there must be a balanced relationship between the teacher and the students. Finally, in a positive classroom climate all students—boys and girls, minorities and nonminorities—feel capable of learning science.

In the section on classroom organization, we discussed aspects of physical facilities, the structure of the school day, and safety. We considered specific strategies for managing a project environment.

In the section on management strategies, we focused on before-teaching considerations such as establishing rules, using contracts, or anticipating problems; during-instruction considerations such as distributing materials, making transitions, dealing with disturbances, and working with multiple instances of activities; and after-instruction considerations such as reinforcing classroom norms, revisiting and reflecting upon norms, and evaluating progress. We also touched on ways that teachers might collaborate with others to discuss classroom management strategies.

CHAPTER HIGHLIGHTS

- Many unwelcome classroom behaviors can often be traced to the larger classroom context and the curriculum.
- A constructivist classroom environment asks students to reflect on what they should do and to solve problems together.
- In a positive classroom climate
  - Students have real choices.
  - Teachers are role models for good behavior and science inquiry.
  - Instructional planning focuses on good curriculum.
  - Teachers exude a positive attitude toward science.
  - Teachers promote positive affective factors such as curiosity, excitement, persistence, enthusiasm, skepticism, and open-mindedess.
- Maintaining a balanced teacher-student relationship helps create a classroom learning community where students feel safe.
- Teachers ensure equality by focusing on classroom practices that help all students learn.
- A well-planned classroom arrangement supports project-based science through
  - Creating an effective physical arrangement.
  - Keeping high traffic areas free of congestion.
  - Ensuring that students can be seen by the teacher.
  - Keeping frequently used materials and supplies readily accessible.
  - Being certain students can see displays as well as see and hear presentations.

- The structure of the school day influences classroom management through
  - The number of minutes allocated to a subject area,
  - The delivery of science as a subject area, and
  - The daily schedule of activities or lessons.
- A safe classroom helps ensure that all students learn.
- In a safe classroom
  - Animals and plants are healthy and well cared for and do not harm students.
  - Goggles are used in science classrooms.
  - Shelving, supplies, and materials are safely stored.
  - Students learn the safe use of electricity.
  - Sources of fire are eliminated or controlled.
  - Glassware is replaced with plastic or its use is carefully monitored.
  - Field trips are well planned to ensure safety and learning by all students.
  - Teachers are familiar with first aid procedures.
- Management strategies are used to help develop welcoming classroom learning communities where students can learn effectively.
- Teachers need to focus on classroom management before instruction, during instruction, and after instruction.
- To create a positive classroom before instruction
  - Establish norms for acceptable student behavior.
  - Establish an atmosphere that fosters "good" behavior.
  - Reward students by focusing on effort.
  - Use caution when using "rewards" because they are viewed by some to be coercive.
  - Set up contracts with students to promote self-responsibility.
- Effective classroom teachers anticipate problems before they occur and plan accordingly.
- Several factors to consider during instruction are
  - The distribution of materials and supplies.
  - Making transitions.
  - Dealing with disturbances.
  - Handling multiple instances of the same activities.
  - Handling multiple instances of different activities at the same time.
- Teachers need to continually reinforce classroom norms, revisit classroom norms, and evaluate progress before, throughout, and after the project.
- After instruction, students and teachers should reflect on classroom norms, on the effectiveness of instruction, and on student behavior.
- Teachers can collaborate with their peers to develop good classroom management strategies.

KEY TERMS

accountability (430)

affective factors (391)

atmosphere (420)

attitudes (391)

behavior tree (418)

classroom management (416)

classroom organization (397)

classroom rules (417)

climate (386)

consequences (425)

downtime (423)

dropouts (428)

fish-bone model (423)

flexible (409)

ground rules (418)

high traffic areas (398)

learning contracts (421)

norms (416)

physical arrangements (397)

real choices (389)

reinforcement (420)

rewards (420)

role models (390)

safety (409)

transitions (425)

REFERENCES

Ajzen, I., and M. Fishbein. 1980. *Understanding attitudes and predicting social behavior*. Englewood Cliffs, N.J.: Prentice Hall.

Baker, D. April. 1988. Teaching for gender differences. *Research matters to the science teacher*. Columbus, Ohio: National Association for Research in Science Teaching.

Bandura, A. 1986. *Social foundations of thought and action: A social cognitive theory*. Englewood Cliffs, N.J.: Prentice Hall.

Barman, C. 1996. How do students really view science and scientists? *Science and Children* 34:30-33.

Bazler, J. A., and D. A. Simonis. 1992. Are women out of the picture? Sex discrimination in science texts. In *OPTIONS for girls: A door to the future*, ed. M. Wilson. Austin, Texas: Pro.Ed.

Boylan, C. R., D. M. Hill, A. R. Wallace, and A. E. Wheeler. 1992. Beyond stereotypes. *Science Education* 76(5):465-76.

Brooks, J. G., and M. G. Brooks. 1993. *The case for constructivist classrooms*. Alexandria, Va.: Association for Supervision and Curriculum Development.

Campbell, J. 1999. *Student discipline and classroom management*. Springfield, Ill.: Charles C. Thomas, Publisher.

Campbell, P. 1996. www.tiac.net/users/ckassoc/.

Dean, R., M. M. Dean, J. A. Gerlovich, and V. Spiglanin. 1993. *Safety in the elementary science classroom*. Washington D.C.: National Science Teachers Association.

Evertson, C. M., E. T. Emmer, B. S. Clements, J. P. Sanford, and M. E. Worsham. 1984. *Classroom management for elementary teachers*. Englewood Cliffs, N.J.: Prentice Hall.

Evertson, C. M., E. T. Emmer, B. S. Clements, and M. E. Worsham. 2000. *Classroom management for elementary teachers*. Boston: Allyn and Bacon.

Garrick-Duhaney, L. M. 2000. Culturally sensitive strategies for violence prevention. *Multicultural Education* 7(4): 10-17.

Guzzetti, B. J., and W. O. Williams. 1996. Gender, text, and discussion: Examining intellectual safety in the science classroom. *Journal of Research in Science Teaching* 33:5-20.

Haberman, M. 1995. *STAR teachers of children in poverty*. West Lafayette, Ind.: Kappa Delta Pi.

Hardin, C. J., and E. A. Harris. 2000. *Managing classroom crises*. Bloomington, Ind.: Phi Delta Kappa Educational Foundation.

Hardin, J., and C. J. Dede. 1992. Discrimination against women in science education: Even Frankenstein's monster was male. In *OPTIONS for girls: A door to the future*, ed. M. Wilson. Austin, Texas: Pro.Ed.

Horsch, P., Q. Chen, and D. Nelson. 1999. Rules and rituals: Tools for creating a respectful, caring learning community. *Phi Delta Kappan* 81(3): 223-27.

Huber, R. A., and G. M. Burton. 1995. What do students think scientists look like? *School Science and Mathematics* 95(7):371-76.

Kahle, J., and M. Lakes. 1983. The myth of equality in science classrooms. *Journal of Research in Science Teaching* 20(2): 131–40.

Kamii, C. 1984. Obedience is not enough. *Young Children* 39:11–14.

Kamii, C. 1991. Toward autonomy: The importance of critical thinking and choice making. *School Psychology Review* 20:382–88.

Kamii, C., F. B. Clark, and A. Dominick. 1994. The six national goals: A road to disappointment. *Phi Delta Kappan*, 75: 672–77.

Katz, L. G. 1984. The professional early childhood teacher. *Young Children* 39:3–9.

King, J. E., E. R. Hollins, and W. C. Hayman. 1997. *Preparing teachers for cultural diversity*. New York: Teachers College Press.

Kohn, A. 1996. *Beyond discipline: From compliance to community*. Alexandria, Va.: Association for Supervision and Curriculum Development.

Lynch, S. J. 2000. *Equity and Science Education*. Mahwah, N.J.: Lawrence Erlbaum.

McEwan-Landau, B, and P. Gathercoal. 2000. Creating peaceful classrooms: Judicious discipline and class meetings. *Phi Delta Kappan* 81(6): 450–454.

Mead, M., and R. Metraux. 1957. Image of the scientist among high school students. *Science* 126:387.

National Council for Research on Women. 2001. *Balancing the equation: What we know and what we need*. Author. www.ncrw.org/research/scifacts/htm.

National Research Council. 1996. *National science education standards*. Washington, D.C.: National Academy of Sciences.

Nelson, B. H., I. R. Weiss, and J. Capper. 1990. *Science and mathematics education briefing book, volume II*. Chapel Hill, N.C.: Horizon Research, Inc.

Nelson, B. H., I. R. Weiss, and L.E. Conaway. 1992. *Science and mathematics education briefing book, volume III*. Chapel Hill, N.C.: Horizon Research, Inc.

Pajares, F. M. 1992. Teacher's beliefs and educational research: Cleaning up a messy construct. *Review of Educational Research* 62(3):307–32.

Pollina, A. 1995. Gender balance: Lessons from girls in science and mathematics. *Educational Leadership* 53(1):30–33.

Rampal, A. 1992. Images of science and scientists: A study of school teachers' views. I. Characteristics of scientists. *Science Education* 76(4):415–36.

Rosser, S. V. 1990. *Female friendly science*. New York: Permagon Press.

Rutherford, F. J., and A. Ahlgren. 1990. *Science for all Americans*. New York: Oxford University Press.

Sadker, M., and D. Sadker. 1992. Sexism in the classroom: From grade school to graduate school. In *OPTIONS for girls: A door to the future*, ed. M. Wilson. Austin, Texas: Pro.Ed.

Sanders, J. 1994. *Lifting the barriers: 600 strategies that really work to increase girls' participation in science, mathematics, and computers*. Port Washington, N.Y.: Jo Sanders Publications.

Schmidt, W. H., C. C. McKnight, R. T. Houang, H. C. Wang, D. E. Wiley, L. S. Cogan, and R. G. Wolfe. 2001. *Why schools matter: A cross-national comparison of curriculum and learning*. San Francisco, CA.: Jossey-Bass.

Sumrall, W. J. 1995. Reasons for the perceived images of scientists by race and gender of students in grades 1–7. *School Science and Mathematics* 95(2): 83–90.

Taylor, P. C. S., B. J. Fraser, and L. R. White. March 1994. *A classroom environment questionnaire for science educators interested in the constructivist reform of school science*. Paper presented at the annual meeting of the National Association for Research in Science Teaching, Anaheim, Calif.

Third International Mathematics and Science Study. 1998. http://timss.bc.edu.

Tobias, R. 1992. *Nurturing at-risk youth in math and science: Curriculum and teaching considerations*. Bloomington, Ind.: National Educational Service.

Weiss, I. 1987. *1985–86 National survey of science and mathematics education*. Research Triangle Park, N.C.: Research Triangle Institute.

Weiss, I. 1978. *Report of the 1977 National Survey on Science, Mathematics, and Social Sciences*. Research Triangle Park, N.C.: Center for Educational Research and Evaluation, Research Triangle Institute.

Wilson, M. 1992. *OPTIONS for girls: A door to the future*. Austin, Texas: Pro.Ed.

Chapter 11

How Do I Plan a Project-Based Curriculum?

INTRODUCTION

DEVELOPING A PROJECT

SELECTING AND OBTAINING RESOURCES

INTEGRATED CURRICULUM

CHAPTER LEARNING PERFORMANCES

- *Explain the important factors teachers must consider when planning a project.*
- *Justify why concept mapping is critical to planning.*
- *Describe how a teacher can use a variety of resources to plan a project.*
- *Create a project-based unit of study.*
- *Compare and contrast strategies that can be used to help all students learn.*
- *Explain the value of integrating science across the curriculum.*

INTRODUCTION

Teaching with a project-based science approach is rewarding and exciting, but it takes thought and time. You may have questions about implementing project-based science in a classroom: *How do I plan a project? How do I modify existing curriculum materials to fit a project approach? What resources are needed in a project environment? Where can I get help in finding resources? How do I help all students learn science?* This chapter focuses on answering these types of questions and walks you through the process of planning a project-based curriculum using an insect project as an illustration of the process. We will discuss how to develop a project, including deciding on concepts and learning performances and developing a driving question, benchmark lessons, investigations, assessments, and a calendar of activities. Next we will discuss how to select and obtain resources from a variety of sources, including commercial suppliers, noncommercial suppliers, local stores, and community resources. Because a project-based curriculum is not limited to science, we will discuss how project-based science supports curriculum integration. We will consider concept mapping as a way to plan science integration with other subject areas. We'll begin by observing three teachers as they plan an insect project.

Scenario: Planning the Curriculum

Imagine three teachers planning a unit on insects. Scattered in front of them are their district's curriculum framework, the textbook adopted by the school, the *National Science Education Standards* (NRC, 1996), *Science for All Americans* (AAAS, 1990), *Benchmarks for Scientific Literacy* (AAAS, 1993), *Atlas of Science Literacy* (AAAS and NSTA, 2001), and other curriculum resources.

"Well, our curriculum framework requires us to cover information about insects. I think we should cover this chapter in the spring when the insects reappear," says Holly.

Martino, looking at the district's curriculum framework, says, "Yeah. We could teach about metamorphosis, insect classification, and predator/prey relationships. Butterflies and other insects would be hatching in the spring."

Judy says, "To show metamorphosis, the kids could raise their own butterflies."

"No, we can just use this chapter. It has lots of nice photographs of butterfly metamorphosis," replies Martino. "If you really want, we could go to the zoo's insect exhibit for the kids to see insects at different stages."

Holly exclaims, "Shouldn't we worry about what the children should learn? What do we want them to be able to do?"

Martino agrees and states, "Right, we should begin by clearly defining what we want students to learn. How about, Students, describe the life cycle of a butterfly?"

Judy then replies, "But that is too low level of a learning performances. How about, Draw and explain the life cycle of a butterfly?"

Holly exclaims, "I like that! What else do we want students to be able to do? Maybe we should identify four of the concepts?"

Judy says, "Well, how are we going to meet our inquiry objectives?"

Holly says, "Right. We have to worry about that."

Judy leans forward in her chair. "I've been learning about project-based science in this course I'm taking and I think we can cover many of our learning performances using this approach. We just turn this insect chapter into an interesting driving question."

"But how can we do that?" asks Holly.

"Yeah and what's a driving question?"

"Well, it's a question like 'What kinds of insects live in our neighborhood?' We could get kids interested in studying insects by taking them outside on a walk and looking for and collecting bugs. This way, kids could become really interested in the topic and learn lots about it."

Holly still isn't sure. "But aren't we supposed to use the school's adopted book? This textbook is what I think we're supposed to use."

"Sure. We could assign sections of the book for kids to read. And you're right; it has some nice pictures that kids could refer to. One of the things I learned in this course is that we need to cover basic science content through *benchmark lessons.* We could use this chapter to cover metamorphosis and animal classification."

Martino is worried. "But we have lots of other curriculum objectives to cover, and those objectives are going to be covered on the proficiency tests. I have to worry about the low scores of some of my students."

"Well, remember, like I said before, one of our curriculum objectives that is on the proficiency exam has to do with kids doing inquiry. By using a project approach, the kids can work together to investigate insects in the neighborhood. They can make posters, presentations, and maybe videos about insects. These things can demonstrate what the kids are learning. They can show that they know how to collect and analyze data, communicate information, and make conclusions. Those are objectives we're supposed to cover, too. And in my class I learned that girls and minorities traditionally left behind respond more positively to this approach."

"Yeah, but what do we use for these investigations?" Martino is still feeling anxious.

Judy explains how project investigations work: "In a project approach, students are working on many different subquestions, so we can draw from lots of different resources. This STC kit on *The Life Cycle of Butterflies* (National Science Resources Center, 1992) is very good for teaching about metamorphosis. We can get butterfly eggs, raise caterpillars, and watch them grow into butterflies. This would make a great lesson to teach the objectives in our curriculum. The kids will also come up with some of their own ideas for the investigations in the project."

"Well, I think I'd like to try this. It sounds like a good way to teach these objectives," says Holly.

Martino says, "Well, I'm not sure."

Judy takes this as a green light, "Okay, let's start by mapping out our content and inquiry learning performances. I think you'll see that we can also get in some math and language arts stuff, too."

DEVELOPING A PROJECT

As the scenario with Judy, Martino, and Holly illustrated, instructional planning is never an easy task, and planning project-based instruction is especially challenging. Teachers must do more than plan individual investigations, artifacts, and classroom activities; they must also interrelate these instructional components in such a way that they

CONNECTING TO
NATIONAL SCIENCE EDUCATION STANDARDS

Science Education Teaching Standards
The plans of teachers provide opportunities for all students to learn science. Therefore, planning is heavily dependent on the teacher's awareness and understanding of the diverse abilities, interests, and cultural backgrounds of students in the classroom. Planning also takes into account the social structure of the classroom and the challenges posed by diverse student groups. Teachers plan activities that they and the students will use to access the understanding and abilities that students hold when they begin a learning activity (p. 32).

complement each other and build toward assessment goals for all students. There are many different planning styles; we will examine one method for developing a project.

Identifying Concepts, Specifying Learning Performances, and Matching to Curriculum Objectives

The decision to help students meet various learning performances and cover certain concepts at a particular grade level is usually not one that teachers make by themselves. Day-to-day lessons are usually guided by the need to cover basic concepts and curriculum objectives that a school district has for its students. At the national level, the *National Science Education Standards* were published in 1996 (NRC), and the American Association for the Advancement of Science established guidelines for school curriculum in *Benchmarks for Scientific Literacy* (AAAS, 1993). Many school districts adopted these ideas and formed curricula based on these sets of standards. Some states established state-mandated curricula that spell out essential knowledge and skills. Therefore, although curriculum objectives may vary from state to state or from school district to school district, you will find a great deal of similarity among concepts and objectives covered at most grade levels around the country. You may want to compare state and national guidelines using a computer program called *Curriculum Orchestrator* (Rose, London, Young, Mucci, & Jay, 1998) by MediaSeek Technologies, Inc.

What learning performances and concepts do you plan students to learn by engaging in a particular project? To answer this question, start by examining local and state guidelines (if they exist), and national guidelines such as The *National Science Education Standards* (NRC, 1996), *Benchmarks for Scientific Literacy* (AAAS, 1993), and *Atlas of Science Literacy* (AAAS and NSTA, 2001). Determine which local, state, or national objectives you plan to meet.

Imagine that the grade level you teach is required by your state to learn about various concepts related to insects. This is a common standard in the primary grades. The *National Science Education Standards* (NRC, 1996) lists "life cycles of organisms" as a content standard for grades K-4. At this point you might want to clarify your own understanding of this standard. You might read what the *National Science Education Standards* or the *Science for All Americans* say about this standard. You could consult various trade books and textbooks. Your reading will help clarify the important concepts and ideas involved in meeting this standard. Make a list of important science concepts associated with this and other standards.

Once you have identified and made a list of concepts, create a concept map of the major concepts. Connect the concepts with linking words. A concept map on insects might look like the one pictured in Figure 11.1.

Concept mapping was described more thoroughly in Chapter 7. You will notice that the teachers described in the opening scenario were using a variety of resources including the *National Science Education Standards* and their curriculum framework. They also started by creating a concept map and thinking about the needs of their own students.

After you have mapped the concepts, create learning performances you plan for students to learn through engaging in the project. For instance, you might write learning performances that state: Students will draw the stages of the life cycle of a butterfly. Students will explain the life cycle of a butterfly. Students will describe the parts of an insect's body. Learning performances are further explained in Chapter 7. Sometimes, your local school district's objectives might be written in a way that specifies learning

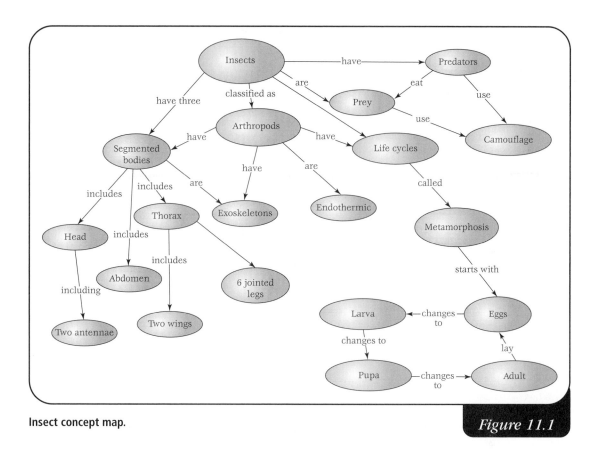

Insect concept map.

Figure 11.1

performances. For example, the concept "life cycles" may be listed in a school's curriculum objectives as "Each fourth grade student will describe the stages of the life cycle of a butterfly in correct sequence." However, your school district's objectives may be written in terms of "Students will know . . ." or "Students will understand . . ." In any case, once you have written learning performances, match them up with your local or state curriculum objectives. Identifying concepts, specifying learning performances, and matching them to curriculum objectives is actually a very iterative process. For example, you might ask yourself, "What concepts will students be learning if they explore this curriculum objective?" or "What curriculum objective will I cover if students learn this concept?" Portfolio Activity 11.1 will get you started planning a project by having you select concepts, specify learning performances, and match objectives.

Developing the Driving Question

Often after identifying concepts, learning performances, and curriculum objectives, teachers brainstorm several driving questions that will allow students to explore the concepts selected. Sometimes, however, teachers will brainstorm driving questions before even starting the concept map.

> ### Key Idea
>
> Teachers often brainstorm driving questions that will support learning of concepts and learning performances.

Portfolio Activity 11.1

IDENTIFYING CONCEPTS, SPECIFYING LEARNING PERFORMANCES, AND MATCHING TO CURRICULUM OBJECTIVES

Materials Needed:
- The curriculum objectives from a local school district
- A copy of the *National Science Education Standards* (NRC, 1996)
- A copy of *Benchmarks for Scientific Literacy* (AAAS, 1993) and *Atlas for Science Literacy* (AAAS/NSTA, 2001)

A. Select a topic to teach to elementary or middle grade students.

B. Consult the *National Science Education Standards* (NRC, 1996), *Atlas for Science Literacy* (AAAS/NSTA, 2001), or *Benchmarks for Scientific Literacy* (AAAS, 1993) to identify the concepts related to this topic.

C. Consult the curriculum from a local school district to find out what objectives need to be covered related to this topic.
- Using this list, create a concept map.
- Using the concept map, specify learning performances your students will accomplish.
- Match the concepts and learning performances to the school's curriculum objectives.

D. In your portfolio, file your concept map, your learning performances, and your comparison of objectives. You will be using them throughout this chapter.

Developing good driving questions takes time and thought. Don't worry if a good question doesn't pop into your mind immediately. Driving questions can always be modified as project development progresses. As we discussed in Chapter 3, there are many sources for driving questions: personal experiences, students' interests and culture, hobbies and personal interests, the newspaper or television, other teachers, textbooks and other curriculum materials, and the World Wide Web.

Here are some initial examples of driving questions related to insects:

- What insects live on our playground? (The idea for this question came from a fellow teacher.)
- What are the names of common insects? (The idea for this question came from a commercial curriculum publisher.)
- How do insects grow and change? (The idea for this question came from a school's curriculum.)
- What insects did you see this morning on the way to school? (The idea for this question came from personal experiences.)
- Where do insects go in the winter? (The idea for this question came from a child.)
- Why are they spraying insecticide to kill gypsy moths? (The idea for this question came from a news story reported in the local paper.)

Of these possible driving questions, the best for elementary students is most likely "What insects live on our playground?" This question meets all of the features of a good driving question (discussed in Chapter 3):

- *Feasibility*. Students can design and perform investigations about insects that live
  on the playground. For example, they can
  plot out a section of the playground to
  study the variety of insects that live on it.
- *Worth*. Students can learn science concepts
  related to the district's curriculum standards such as *metamorphosis, classification, predator and prey*, and *camouflage*.
- *Contextualization*. The question is a real-
  world question for students because it relates to their own physical environment—
  their playground.
- *Sustainability*. Students can learn about insects on the playground throughout the
  school year by studying subquestions such
  as "Which insects are around in the fall?"
  "Where do they go in the winter?" and
  "Which reappear earliest in the spring?"
- *Ethical*. Students can observe insects without harming the insects or themselves.
- *Meaning*. Insects are interesting and
  exciting to most children because they
  have strange defense mechanisms, use
  camouflage in fascinating ways, and have
  interesting life cycles.

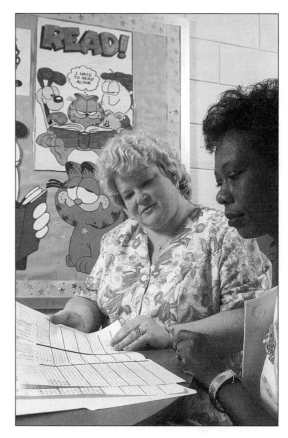

Teachers work together to create interesting driving questions.

Each of the other questions lacks fundamental features of a good driving question. For example, "What
are the names of common insects?" is not sustainable
over time. Students can learn the names of insects in a
very short period of time, and then they will likely become bored. Learning the names of insects is also un-
likely to be meaningful to most children. "How do insects grow and change?" is
feasible—students can design and perform investigations to watch insects grow and
change. However, the question may not be contextualized in students' lives. Studying the
growth of an insect students never see in their own environment might cause some children to lose interest in the topic. This question also can be subsumed as a subquestion
under a broader driving question. "What insects did you see this morning on the way to
school?" is contextualized, but it may not be worthwhile because important concepts in
the curriculum are unlikely to be covered in a study of insects seen on the way to school
one day. This question, too, can be subsumed under a broader driving question. "Where
do insects go in the winter?" might seem sustainable since it covers a longer period of the
year. However, the question may not be feasible because students may not be able to design an investigation that they can conduct outdoors in the winter. Finally, "Why are they
spraying insecticide to kill gypsy moths?" may be contextualized because it is related to
students' lives, but for safety reasons children should not be handling insecticide and,
therefore, there is no investigation students can conduct related to the question. In Portfolio Activity 11.2 you develop a driving question for your project.

Portfolio Activity 11.2

TURNING CONCEPTS, LEARNING PERFORMANCES, AND CURRICULUM OBJECTIVES INTO DRIVING QUESTIONS

Materials Needed:
- The list of concepts, learning performances, and curriculum objectives generated in Portfolio Activity 11.1

A. Take the list of concepts, learning performances, and curriculum objectives generated in Portfolio Activity 11.1 and brainstorm several driving questions from it.

B. Share this list with a colleague or classmate to try to generate additional driving questions.

C. Evaluate each question for
- Feasibility.

- Worth.
- Contextualization.
- Sustainability.
- Meaning.
- Ethical

D. Select one driving question that you will develop into a project throughout the rest of this chapter. Write an argument about why you are selecting this question over others you brainstormed.

E. File the argument and the driving question in your portfolio.

Developing Benchmark Lessons

After teachers have identified concepts, learning performances, and a driving question, they might begin to develop benchmark lessons (sometimes teachers design an investigation before developing benchmark lessons). Remember that the role of benchmark lessons in project-based science is to help students learn difficult concepts, illustrate a laboratory technique, build new inquiry abilities, model thinking, or stimulate curiosity. The teachers described in the opening scenario were worried about covering important objectives and meeting their students' needs, two other reasons to use benchmark lessons.

Don't expect to develop benchmark lessons from scratch. Original ideas are rare. You might come up with some original ideas, but more likely you will modify activities that have already been developed to meet the needs of your own students and to ensure that *all* students in your class learn. For our insect project, there are several good resources that we could use to develop benchmark lessons.

The FOSS *Insects* kit is valuable for teaching about the structure and life cycle of several different insects: mealworms, waxworms, milkweed bugs, silkworms, and butterflies (FOSS, 1993). The FOSS kit *Environments* has several lessons about insects. In one lesson, students investigate the environments (moisture and darkness) preferred by isopods and beetles. In another lesson, students investigate the level of salinity needed for brine shrimp to hatch (FOSS, 1993).

Another useful curriculum is the Science and Technology for Children (National Science Resources Center, 1992) curriculum *The Life Cycle of Butterflies*. Intended for second graders, this material can generate several benchmark lessons. Students raise painted lady butterflies to learn about metamorphosis; they use observation and recording skills to raise caterpillars and butterflies; they learn about caterpillars' basic needs for air, water, food, and shelter; and they learn about insect body parts and function.

Key Idea

Numerous resources help teachers develop benchmark lessons.

The Ranger Rick series entitled *Incredible Insects* (Braus, 1989) is filled with interdisciplinary activities related to insect classification, metamorphosis, habitats, and adaptations for survival and the influence of insects on our lives. One activity that comes from *Incredible Insects* is a butterfly metamorphosis role-play.

The Lawrence Hall of Science GEMS series contains two useful books: *Hide a Butterfly* (Echols, 1993) and *Ladybugs* (Echols, 1993). *Hide a Butterfly*, designed for preschool through kindergarten, focuses on skills (observing, communicating, comparing, and matching), concepts (camouflage and predator/prey), and themes (systems and interactions, models and simulations, scale, structure, evolution, and diversity and unity). *Ladybugs*, which also focuses on skills, concepts, and themes, covers body structure, life cycles, defense mechanisms, predatation, and the environmental role of ladybugs.

Guest lecturers and field trips are also benchmark lesson sources. An entomologist from a local university could provide students with useful information and resources. A field trip to the zoo's insect exhibit would provide information and expose students to a variety of insects.

Children's literature is another rich resource for a benchmark lesson. The following books teach about insect metamorphosis and insect lore:

Livo, L. J., G. McGlathery, and N. J. Livo. 1995. *Of Bugs and Beasts*. Englewood, Colo.: Teacher Ideas Press.

Carle, E. 1969. *The Very Hungry Caterpillar*. New York: Philomel Books.

Ryder, J. 1989. *Where Butterflies Grow*. New York: Lodestar Books, E. P. Dutton.

Using these various resources, we can create a benchmark lesson for second graders. Our lesson will follow this structure, which was introduced in Chapter 7 on benchmark lessons:

- *Learning performances*: What achievement do we expect to accomplish in the benchmark lesson? What concepts or inquiry skills will students develop? Will students develop background experiences for the project?
- *Relationship to the driving question*: How is the lesson related to the driving question of the project?
- *Materials needed*: What materials will you or the students need?
- *Instructional strategies*: What strategies or learning activities, demonstrations, or discussions will you use to help students reach the learning performances?
- *Time required*: How much time will it take for you to complete the benchmark lesson?
- *Cautions*: Are there any dangerous or hazardous components of the activities associated with the lesson? What precautions need to be taken?
- *Instructional sequence*: How will you proceed through this lesson?
  - A. Introducing the lesson.
  - B. Representing the content.
  - C. Establishing links to the driving question.
  - D. Evaluating learning.

Here is the sample benchmark lesson:

- *Learning performances*: Each student will describe that most insects change from egg to adult through a process called *metamorphosis*.

- *Relationship to the driving question*: The driving question "What insects live on our playground?" will be addressed through studying metamorphosis because students may find different stages of insects on the playground at any given time (egg, larvae, pupa, or adult). In order to understand that these different stages are forms of the same insect, students must understand metamorphosis.
- *Materials needed*: Ryder, J. 1989. *Where Butterflies Grow*. New York: Lodestar Books, E. P. Dutton.
- *Instructional strategies*:
  A. Reading a children's literature book
  B. Role-playing butterfly metamorphosis
  C. Drawing pictures for artifacts

- *Time required*: four to five days
- *Cautions*: Make sure students have a clear understanding of behavioral expectations during the role-playing activity.
- *Instructional sequence*:
  A. Introducing the lesson:
    1. Read Ryder, J. 1989. *Where Butterflies Grow*. New York: Lodestar Books, E. P. Dutton.
    2. Discuss what it might be like to change from a caterpillar to a butterfly.
    3. Discuss the stages that a butterfly goes through.
  B. Representing the content:
    1. Show students real butterfly eggs and an adult butterfly (if not available, show photographs of these stages).
    2. Ask the children if they know how the egg changes to a butterfly. Discuss the students' ideas.
    3. Have students role-play the stages of metamorphosis that a butterfly goes through. Ranger Rick's *Incredible Insects* has a good example of a play in which children can participate.
  C. Establishing links to the driving question: See if students can identify other insects on their playground that are simply in different stages of metamorphosis. For example, moths, ants, flies, and bees also go through complete metamorphosis.
  D. Evaluating learning:
    1. Give students a set of photographs or drawings. Have them place them in the correct order of the metamorphosis.
    2. Have collaborative groups of students explain to others how their drawings illustrate complete metamorphosis.
    Portfolio Activity 11.3 asks you to develop a benchmark lesson for your project.

Key Idea

Teachers plan investigations to help children develop their own understandings about a concept.

Developing Investigations

Investigations enable students to plan and conduct experiments that facilitate their construction of partial solutions to important questions. Through investigations, students plan, make decisions, collect and analyze data, draw conclusions, and present results. As you develop your investigations and classroom activities, link them to the driving questions and project concepts.

Portfolio Activity 11.3   DEVELOPING BENCHMARK LESSONS

Materials Needed:
- Access to a variety of curriculum materials and resources
- Access to the Web

A. Consult a variety of curriculum materials for benchmark lesson ideas on your topic.

B. Develop a list of ideas that could be used as benchmark lessons to teach the concepts and skills in your project.

C. Write a lesson plan for one benchmark lesson.

D. File your plan in your portfolio.

After teaching about metamorphosis in a series of benchmark lessons, we might design a class investigation based on the FOSS *Insects* (Lawrence Hall of Science, 1993) curriculum and the STC *The Life Cycle of Butterflies* unit (National Science Resources Center, 1992). One option for an investigation is to have student groups observe the development of a butterfly egg into an adult butterfly. As with the benchmark lesson, to plan this investigation we would have to think about the learning performances, relationship to the driving question, materials needed, instructional strategies, time required, instructional sequence, and cautions.

- *Learning performances:*
  A. Each student will observe and describe butterfly metamorphosis.
  B. Each student will record butterfly metamorphosis by drawing a picture and noting the date of each stage change.
  C. Each student will explain how most insects change from egg to adult through a process called *metamorphosis*.

- *Relationship to the driving question*: The driving question "What insects live on our playground?" will be addressed through studying metamorphosis because students may find different stages of insects on the playground at any given time (egg, larvae, pupa, or adult). In order to understand that these different stages are forms of the same insect, students must understand metamorphosis.

- *Materials needed:*
  A. Butterfly eggs (can be ordered from animal supply houses such as Carolina Biological).
  B. Bug cages.
  C. Drawing paper.
  D. Drawing supplies (colored pencils, markers, or crayons).
  E. Magnifying glasses.
  F. Caterpillar food supply (varies depending upon the stage the butterfly is in and the type of butterfly; for example, Monarch caterpillars eat milkweed).

- *Instructional strategies*:
  A. Investigation to raise butterflies.
  B. Drawing pictures as artifacts.

- *Time required*: four to six weeks.
- *Instructional sequence*:
  A. Have each group of students set up a bug cage with butterfly eggs and caterpillar food.
  B. Each day, have students observe the butterfly's stage of metamorphosis using a magnifying glass. Clean the cage daily. Add food if needed.
  C. Have students draw pictures of the stages and record the date. Have them keep these drawings in their science portfolios.
  D. After students have observed and recorded the complete metamorphosis of the butterfly—egg, larvae (caterpillar), pupa (chrysalis), and adult (butterfly)—have them explain how their butterfly egg changed throughout the last several weeks.
  E. Ask students how this investigation helps them answer the question "What insects live on our playground?" Remind them that when they found a caterpillar and a butterfly, these were actually the same insect. To answer the driving question, they needed to understand that the caterpillar and adult were just in different stages.

- *Cautions*: Always have children wash their hands after touching insects being raised in the classroom. Bring only known species into the room (such as painted ladies, swallowtails, or monarchs).

After students complete the class investigation, we might want groups of students to ask their own questions and design their own investigations. For instance, one group might be interested in finding out what kinds of food caterpillars eat. To answer this subquestion, students would need to plan and conduct an experiment. Students could observe other insects feeding on the playground, or they could research what insects eat. Then they could place monarch caterpillars into different containers holding different foods such as milkweed, carrot tops, grass, and other leaves. Students could determine which foods the caterpillars ate the most by inspecting the leaves or by weighing the leaves before and after the caterpillars had eaten for a day. This investigation could be tied to important concepts of metamorphosis (what animals eat during various life cycle stages), and it would teach basic skills (observation, measurement, recording, and making conclusions). Other groups of students might be interested in the life cycle of other insects such as mealworms and waxworms. Through a series of investigations, these students could compare and contrast the life cycles of various insects. In Portfolio Activity 11.4, you develop an investigation for your project.

Developing Assessments

> **Key Idea**
>
> Teachers link assessment to instruction.

Assessments linked to classroom activities and investigations can be used to gain a complete view of student learning. In Chapters 8 and 9, we discussed many types of assessment strategies that teachers can use to measure student understanding. For our insect project, the following assessment strategies would be effective:

- *Discussion-based observations*: Discuss with students what they have noticed about the changes their butterflies are going through.
- *Anecdotal records*: Make a notation about which students seem to be having difficulty recording daily information about their insect's growth.

Portfolio Activity 11.4   DEVELOPING AN INVESTIGATION

Materials Needed:
- A pencil and paper or a computer

A. For the project topic you have chosen, identify several possible investigations that students could develop.

B. Design a lesson plan for conducting one of the investigations.

C. How does the investigation help students answer the driving question?

D. File your answer in your portfolio.

- *Checklists*: Check off which students have used a magnifying glass to observe insects up close.
- *Clinical interviews*: Talk with students about what they have noticed in their investigation of the foods caterpillars eat.
- *Concept maps*: Have students develop maps to illustrate connections among concepts being studied in the insect project.
- *Performance-based assessment*: Have students design an investigation to explore life cycles of various insects.
- *Student writing samples*: Have students write stories about what it might feel like to be a butterfly.
- *Daily journals*: Have students make daily records of their observations of the life cycle of a butterfly and conclude what the pattern of cycles is for a butterfly.
- *Physical products*: Have students create models illustrating the life cycle of a butterfly.
- *Drawings*: Have students make daily drawings of each day in the life cycle of a butterfly.
- *Music*: Have students adapt songs to describe butterfly metamorphosis.
- *Videos*: Have students make a video explaining their investigation of the foods caterpillars eat and summarizing their findings.
- *Multimedia documents*: Have students create hypermedia documents illustrating the stages of butterfly growth including graphs and photographs of the changes a butterfly goes through.

NSES

CONNECTING TO
NATIONAL SCIENCE EDUCATION STANDARDS

Science Education Teaching Standards
Teachers of science engage in ongoing assessment of their teaching and of student learning (p. 37).

Each of these assessment items can be embedded into instruction and can help teachers determine whether students have met science standards. For example, most of the aforementioned assessments could be used to show whether students know the K–4 AAAS benchmark on understanding life cycles. Many high-stakes assessments, such as state proficiency tests, require students to use higher-level thinking and processing skills

Portfolio Activity 11.5 — DEVELOPING ASSESSMENTS

Materials Needed:
- A pencil and paper or a computer

A. For the project topic you have chosen, identify several possible assessments that could be used to measure student learning.

B. Design plans for carrying out one of the assessments. What would be included? How would it be evaluated?

C. How does the assessment help students show what they have learned about the driving question?

D. Record your assessment plans in your portfolio.

such as writing, analyzing data, and synthesizing information. For example, fourth graders in Ohio are expected to be able to "describe the duration and timing of a pattern given a repetitive pattern in nature" (ODE, 1994, p. 36). Students who can make daily records of observations of the life cycle of a butterfly and conclude what the pattern of cycles is have used important skills such as writing and synthesizing information that can be used on the fourth-grade tests in Ohio. Portfolio Activity 11.5 asks you to develop an assessment for your project.

Developing a Calendar of Activities

Key Idea

A calendar helps a teacher guide the sequence of lessons and plan time frames for instruction.

It is a good idea to develop a **calendar** to guide the sequence of lessons and orchestrate the various components in a time frame. Some teachers like to use a concept map like the one generated earlier to organize the activities, because the hierarchy in the concept map helps define the sequence of concepts students need to learn in benchmark lessons. The calendar is an *estimate* of when each lesson will take place. It almost always gets changed during the course of implementation. Table 11.1 is a sample calendar of activities for our insect project. In Portfolio Activity 11.6, you make a calendar for your project.

Developing a Project

Identifying concepts; specifying learning performances; designing driving questions, benchmark lessons, investigations, and assessments; and creating a calendar of activities is an iterative process. Investigations may lead to new questions that introduce other concepts. Figure 11.2 depicts this iterative process. It shows one possible planning sequence: concepts, learning performances, driving questions, benchmark lessons, investigations, assessments, and calendar of activities. Portfolio Activity 11.7 asks you to revise the project you developed in Portfolio Activities 11.1 through 11.6.

SELECTING AND OBTAINING RESOURCES

As illustrated in the planning sequences described earlier, teachers face many decisions as they design a project-based curriculum. Planning can be supported with a variety of printed and electronic resources such as textbooks, workbooks, kits of materials, slides,

Table 11.1

INSECT PROJECT CALENDAR OF ACTIVITIES.

Monday	Tuesday	Wednesday	Thursday	Friday
2 Introduce driving question "What insects live on our playground?" Read Ryder's story, *Where Butterflies Grow*.	3 Set up insect cages with butterfly eggs and record daily observation of butterflies.	4 Get on Web to find information on monarch butterflies. Record daily observation of butterflies.	5 Take field trip to playground to observe insects. Record daily observation of butterflies.	6 Read Carle's book, *The Very Hungry Caterpillar*. Record daily observation of butterflies. Take photographs or make drawings of insects on the playground in order to identify them.
9 Record daily observation of butterflies and weigh the gain in mass of the caterpillars. Research information about insects found on the playground.	10 Have students design investigations to help answer "What insects live on our playground?" Record daily observation of butterflies.	11 Set up student investigations. Record daily observation of butterflies.	12 Record daily observation of butterflies. Listen to guest speaker on pest control.	13 Record daily observation of butterflies. Take trip to insect exhibit at the zoo.
16 Record daily observation of butterflies. Role-play the stages the butterfly has gone through.	17 Record daily observation of butterflies. Work on investigations. Look on Web for more information about butterflies.	18 Record daily observation of butterflies. Listen to guest speaker–an entomologist from the local university.	19 Record daily observation of butterflies. Work on insect computer program. Use Web to find information related to groups' investigations.	20 Record daily observation of butterflies. Write a song to depict metamorphosis. Try to find insects in different life cycle stages on the playground.
23 Record daily observation of butterflies. Arrange drawings of butterfly stages in portfolio.	24 Record daily observation of butterflies. Revisit playground for additional observations.	25 Record daily observation of butterflies. Revisit playground for observations.	26 Record daily observation of butterflies. Prepare for hypermedia presentation (artifact).	27 Record daily observation of butterflies. Prepare for hypermedia presentation (artifact).
30 Record daily observation of butterflies. Prepare for hypermedia presentation.	31 Give presentation to parents.	1 Give presentation to parents.	2	3

Portfolio Activity 11.6

DEVELOPING A CALENDAR OF ACTIVITIES

Materials Needed:
• A planning calendar

A. Using the ideas you have collected on your topic

throughout this chapter, plan a calendar of activities for the project you are designing.

B. Put this calendar in your portfolio.

Figure 11.2

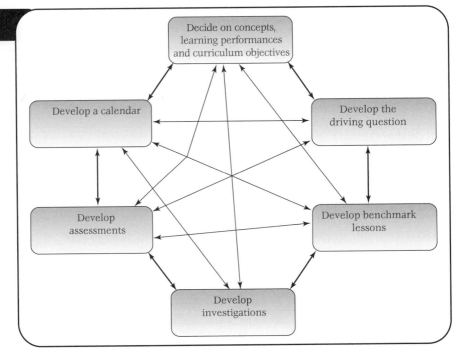

Process of developing a project.

cassettes, transparencies, charts and maps, games, audiotapes, filmstrips, videos, television, computers, CD-ROMs, and electronic notepads. Most communities also offer a wealth of resources through local businesses, organizations, zoos, community centers, and museums. Each type of resource is used for a different reason, offers advantages, and includes disadvantages. You might think of all the available resources as a tool kit for teaching. Several issues revolve around selecting and obtaining resources. In this section, we will discuss these issues.

Portfolio Activity 11.7 — REVISITING YOUR PROJECT DESIGN

Materials Needed:
- Your project design from Portfolio Activities 11.1–11.6

A. Go back through Portfolio Activities 11.1 through 11.6. Think about how you might change your design. What new questions might arise as the project is being implemented?

B. How does your assessment show you how well your instruction is working? What adjustments, if any, might you make if you could? How do you think such changes would improve your project?

C. Share your project design with a classmate or colleague. What new ideas does he or she have for you?

D. Put these ideas in your portfolio.

Selecting Resources

Given the variety of **resources** available to a teacher, it is important to develop or identify criteria for selecting materials to use in a project-based science classroom. Several organizations have published guidelines for selecting resources that can help teachers make good judgments about materials (the National Science Resources Center; Tuomi, 1993; the National Association for the Education of Young Children; Bradekamp, 1987; the National Middle School Association, 1982; Alexander & George, 1981; Wiles & Bondi, 1981; and Barnes & Spector, 1989). Table 11.2 summarizes the common features of these recommendations.

The FOSS *Insects* curriculum meets almost all of the criteria for selecting resources for our insect project. It spans several months, giving students the opportunity to explore the topic in-depth. Children work directly with concrete materials (insects such as mealworms, waxworms, and butterflies) to make their own observations and conclusions. They engage in inquiry to learn about the metamorphoses of various insects. Integration is incorporated in the form of suggested children's literature, writing assignments, and illustrations the children keep. Ongoing assessments occur throughout the unit—children keep observations of their insects, teachers use checklists that focus on process skills, and alternative assessments (such as making models and drawing life cycles) are suggested. Although this unit does not use technology, it is an excellent example of a resource that stresses exploration and depth over coverage of information.

In Portfolio Activity 11.8, you will select resources for the project you are developing throughout this chapter.

Obtaining Resources

Many types of resources are available to help teachers develop a project-based curriculum. A good classroom contains a mixture of inexpensive, everyday household materials as well as commercial and noncommercial materials, magazines, and books. Although

> **Key Idea**
> Effective teachers think carefully about the resources they use in their classrooms.

> **Key Idea**
> Numerous resources can be used in project based science classrooms—commercial and noncommercial materials, everyday household materials, and the community.

Table 11.2

SUMMARY OF CRITERIA FOR SELECTING RESOURCES

Criteria	Rating		
Allows children to explore a science topic in depth	Exceptional 1	Moderate 2	Poor 3
Presents the topic in a manner relevant to students' everyday lives	Exceptional 1	Moderate 2	Poor 3
Lets students engage in direct, purposeful experiences in which they can make their own observations and conclusions	Exceptional 1	Moderate 2	Poor 3
Allows children to work collaboratively	Exceptional 1	Moderate 2	Poor 3
Presents accurate information	Exceptional 1	Moderate 2	Poor 3
Actively engages students in their learning through experiences with concrete materials	Exceptional 1	Moderate 2	Poor 3
Promotes inquiry, problem solving, and critical thinking	Exceptional 1	Moderate 2	Poor 3
Uses technology as a tool to enhance learning	Exceptional 1	Moderate 2	Poor 3
Helps children learn how to learn (establishes a foundation for lifelong learning)	Exceptional 1	Moderate 2	Poor 3
Develops children's self-esteem, sense of competence, and positive feelings toward learning science	Exceptional 1	Moderate 2	Poor 3
Responds to children's individual differences in ability, development, and learning styles (the curricula are novel and varied and use a variety of instructional strategies)	Exceptional 1	Moderate 2	Poor 3
Integrates science across subject areas	Exceptional 1	Moderate 2	Poor 3
Engages children in discussions and conversation that challenge their thinking and help them construct understanding	Exceptional 1	Moderate 2	Poor 3
Stresses skills such as observing, measuring, hypothesizing, and predicting	Exceptional 1	Moderate 2	Poor 3
Uses portfolios, practical assessment, or other forms of alternative assessment	Exceptional 1	Moderate 2	Poor 3
Provides opportunities for physical movement	Exceptional 1	Moderate 2	Poor 3
Stresses exploration and depth over coverage of information	Exceptional 1	Moderate 2	Poor 3

there are numerous sources for obtaining materials, there are a few ideal places to start your search. In the following sections, we will discuss in more detail how to obtain a variety of resources, how to use the community as a resource, and how to use the Web to search for resources.

✎ *Portfolio Activity 11.8*   **SELECTING GOOD RESOURCES**

Materials Needed:
- Table 11.2

A. Find resources that you might use for lesson ideas for the project topic that you have been developing throughout this chapter.

B. Using the criteria listed in Table 11.2, rate the quality of the resources.

C. Record your rating in your portfolio.

By exploring the Eisenhower National Clearinghouse for Mathematics and Science Education, you can identify both commercial and noncommercial resources. This clearinghouse, funded by the U.S. Department of Education, serves to improve access to mathematics and science resources for teachers, students, and parents. The Clearinghouse collects the most up-to-date materials and catalogs them. The materials can be accessed with a database in CD-ROM, in print format, or on the Web. The Clearinghouse is a free resource, and it can save you time. For more information, write to Eisenhower National Clearinghouse for Mathematics and Science Education, Area 200, Research Center, 1314 Kinnear Road, Columbus, OH 43212-1194, call 1-800-621-5785, or visit their website.

Eisenhower National Clearinghouse for Mathematics and Science Education

Commercial Suppliers

The National Science Teachers Association publishes an annual supplement to its journals entitled *NSTA Science Education Suppliers*. This publication is packed with information about commercial companies that sell equipment and supplies (such as microscopes, slides, dissecting kits, tuning forks, and hand generators), software (such as CD-ROMs, and computer disk programs), media (such as maps, games, and kits), curriculum programs (such as FOSS and STC), and tradebooks (such as children's literature). The publication includes addresses, telephone numbers, Web pages, and e-mail addresses of suppliers. It summarizes the type of equipment carried by each company and categorizes it in a number of ways such as by science subject and grade level. You can obtain this publication by either subscribing to the NSTA journals (Scienc*e and Children, Science Scope,* or *Science Teacher*), contacting NSTA at the National Science Teachers Association, 1840 Wilson Boulevard, Arlington, VA 22201-3000, or browsing the resource section on their website.

NSTA

There is no shortage of ideas for teaching science. Teachers' resource books are packed with ideas for hands-on activities that make good benchmark lessons. Many include pages that can be duplicated for children. For example, teacher resource books such as *The Pillbug Project* (Burnett, 1999) can be purchased online at the National Science Teachers Association Web page. This book focuses on the study of the pillbug or sowbug and crustaceans and provides a useful resource to contrast crustaceans with insects.

Noncommercial Suppliers

Noncommercial suppliers include nonprofit groups such as the Audubon Society, businesses such as utility companies, and science parks such as Sea World. These types of suppliers frequently distribute free or inexpensive materials. Most of these materials are

Table 11.3

CRITERIA FOR USING NONCOMMERCIAL RESOURCES

Criteria	Rating		
Furthers my learning performances	Exceptional 1	Moderate 2	Poor 3
Is free from objectionable advertising, propaganda, or bias	Exceptional 1	Moderate 2	Poor 3
Is scientifically accurate	Exceptional 1	Moderate 2	Poor 3
Is interesting	Exceptional 1	Moderate 2	Poor 3
Is intellectually stimulating	Exceptional 1	Moderate 2	Poor 3
Is beneficial for children and classroom use	Exceptional 1	Moderate 2	Poor 3
Meets criteria for selecting resources (Table 11.2)	Exceptional 1	Moderate 2	Poor 3

educationally sound and useful resources for the classroom. However, some businesses create materials for the purpose of conveying the value of their particular products or services. For example, a local utility company might publish free materials on the benefits of nuclear energy. Most of these materials are accurate, but you should watch out for materials that present biased opinions. Table 11.3 shows criteria for evaluating free and inexpensive materials provided by noncommercial suppliers.

Table 11.4 lists some nationally recognized noncommercial suppliers. You may also want to contact local utility companies, fire departments, police departments, zoos, aquariums, botanical gardens, museums, departments of natural resources, environmental organizations, and businesses for science-related information and materials in your region. In Portfolio Activity 11.9, you use the World Wide Web to find resources for the project you are developing.

Everyday Household Materials

Everyday household materials such as cotton balls, cups, vinegar, and baking soda are used in numerous elementary and middle grade investigations and activities. Table 11.5 lists commonly used household materials and identifies places to locate these resources such as drug, hardware, grocery, pet, craft, and toy stores. For example, for our insect unit, food supplies and bug cages can be purchased at pet stores. Hardware stores sell nylon screen and wood for building simple habitats. Grocery stores sell jars and food supplies that can be used for investigations on insects. Portfolio Activity 11.10 asks you to identify local resources you could use in your project.

The Community as a Resource

Community resources provide valuable sites for field trips, are sources of educational materials, and create opportunities for experiences. Besides providing a change of

Portfolio Activity 11.9 FINDING RESOURCES USING THE WEB

Materials Needed:
- Access to the Web

A. Use the URLs provided in Table 11.4 to find resources and ideas for the project you are developing in this chapter.

B. Conduct a search on the Web using a search engine such as Google, Yahoo, or Webcrawler to find additional resources and ideas for your project.

C. File these resources, ideas, and URLs in your portfolio.

NATIONAL NONCOMMERCIAL SUPPLIERS

Table 11.4

Organization	Resources Provided
National Wildlife Federation	*Nature Scope* series of books *Ranger Rick* magazine *My Big Backyard* magazine
Project Wild (5430 Grosvenor Lane, Bethesda, MD 20814, 301-493-5447)	*Project WILD Aquatic* *Project Learning Tree*
NASA Spacelink	Slides, photographs, videotapes, lesson plans
Project WET (201 Culbertson Hall, Montana State University, Bozeman, MT 59717-0057, 406-994-5392)	*Project WET*
TERC	*Hands On!* magazine Papers Innovative projects

Noncommercial Suppliers

Please visit the text's Online Learning Center at www.mhhe.com/krajcik2e to link directly to these websites.

pace, community resources show children how science is relevant to their daily lives. For example, for our insect project, a local public health official or nurse would be a good resource for talking about health hazards (such as Lyme disease) associated with insect bites. Science museums provide students with hands-on displays, interactive experiences, and special programs. Other community resources are local zoos, science centers, parks, hospitals, police stations, courts, radio stations, universities, and businesses. Many teachers find that they can use all of their children's parents as

NSES

CONNECTING TO
NATIONAL SCIENCE EDUCATION STANDARDS

Science Education Teaching Standards
Teachers consider their own strengths and interests and take into account available resources in the local environment (p. 31).

Portfolio Activity 11.10   IDENTIFYING RESOURCES IN LOCAL STORES

Materials Needed:
- Local stores to visit

A.   Visit a local drug, hardware, grocery, pet, craft, and toy store to identify possible resources that could be used in your project.

B.   Keep track of items you could use and their costs.

C.   List them in your portfolio.

community resources. A parent doesn't need to be a doctor or professional to be a resource. A mother who grows houseplants may be an expert in this area as much as any other community member. For the insect project, we could visit the zoo to see insects that are nonindigenous to our region.

The community can also be a wonderful network for providing teachers with free materials. Although schools usually provide teachers with small budgets for purchasing materials, many school budgets are very tight and teachers frequently need to identify creative alternatives for stocking their classrooms. Many schools have joined a trend toward collaborative alliances and partnerships with local businesses. These partnerships provide many advantages: Local businesses become engaged in education, businesses provide schools with needed supplies and materials, and students see the relevance of what they are learning to local businesses. If your school does not have a partnership with local businesses, you might want to consider asking local businesses for donations. Many teachers do this by writing simple letters. A personal follow-up in the form of a telephone call or visit can often secure a donation. Check to make sure your school district's policies allow you to seek donations. Figure 11.3 shows a sample letter requesting donations from businesses. Table 11.5 lists many resources needed in elementary or middle grades science classrooms and identifies likely sources for each.

INTEGRATED CURRICULUM

Curriculum integration has become popular among educators. However, even at the elementary level, it is common for students to move from subject to subject and learn topics in a fragmented, disconnected fashion that bears little resemblance to real life. This frequently leads students to be bored by and overloaded with information. It seems only logical that subject areas should not be separated in schools because they are not separated in the world. Paul DeHart Hurd (1991) in an article entitled "Why We Must Transform Science" wrote,

> Science today is characterized by some 25,000 to 30,000 research fields. Findings from these fields are reported in 70,000 journals, 29,000 of which are new since 1978. Traditional disciplines have been hybridized into such new research areas as biochemistry, biophysics, geochemistry, and genetic engineering. . . . These changes in the way modern science is organized have yet to be reflected in science courses. There is little recognition

Figure 11.3

Dear Local Grocery Store Owner:

I am a fifth-grade teacher at Kenwood Elementary School, and I am very interested in improving the science skills of my students. As a member of our community and a business leader, you are, I am sure, also concerned about the quality of our students' science education. Most science activities in the elementary grades require only simple household items. However, with limited financial resources at our school, we cannot purchase these items. I am asking that you consider donating to our school the items listed below. These materials will be used in a series of lessons to teach students about insects.

  10 aluminum pans
   5 lbs. of flour
     rolls of netting
  10 plastic jars
  10 sets of mixing spoons
  10 measuring cups
   2 bags of potting soil
   1 bag of cornmeal
   5 flashlights
100 Styrofoam cups

     I will call you in a week to see if you are interested in meeting to discuss this donation. Thank you for your interest in our students' educational needs.

Sincerely,

Teacher's Name

Letter requesting donations from local businesses.

that in recent years the boundaries between the various natural sciences have become more and more blurred and major concepts more unified.

Hurd stresses the need for greater integration of school subjects and the integration of science with social issues, technology, and other school subjects.

Consistent with Hurd's recommendations, most national reform efforts currently stress the need to integrate the curriculum (National Council of Teachers of Mathematics, 1989; National Research Council, 1996; International Reading Association, 1996; National Council of Teachers of English, 1996; and National Council of Social Studies, 1994). Integration is a major focus in such science reform initiatives as *Science for All Americans* (Rutherford & Ahlgren, 1990) and the *National Science Education Standards* (NRC, 1996). Curriculum integration is also stressed by the National Association for the Education of Young Children (NAEYC), an organization that specializes in instructional practices appropriate for the education of the young child, and the National

CONNECTING TO
NATIONAL SCIENCE EDUCATION STANDARDS

Science Education Teaching Standards
Schools must restructure schedules so that teachers can use blocks of time, interdisciplinary strategies, and field experiences to give students many opportunities to engage in serious scientific investigation as an integral part of their science learning (p. 44).

Table 11.5

RESOURCES FOR MATERIALS NEEDED IN AN ELEMENTARY OR MIDDLE GRADES SCIENCE CLASSROOM

Source

Item	Drugstore	Hardware Store	Grocery Store	Commercial Supplier	Noncommercial Supplier	Pet Store	Craft Store	Toy Store
Alcohol—rubbing	X		X	X				
Aluminum foil			X	X				
Aluminum pans		X	X	X			X	
Ammonia		X	X	X				
Aquariums/fish supplies			X	X		X		
Baking soda			X	X				
Balances—pan				X				
Balances/scales				X				
Balances—triple beam				X				
Ball and ring heating apparatus				X				
Ball bearings		X		X			X	
Balloons	X		X	X			X	X
Battery clips				X				
Bell wire		X		X				
Benedict's solution				X				
Bimetal strip heating apparatus					X			
Bleach			X	X				
Bones—sets of animals				X				
Bulb holders (small)				X				
Bulbs—flashlight size	X	X	X	X				
Bulbs—household size		X		X			X	
Bulb socket holders				X				
Candles	X		X	X			X	
Cellophane			X	X			X	
Cheesecloth	X	X	X	X			X	
Clothespins		X	X	X			X	
Compass		X		X				
Construction paper			X	X		X	X	
Convex and concave lenses				X				
Copper wire		X		X				
Corks		X		X			X	
Cornstarch			X	X				
Cotton balls	X		X	X			X	
Cotton swabs	X		X	X			X	
Cover slips for microscope slides				X				
Cups			X	X			X	
Diffraction gratings				X				
Dissecting kits and trays				X				
Dropping bottles				X				X
Dry cells (1.5 volt)		X	X	X				
Dry cells (12 volt)		X	X	X				
Electrical switches		X		X				
Electric motors		X		X				
Electronic scale				X				
Elmer's glue		X	X	X			X	
Eyedroppers	X		X	X				
Eye wash				X				
Feathers				X			X	
Filter paper			X	X				
Fire blanket				X	X			
Fire box				X	X			
Fishing line		X		X				
Fishing weights		X		X				

Table 11.5

(CONTINUED)
Source

Item	Drugstore	Hardware Store	Grocery Store	Commercial Supplier	Noncommercial Supplier	Pet Store	Craft Store	Toy Store
Flashlights		x	x	x				
Flour			x					
Food coloring			x	x				
Forceps				x				
Friction boards				x				
Fuses		x		x				
Gear kits				x				
Genecon hand generators				x				
Glassware				x	x			
Glue		x	x	x			x	
Goggles				x				
Graduated cylinders				x				
Gravel		x		x			x	
Hole punchers			x	x				
Hot plates		x		x				
Ice cream salt			x					
Incandescent lightbulbs	x	x	x	x				
Ink			x	x				
Iodine	x		x	x				
Iron filings				x				
Lab glassware drying rack				x				
Lamp sockets—household size		x	x	x				
Large poster paper				x			x	
Magnets—bar				x				
Magnets—circle				x				
Magnets—horseshoe				x				
Magnets—marble				x				
Magnet wire				x				
Magnifying lenses		x		x				
Marbles				x				x
Markers			x	x			x	
Masking tape			x	x			x	
Matches		x	x	x				
Metal rods—brass, copper, aluminum		x		x				
Meter sticks				x				
Microscopes				x				
Microscope—stereoscope				x				
Microscope slides—blank				x				
Microscope slides—prepared				x				
Mirrors (convex and concave)				x				
Mirrors (plane)		x		x			x	
Modeling clay				x			x	x
Motors				x				
Nails		x		x				
Netting		x		x			x	
Newsprint				x			x	
Owl pellets				x	x			
Paper clips				x			x	
Paper cups			x	x				
Paraffin			x	x			x	
Pencils			x	x			x	
Petri dishes				x				
Petroleum jelly	x		x	x				

Table 11.5

(CONCLUDED)
Source

Item	Drugstore	Hardware Store	Grocery Store	Commercial Supplier	Noncommercial Supplier	Pet Store	Craft Store	Toy Store
Ping-Pong balls				x				x
Pipe cleaners				x			x	
Plastic aquariums with lids				x		x		
Plastic gloves		x	x	x				
Plaster of Paris		x		x			x	
Plastic spoons			x	x				
Plastic storage tubs		x	x	x				
Poster board				x			x	
Potting soil		x		x				
Prism				x				
Pulleys		x		x				
Razor blades		x	x	x			x	
Rubberbands		x	x	x			x	
Rubber cement			x	x			x	
Rubber stoppers		x		x				
Rubber tubing		x		x				
Rulers		x	x	x				
Salt			x	x				
Sandpaper		x		x			x	
Scissors		x	x	x			x	
Soap—bar and liquid dish			x	x				
Spatulas			x	x				
Sponges	x	x	x	x			x	
Spoons—plastic and silverware			x	x				
Spring scales				x				
Steel wool		x		x				
Sterno can		x	x	x				
Stopwatch		x		x				
Storage bags (various sizes)		x	x	x				
Strainers			x	x				
Straws			x	x				
Straws—clear			x	x			x	
String		x		x			x	
Styrofoam cups		x	x	x				
Sugar			x	x				
Sulfur				x				
Surface boards (sandpaper, rubber, etc.)				x				
Tape—clear, 1″ wide			x	x		x		
Test tube holders				x				
Test tube racks				x				
Test tubes				x	x			
Thermometers		x		x				
Thread				x			x	
Toothpicks			x	x				
Tuning forks				x				
Vegetable oil				x				
Vinegar			x	x				
Wax			x	x				
Wax paper			x	x				
Weather instruments				x	x			
Wire—copper (insulated)		x		x				
Wire—copper (uninsulated)		x		x				
Wire—electrical, variety of gauges		x		x				

Middle School Association (NMSA), an association that focuses on young and early adolescents.

Howard Gardner (1983, 1993, 1999) challenged our conventional thinking about intelligence by identifying eights forms of intelligence, or **multiple intelligences**: mathematical-logical, linguistic, spatial, bodily kinesthetic, musical, interpersonal, intrapersonal, and naturalist. In classrooms, learners use multiple intelligences to execute complex tasks. Armstrong (1994) suggested that students become active learners when they use most of their intelligences. Teachers now use Gardner's multiple intelligence theory to support multidimensional instruction, integrated curriculum, and assessments that match students' strengths. Gardner described the eight intelligences as follows:

Integration helps students see how science relates to real world contexts.

- **Linguistic intelligence** is characterized by the capacity to use language (written or oral). Students with linguistic intelligence learn best by speaking, hearing, and seeing. Science teachers capitalize on this by using strategies and techniques such as debates, writing, tape recordings, and books.
- **Logical-mathematical intelligence** uses numbers and logic. Students with this intelligence solve puzzles, explore patterns and relationships, work with numbers and data, use logical reasoning, classify, and use time sequencing. Science teachers have these students manipulate numbers, find patterns in data, and make conclusions based on data.
- People with **visual-spatial intelligence** think in terms of physical space. They use graphic images, drawings, and pictures. They learn best by visualizing objects and working with colors, photographs, visual diagrams, concept maps, charts, and 3D models.
- Students with **musical intelligence** are sensitive to sound, pitch, and rhythm. They like to sing, hum, listen to music, and play an instrument. Teachers help them learn science through songs and jingles, by writing songs, and by listening to the radio and CDs.
- **Body-kinesthetic intelligence** involves the use of movement in learning. They like to make things, touch objects, talk, use body language, dance, act, and participate in sports. Teachers help them learn science through acting and role-plays, demonstrating to others, and using physical games.
- **Interpersonal intelligence** is the ability to understand and interact with other people. People with interpersonal intelligence tend to have many friends, talk a great deal, and understand others. Science teachers engage these students in collaborative learning, interviews, and activities in which they can write to or talk with others.
- **Intrapersonal intelligence** is the ability to understand oneself. Students with strong intrapersonal intelligence like to work alone and explore their own interests. They are focused inward on dreams and goals. They work well

> ### Key Idea
>
> Integrated curriculum more closely matches the way information is presented in real life and matches students' intelligences.

Table 11.6

STRATEGIES TO ADAPT TEACHING ACTIVITIES TO MEET STUDENTS' MULTIPLE INTELLIGENCES

Linguistic Intelligence	Logical-Mathematical Intelligence	Visual-Spatial Intelligence	Muscial Intelligence	Body-Kinesthetic Intelligence	Interpersonal Intelligence	Intrapersonal Intelligence	Naturalist Intelligence
Tape recordings	Formulas	Drawings and paintings	Songs, raps, jingles	Field trips	Team tasks	Reflective journals	Examining patterns in nature
Biographies	Puzzles	Photos	Choral reading	Role-playing	Collaborative learning	Self-evaluation	Outdoor education
Poetry	Timelines	Storyboards	Writing songs	Sports and physical games	E-mail and chat room discussions	Independent studies	Nature walks
Books	Venn diagrams	Props and scenes for plays	Tone and rhythmic patterns	Simulations	Group projects	Personal goal setting	Photographing nature
Journals	Data analysis	Posters	Background music for meditation or concentration	Dances	Group and class discussions	Problem solving	Outdoor field trips; trips to the zoo, museums, etc.

on self-paced, individualized projects. Science teachers frequently have them keep personal journals or work on independent study projects.

- **Naturalist intelligence** is a person's ability to identify and classify patterns in nature. People who are sensitive to changes in weather patterns or who are good at seeing relationships and patterns among plants and animals may be expressing naturalist intelligence abilities.

Many schools have adopted integrated curriculum techniques in response to Howard Gardner's theory of multiple intelligences. The process of blending a topic across different subject areas such as science, art, music, and drama helps teachers engage students' multiple intelligences. In addition, technology tools facilitate the use of many different intelligences. When students create a multimedia document, for example, they might use logical thinking to organize the document, visual-spatial skills to design the project, music to add special effects, charts and data to present an argument, and written words to tell a story.

Table 11.6 illustrates how a teacher might plan activities on the topic of insects using Howard Gardner's multiple intelligences theory. Table 11.7 shows how a teacher might adapt such activities to a project on insects.

Research on females and minorities in science indicates that an integrated focus helps spark interest in science (Bianchini, Cavazos, & Helms, 2000). Teachers need to emphasize how technology and science can be integrated with other fields with a human interest such as ecology, health, and sociology (National Council for Research on Women, 2001). Haberman (1995) also stresses the importance of an integrated, project approach related to

Table 11.7

SAMPLE MULTIPLE INTELLIGENCES LESSONS ON INSECTS

Linguistic Intelligence	Logical-Mathematical Intelligence	Visual-Spatial Intelligence	Muscial Intelligence	Body-Kinesthetic Intelligence	Interpersonal Intelligence	Intrapersonal Intelligence	Naturalist Intelligence
Read a book about insects.	Use measurements and data to compare and contrast insects found in different environmental areas.	Draw pictures of various insects.	Listen to a song about insects or go to the children's section of a local music store for songs.	Take a field trip to learn more about insects.	Work with team member to learn more about insects.	Keep a reflective journal about insect findings.	Examine patterns found in insect environments.
Discuss a book with others.	Design a puzzle about insect taxonomy.	Photograph insects in their natural habitats.	Participate in a choral reading about insects.	Role-play insect movement.	Design a collaborative learning investigation on insects.	Conduct a self-evaluation on what has been learned about insects.	Learn how insects are adapted to survive in their environment.
Write a play about insects.	Keep a timeline documenting insect activity.	Create a storyboard depicting insect metamorphosis.	Write lyrics about insects to the tune of a popular song.	Design and play a physical game to depict an insect concept.	Share data on insects with others over e-mail.	Design and complete an independent study to learn more about a particular insect.	Take a nature walk around the school to look for insects.
Listen to an entomologist guest speaker.	Compare and contrast insects with other animal classifications.	Design props for a play about insects.	Note rhythmic patterns in nature.	Simulate insect metamorphosis.	Work with others on a group project on insects.	Set a personal goal for overcoming fear of insects.	Photograph insects in nature.
Write a report on insects.	Analyze data collected on insect observations throughout the school year.	Design a poster to display findings related to an insect investigation.	Play background music while students are investigating insects.	Create a dance to teach a concept related to insects.	Have a whole class discussion about insect investigation.	Figure out how to safely control insects in a garden.	Go to the zoo exhibit on insects.

real life for working with children in poverty. Calabrese-Barton and Yang (2000) stress that teachers need to present science in such a way that encourages all students to participate in science. Teachers need to integrate science into students' daily lives and help students learn science in nontraditional ways that meet their interests and cultures (Barton, 1998). For example, Western science does not traditionally recognize traditional folk medicine, yet long before the discovery of aspirin in 1853, Hispanic families knew that that tea made from the flower of the daisy fleabane could be used to treat aches and pains (Meyer-Monhardt, 2000). These flowers contain acetylsalicylic acid (aspirin). Educators also stress the importance of culturally relevant curriculum for American Indian students. Davison and Miller (1998) write that curriculum can be made culturally relevant for American Indian

Portfolio Activity 11.11

INVESTIGATING YOUR BELIEFS ABOUT CURRICULUM INTEGRATION

Materials Needed:
- An elementary or middle grade science textbook
- Pencil and paper

A. Examine a fourth-grade science textbook for a selected topic. A traditional textbook will usually contain topics such as the human body, electricity, magnetism, sound, light, animals, plants, machines, the earth's crust, volcanoes, earthquakes, and the solar system.

B. Form a team with four other classmates and assign yourselves the roles of particular subject matter specialists (science teacher, mathematics teacher, social studies teacher, language/reading teacher, and art teacher). Take the topic selected and together design a set of integrated lesson ideas for teaching the topic.

C. After you have finished planning, individually critique the lessons using the following criteria. This should establish what you personally believe about integrated

planning. Then, have your group critique the lesson ideas using the same criteria. Make sure your group comes to a consensus.

1. What prior knowledge and experiences do students need before engaging in integrated lessons?
2. Will important content and inquiry objectives be met? If not, what is missing? Explain.
3. If a teacher teaches this way for the entire school year, will there be important topics that are not covered? Standards that are not met?
4. Are the learning performances watered down or less meaningful in these lessons? Explain.
5. Should the topic stay as it is in the textbook (taught separately by subject matter)? Why or why not?
6. Is curriculum integration beneficial? Why or why not?
7. Do you know enough about each subject area to teach this way? Explain.

D. Put your ideas in your portfolio.

students by presenting it in an integrated fashion. An integrated approach that focuses on cultural understanding can help minority students become engaged in science.

Before we continue discussing the integrating of school subject areas, think about your beliefs about curriculum integration with the help of Portfolio Activity 11.11.

The Definition of *Integration*

Key Idea

Integration is the crossing of subject matter boundaries.

Sometimes educators use the terms *integrated, interdisciplinary*, and *thematic* synonymously. Lederman and Niess (1997) define **integrated** as a blending in which the separate parts are not discernible. They use the metaphor of tomato soup; you cannot discern the tomatoes in the soup. They define **interdisciplinary** as a mixture of subjects connected but still identifiable. The metaphor they use is chicken noodle soup; it's a soup but you can still recognize the broth, chicken, and noodles. Similarly, Jacobs (1989) defines *interdisciplinary* as "a knowledge view and curriculum approach that consciously applies methodology and language from more than one discipline to examine a central theme, issue, problem, topic, or experience." Finally, Lederman and Niess (1997) define **thematic** as a unifying topic or subject transcending traditional subject boundaries. For purposes of this book, we use the word *integrated* to define the crossing of subject matter boundaries.

Beane (1995) suggests that curriculum integration, like project-based science, begins with "problems, issues, and concerns posed by life itself" (p. 616). Integrated curriculum, according to Beane (1996), has four characteristics: (1) it is organized around problems and issues that have personal and social significance in the real world, (2) it uses pertinent knowledge in the context of topic without regard for subject lines, (3) it is used to study current problems rather than for a test or grade level outcome, and (4) it emphasizes projects and activities with real application of knowledge and problem solving. Hopkins (1937, as cited in Beane, 1996) defined *integration* similarly—as cooperatively planned, problem-centered, and integrated knowledge. These definitions of curriculum *integration* are consistent with our view of project-based learning as crossing curricular subject areas.

CONNECTING TO
NATIONAL SCIENCE EDUCATION STANDARDS

Science Education Content Standards
The standard for unifying concepts and processes is presented for grades K–12, because the understanding and abilities associated with major conceptual and procedural schemes need to be developed over an entire education, and the unifying concepts and processes transcend disciplinary boundaries (p. 104).

How Project-Based Science Supports Curriculum Integration

Rakow and Vasquez (1998) write, "Project-based integration may be the most authentic form of cross-curricular integration because it involves students in real-world learning experiences. In project-based integration, students investigate real issues in real contexts." Project-based science's key features (driving questions, student engagement in investigations, communities of learners collaborating together, use of technology, and creation of artifacts) are all congruent with curriculum integration. As students answer driving questions, they develop deeper understandings because they make connections among the central concepts of a variety of subject areas. Driving questions are contextualized; they are anchored in the lives of learners and deal with important, real-world issues. Real-world questions are not separated into different subject areas.

> ### Key Idea
> Project-based science supports curriculum integration because driving questions focus on real-world questions that are not separated into different subject areas.

Integration builds understanding of concepts. When science topics involve people, as they usually do, social studies concepts such as economics, politics, culture, and history come into play. Teachers can use children's literature of all types (realistic fiction, historical fiction, fantasy, plays, newspapers, science fiction, traditional or classical literature, poetry, trade books, and biographies) to teach about science topics. Many science investigations make use of the arts: painting, sketching, drawing, collages, sculpture, drama, role-playing, pantomime, charades, skits, movies, puppets, improvisation, music, songs, instruments, and jingles. Integrating mathematics into science allows students to use computation, measurement, ratios, proportion, graphing, and geometry in their investigations. For example, students studying the question "Where does all the garbage go?" will study science concepts such as decomposition and pollution. However, the question does not fit neatly into the school subject of science. The question flows over to social studies because it involves laws, regulations, ethics, value judgments, and decisions. Mathematics comes into play when the amount of garbage is extrapolated for every human on earth over the next few years at present rates. Language, reading, and communication are used to find information, debate issues, discuss possible solutions to our garbage problem, and communicate findings.

When students engage in investigations in project-based science, they use many skills that cross the curriculum. For example, they ask questions, look for relationships, organize procedures, consider multiple factors, take notes, use reference materials, record data, summarize information, interpret data, formulate conclusions, and communicate results. These skills are also used in other subject areas such as mathematics, language arts, and social studies.

Project-based science emphasizes communities of learners collaborating together. Such collaboration allows students to integrate understandings from a variety of careers and subject areas. For example, students investigating the topic of insects might interact with an entomologist from a local university to learn about biological research on insects, cultural norms regarding insects, and mathematical models associated with insect population control.

Use of technology is an integral component of project-based science. Technology is rarely separated along subject area lines. Software programs frequently include digital photographs, sound, and music, for example. Many provide students with opportunities to read and write. Some include mathematics concepts and social studies concepts. For example, a popular software program called *Great Ocean Rescue* (Tom Snyder Productions, 1992, 1994) integrates the sciences and tackles social issues related to oceans such as pollution and coral reef destruction. The Web is not separated into subject areas; topics are organized as they are in the real world around themes. For example, if you were to conduct an Internet search on acid rain, you would uncover a host of subjects: coal mining, air pollution laws, industrial regulations, sulfur in coal, and mutations in frogs.

As students create artifacts, they use all types of knowledge and skills from other subject areas such as music, art, mathematics, and language arts. Students might develop posters or make models from recycled materials. They might write songs, write reports of their results, or give oral presentations. Students might mix written work, sound, video, and graphics in hypermedia artifacts.

A Word of Warning

Key Idea

Integration should focus on enhancing student understanding rather than integrating for the sake of integrating.

Lonning and DeFranco (1997) argue that integration can be justified only when connecting subjects enhances the understanding of them. In other words, teachers should not force integration for the sake of integration. We have seen teachers create integrated units of study around topics such as "teddy bears." Although this topic may encourage reading and writing in language arts, it provides little opportunity for students to engage in meaningful science learning. Driving questions in project-based science should be feasible (students should be able to design and perform investigations to answer the questions), worthwhile (they should contain rich content, relate to what scientists and professionals really do, and be able to be broken down into subquestions), contextualized (they should be of the real world, nontrivial, and important), meaningful (they should be interesting and exciting to learners), ethical (not harm the environment), and sustainable (students should be able to pursue detailed answers to them over time). Good driving questions will help you to integrate curriculum in a meaningful way.

Another way to judge the worth of curriculum integration is to use the rubric in Table 11.8, which lists standards of the *National Science Education Standards* (NRC, 1996), the National Council for the Social Studies (NCSS, 1994), the National Council of Teachers of English/International Reading Association (1996), and the National Council of Teachers of Mathematics (1989).

An Example of Curriculum Integration

The driving question "What kinds of insects live in our neighborhood?" offers many opportunities for teachers to integrate the curriculum:

Table 11.8

RUBRIC FOR EVALUATING INTEGRATED CURRICULUM

Project topic: _____

Rating scale   4 = Strong   3 = Adequate   2 = Weak   1 = No evidence

NATIONAL STANDARDS IN SCIENCE ARE FOLLOWED (FOR GRADES 5–8)

4 3 2 1   •   The activities support unifying concepts and processes (systems, order, and organization; evidence, models, and explanation; constancy, change, and measurement; evolution and equilibrium; and form and function).

4 3 2 1   •   The activates support scientific inquiry (abilities to do scientific inquiry and understand scientific inquiry).

4 3 2 1   •   The activities develop understanding in physical science (properties and changes of properties in matter; motions and forces; and transfer of energy), life science (structure and function in living systems; reproduction and heredity; regulation and behavior; populations and ecosystems; diversity and adaptations of organisms), and/or earth-space science (structure of the earth system; earth's history; and earth in the solar system).

4 3 2 1   •   The activities connect science with technology (students have understandings about science and technology , and they have abilities of technological design).

4 3 2 1   •   Science is presented as it relates to personal and societal perspectives (personal health; populations, resources, and environments; natural hazards; risks and benefits; and science and technology in society).

4 3 2 1   •   The history and nature of science are presented to students (science as a human endeavor, nature of science, and history of science).

NATIONAL STANDARDS IN MATHEMATICS ARE FOLLOWED

4 3 2 1   •   The activities support mathematical communications.

4 3 2 1   •   The activities support mathematical connections.

4 3 2 1   •   The activities support mathematical problem solving.

4 3 2 1   •   The activities support mathematical reasoning.

NATIONAL STANDARDS IN LANGUAGE ARTS/READING ARE FOLLOWED

4 3 2 1   •   Students have opportunities to read a variety of print and nonprint materials.

4 3 2 1   •   Students are able to write for a variety of purposes.

4 3 2 1   •   Students are able to adjust their spoken language for a variety of audiences.

4 3 2 1   •   Students use the language arts—reading, writing, listening, and speaking—to nurture their learning through research.

NATIONAL STANDARDS IN SOCIAL STUDIES ARE FOLLOWED

4 3 2 1   •   The activities provide for the study of culture and cultural diversity.

4 3 2 1   •   The activities provide for the study of time, continuity, and change.

4 3 2 1   •   The activities provide for the study of people, places, and environments.

4 3 2 1   •   The activities provide for the study of individual development and identity.

4 3 2 1   •   The activities provide for the study of individuals, groups, and institutions.

4 3 2 1   •   The activities provide for the study of power, authority, and governance.

4 3 2 1   •   The activities provide for the study of production, distribution, and consumption.

4 3 2 1   •   The activities provide for the study of science, technology, and society.

4 3 2 1   •   The activities provide for the study of global connections.

4 3 2 1   •   The activities provide for the study of civic ideas and practices.

LESSONS INCLUDE CONNECTIONS ACROSS THE CURRICULUM

4 3 2 1   •   The lessons integrate science, mathematics, social studies, and/or language arts.

4 3 2 1   •   The learning of concepts and skills is enhanced because of the connections made across the curriculum.

4 3 2 1   •   The unit allows students to see one subject from the viewpoint of another subject (multiple perspectives).

Source: This rubric is modified from various professional standards (NRC, 1996; NCSS, 1994; NCTE-IRA, 1996; & NCTM, 1989, 2000). It was used in an Eisenhower Professional Development Grant entitled PRISM-CLASS (Project for Integrating Science and Mathematics Curriculum with Language Arts and Social Studies) at the University of Toledo.

- In science, students can study camouflage, metamorphosis, classification, body structure, and predator/prey relationships.
- Mathematics can come into play in several ways. Students might investigate the area of an insect's territory. They might graph the number of insects found in different areas of the playground or graph the weight of the insects during different stages of development. They might use ratio and proportion to contrast the weight of an ant with the mass it can carry. Students might calculate the length of tunnels that ants build. They might explore the geometric shapes found in nature's insect populations or find the average number of days it takes for insects to complete metamorphosis.
- Social studies are involved when students learn about the historical impact of insects (such as locusts) and the development of insecticides to limit insect populations. Students might study the cultural behaviors (such as eating insects) of people in other countries.
- Language arts are involved when students write reports, communicate findings, give each other feedback, and read and discuss insect-related stories. What follows are some stories that could be used in an insect science–language arts activity project:

  Livo, L. J., G. McGlathery, and N. J. Livo. 1995. *Of Bugs and Beasts*. Englewood, Colo.: Teacher Ideas Press.

  Carle, E. 1969. *The Very Hungry Caterpillar*. New York: Philomel Books.

  Ryder, J. 1989. *Where Butterflies Grow*. New York: Lodestar Books, E. P. Dutton.

Concept Mapping to Plan Integrated Projects

Key Idea

Concept mapping can be used to organize the integration of a project across the curriculum.

In Chapter 10, we discussed the integration of disciplines and how it impacts the structure of a school day. In Chapter 7, we explored the use of concept mapping in planning a lesson. Earlier in this chapter, we again discussed concept mapping as a way to identify and organize important concepts in a project. Concept mapping can also be used to organize the integration of a project across the curriculum.

A teacher in a *self-contained classroom* (with one group of students all day) can use concept mapping to develop lessons across subject areas. Teachers in **departmentalized** (separated by subject area) schools can use concept mapping to plan together to integrate a theme or topic across their disciplines. Frequently, intermediate and middle schools (usually grades 4–8) purposefully place teachers in teams so that they can plan integrated lessons together. Regardless of how you plan integrated lessons, you will find that using an integrated approach provides an exciting way to teach science that is consistent with current reform efforts in science education. However, few people are knowledgeable in all subject areas. An excellent resource to help teachers grow professionally by learning more about topics that can be included in a concept map is the *Atlas of Science Literacy* (AAAS and NSTA, 2001). Figure 11.4 is a sample concept map for the integration of science with language arts, reading, mathematics, and social studies in our insect project. Portfolio Activity 11.12 asks you to integrate the project you have developed with other disciplines.

CONNECTING TO
NATIONAL SCIENCE EDUCATION STANDARDS

Science Education Teaching Standards
Individual and collective planning is a cornerstone to science teaching; it is a vehicle for professional support and growth. In the vision of science education described in the *Standards,* many planning decisions are made by groups of teachers at grade and building levels to construct coherent and articulated programs within and across grades (p. 32).

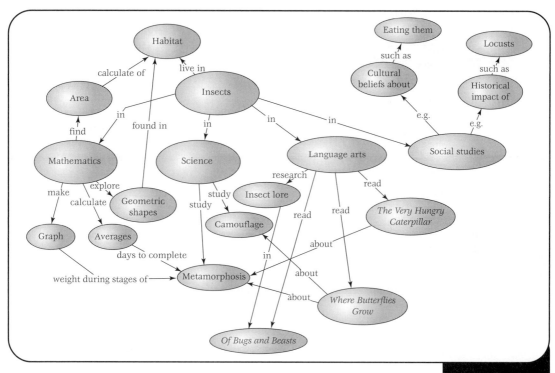

Concept map for science integration.

USING TECHNOLOGY TOOLS TO PLAN PROJECTS

In the opening scenario in this chapter three teachers planned together. Although collaboration is the ideal professional context for teachers, not all teachers have a group of colleagues with whom to work. Some teachers must "swim against the tide" to begin project work. A teacher in a small school may be the only one teaching at his or her grade level. Teachers' planning times might not facilitate optimal planning.

Teachers who don't have a team of colleagues to work with at school need to reach out to others outside of the school. A teacher working in isolation needs to develop a professional network of colleagues by attending conferences or communicating electronically with peers through sites such as the one maintained by the National Science Teachers Association. This site, for example, includes an NSTA Community section in which teachers can talk with colleagues in a discussion forum. Additional science websites where teachers can communicate with other colleagues are Web-based Inquiry Science Environment (WISE) and One Sky, Many Voices.

Other websites include helpful teacher information, lesson plans, and extension ideas. For example, the Carolina Biological site includes teacher resources (tips, science news, answers to frequently asked questions) and a place where teachers can ask professors science questions.

Many teachers use the Web to seek out ideas for lesson plans and curriculum resources. The Eisenhower National Clearinghouse is an excellent place to get answers to questions, search for curriculum resources, read up-to-date research, find lesson plans,

> ### Key Idea
>
> Technology tools can help teachers collaborate with others, locate resources, and find lesson ideas.

Professional Resources

Portfolio Activity 11.12   **DEVELOPING INTEGRATED CURRICULUM**

Materials Needed:

- The National Council of Teachers of Mathematics (2000) standards
- The National Research Center (1996) science standards
- The International Reading Association (1996) standards
- The National Council of Teachers of English (1996) standards
- The National Council of Social Studies (1992) standards
- The AAAS/NSTA (2001) *Atlas of Science Literacy*

A. Compare and contrast the science concepts and skills that need to be covered in the project you have been developing throughout this chapter with important content in the NCTM, NRC, IRA, NCTE, and NCSS standards.

B. What reading, language arts, mathematics, and social studies content might be covered in this project?

C. To the concept map you developed earlier add integrated reading, language arts, social studies, and mathematics content. You might also add art, music, and drama content to your map.

D. Outline several lesson ideas that can be integrated with mathematics, social studies, reading, and language arts.

E. File your revised concept map and lesson ideas in your portfolio.

and talk with other teachers. Other technology tools, such as grade books, help teachers increase their productivity.

ONLINE LEARNING CENTER

CHAPTER REVIEW   www.mhhe.com/krajcik2e

Go to the Online Learning Center at **www.mhhe.com/krajcik2e** to review important content from the chapter and key terms, take a chapter assessment, and link to the chapter's websites.

CHAPTER SUMMARY

Planning is a critical aspect of developing a project environment. This chapter focused on several steps that teachers typically take to plan a project-based curriculum.

Throughout the chapter we developed an insect project. First, we identified concepts and selected learning performances. We matched concepts and learning performances to local, state, and national standards. We used concept mapping to organize the concepts.

Second, we discussed ways that teachers can develop a driving question, benchmark lessons, investigations, assessments, and a calendar of activities. Because the process for developing a project is iterative, we considered a model in which these steps operate in a back-and-forth process.

Third, we examined some ways to locate commercial, noncommercial, household, and community resources because resources are important in any project.

Fourth, we discussed the reasons for the natural support of curriculum integration in a project-based environment. Once again, we used concept mapping as a planning tool for integrating the curriculum.

Fifth, we discussed how technology tools can help facilitate planning.

CHAPTER HIGHLIGHTS

- There are many factors that influence teachers' decisions about the concepts and learning performances to be covered in a project
  - State and national standards.
  - Adopted curricula.
  - Students' interests and culture.
- After identifying concepts and selecting learning performances, teachers brainstorm several driving questions that will allow students to explore the concepts selected.
- Driving questions are
  - Feasible.
  - Worthwhile.
  - Contextualized.
  - Sustainable.
  - Ethical.
  - Meaningful.
- Teachers develop investigations to help students plan and conduct experiments that facilitate their construction of partial solutions to important questions.
- Various assessments that are linked to classroom activities and investigations can be used to gain a complete view of student learning.
- A calendar, although only an estimate of time, helps to guide the sequence of lessons and orchestrate the various components in a time frame.
- Some teachers like to use a concept map to organize a project's activities, because the hierarchy in the concept map helps define the sequence of concepts students need to learn in benchmark lessons.
- Teachers use many resources to help plan benchmark lessons
  - Commercial suppliers.
  - Noncommercial materials.
  - Everyday household materials.
  - Magazines and journals.
  - Teacher trade books.
  - Guest lecturers, field trips, and other community resources.
  - Children's literature.
- Curriculum integration is the crossing of curricular subject areas.
- Curriculum integration has become a popular reform movement for several reasons
  - It resembles real life more closely.
  - National standards are calling for curriculum integration.
  - Integration helps teachers teach to children's multiple intelligences.
  - Curriculum integration has been found to help girls and minorities learn science.
- Project-based science supports curriculum integration because its key features (driving questions, student engagement in investigations, communities of learners collaborating together, use of technology, and creation of artifacts) are all congruent with curriculum integration.
- Teachers do not integrate for the sake of integrating. Rather, they integrate across subjects to enhance learning for all students.
- Concept mapping is a useful tool for planning an integrated curriculum project.
- Technology tools help teachers plan project-based curriculum.

KEY TERMS

body-kinesthetic
    intelligence (465)
calendar (452)
curriculum
    integration (460)
departmentalized (472)
integrated (468)
interdisciplinary (468)
interpersonal
    intelligence (465)

intrapersonal
    intelligence (465)
linguistic
    intelligence (465)
logical-mathematical
    intelligence (465)
multiple
    intelligences (465)
musical
    intelligence (465)

naturalist
    intelligence (465)
resources (455)
thematic (468)
visual-spatial
    intelligence (465)

REFERENCES

Alexander, W. M., and P. S. George. 1981. *The exemplary middle school*. New York: Holt, Rinehart and Winston.

American Association for the Advancement of Science. 1993. *Benchmarks for science literacy*. New York: Oxford University Press.

American Association for the Advancement of Science. 2001. *Atlas of Science Literacy*. Washington, D.C.: American Association for the Advancement of Science and National Science Teachers Association Press.

Armstrong, T. 1994. *Multiple intelligences in the classroom*. Alexandria, Va.: Association for Supervision and Curriculum Development.

Barnes, M. B., T. J. Shaw, and B. S. Spector. 1989. *How science is learned by adolescents and young adults*. Dubuque, Iowa: Kendall/Hunt.

Barton, A. C. 1998. *Feminist science education*. New York: Teachers College Press.

Barton, A. C., and K. Yang, 2000. The culture of power and science education: Learning from Miguel. *Journal of Research in Science Teaching* 37(8): 871–89.

Beane, J. 1995. Curriculum integration and the disciplines of knowledge. *Phi Delta Kappan* 76:616–22.

Beane, J. 1996. On the shoulders of giants! The case for curriculum integration. *Middle School Journal* 28:6–11.

Bianchini, J.A., L. M. Cavazos, and J.V. Helms. 2000. From professional lives to inclusive practice: Science teachers and scientists' views of gender and ethnicity in science education. *Journal of Research in Science Teaching* 37(6): 511–47.

Bradekamp, S. 1987. *Developmentally appropriate practice in early childhood programs serving children from birth through age 8*. Washington, D.C.: National Association for the Education of Young Children.

Braus, J., ed. 1989. *Ranger Rick's nature scope: Incredible insects*. Washington, D.C.: National Wildlife Federation.

Burnett, R. 1999. *The pillbug project: A guide to investigation*. Washington, D.C.: National Science Teachers Association.

Davison, D. M., and K. W. Miller. 1998. An ethnoscience approach to curriculum issues for American Indian students. *School Science and Mathematics* 98(5):260–65.

Echols, J. C. 1986. *Hide a butterfly*. Berkeley, Calif.: Lawrence Hall of Science.

Echols, J. C. 1993. *Ladybugs*. Berkeley, Calif.: Lawrence Hall of Science.

Gardner, H. 1983. *Frames of mind: The theory of multiple intelligence*. New York: Basic Books.

Gardner, H. 1993. *Multiple intelligence: The theory into practice*. New York: Basic Books.

Gardner, H. 1999. *The disciplined mind*. New York: Simon & Schuster.

Haberman, M. 1995. *STAR teachers of children in poverty*. West Lafayette, Ind.: Kappa Delta Pi.

Hurd, P. D. 1991. Why we must transform science education. *Educational Leadership* 49(2):33–35.

Jacobs, H. H. J. 1989. *Interdisciplinary curriculum: Design and implementation*. Alexandria, Va.: Association for Supervision and Curriculum Development.

Lawrence Hall of Science. 1993. *Full option science system (FOSS)*. Chicago, Ill.: Encyclopedia Britannica Educational Corporation.

Lederman, N. G., and M. L. Niess. 1997. Integrated, interdisciplinary, or thematic instruction? Is this a question or is it questionable semantics? *School Science and Mathematics* 97(2):57–58.

Lonning, R. A., and T. C. DeFranco. 1997. Integration of science and mathematics: A theoretical model. *School Science and Mathematics* 97(4):212–15.

Meyer-Monhardt, R. 2000. Fair play in science education: Equal opportunities for minority students. *The Clearing House* 74 (1): 18–22.

National Council for Research on Women. 2001. *Balancing the equation: What we know and what we need*. www.ncrw.org/research/scifacts/htm.

National Council for the Social Studies. 1994. *Curriculum standards for social studies*. Washington, D.C.: Author.

National Council of Teachers of English/International Reading Association (IRA).

1996. *Standards for English language arts*. Newark, Del.: Author.

National Council of Teachers of Mathematics. 2000. *Principle and standards for school mathematics*. Reston, Va.: National Council of Teachers of Mathematics.

National Middle School Association. 1982. *This we believe*. Columbus, Ohio: Author.

National Research Council. 1996. *National science education standards*. Washington, D.C.: National Academy Press.

National Science Resources Center. 1992. *The life cycle of butterflies*. Burlington, N.C.: Carolina Biological.

National Science Resources Center. 1994. *STC: Science and technology for children*. Washington, D.C.: National Academy of Sciences.

Ohio Board of Education. 1994. *Science: Ohio's model competency-based program*. Columbus, Ohio: Author.

Rakow, S. J., and J. Vasquez. 1998. Integrated instruction: A trio of strategies. *Science and Children* 35(6): 18–22.

Rose, C., D. London, D. Young, G. Mucci, and M. Jay. 1998. *Curriculum orchestrator*. Bellingham, Wash.: MediaSeek Technologies, Inc.

Rutherford, J., and A. Ahlgren. 1989. *Science for All Americans: Project 2061*. New York: Oxford University Press.

Tom Snyder Productions. 1992, 1994. *The great ocean rescue*. Watertown, Mass.: Author.

Tuomi, J. Fall. 1993. *Effective materials for science instruction*. *NSRC Newsletter*. Washington, D.C.: National Science Resources Center.

Wiles, J., and J. Bondi. 1981. *The essential middle school*. Columbus, Ohio: Merrill.

Chapter 12

What Are the Next Steps?

INTRODUCTION

SUMMARY OF PROJECT-BASED SCIENCE

BENEFITS OF PROJECT-BASED SCIENCE

CHALLENGES OF PROJECT-BASED SCIENCE

CONTINUING YOUR PROFESSIONAL GROWTH

INQUIRY INTO YOUR TEACHING

CHAPTER LEARNING PERFORMANCES

- *Summarize the key features of project-based science.*
- *Explain the important benefits of using project-based science.*
- *Describe how a teacher can continue his or her professional development.*
- *Create a professional development plan.*
- *Compare and contrast the challenges to implementing a project-based curriculum and specify strategies that can be used to overcome challenges.*
- *Critique how you have grown professionally by examining your portfolio.*

INTRODUCTION

Even though you have learned so much about project-based science, you probably still have questions about this approach: *What challenges will I face when I first implement project-based science? What are the benefits of project-based science? How will I improve my science teaching? What did I learn as I read this book?* This chapter summarizes features of project-based science and some of the benefits of this approach. Project-based science also presents challenges, so we will discuss ways to overcome a number of them. Since one way to overcome challenges is to continue your professional growth, we will examine some strategies for becoming a professional teacher who is a lifelong learner. The chapter concludes with an analysis of the portfolio you have kept as you have read this book. This will help you reflect on your beliefs and analyze what you learned.

SUMMARY OF PROJECT-BASED SCIENCE

Key Idea

Project-based science engages learners in exploring important and meaningful questions through a process of investigation and collaboration.

Although teaching science to young students is a complex task, it is also very rewarding. As we have discussed, one of the most rewarding ways to teach science is a method known as **project-based science**. This approach engages young learners in exploring important and meaningful questions through a process of investigation and collaboration. Students ask questions, make predictions, design investigations, collect and analyze data, make products, and share ideas. As they explore, students learn fundamental science concepts and principles that they apply to their daily lives. Project-based science is an approach that can help all students, regardless of culture, race, or gender, engage in science learning.

As we have discussed throughout this book, project-based science has numerous fundamental features:

- The *driving question* serves to organize and drive instructional tasks and activities. Driving questions are meaningful and important to learners, and they are one vehicle for contextualizing the learning of science. Driving questions are critical to initiating, implementing, and sustaining inquiry. Driving questions need to be feasible, worthwhile, contextualized, meaningful, ethical, and sustainable.
- To answer driving questions, students engage in *investigations*. The process of carrying out an investigation is known as the *investigation web*. Children need to be supported in the process of doing investigations. They find solutions to questions by messing about with ideas, asking and refining questions, finding information, planning and designing, building apparatus, collecting data, analyzing data, making conclusions, and communicating findings.
- As we discussed, learning occurs in a *social context* and children can learn more from more knowledgeable others, including peers, than they can on their own. Project-based science involves students, teachers, and members of a community collaborating to investigate questions. Collaboration involves sharing ideas to find resolutions to questions. Collaboration helps to build learning

communities in which students express ideas, debate the viability of evidence, and come to a resolution about ideas, concepts, and theories.

- *Technology* tools can support science teaching and learning. In a project-based science environment, students can use technology to investigate, develop artifacts or products, collaborate, and access information. Students use technology to access current data on the Web, expand interaction and collaboration with others via networks (such as e-mail), use tools to gather data (such as temperature and pH probes), employ graphing and visualization tools to analyze data, and produce multimedia products.

- *Assessment* is a critical component of teaching and learning. In a project environment, students create various artifacts, or products, that address the driving question and show what they have learned. Often, teachers have students share their artifacts with other class members, teachers, parents, and members of the community. In project environments, students can create a range of artifacts, from posters to multimedia documents.

- Another critical component of teaching and learning, especially in a project-based classroom, is *scaffolding*. This is a process in which a more knowledgeable individual provides support to other learners. We examined diagrams, figures, and tables that showed ways to support children in project-based science.

- Because children frequently lack the knowledge or skills required to investigate a question for any length of time, the teacher needs to introduce *benchmark lessons*. Benchmark lessons are teacher-directed classroom activities that present concepts, principles, or skills necessary for students to understand the work of a project. Benchmark lessons may include demonstrations, discussions, role-plays, presentations of information, concept mapping, field trips, and the use of literature. Benchmark lessons help students learn difficult concepts, illustrate laboratory techniques, build new inquiry abilities, model thinking, and stimulate curiosity.

- Managing a project-based science classroom creates many unique challenges. To be successful, a teacher needs to create a learning environment of trust and self-responsibility. Establishing a *positive learning environment* is essential to the success of project-based teaching. Fortunately, a variety of management skills can be used to help create this positive learning environment for all students. For example, teachers can set expectations for acceptable student behavior, distribute materials and supplies in a manner that reduces classroom disruptions, and keep students accountable to classroom norms.

- Finally, *planning* is key to the success of any curriculum. When planning, teachers must select learning concepts and learning performances, and carry out steps to develop a project (develop a driving question, present benchmark lessons, lead investigations, conduct assessments, and generate a calendar of activities). Teachers need to be cognizant of criteria for selecting and obtaining good resources for a project environment. Resources need to be relevant to students' daily lives, must be worthwhile, and should actively engage students in inquiry. Planning for integration across the curriculum is also important so that students see connections between science, other subject areas, and their own interests and culture.

BENEFITS OF PROJECT-BASED SCIENCE

Teaching is hard work. Nevertheless, you will find there are many benefits to running a project-based classroom:

- Because your students are pursuing solutions to important and meaningful questions, you too will find the work interesting and motivating. Your teaching will vary each year since you will be exploring new projects with each new group of students. Even within a project, students are exploring several sub-questions, making daily lessons novel and varied. Finally, because students are interested in and excited about the questions they are investigating, you will find teaching a pleasurable experience.

- Often, as your students pursue answers to questions, they explore interesting content. A second benefit of teaching in a project-based manner is that you continually learn new ideas about how the world works. This makes you a lifelong learner.

- In project-based science, classroom management is facilitated. Because students are interested and motivated, discipline problems are minimized. This doesn't mean that you don't need good classroom management skills. As we discussed in Chapter 10, good classroom management is essential. However, when students are interested and their minds are active, they are less likely to cause discipline problems. The best way to manage classrooms is to keep children intellectually engaged in the work.

- In a project-based classroom, your teaching and student learning will match the reform efforts in science education including *the National Science Education Standards* (National Research Council, 1996), *Project 2061: Science for All Americans* (Rutherford & Ahlgren, 1989), *Benchmarks for Science Literacy* (AAAS, 1993), and the National Science Teachers Association recommendations for elementary science (NSTA, 1991). For example, the National Research Council (1996) argues that "there needs to be new emphasis placed on inquiry-based learning focusing on having students develop a deep understanding of science embedded in the everyday world." Many states have structured their objectives and high-stakes tests to correspond with these national standards. For example, many state tests now ask students to make conclusions from data, write responses to situations, and demonstrate skills on performance-based components.

- Through engaging in project-based science, learners develop deep, integrated understanding of content and process. Learners build meaningful relationships with and connections between ideas that they can use to understand their world. Students also learn the process of science, which can be used to solve problems in a variety of contexts. For example, students can apply the ability to ask good questions, plan and design investigations, and draw conclusions about everyday problems.

- In project-based science, students learn to work together to solve problems. In order to be successful in the real world, students need to know how to work with people from different backgrounds. Collaborative skills such as being able to listen to others, debate ideas respectfully, and share ideas are abilities that can be used in many contexts at all ages. Moreover, these are important abilities that employers seek in order to create a productive workforce.

- Project-based science promotes responsibility and independent learning. As students come up with their questions and design investigations, they learn to take responsibility for their own learning. In an investigation, students learn to find information from a variety of different sources, follow through on data collection procedures, and take responsibility for gathering necessary materials. Teachers encourage students to engage in self-evaluation strategies, such as assessing progress in their portfolios, which encourages reflection and self-improvement.

Even at a very young age, children in a project-based science classroom learn to work together.

Group and individual accountability are enhanced by collaboration.

- Project-based science is sensitive to the needs of a diverse group of students. Project-based science meets the needs of male and female students of varied cultures, races, and academic abilities by focusing on issues and questions important in their lives. Because project-based science actively engages students in different types of tasks, it meets the varied learning needs of many different students. Multidimensional assessment techniques allow students to demonstrate their understandings in a variety of formats, formats that work for them. Collaboration teaches students to work together despite their differences—in fact, project-based science puts these differences to work.

In Portfolio Activity 12.1 you will further explore the benefits of project-based science.

CHALLENGES OF PROJECT-BASED SCIENCE

Elementary and middle school teachers face a number of **challenges** when implementing project-based science for the first time. In previous chapters, we discussed some challenges of implementing project-based science and some strategies for dealing with these challenges. For example, obtaining resources can be challenging. Some of the strategies for dealing with this challenge are using free and inexpensive materials such as 2-liter soda bottles and finding a local company or university that is willing to donate equipment. Another challenge is getting students to debate ideas. One strategy for dealing

> ### *Key Idea*
>
> Project-based science helps keep teaching interesting, enables teachers to learn new ideas, facilitates classroom management, matches curriculum reforms, improves learning, enhances collaboration, encourages students to become independent learners, and meets the needs of diverse students.

Portfolio Activity 12.1   **BENEFITS OF PROJECT-BASED SCIENCE**

Materials Needed:
- A pencil and paper

A. Of the eight benefits of project-based science listed, which are the most important to you. Why?

B. What additional benefits do you see for project-based teaching?

C. Share your ideas with a classmate. How are your ideas similar or different?

D. Record your ideas in your portfolio.

Key Idea

Teachers may be uncomfortable with science content and process, but there are many ways to overcome these challenges.

with this challenge is building collaborative skills and building trust. Conflict management strategies are also helpful.

You may be confronted by additional challenges not addressed in this book. For example, you might feel that your science background is not strong enough and you might feel uncomfortable with the subject matter involved. You might feel uncomfortable helping your students carry out an investigation if you have never carried out one yourself. Although these are critical issues, there are a number of positive steps you can take to overcome them.

We will discuss a number of challenges—teachers' content knowledge and knowledge of the process of science, limited student experience, lack of time, and real or perceived external pressures. We will consider a number of recommendations for meeting these challenges. However, don't expect to meet all potential challenges your first year of teaching in a project environment. Teaching is lifelong learning. Even after twenty years of teaching, you will still wrestle with how to improve many aspects of your teaching, each year showing more improvement. Any ideas we consider here are just a start. You will need to continue your professional development throughout your career. For this reason, we will also discuss strategies for continuing your professional development.

Teacher Discomfort with Content Knowledge

Numerous reports claim that teachers' lack of content knowledge limits the teaching of science at the K–8 level (Weiss, 1978; 1987). Certainly teachers need to understand what they are teaching, and feeling uncomfortable with content is a major reason that science is cut out of the curriculum. Although you might feel a little shaky during your first attempts to teach science, as we all did, there are ways to increase your science knowledge and increase your comfort level with science:

- Scientific knowledge expands daily. Neither you nor anyone else can know everything. On many occasions, we have been confronted by students' questions to which we did not know the answers. It is okay to say, "I don't know," and then to model how to find the answer. Showing your students that you are interested in learning more and how to learn is more important than demonstrating that you know everything. Demonstrate to students how you can use reference books, the Web, and local experts to find answers to questions.

CONNECTING TO
NATIONAL SCIENCE EDUCATION STANDARDS
Standards for Professional Development
Professional development for teachers of science requires learning essential science content through the perspectives and methods of inquiry (p. 59).

- Like your students, use each project to learn more about a science topic and about engaging in the process of science. If you take this approach, you will gradually become more comfortable with science content. This gradual, "learn as you go" approach is less intimidating than trying to learn a great deal of new information at one time.

- Develop the habit of reading science magazines and books. Reading is a wonderful way to learn. Magazines such as *Science Scope* and *Science and Children*, published by the National Science Teachers Association, and *Nature Scope*, published by the National Wildlife Federation, are excellent, nonthreatening choices. Often, the articles in them give additional sources of reading materials. Also, develop your own personal library of books. For instance, *The PillBug Project* by Robin Burnett will give you some good background knowledge of pillbugs as well as a sense of how to carry out investigations. Finally, the National Science Foundation distributes a number of books that you will find valuable both for your learning and your classroom teaching. Table 12.1 gives the addresses of several professional organizations that publish journals.

- Attending science classes, workshops, and local, regional, and national science conferences will help you learn new science content. Local school districts, a local university, a local environmental group, or a state organization may offer some workshops. You will find these types of classes and conferences extremely valuable; you will not only get new ideas for teaching and learn some science, but you will also meet others who are as interested as you are in improving teaching and learning. (We will discuss more thoroughly how to join professional organizations in the section on professional development.) Once you join a professional development organization, you will receive in the mail information about workshops and conferences.

- Community members and parents can be guest speakers who provide science content expertise. You and your students can learn valuable science knowledge when guest speakers come to your class. For example, if your class is carrying out a project on water quality and some of your students want to perform chemical tests that you don't understand, there is likely to be a parent or other community member who would be very willing to volunteer time to talk with your class and help with a demonstration.

- The World Wide Web is a valuable source of science information. Although you might have to do a little digging, you will find that the Web is filled with a number of very useful pages that help you and your students learn content. For instance, the Great Lakes Information Network provides a wealth of information about the Great Lakes region and its economy, environment, tourism, news, events, and weather. Volcano World contains all the information you could want about all aspects of volcanoes. You can even send a question to a volcanologist via the website. Finally, The National Science Foundation offers many online documents with up-to-date science information.

Useful Science Content Sites

Table 12.1

PROFESSIONAL SCIENCE EDUCATION ORGANIZATIONS

Name of Organization	Mailing Address	E-Mail Address	Focus
National Science Teachers Association	1840 Wilson Blvd. Arlington, VA 22201-3000 703-243-7100	www.nsta.org	Science education at all ages
School Science and Mathematics Association	Department of Curriculum and Foundations Bloomsburg University 400 East Second Street Bloomsburg, PA 17815-1301	www.ssma.org	Science and mathematics education; integration of science and mathematics
AIMS Education Foundation	1595 S. Chestnut Ave. Fresno, CA 93702 209-225-4094 Fax: 209-255-6396	www.aimsedu.org	Activities for integration of science and mathematics at the elementary level
American Association of Physics Teachers	AAPT Membership Dept. One Physics Ellipse College Park, MD 20740 Fax: 301-209-0845	www.aapt.org	Physical science teaching and learning
Chemical Educational Foundation	1525 Wilson Blvd, Suite 750 Arlington, VA 22209 703-527-6223 Fax: 703-527-7747	www.chemed.org	Chemistry education
National Association of Biology Teachers	11250 Roger Bacon Drive 19 Reston, VA 20190-5202 703-471-1134 800-406-0775 Fax: 703-435-5582	www.nabt.org	Biology teaching and learning
Geological Society of America	P.O. Box 9140 Boulder, CO 80301-9140 303-447-2020 Fax: 303-447-1133	www.geosociety.org	Geology and geology education
National Association for Research in Science Teaching	Executive Secretary c/o John Tillotson Syracuse University 101 Heroy Geology Lab Syracuse, NY 13244-1070	www.educ.sfu.ca/narsite/	Research in science teaching and learning

Please visit the text's Online Learning Center at www.mhhe.com/krajcik2e to link directly to these websites and for updates to these URLs.

Teacher Discomfort with the Process of Science

Many of us have performed cookbook activities, following steps to complete science-related tasks, but these are not investigations. Unfortunately, few of us have had experiences conducting investigations. Like a lack of content knowledge, a lack of experience and understanding of how to carry out investigations can inhibit your ability and willingness to help students engage in the process of investigation. The best way to learn how to carry out an investigation is to do it—ask questions, make observations, manipulate variables, and analyze data. If you take an active role in your students' projects, you will soon develop a level of comfort. As in baking a cake, you don't become good at it unless you do it.

Belonging to professional organizations also will help you become comfortable with the process of science. At conferences, speakers present sessions that focus on inquiry. These presentations can help you learn how to support students in the process of investigations. Further, at conferences expert teachers frequently model inquiry activities they use with their own students, and you may be able to talk with these teachers after such sessions.

Another very valuable mechanism to improve your teaching is observation of an expert teacher carrying out an investigation with his or her class. Notice how a knowledgeable teacher supports students in the process of inquiry. Discuss the lesson with the teacher after class to learn the reasons behind the approach.

It is perhaps more important to invite an expert teacher in to observe and critique your teaching. This will be difficult to do at first. We all are hesitant to invite others to critique us, but commentary from an experienced teacher can be very valuable. If you can establish a long-term mentor arrangement with an expert teacher, you will profit even more. Another way to get feedback on your teaching is to videotape it. You can show the videotape to a colleague or critique it yourself. How are you supporting students? In what ways are you promoting understanding of science?

The Web also provides opportunities for teachers and students to learn more about the process of science. For example, the Center for Highly Interactive Computing in Education provides information about projects that students in the Ann Arbor and Detroit areas are investigating. Lab-Net allows students, teachers, and professionals to interact in a virtual environment to gain information about scientific investigations. Resources like these can help you learn more about the process of science and generate confidence-building relationships with others who are conducting investigations.

Science Processes

Finally, field trips and internships in science settings can help you learn about the process of science as it is actually carried out in the real world. Field trips to governmental and commercial research laboratories, local university science laboratories, and medical hospitals can provide valuable insight into the process of science. Sometimes these institutions offer summer paid or volunteer internships.

Limited Student Experience

Carrying out an investigation is difficult cognitive work. You are challenging your students with such activities. Many students see the purpose of school as learning content knowledge. As students advance through grade levels, they become more regimented in their learning. At-risk children are frequently exposed to lots of "kill and drill" strategies that focus on memorizing low-level factual knowledge. Many students develop good strategies for memorizing information, and they may resist new ways of learning that require them to think in more cognitively challenging ways. Although memorizing is an important learning strategy, finding information, analyzing data, making plans, carrying out investigations, developing concept maps, and making products that synthesize understanding cannot be done through memorization.

Children will sometimes ask, "Why can't we just read from the book?" or "Why can't we just answer the questions at the end of the chapter?" These children have likely learned strategies that require very little effort. They read from the book, look for reading cues (such as bold-print words, topic sentences, or summary sentences), and easily identify the answers to questions at the end of the chapter. Although reading for information is a central component of project-based science, it can be easier for some students to find answers at the end of a chapter than to develop a design for an investigation.

You can take several positive measures to overcome this resistance to learning in a more active manner:

- Make your expectations clear to your class. Stress to children that, although they may have done activities differently in other years, this is the way your classroom works.
- Explain to children that they are working the way scientists work. Scientists find information, ask questions, analyze data, and collaborate with others. Explain that just reading and finding answers distorts what science is all about. Science is about inquiry, and that is what students will do in your class. Interactions with scientists, parents, and others in the community will reinforce this spirit of inquiry.
- Point out to your students how the work they are doing in class helps find solutions to real problems and issues. Most children, especially pre- and young adolescents, have a strong desire to engage in meaningful activities.
- Encourage students to take risks, ask questions, and plan designs, even if they don't work. Young inquirers will go down a number of wrong paths, as do real scientists, and students need to know this is okay.

Lack of Time

Having students learn science through inquiry takes time. There is no way around this. It will take your time and it will take classroom time. We are interested in creating useful science knowledge, knowledge that students will retain, and investigations and projects, as time-consuming as they are, foster such knowledge. The National Science Education Standards (NRC, 1996, p. 219) suggest that time is a major resource that must be allotted in the school day. A few suggestions for finding time in the day to teach science are described below.

Often there are downtimes during an investigation—while the plants are growing, material is decomposing, or metal is rusting. Science teachers should use these downtimes productively, slipping benchmark lessons into them. For example, while plants are growing, the class could be learning how to take measurements of plant growth using rules or calipers. These downtimes are also periods in which elementary teachers can teach lessons in other subject areas.

Another way to make maximal use of time is to integrate the curriculum. In Chapter 11, we discussed how project-based science supports curriculum integration. Curriculum integration can be a time-saving device, because it allows many academic objectives to be reached at once. For example, curriculum integration would blend the following objectives into a project designed to answer "Where does all of our garbage go?": (1) students will be able to discern why people make laws (in social studies, students could learn why recycling laws were created in their state); (2) students will be able to discern fact from opinion (in reading, students could debate whether it is a fact or an opinion that recycling makes a difference); and (3) students will be able to find the volume of a container (in mathematics, students can calculate the amount of garbage that fills a trash dumpster outside of the school building during a week's time). Coordinating subject areas to save time is also suggested in the National Science Education Standards (NRC, 1996, p. 214).

One common complaint is how time-consuming it is to set up investigations and clean up after them. Don't deny your students the opportunity to learn through inquiry because of these problems. One solution is to assign class jobs. Some teachers have students help pass out materials at the beginning of class, and they save five minutes or so at the end of every class session by having the entire class help clean up. Teachers of young elementary students frequently rely on the help of volunteer parents or older students in the school.

Another technique that has worked for many schools is block scheduling (creating longer class periods of time such as ninety-minute blocks instead of forty-five–minute segments) or flexible scheduling, which creates extended time periods for students to work on the projects. Since much class time is devoted to setting up and cleaning up project work, longer work periods save the time of setting up and cleaning up for numerous shorter periods. In an elementary school where you teach several subjects, it will be easier for you to build in extended periods of time to work on projects.

At the middle school level, where subject matter classes are forty-five to fifty-five minutes long, you might take a proactive approach, as some teachers have, to lead efforts to shift your school to a block schedule. In block scheduling, classes meet for double periods for two or three days each. If your students move from class to class as a group, which is common in middle schools, you might also arrange to trade classes with a teacher who teaches in the time slot before or after you so that you can have a longer period of time for a science investigation.

> ### Key Idea
>
> Careful planning and schedule changes can overcome time issues experienced in schools.

Real or Perceived External Pressures

Because project-based science is built around meaningful, hands-on science investigations that extend over time, it can create tension between breadth (superficial coverage of many topics and objectives) and depth (extensive coverage of a few topics). Meaningful, in-depth learning of limited but question-relevant content is preferable to superficial surveys of a wide body of content, which is the approach of most science survey texts. Doing science is more important than being exposed to a wide body of meaningless science content that is likely to be forgotten. This position is supported by the Third International Mathematics and Science Study (TIMSS, 2001), which suggests that students would learn more if the curriculum covered fewer topics in a more in-depth manner. Engaging learners in investigations is now strongly supported by a number of prominent national organizations like the National Research Council (1996) and the American Association for the Advancement of Science (1993). These organizations have taken strong "less is more" stances and advocate sustained, project-oriented science teaching. A number of local school districts and state education agencies are becoming more sensitive to these new ideas in education and are beginning to stress cognitive strategies, such as planning and analyzing data, on state examinations.

Unfortunately, curriculum in the United States has, for many years, taken the breadth approach, and it has only been in the last few years that educators have been moving toward covering fewer subjects in a school year. As a result, many principals, parents, and school board members are more familiar with learning science the old way, reading about numerous topics in a textbook, than they are with learning a few science topics in-depth through long-term inquiry. This difference in viewpoint can cause problems for a teacher trying to implement a project-based approach.

Parents, administrators, colleagues, and even the janitor may question what you are doing. This is only natural, since you are doing something new. To counteract this questioning, take positive steps:

Key Idea

Internal and external pressures can be a challenge to implementing project-based science, but teachers can generate support by helping others understand the benefits of project-based science.

National Academy Press

Science Teaching Resources

- Gain the support of administrators and colleagues. Talk to your principal and administrators about how you plan to do science and explain the project-based science approach. You might share a copy of the *National Science Education Standards* (NRC, 1996) with them to show them how this approach is supported in national reform efforts. Extend an open invitation to your principal to visit your class. Share with your colleagues your methods of teaching science and invite them into your classroom as well.

- Hold a science open house to inform parents and members of the community of your science practices. Create a school or class newsletter that includes information about your science class, write information sheets to parents about specific projects students are working on, and extend open invitations to parents to visit your class. Some teachers have even made videos of their teaching and shared it with parents to illustrate how the approach motivates students to learn and how the teaching objectives match state-mandated tests or curriculum standards. You could also lend a copy of *Every Child a Scientist: Achieving Literacy for All* to parents. This is a useful resource for parents, showing them how they can help implement science standards. It is available from the National Research Council and can be ordered by calling 1-800-624-6242 or 202-334-3313, or it can be ordered online at the website of National Academy Press. Teachers who have used these techniques have found them to be very successful.

- You need to inform people in your school community of your teaching approach and educate them about the importance of in-depth coverage of topics through long-term inquiry. Several resources can help you educate others about your position:

  - The *National Science Education Standards* (NRC, 1996) support project-based science. This book can be ordered from the National Academy Press, 2101 Constitution Ave., NW, Box 285, Washington, DC, 1-800-624-6242 or 202-334-3313. Information about the *National Science Education Standards* can also be found online at the website of National Academy Press.

  - Other excellent resources that can be used to educate others about effective science teaching are the National Science Teachers Association position papers. Position papers are available on a number of topics such as the use of computers, elementary science, multicultural science education, research in science education, and parent involvement in science education. These position papers are available online at the National Science Teachers Association website.

  - The Eisenhower National Clearinghouse contains a wealth of information including interesting articles, standards frameworks, findings from educational research, and information about reform efforts.

Portfolio Activity 12.2   YOUR CHALLENGES

Materials Needed:
- A paper and pencil

A. Of the challenges listed, which one is the most critical for you to overcome? Why?

B. What other challenges do you think you might experience as you implement project-based science?

C. How might you resolve these challenges?

D. Work with a few colleagues. What are their suggestions for resolving these challenges?

E. File these ideas in your portfolio.

- The National Association for Research in Science Teaching (NARST) publishes a series entitled *What Research Says to the Science Teacher* that can be obtained by writing to NARST, John W. Tillotson, Ph.D., Executive Secretary, Department of Science Teaching, Syracuse University, 101 Heroy Geology Lab, Syracuse, NY 13244-1070. These papers provide useful information about a variety of topics such as gender equity in science, inquiry, and constructivism. NARST and the National Science Teachers Association (NSTA) have also partnered to publish research-based information for classroom teachers.

NARST

Portfolio Activity 12.2 asks you to further explore each of these challenges.

CONTINUING YOUR PROFESSIONAL GROWTH

Teaching presents challenges, but it also gives rewards. Perhaps one of the best rewards is becoming part of a community that cares about the learning of children. As a teacher, you will need to continue your professional growth by joining professional organizations, attending conferences, subscribing to journals, and getting information from the World Wide Web. Many teachers use these types of resources to help them become National Board–certified teachers.

National Board for Professional Teaching Standards

Joining Professional Organizations

Joining **professional organizations** is essential to being a professional. It is one of the best ways to continue your development as a teacher. Joining national, state, and local organizations will allow you to build connections with other teachers who may have many of the same questions and issues that you do. These organizations, through their publications, conferences, newsletters, and

NSES

CONNECTING TO
NATIONAL SCIENCE EDUCATION STANDARDS

Standards for Professional Development
Becoming an effective science teacher is a continuous process that stretches from preservice experiences in undergraduate years to the end of a professional career (p. 55).

websites, are also sources of information on content and instruction. They can also inform you about national policy and upcoming events.

At the national level, join the National Science Teachers Association (NSTA), which focuses on teaching science to children at all levels. Many states have science education organizations affiliated with NSTA. You can find out about them by contacting NSTA. State Departments of Education employ science consultants who are good sources of information about professional organizations in your state. If you live in a large urban area, there may be local science teacher organizations that you can join. If your school district has a curriculum director, this person should be knowledgeable about local organizations. Principals and other school administrators are also helpful sources of information. Table 12.1 lists national organizations you may want to join.

Attending Conferences

Membership in professional organizations such as those listed in Table 12.1 will give you opportunities to attend their **conferences.** Conferences are exciting because they connect you with other educators. In the process, you get to learn about what others are doing in their teaching. You can also attend presentations by nationally known scientists and educators. At most conferences, you can attend the exhibit hall, where you can see some of the newest commercially available materials. Free materials are often distributed at these conferences. As you become comfortable in your own teaching, you might want to share some of your project ideas with others by presenting at professional conferences yourself. Many teachers find it more comfortable to first present at local or state conferences to gain more experience and confidence.

Subscribing to Publications

Many professional organizations also create associated **publications.** For example, NSTA offers a number of important publications including *Science and Children* (for elementary teachers) and *Science Scope* (for middle grade teachers). These publications are filled with articles written by educators, science teaching ideas, information about science education reform, reviews of curriculum materials and software, and conference information. State and local organizations usually publish newsletters with helpful teaching hints and important local information. Table 12.2 lists the publications associated with each organization.

NSES

CONNECTING TO
NATIONAL SCIENCE EDUCATION STANDARDS

Standards for Professional Development
Science learning experiences for teachers must introduce teachers to scientific literature, media, and technological resources that expand their science knowledge and their ability to access further knowledge (p. 59).

USING TECHNOLOGY TOOLS FOR PROFESSIONAL DEVELOPMENT

As we have discussed throughout this book, the World Wide Web can be used as a source of both content and instructional resources. It also can serve as a source of **professional development**, because it is filled with numerous sites that can give you helpful information regarding various education and science topics. For example, the National Eisenhower Clearinghouse contains information about science and mathematics

Table 12.2

PROFESSIONAL PUBLICATIONS

Name of Organization	Mailing Address	E-Mail Address	Title of Journal
The National Science Teachers Association	1840 Wilson Blvd. Arlington, VA 22201-3000 703-243-7100	www.nsta.org	*Science and Children Science Scope Science Teacher*
School Science and Mathematics Association	Margie and Bill Hunts SSMA Co-Executive Directors 16734 Hamilton Court Strongville, OH 44149-5701 1-800-227-SSMA	www.ssma.org	*School Science and Mathematics*
National Association for the Education of Young Children	1509 16th Street, NW Washington, DC 20036	www.naeyc.org	*Young Children*
National Middle School Association	2600 Corporate Exchange Dr., 370 Columbus, OH 43231 10800-528-NMSA	www.nmsa.org	*Middle School Journal Middle Ground*
Association for Supervision and Curriculum Development	1250 N. Pitt Street Alexandria, VA 22314-1453 1-800-933-ASCD FAX: 703-299-8631	www.ascd.org	*Educational Leadership*
Phi Delta Kappa	408 N. Union P.O. Box 789 Bloomington, IN 47402	www.pdkintl.org/ kappan/kappan/htm	*Kappan*

Please visit the text's Online Learning Center at www.mhhe.com/krajcik2e to link directly to these websites and for updates to these URLs.

reform, research findings in education, lesson plans, and curriculum materials. Table 12.3 lists the Web addresses of several organizations that can provide you with information that will help you continue your professional development.

INQUIRY INTO YOUR TEACHING

One of the best ways to improve your teaching is to reflect on and to engage in inquiry about your own teaching. In this book, you have often been asked to reflect on your beliefs and past experiences. You can continue to use *reflection* throughout your professional career to improve your teaching. This book has also stressed the importance of inquiry to learn about the world. You can use a form of inquiry, called *action research*, to learn about your own teaching.

Table 12.3

USEFUL SCIENCE PROFESSIONAL WWW ADDRESSES

Name	E-Mail Address	Focus
The National Science Teachers Association	www.nsta.org	Science teaching and learning at all ages
Eisenhower National Clearinghouse	www.enc.org	Information about science and mathematics education
The National Science Foundation	www.nsf.gov	Science research and funding
National Center for Education Statistics	http://nces.ed.gov/timss/	Findings from the Third International Science and Mathematics Study
The American Association for the Advancement of Science	www.aaas.org	Advancement of science; publisher of *Science for All Americans and Benchmarks for Scientific Literacy*
National Academy of Science	www.nas.edu www.nap.edu	Advice on scientific issues; author of the *National Science Education Standards*

Please visit the text's Online Learning Center at www.mhhe.com/krajcik2e to link directly to these websites and for updates to these URLs.

CONNECTING TO NATIONAL SCIENCE EDUCATION STANDARDS

Standards for Professional Development

Professional development activities must provide opportunities for teachers to learn and use various tools and techniques for self-reflection and collegial reflection, such as peer coaching, portfolios, and journals (p. 68).

Reflection can be defined as a voluntary effort to share and critique ideas about teaching, assess one's teaching and students' learning, formulate aims and goals about the curriculum through collaboration, and take responsibility for actions and the consequences of actions (Baird, 1992; Barnes, 1992; Putnam & Grant, 1992). The *National Science Education Standards* (NRC, 1996) promotes reflective practices in science education: "Teachers of science engage in ongoing assessment of their teaching and of student learning. In doing this, teachers use student data, observations of teaching, and interactions with colleagues to reflect on and improve teaching practice" (p. 37).

Action research, like the inquiry process, involves asking questions, making plans, carrying out the plans, and analyzing and making use of what was learned. The process is similar to the investigation web described in Chapter 4. The main difference is that action research is not for the purpose of generating findings to share with others but to generate information to put into practice in your own teaching. For example, a teacher might want to investigate whether collaborative learning increases motivation among students in her class. She would make a plan to answer this question, carry out an investigation, and analyze whether collaboration changed motivation levels. Put differently, teachers are engaging in project-based work to investigate their own teaching. Dick Arends (2001), in his book *Learning to Teach*, provides great detail about inquiry into and reflection on one's own teaching.

The following strategies are part of reflection and action research:

- *Keep a journal.* Keeping a journal and taking notes of what works and what doesn't work is one form of action research. For example, you might want to keep notes on the types of driving questions that students seem to find meaningful. In what types of questions do children seem to be interested?
- *Make a video of your teaching.* Another way you can examine your own teaching is to video it. Many people dislike seeing themselves on video, but making a video of your teaching and then analyzing it is an excellent way of improving your teaching—athletes watch videos of themselves constantly to learn how they can maximize their performance. Keeping a record also can show how you change over time.
- *Collaborate with colleagues.* Colleagues can be excellent sources of help for reflection and action research. They can serve as mentors who can provide helpful suggestions to improve your teaching, and they can be good role models. Visiting the classrooms of others can provide you with new ideas and practical suggestions for improving your teaching. Letting others critique your teaching by visiting your classroom or watching you on video can provide you with valuable insight, insight that you might not have on your own.
- *Have students fill out questionnaires.* Many teachers ask their students to fill out questionnaires about their teaching. These questionnaires can be simple open-ended statements like, "The thing I liked most about this lesson was …" or "One thing I would change about this project is …." Questionnaires can also be simple scales: "The acid rain project was 1 (excellent), 2 (good), 3 (satisfactory), 4 (bad)." Teachers of younger students often use "smile faces" on their questionnaires—students circle a picture of a smile, a neutral face, or a frowning face next to pictures or statements such as "growing plants," "using a magnifying glass," and "recording our results."

Looking back at what we have done can also lead to improvements in teaching. In Portfolio Activity 12.3, you will reexamine some of your initial ideas about teaching and learning. In Portfolio Activity 12.4, you will examine the items you put in your portfolio to help you summarize what you learned as you read this book.

CHAPTER REVIEW   **www.mhhe.com/krajcik2e**

ONLINE LEARNING CENTER

Go to the Online Learning Center at **www.mhhe.com/krajcik2e** to review important content from the chapter and key terms, take a chapter assessment, and link to the chapter's websites.

Portfolio Activity 12.3

REVISITING INITIAL IDEAS IN YOUR PORTFOLIO

Materials Needed:
- Your portfolio

A. In Portfolio Activity 1.5, you identified your science teaching goals. Have these goals changed since you completed this activity? How so?

B. Examine your response to Portfolio Activity 1.4. How have your beliefs about why children should learn science changed since the beginning of this book?

C. Throughout this book, you have encountered a number of ideas about teaching science to children. Examine your beliefs now about these ideas.
- What are your beliefs about the role of investigations now? How have they changed since you read the book?
- What are your views on collaboration? Have they changed? How? What will you do differently in your classroom in the future?

- What were your views about covering basic science content and skills before exploring the ideas in this book? Have they changed? How will this affect your teaching?
- What were your views about assessment before reading this book? Have your views changed? How will this affect your teaching in the future?
- What were your beliefs about classroom management before reading this book? Have they changed? How so? How will they affect your teaching in the future?
- What did you think about curriculum integration prior to exploring the ideas in this book? Explain your beliefs now. How will your teaching be affected?

D. How has this book informed your teaching practices? What will you try to change? What will you keep about your current teaching?

E. Record your thoughts in your portfolio.

Portfolio Activity 12.4

REEXAMINING YOUR PORTFOLIO

Materials Needed:
- Your portfolio

A. Go back to Portfolio Activity 1.7. Have your top three or four driving questions about teaching elementary or middle grade science been answered by this book? How so? What questions remain unanswered? How might you resolve them?

B. Go back to Portfolio Activity 9.5. What items have you included in your portfolio? Why have you included these specific artifacts? How do they show what you have learned?

CHAPTER SUMMARY

This book has presented a new approach to teaching elementary and middle school science, an approach called *project-based science*. We started this last chapter by reviewing the key features of project-based science and considering some of the benefits of this approach. This approach can present a number of challenges for the teacher. Some teachers are not comfortable with the science content knowledge necessary to carry out projects. Some do not know how to conduct an investigation with students. Time is always a problem in teaching, but it can be a bigger problem for teachers who are trying to carry out long-term investigations. Finally, because using a project-based approach may be new to parents, colleagues, administrators, and community members, this approach may be met with resistance. These real or perceived pressures can affect a teacher who is trying to implement this new teaching approach.

In this chapter, we discussed these challenges and ways to overcome them. One way to become a better teacher who can implement a project approach is to continue your professional development. We discussed several ways to do this: join professional organizations, attend conferences, read professional publications, and access information on the Web. Finally, we examined the notion of inquiry into your teaching and reexamined your portfolio.

We hope you will continue to grow as a teacher, and we wish you luck as you begin using a project approach in your teaching.

CHAPTER HIGHLIGHTS

- One of the most rewarding ways to teach science is a method known as *project-based science*.
- Project-based science has many benefits
  - Teachers find the work interesting and motivating.
  - Teachers become lifelong learners.
  - Classroom management is facilitated.
  - Project-based science matches the reform efforts in science education.
  - Learners develop deep, integrated understanding of content and process.
  - Students learn to work together to solve problems.
  - Project-based science promotes responsibility and independent learning.
  - Project-based science is sensitive to the needs of a diverse group of students.
- Teachers can face a number of challenges when implementing project-based science for the first time
  - Discomfort with science content knowledge.
  - Discomfort with the process of science.
  - Limited student experience, which might cause some students to resist project work.
  - The length of time required.
  - External pressures that can create tension.

- Professional growth is a continuous process throughout a teacher's career.
- Teachers can continue their professional growth by
  - Joining professional organizations.
  - Attending conferences.
  - Subscribing to journals.
  - Getting information from the World Wide Web.
- Teaching can be improved by reflecting on and engaging in inquiry about one's own teaching.

KEY TERMS

action research (494)

challenges (483)

conferences (492)

professional development (492)

professional organizations (491)

project-based science (480)

publications (492)

reflection (494)

REFERENCES

American Association for the Advancement of Science. 1993. *Benchmarks for science literacy*. New York: Oxford University Press.

Arends, R. 1994. *Learning to teach*. New York: McGraw-Hill, Inc.

Baird, J. R. 1992. Collaborative reflection, systematic inquiry, better teaching. In *Teachers and teaching from classroom to reflection*, ed. T. Russell and H. Munby. Bristol, Penn.: The Falmer Press.

Barnes, D. 1992. The significance of teachers' frames for teaching. In *Teachers and teaching from classroom to reflection*, ed. T. Russell and H. Munby. Bristol, Penn.: The Falmer Press.

National Research Council. 1996. *National science education standards*. Washington, D.C.: National Academy of Sciences.

National Science Teachers Association. 1991. An NSTA position statement: Elementary school science. Washington, D.C.: Author. http://www.nsta.org/.

Putnam, J., and S. S. Grant. 1992. Reflective practice in the multiple perspective program at Michigan State University.

In *Reflective teacher education cases and critiques*, ed. L. Valli. New York: State University of New York Press.

Rutherford, J., and A. Ahlgren. 1989. *Science for All Americans: Project 2061*. New York: Oxford University Press.

Schmidt, W. H., C. C. McKnight, R. T. Houang, H. C. Wang, D. E. Wiley, L. S. Cogan, and R. G. Wolfe, (2001). *Why schools matter: A cross-national comparison of curriculum and learning*. San Francisco, Calif.: Jossey-Bass.

Third International Mathematics and Science Study. 1997. http://nces.ed.gov/TIMSS/.

Third International Mathematics and Science Study. 1998. http://nces.ed.gov/TIMSS/.

Weiss, I. 1978. *Report of the 1977 national survey on science, mathematics, and social sciences*. Research Triangle Park, N.C.: Center for Educational Research and Evaluation, Research Triangle Institute.

Weiss, I. 1987. *1985–86 national survey of science and mathematics education*. Research Triangle Park, N.C.: Research Triangle Institute.

Glossary

accommodation   A permanent change in an individual's mental structure.

accountability   Responsibility for performance or learning.

action research   A process of asking questions, making plans, carrying out the plans and analyzing and making use of what was learned.

active engagement   Students ask and refine questions related to phenomena; they predict and explain phenomena; and they mindfully interact with concrete materials. Active engagement, then is both mental and physical.

adaptation   An individual's attempt to create an accurate view of the world so that she can continue the process of development.

affective factors   Factors related to emotion such as curiosity, excitement, persistence, enthusiasm, flexibility, skepticism, and open-mindedness.

analogy   A comparison between seemingly unlike things points out a similarity between them, and thus infers that they might be alike in other ways as well.

analytic rubrics   A scoring guide that assesses artifacts, performances, or portfolios in a quantitative manner by assigning (or taking away) points for specific traits, dimension, or criteria that are present (or missing).

analyze   To examine a concept or process in detail to better learn more about it.

anecdotal records   Written notes that describe student behaviors made at or near the time that the behaviors occurred.

anxiety   Uneasiness and apprehension.

apply   To make use of something (in this case, make use of scientific understandings); to develop solutions to familiar or new problems.

archival data   Data that scientists collected in the past and then stored for future use.

artifacts   Products that illustrate what one has learned.

assessment   Any method used to judge or evaluate an outcome or help make a decision.

assimilation   An individual fitting new information into existing mental structures or schemes.

atmosphere   The prevailing tone or mood of the classroom.

attestations   Testimonials about a student's work prepared by someone other than the student, such as the teacher, a parent, or a peer.

attitudes   Opinions or feelings.

authentic assessment   Measures meaningful understanding by stressing open-ended answers rather than a single "correct" one.

authentic tasks   Tasks that have meaning for the child beyond the classroom.

base groups   Groups of students who work together on a project.

behavior tree   A diagram in which the teacher and students establish the goals that need to be met during a specific activity and set ground rules that need to be followed to meet the goals.

benchmark lessons   Teacher-directed classroom activities that present concepts, principles, or skills that students need in order to understand the work of a project.

bidirectional zone of proximal development   The fluctuations among group members—sometimes members are the teacher and sometimes they are the learner.

body-kinesthetic intelligence   Intelligence where learners use movement in learning.

calendar   Timetable of dates of events and lessons.

cause and effect questions   Questions that provide opportunities for students to make inferences about how one variable affects another variable.

challenges   A situation or difficulty that tests one's ability to do something.

checklists   A list of items for consideration.

children's literature   Books or other publications intended for a children's audience.

classroom assessments   Assessment used to help teachers evaluate students' progress during a unit of study.

classroom management   Organization or control in a classroom.

classroom organization   Relationships or structure in a classroom.

classroom rules   Governing procedures or conditions in a classroom.

climate   The prevailing conditions or feelings.

clinical interviews   Classroom interviews with students to examine their ideas.

coaching   Providing suggestions to help the student develop knowledge or skills.

cognitive load   Amount of work in acquiring or using knowledge.

cognitive roles   Roles that require a specific type of thinking or specialized knowledge.

collaborate   To work with another person or group on a science topic.

collaboration   A joint intellectual effort of students, peers, teachers, and community members to investigate a question or problem.

concept   An idea or central principle.

concept mapping   The process of making visual representations of the relationships among concepts.

concept maps   Visual representations of the relationships among concepts.

conceptual knowledge   Knowledge of interrelationships, principles, theories, and models.

conceptual models   Models that link the unfamiliar to the familiar by using metaphors and analogies.

concrete operations   A phase of development where children develop the ability to apply logical thought to concrete problems they come across in their environment.

conferences   A meeting of a professional organization, usually lasting several days.

consequences   The result that follows an action.

construct meaning   Create understanding

content knowledge   The central concepts, principles, and theories in an area of study.

contextualization   Anchoring questions in the lives of learners that deal with important, real-world issues.

contextualized   Knowledge cannot easily be separated from the situation in which it is developed.

continuous data   Data when the intervals between the data have meaning.

control variables   Variables that are held constant during an investigation.

convergent   To come from different directions and reach the same conclusion.

create   Produce something; imagine.

creativity   Use one's imagination to develop a new idea or product.

criterion-referenced tests   Tests that grade all students according to a single set of preestablished standards.

cross-links   Links that show the interrelationships among the concepts included on a concept map.

curiosity   Eagerness to learn or know something.

current data   Data collected in the recent past.

curriculum integration   A blending of subject areas such that the separate parts are not discernible.

demonstration   Show or display how something works.

departmentalized   Schools that are organized in a manner that teachers are separated by subject area (teach only their subject area).

dependent variable   Variable that changes as the result of the conditions of the investigation or the "it changed" variable.

descriptive questions   Questions that focus on finding out about the observable characteristics of phenomena.

descriptive statistics   Statistics such as differences, averages, and ranges that help a student make sense of data.

designing   How a student will structure an experiment in order to find an answer to his/her question.

digital cameras   Cameras that take pictures in digital format and can be used as a data collection device by students.

digital divide   Lack of technology access by needy and at-risk students.

digital libraries   Various documents saved in digital format that can be accessed through the World Wide Web.

discrepant event   An event that goes against what students expect and thus provides an open-ended question to stimulate student thought.

discrete data   Data that can be divided into categories and when the intervals between the data have no meaning.

discussions   Talk between or among members of the class and teacher.

divergent   Distinctly separate or increasingly different ideas.

division of labor   A process that occurs when students collaborate, negotiate, compromise, and interface with others to investigate a driving question.

downtime   Time between activities.

drawing   A picture of something made with pencil, pen, markers, etc.

driving question   A question that organizes and drives the diverse activities of a project.

dropouts   Students who lack interest in an activity or who fail to be motivated to complete it.

duped   Trick or persuade someone to do something for you.

elaboration   A stage in the 5-E model where students can gain a deeper understanding of the concept by engaging in additional activities related to the concept.

embedded   Lodged in instruction.

engagement   A stage in the 5-E model where students develop understanding about a concept by engaging in concrete experiences with materials.

equality   The quantity or level of knowledge or ability that members bring to a group.

equilibration   The process of an individual modifying his/her mental structures to fit new experiences he/she encounters.

essay   A short written assignment where students explain or interpret something.

ethical   Scientific moral conduct that is not harmful to living organisms or the environment.

evaluate   To judge or assess.

evaluation   A stage in the 5-E model where students' learning is assessed.

explanation   A stage in the 5-E model where the teacher introduces formal vocabulary or students verbalize understanding about the explorations in which they have been involved.

exploration   A stage in the 5-E model where students develop understanding about a concept by engaging in concrete experiences with materials.

explore   Make an investigation.

factual knowledge   Knowledge of facts and details.

faded   A process where the support is decreased over time.

feasibility   Driving questions that can be carried out by students to perform investigations and are developmentally appropriate.

feedback   Instructional help and information given to a student by teachers or other students for the purpose of improving one's academic work; comments to provide useful information.

fish-bone model   A diagram that lists tasks leading to a goal.

5-E model   An instructional model that has five stages—engagement, exploration, explanation, elaboration, and evaluation.

flexible   Open to change.

formal interviews   Structured interviews.

formal operations   A phase when the child becomes able to apply logical thought to all types of problems— including ones he/she cannot actually experience directly.

formative assessments   Day-to-day assessments used to help teachers evaluate students' progress during a unit of study and make decisions regarding curriculum and instruction.

goals   An endpoint that one wants to achieve.

grading   An interpretation or judgment made from data collected and recorded, thus an extension to evaluation.

ground rules   Basic rules or guidelines.

guide   A person who facilitates students' learning.

hierarchical   To arrange in a ranked order.

high traffic areas   Areas of a room that have a high number of people present or passing through.

higher order   Thinking that requires in-depth analysis or detailed thinking.

holistic rubrics   Rubrics that measure the overall quality of an artifact, performance, or portfolio.

home groups   Groups that are used for critiquing work and supporting each other; may be used the entire school year.

hypermedia   Media that has links to other documents or that has links to other parts of the same document.

hypotheses   Questions stated in testable form that specify how the independent variable will influence the dependent variable.

independent variable   Variable that is purposefully changed by the investigator or the "you changed it" variable.

inert knowledge   Understanding that is stored in the mind but that cannot be retrieved or used in appropriate situations.

inferences   Conclusions drawn from evidences or reasoning.

informal interviews   Less formal interviews that resemble teacher-student discussions.

initial observations   Introductory observations that students make of phenomena that might acquaint them with concepts, pique their curiosity, and motivate them to ask questions.

inquiry   An investigation of a scientific nature.

inquiry-based learning   Learning that focuses on developing a deep understanding of science concepts and principles by systematically exploring the world.

integrated   The crossing of subject matter boundaries.

integration   The combination of science with other subject areas.

interactive multimedia   Technologies that combine video, pictures, graphics, and text in an interactive manner to present information.

interdisciplinary   An approach that consciously applies methodology and language from more than one discipline to examine a central theme, issue, problem, topic, or experience of another.

interest   A topic of curiosity or concern to learn more about.

interpersonal intelligence   Intelligence characterized by the ability to understand and interact with other people.

interpersonal roles   Roles that help students work well among themselves.

interrelationships   Relationships between or among things.

intrapersonal intelligence   Intelligence characterized by the ability to understand oneself.

invent   To think up or make something new.

investigation centers   Areas of a room set up for students to conduct investigations on their own.

investigation web   A process of carrying out an investigation that includes "messing about," asking and refining questions, finding information, planning and designing, building the apparatus and collecting data, analyzing data, making conclusions, and communicating findings.

investigations   Inquiry into a topic using scientific skills.

journals Recordings of personal events, experiences, and reflections.

KWL strategy A method where students are asked to tell what they know about a topic (K), want to know about a topic (W), and have learned about a topic (L).

large-scale assessment District, state, or national assessments used to evaluate school curriculum, school district progress, and programs; sometimes called high-stakes assessment because of the importance placed on the tests.

learning communities A group of students using techniques to help each other learn.

learning contracts An agreement between a student and teacher regarding the type and amount of work to be completed to learn something.

learning cycle An instructional model that consists of phases of instruction that help students learn by providing them with direct experiences with concrete materials, opportunities to construct understanding about concepts, and chances to apply their understanding to new situations.

learning cycle model A three-stage instructional model developed by Robert Karplus—explore, invent, and apply.

learning performances Specification related to what achievement we expect of the students.

learning technologies The use of computers, software, and various peripherals that support students in learning.

less content Fewer topics to be studied, but studied more in-depth.

lesson plan The design of a lesson outlining what will be done.

lines Connections between concepts on a concept map.

linguistic intelligence Intelligence characterized by the capacity to use language (written or oral).

linking words Words written on the line of a concept map that explain or define the relationship between concepts.

listening To pay attention to what someone is saying.

loafer effect A phenomena that occurs when one or more group members allow others to do all the work.

logical-mathematical intelligence Intelligence characterized by the capacity to use numbers and data.

lower order Thinking that requires little analysis or detailed thinking.

managerial roles Roles that help manage time and completion of a task.

manipulation of materials Involving students in building apparatus, taking things apart, or hadling or playing with objects.

marking critical features Identifying necessary or important attributes.

matching Test items that require students to correspond premises made in one column with responses in another column.

mathematical models Models that specify a relationship between the variables described and the behavior of phenomena.

meaning A sense of purpose or significance; interesting and exciting to learners.

meaningful understanding When a learner builds relationships and connections between ideas and blends personal experiences with more formal scientific knowledge.

messing about   A way to initially engage students in exploring, manipulating materials, making initial observations. Reading about phenomena, and taking things apart.

metacognitive knowledge   Having knowledge about cognition in general, as well as awareness and knowledge about one's own cognition.

metaphor   A figure of speech in which a word or phrase that ordinarily designates one thing is used to designate another, making an implicit comparison between the two.

microcomputer-based laboratories (mbls)   Software and probes that allow students to collect various types of data in real time.

microworlds   Software that combines video, pictures, computer graphics, text, and interactivity to present to students situations that otherwise would be inaccessible or too hazardous, time-consuming, or expensive for students to explore.

model   A simplified representation of a phenomenon that suggests how the phenomenon works.

model thinking   To tell out loud what one is thinking in his or her head.

modeling   The process through which a more knowledgeable person illustrates to the learner how to complete a task.

models   Simplified representations of natural phenomena.

multimedia documents   Documents that combine writing, illustrations, photographs, videos, audiotapes, computer applications, and other media.

multiple choice   Test items that include a stem and various options.

multiple intelligences   Forms of intelligence categorized as mathematical-logical, linguistic, spatial, bodily kinesthetic, musical, interpersonal, intrapersonal, and naturalist.

multiple representations   Ideas expressed in more than one medium including text, graphics, images, and video.

multiple resources   More than one source of information.

music   Sound from voices or musical instruments.

musical intelligence   Intelligence characterized by sensitivity to sound, pitch, and rhythm.

mutuality   The common goals of the students.

naturalist intelligence   Intelligence characterized by the ability to identify and classify patterns in nature.

nature of science   The principles and norms that govern the scientific process.

network   A series of connections or branches.

nonlinear   A process that does not happen in a step-by-step, straight-line pattern.

norms   Standards of behavior.

observation   Watching someone or something carefully.

observing   Seeing or noticing.

open-ended questions   Questions structured so that students can fill in their own answer.

operational definition   A definition of a variable in terms of how the variable will be manipulated, measured, or observed.

pact   An agreement between two or more groups or individuals to complete a given amount of work with the least effort.

peer assessment   Assessment of student progress made by other students.

performance-based assessment Methods of directly examining students' knowledge, skills, and dispositions.

physical arrangements The location of objects in a room.

physical models Devices or processes that behave like the phenomena.

planning The process of students thinking about and working out how their investigation will take place, what equipment is needed, and what data do they need to collect.

portfolio assessment A process of collecting representative samples of students' work over time for purposes of documenting and assessing their learning.

portfolios Collections of student artifacts; can be thought of as both objects and methods of assessment. As objects, they are a place for holding materials such as papers, photographs, or drawings that are representative of students' work and progress. As methods of assessment, portfolios provide ways for teachers to continuously collect and assess student work.

positive interdependence The linking of all group members so that one cannot succeed unless the other group members succeed.

predictions A statement of what a student thinks will happen in an investigation .

preoperational thought A phase characterized by the development of language and rapid conceptual development focused on mastering representations without thorough understanding.

primary data sources Original or first-hand sources developed and used by scientists.

primary-source material References or resource materials that are original or first sources of information.

prior experiences Experiences students learned in life before the current topic was introduced.

prior knowledge Knowledge that students gained in life before the current topic was introduced.

probes Electronic instruments connected to computers that allow for the collection of data including temperature, force, motion, and pH.

probing Questions to thoroughly examine students' ideas.

procedural knowledge Knowledge to find solutions to questions, to design an experiment, and to find and evaluate background information related to a question. Knowledge that allows people to know how to do something, conduct an inquiry, or use a skill.

process A series of actions or steps.

product A book, a physical model of some kind, or a working apparatus that a student makes to demonstrate what she has learned.

productions Documents (such items as goal statements, personal reflections, captions, and descriptions of what the items in the portfolio represent) that help explain the contents of a portfolio.

professional development Information or knowledge learned to continue improving one's skills and abilities in a career.

professional organizations An organization of professionals in a particular field or career area.

project-based science A teaching approach that engages young learners in exploring important and meaningful questions through a process of investigation and collaboration. Throughout this dynamic process, students ask questions, make predictions, design investigations, collect and analyze data, make products, and share ideas. As a result, students learn fundamental science concepts and principles that they apply to their daily lives.

proposition Single relationship between two concepts on a concept map.

publications   Printed material to communicate to the members of an organization.

qualitative observations   Detailed descriptions of what is seen.

quantitative observations   Descriptions that can be counted or recorded in a numerical format.

questioning   Asking questions.

quicktrial   Experimental technique in which students try out experimental procedures to see if they work.

real choices   Choices that are meaningful and important to students.

real-time graphs   Graphs generated in real time by computer software as students collect software using probes.

receptional approaches   Transmitting information, and students receiving the information.

redirecting   To take a question or a response to a question and ask a second person to respond to the question or response.

reducing complexity   Withholding complex understandings or tasks until the learner has mastered simpler understandings or subtasks.

reflection   Thinking about alternative questions, considering possible hypotheses, contemplating a variety of answers, speculating on outcomes, deliberating on steps that can be taken, and meditating on conclusions found.

reflective practitioners   Teachers who think about, analyze, and mentally debate what should be done to most effectively teach particular students at any given moment.

reflective   To think about the design of one's practice—such as curriculum and instruction, and ways to revise and adapt lessons.

reinforcement   A reward for a behavior.

relational questions   Questions that allow students to find out about associations between the characteristics of different phenomena.

reliability   How consistently a test measures a student's performance.

reliable assessment   Assessment that provides consistent results across different trials, thus yielding similar results on different occasions.

remember   To recall something from memory.

reproductions   Documents (such as photographs of projects, videos of projects, or audiotapes of presentations) attesting to the learning process—not the actual items produced.

resources   Books, curricula, equipment, supplies, and materials.

rewards   Something desirable given in return for good behavior.

role models   Serving as an example to others.

role-playing   To pretend you are in a different situation or are a different person; to act out a situation.

safety   Protection from harm or injury.

scaffolding   A process in which a more knowledgeable person uses various techniques, such as modeling or coaching, to direct those aspects of the intellectual task that are initially beyond the capacity of the learner.

schemas   Blueprints that guide behavior and reasoning.

science   The study of the physical world.

scientific attitudes   Attitudes of openness, curiosity, skepticism, etc.

scoring rubric   A brief, written description of different levels of quality for student performance that allow one to rank or rate a level of performance.

seeking information   Finding background information essential to an investigation.

selection   Techniques requiring students to select a response from choices provided on the test.

self-assessment   To judge one's own progress.

self-monitoring   Checking on one's self.

sensorimotor intelligence   A phase where the child interacts with the environment through sensory and muscular activity.

sequencing   Breaking a difficult task into much smaller, manageable, step-by-step subtasks.

sharing   Communicating to others your ideas, plans, and progress throughout the investigation, your findings, and your final products.

sharing groups   Groups where students share information about their respective projects.

short answer   Test items that present a problem to students that requires them to answer with (supply) a short response.

simile   A type of metaphor; makes a comparison between two things using the words like or as.

simulations   Software that allows students to explore what it might be like to manipulate variables that would otherwise be just too difficult, impossible, or unethical to do in the real world.

social constructivism   A theory of learning that holds that children learn concepts or construct meaning about ideas through their interactions with and interpretations of their world, including essential interactions with others.

socially induced incompetence   A phenomenon that occurs when members of a group ostracize or disparage a student to the point that he or she feels unable to contribute to the group's work.

status differential effect   A phenomenon that occurs when a high-status member of a group takes control. Higher status can be caused by many things—cliques, socioeconomic status, race, older students working with younger ones, or academic achievement.

subordinate   A lower rank or secondary importance.

subquestions   Questions that come from another, more central question, students' own questions related to the driving question.

summative assessment   Assessment of individual achievement in the form of end-of-unit tests, letter grades, and large-scale assessments.

superordinate   A higher rank or primary importance.

supply   Assessment techniques requiring a student to construct a response to a question or problem.

sustainability   A topic that can be studied or maintained over time.

telecommunication   Students use the World Wide Web to communicate with other students in remote or distant areas.

test anxiety   Nervousness or fear of taking tests.

thematic   A unifying topic or subject transcending traditional subject boundaries.

theories   A body of rules and principles that apply to science; a conjecture or belief about a topic in science.

think critically   Be able to judge and analyze a topic.

transformational approaches   Teaching models that involve teachers supporting students to make sense of material.

transitions   The process or time period between activities.

true and false   Test items that require a student to classify an item as true or false, correct or incorrect, or yes or no.

trust-building skills   Skills or processes that help make all students feel comfortable working in small groups.

understand   To comprehend or be aware of.

using visual tools   Using pictorial prompts that help students understand their own thinking processes.

valid assessment   Assessment that measures what it is supposed to measure and allows the teacher to make accurate generalizations about a student.

validity   Fair and accurate generalizations.

variables   The characteristics that will change in an investigation.

video   Something that has been recorded on videotape, CD, DVD, cassette, or another broadcasting medium.

video camera   A camera that records onto digital or videotape.

visualization tools   Technology tools that enable students to "see," explore, and analyze scientific data.

visual-spatial intelligence   Intelligence characterized by a person's ability to think in terms of physical space.

wait-time   Three to five seconds a teacher waits after asking a question before calling on a student.

worth   Questions that have value by containing rich science content and process that match district curriculum standards.

writing samples   Collection of a student's written work (poems, essays, stories, etc.).

zone of proximal development   The difference in performance between what a learner can accomplish unassisted and what he could accomplish with the assistance of a more knowledgeable or capable other.

Credits

Photos

Chapter 1: *p. 2,* © Barbara Rios/Photo Researchers, Inc.; *p. 18,* © David Young-Wolff/PhotoEdit; *p. 21,* © Richard T. Nowitz/Photo Researchers, Inc.

Chapter 2: *p. 36,* © PhotoDisc; *p. 53,* © David Young-Wolff/PhotoEdit.

Chapter 3: *p. 76,* © Will Hart/PhotoEdit; *p. 88,* © Bill Bachman/Photo Researchers, Inc.; *p. 99,* © David Young-Wolff/PhotoEdit.

Chapter 4: *p. 112,* © Bob Daemmrich/The Image Works; *p. 123,* © Richard T. Nowitz/Photo Researchers, Inc.; *p. 156,* © Bob Daemmrich/The Image Works.

Chapter 5: *p. 166,* © Ellen Senisi/The Image Works.

Chapter 6: *p. 198,* © PhotoDisc; *p. 207,* © Richard Hutchings/Photo Researchers, Inc.; *p. 238,* © Barbara Rios/Photo Researchers, Inc.;

Chapter 7: *p. 248,* © Bob Daemmrich/The Image Works.

Chapter 8: *p. 304,* © PhotoDisc; *p. 321,* © Elizabeth Crews/Stock Boston.

Chapter 9: *p. 334,* © Bob Daemmrich/The Image Works; *p. 355,* © Michael A. Dwyer/Stock Boston.

Chapter 10: *p. 380,* © A. Ramey/PhotoEdit; *p. 400,* © Elizabeth Crews/Stock Boston; *p. 417,* © Davis Barber/PhotoEdit.

Chapter 11: *p. 438,* © Richard Hutchings/Photo Researchers, Inc.; *p. 445,* © Will & Deni McIntyre/Photo Researchers, Inc.; *p. 465,* © Anestis Diakopoulos/Stock Boston.

Chapter 12: *p. 478,* © Lawrence Migdale/Photo Researchers, Inc.; *p. 483,* © Jean-Claude Lejune/Stock Boston.

Line Art, Tables, Text

Chapter 1: *Table 1.1:* Reprinted with permission from American Association for the Advancement of Science.

Chapter 2: *Figure 2.3:* Talsma, V. L. (1998). Student's Scientific Understanding in a Project-Based Science Classroom. Doctoral Dissertation, University of Michigan, Ann Arbor, MI. *Figure 2.4:* Dale's Cone From Audio-Visual Methods in Teaching, 1st edition, by E. Dale © 1969. Reprinted with permission of Wadsworth, an imprint of the Wadsworth Group, a division of Thomson Learning. Fax 800-730-2215.

Chapter 4: *Figures 4.11, 4.12:* Reprinted with permission from Norah Heintz and Alayna Schreier. *Portfolio Activity 4.8:* Reprinted with permission from Ann Novak.

Chapter 5: *Figure 5.1:* Images reprinted by permission from PASCO. *Figure 5.2:* Image reprinted by permission from ImagiWorks, Inc. *Figure 5.3:* Image reprinted with permission from Nancy Songer. *Figure 5.4:* Image reprinted by permission from GoKnow. *Figure 5.5:* The source of this material is *Windows to the Universe,* at http://www.windows.ucar.edu/ at the University Corporation for Atmospheric Research (UCAR). © 1995-1999, 2000 The Regents of the University of Michigan; © 2000-01 University Corporation for Atmospheric Research. All Rights Reserved.

Chapter 7: *Figure 7.4:* Adapted with permission from BSCS, 1992. *Figure 7.5:* Anderson, L. and Krathwohl, D., *A Taxonomy for Learning, Teaching, and Assessing.* Published by Allyn & Bacon, Boston, MA. © 2001 by Pearson Education. Reprinted by permission of the publisher. *Table 7.9:* Bloom, Benjamin S., *Taxonomy of Educational Objectives Book 1: Cognitive Domain.* © 1956 by Allyn & Bacon. Reprinted by permission.

Chapter 8: *Table 8.1:* Anderson, L. and Krathwohl, D., *A Taxonomy for Learning, Teaching, and Assessing.* Published by Allyn & Bacon, Boston, MA. © 2001 by Pearson Education. Reprinted by permission of the publisher.

Chapter 9: *Page 353:* Reprinted with permission from Jodi Haney and Andrew Lumpe.

Chapter 10: *Portfolio Activity 10.4, Mead and Metraux quote:* Reprinted with permission from SCIENCE vol. 126, pg 387. © 1957 American Association for the Advancement of Science.

Chapter 11: *Table 11.8, National Standards Social Studies:* Reprinted from *Expectation of Excellence: Curriculum Standards for Social Studies* with permission from the National Council of Social Studies; *National Standards Math:* Reprinted with permission from the National Council of Teachers of Mathematics; *National Standards Language Arts/Reading:* Reprinted with permission from the National Council of Teachers of English.

Index

('b' indicates boxed material;'i'indicates an illustration;'n' indicates a note;'t' indicates a table)

A

Academic achievement, and collaborative learning, 237
Acceleration, content knowledge, 44
Accommodation, definition of, 49, 52
Accountability, student, 430, 431t
Acid Rain, GEMS books, 98
Action research, 493, 494-495
Active engagement, social constructivist model, 54-56
Activities, benchmark lessons, 281, 284-287
Adaption, definition of, 49
Affective attributes, assessment information, 341, 343b, 343t
Affective factors, promoting positive, 391, 392b, 393t
Alive, understanding of, 39, 55-56, 253-254
American Association for the Advancement of Science (AAAS)
    Atlas of Science Literacy, 25, 120, 440, 442
    Benchmarks for Science Literacy, 4, 22, 24-25, 26, 28
    Project 2061, 4, 22, 24, 26, 28, 440, 461
    on science education, 489
    web site, 494t
American Association of University Women (AAUW), on learning technologies, 191
An NSTA Position Statement: Elementary School Science, 18n, 25
Analogies, presentation technique, 281, 282
Analytic rubrics, 363-365, 364t
Analyze, cognitive process, 264, 265t, 326t-327t
Anecdotal records
    assessment information, 340, 370i
    insect project, 450

Animal care, driving question, 90-91
Animals, classroom safety, 410-411, 415t
Ant Homes, GEMS books, 98
Anxiety, collaborative learning, 239-240
Apparatus, building of, 145
Application
    learning themes, 26
    social constructivist model, 55t, 60
Apply, cognitive process, 264, 265t, 326t-327t
Archival data, sources of, 132
Arends, Richard, 495
Artemis, student web tool, 99, 290
Artifacts
    assembling, 356-361, 362
    benchmark lesson plan, 270i, 271
    description of, 13-14, 354
    presentation of, 361
    student, 354-356
Artifacts production, social constructivist model, 55t, 62
Assessment
    artifacts, 14
    classroom, 313-314
    current practices, 314-332, 318b
    efficiency of, 375, 375b
    information gathering, 338-344
    insect project, 450-452
    investigation, 160-161, 161t
    NSES goals, 22
    NSES standards, 338, 349, 350, 351, 366, 369
    project-based science, 30, 62, 306-309, 372-375, 481
    public attitude toward, 310-311
    purpose of, 309, 310, 310b
    science criteria, 322-325
    teacher self -evaluation, 375, 375b
    techniques of, 362-369, 370i, 371
    types of, 309
    valid/reliable, 316-317, 350
Assimilation, definition of, 49, 52

Association for the Advancement of Science, benchmark lessons, 252
Atlas of Science Literacy,AAAS, 25, 120, 440, 442
Atmosphere, classroom behavior, 420-421
Attestations, portfolio assessment, 361
Attitudes
    learning themes, 27
    project-based science, 30
    promoting positive science, 391
    science education, 19, 21
Audubon, James, 146
Authentic assessment, 313, 322
Authentic tasks, social constructivist model, 55t, 68-70

B

Bakker, Bob, 16
Balloon experiment, 53n, 53-54
Bar graph
    benchmark lessons, 254
    example of, 150i
Base groups, collaborative learning, 212
Basic information questions, 128
Behavior tree, classroom rules, 418-420, 420i
Benchmark lessons
    classroom space, 400-401
    definition of, 250
    description of, 252-255
    identification of, 255-262
    insect project, 446-448
    planning of, 263-264, 265t-273
    project-based science, 481
    scenarios, 250-252
Benchmarks for Science Literacy
    curriculum objectives, 442
    curriculum resources, 440
    goals, 4, 22, 24-25, 26, 28, 89
    scoring rubric design, 365
Berenstain, Jan, 288
Berenstain, Stan, 288
Berg, Craig, 122

Beyond Discipline: From Compliance to Community, 388
Bidirectional zone of proximal development, 64
Biological Science Curriculum Study (BSCS), 5-E model, 271i, 271-272
Blumenfeld, Phyllis, 4, 48-49, 69
Body-kinesthetic intelligence, 465, 466t, 467t
Boiling water experiment, 39, 40i
Bottle Biology, 122
Brainstorming
concept maps 257-258, 292-293
driving question development, 94, 95i, 102-103
Brainstorming wheel, 103i
Brandenburg, Aliki, 288
Brown, Ann, 4
Brown, Deborah, 107
Bruner, Jerome, 4, 4n.
Bubble-ology, GEMS books, 98
Bucklund, William, 15
Building a Presence for Science, NSTA, 329
Burnett, Robin, 485

C
Calculators, learning technologies, 70
Calender of Activities, insect project, 452, 453t, 454b
Campbell, Patricia, 394, 421
Cause and effect questions, 126, 127, 127t, 128
Center for Highly Interactive Computing in Education (hi-ce), 98, 99, 473
Central Idea Diagram, information synthesis, 134, 135i
Checklist for Finding Information, 133t
Checklists
assessment information, 340-341, 341b, 341t, 342t, 343b, 343t, 370i
insect project, 451
student artifacts, 358, 359i
Chemical change, student understanding, 43b
Children
investigation capacity, 117, 120
and science education, 17-18, 21
Children's literature
benchmark lessons, 288, 290b
insect project, 447
Clarification skills, collaborative learning, 222-223
Claris Homepage
findings, 156-157
learning technologies, 184-185
Clark, Eugenie, 118
Class plans/designs, creating, 140t, 143
Classroom assessment, description of, 309
Classroom behavior

potential problems, 422-429, 425b
project-based science, 420-422, 423b
Classroom climate
description of, 385, 386b, 386-387, 388b
effectiveness, 389-396, 392b, 393i, 395b, 396t, 397b
framework for, 388-389
Classroom environment
aspects of, 397, 401t
description of, 385, 386b
driving questions, 101-102
description of, 385, 386b
physical arrangements, 397-401, 401t, 402b
safety, 409-413, 414t-415t, 416b
school day structure, 403-406, 404t, 405b, 407t, 408-409, 410b, 410t
three stages of, 416-432
Classroom rules, 417-418. *See also* Ground rules
Classrooms, science integration, 472
Cleary, Beverly, 271
Clinical interviews
assessment information, 342-344, 370i
insect project, 451
Coaching, teaching strategies, 65
Cognitive learning theories, assessment practices, 319
Cognitive load, collaborative learning, 238-239
Cognitive processes, categories of, 264, 265t
Cognitive roles, collaborative learning, 228
Cognitive task knowledge, definition of, 45, 46
Collaboration
characteristics of, 205-206
constructivism, 52
description of, 12-13, 203-205
professional development, 495
project-based science, 9, 29
scenarios, 200-205
Collaborative environment
creation of, 210-215, 216t, 217-230
learning challenges, 231-235
Collaborative learning
advantages of, 236
types of, 206-210
Collaborative skills
absence of, 230-231
development of, 212-224, 214b
Collaborative Software Laboratory (CSL), 230
Colleagues, driving question development, 93, 96
Commission on Achieving Necessary Skills, new basics, 241
Communication, investigation web, 155-157, 156i, 157i

Communication skills, collaborative learning, 221-222, 222t
Community connections for science education, 413
Community participation, project-based science, 9
Community resources
presentations, 281, 284
suppliers, 458, 461i, 462t-464t
Community-student, collaborative learning, 209-210
Compare/contrast diagram, teaching strategies, 66i, 67
Complexity reduction, teaching strategies, 66
Compromise skills, 222, 224, 224t
Computer lab, technology scenario, 169-170
Computer programs, direct experience, 56
Computer use, technology scenarios, 169-170
Concept
application, learning cycle model, 269
curriculum objectives, 442, 444b
description of, 256b, 256-257, 292
invention, learning cycle model, 268, 269
learning themes, 26
Concept maps
benchmark lessons, 255, 258, 261b
building, 257-259, 259b
chemical change, 257i
computer programs, 181
curriculum objectives, 442, 443i
definition of, 256
food chain, 258, 260i
insect project, 451
learning issues, 292-294
learning technologies, 70, 168
science integration, 472-473, 473i
student assessment, 344-346, 345i, 346i, 370i
Conceptual knowledge
assessment of, 326t
benchmark lessons, 263, 265t
Conceptual learning, benchmark lessons, 252-253
Conceptual model, 152-153
Conclusions, guidelines for, 154-155, 155t
Concrete operations, constructivism, 49
Condensation, understanding of, 39
Conflict-management skills, collaborative learning, 222-224
Connectivity, social constructivist model, 55t, 69
Consequences, student disturbances, 426
Constructive criticism, collaborative learning, 218-221

Constructivism, development of, 52
Content knowledge
    concept maps, 181
    curriculum themes, 27
    description of, 44, 46t
    NSES standards, 61, 101, 124, 125, 135,
        137, 147
    science resources, 485, 486t
Context, assessment practices, 314
Contextualization, project-based science,
    270i, 270
Contextualized driving questions, 78, 82, 84-
    85, 87t, 445
    examples of, 88
Contracts. *See* Learning contracts
Cooties, student web tool, 99
Create, cognitive process, 264, 265t,
    326t-327t
Creativity, learning themes, 27
Crime Lab Chemistry, GEMS books, 98
Criterion-referenced tests, 373
Critical features, teaching strategies, 66
Critical thinking
    learning themes, 26
    science education, 20
Cross-links, concept maps, 256
Cultural diversity. *See* Diversity
Curiosity
    benchmark lessons, 255
    learning themes, 27
    project-based science, 30
Curious Naturalist, The, 290
Current data, information, 132
Curriculum
    collaborative learning, 243b
    driving question development, 92, 93,
        94, 96-98
    education themes, 27
    effective classrooms, 390-391
    insect project, 440-443, 443i, 444b
    learning technologies, 190-191
    model, 24-25, 25t
    planning model, benchmark lessons,
        270-271
Curriculum integration
    advantages of, 466-468
    advocates of, 460-461, 465
    characteristics of, 468-469
    evaluation of, 470, 471t
    and project-based science, 469-470
Curriculum Orchestrator, 442

D
Daily journals
    insect project, 451
    student artifacts, 356, 357-358, 361
Dale's Cone of Experience, 56, 57i, 179
Darwin, Charles, 146

Data
    interpretation of, 147
    techniques, 147-155
    types of, 132
    World Wide Web, 182-183, 183t
Day of the Dinosaur, 288
Dear Mr. Henshaw, 271
Debate, social constructivist model, 55t, 63
Decision making
    science education, 20
    skills, collaborative learning,
        215, 216t
Decisions, Decisions Series, 243b
Decomposition, student investigations,
    158-160
Demonstrations, benchmark lessons,
    273-277
Departmentalized schools, science
    integration, 472
Descriptive questions, investigation web,
    126-128, 127t
Descriptive statistics, data techniques, 147,
    151-152
Design, concept of, 134-135
Dewey, John, 4, 4n., 11
Diagrams
    data techniques, 147
    presentations, 281, 282-283
    social constructivist model, 54
Digging up Dinosaurs, 288
Digital cameras, learning technologies, 187
Digital libraries, 182-183
Dinosaur Babies, 288
Dinosaur Dreams, 288
Dinosaurs, theories about, 15-16
Direct instruction
    description of, 8
    pesticides in food chain, 383-384, 385
Discrepant events, demonstrations, 275-276,
    276b, 277b
Discussion techniques, 278-280
Discussions
    assessment information, 339-340
    value of large group, 277-278
Displays, classroom space, 398, 400, 401t
Disturbances, student problems, 423, 426-
    427, 427i
Divergent questions, 294
Diversity
    assessment practices, 318-319
    collaboration challenges, 233
    curriculum integration, 466-467
    driving question, 78
Downtime, 425
Draw a scientist, 360, 394, 395b
Drawings
    insect project, 451
    student artifacts, 356, 358-360, 361

Driving questions
    benchmark lessons, 253, 271
    definition of, 81
    description of, 11-12
    development of, 92-98, 95i,
        444-445, 446b
    force and motion, 80-81
    insect project, 443-445, 446b, 449
    and investigations, 128-129
    key features of, 78, 82-87, 87t, 445
    project-based science, 4
    project techniques, 108-109
    science education goals, 29
    social constructivist model, 55t,
        68-69
    three examples of, 87-91
    uniqueness of, 91
    value of, 106-108
Duped, fear of being, 232

E
Earth science, NSES standards, 23
Earthquest Explores Ecology, 178-179
Eco-Adventures in the Oceans, 178
Eco-Adventures in the Rainforest, 178
Ecology, simulations, 178-179
Educational goals, and assessment
    practices, 317
Educational Leadership, 493t
Educational television shows, presentations,
    281, 283
Eisenhower National Clearinghouse for
        Mathematics and Science
        Education
    curriculum material, 98, 474
    project resources, 457
    science education, 490
    website, 494t
Elaboration, 5-E model, 271i, 271, 272
Electricity, 5-E model, 271-272
Electronic spreadsheets, learning
    technologies, 70
Elementary school, science education,
    18, 21
Elementary School Studies, planning/
    design, 143
Elementary Science Study (ESS), inquiry-
    focused curriculum, 52
Embedded assessment, project-based
    science, 308-309, 315
Engagement, 5-E model, 271, 271i
Environmental activism, social constructivist
    model, 61
Environments (FOSS), 446
Equality
    collaboration, 205, 206
    effective classrooms, 393, 396t
Equilibrium, definition of, 49

Equipment
    classroom safety, 411
    experimental procedures, 144
Essay exam, student assessment, 348-349
Ethical driving questions, 78, 82, 86, 87t, 445
    examples of, 89, 90-91
Evaluate, cognitive process, 264, 265t,
    326t-327t
Evaluation
    5-E model, 271i, 271, 272
    social constructivist model, 55t, 61-62
    student accountability, 430
Evaporation, understanding of, 39
Every Child a Scientist: Achieving Literacy
    for All, 490
Evidence, social constructivist model, 55t,
    63-64
Experimental procedures
    assessment of, 160-161, 161t
    conclusions, 153-155, 155t
    conduction of, 144-147
    data interpretation, 147-153, 148t, 149i,
        149t, 150i, 152i
    planning/design of, 136-137, 138b-
        139b, 140t, 140-144, 143b, 145b
Explanation, 5-E model, 271i, 271, 272
Exploration
    5-E model, 271i, 271-272
    learning cycle model, 268

F

Facilitator
    project-based science, 29
    science teaching standards, 13
Factual (Content) knowledge
    assessment of, 317, 326t
    benchmark lessons, 263, 265t
Feasible driving questions, 78, 82, 83-84,
    87t, 445
    examples of, 87-88, 89, 90
Feedback
    decomposition investigations, 159, 160
    large group discussions, 277
    planning/design, 144
    project-based science, 307
    teacher assessments, 328-329
Feederwatch Program, 176-178, 178b, 189-
    190, 229
Field Trip to the Rainforest, A, 178-179
Field Trip to the Sea, A, 178-179
Field trips
    classroom safety, 413, 415t
    insect project, 447
    student activities, 281, 287
Findings, formats, 156-157
Fingerprinting, GEMS books, 98
Fire, classroom safety, 412, 415t
First aid, classroom safety, 413

First Law of Motion
    content knowledge, 44
    force and motion, 79n
    and seat belts, 43
Fish-bone model, potential problems, 423,
    424i, 425b
5-E model, 271i, 271-272
Fizz and Martina, 243b
Follow through, experimental procedures,
    143-144
Force, content knowledge, 44
Force/motion, learning scenarios, 79-81
Formal interviews, assessment
    information, 344
Formal operations, constructivism, 49
Formative assessment
    classroom scenario, 337-338
    description of, 309, 329, 356
    use of, 325, 328
Frequency, 48
Full Option Science System (FOSS), kit-
    based curricula, 98, 446
Future Shock, 26

G

Gardner, Howard, 465, 466
Gender
    collaboration challenges, 233
    collaborative learning, 240-241
    group formation, 211-212
    learning technologies, 191-192
    science education, 394
Gender bias, science education, 394-396
Genscope, 179
Geometric Supposer, The, 243b
Girls
    curriculum integration, 466
    science education, 21, 394
Glassware, classroom safety, 412-413,
    414t-415t
Gleason, Chris, 129n, 158, 160
Global Learning and Observations to Benefit
    the Environment (GLOBE)
    driving questions, 98
    learning technologies, 188
*Global Warming and the Greenhouse
    Effect*, GEMS books, 98
Go and Tell software, 187
Goal Sheet
    collaborative learning, 216t
    investigations, 141t
Goals, collaborative learning, 225, 226t
Goggles, classroom safety, 411
Grading, description of, 369, 371
Graphing calculators, 174-175
Graphs
    data techniques, 147, 148-151, 150i
    learning technologies, 70, 168

    presentations, 281, 282-283
    real-time, 173, 175i
*Great Expectations in Math and Science
    (GEMS)*, driving questions,
    97-98
Great Ocean Rescue, 179, 243b, 283, 470
Great Solar System Rescue, 179, 243b
Ground rules, 418, 418b
Group accountability, 430-432, 431t
Groups
    benchmark lessons, 277-280
    formation of, 210-212, 213t
    learning challenges, 231-232
Guest lecturers/speakers
    insect project, 447
    presentations, 281, 284
Guide. *See also* Facilitator
    national goals, 29
    science teaching themes, 28

H

Hide a Butterfly, GEMS, 447
Hierarchical relationships, concept
    maps, 256
High traffic areas, classroom space,
    398-399, 401t
High-stakes assessment, 309, 311,
    312-313, 313b
Higher order questions (convergent), 294
Hobbies/personal interests, driving question
    development, 93, 95-96
Holistic rubrics, description of, 363
Home groups, collaborative learning, 212
Horner, Jack, 15
How Big is a Brachiosaurus?, 288-289
Hurd, Paul DeHart, 27, 460-461
HyperStudio, 184-185
Hypotheses
    description of, 16-17
    investigation web, 129t, 129-130,
        130b, 131b

I

Implementation, investigation web,
    158-160, 160b
Incredible Insects, Ranger Rick, 447, 448
Individual accountability, 430-432, 431t
Inert knowledge, 38, 44, 45i, 324
Informal interviews, assessment
    information, 343
Information
    evaluation of, 133, 133t, 134t
    investigation web, 131
    research process, 132-133, 133t
    synthesis of, 134, 135i
Initial investigations/observations
    magnets, 408t
    web, 121-122

Inquiry
    description of, 12
    NSES definition, 17
    NSES goals, 22
Insect life, driving question example, 87-88
Insects (FOSS), 446, 449, 455
Inspiration, concept maps programs,
        181, 258
Instruction
    classroom space, 398, 400, 401t
    learning technologies, 190-192
    setting scenarios, 382-385
Integrated curriculum
    definition of, 468, 469
    four characteristics of, 468-469
    insect project, 470-471
Integration
    curriculum themes, 27
    project-based science, 29
Intellectual development, constructivism,
        49, 52
Interactive media, learning technologies,
        178-179
Interdisciplinary curriculum
    definition of, 468
    themes, 27
Interest
    learning themes, 27
    project-based science, 30
Interpersonal intelligence, 465, 466t, 467t
Interpersonal roles, collaborative
        learning, 228
Interrelationships, concept maps, 256
Intrapersonal intelligence, 465, 466t, 467t
Investigation centers, student activities, 281,
        286-287
Investigation web
    assessment, 160-161
    components of, 118-120, 119i
    conclusions, 153-155
    conduction of procedures, 144-147
    data interpretation, 147-153, 148t, 149i,
        149t, 150i, 152i
    experimental procedures design, 136-
        137, 138b-139b, 140t, 140-144,
        143b, 145b
    hypothesizing, 129t, 129-130,
        130b, 131b
    implementing investigations,
        158-160, 160b
    information discovery, 131-133
    information evaluation, 133-134,
        133t, 134t
    initial observations, 121-122, 122i
    manipulation of materials, 122
    messing about, 118, 120-121
    planning and design, 134-136
    planning/design critique, 140t, 141-142

predictions, 130-131, 131t, 132t
project-based science, 16-17, 59,
        114, 480
refining questions, 125
sharing information, 155-157, 156i, 157i
teacher's role, 124-126, 132-133, 140t,
        140-144, 141t, 142t, 147, 153
types of questions, 126-128
Investigations
    benchmark lesson plan, 270i, 271
    components of, 114, 115-116
    insect project, 448-450, 451b
    non-linear process, 118-124
    project-based science, 9, 29, 30, 480
    scenarios, 114-116
    social constructivist model, 55t, 59-60
    step-by-step activity, 114-115
    teacher competence, 486-487
    technology scenarios, 170
    trial and error, 115
Invitations to Science Inquiry, discrepant
        events, 275

J
Jasper Woodbury, 283
Journals
    professional development, 494-495
    student artifacts, 356, 357-358, 361

K
Karplus, Robert, 4, 4n., 52, 268
Kids as Global Scientists project, 176,
        177i, 229
Kidspiration, concept maps programs,
        181, 258
Knowledge
    construction, learning themes, 26
    contextualized, 48-49
    current assessment of, 317-325, 327t
    prior, 53-54, 55t, 56, 58-59
    science education, 19
    types of, 44-46, 46t, 263-264, 265t
Knowledge Integration Environment, 180
Kohn, Alfie, 207, 388-389, 390-391, 420-421
Koontz, Trish Yourst, 275
KWL strategy
    benchmark lessons, 255, 256, 260-262,
        261t, 262t
    driving questions, 102

L
Labor division, collaborative learning,
        225-227
Laboratory technique, benchmark
        lessons, 253
Ladybugs, GEMS, 447
Land features, driving question example,
        89-90

Language, social constructivist model, 55t,
        62, 63
Large-scale assessments
    debate over, 310-313
    description of, 309
Lawrence Hall of Science GEMS, 97-98, 447
Learning, education themes, 26-27
Learning communities
    collaborative scenario, 202-203
    learning technologies, 188
    social constructivist model, 55t, 62-68
Learning contracts, 233, 421-422, 422i, 423b
Learning cycle models
    benchmark lessons, 268-270
    instructional, 52
Learning performances
    assessment of, 325, 326t-327t, 328b
    benchmark lessons, 263-264, 265t
    insect project, 442-443, 444b, 448
Learning technologies
    acquiring written information, 289-291
    assessment practices, 329
    classroom management, 432
    collaborative environment, 228-230
    description of, 13, 192
    driving questions, 98
    educational support, 171-172, 175t
    multimedia documents, 372
    planning tools, 473-474
    useful tools, 70, 125
Learning theory, assessment practices,
        319-320
Learning Through Collaborative
        Visualization Project (CoVis),
        98-99
Learning to Teach, 494
Leim, Tik, 275
Lesson plans, benchmark lessons, 264,
        266-268
Life Cycle of Butterflies, The, 441, 446, 449
Life science, NSES standards, 23
Life skills, collaborative learning, 241-242
Line graph, example of, 150i
Lines, concept maps, 256, 293-294
Linguistic intelligence, 465, 466t, 467t
Linking, driving questions, 107-108
Linking words, concept maps, 256, 258,
        258t, 293
Linn, Marcia, 180
Listening, benchmark lessons, 255, 259-260
Loafer effect, collaboration challenges, 232
Logical-mathematical intelligence, 465,
        466t, 467t
Lorax, The, 283
Lower order questions, 294
Lunetta, Vincent, 280

M

Magnetic field, learning cycle model, 268-269

Managerial roles, collaborative learning, 228

Marvin, Frederic, 288-289

Matching, student assessment, 348, 349

Material manipulation, investigation web, 122-124

Materials/supplies
classroom safety, 412
classroom space, 398, 399-400, 401t
distribution problems, 423-425

Mathematical model, 152, 153

McClintock, Barbara, 118

Meaningful driving questions, 78, 82, 85-86, 87t, 106, 445
examples of, 88-90

Meaningful understanding, 43-44, 45i
assessment practices, 320-322

Media, driving question development, 93, 96

Messing about, investigation web, 118, 120-121

Metacognitive knowledge
assessment of, 317, 327t
benchmark lessons, 263-264
definition of, 180-181
description of, 45-46, 46t
learning technologies, 182-183, 184i
self-assessment method, 369

Metaphors, presentations, 281, 282

Microcomputer-based laboratories (MBLs)
learning technologies, 172-175, 174b
school applications, 175, 177b

Microscopes, benchmark scenarios, 250-251

Microworlds, learning technologies, 178, 179

Middle Ground, 493t

Middle school, science education, 18, 21

Middle School Journal, 493t

Middle Years Digital Library Project, 182-183

Mindful interaction, social constructivist model, 55t, 56t

Minorities
collaborative learning, 240, 241
curriculum integration, 466-468
science education, 394, 396, 396t, 397b

Model-It, 99, 179-180, 181i

Modeling
collaborative learning, 236-237
planning and design, 140t, 142-143
teaching strategies, 65

Models
benchmark lessons, 254
data techniques, 147, 152-153
learning technologies, 179-181

Motion probes, 81-82, 82n

Movies, presentations, 281, 283

Multidimensional assessment, current practices, 315-316

Multimedia documents
insect project, 451
student artifacts, 356, 372

Multiple choice tests, student assessment, 348, 349

Multiple intelligences, 286, 465-466, 466t
insect project, 467t

Multiple representations
learning technologies, 184-187
social constructivist model, 55t, 61-62

Multiple resources, social constructivist model, 55t, 59

Music
insect project, 451
student artifacts, 356, 360, 361

Musical intelligence, 465, 466t, 467t

Mutuality, collaboration, 205-206

My Back Yard, archival data, 132, 290

My Visit to the Dinosaurs, 288

Mystery bag game, investigation skills, 124

Mystery Festival, GEMS books, 98

N

National Academy of Science
NSES standards, 22
website, 494t

National Assessment of Educational Progress (NAEP), large-scale testing, 309

National Association for Research in Science Teaching (NARST), 486t, 491

National Association for the Education of Young Children (NAEYC), curriculum integration, 461, 465

National Center for Education Statistics, 494t

National Geographic, archival data, 132, 169

National Middle School Association (NMSA), curriculum integration, 461, 465

National Oceanic and Atmospheric Administration (NOAA), 289

National Research Council (NRC)
benchmark lessons, 252
NSES standards, 22
science assessment, 324
science education, 489, 490

National Science Education Standards, The (NSES)
curriculum integration, 461
curriculum objectives, 442
curriculum resource, 440
executive summary, 312, 316
force/motion scenarios, 82b
formative and summative assessment, 324, 328, 356
goals, 4, 11, 20, 22-23, 26, 28, 237-238

overview, 315
principles and definitions, 15, 17, 253
professional development standards, 491, 492, 494
science education assessment standards, 309, 312, 315, 316
science education content standards, 61, 101, 124, 125, 135, 137, 147, 172, 176, 258, 274, 276
science education design standards, 172, 185
science education program standards, 63, 68, 78, 83, 117-118
science teaching standards, 11, 12, 13, 56, 57, 63, 93, 109, 170, 205, 206, 207, 208, 209, 210, 221, 227, 231, 232, 235, 260, 261, 262, 278, 294, 389, 390, 391, 408, 409, 429, 441, 451, 459, 461, 472
scientific enterprise, 168

National Science Foundation, WISE, 98, 473, 494t

National Science Teachers Association (NSTA)
animal safety guidelines, 410-411
Building a Presence for Science, 329
field trip tips, 413
goals, 4, 22
NSTA Community website, 329, 457, 473
NSTA's Science Education Suppliers, 98, 457
plant safety guidelines, 411
position statement, 18n, 25, 26, 28
professional organization, 486t, 492, 494
Sci Links, 132, 183
science assessment, 324
Science and Children journal, 289, 485, 492, 493t
Science Scope journal, 289, 485, 492, 493t

Naturalist intelligence, 466, 466t, 467t

Nature Scope, 485

Negotiation skills, 222, 223, 223t, 224i
T-Chart, 213t, 214

Network, concept maps, 256

Networking, assessment practices, 329

Nolan, Dennis, 288

Norms, 416, 429-430

Novak, Ann, 129n, 158, 160

Novak, Joseph, 292

NSTA Community website, 329, 457, 473

O

Observation
assessment information, 339, 370i

benchmark lessons, 255, 259-260
insect project, 450
vs. inference, 124-125
Observations
experimental procedures, 146
question generation, 125-126, 126t
Of Bugs and Beasts, 447, 472
Ogle, Debra, 102
One Sky, Many Voices, 188, 473
Online Learning Center, 31, 71, 109, 162,
192, 242, 298, 330, 375, 432,
474, 495
Open-ended questions, assessment
information, 344, 370i
Owen, Richard, 16

P
Pacts, collaboration challenges, 233
Palm device
probes, 174, 176i
software, 187
Parents
gender bias, 394-395
project-based science assessment, 374
Participation, collaborative learning, 224-
228, 226t, 227b
Passport Systems, probes, 174, 176i
Peer assessment, student portfolio, 369
Penner, Lucille Recht, 288
Performance-based assessment
description of, 352-353, 370i
insect project, 451
steps of, 353-354, 355b
Personal and social perspectives science,
NSES standards, 23
Personal experience, driving question
development, 93-94
Pfister, Marcus, 217
Photosynthesis, concept of, 41
Physical arrangements, four keys to, 398-
401, 401t, 402b
Physical change, student understanding, 43b
Physical model, 152
Physical products
insect project, 451
student artifacts, 356, 358, 359i, 361
Physical science, NSES standards, 23
Piaget, Jean, intellectual development,
49, 52
Pic Map, concept maps programs, 181, 258
Pictograph technique, 151, 152i
Pictures, presentations, 281, 282-283
Pillbug Project, The
driving questions, 97
resources, 457, 485
Planning, concept of, 134-135
Planning and Design chart, 140t
Plants, classroom safety, 410, 411, 415t
Portfolio Activity 1.1, School Science
Experiences, 6, 7b

Portfolio Activity 1.2, Science Scenarios,
9, 10b
Portfolio Activity 1.3, Film Cannister
exercise, 15, 15b
Portfolio Activity 1.4, Science Education,
18, 19b
Portfolio Activity 1.5, Science Education
Goals, 22, 23b
Portfolio Activity 1.6, Case Study, 30b, 31
Portfolio Activity 1.7, Science Teaching
Questions, 31, 31b
Portfolio Activity 2.1, Science
Understanding, 41, 42b
Portfolio Activity 2.2, Physical and Chemical
Change, 42, 42b-43b
Portfolio Activity 2.3, Recognizing a Social
Constructivist Lesson, 49,
50b-51b
Portfolio Activity 2.4,
Concreteness/Abstractness,
56, 58b
Portfolio Activity 2.5, Preparing a Social
Constructivist Lesson, 70, 70b
Portfolio Activity 3.1, Force/motion
Scenarios, 81, 82b
Portfolio Activity 3.2, Force/motion
Scenarios, 87, 88b
Portfolio Activity 3.3, Evaluating Questions,
91, 92b
Portfolio Activity 3.4, Generating Driving
Questions, 99, 100b
Portfolio Activity 3.5, Developing Driving
Questions, 100, 101b
Portfolio Activity 3.6, Student Driving
Questions, 103, 104b
Portfolio Activity 4.1, Stream Walk,
121, 123b
Portfolio Activity 4.2, Identifying Testable
Questions, 129, 130b
Portfolio Activity 4.3, Hypotheses from
Questions, 129, 131b
Portfolio Activity 4.4, Writing Procedures,
136, 137b
Portfolio Activity 4.5, Variables: Paper
Dragon Races, 137, 138b-139b,
140, 141
Portfolio Activity 4.6, Sprouting Bean Plants,
143b, 144
Portfolio Activity 4.7, Planning and
Designing, 145b
Portfolio Activity 4.8, Performing the
Investigation, 158, 159b
Portfolio Activity 4.9, Implementing
Investigations, 160, 160b
Portfolio Activity 4.10, Comparing
Investigations, 161, 161t, 162b
Portfolio Activity 5.1, Technologies for
Learning, 171, 171b
Portfolio Activity 5.2, Children and
Technology, 171, 171b

Portfolio Activity 5.3, Computer Labs:
Evaporative Cooling, 173, 174b
Portfolio Activity 5.4, Computers Labs:
Classroom use, 176, 177b
Portfolio Activity 5.5, World Wide Web:
Feederwatch Program,
176-178, 178b
Portfolio Activity 5.6, Simulations, 178,
179, 180b
Portfolio Activity 5.7, Model Building,
180, 182b
Portfolio Activity 5.8, World Wide Web:
Digital Libraries, 183, 185b
Portfolio Activity 5.9, Multimedia
Documents, 187, 187b
Portfolio Activity 5.10, New Technologies,
192, 192b
Portfolio Activity 6.1, Classroom
Collaboration, 203, 204b
Portfolio Activity 6.2, Collaborative Skills,
213, 214, 214b
Portfolio Activity 6.3, Making T-Charts,
214, 215b
Portfolio Activity 6.4, Trust Building, 217,
218b-219b
Portfolio Activity 6.5, Cooperative Group
Skills, 218, 220b
Portfolio Activity 6.6, Understanding
Building, 225, 227b
Portfolio Activity 6.7, Facilitating
Collaborative Learning,
228, 229b
Portfolio Activity 6.8, Troubleshooting,
234, 235b
Portfolio Activity 6.9, Explaining
Collaborative Learning,
235, 236b
Portfolio Activity 6.10, Collaborative
Classroom, 239, 240b
Portfolio Activity 6.11, Collaborative
Classroom Change, 242, 242b
Portfolio Activity 6.12, Collaborative
Curriculum Resources,
242, 243b
Portfolio Activity 7.1, What is a Concept?,
256, 256b
Portfolio Activity 7.2, Building a Concept
Map, 258, 259b
Portfolio Activity 7.3, Concept Map for
Benchmark Lessons, 259, 261b
Portfolio Activity 7.4, Planning/Teaching
Benchmark Lessons, 272, 273b
Portfolio Activity 7.5, Heating Water in a
Paper Cup, 275-276, 276b
Portfolio Activity 7.6, The Inverted Jar,
276, 277b
Portfolio Activity 7.7, Leading a
Discussion, 280b
Portfolio Activity 7.8, Images on the World
Wide Web, 283, 283b

Portfolio Activity 7.9, Value of Community Resources, 284, 285b

Portfolio Activity 7.10, Planning/Teaching 2nd Benchmark Lesson, 287, 288b

Portfolio Activity 7.11, Children's Sciences Magazines, 289, 290b

Portfolio Activity 7.12, Identifying Question Levels, 297b

Portfolio Activity 7.13, Analyzing Question Style, 298b

Portfolio Activity 8.1, Purpose of Assessment, 310, 310b

Portfolio Activity 8.2, Teacher Beliefs and Assessment, 310, 311b

Portfolio Activity 8.3, High-Stakes Testing, 313, 313b

Portfolio Activity 8.4, Science Reform and Assessment, 317, 318b

Portfolio Activity 8.5, Traditional Testing Pitfalls, 323b

Portfolio Activity 8.6, Assessment Choice, 325b

Portfolio Activity 8.7, Learning Performance Assessment, 328b

Portfolio Activity 9.1, Skills Checklist Development, 341, 341b

Portfolio Activity 9.2, Assessing Affective Attributes, 341, 343b

Portfolio Activity 9.3, Writing A Classroom Test, 351, 351b

Portfolio Activity 9.4, Performance-Based Assessment Development, 354, 355b

Portfolio Activity 9.5, Creating A Portfolio, 362, 363b

Portfolio Activity 9.6, Scoring Rubric Development, 366, 367b

Portfolio Activity 9.7, Report Card Creation, 371, 371b

Portfolio Activity 9.8, Efficiency of Assessment, 375, 375b

Portfolio Activity 9.9, Assessment Learning, 375, 375b

Portfolio Activity, 10.1, Managing a Science Classroom, 385, 386b-387b

Portfolio Activity, 10.2, Positive Project-Based Science Classroom, 387, 388b

Portfolio Activity, 10.3, Promoting Positive Affective Factors, 393b

Portfolio Activity, 10.4, Draw A Scientist, 395b

Portfolio Activity, 10.5, Equitable Classroom Practices, 396, 397b

Portfolio Activity, 10.6, Arranging A Project-Based Science Classroom, 401, 402b

Portfolio Activity, 10.7, Preplanning Subject Allocation, 405, 405b

Portfolio Activity, 10.8, Scheduling, 409, 410b

Portfolio Activity, 10.9, Conducting a Safety Audit, 413, 416b

Portfolio Activity, 10.10, Establishing Ground Rules, 418, 418b

Portfolio Activity, 10.11, Making a Contract, 422, 423b

Portfolio Activity, 10.12, Anticipating Problems, 423, 425b

Portfolio Activity, 10.13, Rethinking Managing A Project-Based Science Classroom, 432, 432b

Portfolio Activity, 11.1, Concepts, Learning Performances and Curriculum Objectives, 443, 444b

Portfolio Activity, 11.2, Concepts, Learning Performances, Curriculum Objectives and Driving Questions, 445, 446b

Portfolio Activity, 11.3, Developing Benchmark Lessons, 448, 449b

Portfolio Activity, 11.4, Developing An Investigation, 450, 451b

Portfolio Activity, 11.5, Developing Assessments, 452, 452b

Portfolio Activity, 11.6, Calender of Activities, 452, 454b

Portfolio Activity, 11.7, Revisiting Project Design, 452, 455b

Portfolio Activity, 11.8, Selecting Good Resources, 455, 457b

Portfolio Activity, 11.9, Finding Resources Using the Web, 458, 459b

Portfolio Activity, 11.10, Identifying Resources in Local Stores, 458, 460b

Portfolio Activity, 11.11, Beliefs About Curriculum Integration, 468, 468b

Portfolio Activity, 11.12, Developing Integrated Curriculum, 473, 474b

Portfolio Activity 12.1, Project-Based Science Benefits, 483, 484b

Portfolio Activity 12.2, Your Challenges, 491, 491b

Portfolio Activity 12.3, Revisiting Your Portfolio, 495, 496b

Portfolio Activity 12.4, Reexamining Your Portfolio, 495, 496b

Portfolio assessment, process of, 361, 366-369, 371

"Portfolio review," 367

Portfolios, student artifacts, 356

Positive interdependence, communication skills, 225

PowerPoint
communicating findings, 156-157, 156i, 157i

learning technologies, 184-185, 186i

Predict/explain phenomena, social constructivist model, 54, 55t

Predictions, investigation web, 130-131, 131t, 132t

Preoperational thought, constructivism, 49

Presentations, techniques of, 281, 282-284

Primary data sources, World Wide Web, 182

Primary-source material, World Wide Web, 289

Principles/concepts, social constructivist model, 55t, 70

Principles/definitions, NSES standards, 15, 17, 253

Prior experience, 53-54, 55t, 56, 58-59
project-based science, 29
science teaching themes, 28

Prior knowledge, social constructivism, 53-54, 55t, 56, 58-59

Probes
advantages of, 175-176, 177b
learning technologies, 172-174, 176i
sources of, 174

Probing, 60, 279, 339

Problem solving
collaborative learning, 237-238
meaningful understanding, 43
science education, 20

Procedural knowledge
assessment of, 317, 327t
benchmark lessons, 263, 265t
description of, 45, 46t
learning technologies, 172

Process science teaching
description of, 8-9
force and motion, 79-80, 306-307
microscopes, 250-251
pesticides in food chain, 384, 385
teaching themes, 28

Product, description of, 358

Productions, portfolio assessment, 362

Professional publications, 492-493, 493t

Professional science education organizations, 486t, 491-492

Project 2061: Science for All Americans
curriculum integration, 461
goals, 4, 22, 24, 26, 28, 440

Project-based science
assessment, 372-375, 481
benchmark lessons, 252, 270i, 270-271, 481
benefits of, 482-483, 484b
challenges of, 483-491
and curriculum integration, 469-470
description of, 4, 9, 11-14
driving questions, 78, 80-87, 87t, 444-445, 480
embedded assessment, 308-309, 315
flexibility of, 409
ground rules, 418, 418b, 419t

implementation of, 440
insect learning scenario, 251-252
investigation web, 16-17, 59, 114, 480
investigations, 9, 29, 30, 480
key points, 480-481
learning environments, 389, 409, 481
and national goals, 28-30
Online Learning Center, 31, 71, 109, 162, 192, 242, 298, 330, 375, 432, 474, 495
planning, 136-137, 138b-139b, 140t, 140-144, 141t, 142t, 143b, 145b, 270-271, 440-441, 481
reading, 287-288
scaffolding, 481
scoring rubric design, 365-366
social constructionist teaching model, 54-56, 55t, 57i, 58-70, 66i, 67i
social constructivist theory, 38, 49, 52-53
social context, 55t, 63, 64, 480-481
student assessment process, 338, 370i
and technology, 9, 481
traditional testing, 306-307
Project design
creating, 140t, 143
critique of, 140t, 141-142
driving questions techniques, 108-109
experimental procedures, 136-137, 138b-139b, 140t, 140-144, 143b, 145b
insect project, 452, 454i, 455b
and planning, 134-136
revisiting, 452, 455b
student's role, 135-136
teacher's role, 140t, 140-144, 141t, 142t

Q
Questionnaires, professional development, 495
Questions. *See also* Driving questions
benchmark lessons, 294-297, 296t, 297b
classification of, 294-297
investigative web types, 126-128, 127t
open-ended, 344, 370i
probing, 60
project-based science, 9, 11-12, 28-29, 30, 294
refining, investigation web, 125
social constructivist model, 54, 55t
Quicktrials, 144-145

R
Rainbow Fish, The, 217
Rainforest Researchers, 283
Ranger Rick
archival data, 132, 169, 290

insect project, 447, 448
Read about science
description of, 7
force and motion, 79
insects, 250
pesticides in food chain, 382-383, 385
Reading, project-based science, 287-288
Real choices, effective classrooms, 389-390
Real-time graphs, learning technologies, 173, 175i
Receptional teaching, 46, 47
Redirecting, discussion technique, 279-280, 339
Reflection
definition, 493-494
project-based science assessment, 373
social constructivist model, 55t, 60
Reflective practitioners, 314, 429, 494-495
Reinforcement, classroom behavior, 420, 429-430
Relational questions, 126, 127 127t
Relevance
curriculum integration, 466-467
social constructivist model, 55t, 69
Reliable assessment, 317, 350
Remember, cognitive process, 264, 265t, 326t-327t
Report card, creation of, 371, 371b
Reproductions, portfolio assessment, 361
Resources
community availability, 458, 461i, 462t-464t
household material, 458, 460b, 462t-464t
noncommercial suppliers, 457-458, 458t, 459t
obtaining, 455-460
selection criteria, 455, 456t, 457b, 458
types of, 452, 454
Resources Checklist
collaborative learning, 216t
investigations, 142t
Responsibility, science education, 20
Results, project-based science, 9
Revision, experimental procedures, 146-147
Rewards, classroom behavior, 420-421
"Right answer," collaboration challenges, 234
River Cutters, 123
Role models, effective classrooms, 390
Role-playing, student activities, 281, 285-286
Roles, collaborative learning, 228, 229b
Roth, Wolff-Michael, 4
Roup, Richard, 4
Rowe, Mary Budd, 278

S
Safety audit, 413, 416b
Safety, classroom, 409-413, 414t-415t

Safety precautions
demonstrations, 275
science lessons, 413, 414t, 416b
Safety shields, classroom safety, 411
Scaffolding
collaborative learning, 208
concept of, 65
project-based science, 481
strategies, 65-68, 66i, 67i
Scenarios
assessment, 308-309
benchmark lessons, 250-252
classroom assessment, 336-338
collaborative learning, 200-205
curriculum planning, 440-441
driving questions, 79-81, 82b
instructional settings, 382-385
investigations, 114-116
learning communities, 202-203
Portfolio Activity 1.2, 9, 10b
science understanding, 39-41
technology usage, 169-170
Schemas, definition of, 49
Scholastic, archival data, 132
School Science and Mathematics, 493t
Sci Links, data source, 132, 183
Science
components of, 15-17
nature of, 17
NSES definition, 15
social constructivist definition, 63
theories of, 14-15
Science Activities for the Visually Impaired/Science Enrichment for Learners with Physical Handicaps (SAVI/SELPH), 144
Science and Children, NSTA journal, 289, 485, 492, 493t
Science and technology education, NSES standards, 23
Science and Technology for Children (STC), kit-based curricula, 98, 102, 441
Science anxiety, collaborative learning, 239-240
Science Court, driving questions, 97
Science education
advocacy of, 490-491
benefits of, 18-21
growth of, 18
national goals, 28-30
organizations, 486t
primary goals, 4, 20, 21-28
Science education assessment standards (NSES)
classroom assessment, 309, 312, 315, 319, 324
disabled students, 349
formative and summative assessment, 324, 329, 356

portfolios, 338
  process of, 338, 349, 350, 351
  scoring rubric, 365, 366
  student participation, 316, 368, 369
  teacher assistance, 329
Science education content standards (NSES)
  conceptual skills, 258
  data/evidence, 147
  fair test, 137
  motion/force, 306-307
  partial inquiries, 274
  questions, 101, 125
  results presentations, 276
  science and technology, 61
  scientific inquiry, 124
  scientific investigations, 135, 137
  technological tools, 172
Science education design standards (NSES)
  data manipulation, 172
  electronic devices, 172, 185
  information handling devices, 186
Science education program
            standards (NSES)
  authentic questions, 68
  evidence, 63
  inquiry process, 78
  relevance, 83
  scientific inquiry, 117-118
  teacher role, 68
Science education standards (NSES),
            professional development, 491,
            492, 494
Science enterprise, NSES standards, 168
Science for All Americans
  curriculum integration, 461
  goals, 4, 22, 24, 26, 28, 440
Science for Life and Living, 243b
Science history, NSES standards, 23
Science in Action, 283
Science literacy, science education, 20-21
Science program
  daily schedule, 407t, 409, 410b, 410t
  delivery of, 406, 407t, 408, 408t
  time allocation, 403-405, 404t, 405, 405b
Science Scope, NSTA journal, 289, 485,
            492, 493t
Science Seekers, driving questions, 97
Science Teacher, 493t
Science teaching
  education themes, 28
  media attention, 18
  scaffolding techniques, 65-68, 66i, 67i
Science teaching standards
  active learning, 57
  assessment, 14, 374, 451
  collaborative learning, 206, 210, 227,
            232, 235
  communication, 221
  content, 11

curriculum development, 262
discourse, 56
educational restructuring, 461
facilitation, 13, 207
informal discussions, 278
inquiry-based programs, 12, 93,
            294, 390
learning environments, 389, 409, 481
local resources, 459
NSES goals, 23
planning, 16, 408, 441, 472
practices, 429, 459, 493, 494-495
social process, 63, 109, 205
student-teacher relationship, 261
teacher attitudes, 391
teacher role, 68, 208, 209, 260
technology, 170
Science Technology Society (STS),
            environmental activism, 61
Science World, archival data, 132, 290
Scientific World View, *Benchmarks for
            Science Literacy*, 25, 25t
Scoring rubrics, 363-366, 367b
Selection techniques, student
            assessment, 348
Self-assessment, student portfolio, 367-369
Self-knowledge, definition of, 45, 46, 46t
Self-monitoring, project-based science
            assessment, 373
Sensorimotor intelligence,
            constructivism, 49
Sequencing, scaffolding, 65
Seven Blind Mice, 217
Sharing groups, collaborative learning, 212
Short answer test, student assessment,
            348, 349
Simulations
  contrived experience, 56
  learning technologies, 178, 179, 180b
Skill development, benchmark lessons, 254
Social constructivist teaching model, 54-56,
            55t, 57i, 58-70, 66i, 67i
Social constructivist theory
  assessment practices, 319
  development of, 52
  learning model, 49
  tenets of, 52-53, 268
Social context, project-based science, 55t,
            63, 64, 480-481
Socially induced incompetence,
            collaboration challenges, 234
Solutions, project-based science, 17
Space science, NSES standards, 23
Status differential effect, collaboration
            challenges, 232
Steel wool burning experiment, 40-41, 44i
Story of the Three Bears, The, 223
Strategic knowledge, definition of, 45-46
Student assessment

current practices, 316
  project-based science, 338-344
Student visibility, classroom space, 398,
            399, 401t
Student-community, collaborative learning,
            209-210
Student-teacher, collaborative learning,
            208-209
Students
  autonomous learning, 239
  classroom rules, 417-418
  collaborative learning, 206-208
  demonstrations, 276-277
  driving question development, 93, 94,
            100-106, 105i, 107t
  limited experience of, 487-488
  planning and design capabilities,
            135-136
  project-based science assessment, 373
  scientific inquiry, 117-118
  understanding science, 38-42, 42b-43b
Subordinate concepts, concept maps, 256
Subquestions
  description of, 12
  driving questions, 83-84
Summative assessment
  classroom scenario, 336-338
  description of, 309-310, 329, 356
  use of, 328
Superordinate concepts, concept
            maps, 256
Sustainable driving questions, 78, 82, 86, 87t,
            89, 90, 91, 445

T
T-Charts
  creation of, 214, 215b
  elaborating, 222t
  negotiation skills, 213t, 214
  respect-building, 221t
Tables, data techniques, 147, 148, 148t,
            149i, 149t
Talsma, Valerie, 44
Task-completion skills, collaborative
            learning, 213t, 215, 216t, 217
Teacher-student
  collaborative learning, 208-209
  relationship, classroom climate, 392
Teachers
  assessment assistance, 329
  assessment beliefs, 310, 311b
  assessment technique selection, 325b
  collaborative learning, 239-240, 240b
  curriculum integration view,
            468, 468b
  data interpretation role, 153
  decomposition study, 158-160
  discussion techniques, 278-280,
            280b, 281t

driving question development, 92-99, 95i
experimental procedures role, 147
gender bias, 395-396
independent student investigations, 159-160
information resources role, 132-133
information sharing support, 158
investigation competence, 486-487
investigation role, 124-126, 147
learning technologies, 188-192, 192b
multiple instances of different activities, 423, 428-429, 429t
multiple instances of same activities, 423, 427-428
planning/design role, 140t, 140-144, 141t, 142t
portfolio creation, 362, 363b
positive attitudes, 391
presentation techniques, 281-284
presenting demonstrations, 274
professional development strategies, 494-495, 496b
professional growth, 491-493
project-based assessment, 313, 314, 316
project-based science assessment, 373
question style, 297, 298b
as role-models, 390
science content knowledge, 484-485
science education advocacy, 490-491
social constructivist model, 59
student activities, 281, 284-287
written conclusion support, 155, 155t
Teaching
models of, 46-48
social constructivist model, 54-56, 55t, 57i, 58-70, 66i, 67i, 268
Teaching Science to Children: An Inquiry Approach, 275
Team identity, group formation, 212
Technology
project-based science, 9, 481
and society, 27
tools. *See* Learning technologies
Telecommunication, learning technologies, 188
Test anxiety, student assessment, 350-351
Test construction, 347-351, 351b
Test theory, contemporary, 311
Testing
student assessment, 306, 346
criterion-referenced, 373
traditional methods, 321-322, 323b
types of, 348
Textbooks, gender bias, 396
Textual materials, making sense of, 290-291, 291t

Thematic curriculum, definition of, 468
Third International Mathematics and Science Study (TIMSS)
science teaching, 489
student attitudes, 21
Thought, four forms of, 49
Time
science allocation, 403-405, 404t, 405, 405b
science learning, 488-489
Time frame, project-based science, 9, 17, 28-29
Transformation teaching, 46-48
Transition, potential problems, 423, 425-426
True and false tests, student assessment, 348, 349
Trust-building skills, collaborative learning, 217-221, 218b
Twentieth Earth Day Special, 283

U
Understand, cognitive process, 264, 265t, 326t-327t
Understanding
meaningful, 42-43, 44, 45i
science students, 38
Use and application of knowledge, social constructivist model, 55t, 56, 58-61

V
Valid assessment, 316-317, 350
Variables
controlling, 137, 138b-139b, 140
identifying, 136
operational definition, 136-137
Velocity, content knowledge, 44
Venn diagram, negotiation skills, 223, 224i
Very Hungry Caterpillar, The, 447, 472
Vibration, 48
Video cameras, learning technologies, 188
Video Case Studies, planning/design, 143
Videos
insect project, 451
presentations, 281, 283
professional development, 495
student artifacts, 356, 360-361
Visual-spatial intelligence, 465, 466t, 467t
Visual techniques, data techniques, 147, 151
Visual tools, teaching strategies, 66i, 67, 67i
Visualization tools, learning technologies, 176-178, 177i
Voyage of the Mimi, The, 178-179
Vygotsky, Lev
social constructivism, 52
zone of proximal development, 64-65, 204-205, 207, 211, 236-242

W
Wait-time
assessment information, 339
technique of, 60, 278-279
Web-based Inquiry Science Environment (WISE), 98
Websites
AAAS, 494t
driving questions development, 98
Eisenhower National Clearinghouse, 494t
National Academy of Science, 494t
National Center for Education Statistics, 494t
National Science Foundation, 494t
NSTA, 329, 494t
Online Learning Center, 31, 71, 109, 162, 192, 242, 298, 330, 375, 432, 474, 495
professional science education organizations, 486t
Sci Links, 132
What Research Says to the Science Teacher, 491
What's in Our Water?, 243b
Where Butterflies Grow, insect project, 447, 448, 472
Win-Win Chart, 223t
Window to the Universe Project, World Wide Web, 182, 184i
World Wide Web
benchmark lessons, 254
collaborative learning, 229-230
information source, 132, 289-290
learning technologies, 181-183, 183t, 191
planning tools, 473-474
sciences resources, 456, 457, 458, 459b
visual images, 282-283
Worldwatcher program, weather science, 176
Worthwhile driving questions, 78, 82, 84, 87t, 445
examples of, 88, 89
Writing samples
insect project, 451
student artifacts, 356-357, 361

Y
Young Children, 493t
Young, Ed, 217

Z
Zone of proximal development, 64-65, 204-205, 207, 211, 236-242
Zoo Books, 290